Wireless Networking Complete

The Morgan Kaufmann Series in Networking

Series Editor, David Clark, M.I.T.

Network Routing: Algorithms, Protocols, and Architectures
Deepankar Medhi and Karthikeyan Ramaswami

Deploying IP and MPLS QoS for Multiservice Networks: Theory and Practice
John Evans and Clarence Filsfils

Traffic Engineering and QoS Optimization of Integrated Voice & Data Networks
Gerald R. Ash

IPv6 Core Protocols Implementation
Qing Li, Tatuya Jinmei, and Keiichi Shima

Smart Phone and Next-Generation Mobile Computing
Pei Zheng and Lionel Ni

GMPLS: Architecture and Applications
Adrian Farrel and Igor Bryskin

Content Networking: Architecture, Protocols, and Practice
Markus Hofmann and Leland R. Beaumont

Network Algorithmics: An Interdisciplinary Approach to Designing Fast Networked Devices
George Varghese

Network Recovery: Protection and Restoration of Optical, SONET-SDH, IP, and MPLS
Jean Philippe Vasseur, Mario Pickavet, and Piet Demeester

Routing, Flow, and Capacity Design in Communication and Computer Networks
Michał Pióro and Deepankar Medhi

Wireless Sensor Networks: An Information Processing Approach
Feng Zhao and Leonidas Guibas

Communication Networking: An Analytical Approach
Anurag Kumar, D. Manjunath, and Joy Kuri

The Internet and Its Protocols: A Comparative Approach
Adrian Farrel

Modern Cable Television Technology: Video, Voice, and Data Communications, 2e
Walter Ciciora, James Farmer, David Large, and Michael Adams

Policy-Based Network Management: Solutions for the Next Generation
John Strassner

MPLS Network Management: MIBs, Tools, and Techniques
Thomas D. Nadeau

Developing IP-Based Services: Solutions for Service Providers and Vendors
Monique Morrow and Kateel Vijayananda

Telecommunications Law in the Internet Age
Sharon K. Black

Optical Networks: A Practical Perspective, 2e
Rajiv Ramaswami and Kumar N. Sivarajan

Internet QoS: Architectures and Mechanisms
Zheng Wang

TCP/IP Sockets in Java: Practical Guide for Programmers
Michael J. Donahoo and Kenneth L. Calvert

TCP/IP Sockets in C: Practical Guide for Programmers
Kenneth L. Calvert and Michael J. Donahoo

Multicast Communication: Protocols, Programming, and Applications
Ralph Wittmann and Martina Zitterbart

High-Performance Communication Networks, 2e
Jean Walrand and Pravin Varaiya

Internetworking Multimedia
Jon Crowcroft, Mark Handley, and Ian Wakeman

Understanding Networked Applications: A First Course
David G. Messerschmitt

Integrated Management of Networked Systems: Concepts, Architectures, and Their Operational Application
Heinz-Gerd Hegering, Sebastian Abeck, and Bernhard Neumair

Virtual Private Networks: Making the Right Connection
Dennis Fowler

Understanding Networked Applications
David G. Messerschmitt

Wide Area Network Design: Concepts and Tools for Optimization
Robert S. Cahn

For further information on these books and for a list of forthcoming titles, please visit our Web site at http://www.mkp.com.

Wireless Networking Complete

Pei Zheng
Feng Zhao
David Tipper
Jinmei Tatuya
Keiichi Shima
Yi Qian
Larry L. Peterson
Lionel M. Ni
D. Manjunath
Qing Li
Joy Kuri
Anurag Kumar
Prashant Krishnamurthy
Leonidas Guibas
Vijay K. Garg
Adrian Farrel
Bruce S. Davie

ELSEVIER

AMSTERDAM • BOSTON • HEIDELBERG • LONDON
NEW YORK • OXFORD • PARIS • SAN DIEGO
SAN FRANCISCO • SINGAPORE • SYDNEY • TOKYO
Morgan Kaufmann Publishers is an imprint of Elsevier

MORGAN
KAUFMANN

Morgan Kaufmann Publishers is an imprint of Elsevier
30 Corporate Drive, Suite 400, Burlington, MA 01803, USA

Material in the work originally appeared in *Smart Phone & Next Generation Mobile Computing* by Pei Zheng and Lionel Ni (Elsevier Inc. 2006), *Computer Networks, Fourth Edition,* by Larry Peterson and Bruce Davie (Elsevier Inc. 2007), *Wireless Communication & Networking,* by Vijay Garg (Elsevier Inc. 2007), *Wireless Networks,* by Anurag Kumar, D. Manjunath, Joy Kuri (Elsevier Inc. 2008), *Wireless Sensor Networks*, by Feng Zhao and Leonidas Guibas (Elsevier Inc. 2004), *The Internet and Its Protocols,* by Adrian Farrel (Farrel 2004), *IPv6 Advanced Protocols,* by Qing Li, Keiichi Shima, and Jinmei Tatuya (Elsevier Inc. 2007), and *Information Assurance, edited* by Yi Qian, David Tipper, James Joshi and Prashant Krishnamurthy (Elsevier Inc. 2008).

Library of Congress Cataloging-in-Publication Data
A catalog record for this book is available from the Library of Congress.

British Library Cataloguing-in-Publication Data
A catalogue record for this book is available from the British Library.

ISBN: 978-0-12-375077-8

For information on all Morgan Kaufmann publications,
visit our Web site at www.mkp.com or www.elsevierdirect.com

Printed in the United States of America
09 10 11 12 13   5 4 3 2 1

Contents

About This Book

All of the elements about wireless networking are here together in a single resource written by the best and brightest experts in the field. This book consolidates both introductory and advanced topics, thereby covering the gamut of wireless networking—from wireless systems overview to fundamental wireless application protocols to wireless sensor networks and security in wireless systems.

Wireless Networking Complete expertly combines the finest wireless networking material from the Morgan Kaufmann portfolio, with individual chapters contributed by a select group of authors. The chapters have been combined into one comprehensive book in a way that allows it to be used as a reference work for those interested in new and developing aspects of wireless networking. This book represents a quick and efficient way to unite valuable content from leaders in the wireless networking field, thereby creating a definitive, one-stop-shopping opportunity to access information you would otherwise need to round up from disparate sources.

About the Authors

Pei Zheng (Chapter 1) was an Assistant Professor in the Computer Science Department at Arcadia University and a consultant working in the areas of mobile computing and distributed systems during the writing of this book. Dr. Zheng received his Ph.D. degree in Computer Science from Michigan State University in 2003. He was a Member of Technical Staff in Bell Laboratories, Lucent Technologies. He joined Microsoft in 2005. His research interests include distributed systems, network simulation and emulation, and mobile computing. He is also a co-author of *Smart Phone and Next Generation Mobile Computing*, published by Elsevier, 2005.

Feng Zhao (Chapter 9) is a senior researcher at Microsoft, where he manages the Networked Embedded Computing Group. He received his Ph.D. in Electrical Engineering and Computer Science from Massachusetts Institute of Technology (MIT) and has taught at Stanford University and Ohio State University. Dr. Zhao was a principal scientist at Xerox PARC and directed PARC's sensor network research effort. He is serving as the editor-in-chief of ACM Transactions on Sensor Networks. He is also a co-author of *Wireless Sensor Networks*, published by Elsevier, 2004.

David Tipper (Chapter 12) is an Associate Professor of Telecommunications, with a secondary appointment in Electrical Engineering, at the University of Pittsburgh. He is a senior member of IEEE, and has served as both the Technical Program Chair of the Fourth International IEEE Design of Reliable Communication Networks Workshop and as a co-guest editor of the Journal of Network and Systems Management. He is also a co-author of *Information Assurance: Dependability and Security in Networked Systems*, published by Elsevier, 2007.

Jinmei Tatuya (Chapter 11) is a research scientist at Corporate Research & Development Center, Toshiba Corporation. He had been a core developer of the KAME project since the launch of the project through its conclusion. In 2003, he received a Ph.D. degree from Keio University, Japan, based on his work at KAME. He is also a co-author of *IPv6 Advanced Protocols*, published by Elsevier, 2007.

Keiichi Shima (Chapter 11) is a senior researcher at Internet Initiative Japan Inc. He was a core developer of the KAME project from 2001 until the end of the project and developed Mobile IPv6/NEMO Basic Support protocol stack. He is now working on the new mobility stack (the SHISA stack) for BSD operating systems. He is also a co-author of *IPv6 Advanced Protocols*, published by Elsevier, 2007.

Yi Qian (Chapter 12) is an Assistant Professor in the Department of Electrical and Computer Engineering at the University of Puerto Rico at Mayaguez. Prior to joining UPRM, he worked for several companies as a Technical Advisor and a Senior Consultant in the areas of network optimization and network planning. He has been on numerous conference committees, and has most recently served as the General Chair of the 2007 International Symposium on Wireless Pervasive Computing. He is also a co-author of *Information Assurance: Dependability and Security in Networked Systems*, published by Elsevier, 2007.

Larry L. Peterson (Chapter 2) is Professor and Chair of Computer Science at Princeton University. He is Director of the Princeton-hosted PlanetLab Consortium and Chair of the planning group for NSF's GENI Initiative. His research focuses on the design and implementation of networked systems. Peterson is a Fellow of the ACM. He received his Ph.D. degree from Purdue University in 1985. He is also a co-author of *Computer Networks: A Systems Approach*, published by Elsevier, 2007.

Lionel M. Ni (Chapter 1) is Professor and Head of the Computer Science Department at the Hong Kong University of Science and Technology. Dr. Ni earned his Ph.D. degree in Electrical and Computer Engineering from Purdue University, West Lafayette, IN, in 1981. He was professor in Computer Science and Engineering Department at Michigan State University, where he started his academic career in 1981. He has been involved in many projects related to wireless technologies, 2.5G/3G cellular phones, and embedded systems. He is also a co-author of *Smart Phone and Next Generation Mobile Computing*, published by Elsevier, 2005.

D. Manjunath, Ph.D. (Chapters 7 and 8) is a Professor in the Department of Electrical Engineering of the Indian Institute of Technology (IIT) Bombay. He previously served on the faculty at IIT Kanpur. He is also a co-author of *Wireless Networks*, published by Elsevier, 2008.

Qing Li (Chapter 11) is a senior architect at Blue Coat Systems, Inc. leading the design and development efforts of the next-generation IPv6-enabled secure proxy appliances. Qing holds multiple US patents and is the author of multiple books on networked and embedded systems. He is also a co-author of *IPv6 Advanced Protocols*, published by Elsevier, 2007.

Joy Kuri, (Chapters 7 and 8) is an Associate Professor at the Center for Electronics Design and Technology at the Indian Institute of Science, Bangalore. He is also a co-author of *Wireless Networks*, published by Elsevier, 2008.

Anurag Kumar, Ph.D. (Chapters 7 and 8) is a Professor in the Department of Electrical Communication Engineering, and chair of the Electrical Sciences Division in the Indian Institute of Science (IISc), Bangalore. Previously, he was with AT&T Bell Laboratories, Holmdel, New Jersey. Professor Kumar was also the coordinator at IISc of the Education and

Research Network Project (ERNET), India's first wide-area packet network. He is an IEEE Fellow. He is also a co-author of *Wireless Networks*, published by Elsevier, 2008.

Prashant Krishnamurthy (Chapter 12) is an Associate Professor with the Graduate Program in Telecommunications and Networking at the University of Pittsburgh, PA. At Pitt, he regularly teaches courses on wireless communication systems and networks, cryptography, and network security. His research interests are wireless network security, wireless data networks, position location in indoor wireless networks, and radio channel modeling for indoor wireless networks. He has had funding for his research from the National Science Foundation and the National Institute of Standards and Technology. He is the co-author of the book *Principles of Wireless Networks: A Unified Approach and Physical Layer of Communication Systems* (Prentice Hall; 1st edition, December 11, 2001). He served as the chair of the IEEE Communications Society, Pittsburgh Chapter, from 2000–2005. He obtained his Ph.D. in 1999 from Worcester Polytechnic Institute, Worcester, MA. He is also a co-author of *Information Assurance: Dependability and Security in Networked Systems*, published by Elsevier, 2007.

Leonidas Guibas (Chapter 9) heads the Geometric Computation group in the Computer Science Department of Stanford University, where he works on algorithms for sensing, modeling, reasoning about, rendering, and acting on the physical world. He is well-known for his work in computational geometry, computer graphics, and discrete algorithms. Professor Guibas obtained his Ph.D. from Stanford; has worked at PARC, MIT, and DEC/SRC; and was recently elected an ACM Fellow. He is also a co-author of *Wireless Sensor Networks*, published by Elsevier, 2004.

Vijay K. Garg (Chapters 3, 4, 5, and 6) has been a Professor in the Electrical and Computer Engineering Department at the University of Illinois at Chicago since 1999, where he teaches graduate courses in Wireless Communications and Networking. Dr. Garg was a Distinguished Member of Technical Staff at the Lucent Technologies Bell Labs in Naperville, Illinois from 1985 to 2001. He received his Ph.D. degree from the Illinois Institute of Technologies, Chicago, IL in 1973 and his MS degree from the University of California at Berkeley, CA in 1966. Dr. Garg has co-authored several technical books including five in wireless communications. He is a Fellow of ASCE and ASME, and a Senior Member of IEEE. Dr. Garg is a registered Professional Engineer in the state of Maine and Illinois. He is an Academic Member of the Russian Academy of Transport. Dr. Garg was a Feature Editor of Wireless/PCS Series in *IEEE Communication Magazine* from 1996–2001. He is also the author of *Wireless Communications and Networking*, published by Elsevier, 2007.

Adrian Farrel (Chapter 10) has over two decades of experience designing and developing communications protocol software. At Old Dog Consulting he is an industry-leading freelance consultant on MPLS, GMPLS, and Internet routing, formerly working as MPLS Architect for Data Connection Ltd., and as Director of Protocol Development for Movaz

Networks, Inc. He is active within the Internet Engineering Task Force, where he is co-chair of the CCAMP working group responsible for GMPLS, the Path Computation Element (PCE) working group, and the Layer One VPN (L1VPN) working group. Adrian has co-authored and contributed to numerous Internet Drafts and RFCs on MPLS, GMPLS, and related technologies. He is also the author of *The Internet and Its Protocols: A Comparative Approach*, published by Elsevier, 2004.

Bruce S. Davie (Chapter 2) joined Cisco Systems in 1995, where he is a Cisco Fellow. For many years he led the team of architects responsible for Multiprotocol Label Switching and IP Quality of Service. He recently joined the Video and Content Networking Business Unit in the Service Provider group. He has 20 years of networking and communications industry experience and has written numerous books, RFCs, journal articles, and conference papers on IP networking. He is also an active participant in both the Internet Engineering Task Force and the Internet Research Task Force. Prior to joining Cisco, he was director of internetworking research and chief scientist at Bell Communications Research. Bruce holds a Ph.D. in Computer Science from Edinburgh University and is a visiting lecturer at MIT. His research interests include routing, measurement, quality of service, transport protocols, and overlay networks. He is also a co-author of *Computer Networks: A Systems Approach*, published by Elsevier, 2007.

CHAPTER 1

Supporting Wireless Technologies

Pei Zheng
Lionel M. Ni

This chapter provides extensive coverage of existing mobile wireless technologies. Much of the emphasis is on the highly anticipated 3G cellular networks and widely deployed wireless local area networks (LANs), as the next-generation smart phones are likely to offer at least these two types of connectivity. Other wireless technologies that either have already been commercialized or are undergoing active research and standardization are introduced as well. Because standardization plays a crucial role in developing a new technology and a market, throughout the discussion standards organizations and industry forums or consortiums of some technologies are introduced. In addition, the last section of this chapter presents a list of standards in the wireless arena.

1.1 The Frequency Spectrum

The fundamental principle of wireless communication is electromagnetic wave transmission between a transmitter and a receiver. Signals are characterized by their frequencies in use. Multiple signals or noises of the same frequency will cause interference at the receiver. To avoid interference, various wireless technologies use distinct frequency bands with well-controlled signal power which are portions of the so-called frequency spectrum. As a scarce public resource, the frequency spectrum is strictly regulated by governments of countries around the world. In the United States, the Federal Communications Commission (FCC) has the responsibility of regulating civil broadcast and electronic communications, including the use of the frequency spectrum, and the National Telecommunications and Information Administration (NITA) administers the frequency use of the federal government. In Europe, the frequency spectrum is managed on a national basis, and the European Union (EU) members coordinate via the European Conference of Post and Telecommunications Administrations (ECPT) and the Electronic Communications Committee (ECC). Worldwide unified regulation of wireless communication is understandably difficult to achieve for various technological, economic, and political reasons. To this end, the International Telecommunications Union (ITU) has been formed as an international organization of the United Nation. The ITU allows governments and private sectors to coordinate development of telecommunication systems, services, and standards. In almost all countries, portions of the frequency spectrum have been designated as "unlicensed," meaning that a government license is not required for wireless systems operating at these bands. In effect, wireless system manufacturers and service providers are required to obtain an exclusive license for a frequency band from regulatory bodies or resort to the use of the unlicensed spectrum. In either case, the emitted power of the wireless systems must comply with the power constraints associated with the regulations in question. In addition, frequency allocations of a country may change over time. (For the latest information regarding frequency allocation in the United States, see http://www.ntia.doc.gov/osmhome/allochrt.html.)

A radio signal is characterized by wavelength and frequency. In vacuum, the product of wavelength and frequency is the speed of light (about 3×10^8 m/sec); in general, a higher frequency means shorter wavelength. For example, visible light is in the frequency band of 4.3×10^{14} to 7.5×10^{14} Hz, with wavelengths ranging from 0.35 to 0.9 μm. Frequency modulation (FM) radio broadcasts operate within the frequency range of 30 to 300 MHz at wavelengths between 10 and 1 m.

The frequency spectrum can be divided into the following categories: very low frequency (VLF), low frequency (LF), medium frequency (MF), high frequency (HF), very high frequency (VHF), ultra-high frequency (UHF), super-high frequency (SHF), extremely high frequency (EHF), infrared, visible light, ultraviolet, X-ray, gamma-ray, and cosmic ray, each of which represents a frequency band. Figure 1.1 shows the frequency spectrum up to the visible light band. Notice that in the context of electronic communication, there are two categories of transmission medium: guided medium (e.g., copper coaxial cable and twisted pair) and unguided medium (for wireless communication in the air). The guided medium carries signals or waves between a transmitter and a receiver, whereas the unguided medium typically carries wireless signals between an antenna and a receiver (which may also be an antenna). Nevertheless, each medium operates at a specific frequency band of various bandwidth determined by its physical characteristics. For example, coaxial cable uses many portions of frequencies between 1 KHz and 1 GHz for different purposes: television channels 2, 3, and 4 operate at frequencies from 54 to 72 MHz; channels 5 and 6 from 76 to 88 MHz; and channels 7 to 13 from 174 to 216 MHz. The optical fiber uses visible or infrared light as the carrier and operates at frequencies between 100 and 1000 THz.

Wireless communication operates at frequencies in the so-called radio spectrum, which is further divided into VLF, LF, MF, HF, VHF, UHF, SHF, and EHF. In addition, infrared data association (IrDA) is also used for short-range wireless communication. The following text discusses frequency bands at which existing mobile wireless technologies operate; notice that very often the frequency regulations enforce emitted power restrictions to avoid interference among wireless devices operating at the same frequency band.

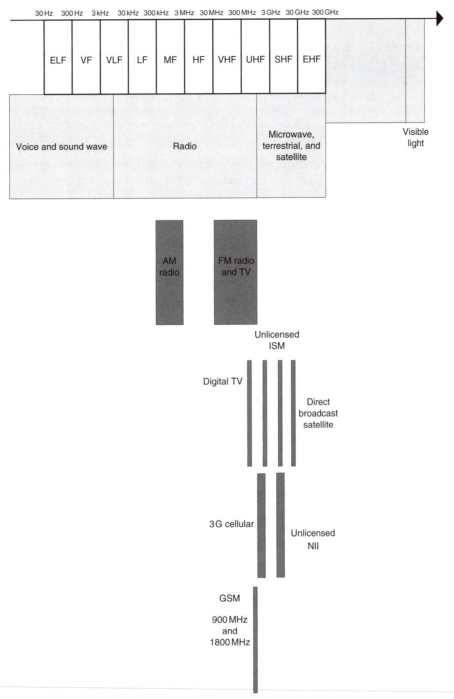

Figure 1.1 The frequency spectrum (refer to the text for the exact frequency band allocated to each system).

1.1.1 *Public Media Broadcasting*

- Amplitude modulation (AM) radio: AM radio stations operate at a frequency band between 520 and 1605.5 KHz.

- FM radio: It uses the frequency band between 87.5 and 108 MHz.

- Shortwave (SW) radio: SW radio uses frequencies between 5.9 and 26.1 MHz within the HF band. The transmission of shortwave radio over a long distance is made possible by ionosphere reflection. HAM amateur radio, a popular activity enjoyed by over three million fans worldwide, relies on the HF band to communicate across the world.

- Conventional analog television: A quite small slice of VHF (30–300 MHz) and UHF (300–3000 MHz) has been allocated for analog television broadcasting. In the United States, each channel occupies a 6-MHz band. The first VHF channel, channel 2, operates at 54–60 MHz, whereas the last UHF channel, channel 69, operates at 800–806 MHz.

- Cable television: The frequency bands of channels 2–13 are exactly the same for both conventional television and cable television. Beyond those channels, cable television requires frequencies from 120 to 552 MHz for channels 13–78.

- Digital cable television: Channels 79 and above are reserved for digital cable broadcasting at frequencies between 552 and 750 MHz.

- Digital audio broadcasting (DAB): DAB is a standard developed by the EU for CD-quality audio transmission at frequencies from 174 to 240 MHz and from 1452 to 1492 MHz. In the United States, a technique called in-band on-channel (IBOC) is used to transmit digital audio and analog radio signals simultaneously with the same frequency band. The resulting services are generally marketed as high-definition radio.

- Direct broadcast satellite (DBS): The upper portion of the microwave Ku band (10.9–12.75 GHz) is used for direct satellite-to-receiver video and audio broadcasting. See Section 1.13 for more details regarding satellite communication.

- Satellite radio: Frequencies from 2320 to 2345 MHz have been allotted for satellite radio services in the United States. See Section 1.13 for more details regarding satellite communication.

1.1.2 *Cellular Communication*

- Global system for mobile (GSM): The two frequency bands used by GSM are 890–960 MHz and 1710–1880 MHz. They are sometimes referred to as the 900-MHz band and the 1800-MHz band.

- Code-division multiple access (CDMA): The IS-95 standard defines the use of the 800- and 1900-MHz bands for CDMA cellular systems.

- 3G wideband CDMA (WCDMA)/universal mobile telecommunications system (UMTS): Three frequency bands are allocated for 3G UMTS services: 1900–1980 MHz, 2020–2025 MHz, and 2110–2190 MHz.

- 3G CDMA 2000: This system reuses existing CDMA frequency bands.

1.1.3 *Wireless Data Communication*

- Wireless LANs: IEEE 802.11b operates at 902–928 MHz and 2400–2483 MHz, and the industrial, scientific, and medical (ISM) radio bands operate at 2.4 GHz in the United States. The IEEE 802.11b operates at 2400–2483 MHz in Europe, and at 2400–2497 MHz in Japan. IEEE 802.11a and HiperLAN2 use 5150–5350 MHz and 5725–5825 MHz, and the unlicensed national information infrastructure (U-NII) band operates at 5.8 GHz in the United States. They operate at 5150–5350 MHz and 5470–5725 MHz in Europe, and at 5150–5250 MHz in Japan. Section 1.10 discusses wireless LANs in more detail.

- Bluetooth: A total of 79 1-MHz channels are allocated from the unlicensed 2.402–2.480 GHz in the United States and Europe for Bluetooth signal transmission. Other countries may have fewer channels but all fall into the 2.4-GHz band. Section 1.11 talks more about the Bluetooth technology.

- WiMax: A wide range from 2 to 11 GHz that includes both licensed and unlicensed bands will be used for 802.116a, and from 11 to 66 GHz can possibly be used by 802.116c. Section 1.14 introduces WiMax as part of the wireless MANs section.

- Ultra-wideband (UWB): In the United States, the FCC mandates that UWB can operate from 1.1 to 10.6 GHz. UWB is further discussed in Section 1.12.

- Radio-frequency identification (RFID): RFID tags operate at the frequency bands of LF (120–140 KHz), HF (13.56 MHz), UHF (868–956 MHz), and microwave (2.4 GHz). Section 1.13 explains RFID technology and its applications.

- IrDA: IrDA uses frequencies around 100 GHz for short-range data communication.

- Wireless sensors: Sensor motes support tunable frequencies in the range of 300 to 1000 MHz and the 2.4-GHz ISM band. In particular, ZigBee, the remote sensor control technology, operates at the 868-MHz band in Europe, 915-MHz band in the United States and Asia, and 2.4-GHz band worldwide.

1.1.4 Other Fixed or Mobile Wireless Communications

- Digital cordless phone: The Digital Enhanced Cordless Telecommunications (DECT) standard in Europe defines the use of the frequency band 1880–1990 MHz for digital cordless phone communication. In the United States, cordless phones use three frequency bands: 900 MHz, 2.4 GHz, and 5.8 GHz, each of which is also intensively used by other short-range wireless communication technologies.

- Global positioning system (GPS): GPS satellites use the frequency bands 1575.42 MHz (referred to as L1) and 1227.60 MHz (L2) to transmit signals.

- Meteorological satellite services: The UHF band from 1530 to 1650 MHz (the L band) is commonly used by meteorological satellites, as well as some global environmental monitoring satellites. Part of the UHF and SHF bands are used for military satellite communication.

- Radio-frequency remote control, such as remote keyless entry systems and garage door openers. These short-range wireless systems, commonly used for automobiles, operate at 27, 128, 418, 433, and 868 MHz in the United States; 315 and 915 MHz in Europe; and 426 and 868 MHz in Japan.

1.2 Wireless Communication Primer

For our in-depth discussion of the many sophisticated mobile wireless network technologies, a basic understanding of wireless communications is necessary. Here, a primer of concepts within the domain of wireless communication is presented. Readers who are interested in further details are referred to Stallings' book on wireless communications and networks [1].

1.2.1 Signal Propagation

A radio signal can be described in three domains: time domain, frequency domain, and phase domain. In the time domain, the amplitude of the signal varies with time; in the frequency domain, the amplitude of the signal varies with frequency; and in the phase domain, the amplitude and phase of the signal are shown on polar coordinates. According to Fourier's theorem, any periodic signal is composed of a superposition of a series of pure sine waves and cosine waves whose frequencies are harmonics (multiples) of the fundamental frequency of the signal; therefore, any periodic signal, no matter how it was originally produced, can be reproduced using a sufficient number of pure waves.

Electronic signals for wireless communication must be converted into electromagnetic waves by an antenna for transmission. Conversely, an antenna at the receiver side is responsible for converting electromagnetic waves into electronic signals. An antenna can be omnidirectional or directional, depending on specific usage scenarios. For an antenna to be effective, it must be of a size consistent with the wavelength of the signals being transmitted or received. Antennas used in cell phones are omnidirectional and can be a short rod on the handset or hidden within the handset. A recent advancement in antenna technology is the multiple-in, multiple out (MIMO) antenna, or smart antenna, which combines spatially separated small antennas to provide high bandwidth without consuming more power or spectrum. To take advantage of multipath propagation (explained on page 8), these small antennas must be separated by at least half of the wavelength of the signal being transmitted or received.

A signal emitted by an antenna travels in the air following three types of propagation modes: ground-wave propagation, sky-wave propagation, and line-of-sight (LOS) propagation. AM radio is a kind of ground-wave propagation, where signals follow the contour of the Earth to reach a receiver. SW radio and HAM amateur radio are examples of sky-wave propagation, where radio signals are reflected by ionosphere and the ground along the way. Beyond 30 MHz, LOS propagation dominates, meaning that signal waves propagate on a direct, straight path in the air. It is noteworthy that radio signals of LOS propagation can also penetrate objects, especially signals of large wavelength (and thus low frequency). Satellite links, infrared light, and communication between base stations of a cellular network are examples of LOS propagation.

1.2.1.1 Attenuation

The strength or power of wireless signals decreases when they propagate in the air, just as visible light does. As soon as radio waves leave the transmitter's antenna, some amount of energy will be lost as the electromagnetic field propagates. The effect will become more evident over a long distance as the signal disperses in space; therefore, the received power of the signal is invariably less than the signal power at the transmitting antenna. In the most ideal circumstances (i.e., in vacuum), signal power attenuation is proportional to d^2, where d denotes the distance between the transmitter and the receiver. This effect is sometimes referred to as *free space loss*. In reality, beside free space loss, a number of other factors have to be considered to determine signal attenuation, such as weather conditions, atmospheric absorption, and space rays. In addition, signal attenuation is more severe at high frequencies · than at low frequencies, resulting in signal distortion.

When it encounters obstacles along the path, a signal may experience more complex attenuation than power reduction. For example, for visible light we are well aware of the following effects: *shadowing*, *reflection*, and *refraction*. Likewise, for high-frequency wireless signals, such effects also exist. Shadowing and reflection occur when a signal encounters an object that is much larger than its wavelength. Though the reflected signal and the shadowed signal are comparatively weak, they in effect help to propagate the signal to spaces where LOS is impossible. For example, when reflection and shadowing are caused by buildings in an urban area, signals from an antenna of a base station may be able to reach cell phone users within a building in the area, although it might be a good idea for the user to walk close to the window for better signal strength (perceived as a number of "bars" displayed on the cell phone screen). Refraction (bending) occurs when a wave passes across the boundary of two media. Moreover, wireless signals are also subject to *scattering* and *diffraction*. Specifically, when the size of an obstacle is on the order of the signal wavelength or less, the signal will be scattered into a number of weaker pieces. Diffraction occurs when a signal hits the edge of an obstacle and is deflected into a number of directions.

1.2.1.2 Noise

The receiver of a wireless communication system must be able to detect transmitted (most likely attenuated and distorted) signals from unwanted noises. Common types of noise are *thermal noise* (white noise) produced by any electronic circuitry; *intermodulation* noise, which occurs when two frequencies of signals are modulated and transmitted over the same medium; *crosstalk* between two channels; and *impulse* noise generated by instantaneous electromagnetic changes. To cope with noises in received signals, a wireless system has to ensure that the transmitted signals are sufficiently stronger than the noises. Another approach is to employ spread spectrum schemes (explained below) that convert a signal over a wide range of frequencies of low power density as random noise. Wireless signals are subject to various impairments or distortion along the way from the transmitter to the receiver. To quantify these effects, the signal-to-noise ratio (SNR) is used to represent the ratio of the power in a signal to the power of the noise. SNR is usually computed in decibels as the product of 10 and the logarithm of the raw power ratio.

1.2.1.3 Multipath Propagation

The receiver of a wireless system is exposed to all radio waves in its surrounding environment; therefore, it may receive indirect signals from different paths, such as reflected signals, shadowed signals, and refracted signals, as well as signals generated by other means of propagation, all carrying the same signal with different levels of attenuation and distortion. These signals may impose some negative effect on the direct signal to a great extent. The most severe effect of multipath propagation is intersymbol interference (ISI). ISI is caused by overlapping of delayed multipath pulses (of a primary pulse) and subsequent primary LOS pulses, where one or multiple pulses represent a bit. The degree of attenuation of these pulses may vary from time to time due to path changes or environmental disturbances, making it more difficult to recover the transmitted bits. To prevent ISI from occurring, the first primary pulse and the second pulse have to be separated by a sufficient time difference such that the delayed multipath pulses of the first can be differentiated from the second LOS pulse. This implies that the symbol rate of the signal and bandwidth of the radio channel are limited by multipath propagation.

1.2.2 Modulation

Signal modulation is a technique used to combine a signal being transmitted with a carrier signal for transmission. The receiver demodulates the transmitted signal and regenerates the original signal. Normally the carrier signal is a sine wave of a high frequency. The input signal could be digital (digital modulation) or analog (analog modulation). In either case, the three basic characteristics of a signal are utilized for modulation. The device that performs this modulation and demodulation is the *modem*. Modulation is often referred to as signal encoding. Analog signals can be modulated by the following methods.

1.2.2.1 Amplitude Modulation

For AM signals, the output signal is a multiplication of the input signal with a carrier wave. The amplitude of the carrier wave is determined by the input analog signal. The frequency of the resulting output signal is centered at the frequency of the carrier. As its name implies, AM radio that operates in the frequency band of 520 to 1605.5 KHz uses AM.

1.2.2.2 Frequency Modulation

Rather than vary the amplitude of the carrier wave, FM alters the transient frequency of the carrier according to the input signal. Again, as its name implies, FM radio that operates within the frequency band of 87.5 to 108 MHz uses FM.

1.2.2.3 Phase Modulation

In phase modulation (PM), the phase of the carrier signal is used to encode the input signal. Like AM, FM and PM shift the frequency of the input signal to a band centered at the carrier frequency. Both FM and PM require higher bandwidths. Analog modulation is necessary for transmitting a wireless analog signal such as voice over a long distance. Directly transmitting the signal itself to the receiver without applying modulation would require a large antenna to be effective, as the frequency of voice signals falls into the range of 30 to 3000 Hz. For digital data, if the medium only facilitates analog transmission (e.g., air), some digital modulation techniques will have to be employed. A carrier wave is also used to carry binary streams being transmitted, according to some keying schemes in digital modulation. Below is a list of digital modulation schemes:

- Amplitude-shift keying (ASK): ASK uses presence of a carrier wave to represent a binary one and its absence to indicate a binary zero. While ASK is simple to implement, it is highly susceptible to noise and multipath propagation effects. Because of that, ASK is primarily used in wired networks, especially in optical networks where the bit error rate (BER) is considerably lower than that of wireless environments.

- Frequency-shift keying (FSK): Similar to FM, FSK uses two or more frequencies of a carrier wave to represent digital data. Binary FSK (BFSK), which employs two carrier frequencies for 0 and 1, is the most commonly used FSK. The resulting signal can be mathematically defined as the sum of two amplitude-modulated signals of different carrier frequencies. If more than two carrier frequencies are used for modulation, each frequency may represent more than one bit, thereby providing a higher bandwidth than ASK.

- Phase-shift keying (PSK): PSK uses the phase of a carrier wave to encode digital data. Binary PSK simply reverses phase when the data bits change. Multilevel PSKs use more evenly distributed phases in the phase domain, with each phase representing two or more bits. One of most commonly used PSK schemes is quadrature PSK, in which the four phases of 0, $\pi/2$, π, and $3\pi/2$ are used to encode two digits. PSK can be implemented in two ways. The first is to produce a reference signal at the receiver side and then compare it with the received signal to decide the phase shift. This method somewhat complicates things at the receiver end, as the transmitter and the receiver must be synchronized periodically to ensure that the reference signal is being generated correctly. Another method is differential PSK (DPSK). In DPSK, the reference signal is not a separated signal but is the one preceding the current wave in question. One of the second-generation cellular systems, Digital-Advanced Mobile Phone Service (DAMPS), uses DPSK.

ASK and PSK can be combined to offer more variations of phase shifts on the phase domain. Quadrature amplitude modulation (QAM) is such a scheme in which multiple levels of amplitudes coupled with several phases provide far more unique symbol shifts over the same bandwidth than used by PSK over the same bandwidth. QAM is widely used in today's modems.

Apart from analog and digital modulation, another category of modulation that should be discussed for wireless communication is analog-to-digital data modulation, a procedure sometimes referred to as *digitization*. Two major digitization schemes are pulse-code modulation (PCM) and delta modulation. PCM samples an input analog signal in short intervals, and each sample is converted into a symbol representing a code. To reconstruct the original input signal from samples, the sampling rate must be higher than twice the highest frequency of the input signal. In other words, given a sample rate of *fs*, a frequency higher than 2*fs* in the input signal will not be recovered in the reconstruction. Delta modulation uses a staircase-like sample function to approximate the input signal. The resulting digital data comprise a series of 1's and 0's indicating the ups and downs, respectively, of the staircase function.

In the wireless world, signals transmitted through the air are primarily high-frequency analog signals. In wireless voice communication, the user's voice is digitalized into digital data and then modulated to analog-based band signals (digital modulation), which are finally modulated with a carrier wave for transmission. For wireless data transmission, the first step of this procedure is not necessary. In either case, the receiver takes the reverse order of these steps to recover the transmitted data or voice.

1.2.3 Multiplexing

Modulations of analog signals or digital data are concerned with a single input signal to be converted efficiently into other forms. In contrast, multiplexing is a collection of schemes that addresses the issue of transmitting multiple signals simultaneously in a wireless system in the hopes of maximizing the capacity of the system. The devices for multiplexing and demultiplexing are multiplexers and demultiplexers, respectively. If signals of the same frequency are spatially separated from each other such that no frequency overlapping occurs at any given place, then multiple signals of different frequencies can be transmitted and received without a problem. Radio stations are an excellent example of this *spatial division multiplexing*: AM and FM radio signals only cover the area in which the radio stations are located, and they cannot interfere with other radio signals on the same frequency in adjacent areas. Apart from spatial division multiplexing, three prominent schemes of multiplexing have been devised.

1.2.3.1 Frequency-Division Multiplexing

In frequency-division multiplexing (FDM), signals from a transmitter are modulated to a fixed frequency band centered at a carrier frequency (i.e., a channel). To avoid inference, these channels have to be separated by a sufficiently large gap (i.e., a guard band) in the frequency domain; hence, transmission and reception of signals in multiple channels can be performed simultaneously but independently. Analog cellular systems use FDM; in these systems, calls are separated by frequency.

1.2.3.2 Time-Division Multiplexing

Time-division multiplexing (TDM) allows multiple channels to occupy the same frequency band but in small alternating slices of time following a sequence known to both the transmitter and the receiver. Each channel makes full use of the bandwidth of the medium but only contributes a portion of the overall data rate. Coordination among the transmitters is necessary to prevent conflicting use of the frequency band. When applied to digital signals, TDM can be done on bit level, byte level, block level, or levels of larger quantities. GSM and D-AMPS both use TDM but in different ways. TDM and FDM can be combined to increase the robustness of the system. In this case, signals from a transmitter are modulated onto different carriers for a certain amount of time and jump to another carrier, effectively creating a "frequency-hopping" phenomenon.

1.2.3.3 Code-Division Multiplexing

Code-division multiplexing (CDM) makes better use of a frequency band than FDM and TDM. Signals from different transmitters are transmitted on the same frequency band at the same time but each has a code to uniquely identify itself. The orthogonal codes mathematically ensure that signals cannot interfere with each other at the receiver. CDM effectively converts the problem of limited frequency space into ample code space but adds the overhead of implementation complexity. The transmitter and receiver must be synchronized such that individual signals can be correctly received and decoded. Compared to FDM, CDM provides greater security against signal tapping because transmitted signals appear as noise if the receiver does not know the code. CDM is the underlying multiplexing scheme of orthogonal frequency-division multiplexing (OFDM). CDMA cellular systems use similar CDM schemes to provide multiple wireless communication channels access to the same frequency band. Another multiplexing scheme, wavelength-division multiplexing (WDM), is very common in optical networks using fiber as the transmission medium. It is actually FDM for fiber, which offers an extremely high bandwidth. In WDM, a fiber can be divided into a number of wavelengths (nanometers), each of which can be assigned to a transmission channel. Dense wavelength-division multiplexing (DWDM) systems support eight or more wavelengths. Because of their high data rate, WDM and DWDM are the predominant multiplexing schemes used by optical networks in the wired Internet backbone.

1.3 Spread Spectrum

Wireless systems transmit data over a specific, quite narrow frequency band that allows a transmitter and a receiver to differentiate the intended signal from background noise when the signal quality is sufficient. Narrowband interference can be avoided by filtering out any other frequencies except the designated ones at the receiver. The major advantage of narrowband signal transmission is, as the term implies, its efficient use of frequency due to only a small frequency band being used for one signal transmission. Its drawback is evident, though, as it requires well-coordinated frequency allocation for different signals, and it is quite vulnerable to signal jamming and interception.

Spread spectrum takes another approach. Instead of applying all transmitting power to a narrow frequency channel, spread spectrum converts the narrowband signals to signals of a much wider band with comparatively lower power density according to a specific signal spreading scheme. Because of the low power density (power per frequency), the converted signal appears to be background noise to others who are unaware of the spreading scheme; only the designated receiver is able to reconstruct the original signal. For data transmission with multiple channels using FM, narrowband signals in each channel can be applied with the spread spectrum technique. To be able to differentiate these channels and reconstruct those signals afterwards, each channel is assigned a code with sufficiently large distance separating it from others in the code space, and the codes are made known to the designated receiver only. The advantages of spread spectrum are as follows:

- CDM has greatly improved channel capacity (i.e., the number of signals that can be transmitted at the same time over a given frequency band) as compared to the narrowband spectrum.

- Spread spectrum offers high resistance against narrowband interference and tolerates narrowband interference because the signal is transmitted over a wide band. Even though some portion of the frequencies is distorted, the original signal can still be recovered with the error detection and correction techniques of the coding mechanism.

- Security against tapping and jamming is greater compared to narrowband spectrum techniques. Signals of spread spectrum are indistinguishable from background noise to anyone who does not know the coding scheme (*language*).

The disadvantage of spread spectrum is its relatively high complexity of the coding mechanism, which results in complex radio hardware designs and higher cost. Nonetheless, because of its remarkable advantages, spread spectrum has been adopted by many wireless technologies, such as CDMA and wireless LANs. Depending on the way the frequency spectrum is used, three types of spread spectrum systems are currently in place: direct-sequence spread spectrum (DSSS), frequency-hopping spread spectrum (FHSS), and OFDM.

1.3.1 Direct-Sequence Spread Spectrum

The DSSS spreads a signal over a much broader frequency band. It employs a "chipping" technique to convert a user signal into a spread signal. Given a user data bit, an XOR computation is performed with the user bit and a special chipping sequence code (digital modulation), which is a series of carefully selected pulses that are shorter than the duration of user bits. The resulting signal (the chipping sequence) is then modulated (radio modulation) with a carrier signal and sent out. On the receiver side, after demodulation, the same chipping sequence code is used to decode the original user bits. The chipping sequence essentially determines how the user signal is spread as pseudorandom noise over a large frequency band. The ratio of the spreading (i.e., the spreading factor) varies for different spread spectrum systems. The longer the chipping sequence, the more likely a user signal can be recovered. A transmitter and a receiver have to stay synchronized during the spreading and despreading.

1.3.2 Frequency-Hopping Spread Spectrum

FHSS uses a frequency-hopping sequence to spread a user signal that is known to both the transmitter and the receiver. User data is first modulated to narrowband signals, then a second modulation takes place—a signal with a hopping sequence of frequency is used as the radio carrier. The resulting spread signal is then sent to the receiver. On the receiver side, two steps of modulations are required: (1) use the same frequency-hopping sequence to recover the narrowband signal, and (2) demodulate the narrowband signal. In effect, the transmitter and the receiver follow the same pattern of synchronized frequency hopping. As a result, only if the hopping sequence is made known to the receiver can it recover the original user data bits; otherwise, the transmitted signals will appear as background noise. FHSS does not take up the entire allotted frequency band for transmission. Instead, at any given moment, only a portion of it is used for hopping. The two types of frequency-hopping systems in use are fast hopping systems and slow hopping systems. Fast hopping systems change frequency several times when transmitting a single bit, whereas in slow hopping systems each hop may transmit multiple bits.

Interestingly, the concept of frequency hopping was invented by a Hollywood actress, Hedy Lamarr, and a composer, George Antheil, during World War II. The idea was to use a piano-roll sequence to hop between 88 channels to make decoding of radio-guided torpedo communications more difficult by enemies. Their idea was not implemented because the U.S. Navy refused to consider developing a military technology based on a musical technique. As George Antheil put it, "The reverend and brass-headed gentlemen in Washington who examined our invention read no further than the words 'player piano.' 'My god,' I can see them saying, 'we shall put a player piano in a torpedo.'" (Source: American Heritage of Invention & Technology, Spring 1997, Volume 12/Number 4).

For both DSSS and FHSS, multiple signals with different sequence codes (either chipping-sequence code or frequency-hopping code) can be multiplexed by CDM. To compare, FHSS is relatively simpler to implement than DSSS, but DSSS makes it much more difficult to recover the signal without knowing the chipping code and is more robust to signal distortion and multipath effects. Both are widely used by a large array of wireless technologies operating on the unlicensed spectrum. For example, the IEEE 802.11b standard for wireless LAN employs DSSS over the 2.4-GHz free spectrum, whereas the Bluetooth standard uses FHSS for simplicity.

1.3.3 Orthogonal Frequency-Division Multiplexing

OFDM is a modulation technique that utilizes multiple subcarriers in parallel to transmit user data. These subcarriers are orthogonal in that they are modulated with their own data independently. OFDM was first conceived in the 1960s in an effort to minimize interference among adjacent channels in a frequency band. Because of multicarrier parallelism, OFDM offers a much higher data rate than single-carrier modulation techniques. In addition, because subcarriers are orthogonal, multipath interference can be largely reduced. In reality, some OFDM systems are actually code OFDM (COFDM), which combines error-control channel coding schemes with OFDM modulation. COFDM has some nice properties, such as being resistant against phase distortion, signal fading, and burst noise. OFDM is used in asymmetric digital subscriber line (ADSL), IEEE 802.11a/g wireless LANs, and the broadband wireless data access technology WiMax. COFDM is predominantly used in Europe for DAB and digital video broadcasting (DVB).

1.4 Global System for Mobile and General Packet Radio Service

Although the world of wireless telecommunication experienced remarkable growth in terms of the number of subscribers at the beginning of the 21st century, some mobile wireless operators soon realized that mobile voice service was not enough. The industry has evolved from analog voice to digital voice, and now it is time to leverage high-speed data access provided by 2.5 and 3 G cellular networks for data-centric applications and services. Second-generation cellular systems can be divided into two categories according to the multiplexing access scheme of the radio interface: TDMA or CDMA. The TDMA systems include GSM, D-AMPS (also referred to as IS-136 to supersede IS-54), and packet data cellular (PDC, used in Japan). The CDMA category is fairly straightforward in that the cellular systems utilizing CDMA are also called CDMA systems and they comply with the IS-95 standard. In this section, we first review two second-generation cellular systems, GSM and CDMA (see Table 1.1), then discuss 2.5 G data services and 3 G cellular networks being rolled out worldwide. The introduction to GSM and CDMA focuses on the functional components and key operations.

1.4.1 Global System for Mobile

The first-generation analog cellular systems are based on frequency-division multiple access (FDMA), where each cell supports a number of channels of equal bandwidth and each mobile connection takes two channels (one up and one down) for full-duplex communication. A user with a mobile device takes up the two channels exclusively over the connection time. The capacity of the first-generation cellular systems is largely limited by the static channel allocation scheme. GSM is a solution to this problem.

GSM can be regarded as a TDMA-based, circuit-switching, digital cellular system (DCS) in that the channels allocated to a cell are shared by several mobile connections in a TDM

Table 1.1 2G Cellular Systems.

2G Cellular System Category	2G Cellular Systems
Time-division multiple access (TDMA)	Global system for mobile (GSM) Digitized advanced mobile phone system (D-AMPS) (IS-136) Packet data cellular (PDC)
Code-division multiple access (CDMA)	CDMA (IS-95)

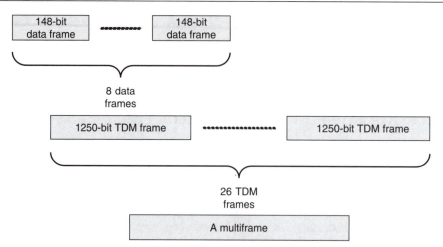

Figure 1.2 GSM data frame structure.

Table 1.2 Frequency Bands of GSM Systems.

GSM Systems	Allocated Frequency Band (MHz)		Deployment
	Uplink	Downlink	
GSM 900	890–915	935–960	Europe, Asia
DCS 1800	1710–1785	1805–1880	United Kingdom
PCS 1900	1850–1910	1930–1990	North America
GSM 400	450–457/478–486	460–467/488–496	Nordic countries

Speech coding of GSM employs the *regular pulse excited–linear predictive coder* (RPE-LPC), which generates a 260-bit block every 20 msec. The modulation scheme of GSM is Gaussian minimum shift keying (GMSK), in which a symbol represents a single bit.

fashion. A mobile connection will use two such simplex channels, each of which is 200 KHz wide, for a time slot of 577 μsec to transmit a 148-bit data frame (see Figure 1.2). Eight such data frames make up a TDM frame of 1250 bits that is sent every 4.615 msec. A multiframe comprises 26 TDM frames, 24 of which are used for data traffic. One of the other two is a control frame and the other is a slot reserved for future use. Accordingly, a shared channel offers a data rate of 270 Kbps, so each user is able to access one-eighth of it, or 33.85 Kbps.

The frequency bands of the first European GSM systems, namely GSM 900, are between 890.2 and 914.8 MHz for cell phone transmissions and between 935.2 and 960.8 MHz for base-station transmissions. Both of these frequency bands are designated for 124,200-KHz channels. Because the frequencies used in adjacent cells cannot overlap in the frequency domain, the total number of channels available in each cell is much smaller than the total number of channels available within the allocated frequency bands. Other GSM systems, such as the DCS 1800, personal communication system (PCS) 1900, and GSM 400, have been deployed in different regions. Table 1.2 outlines the frequency bands of these systems and their deployment worldwide.

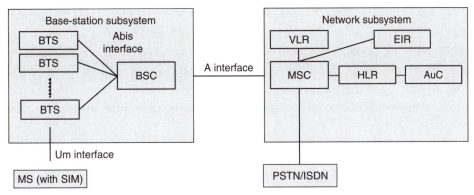

Figure 1.3 GSM architecture.

1.4.1.1 GSM Network Architecture

A GSM network has three components: mobile station, base-station subsystem, and network system (see Figure 1.3). The mobile station comprises cell phones or other portal communication devices that can interface with the base-station subsystem. Each GSM cell phone essentially has two functional components: a mobile environment and a subscriber identity module (SIM) card. A mobile environment is a collection of physical elements for radio transmission and digital signal processing. A SIM card is a small chip that stores the identification of a user (subscriber) and service network information, as well as other data necessary for access authentication and authorization. A SIM card is not built into the cell phone handset; instead, it can be taken out and plugged into other GSM cell phones. As for almost all cellular systems, coverage areas are divided into cell sites. A mobile station in a cell directly communicates with a base transceiver station (BTS), which is responsible for handling all mobile stations within the cell site. The base-station subsystem has one or more BTSs and a base-station controller (BSC). Handoffs among BTSs in the same base-station subsystem are controlled by the BSC.

To cover a large area, a GSM network will build many base-station subsystems, each of which services mobile stations in a smaller area. The network subsystem connects the cellular network to the public switched telecommunication network (PSTN) by means of the mobile switching center (MSC), which also facilitates handoffs of mobile stations among different BSCs. BSCs in an area connect to the responsible MSC, which in turn connects to other MSCs.

The operation of an MSC relies on the home location register (HLR), visitor location register (VLR), authentication center (AuC), and equipment identity register (EIR). The HLR is a central database of mobile stations that maintains updated records of a mobile station's location area and its serving BSC, as well as the mobile subscriber's identification number and subscribed services. The VLR stores a subscriber's current location in terms of a serving MSC. Note that a subscriber always has a home switching center, in which the VLR keeps track of other switching centers (visited switching centers) in the vicinity of the subscriber at that moment. The AuC controls access to the user data and encryption keys of subscribers in the HLR and VLR, as data transfer in GSM systems is encrypted. The EIR is a database of mobile station device identifications, particularly for stolen and malfunctioning devices. In addition to MSCs and these databases, an operation maintenance center (OMC) is set up to monitor and control MSCs in a region. It generates traffic statistics, failure alerts, and security-related reports.

The communication between an MSC and a BSC is defined in the Signaling System No. 7 (SS7). SS7 is a set of protocols of control signaling for circuit switching networks. In a GSM system, many control signaling are based on SS7.

1.4.1.2 Location Area Update

A mobile subscriber is uniquely identified by the phone number, formally known as the mobile station international ISDN number (MSISDN). An MSISDN number comprises three portions: a country code, such as 1 for the United States and 44 for the United Kingdom; a national destination code; and a subscriber number. Within a GSM system, an internal number, the internal mobile subscriber identity (IMSI), is used to identify a mobile subscriber. This number is stored in the SIM card.

A mobile station constantly monitors broadcast messages from its serving BTS. Once a change has been noticed, an update request, together with the subscriber's IMSI and four-byte temporal mobile subscriber identity (TMSI) number, is sent to the new VLR via the new MSC. A temporary mobile station roaming number (MSRN) is allocated and mapped to the mobile's IMSI by the new VLR and sent to the mobile station's HLR. This number contains the new MSC, the subscriber number, and two other codes of the country. Upon receiving the MSRN, the HLR of the mobile station notifies the old VLR to eliminate the previous record of the mobile station. Finally, a new TMSI is allocated and sent to the mobile station to identify it in future paging or call-initiation requests. Throughout this location area update procedure, the MSISDN number of the mobile station is not used at all.

1.4.1.3 Call Routing

Call routing in GSM systems is performed by a procedure similar to that of location area update. There are two cases: mobile terminated call (MTC) and mobile originated call (MOC). An MTC could be initiated by a landline telephone, a cell phone of other cellular networks such as CDMA, or another GSM mobile station. In the first and second cases, a gateway MSC (GMSC) will take the dialed MSISDN number and determine the HLR of that number. The GMSC then uses the MSISDN number to query the HLR, which returns the current MSRN of the dialed number that identifies the current location. Then, the GMSC is able to route the call to the current MSC of the dialed number. Upon receiving notification of an incoming call to a mobile station currently within its control, the MSC queries its VLR for the TMSI of the mobile station by the MSRN number. After that, a paging message is broadcast among all BSCs of the MSC. The BSC that is serving the desired mobile station will reply to the MSC. Finally, two parties of the call are indirectly located, and the call can proceed. If the call is initiated from one mobile station to another (MOC), a GMSC is no longer necessary; instead, the MSC of the caller will take over, and the remaining procedures are the same. An MOC may target a landline phone number or a cell phone number. In this case, a GMSC that connects two types of networks will link the two parties. In either case, the MSC involved must perform additional tasks so as to validate that the mobile subscribers are allowed to utilize the service.

1.4.1.4 Handoff

The mobility of mobile stations requires that a handoff occur when the subscriber carrying the mobile station moves across cells. Depending on the BTS and MSC arrangement of the fixed cellular network infrastructure, the handoff may occur in the following five scenarios, based on the movement of a mobile station: (1) intracell, (2) intercell but intra-BSC, (3) inter-BSC but intro-MSC, (4) inter-MSC but intranetwork, and (5) internetwork.

Intracell handoff is performed when the channels of a mobile station are changed to prevent narrowband interference. This is managed by the BSC and reported to the MSC. Intra-BSC handoff is the most common type and involves two BTSs in the same BSC. During an intra-MSC handoff, two BSCs within the same MSC manage to allocate channels to the mobile station in the new cell and release old channels used in the previous cell. Intranetwork handoff is carried out when the mobile station moves across the border of cells managed by two MSCs. As long as the mobile station remains in the same network, handoff is transparent to the subscriber, and no communication interruption should occur. For internetwork handoffs, such as roaming across GSM networks of two wireless operators, real-time communication will be interrupted and the connection will have to be re-established. These five scenarios deal with GSM networks only. A handoff between two entities of the same type of network is referred to as a *horizontal handoff for micromobility*. Conversely, a *vertical handoff for macromobility* refers to handoffs between two different types of networks such as handoff between a GSM network and a CDMA network. Supporting vertical handoff is a critical issue in next-generation mobile computing when heterogeneous networks converge to allow ubiquitous mobile access.

Issues surrounding mobile station handoff within GSM networks can be summarized as follows.

- *When should the handoff be performed?* Typically, some periodic measurement is done on the serving BTS of the mobile station to monitor the signal strength between them. Generally, a gradual reduction of signal strength might indicate the mobile station is moving away from the BTS. A number of handoff strategies have been devised to make this procedure smooth and fast. Thresholds and handoff margins are used to determine if a handoff is immediately needed and can be done without frequent back-and-forth handoffs. In addition to signal strength, sometimes a set of performance statistics of a cell is also used to decide if a handoff is necessary for better signal quality. In particular, when the call-blocking probability of a cell is considerably high due to heavy traffic load in a cell, the mobile station may choose to handoff to a neighboring cell.

- *How fast is a handoff?* The duration of a handoff is dependent on several factors, including movement speed of the mobile station, signal strength measurement and reporting interval, and handoff thresholds. Handoff may change the frequency and possibly MSRN of the mobile station, yet all necessary operations have to be done without being noticed by the user during a voice call. The GSM standard requires a maximum duration of 60 msec for a handoff.

1.4.2 General Packet Radio Service

GSM was designed for digital voice communication. As the need for data services such as e-mail, web browsing, and text messaging started to grow substantially, the limited data rate of 9.6 to 14.4 Kbps of GSM systems could not meet the increasing bandwidth demands of these applications. Those readers who have used the very first generation of dial-up modems have some idea of how slow the GSM data rate is. Aimed at leveraging the widely deployed existing GSM systems, general packet radio service (GPRS) has been implemented as a 2.5 G cellular system for value-added data services.

1.4.2.1 Packet Switching

Basically, GSM is circuit-switching based, as are landline telephone networks, meaning that when a channel (one of the eight time slots in TDM) is assigned to a user at the beginning of a connection, it will be exclusively used by the user throughout the connection and will not be shared with others, even if there is really nothing going on for some period of time. For voice communications, this is not a serious problem. After all, people will keep talking during a phone call, and the reserved channels (GSM uses two channels for each connection) facilitate reliable voice communication for the two sides; however, data communication is characterized by bursty transmissions rather than steady streams. For example, if a user visits a website, it is very likely that a few hyperlinked web pages will be downloaded from the web server sequentially but not continuously, as the user will take some time to read a page and decide which page to download next. Allocating a channel for a series of intermittent, bursty data transmissions would obviously be wasteful in terms of system utilization and costs.

On the other hand, the maximum data rate of a channel is significantly lower than what the wired Internet can provide, thereby affecting the acceptance of mobile data applications such as wireless application protocol (WAP), which is a standard set of protocols enabling wireless web applications on a cell phone. Simple aggregation of multiple channels for a data transmission will increase the data rate, but it also means that more system capacity is underutilized due to the characteristics of data transmission.

In contrast, GPRS takes a packet-oriented approach for data transmission and a dynamic, on-demand, bundled time-slot allocation approach for a higher data rate. Because it is unnecessary to reserve a channel, no connection has to be established before data transmission and the air interface for data appears to be always on as long as the mobile station remains active in a GSM network. This is one of the most important and marketable features of GPRS. A data-transfer operation from a mobile station to a specific destination could be spread to multiple time slots within a TDM frame, and several such data-transfer operations could possibly share the same eight time slot. Uplinks and downlinks are allocated separately. The GSM standard defines four channel coding schemes: CS-1 of 9.05 Kbps, CS-2 of 13.4 Kbps, CS-3 of 15.6 Kbps, and CS-4 of 21.4 Kbps. The lower the data rate, the higher the error detection and correction capability. If all eight logical channels are used with CS-1 for a GPRS data transmission, the aggregate data rate will reach 72.4 Kbps. GPRS is designed to coexist with traditional voice services; thus, in reality the number of logical channels available for GPRS is always restricted by system load in addition to demanding data transmission. The characteristics of asynchronous data traffic further limit the number of logical channels for uplink data transmission. Furthermore, power consumption will increase rapidly as the data rate of the transmitter on the mobile terminal increases.

1.4.2.2 GPRS Architecture

Two new components have been added to the GSM network architecture for GPRS: serving GPRS support node (SGSN) and gateway GPRS support node (GGSN) (see Figure 1.4). Like MSCs and BSCs, a GSM network generally has many SGSNs and GGSNs, which constitute a GPRS core network. All other existing GSM components are also involved. Additionally, to support GPRS, the mobile station has to incorporate the GPRS terminal functionality. Ideally, for a BTS, only a software upgrade is necessary to enable voice and data communication via the same radio interface; and it can be done remotely. This way the large amount of BTS hardware and the number of antennas do not have to be changed.

On the BSC, a packet control unit (PCU) device is added to deal with data packets from BTSs. It has two functions: (1) separate packet-switched traffic from circuit-switched traffic originating from mobile stations, and (2) multiplex circuit-switched traffic from the GSM core network and packet-switched traffic from the GPRS core network into an intermingled data frame to serving cells. Packet-switched traffic from a PCU on an MSC is sent to the corresponding SGSN, which keeps track of all serving mobile stations. GGSNs are directly connected to packet data networks (PDNs) such as X.25 or the Internet. To the external networks, a GGSN

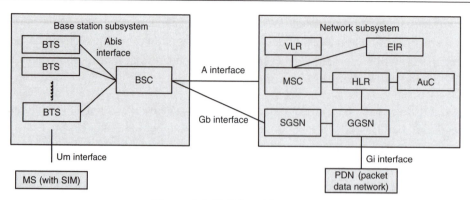

Figure 1.4 GPRS architecture.

appears to be an IP router that takes responsibility for converting and forwarding data packets to destination mobile stations. It achieves this by performing translation between external network node addresses and GPRS mobile addresses and forwarding data to the SGSN responsible for the mobile station in question according to a GPRS tunneling protocol (GTP). Because GPRS data transmission is always initiated from a mobile station, for those mobile stations currently engaged in GPRS data transmission, a GGSN is able to maintain a list of records that map these mobile stations to their serving SGSNs. In reality, IP dominates both the external PDNs and the GPRS core network. GPRS supports both IPv4 and IPv6. The GTP is an IP-based protocol with Transmission Control Protocol (TCP) and User Datagram Protocol (UDP) as transport. As a consequence, the address translation conducted on a GGSN is actually IP network address translation (NAT) that allows mobile stations to use private IP addresses within the GPRS core network. For all mobile stations known to a GGSN, upon leaving the GPRS core network their private IP addresses will be translated into globally unique, routable IP addresses. The GPRS core network may also implement Dynamic Host Configuration Protocol (DHCP) servers and Domain Name System (DNS) servers for dynamic IP assignment and domain name mapping, respectively. The GGSN also performs authentication and collects traffic volume of each subscriber for billing.

1.4.2.3 GPRS Services

GPRS supports both point-to-point (PTP) packet transfer services and point-to-multipoint (PTM) services. The PTP service provides both connectionless mode of PTP connectionless network service (PTP-CLNS) for IP-based data applications and connection-oriented mode of PTP connection-oriented network service (PTP-CONS) for X.25. The PTP-CONS supplies a virtual circuit regardless of the mobile station's location, realized by serving SGSNs and GGSNs. The PTM service essentially offers multicasting among mobile stations in a certain geographic area. To support PTM features, a point-to-multipoint service center (PTM-SC) must be added as well.

1.4.2.4 GPRS Terminals

For mobile stations to use GPRS services, a GPRS terminal that handles packet data transmission via the radio interface is required. A GSM/GPRS cell phone has built-in GPRS terminals. Depending on how these two types of services are offered, three classes of terminals have been defined: class A, which can handle both data and voice simultaneously; class B, which can handle either one but not both at any given time; and class C, which can only attach to one aspect of the services. To date, due to the high cost of class A terminals, most GPRS cell phones are class B terminals on which GPRS data service is suspended during voice calls and short message service (SMS) and resume afterwards. Data-only terminals do not support voice, such as GPRS Personal Computer Memory Card International Association (PCMCIA) cards for laptop computers and personal digital assistants (PDAs).

To identify the capability of a GPRS terminal to use multiple logical channels, 12 multislot classes of GPRS terminals have been defined. Each multislot class specifies the maximum achievable data rates in both uplink and downlink of a data transmission. Written as $d + u$, the first number (d) indicates the number of downlink timeslots and the second number (u) represents the number of uplink timeslots. A third number, the active slots, specifies the total number of time slots that can be used simultaneously for both uplink and downlink data transmission. For example, class 10 represents four downlink slots, three uplink slots, and five active slots. A multislot class and a terminal service class make up a specification of a GPRS terminal. Following the above mentioned example, the class 10/class B designation means that the terminal supports class 10 as the multislot class and can handle both data and voice services but not at the same time (class B).

1.4.2.5 Packet Data Protocol Context

For a mobile station to start a new GPRS session such as WAP browsing, it must obtain a packet data protocol (PDP) address used in the PDN. If the external PDN is the Internet, the mobile station is likely to contact a DHCP server to obtain a dynamic IP address. The key data structure used to map a PDP to the identification of the mobile station is referred to as a PDP context, which consists of the PDP type (e.g., IPv4, or x.25); the PDP address assigned to the mobile station; the requested QoS profile, which specifies the desired service level in terms of delay, throughput, and reliability; and the address of a GGSN that serves as the access point (AP) to the PDN for the mobile station. A PDP context is session-specific and is stored in the mobile station, the SGSN, and the GGSN. The mapping between the PDP and the IMSI of a mobile station allows the GGSN to locate the mobile station with the help of MSCs. For each data session, a different PDP context must be created to allow parallel access to multiple PDNs.

1.4.2.6 Enhanced Data Rates for Global Evolution

Enhanced data rates for global evolution (EDGE) is a further step toward 3G cellular systems by GSM. The objective of EDGE is a high data rate compared to GRPS. EDGE is also known as GSM384, as it can provide a data rate up to 384 Kbps if all eight time slots are used. Recall that GSM/GPRS uses GMSK modulation. EDGE is based on a new modulation scheme, called 8-PSK, that allows a much higher bit rate. In 8-PSK, each symbol transmitted through the air interface carries three bits instead of only one, as in GMSK, thereby greatly improving the data rate. EDGE defines nine coding schemes of different bit data rates. By monitoring the channel-to-interference ratio (C/I), EDGE can automatically switch coding schemes in favor of a higher data rate or reliable transmission. EDGE is also designed to make the convergence of GSM and IS-136 TDMA (D-AMPS) smoother. A major obstacle of this foreseeable convergence is channel bandwidth mismatch. TDMA channels are 30 KHz wide, whereas GSM channels are 200 KHz wide. Compact EDGE was introduced to solve this problem. It uses much fewer frequencies than classic EDGE but has a wider 200-KHz channel. Compact EDGE uses the same modulation scheme as EDGE classic does, with some key exceptions that allow it to be deployed in the spectrum of less than 1 MHz.

1.4.2.7 High-Speed, Circuit-Switched Data

High-speed, circuit-switched data (HSCSD) is an evolutionary technology for GSM systems moving toward 3G UMTS. It can provide a data rate up to 43.2 Kbps using multiple time slots simultaneously. HSCSD allows various error-correction methods to be used, whereas GSM has only one error-correction method to deal with transmission errors in the worst case. HSCSD can also be an option in EDGE and UMTS systems. A major issue that wireless operators must consider while upgrading GSM/GPRS to EDGE or to 3G UMTS/WCDMA is to make the most out of the existing GSM infrastructures. GPRS and EDGE are considered intermediate solutions for early adopters before 3G.

1.5 Code-Division Multiple Access

The notion of CDMA has two distinct meanings: It can refer to the multiplexing scheme of CDMA or it can refer to second-generation cellular systems that use DSSS as the spread spectrum scheme and CDM as the underlying multiplexing technology. Unlike GSM, which is also the name of the standard, the standard for CDMA cellular systems is IS-95.

1.5.1 Code-Division Multiple Access Concept

Section 1.2 introduced CDM. CDMA is actually DSSS utilizing CDM. Like GSM, CDMA uses a dedicated frequency band for multiple simultaneous signal transmission, but what underlies this frequency use scheme is spread spectrum, which essentially spreads a single signal from a transmitter over the entire shared frequency band in such a way that signals will not interfere with each other, thanks to a spreading code assigned to each signal. A single data bit of 1 from a mobile station is mapped to a chip sequence that identifies the mobile station. For a data bit of 0, the complement of the chip sequence is used. The chip sequence is normally 64 or 128 chips long and is pairwise orthogonal, meaning that the normalized inner product (i.e., dot product) of any two distinct chip sequences (they are considered vectors of $+1$ and -1 in mathematical terms) is 0. After the mapping, multiple data bitstreams from different mobile stations are added linearly and transmitted. The intended receiver knows the chip sequence of the individual mobile station and uses it, along with the received aggregated bitstream, to compute data bits of that mobile station. The computation is quite straightforward: Simply compute the normalized inner product of the chip sequence of the desired mobile station and the received bitstream. In this way, the data bits sent by that mobile station will be recovered. Without knowing the correct chip sequence of a transmitter, the computation will yield some pseudorandom bits like noise. An implicit assumption of the decoding procedure is that the receiver and the transmitter are well synchronized in time, which allows the necessary computations for the correct portion of the transmitted bitstream. This is often done by utilizing a special synchronization bit sequence.

The chip sequences assigned to mobile stations can be generated by the Walsh code, an algorithm that produces mathematically orthogonal codes derived from the Walsh matrix. The Walsh-encoded chip sequences appear to be random noise to mobile terminals. Initially, the chip sequences are of equal length. To increase the number of usable chip sequences in the coding space, variable-length chip sequences have been devised and used in today's CDMA systems. Interested readers can refer to A. J. Viterbi's book "CDMA—Principles of Spread Spectrum Communication" for more details of CDMA codes.

1.5.2 IS-95

IS-95 is the underlying standard of CDMA systems. It is worth noting that CDMA is primarily designed and promoted by Qualcomm Inc., which holds key intellectual property rights related to CDMA technology. IS-95 is also commonly referred to as cdmaOne. Table 1.3 outlines key parameters of IS-95.

The forward link refers to the link from a base station to a mobile station, whereas the reverse link is the link from a mobile station to a base station. For both types of links, voice is encoded at a rate of 9600 bps after some error-correction code is added. In a forward link, both data and voice are encoded by a forward error-correction (FEC) scheme, resulting in a doubled bit rate of 19.2 Kbps. In a reverse link, because a different FEC scheme is used, the resulted data rate is 28.8 Kbps. For each forward link, 64 logical channels, each corresponding to a mobile station, are scrambled to prevent repetitive patterns. A reverse link comprises up to 32 logical access channels for paging and 62 logical traffic channels. For both types of links, the DSSS function spreads data of the logical channels over the available frequency range, resulting in an overall 1.228-Mbps data rate. Specifically, a 42-bit-long mask code is used on a reverse link to identify logical traffic channels that are dedicated to connecting mobile stations to a base station. The same mask code is also used to produce a bitstream that will be modulated onto the carrier using orthogonal QPSK or offset QPSK (OQPSK).

Table 1.3 IS-95 Key Parameters.

IS-95 Parameter	Description
Multiple access method	**CDMA with FDM**
Frequency range of downlinks	869–894 MHz
Frequency range of uplinks	824–849 MHz
Number of channels of the frequency range	20
Channel spacing	1.25 MHz
Number of logical channels in forward link	64 (of which 55 can be traffic logical channels)
Number of logical channels in reverse link	94 (of which up to 62 can be traffic channels)
Number of users per channel	798
Voice traffic bit rate	9600 bps
Encoded traffic bit rate in forward link	19.2 Kbps
Encoded data bit rate in reverse link	28.8 Kbps
Chip sequence size	64 bits
Digital modulation scheme of forward link	Quadrature phase shift keying (QPSK)
Digital modulation scheme of reverse link	Orthogonal quadrature phase shift keying (OQPSK)
Channel bit rate	1.2288 Mbps

OQPSK differs from QPSK in that in the implementation of OQPSK one of the two half-rate bitstreams of the original input signal is delayed for one-bit period to reduce phase shift at a time. Because of duplex communication, the total number of reverse-link logical channels for traffic must be the same as the total number of forward-link channels.

1.5.3 Software Handoff

GSM, as well as other TDMA or FDMA systems, uses hard handoff, in which a mobile station will not switch to a new base station until connection to the current mobile station is released. Generally, only when the signal strength of the new base station is sufficiently stronger than that of the current one plus a threshold does the mobile station proceed to connect to the new base station. The reason for utilizing signal strength for hard handoff is frequency reuse among neighbor cells. As a mobile station moves toward a neighboring cell, the signal strength from the new one tends to increase gradually. Unfortunately, such spatial frequency reuse does not exist in CDMA at all. In CDMA, a different handoff approach is used, namely soft handoff. Because all cells essentially use the same frequency band, it is not possible to switch frequency for the handoff. In fact, a mobile station will connect to more than two base stations at a time and constantly monitor the signal strength of them. The handoff will take place only when one of them shows fairly stronger signal strength than others. Before that, all the base stations service the mobile station independently. Soft handoff is advantageous over hard handoff because the mobile station does not lose contact with the cellular network during handoff execution, increasing the possibility of successful handoff. The standard allows up to six base stations to be connected from a mobile station during handoff execution, although in real systems not that many can actually be connected.

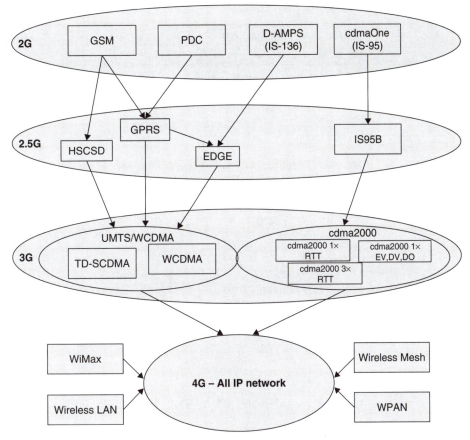

Figure 1.5 Road to 4G.

1.5.4 Road to 4G

IS-95, or cdmaOne, has been designated by Qualcomm as the second-generation digital CDMA cellular system standard. The next generation of cdmaOne is cdma2000, and others are in various stages of development, such as cdma2000 1x RTT, cdma2000 1x EV, cdma2000 1x DV, cdma2000 1x DO, and cdma2000 3x RTT. As mentioned before, the second-generation GSM systems are evolving to a different type of CDMA system: UMTS/ WCDMA. It is quite clear that the concept and underlying technologies of CDMA finally dominate the air interface of the future cellular world, after a long round of debates and remarkable business practices.

Figure 1.5 shows the evolution of 2G cellular systems toward 3G. On the road to 4G, TDMA systems such as GSM, PDC, and D-AMPS may take different paths involving GPRS, EDGE, or HSCSD as 2.5G solutions. Things are much clearer on the CDMA side: cdmaOne (IS-95A) will be first replaced by IS-95B as a 2.5G system, then by cdma2000 systems. The standardization

Table 1.4 Comparison of GSM and CDMA.

Feature	Global System for Mobile (GSM)/ General Packet Radio Service GPRS	Code-Division Multiple Access (CDMA)
Multiple access scheme	Time-division multiple access (TDMA)	CDMA
Duplexing frequency bands	Frequency-division duplex (FDD) 900, 1800, 1900 MHz	FDD 800, 1900 MHz
Channel bandwidth	200 KHz shared by eight time-slotted users	1250 KHz shared by 64 users (codes)
Data rate	Initially 9600 bps, now 38.4 Kbps or 115 Kbps shared by eight users	9.6–14.4 Kbps
Carrier RF spacing	1.25 MHz	200 KHz
Handoff	Hard handoff	Soft handoff
Speech encoding	Fixed rate codec	Variable rate codec
Power control	Open-loop and slow power control	Close-loop and faster power control
Identification	SIM card	Hardwired in the handset
3G	UMTS/WCDMA	cdma2000
Road to 4G	GPRS, EDGE, or HSCSD	cdma2000 1x (IS-95B)
Market	Europe, Asia, Australia, South America, North America, including some U.S. MNOs such as Cingular/AT&T wireless, and T-Mobile	Asia (South Korea and China), Canada, United States; mobile network operators (MNOs) such as Verizon Wireless and Sprint PCS

body supporting UMTS/WCDMA is 3GPP, whereas the counterpart for cdma2000 is 3GPP2. Figure 1.5 also shows wireless networks beyond 3G—the so-called All IP 4G networks.

1.6 GSM Versus CDMA

The two major 2G cellular systems are not compatible with each other. GSM and CDMA networks are both widely used worldwide. For example, in the United States, Verizon Wireless, Sprint PCS, and ALLTEL are CDMA operators, whereas Cingular Wireless, AT&T Wireless (merged with Cingular in 2004), and T-Mobile USA are GSM operators. Another wireless operator, Nextel, uses iDEN, a TDMA technology developed by Motorola. While the Europeans enjoy continent-wide, GSM-dominated wireless services, the world's largest mobile wireless market, China, with a total number of about 398 million subscribers as of 2005 (Source: Computer Industry Almanac Inc.), is basically shared by two companies: China Telecom, which operates a GSM network, and China Unicom, which operates both GSM and CDMA networks. Table 1.4 provides a technical comparison of GSM and CDMA with an emphasis on the data services for next-generation mobile computing. Most differences between the two types of systems have been extensively discussed in the preceding sections, except speech encoding and power control. CDMA employs variable-rate codec for speech encoding, which is more efficient than GSM's fixed-rate codec. Power control of CDMA systems requires a closed-loop approach, thus it is faster than GSM's open-loop approach.

Table 1.5 The 3G Landscape.

3 G Systems	Key Features	IMT Proposal	Radio Interface
Universal mobile telecommunications system (UMTS)/wideband code-division multiple access (WCDMA)	144 Kbps satellite and rural outdoor, 384 Kbps urban outdoor, 2048 Kbps indoor and low range outdoor	IMT 2000 CDMA direct spread by 3GPP	Direct-sequence spread spectrum (DSSS) CDMA; both frequency-division duplex (FDD) and time-division duplex (TDD) are used
cdma2000 1x RTT	Also known as cdma2000 1x MC (multiple carriers); data rate up to 144 Kbps	IMT 2000 CDMA multicarrier by 3GPP2	Uses a 1.25-MHz band, coexistent with IS95
cdma2000 1x EV-DO	Downlink (forward-link) data rates up to 3.1 Mbps and uplink (reverse-link) rates of 154 Kbps		Backward compatible with cdmaOne
cdma2000 1x EV-DV	Downlink (forward-link) data rates up to 3.1 Mbps and uplink (reverse-link) rates of up to 451 Kbps		Backward compatible with cdamOne
cdma2000 3x RTT	2–4 Mbps		Uses three 1.25 MHz bands
TD-SCDMA (Time Division–Synchronous Code Division Multiple Access)	2 Mbps	IMT-2000 CDMA TDD by China	TDMA and CDMA combined

1.7 3G Cellular Systems

There is some debate over which cellular systems are so-called 3G systems, especially with regard to EDGE and some cdma2000 systems. Because GPRS and EDGE are GSM based, it is fairly intuitive to put them into the 2.5G category. In the CDMA camp, one cdma2000 system, called cdma2000 1x RTT, has been arguably considered a 3G system. Generally, all cdma2000 and UMTS/WCDMA systems may be considered 3G systems, as shown in Table 1.5.

The International Telecommunication Union (ITU) made a request for proposal (RFP) in 1997 for cellular technologies for the International Mobile Telecommunication (IMT)-2000 program. A proposal for a UMTS was submitted by the European Telecommunication Standards Institute (ETSI) to ITU. Its radio interface is universal terrestrial radio access (UTRA). In addition to the proposals and systems outlined in Table 1.5, other 3G radio access technologies are listed as follows:

- IMT-2000 TDMA single carrier, originally promoted by the Universal Wireless Communications Consortium (UWCC); EDGE is one of the IMT-2000 TDMA SC technologies.

- IMT-2000 FDMA/TDMA, also known as DECT, the enhanced version of the cordless phone standard.

1.7.1 UMTS/WCDMA Versus cdma2000

A UMTS system works in two modes: Its frequency-division duplex (FDD) mode is the well-known wideband CDMA (WCDMA), whereas its time-division duplex (TDD) mode seems to remain unnoticed by the public. The cdma2000 is the evolution of cdmaOne, the current CDMA system in the United States. In fact, strictly speaking, WCDMA only refers to the radio interface aspect of the entire UMTS system. The same radio interface technology is used by NTT DoCoMo and J-Phone (a subsidiary of Vodafone) as well. As an FDD system, WCDMA does not require time synchronization among base stations. It allows a bit rate up to 384 Kbps, compared with the maximum rate of 2 Mbps in TDD UMTS systems. In particular, China has proposed a TDD UMTS system, called TD-SCDMA, and is vigorously promoting this technology among Chinese telecommunications device manufacturers and wireless operators.

The cdma2000 is a general term representing technical specifications such as cdma2000 1x RTT, cdma200 1x EV-DO, cdma2000 1x EV-DV, and cdma2000 3x RTT. RTT stands for radio transmission technology, EV-DO for evolution-data optimized, and EV-DV for evolution-data and voice. 1x RTT can provide a peak rate of 153.6 Kbps, while 3x RTT may theoretically offer a peak rate of 3.09 Mbps. The first commercial system of cdma2000 1x EV-DO was launched in South Korea in January 2002. The cdma2000 is backward compatible with existing IS95/cdmaOne systems, whereas WCDMA requires an overhaul of existing base stations. There is no synchronization in WCDMA systems, thus sophisticated protocol designs and handoff mechanisms are not required. On the other hand, cdma2000 requires base-station synchronization. In some sense, WCDMA can be seen as an opportunity for operators to challenge Qualcomm's CDMA technology monopoly. Readers interested in the evolution of mobile networks are encouraged to refer to Vriendt et al. [2].

1.7.2 UMTS/WCDMA

A UMTS system comprises three components and two interfaces (see Figure 1.6). The components are the user environment (UE), the UMTS terrestrial radio access network (UTRAN), and the core network (CN). The interface between UE and UTRAN is referred to as Uu. The interface between UTRAN and a Node B is Iub. UMTS introduces Node Bs as base stations (BTSs in GSM) and radio network controllers (RNCs) as BSCs in GSM. Similar to GSM and GPRS, MSCs and SGSNs control RNCs through the Iu interface. In particular, an MSC connects to an RNC through an Iu–CS (circuit-switching) interface, whereas an SGSN connects to an RNC through an Iu–PS (packet-switching) interface. In UMTS, GMSCs and GGSNs connect to PSTN and PDNs. Other components such as HLR and VLR are the same as in GSM but with enhanced functionality for UMTS.

UMTS uses a pair of 5-MHz channels, one in the 1900-MHz range for uplink and one in the 2100-MHz range for downlink. In contrast, cdma2000 uses one or more arbitrary 1.25-MHz

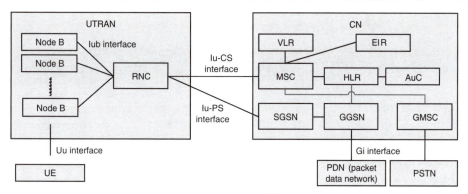

Figure 1.6 UMTS architecture.

channels for each direction of transmission. UMTS is expected to deliver a user data rate of 1920 Kbps, although in reality 384 Kbps is probably what the system can really offer. A future version of UMTS/WCDMA, high-speed downlink packet access (HSDPA), will offer data speeds up to 8–10 Mbps and 20 Mbps MIMO antenna systems. The data modulation scheme is QPSK for uplink and BPSK for downlink. The chip rate is 3 M chips per second.

As a spread spectrum radio interface, WCDMA uses soft handoff just as cdmaOne does for the same reason: It is quite difficult to control power beyond the hysteresis if hard handoff is employed because in CDMA systems forcing a mobile station to operate over some hysteresis level will cause large interference.

The first UMTS network went into operation in the United Kingdom in 2003. AT&T Wireless in the United States deployed UMTS in selected cities in late 2004. Japan's largest telecommunication service provider NTT DoCoMo launched the first WCDMA-based 3G network, dubbed Freedom of Mobile Multimedia Access (FOMA), in 2001.

1.7.3 cdma2000

cdma2000 is another standard under the ITU-2000 program (see Figure 1.7). It comes in two stages: 1x and 3x. Using the existing cdmaOne infrastructure, cdma2000 1x can supply a maximum user data rate of 207 Kbps and a typical data rate of 144 Kbps in general. It doubles the voice capacity of cdmaOne systems and offers six times the capacity of GSM or TDMA systems. cdma2000 3x further improves the user data rate to 2 Mbps.

In cdma2000, three major components exist in the overall network architecture: mobile station, radio access network, and core network. The interface between a mobile station and radio access network is called Um, and the interface between radio access network and core network is called A. In addition, the core network can be further decomposed into two

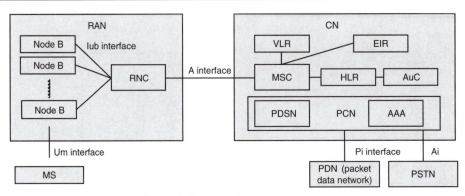

Figure 1.7 cdma2000 architecture.

portions: One portion, the packet core network (PCN), connects to external IP networks via a Pi interface, whereas the other connects to PSTN via an Ai interface. Similar to a UMTS network; the core network of cdma2000 also has MSCs, HLRs, and VLRs. The principal difference between the core network of cdma2000 and those of other cellular systems is the PCN that provides IP network access to mobile stations. A component in PCN, the packet data service node (PDSN), performs roughly the same task as an SGSN in UMTS or GPRS; however, in cdma2000, two IP access methods are provided: simple IP access and mobile IP access. Simple IP access is the traditional way to obtain and retain an IP address within a geographically located subnet. When the mobile station moves to another subnet, it has to redo the DHCP procedure and obtain a new IP address. This is the case when a mobile worker uses a laptop computer to connect to an enterprise network across several buildings. Mobile IP access enables a mobile station to use the same IP address across different regions. In this case, a *home agent* of the mobile station will assume the responsibility of maintaining the same IP address for the mobile station. A *foreign agent* that is part of the PDSN is used to assign a temporary address to the mobile station that just moved in, and tunnels packets from the home agent to the mobile station. Note that GPRS has only a single IP access method: the simple IP access. It has to be emphasized that cdma2000 has better IP support. This is indeed a tremendous advantage of cdma2000 over UMTS, as in the long run the core cellular network will be interoperable with other wired or wireless networks with IP as the underlying network protocol.

Another major task of the PCN is authentication, authorization, and accounting (AAA). Three parties are involved: home AAA (HAAA), broker AAA (BAAA), and visited AAA (VAAA). HAAA stores a subscriber's profile information. Once requested by a VAAA, it will authenticate and authorize a subscriber and send the response back to the VAAA. For accounting, VAAA is able to receive accounting information from HAAA and provides the subscriber's profile to the PDSN. BAAA is used as an intermediate server when VAAA and HAAA are not directly associated with each other.

1.7.4 4G Cellular Systems

As of 2004, UMTS/WCDMA and cdma2000 3G services have been rolled out in a number of countries and continue to gain some ground among business professionals. It is widely agreed that 3G will replace 2G and 2.5G systems in the next several years, providing a seemingly high throughput of several megabits per second for a mobile station. While this data rate seems sufficiently large for popular applications such as text messaging and web browsing on a cell phone, it cannot meet the relentless demand of emerging applications such as full-motion video broadcasting and videoconferencing. In response, researchers have moved on to 4G cellular systems, which provide even higher data rates of 20 to 100 Mbps. It has to be noted that wireless LANs can now provide data rates of up to 54 Mbps, much higher than current and future variants of 3G systems, whether UMTS or cdma2000. On the other hand, a significant effort has been made to coalesce voice and data communication in all 3G systems to leverage the legacy systems as much as possible. As voice over IP technology matures, an all-IP wireless network that supports voice and data over the same packet-switching infrastructure will become technically feasible to build and will be more cost-effective than current 3G frameworks. Emerging technologies for 4G wireless networks are summarized as follows; note that the application of these technologies is not limited to cellular systems:

- Smart antenna technologies exploit spatial separation of signals to allow an antenna to focus on desired signals as a way to reduce interference and improve system capacity.

- MIMO utilizes antenna arrays at both the transmitter end and receiver end to boost the link data rate and system capacity. MIMO takes advantages of multipath propagation of signals by which more data can be sent in a single channel by splitting and recombining data onto multiple paths.

- OFDM, multiple-carrier-code-division multiple access (MC-CDMA), modulation, and multiplexing technologies will improve the robustness of signal transmission and the data rate.

- Software radio or software-defined radio will make it possible to reconfigure channel modulation and multiplexing on the fly.

In a broader vision, 3G cellular systems are merely one type of wireless access in the world of mobile computing. Other wireless access technologies, such as wireless LANs and WiMax, have demonstrated great potential to become a primary means of network access, as shown in Figure 1.5. These technologies may complement each other and may certainly compete head-on with each other in a variety of industry segments, leading to coexistence and integration of these systems and spurring new services and applications. The following section talks about a galaxy of new services and applications in the wireless arena.

1.8 2G Mobile Wireless Services

Aside from traditional voice services, other cellular wireless services have proliferated in some countries. For example, SMS is a vastly successful service in some Asian countries and has become a major revenue source to MNOs. Customized mobile web surfing also gain some ground as WAP and iMode mature. In this section, we will discuss these two types of 2G mobile wireless services.

1.8.1 WAP and iMode

WAP is an open-application layer protocol for mobile applications targeting cell phones and wireless terminals. It was developed by the WAP Forum, which has been consolidated into the Open Mobile Alliance (OMA)[3]. The current release is WAP 2.0. WAP is intended to be the World Wide Web for cell phones. It is independent of the underlying cellular networks in use. To a cell phone or PDA user, WAP is perceived as a small browser application that can be used to browse some specific websites, quite similar to the web browsing experience on a desktop computer but with significant constraints due to the form factor of the mobile terminal. A WAP system employs a proxy-based architecture to overcome the inherent limitations of mobile devices with respect to low link bandwidth and high latency. Below is a list of features that separate WAP from other application protocols:

- Wireless markup language (WML), WML script, and supporting WAP application environment: Together, they are referred to as WAE. WML is an HTML-like markup language specifically devised for mobile terminals that have limited bandwidth, fairly small screen size, limited battery time, and constrained input methods. WSL is a scaled-down scripting language supported by the WAP application environment. In addition, WAP 2.0 supports XHTML language, which allows developers to write applications for both desktop computers and mobile terminals.

- WAP protocol stack: WAP Version 1.0 includes wireless session protocol (WSP), wireless transaction protocol (WTP), wireless transport layer security (WTLS), and wireless datagram protocol (WDP). Version 2.0 incorporates standard Internet protocols into its protocol stack, such as TCP, transport layer security (TLS), and Hyper Text Transport Protocol (HTTP). Both TCP and HTTP are optimized for wireless environments.

- WAP services, such as push and traditional request/response, user agent profile, wireless telephony application, external functionality interface, persistent storage interface, data synchronization, and multimedia messaging service.

WAP 1.0 has proved to be a technological hype; it has been intensively promoted by wireless operators and content providers but has received little, if any, positive feedback from users.

Because of that, WAP has sometimes been referred to as "wait and pay." Interestingly, it is not only the protocol but also the applications utilizing WAP that, as a whole, push users away because of application performance, input methods, and the GUI interface, among other reasons. Moving toward standard IP protocols rather than specialized wireless protocols, WAP 2.0 addresses most of the problems of the protocol stack and the application environment, thereby giving the technology a brighter future.

iMode is a successful wireless application service provided by NTT DoCoMo. It is very similar to WAP in that it defines an architecture of web access on mobile terminals, primarily cell phones. Like WAP 2.0, iMode adopts standard Internet protocols as transport for applications, but iMode does not use any gateways. Instead, it utilizes overlay packet network on top of a cellular network for direct communication. The fundamental difference between WAP and iMode is that iMode requires mobile terminals to be designed to adapt to the services and applications of iMode, while WAP focuses on adapting itself to fit into general mobile terminals. Furthermore, NTT DoCoMo's effective WAP initiative has managed to attract many satisfied providers who can offer a wide array of services and applications to users [4].

1.8.2 Short Message Service

No one ever expected that SMS would be such a tremendous success, one that exemplifies the perfect marriage of a business model with a wireless technology. European and Asian subscribers have been using SMS for years. More than a billion SMS messages are sent each month in some countries. Finally, as of 2004, SMS began to take off in North America. SMS allows two-way transmission of 160-character alphanumeric messages between mobile subscribers and external computing systems such as e-mail systems and paging systems. Because of its increasing popularity, SMS has been extensively combined with many new types of information services in addition to traditional usage. For example, both Google and Yahoo offer Internet searching via SMS. SMS was initially designed to replace alphanumeric paging service with two-way guaranteed messaging and notification services.

Two new types of SMS components have been added to the cellular network: short message service center (SMSC) and signal transfer point (STP). An SMSC is a central controller of SMS services for the entire network. It interfaces with external message sources, such as voice-mail systems, e-mail systems, and the web. Messages sent from a mobile subscriber will also be stored and forwarded by the SMSC. An STP is a general network element connecting two separate portions of the network via SS7 signaling protocol. In the case of SMS, numerous STPs interface with the SMSC, each handling SMS transmission and delivery to and from a large number of mobile stations. No matter where the messages come from, the SMSC will guarantee delivery and inform the transmitter. For the SMSC to locate a mobile station for message delivery, it must utilize the cellular network, especially the HLR, VLR, and MSC of the mobile station.

SMS has been enhanced with new capabilities to support enhanced message service (EMS) and multimedia message service (MMS). If you consider SMS to represent very early plain-text e-mails, you might think of EMS as the fancier HTML e-mails containing pictures, animations, embedded objects such as sound clips, and formatted text. MMS is the next-generation messaging service that supports rich media such as video and audio clips. The wide use of picture messages sent from a camera cell phone is merely one example of MMS in action. MMS consumes more bandwidth so it requires a high data rate for the underlying network and considerable computing capability of the mobile handset. The multimedia service center (MMSC) performs similar tasks as the SMSC for SMS. The following list outlines the necessary steps of an MMS procedure:

- The transmitter sends a message to the MMSC from a cell phone, PDA, or networked computer.

- The MMSC replies to the transmitter with a confirmation of "message sent." In fact, it is not sent to the receiver yet, as the message is stored at the MMSC.

- The MMSC locates the receiver with the help of a number of cellular network elements, such as MSCs, HLRs, and VLRs. If the mobile station of the receiver is ON, the MMSC sends a notification of a new message to it, along with a URL to the new message. Otherwise, it waits and tries again later.

- The receiver can choose to download the message right away or save the URL to download it later.

- The MMSC will be notified by the receiver that the message has been downloaded and presumably read. Then the MMSC notifies the transmitter that the message has been delivered.

MMS is the natural evolution of SMS, with EMS as an optional intermediate messaging service, but it is very unlikely that MMS will replace SMS completely as plain text messages are preferable in many cases. Additionally, MMS does not require 3G; it can be done in 2.5G systems such as GPRS and EDGE. Problems that may hinder the widespread use of MMS include digital rights management of content being exchanged among many mobile subscribers, development of a user-friendly interface design, and sufficiently large bandwidth for message delivery.

1.9 Wireless Technologies Landscape

In the wireless world, aside from cellular technologies, myriad wireless technologies have emerged and matured. At the eve of the new millennium, "wireless" typically referred to the use of cell phones. After only a few years, the dramatic growth of new wireless communication and

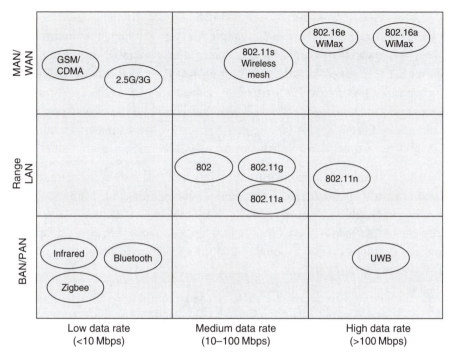

Figure 1.8 Wireless technology landscape.

computing technologies has fundamentally changed our perception of wireless technologies. This section discusses these technologies from an overall perspective. Once again, the emphasis of the discussion is on mobile data access in the greater domain of mobile computing, rather than on wireless communication. Figure 1.8 depicts the landscape of existing and emerging wireless technologies with respect to two significant characteristics pertaining to mobile computing: data rate and signal transmission range. As the figure suggests, cellular systems are positioned in a grid of low data rate and high signal range. Wireless LANs (the 802.11 family) provide medium and high data rates in a local area range. Within the body area network (BAN)/ personal area network (PAN) range, UWB is expected to supply a quite high data rate, whereas Bluetooth, ZigBee, and infrared fall into the low data rate range. For PTP and multipoint wireless communications, 802.16a and 802.16e offer a high data range for communication over a metropolitan area network (MAN). A broad set of applications has been created to make use of the data rates in each range for various cases where wireless communication is preferred.

1.10 802.11 Wireless LANs

A wireless LAN is a LAN that utilizes radio-frequency communication to permit data transmission among fixed, nomadic, or moving computers. Wireless LANs can be divided into two operational modes: infrastructure mode and ad hoc mode, depending on how the network is formed. Most wireless LANs operate in infrastructure mode. In many cases, a wireless LAN is used to avoid the hassle of establishing a wired LAN (e.g., cabling in a multiroom building or a large open space such as a warehouse or a manufacturing plant). Several computers are connected over the air to a central AP that in turn links to the wired network. At the same time, a laptop computer with a wireless LAN interface is able to access the backend wired network across different APs in an intermittent or real-time fashion. In all these scenarios, a wireless LAN infrastructure of networked APs is needed. These APs may connect directly to each other via wireless links or rely on the wired network for interconnection.

Ad hoc mode is more flexible than infrastructure mode in that it does not require any central or distributed infrastructure devices or computers to operate. Instead, computers in an ad hoc wireless LAN temporarily self-organize into a group to serve each other in a peer-to-peer manner. In some cases when it is not feasible to build a network infrastructure for technical or other reasons (e.g., troops on the battlefield or sports spectators in a huge stadium), an ad hoc wireless LAN seems a good solution.

Today, the dominant radio-frequency technology used to build a wireless LAN is a spread spectrum on the unlicensed 2.4-GHz frequency band, as defined in the IEEE 802.11 standards and ETSI HIPERLAN (High-Performance Radio Local Access Network). Other radio-frequency technologies such as infrared wireless LANs and narrowband microwave LANs have faded away following the explosive growth of spectrum wireless LANs. The following is a list of advantages of radio-frequency wireless LANs over infrared; narrowband microwave LANs are not considered because they are primarily used for PTP wireless communication rather than group communication:

- High bandwidth: 802.11 wireless LANs support a link bandwidth up to 11 Mbps for 802.11b and 55 Mbps for 802.11a and HIPER-LAN2, much higher than that of infrared, which is only up to several megabits per second.

- No LOS restriction: Infrared requires LOS for transmission, but radio does not as long as the frequency in use is not too high. This is the major reason why 802.11 wireless LANs are the number one choice for home networking.

- Easy to set up and use: The 802.11 protocols are designed to allow almost zero configuration of the network and the interfaces. Of course, the default setting is by no means secure but it does work.

1.10.1 Architecture and Protocols

According to the IEEE 802.11 standard, a basic service set (BSS) is a number of computers equipped with wireless LAN interfaces connecting to an AP. Multiple APs can be connected to a wired or wireless distribution system (DS), whereas several BSSs interconnected via the DS comprise an extended service set (ESS) uniquely identified by an extended service set identifier (ESSID) or SSID. The APs may broadcast the ESSID such that anyone within its coverage is able to discover it and configure the wireless LAN interface to participate in the ESS. If the ESSID is not broadcast, users have to know it from other sources in order to access the network.

In many ways, wireless LANs are designed to be the wireless equivalent of LANs such as Ethernet; consequently, similar to other 802 LAN standards, these IEEE 802.11 standards define two bottom layers of protocols: physical layer (PHY) and medium access layer (MAC), retaining the upper layers of the TCP/IP stack. These two layers essentially hide the underlying low-level details of data transmission and medium access, supplying the same interface to the logical link control (LLC) sublayer of data link as that of a wired LAN. Hence, applications will not detect any difference when running in a wired LAN or a wireless LAN. The various 802.11 wireless LAN standards differ only in physical layer (i.e., frequency band being used), signal multiplexing schemes, modulation schemes, and data rates.

According to the MAC layer of 802.11, to ensure reliable frame transmission between two stations an acknowledgment (ACK) frame will be sent from a destination station to the source station when the destination receives a data frame from the source. If no ACK is received at the source, it may simply retransmit the data frame. The MAC layer of 802.11 also employs the carrier sense multiple access/collision avoidance (CSMA/CA) medium access mechanism to provide reliable frame transmission service, formally known as the distribution coordination function (DCF), which was defined as a sublayer of MAC. On top of it is a partial sublayer, the point coordination function (PCF), as shown in Figure 1.9. Two traffic services are supported by 802.11: asynchronous data service and time-bounded service. The first is commonly the best effort service, while the latter can guarantee a maximum delay but relies on a centralized polling master to offer contention-free service. DCF supports

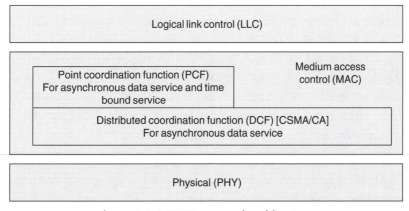

Figure 1.9 802.11 protocol architecture.

asynchronous data services only in either infrastructure mode or ad hoc mode, whereas PCF is used for time-bounded service only in infrastructure mode. In particular, in addition to a general CSMA/CA mechanism, DCF has an optional MAC mechanism that addresses the hidden terminal problem and exposed terminal problem (discussed shortly). On the other hand, the contention-free service offered by PCF is realized by a centralized polling master called the point coordinator. 802.11 defines a time interval called superframe that consists of two separated stages, first for the poll and second for regular asynchronous contention-based access. The resulting effect resembles time-division multiple access, where each station receives an evenly distributed share of the bandwidth.

Radio communication is via a shared medium. To use the shared medium, a station must first sense the communication channel (the carrier) and make sure it is not occupied, a procedure called CSMA. If the channel is idle, it can begin to transmit; otherwise, it will wait for a random amount of time with a contention window and sense the channel again. In addition, the radio communication of wireless LANs is a half-duplex operation in that it cannot transmit and receive at the same time. This is because when the station is transmitting the strength of its own transmission will mask all other signals nearby in the air. Recall that, for Ethernet, collision detection (CD) is used (by monitoring abnormal current of the wire) when a station is sending data. In wireless LANs, such an approach is not possible because a station has no way to detect a collision while sending data; therefore, collision avoidance is used instead of CD and is implemented by a three-way handshake protocol described as follows.

Due to spatial limitations of signal strength, a station may not draw a correct conclusion on the channel usage, leading to signal interference or channel underutilization. Usually, collisions occur when a station is receiving two signals at the same time. This "hidden terminal" problem is depicted in Figure 1.10a. In the figure, station B initiates a transmission to A, and station C also begins transmitting to A at the same time because C, after sensing the channel, is unaware of B's transmission. Hence, two simultaneous transmissions cause interference at A. In this case, C is a hidden terminal to B.

Another problem is the "exposed terminal," where the transmission of station B to station C effectively prevents B's neighbor (A) from transmitting because A senses the channel and finds B is using it; however, A, the exposed terminal, should be able to transmit to D without any problem, as A cannot reach C and the transmission from A to D should not affect the ongoing transmission from B to C. The exposed terminal problem causes channels to be underutilized and thereby reduces the data throughput of the system. Figure 1.10b shows the exposed terminal problem.

To address these problems, some sort of coordination of channel use among stations is needed. The MAC layer of 802.11 solved the problems by introducing a handshake protocol along with small request-to-send (RTS) and clear-to-send (CTS) frames. An RTS frame is first sent from the source to the destination. Then, if the destination is not receiving, it replies

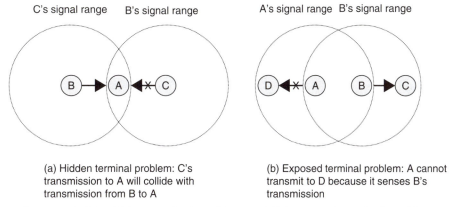

(a) Hidden terminal problem: C's transmission to A will collide with transmission from B to A

(b) Exposed terminal problem: A cannot transmit to D because it senses B's transmission

Figure 1.10 (a) Hidden terminal problem and (b) exposed terminal problem.

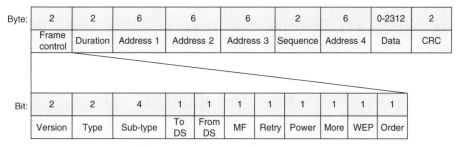

Figure 1.11 802.11 frame format.

with a CTS frame. Upon receiving the CTS frame, data frame transmission can begin. With this enhancement, both the hidden terminal and exposed terminal problems are avoided. For the hidden terminal problem, C will not receive CTS until the transmission from B to A is over. Thus, it will refrain from transmission to A during that period. For the exposed terminal problem, between B and C, B first sends an RTS to C. A also receives this RTS. Then C sends a CTS message to B indicating that B's transmission to C can begin. This CTS message will not reach A, meaning that the RTS it received belongs to a transmission beyond its coverage (B to C, in this case). Thus, A can safely proceed to send frames to D. Note that RTS and its CTS both contain the time duration of the data transmission plus ACK transmission. Stations that must refrain from this imminent data transmission will have to wait until it is over and then contend for the channel (CSMA). Collisions may only occur when multiple stations access the channel by sending RTSs or data frames.

1.10.2 Frame Format

The 802.11 frame format is depicted in Figure 1.11. The figure on the top shows the frame structure of nine fields in bytes. The figure on the bottom shows the first field, the frame control field, in bits. Depending on the control field, some of the other fields may contain specific information:

- Frame control: Indicates the frame type and provides related control information.

- Duration/connection ID: Duration indicates the time in microseconds that the channel is occupied which it can be used for network allocation vector computation during the RTS/CTS exchange. The field may also be used as a station ID for power-save poll messages.

- Address 1–4: Up to four 48-bit addresses can be specified in these four fields. The usage of these four fields depends on the To DS and From DS bits in the frame control for both ad hoc mode and infrastructure mode. These addresses may specify a frame source station, a frame destination station, a transmitting station or AP, and a receiving station or AP.

- Sequence control: Contains a 4-bit fragment number for fragmentation and reassembly and a 12-bit sequence number to detect duplicates.

- Frame data: Up to 2312 bytes of data can be transmitted with one frame.

- CRC: Contains a 32-bit cyclic redundancy check of the frame.

The following fields are defined in the frame control:

- Version: Indicates 802.11 version number (0).

- Type: These two bits indicate frame type: management, control, or data. Management frames are used for communication between stations and APs such as association, dissociation, probing, and beaconing. Control frames are used to provide reliable frame delivery service.

- Subtype: Depending on the type of field, subtype further identifies the function of a frame.

- To DS: This field is set to 1 if the frame is destined to a DS from a station or an AP to another AP.

- From DS: This field is set to 1 if the frame is leaving from a DS for a station or an AP. This field is set when a frame is sent from an AP.

- MF: Indicates that more fragments follow the current one.

- Retry: Indicates that this frame is a retransmission of a previous one that does not has an ACK.

- Power control: This field is set to 1 if the transmission station is in sleep mode; it is set to 0 if it is in active mode.

- More data: Indicates that the transmitter has more data for the intended receiver. If the transmitter is an AP, the field informs a station in sleep mode that more data are buffered at the AP.

- WEP: This field is set to 1 to indicate that the frame body is encrypted using the WEP algorithm (described later).

- Order: This field is set to 1 to inform the receiver that a number of fames are in strict order.

1.10.3 Beacon Frame

802.11 beacon frames are used for a number of purposes including time synchronization, power saving, and AP discovery. Like other types of frames, a beacon frame contains source MAC address and destination MAC address. The source MAC address is the physical address of the AP that sends the beacon, whereas the destination MAC address consists of all 1s for broadcasting. A number of fields make up the beacon frame body, such as beacon interval, timestamp, SSID, supported data rates, wireless LAN capability, and traffic indication map (TIM). Beacon interval and TIM are used for power management. A station may sleep to save power and only wake up periodically to check if the associated AP has some buffered frames destined for it. The beacon interval indicates the next time a beacon from the AP will be sent and whether there are buffered frames at the AP. The TIM will further inform listening stations which ones have buffered unicast frames at the AP. Stations will go back to sleep if no buffered unicast frames are intended for them. Others will stay awake to receive the buffered unicast frames. The timestamp in a beacon frame allows a station to synchronize its local clock with the AP, as time synchronization is needed for DCF and physical layer signal transmission. SSID identifies the underlying ESS. A station can automatically associate to an AP by reading beacon frames from it. Some vendors have an option to disable SSID in beacon frames to enhance security. The supported rates field in a beacon frame tells stations which data rates are supported by the AP. The wireless capability field indicates the requirements of stations that wish to participate in the wireless LAN.

1.10.4 Roaming in a Wireless LAN

Roaming in wireless LANs is conducted in a nomadic way: Connection to the current AP will be lost before a new one is discovered and associated with it. If a mobile station is moving within a set of APs sharing the same ESSID, what is needed is a layer-2 roaming procedure that does not involve IP change. The procedure is also called roaming in a roaming domain or a broadcast domain and is briefly outlined as follows:

- The station senses a roaming operation is necessary based on monitored signal strength, frame acknowledgment, and missed beacons, if any. The client then starts the roaming procedure by looking for adjacent APs.

- The station scans for APs. It can perform active scanning by sending out probe messages on each channel or passive scanning in which it silently listens to beacon messages of an AP. Either approach can be taken before or after the decision to roam. Beacon messages and probe response messages have necessary information used to associate to the new AP.

- The station tries to associate itself with a new AP by sending an association request message. The AP will reply with an association reply message, and the station can then participate in the new BSS.

The 802.11 standard does not specify the algorithm to determine when roaming is needed and the algorithm to scan APs. Products from different vendors are likely to be incompatible in their support of roaming among different APs. To address this issue, the IEEE 802.11f (Inter Access Point Protocol, or IAPP) working group has been formed and a standard for roaming among APs in the same network segment has been devised. The IAPP protocol defines a set of operations for APs to handle roaming stations. It can be implemented using UDP/IP or SNAP (Sub Network Access Protocol). Two basic operations are *announce* and *handover*. The 802.11f does not support cross-subnet roaming, meaning that vendors will still have to design proprietary protocols for wireless handoff and routing.

Roaming across different roaming domains requires layer-3 operations in addition to layer-2 operations because a mobile station will obtain a new IP address while moving to a new network segment. The association process and authentication based on 802.11i may introduce a delay of hundreds of milliseconds. For ongoing data connections, this does not result in noticeable downtime, but for voice traffic it is noticeable. As voice over wireless LAN is gaining some traction, fast roaming that eliminates noticeable disconnections primarily for voice traffic is needed. To speed up authentication, 802.11i has been enhanced with *key caching* and *preauthentication*. Key caching caches a user's credential on the authentication server so users do not need to reenter that information when they return to the system. Preauthentication allows a station to be authenticated to an AP before moving to it. On the other hand, IEEE 802.11r working group was formed to solve the fast roaming problem.

Another imminent problem in this realm is roaming among Wi-Fi hotspots operated by wireless internet service providers (WISPs). The Wi-Fi Alliance has published *WISPr Best Current Practices for Wireless Internet Service Provider (WISP) Roaming*. WISPr recommends that WISPs adopt a web-browser-based universal access method (UAM), which essentially specifies some log-on/log-off web pages for user authentication using a web browser. Remote Authentication Dial in User Service (RADIUS) is the preferred AAA protocol for Wi-Fi roaming. AAA data exchange among WISPs allows users to be authenticated and billed for services by their home entities (the users' WISPs). For details of WISPr, please consult the WISPr document at http://www.wi-fialliance.org/opensection/wispr.asp.

Table 1.6 802.11 Wireless LAN Technologies.

	802.11b	802.11a	802.11g	802.11n
Maximum data rate (Mbps)	Up to 11	Up to 54	Up to 54	108–320 Mbps
Frequency band	2.4 GHz	5 GHz	2.4 GHz	2.4 GHz
Modulation	CCK (Complementary Code Keying)	OFDM	CCK and/or OFDM	OFDM
Number of nonoverlapped channels	3	8–12	3	Not yet specified
Range (meter)	100	50	100	100
Power consumption	Low	High	Low	Low

1.10.5 IEEE 802.11 Family

Within the IEEE 802.11 family, a few wireless LAN technologies represent the evolution and refinement of wireless LANs. Table 1.6 provides a comparison of these technologies. Note that, to the general public, Wi-Fi is probably the term that links to 802.11 wireless LANs. The Wi-Fi Alliance is a nonprofit industry association formed in 1999 to certify the interoperability of wireless LAN products based on IEEE 802.11 specifications. It has over 200 member companies. The goal of the Wi-Fi Alliance is to enhance the user experience through product interoperability and, understandably, promote the wireless technology and products for business interest.

The initial 802.11:1997 standard contained three incompatible options—infrared, FHSS, and DSSS—to support data rates of 1 to 2 Mbps. For FHSS, 79 channels are allocated in the 2.4-GHz ISM band in the United States and Europe. For DSSS, an 11-chip Barker sequence is used. A Barker sequence is a special binary sequence of -1 and $+1$ possessing mathematical characteristics that can be utilized to improve a coding scheme's robustness and error-correction capability. Only a few Barker sequences are known. The one that is 11 in length is used in the initial 802.11 DSSS, which only supports data rates of 1 and 2 Mbps. The updated 802.11b:1999 standard discontinued further specification of infrared and FHSS, focusing instead on only enhancements to DSSS WLANs. 802.11b added new 5.5- and 11-Mbps data rates based on CCK modulation, a new chip sequence using 8-chip complementary code keying. Wi-Fi-certified products implement DSSS as defined by 802.11b:1999, supporting both 1 and 2 Mbps with the Barker code and 5.5–11 Mbps with CCK. 802.11b defines a total number of 14 channels separated by a 5-MHz gap, from 2414 to 2484 MHz, but only 11 are usable due to FCC regulations in the United States. Furthermore, for DSSS to operate, the bandwidth of these channels should be 22 MHz apart in the frequency domain. As a result, only channel 1 (2412 MHz), channel 6 (2437 MHz), and channel 11 (2462 MHz) can be used at the same time. In Europe, these channels are channel 1 (2412 MHz), channel 7 (2442 MHz), and channel 13 (2472 MHz).

In 802.11a, OFDM is used instead of DSSS. 802.11a operates on the UNNI 5-GHz band with a total number of 12 non-overlapping channels. Channel spacing is 20 MHz. Recall that OFDM leverages multiple carriers (52 in the case of 802.11a) of different frequencies to transmit the same bitstream. Each channel of 802.11a leverages 52 subcarriers that are evenly separated by a distance of 312.5 KHz, plus some virtual subcarriers that are not used. The data rates of 802.11a are 6, 9, 12, 18, 24, 36, 49, and 54 Mbps, each of which is realized by a combination of a specific PSK or QAM digital modulation scheme and OFDM symbol setting.

802.11g wireless LANs operate at the 2.4-GHz band but can offer much higher data rates, up to 54 Mbps. To be backward compatible, 802.11g incorporates 802.11b's CCK to achieve bit transfer rates of 5.5 and 11 Mbps in the 2.4-GHz band. To obtain higher data rates at the 2.4-GHz band, it adopts 802.11a's OFDM scheme. Use of the 2.4-GHz ISM band permits 802.11g to have almost the same signal coverage as 802.11b.

802.11n is the latest wireless LAN standard and promises to offer data rates up to 108–320 Mbps at the 2.4-GHz ISM band. As of this writing, no official release has been made by the IEEE 802.11n working group. Two proposals are being considered, and it is unclear which one will finally win. One group, TG n Synch, advocates using a 40-MHz bandwidth for each channel. The competing World Wide Spectrum Efficiency (WWiSE) group wants to retain the 20-MHz bandwidth (as in 802.11b, a, and g) and utilize 2×2 MIMO (two transmitters and two receivers in each device) and OFDM. Recall that MIMO is in essence a spatial-division multiplexing technology that leverages multipath propagation to generate quasi-independent paths in space in order to boost the capacity of the system.

In addition to new wireless LANs, some other 802.11 working groups are focusing on specific issues of general wireless LANs. For example, 802.11c and 802.11d work on wireless switching that enables extension of wireless LANs, while 802.11e emphasizes providing QoS support at the MAC layer for audio and video services. Probably the most notable one is 802.11i, the new security mechanism to replace WEP and intermediate WPA (see below).

HIPERLAN is a wireless standard developed by ETSI. HIPERLAN version 1 offers up to 10 Mbps of data rate within a range of 50 m, targeting the wireless home networking market. HIPERLAN version 2 was actually codeveloped with 802.11a. As a result, HIPERLAN/2 uses the 5-GHz UNNI band and provides data rates up to 54 Mbps. An interesting component of the HIPERLAN/2 is the so-called *convergence layer* defined in its protocol stack. The convergence layer unifies the data-link layer (*data-link control* layer in HIPERLAN terminology) functionality of various wireless access technologies and provides a unified interface and services to the network layer. This enables a HIPERLAN/2 node to interconnect with heterogeneous networks such as UMTS and the Internet. The standard specifies a cell-based convergence layer for ATM networks and a packet-based convergence layer for general packet-switching networks.

1.10.6 Security in Wireless LANs

Security was undoubtedly the biggest problem of wireless LANs. It has been shown that air serves as an excellent field for network-based hacks and attacks targeting wireless LANs. The topmost security issue of wireless LAN is no security at all. Wireless LANs without any security configuration account for most home wireless networks and many enterprise wireless LANs. In most cases, these open wireless LANs allow any computers with a wireless LAN interface to join the network with little or no trouble. Some security professionals have demonstrated this problem by driving around an area in a city and detecting available wireless LANs along the road, an activity called "war driving" [5]. Another major problem of wireless LANs is the security mechanism of 802.11 protocols: wired equivalent privacy (WEP), the first security mechanism implemented in 802.11b, has proved to have a serious flaw in the key scheduling algorithm that may result in unauthenticated access. New security standards have been devised and incorporated in 802.11.

1.11 Bluetooth

1.11.1 Architecture and Protocols

Bluetooth is probably the most widely used Wireless Personal Area Network (WPAN) technology now. A WPAN is a small-scale wireless network that connects a few computing or communication devices in the range of several meters. A WPAN may comprise a wide range of fixed or mobile devices that have been equipped with radio interfaces, such as computers, cell phones, PDAs, mp3 players, portal game devices, digital cameras, digital camcorders, and so on. The vision of mobile computing encompasses a more rapid and broad proliferation of WPAN technologies in our daily lives that renders convenient and high-performance data access among any intelligent electronic devices. This section and the following section introduce two wireless PAN technologies: the widely used Bluetooth and the emerging UWB.

1.11.2 Bluetooth Overview

Harald I. Bluetooth (Danish Harald Blåtand), King of Denmark between 940 and 985 AD, conquered Norway in the year 960 AD. His "bluetooth" was a result of eating too many blueberries. More than 1000 years later, in 1994, his nickname was used to name a wireless technology that connects cell phones or other devices without using cables. The company that took the initiative to invent the short-range, low-power, and low-cost radio technology is Ericsson. In February 1998, an industry consortium, called Special Interest Group (SIG), of Bluetooth was formed by five companies—Ericsson, Nokia, IBM, Toshiba, and Intel—across three different sectors of the industry. Ericsson and Nokia were major cell phone manufacturers, IBM and Toshiba were major laptop computer manufacturers, and

Intel's strength was signal processing (in addition to computer processors). In July 1999, the Bluetooth SIG released a 1500-page specification (Bluetooth 1.0). In 2001, the first Bluetooth-enabled products, primarily cell phones and PDAs, were announced. More than 1500 companies adopted Bluetooth for their products. To date, Bluetooth has become the de facto short-range wireless technology for mobile devices. The IEEE 802.15 working group for personal area networks has adopted Bluetooth as one of the IEEE 802.15 standards: IEEE Std 802.15.1-2002. Other 802.15 standards are 802.15.2 for the coexistence of WPAN and wireless LAN, 802.15.3 and 802.3a for UWB, and 802.15.4 for ZigBee. The features of Bluetooth are summarized as follows:

- Short range: 10 to 100 m.
- Low cost: less than $5.
- Low power: 10 to 100 mW.
- Low data rate: 1 to 2 Mbps.

The interoperable applications of Bluetooth fall into the following categories:

- Cable replacement: Computers are notorious for having cluttered cables for various peripherals such as a keyboard, a mouse, speakers, and a headset. More and more people use an earpiece connected to a cell phone while making a call. It would be far more convenient to have wireless connections between the peripherals and the devices. Bluetooth can be used for this purpose.
- Ad hoc data networking: As more mobile devices are used by the general public, ad hoc networking capability is often desired to facilitate occasional data transfer and interaction. Bluetooth is designed to allow effortless network setup of a number of compatible devices in a short range.

It is worth noting that Bluetooth and wireless LANs are not exactly targeting the same application scenarios of wireless connectivity, even if both of them (i.e., 802.11b wireless LANs and Bluetooth) operate at the same 2.4-GHz band. Bluetooth by and large is used for power-limited mobile devices for data transfer within a person's reach, which is why it is considered a WPAN technology. Wireless LANs, on the other hand, provide much higher bandwidths over a longer distance but consume more power.

1.11.3 Bluetooth Architecture

The basic unit of a Bluetooth network is a piconet consisting of up to eight devices. One of the devices is the designated master, which actually controls all the other slave devices in terms of radio communication, data transfer, and security mechanisms. Bluetooth uses frequency-hopping spreading spectrum for its radio interface. Each slave will be notified with the same frequency-hopping sequence by the master; thus, all devices in a piconet

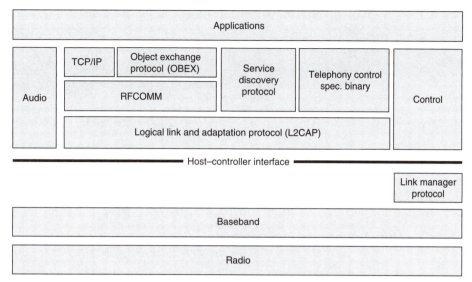

Figure 1.12 Bluetooth protocol stack.

hop simultaneously on the same sequence. Communication between any two of the eight devices has to go through the master in a time-division manner, sharing the 1-Mbps data rate. Multiple piconets can connect together via some overlapping devices, forming a scatternet.

How do two Bluetooth devices communicate with each other? To answer this question, one needs to first look at the Bluetooth protocol stack, which makes up the core portion of the Bluetooth specification. Figure 1.12 shows a simplified protocol stack of Bluetooth. Keep in mind that the official Bluetooth specification has incorporated many new protocols that can be divided into two categories: core specification and profile specification. The core specification is mainly concerned with the physical layer and data-link layer, whereas the profile specification covers the applications and functions required for Bluetooth to support data or voice wireless applications. In addition, the Bluetooth protocol stack architecture has been designed to facilitate the operation of many existing commonly used protocols on top of the core protocols. The basic functions of each component in the Bluetooth protocol stack are summarized in Table 1.7. The "Adopted" category refers to existing protocols. Key components are discussed to explain how Bluetooth supplies desired data services as follows.

1.11.4 Radio and Baseband

The radio layer of Bluetooth utilizes the 2.4-GHz ISM band, the globally free available frequency band, for spread spectrum communication. About 79 MHz of bandwidth is used for frequency hopping, with 1-MHz carrier spacing. The modulation scheme is GFSK at a rate of 1 bit per Hz, providing a data rate of 1 Mbps. The frequency-hopping rate is 1600 hops per

Table 1.7 Bluetooth Protocol Stack Components.

Protocol Stack Component	Category	Description
Radio	Core	Radio signal modulation and transmission
Baseband	Core	Frequency-hopping and time-division multiplexing between a master and its slaves
Link manager protocol (LMP)	Core	Establishment of logical channels, authentication, and power management
Host controller interface	N/A	Software interface to baseband and link manager, as well as Bluetooth hardware status and registers
L2CAP (logical link control and adaptation protocol)	Core	Adaptation of upper layer services and application to the Bluetooth; key component of Bluetooth stack from application developer's point of view
Control	Adopted	Control over link manager protocol
Radio Frequency Communication (RFCOMM)	Cable replacement protocol	Emulation of serial line interface following the widely used EIA-232 (formerly known as RS-232) standard
Service discovery protocol (SDP)	Core	Discovery of services provided on Bluetooth devices
Telephony control specification, binary (TCS-BIN)	Cable replacement protocol	Establishment of speech and data calls between a master and a slave
Object Exchange Protocol (OBEX)	Adopted	Exchange of structured data objects such as calendar, vCard (electronic business card), and calendar entries
Audio	Adopted	Supporting audio communication directly on top of baseband

second with a dwell time of 625 μsec. As a WPAN, the radio interface of Bluetooth imposes strict emitted power control. Three classes of transmitters are defined based on power and signal transmission range.

- Class 1 outputs a maximum of 100 mW and a minimum of 1 mW for the greatest distance (around 100 m without obstacles). Power control is mandatory.
- Class 2 outputs power between 0.25 and 2.4 mW for a range of about 10 m without obstacles. Power control is optional.
- Class 3 outputs around 1 mW with range of a few meters or less.
- The power control algorithm can be implemented in the link control protocol and controlled by the *control* component in the protocol stack.

The baseband layer controls transmission of frames in association with frequency hopping. The master in a piconet takes the channel to transmit in even-numbered hops, and slaves transmit in odd-numbered hops, reflecting a time-division duplex for all devices in a piconet. A single frame can be transmitted in the duration of one, three, or five hops. Depending on the nature of the logical link between a slave and the master, two types of links are offered.

One is the asynchronous connectionless (ACL) link for best-effort packet data transmission. The other is synchronous connection oriented (SCO) for time-critical data such as voice. Frames sent on ACL links may have to be transmitted if lost, whereas frames sent over SCO links will never be retransmitted, necessitating upper layers for error correction.

The baseband layer has defined some types of frames that correspond to various purposes of the baseband frames. Different types of frames can carry different sizes of payload data and error-correction schemes. In particular, the access code field in a baseband frame indicates the purpose of the frame in a special state. For example, a frame with the inquiry access code (IAC) will be sent when a device elects to scan for other devices within the radio range in a series of 32 frequency hops. Bluetooth devices can be configured to periodically hop according to the inquiry scan hopping sequence to scan inquires. When an inquiry is detected, the device, now the slave, will reply with its address and timing information to the master, then the master and the slave begin the paging process to determine a common hopping sequence to establish a connection. Eventually, both the master and the slave will hop on the same sequence of channels for the duration of the connection.

1.11.5 L2CAP and Frame Format

The L2CAP layer loosely matches the data-link layer of the OSI model. Apart from framing and multiplexing of packet streams, it also supplies QoS for the ACL links. Two alternatives services are provided:

- Connectionless service: Datagram-like service without establishing a connection.

- Connection-mode service: A connection is required before a data exchange between the master and a slave.

- Three types of channels are provided by the L2CAP layer. For each type, a channel identification (CID) is assigned to identify the channel in use:
  1. Connectionless: Unidirectional channel used primarily for broadcasting by the master. A slave can only have one connectionless channel to the master. Its CID is 2. Connectionless channels are used to implement connectionless service.
  2. Connection-oriented: Full-duplex channel for connection-mode service. Between a slave and the master there can be multiple connection-oriented channels, each of which is identified by a unique CID larger than 63.
  3. Signaling: This is not for data exchange but for signaling between L2CAP entities.

Protocol Data Units (PDUs) handled by the L2CAP layer are of a similar format across the three types of channels. In addition to the payload data (in the case of a signaling command PDU, the payload is the command representation), a field of PDU length and a field of CID are encapsulated. CIDs of connection-oriented channels are used to conduct multiplexing and demultiplexing of upper layer data sources. For connectionless channels, a PDU that is carried by the channel has a protocol/service multiplexing (PSM) field to indicate its upper layer source. On the transmitter side, the L2CAP-layer PDUs may be fragmented into small segments if the underlying logical channel cannot send packets of that length.

1.11.6 RFCOMM

Radio-Frequency Communications (RFCOMM) is a cable replacement protocol that can be used to connect two Bluetooth devices using a virtual serial line interface. It emulates the 9-pin circuit of an RS-232 interface. Multiple emulated serial connections (up to 60) can be multiplexed into the same Bluetooth connection, while the actual number of connections supported is implementation-specific. A complete communication path involves two applications running on two devices with a communication segment between them. The applications utilizing RFCOMM treat the connection as a regular serial line connection via one of its serial ports.

In Bluetooth, a profile is a set of interrelated protocols and pertinent parameters that are chosen for a specific user case. The profile that accounts for virtual serial line communication is the serial port profile, which includes RFCOMM, service discovery protocol (SDP), LMP, and L2CAP in addition to base band and radio. The serial port profile essentially defines a PTP wireless link between two Bluetooth devices that can be used by the general network layer. The two Bluetooth devices are called *endpoints*, each identified by a unique address. SDP is the protocol used to obtain the address of the other endpoint.

1.11.7 SDP

A service is a shared function that provides some data and performs an operation on behalf of a consumer. Service discovery is a key issue in an ad hoc network environment such as Bluetooth piconet or PTP direct communication. The SDP in Bluetooth defines a simple request-and-response mechanism that uses service records and service classes for service discovery and browsing. A Bluetooth device that is configured to offer a service should implement an SDP server. The service is described in a service record with a number of service attributes. A service record is identified by a 32-bit handle. A service attribute consists of an attribute ID and a value. SDP defines the following attributes: ServiceRecord-Handle, ServiceClassIDList, ServiceRecordState, ServiceID, ProtocolDescriptionList, BrowseGroupList, LanguageBaseAttributeIDList, ServiceInfoTimeToLive, ServiceAvailability, BluetoothProfileDescriptorList, DocumentationURL, ClientExecutibleURL, IconURL, ServiceName, ServiceDescription, and ProviderName. Semantics of the attributes are further structured into service classes. As a result, a service record must have a ServiceClassIDList attribute that contains a list of service classes representing the general and exact descriptions of capabilities of the underlying service. Each class ID is a universally unique identifier (UUID) that is guaranteed to be unique in space and time.

Before service discovery between two Bluetooth devices occurs, they must be powered-on and initialized such that a Bluetooth link between them can be established, which may require the discovery of the address of the other device by initiating an inquiry process and the paging of the other device, as introduced in the previous section. Then a client can search for desirable services using a list of service attributes or browse the services offered by an SDP server by issuing a specific UUID of the BrowseGroupList attribute that represents the root browse service group of the SDP server. All services that may be browsed at the top level are members of the root browse group.

1.11.8 Bluetooth Evolution

Since its inception, the Bluetooth SIG has made significant effort to improve and promote the technology. In response to feedbacks on Bluetooth specification 1.1, the Bluetooth SIG has released versions 1.2 and 2.0 of the specifications. Enhancements of Bluetooth include high data rates, interference resistance, and security. As shown in the protocol stack, Bluetooth supports both voice and data, and audio communication can be built directly on top of baseband. Bluetooth audio communication provides two types of encoding schemes: PCM and continuously variable slope delta (CVSD). The voice channels support 64 Kbps. A piconet can have up to three simultaneous full duplex voice channels. For asymmetric data transmission, the data rate can be as high as 721 Kbps one way and 57.6 Kbps the other way. For symmetric data transmission, the maximum data rate is 432.6 Kbps. Bluetooth 1.2 and 2.0 are expected to support a maximum data rate of 2.1 Mbps. The 2.4-GHz ISM band is used by many wireless enabled devices; thus, the potential interference between Bluetooth devices and others such as wireless LANs has to be addressed. Bluetooth 1.2 incorporates adaptive frequency hopping (AFH), which allows the selection of idle frequencies for frequency hopping, thereby improving resistance to interference.

Bluetooth security has been criticized to some extent due to the user's lack of total control over wireless connections and data transmission. Bluetooth provides link-level authentication and encryption using unit address, a secret authentication key, a secret privacy key, and a random number. A number of concerns have been raised over Bluetooth security mechanisms as a result of a few proof-of-concept attacks on communication and user data, such as Bluesnarfing and Bluejacking.

1.12 Ultra-Wideband

UWB is a disruptive short-range radio-frequency wireless technology that could provide a potential solution to many problems in the WPAN communication and computing domain, such as low data rate and insufficient frequency. Despite the standardization controversy with

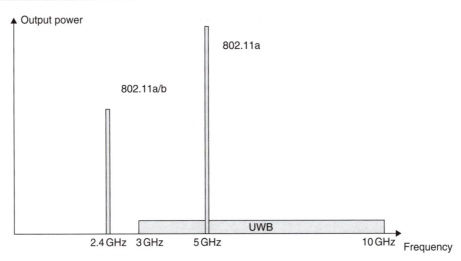

Figure 1.13 Ultra-wideband.

regard to UWB, commercial UWB products were demonstrated at the Consumer Electronics Show in early 2005. Prototypes of UWB-enabled cell phones, HDTVs, DVD players, and music players are expected to hit the market very soon. One example of such an effort is the wireless USB technology, a short-range wireless connectivity technology resembling the wired USB standard. UWB was initially developed in the 1960s for high-resolution radar communication. The primary inventor of UWB was Gerald Ross, who held several patents for this technology. UWB was originally referred to as "baseband," "carrier-free," or "impulse." In 1978, Bennett and Ross published a seminal paper on UWB titled *Time-Domain Electromagnetics and Its Applications*. The year 1986 saw the birth of the first UWB system, and the FCC approved the marketing and operation of UWB in 2002.

The FCC's First Report and Order [6] defines a UWB device as any device-emitting signals over a bandwidth that is 20% greater than the center frequency or a bandwidth of at least 500 MHz at all times of transmission within a frequency band between 3.1 and 10.6 GHz, as shown in Figure 1.13. UWB devices operate by emitting a large number of very short pulses (often of a duration of only nanoseconds or less) of signals over a wide bandwidth within a range of 10 m, resulting in an unprecedented data rate on the level of several hundred megabits per second. UWB does not require any dedicated frequency allocation. Instead, it is designed to operate in frequency spectrum occupied by existing radio technologies. The channel capacity of UWB is linearly proportional to the bandwidth occupied for signal transmission. The advantages of UWB include:

- High data capacity: Due to the use of wide bandwidth, UWB offers very high data capacity, up to several gigabits per second.

Table 1.8 Ultra-Wideband System Comparison.

	802.15.3	802.15.3a Proposals
Frequency allocation	3.1–10.6 GHz	3.1–10.6 GHz
Channel bandwidth	15 MHz	500 MHz–7.5 GHz
Number of radio channels	5	1–15
Spreading	—	Multiband OFDM or DS-CDMA
Digital modulation	QAM and DQPSK	BPSK and QPSK
Range	10 m	2–10 m
Data rate	11 Mbps (QPSK) to 55 Mbps (64 QAM) with a minimum of 22 Mbps	110 Mbps at 10 m, 200 Mbps at 4 m, up to 1300 Mbps at 2 m
Emitted power	200 mW	100 mW or −41.3 dBm/MHz

- Use of a license-exempt frequency band: As a short-range wireless technology, UWB does not require any licensed frequencies to operate.

- Low power: The output power of UWB is at the level of less than 1 mW, compared with tens to a few hundred milliwatts of wireless LAN APs; typically 3 mW is allowed for a cell phone.

- Resilient to multipath fading and distortions: Because the signal is transmitted over a wide bandwidth with sufficient redundancy, fading and distortion are significantly reduced.

- Security: UWB is inherently secure. Like other spread spectrum technologies, the signal appears to be random noise to outsiders.

1.12.1 UWB Standards

The first standard for UWB was IEEE 802.15.3, which was released in 2002. This standard does not offer many advantages for wireless services and applications, as the data rate can be easily obtained in a wireless LAN (see Table 1.8). A new workgroup, IEEE 802.15.3a, was formed to address high data rate UWB standardization. Two major proposals from different groups of companies are under review: multiband OFDM (MB-UWB) and DS-CDMA. Table 1.8 provides a comparison of the 802.15.3 UWB system and the forthcoming 802.15.3a UWB system.

1.12.2 UWB Applications

In addition to military use of the UWB technology, many companies are working to bring UWB to industrial operations and to people's daily lives. The application scenarios of UWB for the consumer market can be summarized as follows:

- High-speed data transfer between mobile devices in a WPAN: Given a data rate of 100 to 500 Mbps at a distance of 1 to 10 m, computers, PDAs, cell phones, and consumer electronic devices are able to exchange data much faster than via other wireless technologies. The first wave of UWB products will probably target wireless home networks, where interconnection between a wide range of computing, communication, and consumer electronic devices has always been a troublesome problem.

- Cable replacement: It may be possible to link an LCD screen or a television to a computer or any other UWB-enabled electronic devices without using a video cable. The data rate may be further improved to 1 to 2.5 Gbps but only within a short distance of several meters. This would allow video streaming over a number of wireless devices, ranging from handheld mobile devices to computers and HDTVs.

- Wireless measurement in a short distance: An example of this application scenario would be measuring the oil level in a storage tank.

- Location and movement detection: Used in vehicular radar systems, UWB devices can detect the locations of fixed or moving objects near a vehicle. Such information can be used for various applications such as collision avoidance in a parking lot.

- Inventory tracking and supply chain management: Products in a warehouse or a store can have embedded UWB RF tags containing a small amount of data, permitting any UWB readers to access such information.

1.13 Radio-Frequency Identification

RFID is a wireless radio-frequency technology that allows objects, persons, and spaces to be remotely identified using low-cost electromagnetic tags. In its simplest form, an RFID tag attached to an object can store data that can be used to identify the existence of the object or maintain other information regarding the object. The RFID technology has been in place for more than 40 years, primarily being used in a very narrow range of industrial and military applications and remaining unnoticed by the mass market. In the last several years, RFID technology has matured in many ways such as a longer signal range, faster data transfer rate, and shorter tag reading intervals. The reduced cost of RF tags has fostered mass deployment and use of this technology. The retail chain company Wal-Mart was arguably the strongest driving force behind the application of RFID technology. The company requires its top 100 suppliers to have RF tags attached to pallets and cases by 2005 following the Electronic Product Code (EPC).

1.13.1 RFID System

The form factor of RF tags varies largely, but the components that make up a tag are usually the same: a transponder, an antenna, and a tiny integrated circuit (IC). For example, some tags are in the form of planar labels with an aluminum spiral coil on a polymer substrate and delivered in reels, and a flip-chip at its center. Figure 1.14 shows four such tags. The antenna

Figure 1.14 High-frequency passive RFID tags. (Photograph courtesy of Texas Instruments; © Copyright 1995–2005 Texas Instruments Incorporated.)

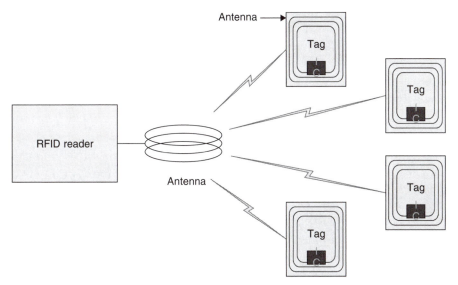

Figure 1.15 An RFID system.

of a tag (the dark lines circling the tag in Figure 1.15) is printed on the tag. Depending on how they are powered, RF tags can be divided into two categories: passive tags and active tags. A passive tag does not have a battery; it relies on the interrogation signal from the reader to transmit data back to the reader using a transponder and a small antenna. An active tag has a battery and an onboard transceiver. Compared with passive tags, active tags provide a long signal range but at a high cost.

A typical RFID system is composed of readers and tags, as shown in Figure 1.15. A reader is electronic equipment composed of a transceiver and an antenna. Some readers can even be

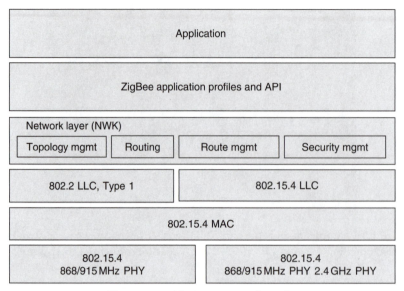

Figure 1.16 ZigBee protocol stack.

integrated into a mobile device such as a PDA or a cell phone. A reader is able to interrogate many tags at a time within its transmission range. Once interrogated, a tag will respond with a unique digital ID. The reader then uses the ID to retrieve corresponding information from a backend database. Examples of potential IDs that can use RFID include bar codes, license plates, student and employee IDs, conference attendee IDs, passports, ISBNs of publications, and software license keys. Some tags allow the reader to "write" or modify the stored information.

The frequency bands used by RFID communication are 100–500 KHz, 10–16 MHz, 850–950 MHz, and 2.4–5.8 GHz. Modern RFID systems choose to operate on high-frequency bands in order to achieve a higher data rate and longer signal range. The downside of choosing a high-frequency band is the LOS requirement. Collision will occur if two tags respond to the same interrogation from a reader; thus, some readers can only read one tag at a time. Others implement anticollision mechanisms to schedule the tags' responses, making it possible to read multiple tags simultaneously. The standard of RFID radio interfaces for different frequency bands is ISO/IEC 18000 created by ISO/IEC/JTC1/SC31.

1.13.2 RFID Applications

RFID technology has already been used by many industry sectors ranging from security systems in a building to automatic toll systems on highways. The cost of each passive tag is expected to eventually drop to less than 5¢, thereby making it cost effective to deploy tags for a vast number of objects for tracking and monitoring that otherwise would be highly error-prone and labor-intensive. Active RFIDs can be used in the following applications:

- Warehouse inventory tracking for logistics and supply chain management (tags can be embedded into pallets, cases, and containers);

- Equipment maintenance in a hospital and part tracking in a factory;

- Vehicle tracking and toll payment, such as EZPass on some U.S. highways;

- Product and book positioning in a store, warehouse, manufacturing plant, etc.

Passive tags are powered by signals from a reader via magnetic induction. Passive tags can be used in the following applications:

- Automated entry in security systems that currently utilize pass-code entry pads and magnetic card swipe machines (tags would be embedded into personal IDs that are scanned wirelessly at the point of entry);

- Product tagging in a store, replacing bar codes and UPCs (e.g., smart grocery stores and smart department stores);

- Wild animal, livestock, and pet tracking on farms and by pet-control organizations;

- Vehicle antitheft systems;

- Luggage tagging in airports;

- Pallet and case tracking for retailers;

- Passport control in customs, airports, and government offices (U.S. passports will soon have embedded RFID tags).

Needless to say many potential applications overlap the two categories. Depending on specific application scenarios and business objectives, users may choose either active tags or passive tags to fulfill their needs in a cost-effective manner. In addition, a smart phone or a smart handheld device with built-in or attached RFID readers can replace specific reader devices in many circumstances. Conversely, a smart phone may contain an RF tag that is mapped to the phone user.

RF tags may be combined with wireless sensors to extend the capability of the RF system. Embedded sensors in tagged objects allow real-time monitoring of some environmental factors within the proximity of the objects. In addition, in the long run, RF tags may use tiny microprocessors and store more valuable data in local memory. They can even self-organize into a network with collaborative ambient intelligence and in-network information processing without readers.

As is true for many pervasive computing technologies, RFID raises some privacy concerns with regard to tagging and our daily lives. Imagine a world where everything is tagged and readers are everywhere. From the point of view of a manufacturer or retailer, real-time supply chain visibility boosts productivity and aids future product development by providing extensive information regarding consumers (e.g., who they are, where they are, and when and how they use the products). But consumers, for the most part, may not want to reveal this information to those manufactures and retailers. Suppose a consumer purchases an electronic shaver that has an embedded RF tag uniquely identifying the shaver. When the consumer travels with the shaver, he may be tracked by any RF readers that can reach the shaver. These privacy issues are very common in the mobile computing domain, as wireless technologies tend to pervade our lives to an unimaginable level of imbedding and integration.

1.14 Wireless Metropolitan Area Networks

Wireless MANs refer to a set of wireless data networks that provide wireless data access in a metropolitan area. The principal advantage of building wireless MANs for data access as opposed to establishing a wired network infrastructure is the cost of copper-wire or fiber optic cable, installation, and maintenance. In rural areas and developing countries where telephone lines and cable televisions are not in place, a wireless data access solution is more cost-effective than a wired network solution. Depending on how wireless technologies are used in the infrastructure, wireless MANs can be categorized into the following types:

- Wireless "last mile" (fixed broadband wireless access),
- Wireless data access for mobile terminals,
- Wireless backbones or wireless mesh.

The first type is still based on a wired network infrastructure; that is, base stations connect directly to a backend wired network. PTM wireless communication replaces wired network communication between a base station and the end-user's computer, the so-called "last mile." Telephone-line-based last-mile access allows dial-up data access and ADSL (with necessary modems), whereas cable-television-based last-mile access permits higher bandwidths and an always-on connection. Dedicated T1 is commonly used by businesses. For the general public, these Internet service providers coined the terms "broadband Internet" or "high-speed Internet access" in order to differentiate high-speed data access services such as ADSL and cable television from traditional dial-up service. In fact, one of the driving forces behind the wireless last-mile technology is that the broadband Internet access of ADSL and cable has grown rapidly in recent years.

The second type of wireless MANs targets mobile data access. In a sense, 2.5G and 3G cellular networks could be considered wireless MANs or wireless WANs as they have provided wide-area mobile data access for cell phone users. On the other hand, it would be natural to speculate on extending wireless LANs to cover a larger area and to allow roaming across areas covered by these base stations. Still, this type of wireless MAN relies on a wired

Table 1.9 IEEE 802.16 Summary.

Feature	Description
Frequency band	10–66 GHz, 2–11 GHz
Range	Up to 40 km (about 30 miles)
Multiplexing/modulation	OFDM, adaptive modulation
Channel data rate	75 Mbps for both uplink and downlink
Antenna	Directional antenna, point-to-multipoint
Multiple access	Demand-assignment multiple access–time-division multiple access (DAMA-TDMA)

network infrastructure to function, as the base stations connect directly to a wired network. Many proprietary wireless MANs have been in operation for years. They mainly target a very narrow business market such as mobile professionals, rather than the general public.

The third type of MAN is a pure wireless network, in which backbones as well as the means of access are both wireless. Base stations are not connected to a backend wired network; instead, they coordinate with adjacent base stations, forming a mesh for data forwarding over a wide area. This is a significant development with regard to providing data access services to underdeveloped areas where no fixed networks exist.

1.14.1 Wireless Broadband: IEEE 802.16

The most noticeable technological development in wireless MANs and wireless WANs are embodied by the IEEE 802.16, 802.20, and ETSI HIPERMAN standards. Based on the open IEEE 802.16 and HIPERMAN, a commercialized technology called WiMax has been devised. The WiMax Forum, an industry consortium of over 100 companies, has been formed to promote the technology and provide certified, interoperable WiMax products. IEEE 802.16 specifies the PHY and MAC layers. It will support higher network layers and transport layer protocols such as ATM, Ethernet, and IP. Characteristics of IEEE 802.16 are listed in Table 1.9.

It is noteworthy that the frequency band of 10 to 66 GHz specified by the initial 802.16 standard requires LOS transmission. Some other frequency bands are also specified in later versions of the standard in order to provide indoor wireless access. The MAC layer portion of 802.16 addresses QoS by introducing a bandwidth request and grant scheme. Terminals can be polled or actively signal the required bandwidth, which is based on traffic QoS parameters. 802.16 employs a public-key infrastructure in conjunction with a digital certificate for authentication.

Extensions of IEEE 802.16 include:

- 802.16a, which specifies a data rate up to 280 Kbps per base station over the 2- to 11-GHz frequency band reaching a maximum of 50 km and mesh deployment.
- 802.16b, which addresses QoS issues surrounding real-time multimedia traffic.

- 802.16c, which defines system profiles that operate at 10–66 GHz for interoperability.
- 802.16d, which represents system profile for 802.16a devices.
- 802.16e, which standardizes handoff across base stations for mobile data access.

The ETSI HIPERMAN standard is similar to 802.16a. It has been developed in very close cooperation with IEEE 802.16, such that the HIPERMAN standard and IEEE 802.16a standard can work together seamlessly. As a result, many of the characteristics of 802.16 are available in HIPERMAN, such as QoS support, adaptive modulation, and strong security. HIPERMAN supports both PTM and mesh network configurations. The differences between HIPERMAN and 802.16 are primarily on the PHY layer. In order to create a single interoperable standard for commercialization, as well as product testing and certification, several leaders in the wireless industry formed the WiMax Forum. Another IEEE working group, called IEEE 802.20 Mobile Broadband Wireless Access (MBWA), uses the 500-MHz to 3.5-GHz frequency band for mobile data access, an application also targeted by 802.16e; however, 802.20 does not have as strong industry support as 802.16 does.

1.14.2 WiMax

The WiMax Forum harmonizes IEEE 802.16 and ETSI HIPERMAN into a WiMax standard. The core components of a WiMax system include the subscriber station (SS), also known as the customer premise environment (CPE), and the base station (BS). A BS and one or more CPEs can form a cell with a point-to-multipoint (PTM) structure, in which the BS acts as central control over participating CPEs. The WiMax standard specifies the use of licensed and unlicensed bands within the 2- to 11-GHz range, allowing non-LOS (NLOS) transmission, which is highly desired for wireless service deployment, as NLOS does not require high antennas in order to reach remote receivers, which reduces site interference and the deployment cost of CPE. NLOS raises multipath transmission issues such as signal distortion and interference. WiMax employs a set of technologies to address these issues [7]:

- *OFDM*: As discussed earlier in this chapter, OFDM uses multiple orthogonal narrowband carriers to transmit symbols in parallel, effectively reducing ISI and frequency-selective fading.

- *Subchannelization*: The subchannelization of WiMax uses fewer OFDM carriers in the upstream link of a terminal, but each carrier operates at the same level of the base station. Subchannelization extends the reach of upstream signals from a terminal and reduces its power consumption.

- *Directional antennas*: Directional antennas are advantageous in fixed wireless systems because they are more powerful in picking up signals than are omnidirectional antennas; hence, a fixed CPE typically uses a directional antenna, while a fixed BS may use directional or omnidirectional antennas.

- *Transmit and receive diversity*: WiMax may optionally employ a transmit and receive diversity algorithm to make use of multipath and reflection using MIMO radio systems.

- *Adaptive modulation*: Adaptive modulation allows the transmitter to adjust modulation schemes based on the SNR of the radio links. For example, if the SNR is 20 dB, 64 QAM will be used to achieve high capacity. If the SNR is 16 dB, 16 QAM will be used, and so on. Other NLOS schemes of WiMax, such as directional antenna and error correction, are also used.

- *Error-correction techniques*: WiMax specifies the use of several error-correction codes and algorithms to recover frames lost due to frequency-selective fading or burst errors. These codes and algorithms are Reed Solomon FEC, convolutional encoding, interleaving algorithms, and Automatic Repeat Request (ARQ) for frame retransmission.

- *Power control*: In a WiMax system, a BS is able to control power consumption of CPEs by sending power-control codes to them. The power-control algorithms improve overall performance and minimize power consumption.

- *Security*: Authentication between a BS and an SS is based on the use of X.509 digital certificates with RSA public key authentication. Traffic is encrypted using Counter Mode with Cipher Block Chaining Message Authentication Code Protocol (CCMP) which uses Advanced Encryption Standard (AES) for transmission security and data integrity authentication. WiMax also supports Triple Data Encryption Standard (3DES).

Initially, the WiMax Forum has focused on fixed wireless access for home and business users using outdoor antennas (CPEs), and indoor fixed access is under development. A base station may serve about 500 subscribers. WiMax vendors have begun to test fixed wireless broadband access in metropolitan areas such as Seattle. Due to its relatively high cost, the major targets of this technology are business users who want an alternative to T1, rather than residential home users. A second goal of the forum is to address portable wireless access without mobility support, and another is to achieve mobile access with seamless mobility support (802.16e). Recall that a Wi-Fi hotspot offers wireless LAN access within a limited coverage of an AP; the WiMax Forum plans to build *MetroZones* that allow portable broadband wireless access. A MetroZone comprises base stations connected to each other via LOS wireless links, and 802.16 interfaces for laptop computers or PDAs that connect to the "best" base station for portable data access. This aspect of WiMax seems more compelling in terms of potential data rate compared with 3G cellular systems.

Like the Wi-Fi forum, the WiMax forum aims at providing certification of WiMax products in order to guarantee interoperability. In March 2005, Alvarion, Airspan, and Redline began to conduct the industry's first WiMAX interoperability test. WiMax chips for fixed CPEs and base stations developed by Intel will be released in the second half of 2005, and WiMax chips for mobile devices will be released in 2007. At the time of this writing, some WiMax systems were expected to go into trial operation in late 2005.

1.15 Satellite

Global wireless communication comprises two elements: terrestrial communication and satellite communication. Cellular networks are primarily terrestrial-based, consisting of a vast number of base stations across heavily populated areas. In some circumstances, such as research laboratories established in the Antarctic, satellite communication is the only means of communication. Some other applications of satellite communication include military satellite espionage, global television broadcast, satellite radio, meteorological satellite imaging, and GPS. In addition, satellites complement cellular networks in reaching far rural areas and have been integrated into worldwide GSM and CDMA systems.

1.15.1 Satellite Communication

Despite the advantage of providing global coverage, satellite communication is known to have significant drawbacks. For one thing, satellite links introduce greater propagation latency than fiber-optic links due to the much longer distance a signal must travel back and forth between a terminal and a satellite. A delay of even half a second when using a geostationary satellite phone is noticeable. Bandwidth is another downside of satellite communication compared to terrestrial wired or wireless communications. Although a single satellite may cover a large geographical area (known as the "footprint"), the cost of the entire system remains extremely high, making its acceptability by the general public economically impossible.

1.15.2 Satellite Systems

Satellites orbit the Earth at different heights in various periods. The higher the satellite, the longer the period of the satellite will be. The orbits can be circles or eclipses. Earlier satellites were composed of transponders that received signals on one frequency and transmitted them on another. Digital technologies were introduced later to allow improved quality of the signals and more reliable communication. Signals transmitted from a satellite to the Earth attenuate proportional to the square of the distance. A variety of atmospheric conditions also influence satellite signal transmission, such as rain absorption and meteors in the space.

Communication satellites can be divided into four categories based on the orbit of the satellite in space: geostationary (GEO) satellite, medium Earth orbit (MEO) satellite, and low Earth orbit (LEO) satellite, as shown in Table 1.10.

GEO satellites remain relatively stationary at a height of about 36,000 km. Three of them are required to cover the entire surface of the Earth. The frequency bands allocated for GEO

Table 1.10 Satellite Systems.

	Geostationary (GEO)	Medium Earth Orbit (MEO)	Low Earth Orbit (LEO)
Orbit height (km)	36,000	5000–20,000	1000–2000
Orbit period (hours)	24	6	1.5–2
Number of satellites required to cover the Earth	3	12	.66
Frequency band	L, S, C, Ku, Ka[a]	L[a]	L[a]

[a]See text for description of frequency bands.

satellite communication by the ITU are L band (1.5-GHz downlink, 1.6-GHz uplink, 15-MHz bandwidth), S band (1.9-GHz downlink, 2.2-GHz uplink, 70-MHz bandwidth), C band (4.0-GHz downlink, 6.0-GHz uplink, 500-MHz bandwidth), Ku band (11-GHz downlink, 14-GHz uplink, 500-MHz bandwidth), and Ka band (20-GHz downlink, 30-GHz uplink, 3500-MHz bandwidth). GEO satellite systems are primarily used for television broadcasting, such as Direct TV and Dish Networks, and mobile communications. The newest member of this family is satellite digital radio, which provides CD-quality music over more than 1000 channels.

MEO satellites orbit the Earth at heights of around 10,000 to 20,000 km. GPS systems use MEO satellites to provide precise location identification with a range of several meters. 24 GPS satellites operated by U.S. Department of Defense orbit the Earth twice a day at a height of about 19,320 km. The civilian use of GPS operates at 1575.42 MHz, part of the L band. A GPS receiver must communicate with at least three GPS satellites in order to compute a specific two-dimensional location via triangulation. With four or more signals from GPS satellites, the receiver is able to calculate a three-dimensional location.

LEO satellites are much closer to the surface of the Earth than MEO and GEO satellites. Their period can be as short as 1 or 2 h. Because of the considerably shorter distance between LEO satellites and receivers, propagation latency is reduced down to about 10 msec; however, to offer global coverage, many more satellites are needed. For example, the Iridium system was originally designed to have 77 satellites in space (element 77 is iridium). The Teledesic project planed to launch 840 LEO satellites. These numbers had to be scaled back in order to keep costs under control. Aimed at reducing the cost of satellites, another system, Globalstar, has 48 satellites and a large number of ground base stations. (It must be noted that Iridium went bankrupt in 1999 as a result of a small user base and high operational cost.) The data rate offered by LEO satellite systems varies from kilobits per second to megabits per second, depending on the target applications.

1.16 Wireless Sensor Networks

Data communication continues to expand in both scope and complexity, from internal communication among the hardware components of an individual computer to intercomputer network communication via wired or wireless BANs, PANs, LANs, MANs, and WANs. At the same time, computers are becoming more closely related to the physical world and human beings, gathering, monitoring, processing, and analyzing data to allow instrumentation and automation and to facilitate decision-making. Wireless sensor networks (WSNs) represent networks that are embedded into our physical environments. A sensor is a tiny electronic device that can respond to a physical stimulus and convert it into numeric data. A WSN is composed of many low-power, low-cost, autonomous sensor nodes interconnected with wireless communication of sensory data. A myriad of measurements can be done by sensors, including environmental properties such as temperatures, humidity, and air pressure; presence, vibration, and motion detection of objects; chemical properties; radiation levels; GPS; light; and acoustic and seismic activities. Data gathering is conducted intermittently at a specified frequency. A sensor node in a WSN possesses sufficient computing power to process sensory data gathered locally or transmitted from other sensor nodes via wireless links. Furthermore, sensor nodes in a WSN self-organize into a network topology, thereby improving robustness and reducing maintenance costs.

1.16.1 WSN Applications

The wide range of sensors and collective instrumental functionality of WSNs, coupled with the underlying wireless networks, make it possible to provide unprecedented levels of data access and associated intelligence, bringing about a new dimension of application for different industry sectors. WSN applications can be divided into three categories [8]: monitoring space, including objects as part of the space; monitoring operation states of objects; and monitoring interactions between objects and space. The first category represents the most common and basic use of WSNs (dealing with physical environments), whereas the second is mainly concerned with a specific entity rather than its surroundings. The third category encompasses more sophisticated monitoring and control over communications and interactions between objects and between an object and its surroundings. Some pilot projects have explored WSNs for a number of different application scenarios. Many potential applications are being developed to leverage WSNs. Some examples are introduced as follows.

1.16.1.1 Environmental Sensing

Using a large number of sensor nodes deployed in a target geographic location, it is possible to derive useful patterns and trends based on datasets collected over time. Examples of environmental sensing are light sensing, microclimate monitoring, traffic monitoring, pollution level monitoring, indoor climate control, and habitat monitoring. Very often users are only concerned with independent characteristics of an entity, such as the number of vehicles passing by during a time period or the propagation speed of some contaminant in a river.

1.16.1.2 Object Sensing

Aside from environmental sensing, sensors can be attached to objects and collect data regarding motion, pressure, or any mechanical, electronic, or biological characteristics of the host. Object sensing is predominantly used in industrial control and maintenance. Examples include structural monitoring of buildings, bridges, vehicles, and airplanes; sensing machinery wear in a factory; industrial asset tracking in warehouses and stores; surveillance in parking lot and streets; crop monitoring; and military-related object sensing in battlefields. In particular, RFID, a scaled-down wireless sensing technology, utilizes small tags of very limited local computing power and storage to identify and inventory objects. Section 13 has presented a detailed introduction to RFID.

1.16.1.3 Sensing with Intelligence

More challenging application scenarios require embedded intelligence that goes beyond raw data sensing, thus requiring the simultaneous sensing of multiple related quantities and in-network processing so as to detect internal interactions between objects. Examples of this category are monitoring wildlife habitats, telemedicine sensing, context-aware pervasive computing using sensors, and disaster management. For instance, researchers at the University of California, Berkeley, and Intel have developed a successful experimental WSN to monitor petrels on an uninhabited island off the coast of Maine [9,10]. The birds being observed are Leach's store petrels, a type of tiny reclusive seabird that burrows in sandy soil and emerges only at night. To ornithologists, monitoring and understanding the comings and goings of these birds in a wild area are not simple tasks, as they would have to dig into the birds' burrows for more information. The WSN deployed on the island consists of 190 wireless sensor nodes called *motes*, some of which are located in burrows and others on the ground, and a solar-powered central computer station that collects sensory data from a gateway mote and reports back to a remote site in real-time via satellite links. Sensors on the motes monitor temperature, humidity, barometric pressure, and ambient light. The temperature reading within a burrow can be used to infer if a petrel is present or not. Other data also contribute to our understanding of the behavior of these petrels and their responses to changes in their surroundings.

1.16.2 Wireless Sensor Node

A sensor node is made up of four basic components: sensing unit, processing unit, transceiver unit, and power unit. The sensing unit usually consists of two components: a sensor and an analog-to-digital converter (ADC). The processing unit acts as a tiny computer: a microprocessor and some RAM. The processing unit runs an embedded operating system and executes WSN applications that control the operations of the sensor and communication between sensor nodes. The transceiver unit is a low-power radio operating on an unlicensed frequency band. The power unit is a battery for regular sensor nodes. Note that in most cases a WSN will have a special sensor node that acts as the gateway for other sensor nodes with respect to ultimate data delivery. The gateway node interfaces to computers via RS232 or Ethernet links. As a result, the gateway node is different from other regular nodes, in both size and processing functionality, thus requiring more power supply.

Following is a list of sensor node characteristics that affect the design of WSN system architectures and applications:

- *Size:* Sensor nodes are very small, due to advancements in semiconductor technologies.
- *Low power:* Sensor nodes are expected to operate for a long time before the battery drains out. In many cases, it is prohibitive to replace batteries.
- *Autonomous, unattended operations:* Once deployed, sensor nodes should self-organize to work as programmed. Remote reprogramming is sometimes possible.
- *Inexpensive:* Their low cost makes it possible to deploy a large number of sensor notes at a moderate cost.
- *Adaptive to environments and themselves:* Sensor nodes are able to adapt to environmental and status changes.

1.16.3 Self-Organized Networks

The physical layer of a WSN is nothing new: radio-frequency transmission at unlicensed bands. LOS is not required. The data-link layer monitors the channels and transmits frames only when the channel is idle. The network layer and transport layer require more discussion. Like ad hoc networks, the routing paths between each two nodes cannot be determined and configured prior to deployment because there is no predefined fixed infrastructure in WSNs. Sensor nodes have to discover multihop routes to relevant nodes themselves. This is often done via routing data dissemination, in which packets that contain the transmitter and the distance to the root are flooded in the network. A sensor node, upon receiving such packets, will be able to find a "parent" who is closer to the root; hence, a distribution tree can be generated. Data collection from sensor nodes can be routed back to the root following the distribution tree.

Task or query dissemination throughout a sensor network is data-centric in association with data aggregation, a routing scheme known as *directed diffusion* [11]. Sensor nodes are not addressed uniformly using numeric identifications; instead, the addressing and naming schemes are correlated with the application. They are identified by "attribute–value" pairs in their data. A task in the form of some attribute inquiry is sent out from some nodes in the hope of obtaining relevant data from other nodes, and then all participating nodes form a routing gradient toward the originators. In the case where a WSN is used as a platform of the sensory database, the applications and underlying routing schemes must support declarative queries, thereby making the detail of in-network query processing and optimization transparent to the user. Power consumption is another crucial factor when it comes to in-network aggregation support of query processing. Sophisticated power-aware query processing and packet routing schemes have been devised to reduce the overall power consumption of a WSN.

Sensory data delivery can be performed in several ways. Sensor node can actively report readings periodically to its parent or only report when an event occurs. The delivery procedure can also be initiated by a user issuing a command that is diffused across the network. Depending on the design objectives, a WSN may apply different data delivery models to different sensor nodes. For example, some high-level roots in the distribution tree may employ a request-and-response mechanism for queries, whereas some low-level sensor nodes may simply report data continuously.

Compared with mobile ad hoc network, network communication over WSNs imposes additional constraints other than node mobility and power consumption. Sensors node are more prone to failure, and their computational capability and memory capacity are greatly limited. When designing a protocol stack of a WSN, these constraints have to be taken into account. Specifically, because complete raw data forwarding is not necessary in many circumstances, data aggregation may be conducted at various levels of the distribution tree to reduce the amount of data being transferred upward to the gateway while still providing sufficient information to other nodes. Furthermore, data aggregation can be combined with applications of the WSN to further improve the efficiency of data collection and dissemination schemes. This reflects one of the most important characteristics of WSNs: cross-layer design. The well-known sensor operating system is TinyOS [12], which is an open-source, event-based embedded operating system developed at the University of California, Berkeley. TinyOS provides a set of components for networking, memory management, and power management, as well as data acquisition and query processing tools. The programming language supported by TinyOS is nesC, a C-like language for embedded network system development.

1.16.4 ZigBee

One of the emerging applications of WSN is wireless monitoring and control. ZigBee is such an application that uses low-power and low-data-rate networked sensors. It was developed by the ZigBee Alliance, an industry association of semiconductor companies and network equipment companies such as Ember, Honeywell, Mitsubishi Electric, Motorola, Samsung, and Philips. It has to be noted that the term *ZigBee* refers to the silent communication between honeybees where the bee dances in a zig-zag pattern to tell others the location, distance, and direction of some newly found food. WSN communication somewhat resembles the ZigBee principle in that they must be simple and effective.

The idea is to take advantage of wireless sensors to monitor environments, objects, and human beings and control devices, appliances, and facilities. Wireless sensors make it possible to remotely and conveniently monitor or be notified of operational states or crucial state change of an object, such as a dying battery in a smoke detector and rapidly increasing temperature in a truck carrying frozen goods. WSNs in ZigBee are not designed to carry large data transfer due to the limited capability of wireless communication; however, these sensors are able to form a fully functional network, self-organize for efficient data routing and in-network processing, and self-heal in the case of node failure. The initial target markets of ZigBee products are home control, building control, industrial automation, personal healthcare, consumer electronics, PC and peripherals control, etc. Key specs of ZigBee include the following:

- Frequency bands: 868 MHz, 915 MHz, and 2.4 GHz;
- Data transfer rate up to 250 Kbps;
- Signal transmission range of 10 to 100 m, depending on the sensors being used;
- AES encryption of data;
- Various ZigBee applications can work with each other;
- Low power usage.

Unlike UWB or Bluetooth, ZigBee specifications do not define radio interface and data-link layer protocols; ZigBee simply uses the IEEE 802.15.4 physical radio standard, as shown in Figure 1.16. The ZigBee network application support layer and application profile are the major components that make up the ZigBee specification. Because ZigBee is a proprietary protocol rather than an open standard like those ratified by IEEE, its fate hinges on how it refines itself to become the de facto industry standard. To this end, standardization battles seem inevitable.

1.17 Standardization in the Wireless World

The advent of next-generation mobile computing calls for open standards and platforms to enable interoperability. As has been discussed in this chapter, a full spectrum of wireless technologies is set to be integrated to allow roaming in on unprecedented levels. Proprietary technologies do not fit into this new era of convergence, as it would be difficult for them to gain ground to a great extent due to the limited number of vendors and compatible products. On the contrary, open, well-crafted standards for the technology will enable and encourage any interested business parties to engage in developing and manufacturing products or offering services that are guaranteed to be interchangeable or compatible. Open standards essentially provide a solid foundation of framework of a technology as well as design constraints, thereby boosting the spread and acceptance of the technology.

A standard is a specification or definition that has been approved by a recognized standards organization such as ITU, IEEE, and ETSI, or is generally accepted as a de facto model by the industry. In the context of computing, standards exist for computer hardware, communication protocols, programming languages, operating systems, and some applications. Network communications have a wide range of standards, such as IEEE 802.3 Ethernet standard for LANs, IEEE 802.11 and ETSI HIPERLAN for wireless LANs, GSM, and IS-95 and IS136.

In addition to communication standard bodies such as ITU, IEEE, and ETSI, some other standard bodies have been founded for specialized technological fields. The American National Standards Institute (ANSI) is primarily responsible for software and programming language standardization; it has created ANSI C and C++. HTML and XML have been adopted by the International Organization for Standardization (ISO) and the World Wide Web Consortium (W3C). The Internet Engineering Task Force (IETF) has released a number of requests for comments (RFCs) that serve as the basis of many network protocols. Many computer peripheral standards such as the PCMCIA, Universal Serial Bus (USB), and compact flash have been created by industrial forums or associations.

1.17.1 Cellular Standard Groups

The two standard bodies behind competing cellular technologies are the Third Generation Partnership Project (3GPP) and Third Generation Partnership Project 2 (3GPP2). 3GPP is an international organization supporting the development of UMTS/WCDMA systems. 3GPP partners include ETSI of Europe, ATIS of the United States, ARIB and TTC of Japan, TTA of Korea, and CCSA of China. 3GPP has released two versions of UMTS standards, namely Release 99 and Release 2000. 3GPP2 is the parallel partnership project for cdma2000 technology. It consists of TIA of the United States, ARIB and TTC of Japan, TTA of Korea, and CCSA of China. ITU is a United Nations organization responsible for maintaining and extending worldwide coordination of different governments and private sectors and managing the radio-frequency spectrum. 3GPP and 3GPP2 are formed under ITU.

1.17.2 IEEE Standards

The Institute of Electrical and Electronic Engineers (IEEE) has been the key standards organization in promoting networking technologies for many years. For wireless technologies, IEEE has established several working groups, mainly under the 802 standard committee. Figure 1.17 shows an overview of 802 standards. Below is a list of such working groups and their tasks:

- IEEE 802.1: LAN/MAN architecture with emphasis on internet working and link security (inactive).

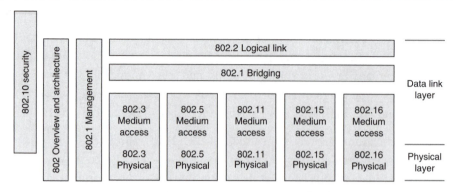

Figure 1.17 IEEE 802 Standards.

- IEEE 802.2: Logical link control, part of the data-link layer protocol of a LAN.
- IEEE 802.3: Ethernet, the dominating LAN technology.
- IEEE 802.4: Token bus, a LAN technology utilizing token rings over coaxial cables.
- IEEE 802.5: Token ring, another token ring LAN technology (inactive).
- IEEE 802.6: Metropolitan area networks, a specification of MANs using Distributed Queue Dual Bus (DQDB) (inactive).
- IEEE 802.7: Broadband TAG (Technical Advisory Group), a broadband LAN.
- IEEE 802.8: Fiberoptic TAG, a fiber-optic LAN standard (inactive).
- IEEE 802.9: Isochronous LAN, an Isochronous Ethernet (IsoEnet) (inactive).
- IEEE 802.10: Security, specifying key management, access control, and data integrity for LANs and WANs (inactive).
- IEEE 802.11: Wireless LAN, a set of protocols for wireless LANs operating on unlicensed 2.4-GHz and 5-GHz bands.
- IEEE 802.12: Demand priority, 100BaseVG-AnyLAN (inactive).
- IEEE 802.13: Not used (for some reason).
- IEEE 802.14: Cable data, a MAC layer specification for multimedia traffic over hybrid fiber and coaxial networks.
- IEEE 802.15: Wireless PAN, a set of protocols for short-range wireless networks, including Bluetooth (802.15.1).
- IEEE 802.16: Broadband wireless access, PHY and MAC layer protocols for PTM broadband wireless access; WiMax is based on 802.16.
- IEEE 802.17: Resilient packet ring (RPR), a protocol to improve resilience for packet data traffic over fiber rings.
- IEEE 802.20: Mobile Broadband Wireless Access, PHY and MAC layer protocols for mobile data access.

1.17.3 Standards War

Emerging innovational technologies usually imply huge business opportunities. Different groups of industry alliances always attempt to influence the standardization of these technologies in favor of their own business interests. This sometimes leads to serious conflicts within a standardization body which inevitably puts the technology in stalemate and affects the promotion of the underlying technology with respect to providing a unified, interoperable solution framework for interested parties. For instance, the IEEE standardization of UWB (802.15.3) has been deadlocked due to proposals from two rivalry groups: the MBOA Alliance (Intel and TI lead) and UWB Forum (Motorola leads). Each side claims its proposal is superior to the other. Seeing no immediate ratification of a standard, both groups are moving forward to advance their approaches in commercial developments, effectively creating a segmented UWB market. The evolution of cellular networks is another example of a standards war. The lack of a global standard of cellular networks has resulted in two dominating 2G GSM and CDMA systems and two ongoing 3G deployments: UMTS/WCDMA and cdma2000, backed up by two organizations, 3GPP and 3GPP2, respectively. If a united standard agreement cannot be reached by the different groups, it is very likely the market will make the final decision. The standards body will supposedly pick the approach that is the most popular in the marketplace. Interestingly and understandably, it is not always the technically superior approach or system that eventually wins the majority of the market. We have seen this happen with Betamax versus VHS, two competing videotape standards back in the 1990s. It would be interesting to see what will happen to those emerging wireless technology standards.

1.18 Summary

Mobile wireless is probably the most active area in the domain of computing and communications. For one thing, the boundary between data networking and voice communication continues to blur, as voice over IP begins to gain some ground in enterprise networks to replace PBX. The dominance of mobile voice communications in the wireless world, including cellular network services, walkie-talkies, and cordless phones, may begin to change as a result of evident growth of mobile data services and applications, enabled by a multitude of wireless technologies operating within the ranges of BAN, PAN, LAN, and WAN. In addition, mobile communications and computing are taking place in many forms, including interperson, intrasystem, intersystem, and person to system. This implies ubiquitous mobile access to a converged mobile wireless infrastructure from everywhere, all the time, and from all mobile devices.

This chapter talked about the technical details of the state-of-the-art of many wireless technologies, including cellular, wireless LANs, wireless MANs, Bluetooth, UWB, satellite, WSNs, and RFID. The emphasis was on explaining how the technology works, how it compares to other competing or complementary technologies, and what the possible applications are that can take advantage of the technology. To readers not familiar with these technologies, thorough basic understanding of these technologies is required before proceeding on to the remaining chapters. The next chapter will focus on hardware and software platforms for smart phones. It will cover topics such as mobile processor, memory and storage, input method, display, existing software solutions, and application development environment.

Further Reading

Federal Communication Commission (FCC) Spectrum page, http://www.fcc.gov/oet/spectrum/; National Telecommunications and Information Administration (NITA) Spectrum page, http://www.ntia.doc.gov/osmhome/osmhome.html.

WAP 2.0, http://www.openmobilealliance.org/tech/affiliates/wap/wapindex.html.

3GPP group, http://www.3gpp.org; MMS specification for stage 1 and stage 2, http://www.3gpp.org/ftp/Specs/html-info/status-report.htm.

IEEE 802.11 work group, http://grouper.ieee.org/groups/802/11/; 802.11 wireless LAN standard download site, http://standards.ieee.org/getieee802/802.11.html.

A good survey on IEEE 802.11 standards is William Stallings' IEEE 802.11: wireless LANs from a to n, IT Prof. Mag. 6 (5) (2004) 32–37.

Official Bluetooth membership website, http://www.bluetooth.org/; specifications download, http://www.bluetooth.org/spec/.

IEEE 802.15 working group for WPAN, http://standards.ieee.org/getieee802/802.15.html.

MBOA (Multi Band OFDM Alliance), UWB industry alliance, http://www.multibandofdm.org/.

UWB forum, another camp of UWB vendors, proposed DS-CDMA, http://www.uwbforum.org/.

EPC Global (RFID code standard body), http://www.epcglobalinc.org/; RFID specifications version 1.0/1.1 can be downloaded from http://www.epcglobalinc.org/standards_technology/specifications.html.

WiMax Forum, http://www.wimaxforum.org; WiMax white papers can be downloaded from http://www.wimaxforum.org/technology/White_Papers/.

Intel's WiMax site, http://www.intel.com/netcomms/technologies/wimax/.

IEEE 802.16 working group, http://grouper.ieee.org/groups/802/16/; a list of 802.16 standards can be accessed at http://grouper.ieee.org/groups/802/16/published.html.

D. Estrin, D. Culler, K. Pister, Connecting the physical world with pervasive networks, IEEE Pervasive Comput. 1 (1) (2002) 59–69 (for a survey on wireless sensor networks and applications).

ZigBee Alliance, http://www.zigbee.org/; ZigBee whitepapers can be downloaded from http://www.zigbee.org/en/resources/#WhitePapers.

IEEE 802 LAN/MAN standards list, http://standards.ieee.org/catalog/olis/lanman.html.

References

[1] W. Stallings, Wireless Communications and Networks, Prentice Hall, Englewood Cliffs, NJ, 2002.

[2] J.D. Vriendt, P. Laine, C. Lerouge, X. Xu, Mobile network evolution: a revolution on the move, IEEE Commun. 40 (2002) 104–111.

[3] WAP Forum, WAP 2.0 Technical White Paper, Open Mobile Alliance, La Jolla, CA, 2002 (http://www.wapforum.org/what/WAPWhite_Paper1.pdf).

[4] S.J. Barnes, S.L. Huff, Rising sun: iMode and the wireless internet, Commun. ACM 46 (11) (2003) 78–84.

[5] H. Berghel, Wireless infidelity. I. War driving, Commun. ACM 47 (9) (2004) 21–26.

[6] FCC, Revision of Part 15 of the Commission's Rules Regarding Ultra-Wideband Transmission Systems, First Report and Order, Federal Communications Commission, Washington, D.C., 2002.

[7] WiMax Forum, WiMax's Technology for LOS and NLOS Environment, White Paper, The WiMax Forum, Hillsboro, OR, 2004.

[8] D. Culler, D. Estrin, M. Srivastrava, Overview of sensor networks, IEEE Comput. 37 (8) (2004) 41–49.

[9] A. Mainwaring, J. Polastre, R. Szewczyk, D. Culler, J. Anderson, Wireless sensor networks for habitat monitoring, in: Proceedings of the ACM International Workshop on Wireless Sensor Networks and Applications (WSNA'02), Atlanta, Georgia, September 28, 2002.

[10] J. Kumagai, Life of birds: wireless sensor network for bird study, IEEE Spectr. 41 (4) (2004) 42–49.

[11] C. Intanagonwiwat, R. Govindan, D. Estrin, Directed diffusion: a scalable and robust communication paradigm for sensor networks, in: Proceedings of the Sixth Annual International Conference on Mobile Computing and Networking (MobiCom'00), Boston, MA, 2000.

[12] TinyOS Forum, TinyOS, 2004 (http://www.tinyos.net).

CHAPTER 2

Wireless Networks

Larry L. Peterson
Bruce S. Davie

Wireless technologies differ in a variety of dimensions, most notably in how much bandwidth they provide and how far apart communicating nodes can be. Other important differences include which part of the electromagnetic spectrum they use (including whether it requires a license) and how much power they consume (important for mobile nodes). In this section we discuss four prominent wireless technologies: Bluetooth (802.15.1), Wi-Fi (more formally known as 802.11), WiMAX (802.16), and third-generation or 3G cellular wireless. In the following sections we present them in order from shortest range to longest range. Table 2.1 gives an overview of these technologies and how they relate to each other.

The most widely used wireless links today are usually asymmetric, i.e., the two endpoints are usually different kinds of nodes. One endpoint, sometimes described as the *base station*, usually has no mobility, but has a wired (or at least high bandwidth) connection to the Internet or other networks as shown in Figure 2.1. The node at the other end of the link—shown here as a "client node"—is often mobile, and relies on its link to the base station for all its communication with other nodes.

Observe that in Figure 2.1 we have used a wavy pair of lines to represent the wireless "link" abstraction provided between two devices (e.g., between a base station and one of its client nodes). One of the interesting aspects of wireless communication is that it naturally

Table 2.1 Overview of Leading Wireless Technologies.

	Bluetooth 802.15.1	Wi-Fi 802.11	WiMAX 802.16	3G Cellular
Typical link length	10 m	100 m	10 km	Tens of km
Typical bandwidth	2.1 Mbps (shared)	54 Mbps (shared)	70 Mbps (shared)	384 + Kbps (per connection)
Typical use	Link a peripheral to a notebook computer	Link a notebook computer to a wired base	Link a building to a wired tower	Link a cell phone to a wired tower
Wired technology analogy	USB	Ethernet	Coaxial cable	DSL

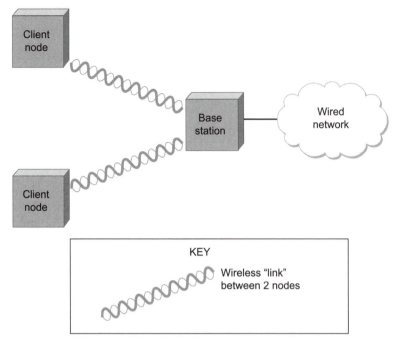

Figure 2.1 A wireless network using a base station.

supports point-to-multipoint communication, because radio waves sent by one device can be simultaneously received by many devices. However, it is often useful to create a point-to-point link abstraction for higher-layer protocols, and we will see examples of how this works later in this section.

Note that in Figure 2.1, communication between nonbase (client) nodes is routed via the base station. This is in spite of the fact that radio waves emitted by one client node may well be received by other client nodes—the common base station model does not permit direct communication between the client nodes.

This topology implies three qualitatively different levels of mobility. The first level is no mobility, such as when a receiver must be in a fixed location to receive a directional transmission from the base station, as is the case with the initial version of WiMAX. The second level is mobility within the range of a base, as is the case with Bluetooth. The third level is mobility between bases, as is the case with cell phones and Wi-Fi.

An alternative topology that is seeing increasing interest is the *mesh* or *ad hoc* network. In a wireless mesh, nodes are peers (i.e., there is no special base station node). Messages may be forwarded via a chain of peer nodes as long as each node is within the range of the preceding node. This is illustrated in Figure 2.2. This allows the wireless portion of a network to extend beyond the limited range of a single radio. From the point of view of competition between technologies, this allows a shorter-range technology to extend its range and potentially

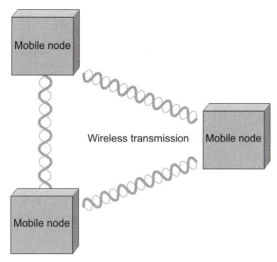

Figure 2.2 A wireless ad hoc or mesh network.

compete with a longer-range technology. Meshes also offer fault tolerance by providing multiple routes for a message to get from point A to point B. A mesh network can be extended incrementally, with incremental costs. On the other hand, a mesh requires nonbase nodes to have a certain level of sophistication in their hardware and software, potentially increasing per-unit costs—and power consumption, a critical consideration for battery-powered devices. Wireless mesh networks are of considerable research interest, but they are still in their relative infancy compared to networks with base stations, and thus we do not cover them further here.

We now turn our attention to the details of the four wireless technologies mentioned above, beginning with the most short-range technology, Bluetooth.

2.1 Bluetooth (802.15.1)

Bluetooth fills the niche of very short-range communication between mobile phones, PDAs, notebook computers, and other personal or peripheral devices. For example, Bluetooth can be used to connect a mobile phone to a headset or a notebook computer to a printer. Roughly speaking, Bluetooth is a more convenient alternative to connecting two devices with a wire. In such applications, it is not necessary to provide much range or bandwidth. This is fortunate for some of the target battery-powered devices, since it is important that they not consume much power.

Bluetooth operates in the license-exempt band at 2.45 GHz. It has a range of only about 10 m. For this reason, and because the communicating devices typically belong to one individual or group, Bluetooth is sometimes categorized as a personal area network (PAN). Version 2.0 provides speeds up to 2.1 Mbps. Power consumption is low.

Bluetooth is specified by an industry consortium called the Bluetooth Special Interest Group. It specifies an entire suite of protocols, going beyond the link layer to define application protocols, which it calls *profiles*, for a range of applications. For example, there is a profile for synchronizing a PDA with a personal computer. Another profile gives a mobile computer access to a wired LAN in the manner of 802.11, although this was not Bluetooth's original goal. The IEEE 802.15.1 standard is based on Bluetooth but excludes the application protocols.

The basic Bluetooth network configuration, called a *piconet*, consists of a master device and up to seven slave devices, as shown in Figure 2.3. Any communication is between the master and a slave; the slaves do not communicate directly with each other. Because slaves have a simpler role, their Bluetooth hardware and software can be simpler and cheaper.

Since Bluetooth operates in a license-exempt band, it is required to use a spread spectrum technique to deal with possible interference in the band. It uses frequency hopping with 79 *channels* (frequencies), using each for 625 µm at a time. This provides a natural time slot for Bluetooth to use for synchronous time-division multiplexing. A frame takes up 1, 3, or 5 consecutive time slots. Only the master can start to transmit in odd-numbered slots. A slave can start to transmit in an even-numbered slot, but only in response to a request from the master during the previous slot, thereby preventing any contention between the slave devices.

A slave device can be *parked*: set to an inactive, low-power state. A parked device cannot communicate on the piconet; it can only be reactivated by the master. A piconet can have up to 255 parked devices in addition to its active slave devices.

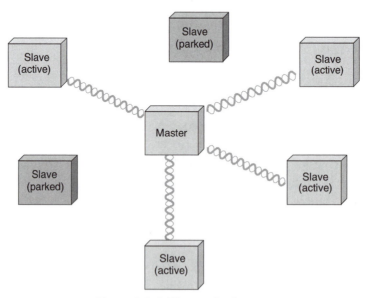

Figure 2.3 A Bluetooth piconet.

ZigBee is a newer technology that competes with Bluetooth to some extent. Devised by the ZigBee alliance and standardized as IEEE 802.15.4, it is designed for situations where the bandwidth requirements are low and power consumption must be very low to give very long battery life. It is also intended to be simpler and cheaper than Bluetooth, making it financially feasible to incorporate in cheaper devices such as a wall switch that wirelessly communicates with a ceiling-mounted fan.

2.2 Wi-Fi (802.11)

This section takes a closer look at a specific technology centered around the emerging IEEE 802.11 standard, also known as *Wi-Fi*. Wi-Fi is technically a trademark, owned by a trade group called the Wi-Fi alliance, that certifies product compliance with 802.11. Like its Ethernet and token ring siblings, 802.11 is designed for use in a limited geographical area (homes, office buildings, campuses), and its primary challenge is to mediate access to a shared communication medium—in this case, signals propagating through space. 802.11 supports additional features (e.g., time-bounded services, power management, and security mechanisms), but we focus our discussion on its base functionality.

2.2.1 Physical Properties

802.11 runs over six different physical layer protocols (so far). Five are based on spread spectrum radio and one on diffused infrared (and is of historical interest only at this point). The fastest runs at a maximum of 54 Mbps.

The original 802.11 standard defined two radio-based physical layer standards, one using frequency hopping (over 79 1-MHz-wide frequency bandwidths) and the other using direct sequence (with an 11-bit chipping sequence). Both provide up to 2 Mbps. Then physical layer standard 802.11b was added. Using a variant of direct sequence, 802.11b provides up to 11 Mbps. These three standards run in the license-exempt 2.4 GHz frequency band of the electromagnetic spectrum. Then came 802.11a, which delivers up to 54 Mbps using a variant of frequency-division multiplexing (FDM) called *orthogonal frequency-division multiplexing (OFDM)*. 802.11a runs in the license-exempt 5-GHz band. On one hand, this band is less used, so there is less interference. On the other hand, there is more absorption of the signal and it is limited to almost the line of sight. The most recent standard is 802.11g, which is backward compatible with 802.11b (and returns to the 2.4-GHz band). 802.11g uses OFDM and delivers up to 54 Mbps. It is common for commercial products to support all three of 802.11a, 802.11b, and 802.11g, which not only ensures compatibility with any device that supports any one of the standards, but also makes it possible for two such products to choose the highest bandwidth option for a particular environment.

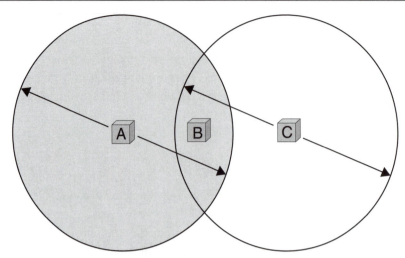

Figure 2.4 The hidden node problem. Although A and C are hidden from each other, their signals can collide at B. (B's reach is not shown.)

2.2.2　Collision Avoidance

At first glance, it might seem that a wireless protocol would follow the same algorithm as the Ethernet—wait until the link becomes idle before transmitting and back off should a collision occur—and to a first approximation, this is what 802.11 does. The additional complication for wireless is that, while a node on an Ethernet receives every other node's transmissions, a node on an 802.11 network may be too far from certain other nodes to receive their transmissions (and vice versa).

Consider the situation depicted in Figure 2.4, where A and C are both within range of B but not each other. Suppose both A and C want to communicate with B and so they each send it a frame. A and C are unaware of each other since their signals do not carry that far. These two frames collide with each other at B, but unlike an Ethernet, neither A nor C is aware of this collision. A and C are said to be *hidden nodes* with respect to each other.

A related problem, called the *exposed node problem*, occurs under the circumstances illustrated in Figure 2.5, where each of the four nodes is able to send and receive signals that reach just the nodes to its immediate left and right. For example, B can exchange frames with A and C but it cannot reach D, while C can reach B and D but not A. Suppose B is sending signal to A. Node C is aware of this communication because it hears B's transmission. It would be a mistake, however, for C to conclude that it cannot transmit to anyone just because it can hear B's transmission. For example, suppose C wants to transmit to node D. This is not a problem since C's transmission to D will not interfere with A's ability to receive from B. (It would interfere with A sending to B, but B is transmitting in our example.) 802.11 addresses these two problems with an algorithm called *multiple access with collision avoidance (MACA)*.

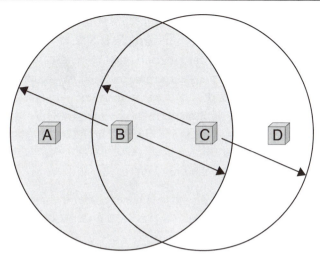

Figure 2.5 The exposed node problem. Although B and C are exposed to each other's signals, there is no interference if B transmits to A while C transmits to D. (A's and D's reaches are not shown.)

The idea is for the sender and receiver to exchange control frames with each other before the sender actually transmits any data. This exchange informs all nearby nodes that a transmission is about to begin. Specifically, the sender transmits a request-to-send (RTS) frame to the receiver; the RTS frame includes a field that indicates how long the sender wants to hold the medium (i.e., it specifies the length of the data frame to be transmitted). The receiver then replies with a clear-to-send (CTS) frame; this frame echoes this length field back to the sender. Any node that sees the CTS frame knows that it is close to the receiver, and therefore cannot transmit for the period of time it takes to send a frame of the specified length. Any node that sees the RTS frame but not the CTS frame is not close enough to the receiver to interfere with it, and so is free to transmit.

There are two more details to complete the picture. Firstly, the receiver sends an acknowledgment (ACK) to the sender after successfully receiving a frame. All nodes must wait for this ACK before trying to transmit. Secondly, should two or more nodes detect an idle link and try to transmit an RTS frame at the same time, their RTS frames will collide with each other. 802.11 does not support collision detection, but instead the senders realize the collision has happened when they do not receive the CTS frame after a period of time, in which case they each wait a random amount of time before trying again. The amount of time a given node delays is defined by the same exponential backoff algorithm used on the Ethernet.

2.2.3 Distribution System

As described so far, 802.11 would be suitable for a network with a mesh (ad hoc) topology, and development of a 802.11s standard for mesh networks is nearing completion. At the current time, however, nearly all 802.11 networks use a base-station-oriented topology.

Instead of all nodes being created equal, some nodes are allowed to roam (e.g., your laptop) and some are connected to a wired network infrastructure. 802.11 calls these base stations access points (APs), and they are connected to each other by a so-called *distribution system*. Figure 2.6 illustrates a distribution system that connects three APs, each of which services the nodes in some region. The details of the distribution system are not important to this discussion—it could be an Ethernet or a token ring, for example. The only important point is that the distribution network runs at layer-2 of the ISO architecture (the link layer), i.e., it operates at the same protocol layer as the wireless links. In other words, it does not depend on any higher-level protocols (such as the network layer).

Although two nodes can communicate directly with each other if they are within reach of each other, the idea behind this configuration is that each node associates itself with one AP. For node A to communicate with node E, e.g., A first sends a frame to its AP (AP-1), which forwards the frame across the distribution system to AP-3, which finally transmits the frame to E. How AP-1 knew to forward the message to AP-3 is beyond the scope of 802.11. What 802.11 does specify is how nodes select their APs and, more interestingly, how this algorithm works in light of nodes moving from one cell to another.

The technique for selecting an AP is called *scanning* and involves the following four steps:

1. The node sends a **Probe** frame;
2. All APs within reach reply with a **Probe Response** frame;
3. The node selects one of the APs, and sends that AP an **Association Request** frame;
4. The AP replies with an **Association Response** frame.

A node engages this protocol whenever it joins the network, as well as when it becomes unhappy with its current AP. This might happen, e.g., because the signal from its current AP

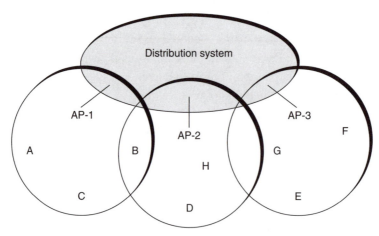

Figure 2.6 Access points connected to a distribution network.

has weakened due to the node moving away from it. Whenever a node acquires a new AP, the new AP notifies the old AP of the change (this happens in step 4) via the distribution system.

Consider the situation shown in Figure 2.7, where node C moves from the cell serviced by AP-1 to the cell serviced by AP-2. As it moves, it sends **Probe** frames, which eventually result in **Probe Response** frames from AP-2. At some point, C prefers AP-2 over AP-1, and so it associates itself with that AP.

The mechanism just described is called active scanning since the node is actively searching for an AP. APs also periodically send a **Beacon** frame that advertises the capabilities of the AP; these include the transmission rates supported by the AP. This is called passive scanning, and a node can change to this AP based on the Beacon frame simply by sending an **Association Request** frame back to the AP.

2.2.4 Frame Format

Most of the 802.11 frame format, which is depicted in Figure 2.8, is exactly what we would expect. The frame contains the source and destination node addresses, each of which are 48-bit long, up to 2312 bytes of data, and a 32-bit CRC. The **Control** field contains three subfields of interest (not shown): a 6-bit **Type** field that indicates whether the frame carries data, is an RTS or CTS frame, or is being used by the scanning algorithm; and a pair of 1-bit fields—called **ToDS** and **FromDS**—that are described below.

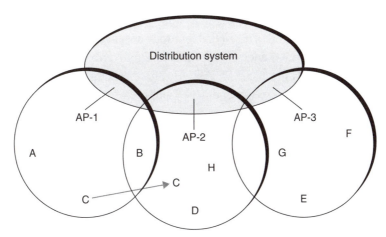

Figure 2.7 Node mobility.

16	16	48	48	48	16	48	0–18,496	32
Control	Duration	Addr1	Addr2	Addr3	SeqCtrl	Addr4	Payload	CRC

Figure 2.8 802.11 frame format.

The peculiar thing about the 802.11 frame format is that it contains four, rather than two, addresses. How these addresses are interpreted depends on the settings of the **ToDS** and **FromDS** bits in the frame's **Control** field. This is to account for the possibility that the frame had to be forwarded across the distribution system, which would mean that the original sender is not necessarily the same as the most recent transmitting node. Similar reasoning applies to the destination address. In the simplest case, when one node is sending directly to another, both the **DS** bits are 0, **Addr1** identifies the target node, and **Addr2** identifies the source node. In the most complex case, both **DS** bits are set to 1, indicating that the message went from a wireless node onto the distribution system, and then from the distribution system to another wireless node. With both bits set, **Addr1** identifies the ultimate destination, **Addr2** identifies the immediate sender (the one that forwarded the frame from the distribution system to the ultimate destination), **Addr3** identifies the intermediate destination (the one that accepted the frame from a wireless node and forwarded it across the distribution system), and **Addr4** identifies the original source. In terms of the example given in Figure 2.6, **Addr1** corresponds to E, **Addr2** identifies AP-3, **Addr3** corresponds to AP-1, and **Addr4** identifies A.

2.3 WiMAX (802.16)

WiMAX, which stands for Worldwide Interoperability for Microwave Access, was designed by the WiMAX Forum and standardized as IEEE 802.16. It was originally conceived as a last-mile technology. In WiMAX's case that "mile" is typically 1–6 miles, with a maximum of about 30 miles, leading to WiMAX being classified as a metropolitan area network (MAN). In keeping with a last-mile role, WiMAX does not incorporate mobility at the time of this writing, although efforts to add mobility are nearing completion as IEEE 802.16e. Also in keeping with the last-mile niche, WiMAX's client systems, called *subscriber stations*, are assumed to be not end-user computing devices, but rather systems that multiplex all the communication of the computing devices being used in a particular building. WiMAX provides up to 70 Mbps to a single subscriber station.

In order to adapt to different frequency bands and different conditions, WiMAX defines several physical layer protocols. The original WiMAX physical layer protocol is designed to use frequencies in the 10- to 66-GHz range. In this range waves travel in straight lines, so communication is limited to line-of-sight (LOS). A WiMAX base station uses multiple antennas pointed in different directions; the area covered by one antenna's signal is a *sector*. To extend WiMAX to near-LOS and non-LOS situations, several physical layer protocols were added that use the frequencies below 11 GHz (in the 10- to 11-GHz range, WiMAX can use either the original physical layer or one of the newer ones). Since this range includes both licensed and license-exempt frequencies, each of these physical layer protocols defines a variant better adapted to the additional interference and the regulatory constraints of the license-exempt frequencies.

The physical layer protocols provide two ways to divide the bandwidth between upstream (i.e., from subscribers to base station) and downstream traffic: time-division duplexing (TDD) and frequency-division duplexing (FDD). TDD is simply STDM of the two streams; they take turns using the same frequency, and the proportion of upstream to downstream time can be varied dynamically, *adaptively*, by the base station. FDD is simply FDM of the two streams: one frequency is used for upstream and another for downstream. In license-exempt bands, the protocols use only TDD.

Both channels, upstream and downstream, must be shared not just among the many subscriber stations in a given sector, but also among the many WiMAX *connections* that each subscriber can have with the base station. WiMAX—unlike 802.11 and Ethernet—is connection-oriented. One reason for this is to be able to offer a variety of QoS guarantees regarding properties such as latency and jitter, with the aim of supporting high-quality telephony and high-volume multimedia in addition to bursty data traffic. This is conceptually similar to some of the wired last mile technologies (such as DSL) with which WiMAX is intended to compete.

Sharing of the upstream and downstream channels is based on dividing them into equal-sized time slots. A WiMAX frame generally takes up multiple slots, with different frames taking different numbers of slots. The downstream channel (from base to subscribers) is relatively easy to subdivide into connections since only the base station sends on that channel. The base station simply sends addressed frames, one after the other. Each subscriber station in the sector receives all the frames, but ignores those not addressed to one of its connections.

In the upstream direction, how a connection gets handled depends on its QoS parameters. Some connections get slots at a fixed rate, some get polled to determine how many slots they need currently, and some must request slots whenever they need them. Connections in this last category must contend to place their requests in a limited number of upstream slots set aside for contention. They use an exponential backoff algorithm to minimize the chance of a collision, even on the first attempt.

A European alternative to WiMAX is HIPERMAN, which stands for high-performance radio metropolitan area network and uses the 2- to 11-GHz range. South Korea's WiBro (for wireless broadband) technology operates at 2.3 GHz, and is being brought into line with the emerging IEEE 802.16e standard for mobile WiMAX.

2.4 Cell Phone Technologies

Cell phone technology seems an obvious approach to mobile computer communication, and indeed data services based on cellular standards are commercially available. One drawback is the cost to users, due in part to cellular's use of licensed spectrum (which has historically been sold off to cellular phone operators for astronomical sums). The frequency bands that are used for cellular telephones (and now for cellular data) vary around the world. In Europe, e.g., the main bands for cellular phones are at 900 and 1800 MHz. In North America, 850- and 1900-MHz bands are used. This global variation in spectrum usage creates problems for users who want to travel from one part of the world to another, and has created a market for phones that can operate at multiple frequencies (e.g., a tri-band phone can operate at three of the four frequency bands mentioned above). That problem, however, pales in comparison to the proliferation of incompatible standards that have plagued the cellular communication business. Only recently have some signs of convergence on a small set of standards appeared. And finally, there is the problem that most cellular technology was designed for voice communication, and is only now starting to support moderately high-bandwidth data communication.

Like 802.11 and WiMAX, cellular technology relies on the use of base stations that are part of a wired network. The geographic area served by a base station's antenna is called a *cell*. A base station could serve a single cell or use multiple directional antennas to serve multiple cells. Cells do not have crisp boundaries, and they overlap. Where they overlap, a mobile phone could potentially communicate with multiple base stations. This is somewhat similar to the 802.11 picture shown in Figure 2.6. At any time, however, the phone is in communication with, and under the control of, just one base station. As the phone begins to leave a cell, it moves into an area of overlap with one or more other cells. The current base station senses the weakening signal from the phone, and gives control of the phone to whichever base station is receiving the strongest signal from it. If the phone is involved in a call at the time, the call must be transferred to the new base station in what is called a *handoff*.

As we noted above, there is not one unique standard for cellular, but rather a collection of competing technologies that support data traffic in different ways and deliver different speeds. These technologies are loosely categorized by "generation." The first generation (1G) was analog, and thus of limited interest from a data communications perspective. Most of the cell phone technology currently deployed is considered second generation (2G) or "2.5G" (not quite worthy of being called 3G, but more advanced than 2G). The 2G and later technologies are digital. The most widely deployed 2G technology is referred to as GSM—the Global System for Mobile Communications—which is used in more than 200 countries. North America, however, is a late adopter of GSM, which helped prolong the proliferation of competing standards.

Most 2G technologies use one of two approaches to sharing a limited amount of spectrum between simultaneous calls. One way is a combination of frequency-division multiplexing (FDM) and time-division multiplexing (TDM). The spectrum available is divided into disjoint frequency bands, and each band is subdivided into time slots. A given call is allocated every nth slot in one of the bands. The other approach is code division multiple access (CDMA). CDMA does not divide the channel in either time or frequency, but rather uses different chipping codes to distinguish the transmissions of different cell phone users.

The 2G and later cell phone technologies use compression algorithms tailored to human speech to compress voice data to about 8 Kbps without losing quality. Since 2G technologies focus on voice communication, they provide connections with just enough bandwidth for that compressed speech—not enough for a decent data link. One of the first cellular data standards to gain widespread adoption is the General Packet Radio Service (GPRS), which is part of the GSM set of standards and is often referred to as a 2.5G technology.

GSM networks make use of a multiplexing technique called time-division multiple access (TDMA). (Confusingly, there is also a particular cellular *standard* that is sometimes called TDMA, but is known formally as IS-136.) You can think of TDMA as being like TDM—traditionally used for telephone services—with the additional feature that the timeslots can be dynamically allocated to users or devices that need them (and deallocated from devices that no longer need them). The number of timeslots that are available for GPRS at a given frequency depends on how many cellular voice calls are currently in progress, since voice calls also consume timeslots. As a result, GPRS data rates tend to be lower in busy cells. In practice, users often get between 30 and 70 Kbps—coincidentally, just about the same as a user of a dial-up modem on a landline. Nevertheless, GPRS has proven quite useful and popular in some parts of the world as a way to communicate wirelessly when faster connection methods (such as 802.11) are not available. Other 2.5G data standards have also become available and some manage to be quite a bit higher in bandwidth than GPRS.

The concept of a third generation (3G) was established before there was any implementation of 3G technologies, with the aim of shaping a single international standard that would provide much higher data bandwidth. Unfortunately, at the time of writing, several mutually incompatible 3G standards are emerging. Thus, the possibility that cellular standards will continue to diverge seems quite realistic. Interestingly, all the 3G standards are based on variants of CDMA. For example, the Universal Mobile Telecommunications System (UMTS) is based on wideband CDMA (W-CDMA). UMTS appears poised to be the successor to GSM, and in fact is sometimes referred to as 3GSM (i.e., the third-generation version of GSM). UMTS is intended to support data transfer rates of up to 1.92 Mbps, although real network conditions will probably result in lower rates in practice. Nevertheless, it should represent a significant performance improvement over GPRS. And like GSM, it should have quite widespread (if not actually universal) adoption around the world.

There are a number of commercial UMTS networks in operation at the time of writing with many more announced or planned. And to make it quite clear that work in this field is far from complete, we note that 3.5G and 4G standards are also in the works.

Finally, it should be noted that there is a class of mobile phones that are not cellular phones but satellite phones, or *satphones*. Satphones use communication satellites as base stations, communicating on frequency bands that have been reserved internationally for satellite use. Consequently, service is available even where there are no cellular base stations. Satphones are rarely used where cellular is available, since service is typically much more expensive. Satphones are also larger and heavier than modern cell phones because of the need to transmit and receive over much longer distances, to reach satellites rather than cellphone towers. Satellite communication is more extensively used in television and radio broadcasting, taking advantage of the fact that the signal is broadcast, not point-to-point. High-bandwidth data communication via satellite are commercially available, but its relatively high price (for both equipment and service) limits its use to regions where no alternative is available.

Further Reading

One of the most important contributions in computer networking over the last 20 years is the original paper by Metcalf and Boggs (1976) introducing the Ethernet. Many years later, Boggs, Mogul, and Kent (1988) reported their practical experiences with Ethernet, debunking many of the myths that had found their way into the literature over the years. Both papers are must reading. The third and fourth papers discuss the issues involved in integrating high-speed network adaptors with system software.

- R. Metcalf, D. Boggs, Ethernet: distributed packet sitching for local computer networks, Commun. ACM 19 (7): (1976), 395–403.

- D. Boggs, J. Mogul, C. Kent. Measured capacity of an ethernet, Proc. SIGCOMM 88 Symposium, August 1988, pp. 222–234.

- R. Metcalf, Computer/network interface design lessons from arpanet and ethernet, IEEE J. Select. Areas Commun. (JSAC) 11 (2): (1993), 173–180.

- P. Druschel, M. Abbott, M. Pagels, L. L. Peterson, Network subsystem design, IEEE Network (Special Issue on End-System Support for High-Speed Networks) 7 (4): (1993), 8–17.

There are countless textbooks with a heavy emphasis on the lower levels of the network hierarchy, with a particular focus on *telecommunications*—networking from the phone company's perspective. Books by Spragins et al., and Minoli are two good examples. Several other books concentrate on various local area network technologies. Of these, Stallings's book is the most comprehensive, while Jain gives a thorough description of FDDI. Jain's book also gives a good introduction to the low-level details of optical communication. Also, a comprehensive overview of FDDI can be found in Ross's article.

For an introduction to information theory, Blahut's book is a good place to start, along with Shannon's seminal paper on link capacity.

For a general introduction to the mathematics behind error codes, Rao and Fujiwara is recommended. For a detailed discussion of the mathematics of CRCs in particular, along with some more information about the hardware used to calculate them, see Peterson and Brown.

On the topic of network adaptor design, much work was done in the early 1990s by researchers trying to connect hosts to networks running at higher and higher rates. In addition to the two examples given in the reading list, see Traw and Smith, Ramakrishnan, Edwards et al., Druschel et al., Kanakia and Cheriton, Cohen et al., and Steenkiste. Recently, a new generation of interface cards, ones that utilize *network processors*, is coming onto the market. Spalink et al., demonstrate how these new processors can be programmed to implement various network functionalities.

For general information on computer architecture, Hennessy and Patterson's book is an excellent reference.

Finally, we recommend the following live reference: http://standards.ieee.org/

CHAPTER 3

An Overview of Wireless Systems

Vijay K. Garg

3.1 Introduction

The cellular system employs a different design approach than most commercial radio and television systems use [1,2]. Radio and television systems typically operate at maximum power and with the tallest antennas allowed by the regulatory agency of the country. In the cellular system, the service area is divided into cells. A transmitter is designed to serve an individual cell. The system seeks to make efficient use of available channels by using low-power transmitters to allow frequency reuse at much smaller distances. Maximizing the number of times each channel can be reused in a given geographic area is the key to an efficient cellular system design.

During the past three decades, the world has seen significant changes in the telecommunications industry. There have been some remarkable aspects to the rapid growth in wireless communications, as seen by the large expansion in mobile systems. Wireless systems consist of wireless wide area networks (WWANs) (i.e., cellular systems), wireless local area networks (WLANs) [3], and wireless personal area networks (WPANs) (see Figure 3.1) [4]. The handsets used in all of these systems possess complex functionality, yet they have become small, low-power-consuming devices that are mass produced at a low cost, which has in turn accelerated their widespread use. The recent advancements in Internet technology have increased network traffic considerably, resulting in a rapid growth of data rates. This phenomenon has also had an impact on mobile systems, resulting in the extraordinary growth of the mobile Internet.

Wireless data offerings are now evolving to suit consumers due to the simple reason that the Internet has become an everyday tool and users demand data mobility. Currently, wireless data represents about 15 to 20% of all air time. While success has been concentrated in vertical markets such as public safety, health care, and transportation, the horizontal market (i.e., consumers) for wireless data is growing. In 2005, more than 20 million people were using wireless e-mail. The Internet has changed user expectations of what data access means. The ability to retrieve information via the Internet has been "an amplifier of demand" for wireless data applications.

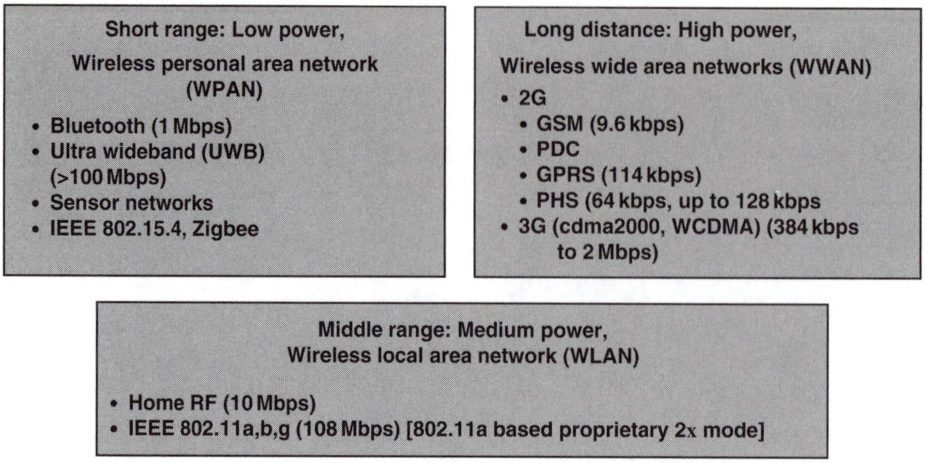

Short range: Low power, Wireless personal area network (WPAN)	Long distance: High power, Wireless wide area networks (WWAN)

• Bluetooth (1 Mbps)
• Ultra wideband (UWB) (>100 Mbps)
• Sensor networks
• IEEE 802.15.4, Zigbee
	• 2G
	  • GSM (9.6 kbps)
	  • PDC
	  • GPRS (114 kbps)
	  • PHS (64 kbps, up to 128 kbps
	• 3G (cdma2000, WCDMA) (384 kbps to 2 Mbps)

Middle range: Medium power, Wireless local area network (WLAN)

• Home RF (10 Mbps)
• IEEE 802.11a,b,g (108 Mbps) [802.11a based proprietary 2x mode]

PDC: Personal Digital Cellular (Japan)
GPRS: General Packet Radio Service
PHS: Personal Handy Phone System (Japan)

Figure 3.1 Wireless networks.

More than three-fourths of Internet users are also wireless users and a mobile subscriber is four times more likely to use the Internet than a nonsubscriber to mobile services. Such keen interest in both industries is prompting user demand for converged services. With more than a billion Internet users expected by 2008, the potential market for Internet-related wireless data services is quite large.

In this chapter, we discuss briefly 1G, 2G, 2.5G, and 3G cellular systems and outline the ongoing standard activities in Europe, North America, and Japan. We also introduce broadband (4G) systems (see Figure 3.2) aimed on integrating WWAN, WLAN, and WPAN.

3.2 First- and Second-Generation Cellular Systems

The first- and second-generation cellular systems are the WWAN. The first public cellular telephone system (first-generation, 1G), called Advanced Mobile Phone System (AMPS) [5,6], was introduced in 1979 in the United States. During the early 1980s, several incompatible cellular systems (TACS, NMT, C450, etc.) were introduced in Western Europe. The deployment of these incompatible systems resulted in mobile phones being designed for one system that could not be used with another system, and roaming between the many countries of Europe was not possible. The 1G systems were designed for voice applications. Analog frequency modulation (FM) technology was used for radio transmission.

In 1982, the main governing body of the European post telegraph and telephone (PTT), la Conférence européenne des Administrations des postes et des télécommunications (CEPT),

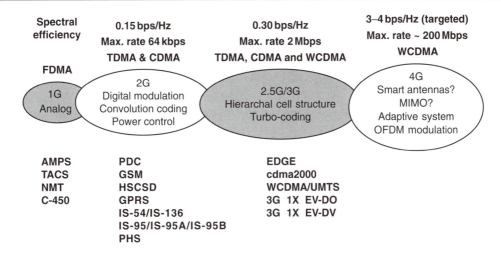

PHS: Personal handy phone system (Japan)
MIMO: Multi-input and multi-output
OFDM: Orthogonal frequency division multiple access

Figure 3.2 Wireless network from 1G to 4G.

set up a committee known as Groupe Special Mobile (GSM) [7], under the auspices of its Committee on Harmonization, to define a mobile system that could be introduced across western Europe in the 1990s. The CEPT allocated the necessary duplex radio frequency bands in the 900 MHz region.

The GSM (renamed Global System for Mobile Communications) initiative gave the European mobile communications industry a home market of about 300 million subscribers, but at the same time provided it with a significant technical challenge. The early years of the GSM were devoted mainly to the selection of radio technologies for the air interface. In 1986, field trials of different candidate systems proposed for the GSM air interface were conducted in Paris. A set of criteria ranked in the order of importance was established to assess these candidates.

The interfaces, protocols, and protocol stacks in GSM are aligned with the Open System Interconnection (OSI) principles. The GSM architecture is an open architecture which provides maximum independence between network elements such as the Base Station Controller (BSC), the Mobile Switching Center (MSC), the Home Location Register (HLR), etc. This approach simplifies the design, testing, and implementation of the system. It also favors an evolutionary growth path, since network element independence implies that modification to one network element can be made with minimum or no impact on the others. Also, a system operator has the choice of using network elements from different manufacturers.

GSM 900 (i.e., GSM system at 900 MHz) was adopted in many countries, including the major parts of Europe, North Africa, the Middle East, many East Asian countries, and Australia.

In most of these cases, roaming agreements exist to make it possible for subscribers to travel within different parts of the world and enjoy continuity of their telecommunications services with a single number and a single bill. The adaptation of GSM at 1800 MHz (GSM 1800) also spreads coverage to some additional East Asian countries and some South American countries. GSM at 1900 MHz (i.e., GSM 1900), a derivative of GSM for North America, covers a substantial area of the United States. All of these systems enjoy a form of roaming, referred to as Subscriber Identity Module (SIM) roaming, between them and with all other GSM-based systems. A subscriber from any of these systems could access telecommunication services by using the personal SIM card in a handset suitable to the network from which coverage is provided. If the subscriber has a multiband phone, then one phone could be used worldwide. This globalization has positioned GSM and its derivatives as one of the leading contenders for offering digital cellular and Personal Communications Services (PCS) worldwide. A PCS system offers multimedia services (i.e., voice, data, video, etc.) any time and anywhere. With a three band handset (900, 1800, and 1900 MHz), true worldwide seamless roaming is possible. GSM 900, GSM 1800, and GSM 1900 are second-generation (2G) systems and belong to the GSM family. Cordless Telephony 2 (CT2) is also a 2G system used in Europe for low mobility.

Two digital technologies, Time Division Multiple Access (TDMA) and Code Division Multiple Access (CDMA) [8] emerged as clear choices for the newer PCS systems. TDMA is a narrowband technology in which communication channels on a carrier frequency are apportioned by time slots. For TDMA technology, there are three prevalent 2G systems: North America TIA/EIA/IS-136, Japanese Personal Digital Cellular (PDC), and European Telecommunications Standards Institute (ETSI) Digital Cellular System 1800 (GSM 1800), a derivative of GSM. Another 2G system based on CDMA (TIA/EIA/IS-95) is a direct sequence (DS) spread spectrum (SS) system in which the entire bandwidth of the carrier channel is made available to each user simultaneously. The bandwidth is many times larger than the bandwidth required to transmit the basic information. CDMA systems are limited by interference produced by the signals of other users transmitting within the same bandwidth.

The global mobile communications market has grown at a tremendous pace. There are nearly one billion users worldwide with two-thirds being GSM users. CDMA is the fastest growing digital wireless technology, increasing its worldwide subscriber base significantly. Today, there are already more than 200 million CDMA subscribers. The major markets for CDMA technology are North America, Latin America, and Asia, in particular Japan and Korea. In total, CDMA has been adopted by almost 50 countries around the world.

The reasons behind the success of CDMA are obvious. CDMA is an advanced digital cellular technology, which can offer six to eight times the capacity of analog technologies (AMP) and up to four times the capacity of digital technologies such as TDMA. The speech quality provided by CDMA systems is far superior to any other digital cellular system, particularly in difficult radio frequency (RF) environments such as dense urban areas and mountainous regions. In both initial deployment and long-term operation, CDMA provides the most cost-effective solution for cellular operators. CDMA technology is constantly evolving to offer customers new and advanced services. The mobile data rates offered through CDMA phones have increased and new voice codecs provide speech quality close to the fixed wire-line. Internet access is now available through CDMA handsets. Most important, the CDMA network offers operators a smooth migration path to third-generation (3G) mobile systems [9,10,11,12].

3.3 Cellular Communications from 1G to 3G

Mobile systems have seen a change of generation, from first to second to third, every 10 years or so (see Figure 3.3). At the introduction of 1G services, the mobile device was large in size, and would only fit in the trunk of a car. All analog components such as the power amplifier, synthesizer, and shared antenna equipment were bulky. 1G systems were intended to provide voice service and low rate (about 9.6 kbps) circuit-switched data services. Miniaturization of mobile devices progressed before the introduction of 2G services (1990) to the point where the size of mobile phones fell below 200 cubic centimeters (cc). The 1G handsets provided poor voice quality, low talk-time, and low standby time. The 1G systems used Frequency Division Multiple Access (FDMA) technology and analog frequency modulation [5,13].

The 2G systems based on TDMA and CDMA technologies [14] were primarily designed to improve voice quality and provide a set of rich voice features. These systems supported low rate data services (16–32 kbps).

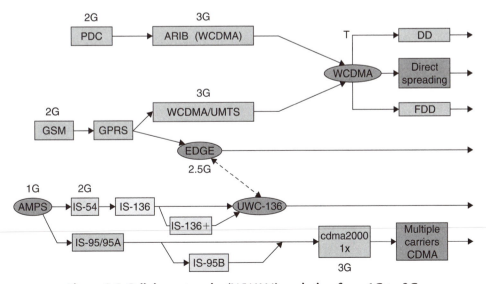

Figure 3.3 Cellular networks (WWAN) evolution from 1G to 3G.

For 2G systems three major problems impacting system cost and quality of service (QoS) remained unsolved. These include what method to use for band compression of voice, whether to use a linear or nonlinear modulation scheme, and how to deal with the issue of multipath delay spread caused by multipath propagation of radio waves in which there may not only be phase cancellation but also a significant time difference between the direct and the reflected waves.

The swift progress in Digital Signal Processors (DSPs) was probably fueled by the rapid development of voice codecs for mobile environments that dealt with errors. Large increases in the numbers of cellular subscribers and the worries of exhausting spectrum resources led to the choice of linear modulation systems.

To deal with multipath delay spread, Europe, the United States, and Japan took very different approaches. Europe adopted a high transmission rate of 280 kbps per 200 kHz RF channel in GSM [15,16] using a multiplexed TDMA system with 8–16 voice channels, and a mandatory equalizer with a high number of taps to overcome intersymbol interference (ISI). The United States used the carrier transmission rate of 48 kbps in 30 kHz channel, and selected digital advanced mobile phone (DAMP) systems (IS-54/IS-136) to reduce the computational requirements for equalization, and the CDMA system (IS-95) to avoid the need for equalization. In Japan the rate of 42 kbps in 25 kHz channel was used, and equalizers were made optional.

Taking into account the limitations imposed by the finite amount of radio spectrum available, the focus of the 3G mobile systems has been on the economy of network and radio transmission design to provide seamless service from the customers' perspective. The 3G systems provide their users with seamless access to the fixed data network [17,18]. They are perceived as the wireless extension of future fixed networks, as well as an integrated part of the fixed network infrastructure. 3G systems are intended to provide multimedia services including voice, data, and video.

One major distinction of 3G systems relative to 2G systems is the hierarchical cell structure designed to support a wide range of multimedia broadband services within the various cell types by using advanced transmission and protocol technologies. The 2G systems mainly use one-type cell and employ frequency reuse within adjacent cells in such a way that each single cell manages its own radio zone and radio circuit control within the mobile network, including traffic management and handoff procedures. The traffic supported in each cell is fixed because of frequency limitations and little flexibility of radio transmission which is mainly optimized for voice and low data rate transmissions. Increasing traffic leads to costly cellular reconfiguration such as cell splitting and cell sectorization.

The multilayer cell structure in 3G systems aims to overcome these problems by overlaying, discontinuously, pico- and microcells over the macrocell structure with wide area coverage.

Global/satellite cells can be used in the same sense by providing area coverage where macrocell constellations are not economical to deploy and/or support long distance traffic.

With low mobility and small delay spread profiles in picocells, high bit rates and high traffic densities can be supported with low complexity as opposed to low bit rates and low traffic load in macrocells that support high mobility. The user expectation will be for service selected in a uniform manner with consistent procedures, irrespective of whether the means of access to these services is fixed or mobile. Freedom of location and means of access will be facilitated by smart cards to allow customers to register on different terminals with varying capabilities (speech, multimedia, data, short messaging).

The choice of a radio interface parameter set corresponding to a multiple access scheme is a critical issue in terms of spectral efficiency, taking into account the ever-increasing market demand for mobile communications and the fact that radio spectrum is a very expensive and scarce resource. A comparative assessment of several different schemes was carried out in the framework of the Research in Advanced Communications Equipment (RACE) program. One possible solution is to use a hybrid CDMA/TDMA/FDMA technique by integrating advantages of each and meeting the varying requirements on channel capacity, traffic load, and transmission quality in different cellular/PCS layouts. Disadvantages of such hybrid access schemes are the high-complexity difficulties in achieving simplified low-power, low-cost transceiver design as well as efficient flexibility management in the several cell layers.

CDMA is the selected approach for 3G systems by the ETSI, ARIB (Association of Radio Industries and Business, Japan), and Telecommunications Industry Association (TIA). In Europe and Japan, Wideband CDMA [WCDMA/UMTS (Universal Mobile Telecommunication Services)] was selected to avoid IS-95 intellectual property rights. In North America, cdma2000 uses a CDMA air interface based on the existing IS-95 standard to provide wire-line quality voice service and high-speed data services at 144 kbps for mobile users, 384 kbps for pedestrians, and 2 Mbps for stationary users. The 64 kbps data capability of CDMA IS-95B provides high-speed Internet access in a mobile environment, a capability that cannot be matched by other narrowband digital technologies.

Mobile data rates up to 2 Mbps are possible using wide band CDMA technologies. These services are provided without degrading the systems' voice transmission capabilities or requiring additional spectrum. This has tremendous implications for the majority of operators that are spectrum constrained. In the meantime, DSPs have improved in speed by an order of magnitude in each generation, from 4 MIPs (million instructions per second) through 40 MIPs to 400 MIPs.

Since the introduction of 2G systems, the base station has seen the introduction of features such as dynamic channel assignment. In addition, most base stations began making shared use of power amplifiers and linear amplifiers whether or not modulation was linear. As such there has been an increasing demand for high-efficiency, large linear power amplifiers instead of nonlinear amplifiers.

At the beginning of 2G, users were fortunate if they were able to obtain a mobile device below 150 cc. Today, about 10 years later, mobile phone size has reached as low as 70 cc. Furthermore, the enormous increase in very large system integration (VLSI) and improved CPU performance has led to increased functionality in the handset, setting the path toward becoming a small-scale computer.

3.4 Road Map for Higher Data Rate Capability in 3G

The 1G and 2G cellular systems were primarily designed for voice services and their data capabilities were limited. Wireless systems have since been evolving to provide broadband data rate capability as well.

GSM is moving forward to develop cutting-edge, customer-focused solutions to meet the challenges of the 21st century and 3G mobile services. When GSM was first designed, no one could have predicted the dramatic growth of the Internet and the rising demand for multimedia services. These developments have brought about new challenges to the world of GSM. For GSM operators, the emphasis is now rapidly changing from that of instigating and driving the development of technology to fundamentally enable mobile data transmission to that of improving speed, quality, simplicity, coverage, and reliability in terms of tools and services that will boost mass market take-up.

People are increasingly looking to gain access to information and services whenever they want from wherever they are. GSM will provide that connectivity. The combination of Internet access, web browsing, and the whole range of mobile multimedia capability is the major driver for development of higher data speed technologies.

GSM operators have two nonexclusive options for evolving their networks to 3G wide band multimedia operation: (1) they can use General Packet Radio Service (GPRS) and Enhanced Data rates for GSM Evolution (EDGE) (also known as 2.5G) in the existing radio spectrum, and in small amounts of new spectrum; or (2) they can use WCDMA/UMTS in the new 2 GHz bands [19,20,21]. Both approaches offer a high degree of investment flexibility because roll-out can proceed in line with market demand and there is extensive reuse of existing network equipment and radio sites.

The first step to introduce high-speed circuit-switched data service in GSM is by using High-Speed Circuit-Switched Data (HSCSD). HSCSD is a feature that enables the co-allocation of multiple full rate traffic channels (TCH/F) of GSM into an HSCSD configuration. The aim of HSCSD is to provide a mixture of services with different user data rates using a single physical layer structure. The available capacity of an HSCSD configuration is several times the capacity of a TCH/F, leading to a significant enhancement in data transfer capability.

Ushering faster data rates into the mainstream is the new speed of 14.4 kbps per time slot and HSCSD protocols that approach wire-line access rates of up to 57.6 kbps by using multiple 14.4 kbps time slots. The increase from the current baseline of 9.6 kbps to 14.4 kbps is due to a nominal reduction in the error-correction overhead of the GSM radio link protocol, allowing the use of a higher data rate.

The next phase in the high-speed road map is the evolution of current short message service (SMS), such as smart messaging and unstructured supplementary service data, toward the new GPRS, a packet data service using TCP/IP and X.25 to offer speeds up to 115.2 kbps. GPRS has been standardized to optimally support a wide range of applications ranging from very frequent transmissions of medium to large data volume. Services of GPRS have been developed to reduce connection set-up time and allow an optimum usage of radio resources. GPRS provides a packet data service for GSM where time slots on the air interface can be assigned to GPRS over which packet data from several mobile stations can be multiplexed.

A similar evolution strategy, also adopting GPRS, has been developed for DAMPS (IS-136). For operators planning to offer wide band multimedia services, the move to GPRS packet-based data bearer service is significant; it is a relatively small step compared to building a totally new 3G network. Use of the GPRS network architecture for IS-136 packet data service enables data subscription roaming with GSM networks around the globe that support GPRS and its evolution. The IS-136 packet data service standard is known as GPRS-136. GPRS-136 provides the same capabilities as GSM GPRS. The user can access either X.25 or IP-based data networks.

GPRS provides a core network platform for current GSM operators not only to expand the wireless data market in preparation for the introduction of 3G services, but also a platform on which to build UMTS frequencies, should they acquire them.

GPRS enhances GSM data services significantly by providing end-to-end packet-switched data connections. This is particularly efficient in Internet/intranet traffic, where short bursts of intense data communications are actively interspersed with relatively long periods of inactivity. Since there is no real end-to-end connection to be established, setting up a GPRS call is almost instantaneous and users can be continuously on-line. Users have the additional benefits of paying for the actual data transmitted, rather than for connection time.

Because GPRS does not require any dedicated end-to-end connection, it only uses network resources and bandwidth when data are actually being transmitted. This means that a given amount of radio bandwidth can be shared efficiently between many users simultaneously.

The significance of EDGE (also referred to as 2.5G system) for today's GSM operators is that it increases data rates up to 384 kbps and potentially even higher in good quality radio environments that are using current GSM spectrum and carrier structures more efficiently. EDGE will both complement and be an alternative to new WCDMA coverage. EDGE will also have the effect of unifying the GSM, DAMPS, and WCDMA services through the use of dual-mode terminals.

GSM operators who win licenses in new 2 GHz bands will be able to introduce UMTS wideband coverage in areas where early demand is likely to be greatest. Dual-mode EDGE/UMTS mobile terminals will allow full roaming and handoff from one system to the other, with mapping of services between the two systems. EDGE will contribute to the commercial success of the 3G system in the vital early phases by ensuring that UMTS subscribers will be able to enjoy roaming and interworking globally.

While GPRS and EDGE require new functionality in the GSM network with new types of connections to external packet data networks, they are essentially extensions of GSM. Moving to a GSM/UMTS core network will likewise be a further extension of this network.

EDGE provides GSM operators—whether or not they get a new 3G license—with a commercially attractive solution for developing the market for wide band multimedia services. Using familiar interfaces such as the Internet, volume-based charging and a progressive increase in available user data rates will remove some of the barriers to large-scale take-up of wireless data services. The move to 3G services will be a staged evolution from today's GSM data services using GPRS and EDGE. Table 3.1 provides a comparison of GSM data services.

The use of CDMA technology began in the United States with the development of the IS-95 standard in 1990. The IS-95 standard has evolved since to provide better voice services and applications to other frequency bands (IS-95A), and to provide higher data rates (up to 115.2 kbps) for data services (IS-95B). To further improve the voice service capability and provide even higher data rates for packet- and circuit-switched data services, the industry developed the cdma2000 standard in 2000. As the concept of wireless Internet gradually

Table 3.1 Comparison of GSM Data Services.

Service Type	Data Unit	Maximum Sustained User Data Rate	Technology	Resources Used
Short message service (SMS)	Single 140 octet packet	9 bps	Simplex circuit	SDCCH or SACCH
Circuit-switched data	30 octet frames	9.6 kbps	Duplex circuits	TCH
HSCSD	192 octet frames	115 kbps	Duplex circuits	1–8 TCH
GPRS	1600 octet frames	115 kbps	Virtual circuit packet switching	PDCH (1–8 TCH)
EDGE (2.5G)	Variable	384 kbps	Virtual circuit/ packet switching	1–8 TCH

Note: SDCCH: Stand-alone Dedicated Control Channel; SACCH: Slow Associated Control Channel; TCH: Traffic Channel; PDCH: Packet Data Channel (all refer to GSM logical channels).

turns into reality, the need for an efficient high-speed data system arises. A CDMA high data rate (HDR) system was developed by Qualcomm. The CDMA-HDR [now called 3G 1X EV-DO (3G 1X Enhanced Version Data Only)] system design improves the system throughput by using fast channel estimation feedback, dual receiver antenna diversity, and scheduling algorithms that take advantage of multi-user diversity. 3G 1X EV-DO has significant improvements in the downlink structure of cdma2000 including adaptive modulation of up to 8-PSK and 16-quadrature amplitude modulation (QAM), automatic repeat request (ARQ) algorithms, and turbo coding. With these enhancements, 3G 1X EV-DO can transmit data in burst rates as high as 2.4 Mbps with 0.5–1 Mbps realistic downlink rates for individual users. The uplink design is similar to that in cdma2000. Recently, the 3G 1X EV-Data and Voice (DV) standard was finalized by the TIA and commercial equipment is currently being developed for its deployment. 3G 1X EV-DV can transmit both voice and data traffic on the same carrier with peak data throughput for the downlink being confirmed at 3.09 Mbps.

As an alternative, Time Division-Synchronous CDMA (TD-SCDMA) has been developed by Siemens and the Chinese government. TD-SCDMA uses adaptive modulation of up to quadrature phase shift keying (QPSK) and 8-PSK, as well as turbo coding to obtain downlink data throughput of up to 2 Mbps. TD-SCDMA uses a 1.6 MHz time-division duplex (TDD) carrier whereas cdma2000 uses two 1.25 MHz frequency-division duplex (FDD) carriers (2.5 MHz total). TDD allows TD-SCDMA to use the least amount of spectrum of any 3G technologies.

Table 3.2 lists the maximum data rates per user that can be achieved by various systems under ideal conditions. When the number of users increases, and if all the users share the same carrier, the data rate per user will decrease.

One of the objectives of 3G systems is to provide access "anywhere, any time." However, cellular networks can only cover a limited area due to high infrastructure costs. For this reason, *satellite* systems will form an integral part of the 3G networks. Satellite will provide extended wireless coverage to remote areas and to aeronautical and maritime mobiles. The level of integration of the satellite system with the terrestrial cellular networks is under investigation. A fully integrated solution will require mobiles to be dual mode terminals to allow communications with orbiting satellite and terrestrial cellular networks. Low Earth orbit (LEO) satellites are the most likely candidates for providing worldwide coverage. Currently, several LEO satellite systems are being deployed to provide global telecommunications.

3.5 Wireless 4G Systems

4G networks can be defined as wireless ad hoc peer-to-peer networking with high usability and global roaming, distributed computing, personalization, and multimedia support. 4G networks will use distributed architecture and end-to-end Internet Protocol (IP). Every device will be

Table 3.2 Network Technology Migration Paths and Their Associated Data Rates.

Technology	Carrier Width (MHz)	Duplexing	Multiplexing	Modulation	Maximum Data Rates	End-user Data Rates
Analog CDPD (1G) GSM circuit Switched data (2G) GPRS	0.20 0.20	FDD FDD	TDMA TDMA	GMSK GMSK	9.6 kbps 19.2 kbps 9.6–14.4 kbps up to 115.2 kbps (8 channels)	4.8–9.6 kbps about 16 kbps about 12 kbps 10–56 kbps
EDGE (2.5G) WCDMA (3G)	0.20 5.00	FDD FDD	TDMA CDMA	GMSK, 8-PSK QPSK	384 kbps 2 Mbps (stationary); 384 kbps (mobile)	About 144 kbps 50 kbps uplink; 150–200 kbps downlink
IS-54/IS-136 TDMA Circuit-switched data (2G)	0.03	FDD	TDMA	QPSK	14.4 kbps	About 10 kbps
EDGE (2.5G) for North American TDMA system	0.20	FDD	TDMA	GMSK, 8-PSK	64 kbps uplink (initial roll out) 384 kbps	Initial roll out in 2001/2002: 45–50 kbps uplink; 80–90 kbps downlink 2003: 45–50 kbps uplink; 150–200 kbps downlink
cdma2000 (3G) 1X	1.25	FDD	CDMA	QPSK	153 kbps	90–130 kbps (depending on the number of users and distance from BS)
3G 1X EV-DO (data only)	1.25	FDD	TD-CDMA	QPSK, 8-PSK, 16-QAM	2.4 Mbps	700 kbps
3G 1X EV-DV (data and voice)	1.25	FDD	TD-CDMA	QPSK, 8-PSK, 16-QAM	3–5 Mbps	>1 Mbps
TD-SCDMA	1.60	TDD	TD-CDMA	QPSK, 8-PSK	2 Mbps	1.333 Mbps

Note: FDD: Frequency-division duplex; TDD: Time-division duplex; PSK: Phase shift keying; QPSK: Quadrature phase shift keying; GMSK: Gaussian minimum shift keying; QAM: Quadrature amplitude modulation.

both a transceiver and a router for other devices in the network eliminating the spoke-and-hub architecture weakness of 3G cellular systems. Network coverage/capacity will dynamically change to accommodate changing user patterns. Users will automatically move away from congested routes to allow the network to dynamically and automatically self-balance.

Recently, several wireless broadband technologies [13] have emerged to achieve high data rates and QoS. Navini Networks developed a wireless broadband system based on TD-SCDMA. The system, named Ripwave, uses beamforming to allow multiple subscribers in different parts of a sector to simultaneously use the majority of the spectrum bandwidth. Beamforming allows the spectrum to be effectively reused in dense environments without having to use excessive sectors. The Ripwave system varies between QPSK, 16- and 64-QAM, which allows the system to burst up to 9.6 Mbps using a single 1.6 MHz TDD carrier. Due to TDD and 64-QAM modulation the Ripwave system is extremely spectrally efficient. Currently, Ripwave is being tried by several telecom operators in the United States. The Ripwave Customer Premise Equipment is about the size of a cable modem and has a self-contained antenna. Recently, PC cards for laptops have become available allowing greater portability for the user.

Flarion Technologies is promoting their proprietary Flash-orthogonal frequency-division multiple (OFDM) as a high-speed wireless broadband solution. Flash-OFDM uses frequency-hopping spread spectrum (FHSS) to limit interference and allows a reuse pattern of one in an OFDM access environment. Flarion's Flash-OFDM system uses 1.25 MHz FDD carriers with QPSK and 16-QAM modulation. Peak speeds can burst up to 3.2 Mbps with sustained rates leveling off at 1.6 Mbps on the downlink. Flarion has not implemented an antenna-enhancement technology that may further improve data rates.

BeamReach is a wireless broadband technology based on OFDM and beamforming. It uses TDD duplexed 1.25 MHz paired carriers. SS is used to reduce interference over the 2.5 MHz carriers allowing a frequency reuse of one. Individual users can expect downlink rates of 1.5, 1.2, and 0.8 Mbps using 32-QAM, 16-QAM, and 8-PSK modulation, respectively. The aggregate network bandwidth is claimed to be 88 Mbps in 10 MHz of spectrum or 220 Mbps in 24 MHz of spectrum, which equates to a high spectral efficiency of 9 bps/Hz. It should be noted that the system uses either four or six sectors and these claims are based on those sectoring schemes. For any technology with a reuse number of 1 to achieve 9 bps/Hz per cell with four or six sectors, the efficiency in each sector would need to be a reasonable 2.3 or 1.5 bps/Hz, respectively.

IPWireless is the broadband technology based upon UMTS. It uses either 5 or 10 MHz TDD carriers and QPSK modulation. The theoretical peak transmission speeds for a 10 MHz deployment are 6 Mbps downlink and 3 Mbps uplink. The IPWireless system only uses QPSK modulation and no advanced antenna technologies. With the inclusion of advanced antenna technologies and the development of High-Speed Downlink Packet Access (HSDPA), IPWireless has significant potential.

SOMA networks has also developed a wireless broadband technology based on UMTS. Like UMTS, SOMA's technology uses 5 MHz FHSS carriers. Peak throughput is claimed to be as high as 12 Mbps, making SOMA one of the faster wireless broadband technologies.

Table 3.3 Non-Line-of-Sight (LOS) Wireless Broadband Technologies.

Developer	Technology	Multiplexing	Duplexing	Carrier (MHz)	Modulation	System DL Peak (Mbps)	System DL LOM (Mbps)	Avg. DL efficiency (bps/Hz)
Navini	TD-SCDMA	TD-CDMA	TDD	1.6	QPSK to 64-QAM	8.0	2.0	2.5
IP wireless	TD-WCDMA	TD-CDMA	TDD	5.0	QPSK	3.0	3.0	1.2
Flarion	Flash-OFDM	FHSS-OFDM	FDD	1.25	QPSK, 16-QAM	3.2	1.6	1.28
SOMA	UMTS	CDMA	FDD	5.0	QPSK, 16-QAM	12.0	6.0	1.2
Beam Reach	AB-OFDM	DSSS-OFDM	TDD	2.5	8-PSK, 16-, 32-QAM	3.33	2.0	1.6

Note: TDD carriers need one carrier for Tx and Rx, thus efficiency is doubled; BeamReach system throughput includes six sectors, thus it was divided by six; LOM: sustained system throughput estimated using lowest order modulation.

Table 3.3 compares the wireless broadband technologies and their lowest order modulation data throughput.

3.6 Future Wireless Networks

As mobile networks evolve to offer both circuit- and packet-switched services, users will be connected permanently (always on) via their personal terminal of choice to the network. With the development of intelligence in core network (CN), both voice and broadband multimedia traffic will be directed to their intended destination with reduced latency and delays. Transmission speeds will be increased and there will be far more efficient use of network bandwidth and resources. As the number of IP-based mobile applications grows, 3G systems will offer the most flexible access technology because it allows for mobile, office, and residential use in a wide range of public and nonpublic networks. The 3G systems will support both IP and non-IP traffic in a variety of modes, including packet-, circuit-switched, and virtual circuit, and will thus benefit directly from the development and extension of IP standards for mobile communications. New developments will allow parameters like QoS, data rate, and bit error rate (BER)—vital for mobile operation—to be set by the operator and/or service provider.

Wireless systems beyond 3G (e.g., 4G) will consist of a layered combination of different access technologies:

- Cellular systems (e.g., existing 2G and 3G systems for wide area mobility);
- WLANs for dedicated indoor applications (such as IEEE 802.11a, 802.11b, 802.11g);
- Worldwide interoperability for microwave access (WiMAX) (IEEE 802.16) for metropolitan areas;
- WPANs for short-range and low-mobility applications around a room in the office or at home (such as Bluetooth).

These access systems will be connected via a common IP-based core network that will also handle interworking between the different systems. The core network will enable inter- and intra-access handoff.

The peak data rates of 3G systems are around 10 times more than 2G/2.5G systems. The 4G systems may be expected to provide a data rate 10 times higher than 3G systems. User data rates of 2 Mbps for vehicular and 20 Mbps for indoor applications are expected. The 4G systems will also meet the requirements of next generation Internet through compliance with IPv6, Mobile IP, QoS control, and so on.

3.7 Standardization Activities for Cellular Systems

The standardization activities for PCS in North America were carried out by the joint technical committee (JTC) on wireless access, consisting of appropriate groups from within the T1 committee, a unit of the Alliance for Telecommunications Industry Solutions (ATIS), and the engineering committee TR46, a unit of the Telecommunications Industry Association (TIA). The JTC was formed in November of 1992, and its first assignment was to develop a set of criteria for PCS air interfaces. The JTC established seven technical ad hoc groups (TAGs) in March 1994, one for each of the selected air interface proposals. The TAGs drafted the specifications document for the respective air interface technologies and conducted validation and verification to ensure consistency with the criteria established by the JTC. This was followed by balloting on each of the standards. After the balloting process, four of the proposed standards were adopted as ANSI standards: IS-136-based PCS, IS-95-based PCS, GSM 1900 (a derivative of GSM), and Personal Access Communication System (PACS). Two of the proposed standards—composite CDMA/TDMA and Oki's wide band CDMA—were adopted as trial use standards by ATIS and interim standards by TIA. The Personal Wireless Telecommunications-Enhanced (PWT-E) standard was moved from JTC to TR 46.1 which, after a ballot process, was adopted in March 1996. Table 3.4 provides a comparison of seven technologies using a set of parameters which include access methods, duplex methods, bandwidth per channel, throughput per channel, maximum power output per subscriber unit, vocoder, and minimum and maximum cell ranges.

The 3G systems were standardized under the umbrella of the International Telecommunications Union (ITU). The main proposals to the ITU International Mobile Telecommunications-2000 (IMT-2000) are: ETSI UMTS Terrestrial Radio Access (UTRA), ARIB WCDMA, TIA cdma2000, and TD-SCDMA. These 3G systems will provide the necessary quality for multimedia communications. The IMT-2000 requirements are: 384 kbps for full area coverage (144 kbps for fast-moving vehicles between 120 km per hour and 500 km per hour) and 2 Mbps for local coverage. It is, therefore, important to use packet-switched data service to dynamically allocate and release resources based on the current needs of each user.

Table 3.4 Technical Characteristics of North American PCS Standards.

	TAG-1	TAG-2	TAG-3	TAG-4	TAG-5	TAG-6	TAG-7
Standard	Composite CDMA/TDMA	IS-95 based PCS	PACS	IS-136 based PCS	GSM 1900	PWT-E	Oki's wide band CDMA
Access	CDMA/ TDMA/FDMA	CDMA	TDMA	TDMA	TDMA	TDMA	CDMA
Duplex method	TDD	FDD	FDD	FDD	FDD	TDD	FDD
Frequency reuse	3	1	16 × 1	17 × 3	7 × 1, 3 × 3	Portable selected	1
Bandwidth/ channel	2.5/5 MHz	1.25 MHz	300 kHz	30 kHz	200 kHz	1 kHz	5, 10, 15 MHz
Throughput/ channel (kb/s)	8	8.55/13.3	32	8	13	32	32
Maximum power/ subscriber unit	600 mW	200 mW	200 mW	600 mW	0.5–2.0 W	500 mW	500 mW
Vocoder	PHS HCA	CELP ADPCM	VCELP/ ACELP	RPE-LTE ACELP	ADPCM	ADPCM	
Maximum cell range (km)	10.0	50.0	1.6	20.0	35.0	0.15	5.0
Minimum cell range (km)	0.1	0.05	0–1	0.5	0.5	0.01	0.05

The ETSI agreed on a WCDMA solution using FDD mode. In Japan, a WCDMA solution was adopted for both TDD and FDD modes. In Korea, two different types of CDMA solutions were proposed—one based on WCDMA similar to that of Europe and Japan and the other similar to the cdma2000 proposed in North America.

A number of groups working on similar technologies pooled their resources. This led to the creation of two standards groups—the third-generation partnership project (3GPP) and 3GPP2. 3GPP works on UMTS, which is based on WCDMA, and 3GPP2 works on cdma2000.

The IEEE standard committee 802.11 is responsible for the WLAN standard. There are two IEEE standards committees that are involved in certification of wireless broadband technologies. The 802.16x committee focuses on the wireless metropolitan area network (WMAN) using CDMA and OFDM technologies. 802.16x allows for portability and data rates above 1 Mbps. The newly formed IEEE 802.20 committee, evolved from the 802.16e committee, focuses on mobile wide area network (MWAN). Several key performance requirements include megabit data rates and mobile handoff at speeds of up to 250 km per hour.

The Worldwide Interoperability for Microwave Access (WiMAX) Forum is a nonprofit organization formed by equipment and component suppliers to promote the adoption of IEEE 802.16-compliant equipment by operators of broadband wireless access systems. The organization is working to facilitate the deployment of broadband wireless networks based on IEEE 802.16 standards by helping to ensure the compatibility and interoperability of broadband wireless access equipment.

3.8 Summary

In this chapter, we presented the scope of wireless networks and gave an overview. We briefly discussed 1G, 2G/2.5G, and 3G cellular systems. The advantage of wireless data networking is apparent. Wireless data network users are not confined to the locations of "wired" data jacks, and enjoy connectivity that is less restrictive and therefore well-suited to meet the needs of today's mobile users. Wireless network deployment in three service classifications—wireless personal access network (WPAN), WLAN, and wireless wide area network (WWAN)—was discussed. Today, the core technology behind the wireless service in each of these service classifications is unique and, more important, not an inherently integrated seamless networking strategy. As an example, a user of a personal digital assistant (PDA), such as a PALM (XXX) connecting to the Internet via a WWAN service provider will not be able to directly connect to a WLAN service. Simply stated, they are different services, with different hardware requirements, and have fundamentally different service limitations. In the future, wireless networks have to evolve to provide interoperability of WPAN, WLAN, and WWAN systems.

Problems

1.1 Name the wireless access techniques used in 1G, 2G, and 3G wireless systems.
1.2 What are the three classes of wireless data networking?
1.3 Define the roles of WPAN technology in wireless data networking.
1.4 List the main features of 3G systems.
1.5 What is the role of GPRS in enhancing 2G GSM systems?
1.6 Show how CDMA IS-95 systems are moving to provide 3G services.
1.7 Show how 2G GSM systems are moving to achieve 3G services.
1.8 What are the data rate requirements for 3G systems?
1.9 Define IPWireless technology.
1.10 What are the goals of 4G systems?

References

[1] D.M. Balston, R.C.V. Macario, Cellular Radio Systems, Artech House, Norwood, MA, 1993.

[2] D.M. Balston, The Pan-European cellular technology, IEE Conference Publication, 1988.

[3] B.P. Crow, I. Widjaja, L.G. Kim, P.T. Sakai, IEEE 802.11 wireless local area networks, IEEE Commun. Mag. (1998) 116–126.

[4] K. Negus, A. Stephens, J. Lansford, Home RF: wireless networking for the connected home, IEEE Pers. Commun. (2000) 20–27.

[5] V.K. Garg, J.E. Wilkes, Wireless and Personal Communications Systems, Prentice Hall, Upper Saddle River, NJ, 1996.

[6] W.R. Young, Advanced mobile phone services—Introduction, background and objectives, Bell Syst. Tech. J. 58 (1979) 1–14.

[7] V.K. Garg, J.E. Wilkes, Principles and Applications of GSM, Prentice Hall, Upper Saddle River, NJ, 1998.

[8] V.K. Garg, CDMA IS-95 and cdma2000, Prentice Hall, Upper Saddle River, NJ, 2000.

[9] J. Cai, D.J. Goodman, General packet radio service in GSM, IEEE Commun. Mag. 35 (10) (1997) 121–131.

[10] J.S. Dasilva, D. Ikonomou, H. Erben, European R&D programs on third-generation mobile communications systems, IEEE Pers. Commun. 4 (1) (1997) 46–52.

[11] The European path towards UMTS, IEEE Pers. Commun., Special Issue, February 1995.

[12] 3GPPweb third generation partnership project website: http://www.3gpp.org.

[13] M. Shafi, S. Ogose, T. Hattori (Eds.), Wireless Communication in the 21st Century, Wiley-Interscience, 2002.

[14] E.H. Dinan, B. Jabbari, Spreading codes for direct sequence CDMA and wide band CDMA cellular networks, IEEE Commun. Mag., September 1998.

[15] N. Marley, GSM and PCN Systems and Equipment, JRC Conference, Harrogate, 1991.

[16] M. Mouly, M.-B. Pautet, The GSM System for Mobile Communications, Palaiseau, France, 1992.

[17] R. Pirhonen, T. Rautava, J. Pentinen, TDMA convergence for packet data services, IEEE Pers. Commun. Mag. 6 (3) (1999) 68–73.

[18] J. Rapeli, UMTS: targets, system concepts, and standardization in a global framework, IEEE Pers. Commun. (1995).

[19] 3GPP2web third generation partnership project-2 website: http://www.3gpp2.org.

[20] N. Nakajma, Future mobile communications systems in Japan, Wireless Pers. Commun. 17 (2–3) (2001) 209–223.

[21] E. Nikula, A. Toshala, E. Dahlman, L. Girard, A. Klein, FRAMES multiple access for UMTS and IMT-2000, IEEE Pers. Commun. Mag. (1998) 16–24.

CHAPTER 4

Wireless Application Protocol

Vijay K. Garg

4.1 Introduction

Wireless application protocol (WAP) [1, 2] is a set of protocols that allows wireless devices such as cell phones, PDAs, and two-way radios to access the Internet. It is designed to work with small screens and with limited interactive controls. WAP incorporates wireless markup language (WML) [3], which is used to specify the format and presentation of text on the screen. WAP is a standard developed by the WAP forum [now the open mobile alliance (OMA)], and defines a communications protocol as well as an application environment. It is a standardized technology for cross-platform, distributed computing. WAP is very similar to the combination of hyper text markup language (HTML) and hyper text transport protocol (HTTP) except that it adds one very important feature: optimization for low-bandwidth, low-memory, and low-display capability environment. These types of environments include PDAs, wireless phones, pagers, and virtually any other communications device.

The imode is a proprietary mobile Internet service provider (ISP) and portal service from NTT DoCoMo, Japan. In this chapter we focus on WAP and discuss WAP programming model, WAP protocol stack, and WAP architecture. The goal of imode and its protocol stack is also presented and compared with the WAP.

4.2 WAP and the World Wide Web (WWW)

From a certain viewpoint, the WAP approach to content distribution and the web approach are virtually identical in concept. Both concentrate on distributing content to remote devices using inexpensive, standardized client software. Both rely on back-end servers to handle user authentication, database queries, and intensive processing. Both use markup languages derived from standard generalized markup language (SGML) for delivering content to the client. In fact, as WAP continues to grow in support and popularity, it is highly likely that WAP application developers will make use of their existing web infrastructure (in the form of application servers) for data storage and retrieval. WAP allows a further extension of the concept as existing "server" layers can be reused and extended to reach out to the vast array of wireless devices in business and personal use today. Extensible markup language (XML), as opposed to HTML, contains no screen formatting instructions; instead, it concentrates on returning structured data that the client can use as it sees fits.

4.3 Introduction to Wireless Application Protocol

WAP has become the de facto global industry standard for providing data to wireless hand-held mobile devices [4–10]. WAP takes a client/server approach and incorporates a relatively simple microbrowser into the mobile phone, requiring only limited resources on mobile phones. WAP puts the intelligence in the WAP Gateways while adding just a microbrowser to the mobile phones themselves. Microbrowser-based services and applications reside temporarily on servers, not permanently in phones. The WAP is aimed at turning mass-market phones into a *network-based smart phone*. The philosophy behind WAP's approach is to use as few resources as possible on the hand-held device and compensate for the constraints of the device by enriching the functionality of the network.

WAP specifies a thin-client microbrowser using a new standard called *wireless markup language* (*WML*) that is optimized for wireless hand-held mobile devices. WML is a stripped down version of HTML.

WAP specifies a proxy server that acts as a gateway between the wireless network and the wire-line Internet, providing protocol translation and optimizing data transfer for the wireless handset. WAP also specifies a computer-telephony integration *application programming interface* (*API*), called *wireless telephony application interface* (*WTAI*), between data and voice. This enables applications to take full advantage of the fact that this wireless mobile device is most often a phone and a mobile user's constant companion. On-board memory on a WAP phone can be used for off-line content, enhanced address books, bookmarks, and text input methods.

The importance of WAP can be found in the fact that it provides an evolutionary path for application developers and network operators to offer their services on different network types, bearers, and terminal capabilities. The design of the WAP standard separates the application elements from the bearer being used. This helps in the migration of some applications from short message service (SMS) or circuit-switched (CS) data to general packet radio service (GPRS), for example. WAP 1.0 was optimized for early WAP-phones.

The WAP cascading style sheet (WAP CSS) is the mobile version of a cascading style sheet. It is a subset of CSS2 (the cascading style sheet language of the WWW) plus some WAP-specific extensions. CSS2 features and properties that are not useful for mobile Internet applications are not included in WAP CSS. WAP CSS is the companion of XHTML Mobile Profile (XHTML MP). Both of them are defined in the WAP 2.0 specification, which was created by the WAP forum. XHTML MP is a subset of XHTML, which is the combination of HTML and XML. There are many WAP 2.0-enabled cell phones on the market currently.

Before creating WAP 2.0, developers used WML to build WAP sites and HTML/XHTML/CSS to build web sites. Now with WAP 2.0 they can make use of the same technologies to create both web sites and WAP sites. Documents written in XHTML MP/WAP CSS are viewable on ordinary PC web browsers, since XHTML MP and WAP CSS are just the subsets of XHTML and CSS.

The following are the goals of WAP:

- Independent of wireless network standards;
- Interoperability: Terminals from different manufacturers must be able to communicate with services in the mobile network;
- Adaptation to bounds of wireless networks: Low bandwidth, high latency, less connection stability;
- Adaptation to bounds of wireless devices: Small display, limited input facilities, limited memory and CPU, limited battery power;
- Efficient: Provide quality of service (QoS) suitable to the behavior and characteristics of the mobile world;
- Reliable: Provide a consistent and predictable platform for deploying services;
- Secure: Enable services to be extended over potentially unprotected mobile networks while preserving the integrity of data;
- Applications scale across transport options;
- Applications scale across device types;
- Extensible over time to new networks and transport.

WAP is envisaged as a comprehensive and scalable protocol designed for use with:

- Any mobile device from those with a one-line display to a smart phone;
- Any existing or planned wireless service such as the SMS, CS data, unstructured supplementary services data (USSD) and GPRS;
- Any mobile network standard such as code division multiple access (CDMA), global system of mobile communications (GSM), or universal mobile telephone system (UMTS); WAP has been designed to work with all cellular standards and is supported by major worldwide wireless leaders such as AT&T wireless and NTT DoCoMo;
- Multiple input terminals such as keypads, keyboards, touch-screens, etc.

4.4 The WAP Programming Model

Before presenting the WAP programming model, we briefly discuss the WWW model that is the basis for the WAP model.

4.4.1 The WWW Model

The Internet WWW architecture provides a flexible and powerful programming model. Applications and content are presented in standard data formats, and are browsed by applications known as web browsers. The web browser is a network application, i.e., it sends requests for named data objects to a network server and the network server responds with encoded data using the standard formats.

The WWW standards specify several mechanisms necessary to build a general-purpose application environment which includes:

- **Standard naming model.** All servers and content on the WWW are named with an Internet-standard *Uniform Resource Locator (URL)*.

- **Content typing.** All content on the WWW is given a specific type, thereby allowing web browsers to correctly process the content based on its type.

- **Standard content formats.** All web browsers support a set of standard content formats. These include (HTML), JavaScript scripting language (ECMAScript, JavaScript), and a large number of other formats.

- **Standard protocols.** Standard networking protocols allow any web browser to communicate with any web server. The most commonly used protocol on the WWW is the HTTP. This infrastructure allows users to easily reach a large number of third-party applications and content services. It also allows application developers to easily create applications and content services for a large community of clients.

The WWW protocols define three classes of servers:

1. *Origin server:* The server on which a given resource (content) resides or is to be created.

2. *Proxy:* An intermediary program that acts as both a server and a client for the purpose of making requests on behalf of other clients. The proxy typically resides between clients and servers that have no means of direct communication (e.g., across a firewall). Requests are either serviced by a proxy program or passed on with possible translation to other servers. A proxy must implement both the client and the server requirements of WWW specifications.

3. *Gateway:* A server which acts as an intermediary for some other server. Unlike a proxy, a gateway receives requests as if it were the origin server for the requested resource. The requesting client may not be aware that it is communicating with a gateway.

4.4.2 The WAP Model

The WAP programming model (see Figure 4.1) is similar to the WWW programming model. This provides several benefits to the application developer community, including a familiar

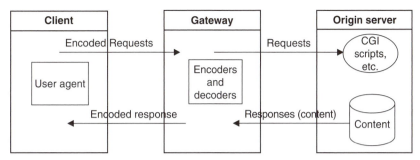

Figure 4.1 WAP programming model.

programming model, a proven architecture, and the ability to leverage existing tools (e.g., web servers, XML tools, etc.). Optimization and extensions have been made in order to match the characteristics of the wireless environment. Wherever possible, existing standards have been adopted or have been used as the starting point for the WAP technology.

WAP content and applications are specified in a set of well-known content formats based on WWW content formats. Content is transported using a set of standard communication protocols based on WWW communication protocols. A microbrowser in the wireless terminal coordinates the user interface and is analogous to a standard web browser. WAP defines a set of standard components that enable communication between mobile terminals and network servers, including:

- *Standard naming model*: WWW-standard URLs are used to identify WAP content on origin servers. WWW-standard URLs are used to identify local resources in a device (e.g., call control functions).

- *Content typing*: All WAP content is given a specific type consistent with WWW typing. This allows WAP user agents to correctly process the content based on its type.

- *Standard content formats*: WAP content formats are based on WWW technology and include display markup, calendar information, electronic business card objects, images, and scripting language.

- *Standard protocols*: WAP communication protocols enable the communication of browser requests from the mobile terminal to the network web server. The WAP content types and protocols have been optimized for mass market, hand-held wireless devices. WAP utilizes proxy technology to connect between the wireless domain and the WWW.

The WAP proxy typically comprises the following functionality:

- *Protocol gateway*: The protocol gateway translates requests from the WAP protocol stack to the WWW protocol stack (HTTP and TCP/IP).

- *Content encoders and decoders*: The content encoders translate WAP content into compact encoded formats to reduce the size of data over the network. This infrastructure ensures that mobile terminal users can browse a wide variety of WAP content and applications, and that the application author is able to build content services and applications that run on a large base of mobile devices. The WAP proxy allows content and applications to be hosted on standard WWW servers and to be developed using proven WWW technologies such as cell global identity (CGI) scripting. While the nominal use of WAP includes a web server, WAP proxy, and WAP client, WAP architecture can easily support other configurations. It is possible to create an origin server that includes WAP proxy functionality. Such a server might be used to facilitate end-to-end security solutions, or applications that require better access control or a guarantee of responsiveness.

4.5 WAP Architecture

WAP architecture [11–15] provides a scalable and extensible environment for the application development of mobile communication devices. This is achieved using a layered design of the entire protocol stack (see Figure 4.2). Each of the layers of architecture is accessible by layers above, as well as by other services and applications. WAP layered architecture enables other services and applications to utilize the features of the WAP stack through a set of well-defined interfaces. External applications may access the session, transaction, security, and transport layers directly. The layered design and functions of the WAP protocol stack resemble the layers of the open system interconnection model. In Figure 4.3, WAP and Internet protocol

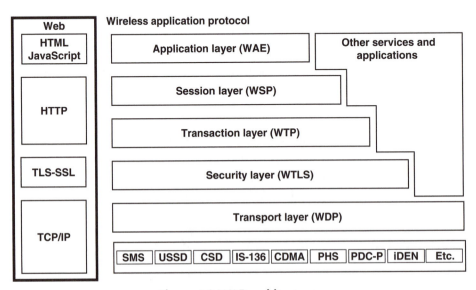

Figure 4.2 WAP architecture.

stacks are compared. The following sections provide a description of the various elements of the WAP protocol.

4.5.1 Wireless Application Environment

The uppermost layer in the WAP stack, the wireless application environment (WAE), is a general-purpose application environment based on a combination of WWW and mobile telephony technologies. The primary objective of the WAE is to establish an interoperable environment that allows operators and service providers to build applications and services that can reach a wide variety of different wireless platforms in an efficient and useful manner. Various components of the WAE are:

*   *Addressing model:* WAP uses the same addressing model as the one used on the Internet (i.e., URL). A URL uniquely identifies a resource on a server that can be retrieved using well-known protocols. WAP also uses Uniform Resource Identifiers

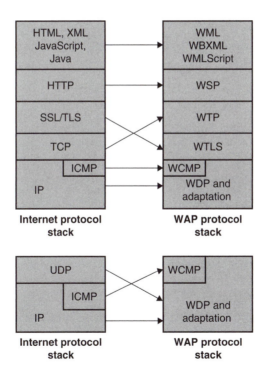

WML: Wireless markup language
WSP: Wireless session protocol
WTP: Wireless transport protocol
WTLS: Wireless transport layer security
WCMP: Wireless control management protocol
WDP: Wireless datagram protocol

Figure 4.3 WAP and Internet protocol stacks.

(URI). A URI is used for addressing resources that are not necessarily accessed using known protocols. An example of using a URI is local access to a wireless device's telephony functions.

- *WML:* It is WAP's analogy to HTML and is based on XML. It is WAP's answer to problems such as creating services that fit on small hand-held devices, low bandwidth wireless bearers, etc. WML uses a deck/card metaphor to specify a service. A card is typically a unit of interaction with the user (i.e., either presentation of information or request for information from the user). A collection of cards is called a deck, which usually constitutes a service. This approach ensures that a suitable amount of information is displayed to the user simultaneously since interpage navigation can be avoided to the maximum possible extent. Key features of WML include variables, text formatting features, support for images, support for soft-buttons, navigation control, control of browser history, support for event handling (e.g., telephony services) and different types of user interactions (e.g., selection lists and input fields). One of the key advantages of WML is that it can be binary encoded by the WAP Gateway/Proxy in order to save bandwidth in the wireless domain.

- *WMLScript:* It is used for enhancing services written in WML. WMLScript can be used for validation of user input. Since WML does not provide any mechanisms for achieving this, a round trip to the server would be needed in order to determine whether user input is valid if scripting was not available. Access to local functions in a wireless device is another area in which WMLScript is used (e.g., access to telephony related functions). WMLScript libraries contain functions that extend the basic WMLScript functionality. This provides a means for future expansion of functions without having to change the core of WMLScript. Just as with WML, WMLScript can be binary encoded by the WAP Gateway/Proxy in order to minimize the amount of data sent over the air.

4.5.2 Wireless Telephony Application

The wireless telephony application (WTA) environment provides a means to create telephony services using WAP. WTA utilizes a user-agent, which is based on the WML user-agent, but extends its functionality that meets special requirements for telephony services. This functionality includes.

- *WTAI:* An interface toward a set of telephony-related functions in a mobile phone that can be invoked from WML and/or WMLScript. These functions include call management, handling of text messages, and phone book control. WTAI enables access to functions that are not suitable for allowing common access to them, e.g., setting up calls and manipulating the phone book without user acknowledgment.

- *Repository:* Since it is not feasible to retrieve content from a server every now and then, repository makes it possible to store WTA services in the device in order to enable access to them without accessing the network.

- *Event handling:* Typical events in a mobile network are incoming calls, call disconnect, and call answered. The event handling within WTA enables WTA services stored in the repository to be started in response to such events.

- *WTA service indication:* It is a content type that allows a user to be notified about events of different kinds (e.g., new voice mails) and be given the possibility to start the appropriate service to handle the event. In the most basic form, the WTA service indication makes it possible to send a URL and a message to a wireless device.

The WTA framework relies on a dedicated WTA user-agent to carry out these functions. Only trusted content providers should be able to make content available to the WTA user-agent. Thus, it must be possible to distinguish between servers that are allowed to supply the user-agent with services containing these functions and those who are not. To accomplish this, the WTA user-agent retrieves its services from the WTA domain, which, in contrast to the Internet, is controlled by the network operator. WTA services and other services are separated from each other using WTA access control based on port numbers.

4.5.3 Wireless Session Protocol

Wireless session protocol (WSP) provides a means for the organized exchange of content between cooperating client/server applications. Its functions are to:

- Establish a reliable session from the client to the server and release the session in an orderly manner.
- Agree on a common level of protocol functionality using capability negotiation.
- Exchange content between client and server using compact encoding.
- Suspend and resume the session.
- Provide HTTP 1.1 functionality.
- Exchange client and server session headers.
- Interrupt transactions in process.
- Push content from server to client in an unsynchronized manner.
- Negotiate support for multiple, simultaneous asynchronous transactions.

The core of the WSP design is a binary form of HTTP. Consequently, all methods defined by HTTP 1.1 are supported. In addition, capability negotiation can be used to agree on a set of extended request methods, so that full compatibility to HTTP applications can be retained. HTTP content headers are used to define content type, character set encoding, language, etc., in an extensible manner. However, compact binary encoding is defined for the well-known headers to reduce protocol overhead.

The life cycle of a WSP is not tied to the underlying transport protocol. A session can be suspended while the session is idle to free up network resources or save battery power. A lightweight session re-establishment protocol allows the session to be resumed without the overload of full-blown session establishment. A session may be resumed over a different bearer network.

WSP allows extended capabilities to be negotiated between peers (as an example this allows for both high-performance, feature-full implementation as well as simple, basic, and small implementations). WSP provides an optimal mechanism for attaching header information to the acknowledgment of a transaction. It also optionally supports asynchronous requests so that a client can submit multiple requests to the server simultaneously. This improves utilization of air time and latency as the result of each request can be sent to the client when it becomes available.

4.5.4 Wireless Transaction Protocol

Wireless transaction protocol (WTP) does not have security mechanisms. WTP has been defined as a light-weight transaction-oriented protocol that is suitable for implementation in "thin" clients and operates efficiently over wireless datagram networks. Reliability is improved through the use of unique transaction identifiers, acknowledgments, duplicate removal, and retransmissions. There is an optional user-to-user reliability function in which WTP user can confirm every received message. The last acknowledgment of the transaction, which may contain out-of-band information related to the transaction, is also optional. WTP has no explicit connection set-up or tear-down phases. This improves efficiency over connection-oriented services. The protocol provides mechanisms to minimize the number of transactions being replayed as a result of duplicate packets.

WTP is designed for services oriented toward transactions, such as browsing. The basic unit of interchange is an entire message and not a stream of bytes. Concatenation may be used, where applicable, to convey multiple packet data units (PDUs) in one service data unit (SDU) of the datagram transport. WTP allows asynchronous transactions. There are three classes of transaction service:

- Class 0: Unreliable "send" with no result message. No retransmission if the sent message is lost.

- Class 1: Reliable "send" with no result message. The recipient acknowledges the sent message; otherwise the message is resent.

- Class 2: Reliable "send" with exactly one reliable result message. A data request is sent and a result is received which is finally acknowledged by the initiating part.

Note: For reliable "send," both success and failure are reported.

4.5.5 Wireless Transport Layer Security

The purpose of wireless transport layer security (WTLS) is to provide transport layer security between a WAP client and the WAP Gateway/Proxy. WTLS is a security protocol based on the industry standard transport layer security (TLS) protocol with new features such as datagram support, optimized handshake, and dynamic key refreshing. The WTLS layer is modular and depends on the required security level of the given application, or characteristics of the underlying network, whether it is used or not. WTLS is optional and can be used with both the connectionless and the connection mode WAP stack configuration. In addition, WTLS provides an interface for managing secure connections. The primary goal of WTLS is to provide the following features between two communicating applications:

- *Data integrity:* WTLS contains facilities to ensure that data sent between the terminal and an application server are unchanged and not corrupted.

- *Privacy:* WTLS contains facilities to ensure that data transmitted between the terminal and an application server is private and cannot be understood by any intermediate parties that may have intercepted the data stream.

- *Authentication:* WTLS contains facilities to establish the authenticity of the terminal and application server.

- *Denial-of-service protection:* WTLS contains facilities for detecting and rejecting data that are replayed or not successfully verified. WTLS makes many typical denial-of-service attacks harder to accomplish and protects the upper protocol layers.

WTLS protocol is optimized for low-bandwidth bearer networks with relatively long latency. These features make it possible to certify that the sent data have not been manipulated by a third party, that privacy is guaranteed, that an author of a message can be identified, and that both parties cannot falsely deny having sent their messages.

4.5.6 Wireless Datagram Protocol

Wireless datagram protocol (WDP) offers a consistent service to the upper layer protocols of WAP and communicates transparently over one of the available bearer services. The services offered by WDP include application addressing by port numbers, optional segmentation and reassembly, and optional error detection.

WDP supports several simultaneous communication instances from a higher layer over a single underlying WDP bearer service. The port number identifies the higher layer entity above the WDP. Reusing the elements of the underlying bearers and supporting multiple bearers, WDP can be optimized for efficient operation within the limited resources of a mobile device.

The WDP adaptation layer is the layer of the WDP that maps the WDP functions directly onto a specific bearer. The adaptation layer is different for each bearer and deals with the specific capabilities and characteristics of that particular bearer service. At the gateway, the adaptation layer terminates and passes the WDP packets on to a WAP proxy/server via a tunneling protocol.

If WAP is used over a bearer UDP, the WDP layer is not needed. On other bearers, such as GSM SMS, the datagram functionality is provided by WDP. This means that WAP uses a datagram service, which hides the characteristics of different bearers and provides port number functionality.

Processing errors can occur when the WDP datagrams are sent from one WDP provider to another. For example, a wireless data gateway is unable to send a datagram to the WAP gateway, or the receiver does not have enough buffer space to receive large messages. The wireless control message protocol (WCMP) provides an efficient error-handling mechanism for WDP.

4.5.7 Optimal WAP Bearers

The WAP is designed to operate over a variety of different services, including SMS, circuit-switched data (CSD), and packet-switched data (PSD). The bearers offer differing levels of QoS with respect to throughput, error rate, and delays. The WAP is designed to compensate for or tolerate these varying levels of service:

- *SMS:* Given its limited length of 160 characters per short message, the overhead of the WAP that would be required to be transmitted in an SMS message would mean that even for the simplest of transactions several SMS messages may have to be sent.

- *CSD:* Most of the trial-based services use CSD as the underlying bearer. CSD lacks immediacy—a dial-up connection taking about 10 sec is required to connect the WAP client to the WAP gateway; and this is the best case scenario when there is a complete end-to-end digital call.

- *USSD:* It is a means of transmitting information or instructions over a GSM network. In USSD a session is established and the radio connection stays open until the user, application, or time-out releases it. USSD text messages can be up to 182 characters in length. USSD can be an ideal bearer of WAP on GSM networks. USSD is preferable due to the following advantages:
  1. Turnaround response times for interactive applications are shorter for USSD.
  2. Users need not access any particular phone menu to access services with USSD but they can enter the command directly from the initial mobile phone screen.

- *GPRS:* GPRS is a new bearer because it is immediate, relatively fast, and supports virtual connectivity, allowing relevant information to be sent from the network as and when it is generated. There are two efficient means of delivering proactively sending (pushing) content to a mobile phone: by SMS (which is, of course, one of the WAP bearers) or by the user maintaining more or less a permanent GPRS session with the content server. WAP incorporates two different connection modes—WSP connection mode or WSP connection protocol. This is similar to the two GPRS point-to-point services— connection-oriented and connectionless. For the interactive menu-based information exchanges that WAP anticipates, GPRS and WAP can be ideal bearers for each other.

4.6 Traditional WAP Networking Environment

WAP allows the presentation and delivery of information and services to wireless devices such as mobile telephone or hand-held computer. The major players in WAP space are the wireless service provider (WSP) and the enterprise (see Figure 4.4). The WSP is the wireless equivalent of an ISP. The role of the WSP is to provide access to back-end resources for wireless users. The WSP provides additional service because wireless users must transition from a wireless to a wired environment (unlike an Internet environment where the user is already "on" on the Internet). The WSP's space contains a modem bank, remote access service (RAS) server, router, and potentially a WAP gateway. The environment is similar to the wired environment, where all connection type services are provided by the WSP. The WSP handles the processing associated with incoming WAP communications, including the translation of wireless communication from the WAP device through the transmission towers

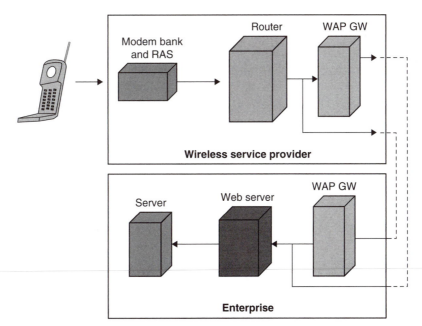

Figure 4.4 Traditional WAP networking environment.

to a modem bank and RAS and on to the WAP gateway. The modem bank receives incoming phone calls from the user's mobile device, the RAS server translates the incoming calls from a wireless packet format to a wired packet format, and the router routes these packets to correct destinations. The WAP gateway is used to translate the WAP into traditional Internet protocol (TCP/IP). The WAP gateway is based on proxy technology. Typical WAP gateways provide the following functionality:

- Domain name server (DNS) service (e.g., to resolve domain names used in URLs).
- A control point for management of fraud and service utilization.
- Act as a proxy, translating the WAP protocol stack to the Internet protocol stack.

Many gateways also include a transcoding function that will translate an HTML page into a WML page that is suited to a particular device type. The enterprise space contains the backed web and application servers that provide the enterprises' transactions. Generally, the WSP maintains and manages the WAP gateway, but there are circumstances under which this is not desirable. This is due to the presence of an encryption gap caused by the ending of the WTLS session at the gateway. The data are temporarily in clear text on the gateway until they are re-encrypted under the SSL session established with the enterprise's web server. In such cases, the WAP gateway should be maintained at the enterprise. The problem with this solution is the absence of the DNS client at the mobile device, which would require the storage of profiles for every target on the mobile device. This also requires that the enterprise set up a relationship with service provider whereby all incoming packets destined for the enterprise (identified by the IP address) are immediately routed by the WSP directly to the enterprise and are never sent to the WSP's gateway.

4.7 WAP Advantages and Disadvantages

The following are the advantages of WAP:

- Implementation near to the Internet model;
- Most modern mobile telephone devices support WAP;
- Real-time send/receive data;
- Multiplatform functionality (little change is needed to run on any web site since XML is used);
- No hardware obsolescence.

The following are some of the advantages of using WAP CSS on mobile Internet sites:

- Because of WAP 2.0 (XHTML MP/WAP CSS), web programming and WAP programming converge. Learning WAP programming does not require much effort if you already know how to program the web. Web developers can continue to use their familiar web authoring tools and PC web browsers for building mobile Internet sites. This is one major advantage of XHTML MP/WAP CSS over WML.

- You can have greater control on the appearance of WAP pages with WAP CSS than with WML. For example, you can specify the colors, fonts, background, borders, margins, and padding of various elements with WAP CSS.

- If you apply a single CSS to the whole mobile Internet site, a mobile device will download the CSS only once the first time the mobile Internet site is visited. The CSS will then be stored in the cache and it can be accessed later without connecting to the server.

- The file sizes of XHTML MP documents can become smaller if the layout and formatting information is moved to an external WAP CSS style sheet. A small file size has the advantage of a shorter download time.

- Using WAP CSS has the advantage that the content and presentation can be separated. This means you can:
  1. Match the layout and style of the same content to the characteristics of different wireless devices easily.
  2. Match the layout and style of the same content for different user agents easily.
  3. Minimize the effort to maintain a WAP site. When new mobile phone models come onto the market, you can write new WAP CSS style sheets to optimize the layout of the WAP site on these new mobile phones. The content files do not need to be modifed.
  4. Apply a single WAP CSS style sheet to multiple WAP pages. Later if you want to change the look and feel of the whole WAP site, just modify the WAP CSS.
  5. Reuse the style code in multiple projects.
  6. Remotely divide work—someone can focus on look and feel WAP, whereas others can concentrate on contents.

Some of the disadvantages of the WAP are the following:

- Low speeds, security, and very small user interface;
- Not very familiar to the users;
- Business model is expensive;
- Forms are hard to design;
- Third party is included.

Some of the disadvantages of using WAP CSS style sheets on mobile Internet sites are:

- Different WAP browsers have varied levels of support for WAP CSS. One property supported on one WAP browser may not be available on another WAP browser.

- An external WAP CSS style sheet can increase the time required for a page to be completely loaded the first time the WAP site is visited because of the following reasons:

  1. The external WAP CSS style sheet does not exist in the cache of the mobile phone at the first visit, which means the mobile phone has to download it from the server.

  2. An XHTML MP document and its external WAP CSS style sheet have to be downloaded in separate requests.

  3. If you make use of a single WAP CSS file to specify all the presentation information about the mobile Internet site, the file size of the WAP CSS file can be quite large.

  4. The WAP browser needs to parse the CSS in addition to the XHTML MP document.

4.8 Applications of WAP

The first and foremost application of WAP is accessing the Internet from mobile devices. This is already in use in many mobile phones. This application is gaining popularity daily, and many web sites already have a WAP version of their site. An application, which is out, is sending sale offers to mobile customers through WAP. The user's phone will be able to receive any sale prices and offers from the web site of a store.

Games can be played from mobile devices over wireless devices. This application has been implemented in certain countries and is under development in many others. This is an application which has been predicted to gain high popularity.

Application to access time sheets and filing expenses claims via mobile handsets are currently being developed. These applications, when implemented, will be a breakthrough in the business world.

Applications to locate WAP customers geographically have been developed. Applications to help users who are lost or stranded by guiding them using their locations are under consideration.

WAP also provides short messaging, e-mail, weather, and traffic alerts based on the geographic location of the customer. These applications are available in some countries but will soon be provided in all countries.

One of the biggest applications of WAP under consideration is banking from mobile devices. These applications will be very popular if they are implemented in a secure manner.

The mobile industry appears to be moving forward, putting aside the issues of network and air interface standards, and instead concentrating on laying the foundations for service development, regarded by many as the key driver to multimedia on the move and third-generation mobile systems. From that point of view, in the near future WAP and Bluetooth will play fundamental roles.

4.9 imode

imode is a proprietary mobile ISP and portal service from NTT DoCoMo, Japan, with about 50 million subscribers. For imode, DoCoMo adopted the Internet model and protocol. imode uses compact HTML (cHTML) as a page description language. The structure of cHTML means that the user can view traditional HTML and imode sites can be inspected with ordinary Internet web browsers. This is in contrast to WAP, where HTML pages must be translated to WML. imode provides Internet service using personal digital cellular-packet (PDC-P) and a subset of HTML 3.0 for content description.

imode is a packet-switched service (always connected, as long as the user's handset is reached by imode signal) which includes images, animated images, and colors. In imode, users are charged per packet of downloaded information. imode allows application/content providers to distribute software to cellular phones and also permits users to download appilets (e.g., games). imode uses packet-switched technology for the wireless part of the communication. The wired part of the communication is carried over TCP/IP.

Packet-switched services send and receive information by dividing messages into small blocks called packets and adding headers containing address and control information to each packet. This allows multiple communications to be carried on a communication channel, giving efficient channel usage with low cost. Dopa, DoCoMo's dedicated data communications service, offers connections to location area network (LAN) and ISPs. The mobile packet communications system has a network configuration in which a packet communications function is added and integrated into PDC, the digital system for portable and automobile telephones. DoCoMo has developed a data transmission protocol specific to imode. This protocol is used with the PDC-P system. The PDC-P network includes a mobile message packet gateway (M-PGW) to handle conversions between the two protocol formats. Connection between the imode server and the Internet uses TCP/IP. The imode server is a regular web server which can reside at NTT DoCoMo or at the enterprise. DoCoMo has been acting as a 1717 portal and normally maintains the imode server. Figure 4.5 shows the imode protocol stack.

imode relies on Internet security as provided by SSL/TLS and does not have the ability to handle server-side authenticated SSL sessions. imode phones are preconfigured with root collision avoidance keys from public key infrastructure. This will allow for establishment of a server-side authenticated SSL session between the imode device and imode server hosted by the enterprise. imode does not have the capability of handling client-side certificates which

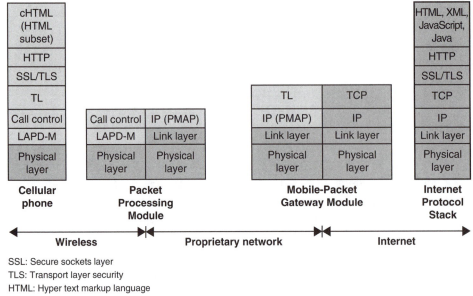

Figure 4.5 imode protocol stack.

means that nonrepudiation is not possible with the current implementation of imode. Figure 4.6 shows a typical imode wireless networking environment.

4.10 imode Versus WAP

imode is available only in Japan, whereas Europe and other big markets for 3G mobile service providers are completely WAP-based. In the United States, most service providers have chosen WAP.

The most basic difference between imode and WAP is the different graphic capabilities; imode only supports simple graphics, which is far more than what WAP allows. The imode packet-switched data network is more suited for transferring data than the WAP CS network.

Another major difference is the "always-on" capabilities of imode. Since users are not charged for the time they spend on-line, it is more convenient and also less expensive. Since there is no need to dial up before using the various IP-based services, e-mail becomes as instant as SMS. imode uses cHTML, a subset of HTML, while WAP uses WML, a subset of XML. cHTML, while certainly easier to develop from a web-designer standpoint, has its limitations. The downside of WML, on the other hand, is similarly obvious—currently a WAP gateway is required to translate between HTML and WML for almost every data transfer. On the other hand, since WML is derived from XML, it is much more extensible. XML allows

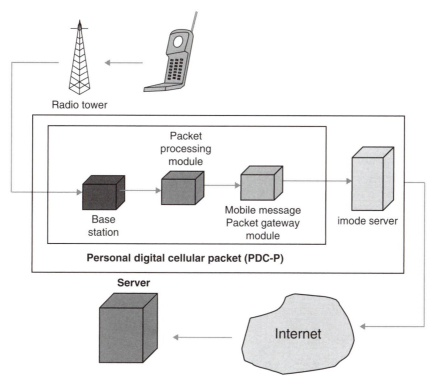

Figure 4.6 imode wireless networking environment.

for more dynamic content and various different applications. In the future, a WML-based service will be of more advantage than an HTML-based one. So while WAP may currently require more complicated technology, in the long run, it may enable the user to do more with his or her device.

4.11 Summary

In this chapter we discussed WAP. WAP specifies a thin-client microbrowser using a new standard called wireless markup language (WML) that is optimized for wireless hand-held mobile devices. WML is a stripped-down version of HTML. NTT DoCoMo imode provides Internet service using PDC-P and a subset of HTML 3.0 for content description. imode allows application/content providers to distribute software to cellular phones. We concluded the chapter by providing basic differences between WAP and imode.

Problems

4.1 What is WAP? Discuss briefly.
4.2 Discuss WAP architecture.

4.3 What is wireless transport layer security in WAP?

4.4 What is imode? Discuss briefly.

4.5 What is WAP 2.0?

4.6 What are the major differences between WAP and imode?

References

[1] S. Buckingham, "Introduction to WAP." http://www.gsmworld.com/technology/yes2wap.htm.

[2] M. Van Der Heijden, M. Taylor, Understanding WAP, Wireless Applications, Devices and Services. Artech House Publishers, 2000.

[3] http://www.wapforum.org/.

[4] http://www.wap.de/.

[5] http://www.w3c.org/.

[6] http://www.wap.com/.

[7] J. Kanjilal, "WAP: Internet over Wireless Networks." http://www.Infocommworld.com//99sep/cover02.htm.

[8] Laurence, Lee Min En. "Introduction to WAP Architecture." http://www.fit.qut.edu.au//DataComms/itn540/gallery/a100/lee/INTROD~1.HTM.

[9] R. Shah, "Wireless Application Protocol set to take over." http://www.sunworld.com/sunworldonline/swol-01-2000/swol-01-connectivity.htm.

[10] W. Simpson, Ed. "The Point-to-Point Protocol (PPP)." STD 50, RFC1661, Day-dreamer, July 1994.

[11] W. Simpson, Ed. "PPP in HDLC Framing." STD 51, RFC1662, Day-dreamer, July 1994.

[12] WAP Forum. "Wireless Application Protocol White Paper." http://www.wapforum.org/what/WAPwhitepages.pdf.

[13] Wireless Application Protocol Forum. "Wireless Application Protocol (WAP)." Bluetooth Special Interest Group, version 1.0, 1998.

[14] Wireless Application Protocol Forum. "WAP Conformance." Draft version 27, May 1998.

[15] Wireless Markup Language (WML). http://www.cellular.co.za/wml.htm.

CHAPTER 5

Wireless Local Area Networks

Vijay K. Garg

5.1 Introduction

With the success of wired local area networks (LANs), the local computing market is moving toward wireless LAN (WLAN) with the same speed as current wired LAN. WLANs are flexible data communication systems that can be used for applications in which mobility is required. In the indoor business environment, although mobility is not an absolute requirement, WLANs provide more flexibility than that achieved by the wired LAN. WLANs are designed to operate in industrial, scientific, and medical (ISM) radio bands (see Table 5.1) and unlicensed-national information infrastructure (U-NII) bands. In the United States, the Federal Communications Commission (FCC) regulates radio transmissions; however, the FCC does not require the end-user to buy a license to use the ISM or U-NII bands. Currently, WLANs can provide data rates up to 11 Mbps, but the industry is making a move toward high-speed WLANs. Manufacturers are developing WLANs to provide data rates up to 54 Mbps or higher. High speed makes WLANs a promising technology for the future data communications market [1].

The IEEE 802.11 committee is responsible for WLAN standards. WLANs include IEEE 802.11a (Wi-Fi 5), IEEE 802.11b (Wi-Fi), IEEE 802.11g, and IEEE 802.11n (see Figure 5.1). The deployment of WLANs can provide connectivity in homes, factories, and hot-spots. The IEEE 802.16 group is responsible for wireless metropolitan area network (WMAN) standards. This body is concerned with fixed broadband wireless access systems, also known as "last mile" access networks. In this chapter, we focus on different types of

Table 5.1 Industrial, Scientific, and Medical (ISM) Bands.

No.	Band (GHz)	Bandwidth (MHz)	Power Level	Spread Spectrum
1	0.902–0.928	26	1 W	FHSS, DSSS
2	2.4–2.4835	83.5	1 W	FHSS, DSSS
3	5.725–5.850	125	1 W	FHSS, DSSS
4	24.0–24.5	250	50 mW/m @ 3 m	Not Applicable

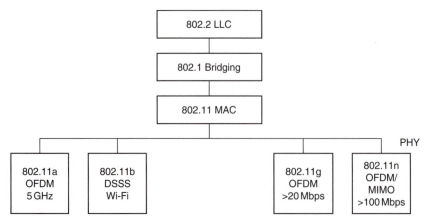

Figure 5.1 IEEE 802.11 WLAN standards.

Table 5.2 IEEE 802.11 Subgroups.

802.11a	High-speed physical layer in 5 GHz band
802.11b	Higher-speed physical layer extension of wireless in 2.4 GHz band
802.11d	Local and metropolitan area wireless
802.11g	Broadband wireless
802.11i	Security
802.11n	Wideband service

WLANs and introduce IEEE 802.16 standards including WiMAX (high-speed WLAN) [2–4]. Table 5.2 lists all subgroups of IEEE 802.11.

WLANs are flexible data communications systems implemented as an extension or as an alternative for wired LANs. Using radio frequency (RF) technology, WLANs transmit and receive data over the air, minimizing the need for wired connections. Thus, WLANs combine data connectivity with user mobility [5–12].

Recently, manufacturers have deployed WLANs for process and control applications. Retail applications have expanded to include wireless point of sale (WPOS). The health-care and education industry are also fast-growing markets for WLANs. WLANs provide high-speed, reliable data communications in a building or campus environment as well as coverage in rural areas. WLANs are simple to install. Figure 5.2 provides application fields of WLANs.

Figure 5.2 WLAN application.

In WLANs, the connection between the client and the user is accomplished by the use of a wireless medium such as RF or infrared (IR) communications instead of a cable. This allows a remote user to stay connected to the network while mobile or not physically attached to the network. The wireless connection is usually accomplished by the user having a hand-held terminal or laptop that has an RF interface card installed inside the terminal or through the PC card slot of the laptop. The client connection from the wired LAN to the user is made through an access point (AP) that can support multiple users simultaneously. The AP can reside at any node on the wired network and acts as a gateway for wireless users' data to be routed onto the wired network.

The range of a WLAN depends on the actual usage and environment of the system. It may vary from 100 ft inside a solid walled building to several thousand feet in an outdoor environment with direct line-of-sight. Much like cellular phone systems, WLANs are capable of roaming from the AP and reconnecting to the network through other APs residing at other points in the network. This can allow the wired LAN to be extended to cover a much larger area than the existing coverage by the use of multiple APs.

An important feature of WLANs is that they can be used independently of wired networks. They can be used as stand-alone networks anywhere to link multiple computers together without having to build or extend wired networks. The network communications take place in a part of the radio spectrum that is designed as *license-free.* In this band, 2.4–2.5 GHz users can operate without a license so long as they use equipment that has been of the type approved for use in the license-free band. The 2.4–2.5 GHz band has been designated as license-free by the International Telecommunications Union (ITU), and is available as license-free in most countries of the world.

Standard WLANs are capable of operating at speeds in the range of 1–2 Mbps depending on the actual system; both of these speeds are supported by the standard for WLANs defined by the IEEE. The fastest WLANs use 802.11b high-rate standard to move data through air at a maximum speed of 11 Mbps. The IEEE established the 802.11b standard for wireless networks and the wireless compatibility Ethernet alliance to assure that WLAN products are interoperable from manufacturer to manufacturer. Any LAN application, network operating systems, or protocol, including transmission control protocol/Internet protocol (TCP/IP) will run on 802.11b-compliant WLANs as easily as they run over the Ethernet.

The following are a few advantages of deploying WLANs:

- Mobility improves productivity with real-time access to information, regardless of worker location, for faster and more efficient decision-making;
- Cost-effective network setup for hard-to-wire locations such as older buildings and solid wall structures;
- Reduced cost of ownership, particularly in a dynamic environment requiring frequent modification due to minimal wiring and installation costs per device and per user.

However, there are several issues that should be considered in deploying the WLAN including:

- *Frequency allocation*: Operation of a wireless network requires that all users operate in a common frequency band. The frequency band must be approved in each country.

- *Interference and reliability*: In a wired LAN, one hears only the terminals connected to the network. In a WLAN, interference is caused by simultaneous transmission of information in the shared frequency band and by multipath fading. The reliability of a communication channel is measured by bit error rate (BER). Automatic repeat request (ARQ) and forward error correction (FEC) techniques are used to increase reliability.

- *Security*: Radio waves are not confined to the boundary of buildings or campuses. There exists the possibility of eavesdropping and intentional interference. Data privacy over a radio medium is usually accomplished by using encryption.

- *Power consumption*: WLANs are typically related to mobile applications. In these applications, battery power is a scarce resource. Therefore, the devices must be designed to be energy-efficient.

- *Mobility*: One of the advantages of a WLAN is the freedom of mobility. The devices should accommodate handoff at transmission boundaries to route data calls to mobile users.

- *Throughput*: To support multiple transmissions simultaneously, spread spectrum (SS) techniques are often used.

5.2 WLAN Equipment

There are three main links that form the basis of the wireless network. These are:

- *LAN adapter*: Wireless adapters are made in the same basic form as their wired counterparts: PCMCIA, Card bus, PCI, and USB. They also serve the same function, enabling end-users to access the network. In a wired LAN, adapters provide an interface between the network operating system and the wire. In a WLAN, they provide the interface between the network operating system and an antenna to create a transparent connection to the network.

- *AP*: The AP is the wireless equivalent of a LAN hub. It receives, buffers, and transmits data between the WLAN and the wired network, supporting a group of wireless user devices. An AP is typically connected with the backbone network through a standard Ethernet cable, and communicates with wireless devices by means of an antenna. The AP or antenna connected to it is generally mounted on a high wall or on the ceiling. Like cells in a cellular network, multiple APs can support handoff from one AP to another as the user moves from area to area. APs have a range from 20 to 500 m. A single AP can support between 15 to 250 users, depending on technology, configuration, and use. It is relatively easy to scale a WLAN by adding more APs to reduce network congestion and enlarge the coverage area. Large networks requiring multiple APs deploy them to create overlapping cells for constant connectivity to the network. A wireless AP can monitor movement of a client across its domain and permit or deny specific traffic or clients from communicating through it.

- *Outdoor LAN bridges*: Outdoor LAN bridges are used to connect LANs in different buildings. When the cost of buying a fiber optic cable between buildings is considered, particularly if there are barriers such as highways or bodies of water in the way, a WLAN can be an economical alternative. An outdoor bridge can provide a less expensive alternative to recurring leased-line charges. WLAN bridge products support fairly high data rates and ranges of several miles with the use of line-of-sight directional antennas. Some APs can also be used as a bridge between buildings of relatively close proximity.

5.3 WLAN Topologies

WLANs can be built with either of the following topologies:

- Peer-to-peer (ad hoc) topology;
- AP-based topology;
- Point-to-multipoint bridge topology.

In peer-to-peer topology, client devices within a cell communicate directly to each other as shown in Figure 5.3.

AP-based technology uses APs to bridge traffic onto a wired (Ethernet or Token Ring) or a wireless backbone as shown in Figure 5.4. AP enables a wireless client device to communicate with any other wired or wireless device on the network. Ap-based topology is

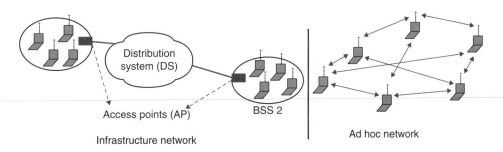

Figure 5.3 Peer-to-peer topology (ad hoc network).

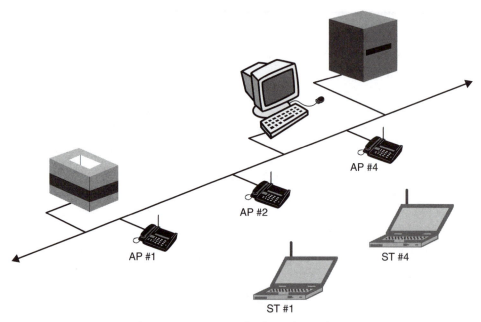

Figure 5.4 Access point-based topology.

more commonly used and demonstrates that the WLAN does not replace the wired LAN; it extends connectivity to mobile devices.

Another wireless network topology is the point-to-multipoint bridge. Wireless bridges connect LANs in one building to LANs in another building even if the buildings are miles apart. These conditions receive a clear line-of-sight between buildings. The line-of-sight range varies based on the type of wireless bridge and antenna used as well as environmental conditions.

5.4 WLAN Technologies

The technologies available for use in a WLAN include IR, UHF (narrowband), and SS implementation. Each implementation comes with its own set of advantages and limitations.

5.4.1 IR Technology

IR is an invisible band of radiation that exists at the lower end of the visible electromagnetic spectrum. This type of transmission is most effective when a clear line-of-sight exists between the transmitter and the receiver.

Two types of IR WLAN solutions are available: diffused-beam and direct-beam (or line-of-sight). Currently, direct-beam WLANs offer a faster data rate than the diffused-beam

Table 5.3 Considerations for Choosing Infrared Technology.

Advantages	No government regulations controlling use
	Immunity to electro-magnetic (EM) and RF interference
Disadvantages	Generally a short-range technology (30–50 ft radius under ideal conditions)
	Signals cannot penetrate solid objects
	Signal affected by light, snow, ice, fog
	Dirt can interfere with infrared

networks. Direct-beam is more directional since diffused-beam technology uses reflected rays to transmit/receive a data signal. It achieves lower data rates in the 1–2 Mbps range.

IR is a short-range technology. When used indoors, it can be limited by solid objects such as doors, walls, merchandise, or racking. In addition, the lighting environment can affect signal quality. For example, loss of communication may occur because of the large amount of sunlight or background light in an environment. Fluorescent lights also may contain large amounts of IR. This problem may be solved by using high signal power and an optimal bandwidth filter, which reduces the IR signals coming from an outside source. In an outdoor environment, snow, ice, and fog may affect the operation of an IR-based system. Table 5.3 gives considerations for choosing IR technology.

5.4.2 UHF Narrowband Technology

UHF wireless data communication systems have been available since the early 1980s. These systems normally transmit in the 430–470 MHz frequency range, with rare systems using segments of the 800 MHz range. The lower portion of this band—430–450 MHz—is referred to as the unprotected (unlicensed), and 450–470 MHz is referred to as the protected (licensed) band. In the unprotected band, RF licenses are not granted for specific frequencies and anyone is allowed to use any frequencies, giving customers some assurance that they will have complete use of that frequency.

Because independent narrowband RF systems cannot coexist on the same frequency, government agencies allocate specific RFs to users through RF site licenses. A limited amount of unlicensed spectrum is also available in some countries. In order to have many frequencies that can be allocated to users, the bandwidth given to a specific user is very small.

The term *narrowband* is used to describe this technology because the RF signal is sent in a very narrow bandwidth, typically 12.5 or 25 kHz. Power levels range from 1 to 2 W for narrowband RF data systems. This narrow bandwidth combined with high power results in larger transmission distances than are available from 900 MHz or 2.4 GHz SS systems, which have lower power levels and wider bandwidths. Table 5.4 lists the advantages and disadvantages of UHF technology.

Table 5.4 Considerations for Choosing UHF Technology.

Advantages	Longest range
	Low cost solution for large sites with low to medium data throughput requirements
Disadvantages	Large radio and antennas increase wireless client size
	RF site license required for protected bands
	No multivendor interoperability
	Low throughput and interference potential

Many modern UHF systems are synthesized radio technology. This refers to the way channel frequencies are generated in the radio. The crystal-controlled products in legacy UHF products require factory installation of unique crystals for each possible channel frequency. Synthesized radio technology uses a single, standard crystal frequency and drives the required channel frequency by dividing the crystal frequency down to a small value, then multiplying it up to the desired channel frequency. The division and multiplication factors are unique for each desired channel frequency, and are programmed into digital memory in the radio at the time of manufacturing. Synthesized UHF-based solutions provide the ability to install equipment without the complexity of hardware crystals. Common equipment can be purchased and specific UHF frequency used for each device can be tuned based upon specific location requirements. Additionally, synthesized UHF radios do not exhibit the frequency drift problem experienced in crystal-controlled UHF radios.

Modern UHF systems allow APs to be individually configured for operation on one of the several preprogrammed frequencies. Terminals are programmed with a list of all frequencies used in the installed APs, allowing them to change frequencies when roaming. To increase throughput, APs may be installed with overlapping coverage but use different frequencies.

5.4.3 Spread Spectrum Technology

Most WLANs use SS technology, a wideband RF technique that uses the entire allotted spectrum in a shared fashion as opposed to dividing it into discrete private pieces (as with narrowband). The SS system spreads the transmission power over the entire usable spectrum. This is obviously a less efficient use of the bandwidth than the narrowband approach. However, SS is designed to trade off bandwidth efficiency for reliability, integrity, and security. The bandwidth trade-off produces a signal that is easier to detect, provided that the receiver knows the parameters of the SS signal being broadcast. If the receiver is not tuned to the right frequency, a SS signal looks like background noise.

By operating across a broad range of radio frequencies, a SS device could communicate clearly despite interference from other devices using the same spectrum in the same physical location. In addition to its relative immunity to interference, SS makes eavesdropping and jamming inherently difficult.

In commercial applications, SS techniques currently offer data rates up to 2 Mbps. Because the FCC does not require site licensing for the bands used by SS systems, this technology has become the standard for high-speed RF data transmission. Two modulation schemes are commonly used to encode SS signals: direct sequence SS (DSSS) and frequency-hopping SS (FHSS).

FHSS uses a narrowband carrier that changes frequency in a pattern known to both transmitter and receiver. Properly synchronized, the net effect is to maintain a single logical channel. To an unintended receiver, FHSS appears to be a short-duration impulse noise.

DSSS generates a redundant bit pattern for each bit to be transmitted. This bit pattern is called a *spreading code*. The longer the code, the greater the probability that the original data can be recovered (and, of course, the more bandwidth will be required). To an unintended receiver DSSS appears as low-power wideband noise and is rejected by most narrowband receivers.

5.5 IEEE 802.11 WLAN

In 1997 the IEEE developed an international standard for WLANs: IEEE 802.11-1997. This standard was revised in 1999. Like other IEEE 802 standards, the 802.11 standard focuses on the bottom two layers of the OSI model: the physical layer (PHY) and data link layer (DLL). Because of the common interface provided to upper layers, any LAN application, network operating system, or protocol including TCP/IP and Novell Netware will run on an 802.11-compliant WLAN. The objective of the IEEE 802.11 standard was to define a medium access control (MAC) sublayer, MAC management protocols and services, and three PHYs for wireless connectivity of fixed, portable, and moving devices within a local area. The three physical layers are an IR baseband PHY, an FHSS radio in the 2.4 GHz band, and a DSSS radio in the 2.4 GHz. All three PHYs support both 1 and 2 Mbps operations.

WLANs support asynchronous data transfers that refer to the traffic that is relatively insensitive to time delays such as e-mail and file transfers. Optionally WLANs can also support the traffic, which is bounded by the specified time delay, to achieve an acceptable quality of service (QoS), such as packetized voice and video.

5.5.1 IEEE 802.11 Architecture

The architecture of the IEEE 802.11 WLAN is designed to support a network where most decision-making is distributed to mobile stations. This type of architecture has several advantages. It is tolerant of faults in all of the WLAN equipment and eliminates possible bottlenecks a centralized architecture would introduce. The architecture is flexible and can easily support both small, transient networks and large, semipermanent or permanent networks. In addition, the architecture and protocols offer significant power saving and prolong the battery life of mobile equipment without losing network connectivity.

Two network architectures are defined in the IEEE 802.11 standard:

- *Infrastructure network:* An infrastructure network is the network architecture for providing communication between wireless clients and wired network resources. The transition of data from the wireless to wired medium occurs via an AP. An AP and its associated wireless clients define the coverage area. Together all the devices form a basic service set (see Figure 5.5).

- *Point-to-point (ad hoc) network:* An ad hoc network is the architecture that is used to support mutual communication between wireless clients. Typically, an ad hoc network is created spontaneously and does not support access to wired networks. An ad hoc network does not require an AP.

IEEE 802.11 supports three basic topologies for WLANs: the independent basic service set (IBSS), the basic service set, and the extended service set (ESS). The MAC layer supports implementations of IBSS, basic service set, and ESS configurations.

- The IBSS configuration is referred to as an independent configuration or an ad hoc network. An IBSS configuration is analogous to a peer-to-peer office network in which no single node is required to act as a server. IBSS WLANs include a number of nodes or wireless stations that communicate directly with one another on an ad hoc,

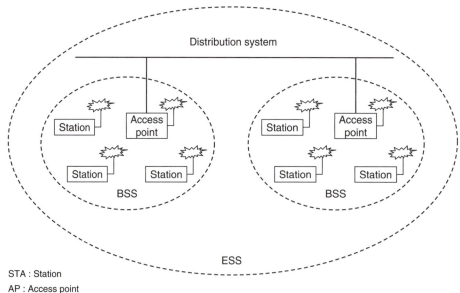

STA : Station
AP : Access point
BSS : Basic service set
ESS : Extended service set

Figure 5.5 BSS and ESS configuration of IEEE 802.11 WLAN.

peer-to-peer basis. Generally, IBSS implementations cover a limited area and are not connected to any large network. An IBSS is typically a short-lived network, with a small number of stations, that is created for a particular purpose.

- The basic service set configuration relies on an AP that acts as the logical server for a single WLAN cell or channel. Communications between station 1 and station 4 actually flow from station 1 to AP1, then from AP1 to AP2, then from AP2 to AP4, and finally from AP4 to station 4 (refer to Figure 5.4). An AP performs a bridging function, connects multiple WLAN cells or channels, and connects WLAN cells to a wired enterprise LAN.

- The ESS configuration consists of multiple basic service set cells that can be linked by either wired or wireless backbones called a distributed system. IEEE 802.11 supports ESS configurations in which multiple cells use the same channel, and configurations in which multiple cells use different channels to boost aggregate throughput. To network the equipment outside of the ESS, the ESS and all of its mobile stations appear to be a single MAC-layer network where all stations are physically stationary. Thus, the ESS hides the mobility of the mobile stations from everything outside the ESS (see Figure 5.5).

5.5.2 802.11 Physical Layer (PHY)

At the PHY, IEEE 802.11 defines three physical characteristics for WLANs: diffused IR (baseband), DSSS, and FHSS. All three support a 1–2 Mbps data rate. Both DSSS and FHSS use the 2.4 GHz ISM band (2.4–2.4835 GHz). The PHY provides three levels of functionality. These include: (1) frame exchange between the MAC and PHY under the control of the physical layer convergence procedure (PLCP) sublayer; (2) use of signal carrier and SS modulation to transmit data frames over the media under the control of the physical medium dependent (PMD) sublayer; and (3) providing a carrier sense indication back to the MAC to verify activity on the media (see Figure 5.6).

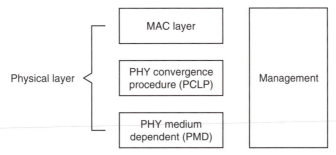

Figure 5.6 OSI model for IEEE 802.11 WLAN.

Each of the PHYs is unique in terms of the modulation type, designed to coexist with each other and operate with the MAC. The specifications for IEEE 802.11 meet the RF emissions guidelines of FCC, ETSI, and the Ministry of Telecommunications.

5.5.2.1 DSSS PHY

In the DSSS PHY, data transmission over the media is controlled by the PMD sublayer as directed by the PLCP sublayer. The PMD sublayer takes the binary information bits from the PLCP protocol data unit (PPDU) and converts them into RF signals by using modulation and DSSS techniques (see Figure 5.7). Figure 5.8 shows the PPDU frame, which consists of a PLCP preamble, PLCP header, and MAC protocol data unit (MPDU). The PLCP preamble and PLCP header are always transmitted at 1 Mbps, and the MPDU can be sent at 1 or 2 Mbps.

The start of frame delimiter (SFD) contains information that marks the start of the PPDU frame. The SFD specified is common for all IEEE 802.11 DSSS radios.

The *signal field* indicates which modulation scheme should be used to receive the incoming MPDU. The binary value in this field is equal to the data rate multiplied by 100 kbps. Two

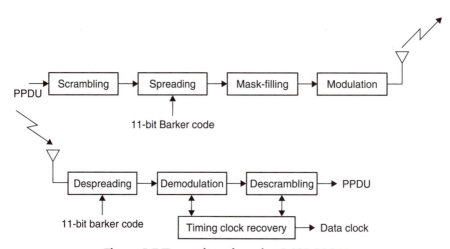

Figure 5.7 Transmit and receive DSSS PPDU.

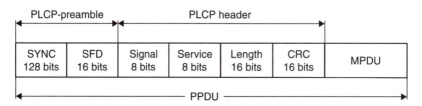

Figure 5.8 DSSS PHY PPDU frame.

modulation schemes, differential binary phase shift keying (DBPSK)—for 1 Mbps—and differential quadrature phase shift keying (DQPSK)—for 2 Mbps—are available.

The *service field* is reserved for future use. The *length field* indicates the number of microseconds necessary to transmit the MPDU. The MAC layer uses this field to determine the end of a PPDU frame.

The *cycle redundancy check (CRC) field* contains the results of a calculated frame check sequence (FCS) from the sending station. The ITU CRC-16 error-detection algorithm is used to protect the signal, service, and length field.

The *SYNC field* is 128 bits (symbols) in length and contains a string of 1s which is scrambled prior to transmission. The receiver uses this field to acquire the incoming signal and to synchronize the receiver's carrier tracking and timing prior to receiving the SFD. The SFD field contains information to mark the start of the PPDU frame. The SFD specified is common for all IEEE 802.11 DSSS radios.

All information bits transmitted by the DSSS PMD are scrambled using a self-synchronizing seven-bit polynomial. An 11-bit Barker code $(1, -1, 1, 1, -1, 1, 1, 1, -1, -1, -1)$ is used for spreading. In the transmitter, the 11-bit Barker code is applied to a modulo-2 adder together with each of the information bits in the PPDU. The output of the modulo-2 adder results in a signal with a data rate that is 10 times higher than the information rate. The result in the frequency domain is a signal that is spread over a wide bandwidth at a reduced RF power level. Every station in the IEEE 802.11 network uses the same 11-bit sequence. At the receiver, the DSSS signal is convolved with the same 11-bit Barker code and correlated. The minimum requirement for processing gain (G_p) in North America and Japan is 10 dB.

Each DSSS PHY channel occupies 22 MHz of bandwidth and allows for three noninterfering channels spaced 25 MHz apart in the 2.4 GHz frequency band (see Figure 5.9). With this

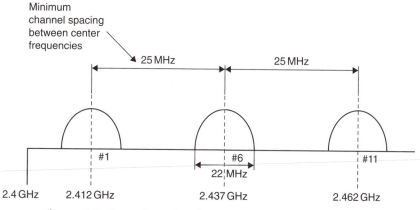

Figure 5.9 Channel spacing for IEEE 802.11 DSSS networks.

Table 5.5 DSSS Channels for Different Parts of the World.

Channel Number	Frequency (GHz)	North America	Europe	Spain	France	Japan
1	2.412	x	x			
2	2.417	x	x			
3	2.422	x	x			
4	2.427	x	x			
5	2.432	x	x			
6	2.437	x	x			
7	2.442	x	x			
8	2.447	x	x			
9	2.452	x	x			
10	2.457	x	x	x	x	
11	2.462	x	x	x	x	
12	2.467		x		x	
13	2.472		x		x	
14	2.483					x

Table 5.6 Maximum Allowable Transmit Power.

Country	Power
North America	1000 mW
Europe	100 mW
Japan	10 mW/Hz

channel arrangement, a user can configure multiple DSSS networks to operate simultaneously in the same area. Table 5.5 lists the DSSS channels used in different parts of the world. A total of 14 frequency channels are defined for operation across the 2.4 GHz frequency band. In North America, 11 frequencies are used ranging from 2.412 to 2.462 GHz. In Europe, 13 frequencies are allowed between 2.412 and 2.472 GHz. In Japan only channels at the 2.483 GHz frequency are permitted.

The maximum allowable radiated power for DSSS PHY varies from region to region (refer to Table 5.6). The transmit power is directly related to the range that a particular implementation can achieve.

■ Example 5.1

A QPSK/DSSS WLAN is designed to transmit in the 902–928 MHz ISM band. The symbol transmission rate is 0.5 Megasymbols/sec. An orthogonal code with 16 symbols is used. A BER of 10^{-5} is required. How many users can be supported by the WLAN? A sector antenna with a gain of 2.6 is used. Assume interference factor $\beta = 0.5$

to account for the interference from users in other cells and power control efficiency $\alpha = 0.9$. What is the bandwidth efficiency?

Solution

$$B_w = 928 - 902 = 26\,\text{MHz}$$

$$R_b = R_s \log_2 16 = 2\,\text{Mbps}$$

$$G_p = \frac{26}{2} = 13$$

$$P_b = 10^{-5} = \frac{1}{2}\text{erfc}\sqrt{\frac{E_b}{N_0}}$$

$$\therefore \frac{E_b}{N_0} = 10\,\text{dB}$$

$$M = \frac{G_p}{(E_b/N_0)} \times \frac{1}{1+\beta} \times \alpha \times \lambda = \frac{13}{10} \times \frac{1}{1+0.5} \times 2.6 \times 0.9 \approx 2$$

$$\eta = \frac{2 \times 2}{26} = 0.16\,\text{bps/Hz}$$

5.5.2.2 FHSS PHY

In FHSS PHY, data transmission over media is controlled by the FHSS PMD sublayer as directed by the FHSS PLCP sublayer. The FHSS PMD takes the binary information bits from the whitened PLCP service data unit (PSDU) and converts them into RF signals by using carrier modulation and FHSS techniques (see Figure 5.10).

The format of the PPDU is shown in Figure 5.11. It consists of the PLCP preamble, PLCP header, and PSDU. The PLCP preamble is used to acquire the incoming signal and synchronize the receiver's demodulator. The PLCP header contains information about PSDU from the sending PHY. The PLCP preamble and header are transmitted at 1 Mbps.

The *sync field* contains a string of alternating 0's and 1's pattern and is used by the receiver to synchronize the receiver's packet timing and correct for frequency offsets.

The *SFD field* contains information marking the start of a PSDU frame. FHSS radios use a 0000110010111101 bit pattern. The leftmost bit is transmitted first.

The *PLCP length word (PLW) field* specifies the length of the PSDU in octets and is used by the MAC layer to detect the end of a PPDU frame.

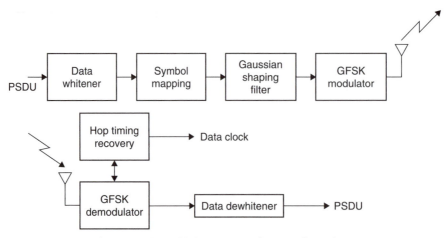

Figure 5.10 FHSS PHY transmitter and receiver.

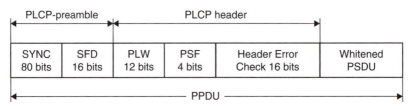

Figure 5.11 FHSS PHY PPDU frame.

The *PLCP signaling field* (*PSF*) identifies the data rate of the whitened PSDU ranging from 1 to 4.5 Mbps in increments of 0.5 Mbps.

The *header error check field* contains the results of a calculated FCS from the sending station. The ITU CRC-16 error-detection algorithm is used to protect the PSF and PLW fields.

Data whitening is used for the PSDU before transmission to minimize DC bias on the data if long strings of 1's or 0's are contained in the PSDU. The PHY stuffs a special symbol every four octets of the PDSU in a PPDU frame. A 127-bit sequence generator using the polynomial $x^7 + x^4 + 1$ and a 32/33 bias-suppression encoding algorithm are used to randomize and whiten the data.

The FHSS PMD uses two-level Gaussian frequency shift key (GMSK) modulation to transmit the PSDU at the basic rate of 1 Mbps. Four-level GFSK is an optimal modulation scheme defined in the standard that enables the whitened PSDU to be transmitted at a higher rate. The value in the PSF field of the PLCP header is used to determine the data rate of the PSDU.

In GFSK modulation, the frequency is shifted on either side of the carrier hop frequency depending on whether the binary symbol from the PSDU is either a 1 or a 0. For two-level GFSK, a binary 1 represents the upper deviation frequency ($f_c + \Delta f$) from the hopped carrier, and binary 0 represents the lower deviation frequency ($f_c - \Delta f$), where f_c is the carrier hopped frequency and Δf the deviation frequency. The deviation frequency should be greater than 110 kHz for IEEE 802.11 FHSS radios. Four-level GFSK is similar to two-level GFSK and is used to achieve a data rate of 2 Mbps in the same occupied frequency bandwidth. The symbol pairs (10, 11, 01, 00) generate four frequency deviations from the hopped carrier frequency, two upper and two lower.

A set of hop sequences is defined in IEEE 802.11 for use in the 2.4 GHz frequency band. The channels are evenly spaced across the band over a span of 83.5 MHz. In North America and Europe (except France and Spain) the number of hop channels is 79. The number of hop channels for Spain and France are 23 and 35, respectively. In Japan the required number of hop channels is 23. The hop channels are spaced uniformly across the 2.4 GHz frequency band occupying a bandwidth of 1 MHz. In North America and Europe (except Spain and France) the hop channels operate from 2.402 to 2.480 GHz and in Japan, 2.473 to 2.495 GHz. In Spain the hop channels operate from 2.447 to 2.473 GHz, and in France from 2.448 to 2.482 GHz. Channel 2 is the first hop channel located at the center frequency of 2.402 GHz and channel 95 is the last hop frequency channel at 2.495 GHz in the 2.4 GHz band.

Channel hopping is controlled by FHSS PMD. The FHSS PMD transmits the whitened PSDU by hopping from channel to channel in a pseudo-random fashion using one of the hopping sequences. In the United States, FHSS radios hop a minimum 2.5 hops/sec for a minimum hop distance of 6 MHz.

The hopping sequences for IEEE 802.11 are grouped in hopping sets for worldwide operation: Set 1, Set 2, and Set 3. The sequences are selected when FHSS basic service set is configured for a WLAN. The hopping sets are designed to minimize interference between neighboring FHSS radios in a set. The following hop sets are valid IEEE 802.11 hopping sequences in North America and most of Europe (except Spain and France).

- **Set 1**: (0, 3, 6, 9, 12, 15, 18, 21, 24, 27, 30, 33, 36, 39, 42, 45, 48, 51, 54, 57, 60, 63, 66, 69, 72, 75);
- **Set 2**: (1, 4, 7, 10, 13, 16, 19, 22, 25, 28, 31, 34, 37, 40, 43, 46, 49, 52, 55, 58, 61, 64, 67, 70, 73, 76);
- **Set 3**: (2, 5, 8, 11, 14, 17, 20, 23, 26, 29, 32, 35, 38, 41, 44, 47, 50, 53, 56, 59, 62, 65, 68, 71, 74, 77).

5.5.2.3 *802.11a—Orthogonal Frequency-Division Multiplexing (OFDM)*

The OFDM PHY provides the capability to transmit PSDU frames at multiple data rates up to 54 Mbps for a WLAN where the transmission of multimedia content is a consideration. The OFDM PHY defined for IEEE 802.11a is similar to the OFDM PHY specification of ETSI-HIPERLAN 2.

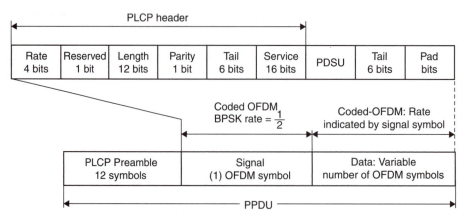

Figure 5.12 OFDM PLCP preamble, header, and PSDU.

The PPDU is unique to the OFDM PHY. The PPDU frame consists of a PLCP preamble and signal and data fields (see Figure 5.12). The receiver uses the PLCP preamble to acquire the incoming OFDM signal and synchronize the demodulator. The PLCP header contains information about the PSDU from sending OFDM PHY. The PLCP preamble and the signal fields are always transmitted at 6 Mbps, BPSK-OFDM modulated using a convolutional encoding rate $R = 1/2$.

PLCP preamble field is used to acquire the incoming signal and train and synchronize the receiver. The PLCP preamble consists of 12 symbols, 10 of which are short symbols, and 2 long symbols. The short symbols are used to train the receiver's automatic gain control (AGC) and obtain a coarse estimate of the carrier frequency and the channel. The long symbols are used to fine-tune the frequency and channel estimates. A total of 12 subcarriers are used for the short symbols and 53 for the long. The training of an OFDM is accomplished in 16 μs. The PLCP preamble is BPSK-OFDM modulated at 6 Mbps.

The *signal* is a 24-bit field that contains information about the rate and length of the PSDU. The signal field is convolutional encoded rate $R = 1/2$, BPSK-OFDM modulated. Four bits are used to encode the rate, 11 bits are used to define the length, one reserved bit, a parity bit, and six 0 tail bits (see Table 5.7).

The *length field* is an unsigned 12-bit integer to indicate the number of octets in the PSDU.

The *data field* contains the service field, PSDU, tail bits, and pad bits. A total of six tail bits containing 0's are appended to the PPDU to ensure that the convolutional encoder is brought back to the zero state.

All the bits transmitted by the OFDM PMD in the data portion are scrambled using a frame-synchronous 127-bit sequence generator. Scrambling is used to randomize the service, PSDU, pad bit, and data patterns, which may contain long strings of binary 1's or 0's. The tail bits are not scrambled.

Table 5.7 PSDU Data Rate.

Rate (Mbps)	Modulation	Coding Rate	Signal Bits
6	BPSK	$R = 1/2$	1101
9	BPSK	$R = 3/4$	1111
12	QPSK	$R = 1/2$	0101
18	QPSK	$R = 3/4$	0111
24	16-QAM	$R = 1/2$	1001
36 (optional)	16-QAM	$R = 3/4$	1011
48 (optional)	64-QAM	$R = 2/3$	0001
54 (optional)	64-QAM	$R = 3/4$	0011

All information contained in the service, PSDU, tail, and pad are encoded using convolutional encoding $R = 1/2$, 2/3, or 3/4 corresponding to the desired data rate. Puncture codes are used for the higher data rates.

In OFDM modulation, the basic principal of operation is to divide a high-speed binary signal to be transmitted into a number of lower data rate subcarriers. There are 48 data subcarriers and 4 carrier pilot subcarriers for a total of 52 nonzero subcarriers defined in IEEE 802.11a. Each lower data rate bit stream is used to modulate a separate subcarrier from one of the channels in the 5 GHz band. Intersymbol interference is generally not a concern for a lower speed carrier; however, the subchannels may be subjected to frequency-selective fading. Therefore, bit interleaving and convolutional encoding is used to improve the BER performance. The scheme uses integer multiples of the first subcarrier, which are orthogonal to each other. Prior to transmission, the PPDU is encoded using a convolutional coded rate $R = 1/2$, and the bits are reordered and bit interleaved for the desired data rate. Each bit is then mapped into a complex number according to the modulation type and subdivided into 48 data subcarriers and 4 pilot subcarriers. The subcarriers are combined using an inverse fast Fourier transform and transmitted. At the receiver, the carrier is converted back to a multicarrier lower data rate form using a fast frequency transform (FFT). The lower data subcarriers are combined to form the high-rate PPDU. Figure 5.13 shows IEEE 802.11a OFDM PMD.

The 5 GHz frequency band is segmented into three 100 MHz bands for operation in the United States. The lower band ranges from 5.15 to 5.25 GHz, the middle band ranges from 5.25 to 5.35 GHz, and the upper band ranges from 5.725 to 5.825 GHz. The lower and middle bands accommodate eight channels in a total bandwidth of 200 MHz and the upper band accommodates four channels in a 100 MHz bandwidth. The frequency channel center frequencies are spaced 20 MHz apart. The outermost channels of the lower and middle bands are centered 30 MHz from the outer edges. In the upper band the outermost channel centers are 20 MHz from the outer edges. The channel frequencies and numbering defined in 802.11a start at 5 GHz and each channel is spaced 5 GHz apart (see Table 5.8).

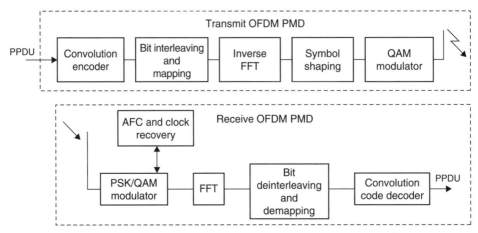

Figure 5.13 IEEE 802.11a transmits and receives OFDM PMD.

Table 5.8 Channel Frequencies and Channel Numbers in the United States.

Regulatory Domain	Frequency Band	Channel Number	Center Frequencies (GHz)
USA	Lower band 5.15–5.25 GHz	36	5.180
		40	5.220
		44	5.220
		48	5.240
USA	Middle band 5.25–5.35 GHz	52	5.26
		56	5.280
		60	5.300
		64	5.320
USA	Upper band	149	5.745
		153	5.765
		157	5.785
		161	5.805

Table 5.9 Transmit Power Levels for North American Operation.

Frequency Band	Maximum Transmit Power with 6 dBi Antenna Gain
5.150–5.250 GHz	40 mW (2.5 mW/MHz)
5.250–5.350 GHz	200 mW (12.5 mW/MHz)
5.725–5.825 GHz	800 mW (50 mW/MHz)

Three transmit RF power levels are specified: 40, 200, and 800 mW (see Table 5.9). The upper band defines RF transmit power levels suitable for bridging applications while the lower band specifies a transmit power suitable for short-range indoor home and small office environments.

■ Example 5.2

Consider an FH/MFSK WLAN system, in which a pseudo-random noise (PN) generator is defined by a 20-stage linear feedback shift register with a maximal length sequence. Each state of the register dictates a new center frequency within the hopping band. The minimum step-size between center frequencies (hop to hop) is 200 Hz. The register clock rate is 2 kHz. 8-ary FSK modulation is used and the data rate is 1.2 kbps.
(a) What is the hopping bandwidth? (b) What is the chip rate? (c) How many chips are there in each data symbol? (d) What is the processing gain?

Solution

$\Delta f = 200 \, Hz$

Minimum number of chips $= 20$

Number of tones contained in spreading bandwidth $(B_{ss}) = 2^{20} = 1{,}048{,}576$

$$1{,}048{,}576 = \frac{B_{ss}}{200}$$

$$\therefore B_{ss} = 209{,}715{,}200 = 209.715 \, MHz$$

$$\text{Chip rate} = 1.2 \times 20 = 24 \, kchip/sec$$

$$\text{Processing gain } (G_p) = \frac{209.715 \times 10^6}{1.2 \times 10^3} = 174{,}762.5$$

$$\text{Symbol rate} = \frac{1.2 \times 10^3}{3} = 400 \, symbols/sec$$

$$\text{Number of chips per symbol} = \frac{24 \times 10^3}{400} = 60$$

■ Example 5.3

The IEEE 802.11a WLAN uses a 64-subchannel implementation of multicarrier modulation (MCM, i.e., OFDM). A total of 48 subcarriers are used for information transmission, 4 subcarriers for pilot tones are used for synchronization, and 12 are reserved. Each subchannel has a symbol rate of 250 kilo symbols per second (ksps). The occupied bandwidth is 20 MHz. Find the bandwidth of a subchannel. What is modulation efficiency? What is a user symbol rate? If 16-QAM modulation is used, what is the user data rate if the information bits are encoded with a rate of 3/4? If the guard time between two transmitted symbols is 800 ns, what is the time utilization efficiency of the system?

Solution

- Total number of subcarriers $= 48 + 12 + 4 = 64$

- Bandwidth of subchannels $= \dfrac{20 \times 10^6}{64} = 312.5\,\text{kHz}$

- Modulation efficiency $= \dfrac{250}{312.5} = 0.8\,\text{symbols/sec/Hz}$

- User symbol transmission rate $= 48 \times 250 = 1.2\,\text{Msps}$

- User bit per symbol $= 4$ for 16-QPSK modulation

- User data rate $= \dfrac{3}{4} \times 4 \times 12 = 36\,\text{Mbps}$

- Symbol duration $= \dfrac{1}{250 \times 10^3} = 4000\,\text{ns}$

- Time utilization efficiency $= \dfrac{4000}{4800} = 0.83$

∎

■ Example 5.4

A WLAN is required to have the minimum E_b/N_0 of 10 dB in an indoor office environment. The background noise at 2.4 GHz is -120 dBM. If the transmit power is 20 mW and there is no line-of-sight (NLOS) between the AP and mobile terminals, what is the coverage of the AP? Assume a data rate of 1 Mbps and channel bandwidth of 0.5 MHz. Use the Joint Technical Committee (JTC) path loss model in which for NLOS conditions in the indoor office environment, path loss at the first meter (A) is 37.7 dB and path loss exponent, γ, is 3.3. Assume power loss from the floors to be 19 dB and a shadow effect of 10 dB.

Solution

- Required $\dfrac{S}{N} = \dfrac{E_b}{N_0} \times \dfrac{R}{B_w} = 10 \times \dfrac{1}{0.5} = 20\,\text{dB}$

- Transmit power $= 10 \log 20 = 13\,\text{dBm}$

- Receiver sensitivity $= -120 + 20 = -100\,\text{dBm}$
- Maximum allowable path loss $= 13 - (-100) = 113\,\text{dB}$
- $L_p = A + 10\gamma \log d + L_f(n) + X_\sigma$

where A is the path loss at the first meter, γ is the path loss exponent, L_f the function relating power loss with number of floors n, X_σ the lognormally distributed random variable representing the shadow effect, d the distance between AP and mobile terminal:

$$113 = 37.7 + 33 \log d + 19 + 10$$
$$\therefore d = 25.3\,\text{meters}$$

■

5.5.3 IEEE 802.11 Data Link Layer

The DLL within 802.11 consists of two sublayers: logical link control (LLC) and media access control (MAC). 802.11 uses the same 802.2 LLC and 48-bit addressing as the other 802 LAN, allowing for simple bridging from wireless to IEEE wired networks, but the MAC is unique to WLAN. The sublayer above MAC is the LLC, where the framing takes place. The LLC inserts certain fields in the frame such as the source address and destination address at the head end of the frame and error-handling bits at the end of the frame.

The 802.11 MAC is similar in concept to 802.3, in that it is designed to support multiple users on a shared medium by having the sender sense the medium before accessing it. For the 802.3 Ethernet LAN, the carrier-sense multiple-access with collision detection (CSMA/CD) protocol regulates how Ethernet stations establish access to the network and how they detect and handle collisions that occur when two or more devices try to simultaneously communicate over the LAN. In an 802.11 WLAN, collision detection is not possible due to the *near/far* problem. To detect a collision, a station must be able to transmit and listen at the same time, but in radio systems the transmission drowns out the ability of a station to hear a collision.

5.5.4 IEEE 802.11 Medium Access Control

Wireless LANs operate using a shared, high bit rate transmission medium to which all devices are attached and information frames relating to all calls are transmitted. MAC sublayer defines how a user obtains a channel when he or she needs one.

MAC schemes include random access, order access, deterministic access, and mixed access. The random access MAC protocols are: ALOHA (asynchronous, slotted), CSMA/collision-detection (CD), CSMA/collision-avoidance (CA), nonpersistent, and p-persistent. The maximum throughput of slotted ALOHA protocol is about 36% of the data rate of the channel. It is simple, but not very efficient. Most WLANs implement a random access protocol, CSMA/CA with some modification, to deal with the *hidden node* problem. The

CSMA peaks at about 60%. When the traffic becomes heavy, it degrades badly. The way of dealing with that situation is to use p-persistent. Most mobile data networks also use random access protocol, usually one that is simpler than CSMA, namely slotted ALOHA. Table 5.10 provides a comparison of MAC schemes for wireless networks.

Deterministic MAC schemes improve throughput and response time when traffic is heavy. They offer the guaranteed bandwidth for isochronous traffic. In mixed cases such as CSMA/TDMA, the frame is divided into a random access part and a reserved part. When the traffic is light, it is left to be mostly random. When the traffic is heavy and throughput is in danger of declining or if a node requires isochronous bandwidth, the control point allocates bandwidth deterministically. CSMA/TDMA approaches CSMA performance under light traffic, so it has fast access time. It approaches TDMA performance when the traffic becomes heavy, so its throughput can rise close to 100% of the data rate.

IEEE 802.11 uses a modified protocol known as *carrier-sense multiple-access with collision avoidance* (*CSMA/CA*) or distributed coordination function (DCF). CSMA/CA attempts to avoid collisions by using *explicit packet acknowledgment* (ACK), which means an ACK packet is sent by the receiving station to confirm that the data packet arrived intact.

The CSMA/CA protocol is very effective when the medium is not heavily loaded since it allows stations to transmit with minimum delay. But there is always a chance of stations simultaneously sensing the medium as being free and transmitting at the same time, causing a collision. These collisions must be identified so that the MAC layer can retransmit the packet by itself and not by the upper layers, which would cause significant delay. In the Ethernet with CSMA/CD the collision is recognized by the transmitting station, which goes into a retransmission phase based on an exponential random backoff algorithm. While these collision-detection mechanisms are a good idea on a wired LAN, they cannot be used on a WLAN environment for two main reasons:

- Implementing a collision detection mechanism would require the implementation of a full duplex radio capable of transmitting and receiving at the same time, an approach that would increase the cost significantly.

Table 5.10 Comparison of MAC Access Schemes in Wireless Networks.

Access	Protocols	Characteristics
Random	CSMA	Under light load—fast response time
		Under heavy load—throughput declines
		Simple to implement
Deterministic	FDMA	Able to provide guaranteed bandwidth
	TDMA	Larger average delay compared to random access
	CDMA	Smaller delay variance
Mixed	CSMA/TDMA	Under light load—fast response time
		Under heavy load—throughput approaches TDMA
		Higher overhead compared to random and deterministic access

- In a wireless environment we cannot assume that all stations hear each other (which is the basic assumption of the collision detection scheme), and the fact that a station wants to transmit and senses the medium as free does not necessarily mean that the medium is free around the receiver area.

To overcome these problems, the 802.11 uses a CA mechanism together with a positive ACK. The MAC layer of a station wishing to transmit senses the medium. If the medium is free for a specified time, called *distributed inter-frame space* (DIFS), then the station is able to transmit the packet; if the medium is busy (or becomes busy during the DIFS interval) the station defers using the *exponential backoff algorithm*.

This scheme implies that, except in cases of very high network congestion, no packets will be lost because retransmission occurs each time a packet is not acknowledged. This entails that all packets sent will reach their destination in sequence.

The 802.11 MAC layer provides for two other robustness features: *CRC checksum* and *packet fragmentation*. Each packet has a CRC checksum calculated and attached to ensure that the data was not corrupted in transmittance. This is different from the Ethernet, where higher-level protocols such as TCP handle error checking.

Packet fragmentation allows large packets to be segmented into smaller units when sent over the medium. This is useful in very congested environments or when interference is a factor, since large packets have a better chance of being corrupted. This technique reduces the need for retransmission in many cases and improves overall wireless network performance. The MAC layer is responsible for reassembling fragments received, rendering the process transparent to higher-level protocols. The following are some of the reasons it is preferable to use smaller packets in a WLAN environment:

- Due to higher BER of a radio link, the probability of a packet getting corrupted increases with packet size.
- In the case of corrupted packets (either due to collision or interference), smaller packets cause less overhead.
- On an FHSS system the medium is interrupted periodically for hopping. With smaller packets the chance that the transmission will be postponed after dwell time is reduced.

A simple *send-and-wait* algorithm is used at the MAC sublayer. In this mechanism the transmitting station is not allowed to transmit a new packet until one of the following happens:

- Receives an ACK for the packet.
- Decides that packet was retransmitted too many times and drops the whole frame.

5.5.4.1 Exponential Backoff Algorithm

Backoff is a scheme commonly used to resolve contention problems among different stations wishing to transmit data at the same time. When a station goes into the backoff state, it waits an additional, randomly selected number of time slots [in 802.11b a slot has a 20 μs duration and the random number must be greater than 0 and smaller than a maximum value referred to as the contention window (CW)]. During the wait, the station continues sensing the medium to check whether it remains free or another transmission begins. At the end of its contention window, if the medium is still free the station can send its frame. If during the contention window another station begins transmitting data, the backoff counter is frozen and counting down starts again when the channel returns to the idle state.

There is a problem related to the CW dimension. With a small CW, if many stations attempt to transmit data at the same time, it is very possible that some of them may have the same backoff interval. This means that there will continuously be collisions, with serious effects on the network performance. On the other hand, with a large CW, if few stations wish to transmit data they will likely have long backoff delays resulting in the degradation of the network performance. The solution is to use an exponentially growing CW size. It starts from a small value (CW_{min} = 31) and doubles after each collision, until it reaches the maximum value CW_{max} (CW_{max} = 1023). In 802.11 the backoff algorithm must be executed in three cases:

- When the station senses that the medium is busy before the first transmission of a packet;
- After each retransmission;
- After a successful transmission.

This is necessary to avoid a single host wanting to transmit a large quantity of data, occupying the channel for too long a period, and denying access to all other stations. The backoff mechanism is not used when the station decides to transmit a new packet after an idle period and the medium has been free for more than the DIFS (see Figure 5.14):

$$\text{The transmission time for a data frame} = \left(\text{PLCP} + \frac{D}{R}\right)\mu s$$

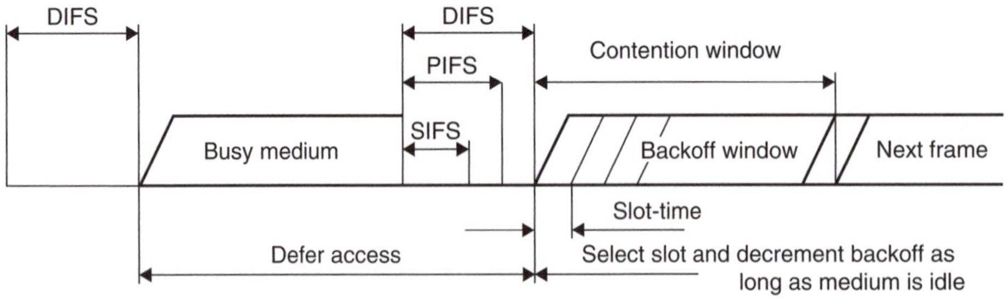

Figure 5.14 CSMA/CA in IEEE 802.11b.

where PLCP is the time required to transmit the PHY convergence protocol (PLCP), D is the frame size, R the channel bit rate:

$$\text{CSMA/CA packet transmission time} = \text{BO} + \text{DIFS} + 2\text{PLCP} + \frac{D}{R} + \text{SIFS} + \frac{A}{R}\mu s$$

where A is the ACK frame size, BO is the backoff time, DIFS the distributed interframe space, SIFS the short interframe space.

The loss of performance strongly depends on the packet size and data rate, but a 30% loss is more than likely to occur. The smaller the packets, the larger will be the impact of CSMA/CA on network performance. To evaluate the performance impact of CSMA/CA it is important to know how the various interframe spaces are defined. The 802.11 standard defines the following four interframe spaces to provide different priorities.

- *Short interframe space (SIFS):* It is used to separate transmissions belonging to a single dialog (e.g., fragment-ACK), and is the minimum interframe space. There is always at most one single station to transmit at any given time, therefore giving it priority over all other stations. This value is fixed per PHY and is calculated in such a way that the transmitting station will be able to switch back to receive mode and be capable of decoding the incoming packet. For the 802.11 DSSS PHY the value is $10\,\mu s$.

- *Point coordinate interframe space (PIFS):* It is used by the AP to gain access to the medium before any other station. This value is SIFS plus a slot time (i.e., $30\,\mu s$).

- *Distributed interframe space (DIFS):* It is the interframe space used for a station willing to start a new transmission. It is calculated as PIFS plus one slot time (i.e., $50\,\mu s$).

- *Extended interframe space (EIFS):* It is the longer interframe space used by a station that has received a packet which it could not understand. This is required to prevent the station (which could not understand the duration information for the virtual carrier sense) from colliding with a future packet belonging to the current dialog.

5.5.4.2 Hidden and Exposed Node Problem

Another major MAC layer problem specific to a WLAN is the *hidden node* issue in which two stations on opposite sides of an AP can both hear activity from an AP, but not from each other, usually due to distance or an obstruction (see Figure 5.15a). To solve this problem, 802.11 specifies an optional *request-to-send/clear-to-send* (RTS/CTS) protocol at the MAC layer. When this feature is in use, a sending station transmits an RTS and waits for the AP to reply with a CTS. Since all stations in the network can hear the AP, the CTS causes them to delay any intended transmissions, allowing the sending station to transmit and receive a

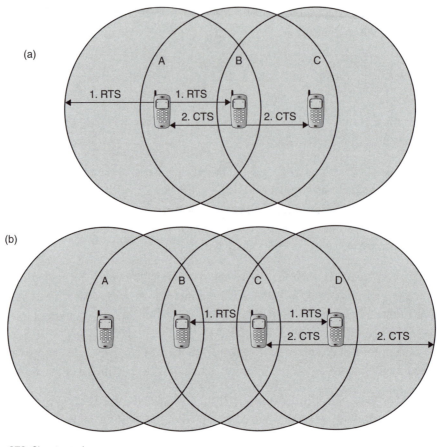

(a)

(b)

CTS: Clear to send
RTS: Request to send

Figure 5.15 (a, b) Hidden and exposed node problems.

packet ACK without any chance of collision. Since RTS/CTS adds additional overhead to the network by temporarily reserving the medium, it is typically used only on the largest-sized packets, for which transmission would be expensive from a bandwidth standpoint. This mechanism reduces the probability of a collision on the receiver area by a station that is hidden from the transmitter to the short duration of the RTS transmission, because all stations hear the CTS and make the medium busy until the end of the transaction. The duration information on the RTS also protects the transmitter area from collisions during the ACK (from stations that are out of range of the acknowledged station). It should also be noted that, due to the fact that RTS and CTS are short frames, the mechanism also reduces the overhead of collisions, since these frames are recognized faster than if the whole packet were to be transmitted. The mechanism is controlled by a parameter called RTS threshold, which, if used, must be set on both the AP and the client side.

The time required to transmit a frame, taking into account the RTS/CTS four-way handshake is given as:

$$BO + DIFS + 4\,PLCP + \frac{RTS + CTS + D + A}{R} + 3\,SIFS\,\mu s$$

where BO is the backoff time (μs), DIFS is the distributed interframe space (50 μs), PLCP the time required to transmit PHY convergence protocol (μs), RTS is the request-to-send frame size (bits), CTS the clear-to-send frame size (bits), D the frame size (bits), A the ACK frame size (bits), R the channel bit rate (bits per second), SIFS the short interframe space (10 μs).

We refer to Figure 5.15b and assume that nodes B and C intend to transmit data only without receiving data. When node C is transmitting data to node D, node B is aware of the transmission. This is because node B is within the radio coverage of node C. Without exchanging RTS and CTS frames, node B will not initiate data transmission to node A because it will detect a busy medium. The transmission between node A and node B, therefore, is blocked even if both of them are idle. This is referred as the *exposed node problem*. To alleviate this problem, a node must wait a random backoff time between the two consecutive new packet transmission times.

5.5.5 IEEE 802.11 MAC Sublayer

In IEEE 802.11, the MAC sublayer is responsible for asynchronous data service [e.g., exchange of MAC service data units (MSDUs)], security service (confidentiality, authentication, access control in conjunction with layer management), and MSDU ordering.

The MAC sublayer accepts MSDUs from higher layers in the protocol stack to send them to the equivalent layer of the protocol stack in another station. The MAC adds information to the MSDU in the form of headers and trailers to generate an MPDU. The MPDU is then passed to the PHY to be sent over the wireless medium to other stations. The MAC may fragment MSDUs into several frames to increase the probability of each individual frame being delivered successfully. The MAC frame contains addressing information, information to set the network allocation vector (NAV), and a FCS to verify the integrity of the frame. The general IEEE 802.11 MAC frame format is shown in Figure 5.16.

The MAC frame format contains four address fields. Any particular frame type may contain one, two, three, or four address fields. The address format in IEEE 802.11-1997 is a 48-bit address, used to identify the source and destination of MAC addresses contained in a frame, as IEEE 802.3. In addition to the source address (SA) and the destination address (DA), three additional address types are defined: the transmitter address, the receiver address (RA), and the basic service set identifier (BSSID). The BSSID is a unique identifier for a particular basic service set of the IEEE 802.11 WLAN. In an infrastructure basic service set, the BSSID is the MAC address of the AP.

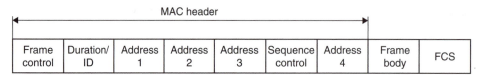

Figure 5.16 IEEE 802.11 MAC frame format.

The *transmitter address* is the address of the MAC that transmitted the frame onto the wireless medium. This address is always an individual address. The transmitter address is used by stations receiving a frame to identify the station to which any responses in the MAC frame exchange protocol will be sent.

The *RA* is the address of the MAC to which the frame is sent over the wireless medium. This address may be either an individual or a group address.

The *SA* is the address of the MAC that originated the frame. This address is always an individual address. This address does not always match the address in the transmitter address field because of the indirection that is performed by the distribution system of an IEEE 802.1 WLAN. It is the SA field that should be used to identify the source of a frame when indicating that a frame has been received to higher layer protocols.

The *DA* is the address of the final destination to which the frame is sent. This address may be either an individual or a group address. This address does not always match the address in the RA field because of the indirection that is performed by the DS.

The *sequence control field* is a 16-bit field that consists of two subfields. The subfields are a 4-bit fragment number and a 12-bit sequence number. This field is used to allow a receiving station to eliminate duplicate received frames. The *sequence number subfield* contains numbers assigned sequentially by the sending station to each MSDU. This sequence number is incremented after each assignment and wraps back to zero when incremented from 4095. The sequence number for a particular MSDU is transmitted in every data frame associated with the MSDU. It is constant over all transmissions and retransmissions of the MSDU. If the MSDU is fragmented, the sequence number of the MSDU is sent with each frame containing a fragment of the MSDU. The *fragment number subfield* contains a 4-bit number assigned to each fragment of an MSDU. The first, or only, fragment of an MSDU is assigned a fragment number of zero. Each successive fragment is assigned a sequentially incremented fragment number. The fragment number is constant in all transmissions or retransmissions of a particular fragment.

The *frame body field* contains the information specific to the particular data or management frames. This field is variable in length. It may be as long as 2034 bytes without encryption or 2312 bytes when the frame body is encrypted. The value of 2304 bytes as the maximum length of this field was chosen to allow an application to send 2048-byte pieces of information, which can be encapsulated by as many as 256 bytes of upper layer protocol headers and trailers.

The *FCS field* is 32 bits in length. It contains the result of applying the C-32 polynomial to the MAC header and frame body.

The original 802.11 standard suffers from some serious limitations which prevent it from becoming a leading technology and a serious alternative to wired LAN. The following are some of the problems:

- The 802.11 protocol imposes very high overhead to all packets that reduce real data rate significantly.
- No QoS guarantees.

Several extensions to the basic 802.11 standard have been introduced by IEEE to provide higher data rates or QoS guarantees. 802.11a, 802.11b, and 802.11g focus on higher data rates whereas 802.11e is aimed at providing QoS guarantees.

5.6 Joining an Existing Basic Service Set

The 802.11 MAC sublayer is responsible for how a station associates with an AP. When an 802.11 station enters the range of one or more APs, it chooses an AP to associate with (also known as joining a basic service set), based on signal strength and observed packet error rates. Once accepted by the AP, the station tunes to the radio channel to which the AP is set. Periodically it surveys all 802.11 channels in order to access whether a different AP would provide it with better performance characteristics. If it determines that this is the case, it reassociates with the new AP, tuning to the radio channel to which that AP is set. Reassociating usually occurs because the wireless station has physically moved away from the original AP, causing the signal to be weakened. In other cases, reassociating occurs due to changes in radio characteristics in the building, or due to high network traffic on the original AP. In the latter case this function is known as load balancing, since its primary function is to distribute the total WLAN load most efficiently across the available wireless infrastructure.

The process of dynamically associating and reassociating with APs allows network managers to set up WLANs with very broad coverage by creating a series of overlapping 802.11b cells throughout a building or across a campus. To be successful, the IT manager ideally will employ channel reuse, taking care to set up each AP on an 802.11 DSSS channel that does not overlap with a channel used by a neighboring AP (see Figure 5.17).

As noted above, while there are 14 partially overlapping channels specified in 802.11 DSSS, there are only three channels that do not overlap at all and these are the best to use for multicell coverage (refer to Table 5.5). If two APs are in range of one another and are set to

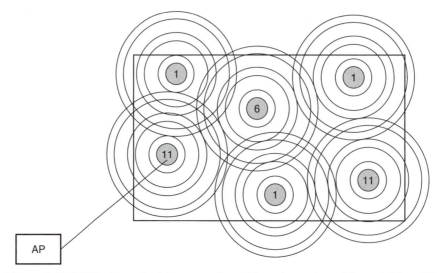

Figure 5.17 DSSS channel without overlap with a channel used by neighbor AP.

the same or partially overlapping channels, they may cause some interference for one another, thus lowering the total available bandwidth in the area of overlap.

When a station wishes to access an existing basic service set, it needs to get synchronization information from the AP. The station can get this information in one of two ways:

- *Passive scanning:* In this case the station waits to receive a beacon frame from the AP. The beacon frame is a frame sent out periodically by the AP containing synchronization information.

- *Active scanning:* In this case the station tries to locate an AP by transmitting *probe request frame* and waits for *probe response* from the AP.

A method is chosen according to the power consumption/performance trade-off. Once the station has located an AP and decides to join its basic service set, it goes through the authentication process. This is the interchange of information between the AP and the station, where each side proves the knowledge of a given password. This is necessary because WLANs have limited physical security to prevent unauthorized access. The goal of authentication is to provide access control equal to a wired LAN. The authentication service provides a mechanism for one station to identify another station. Without this proof of identity, the station is not allowed to use the WLAN for data delivery. All 802.11 stations, whether they are part of an IBSS or ESS network, must use the authentication process prior to communicating with another station. IEEE 802.11 uses authentication services defined in IEEE 802.11i.

Once the station is authenticated, it then starts the association process. It is used to make a logical connection between a mobile station and an AP and to exchange information about the station and basic service set/capabilities, which allows the distribution system service (DSS) to know about the current position of the station. This is necessary so that the AP can know where and how to deliver data to the mobile station. A station is allowed to transmit data frames through the AP only after the association process is completed.

When a station determines that the existing signal is poor, it begins scanning for another AP. This can be done by passively listening or actively probing each channel and waiting for a response. Once information has been received, the station selects the most appropriate signal and sends an association request to the new AP. If the new AP sends an association response, the client connects to the new AP. This feature is known as *roaming* and is similar to the cellular handover, with two main differences:

- On a packet-based LAN system, the transition from cell to cell may be performed between packet transmissions as opposed to a cellular system where the transition may occur during a phone conversation. This makes WLAN roaming a little easier.

- On a voice system, a temporary disconnection may not affect the conversation, while in a packet-based data system it significantly reduces performance because retransmission is performed by the upper layer protocols.

The 802.11 standard does not define how roaming should be performed, but defines the basic tools including active/passive scanning and a reassociation process, in which a station roaming from one AP to another becomes associated with the new AP.

The 802.11 standard also provides a mechanism to remove a station from the basic service set. The process is called de-authentication. De-authentication is used to prevent a previously authenticated station from using the network any further. Once a station is de-authenticated, it is no longer able to access the WLAN without performing the authentication process again. De-authentication is a notification and cannot be refused. When a station wishes to be removed from a basic service set, it can send a de-authentication management frame to the associated AP. An AP could also de-authenticate a station by sending a de-authentication frame to the station.

5.7 Security of IEEE 802.11 Systems

The IEEE 802.11 provides for MAC access control and encryption mechanisms. Earlier, the *wireline equivalent privacy* (WEP) algorithm was used to encrypt messages. WEP uses a Rivest Cipher 4 (RC4) pseudo-random number generator with two key structures of 40 and 128 bits. Because of the inherent weaknesses of the WEP, the IEEE 802.11i committee developed a new encryption algorithm and worked on the enhanced security and authentication mechanisms for 802.11 systems.

For access control, ESSID (also known as a WLAN service area ID) is programmed into each AP and is required in order for a wireless client to associate with an AP. In addition, there is provision for a table of MAC addresses called an *access control list* to be included in the AP, restricting access to stations whose MAC addresses are not on the list.

Beyond layer-2, 802.11 WLANs support the same security standards supported by other 802 LANs for access control (such as network operating system logins) and encryption (such as IPSec or application-level encryption). These higher-level technologies can be used to create end-to-end secure networks encompassing both wired LAN and WLAN components, with the wireless piece of the network gaining additional security from the IEEE 802.11i feature set.

5.8 Power Management

Power management is necessary to minimize power requirements for battery-powered portable mobile units. The standard supports two power-utilization modes, called *continuous aware mode* and *power-save polling mode*. In the former, the radio is always ON and draws power, whereas in the latter, the radio is dozing with the AP and is queuing any data for it.

A power-saver mode or sleep mode is defined when the station is not transmitting in order to save battery power. However, critical data transmissions cannot be missed. Therefore APs are required to have buffers to queue messages. Sleeping stations are required to periodically wake up and retrieve messages from the AP. Power management is more difficult for peer-to-peer IBSS configurations without central AP. In this case, all stations in the IBSS must be awakened when the periodic beacon is sent. Stations randomly handle the task of sending out the beacon. An announcement traffic information message window commences. During this period, any station can go to sleep if there is no announced activity for it during this short period.

5.9 IEEE 802.11b—High-Rate DSSS

In September 1999, IEEE ratified the 802.11b *high-rate* amendment to the standard, which added two higher speeds (5.5 and 11 Mbps) to 802.11. The key contribution of the 802.11b addition to the WLAN standard was to standardize the PHY support to two new speeds, 5.5 and 11 Mbps. To accomplish this, DSSS was selected as the sole PHY technique for the standard, since frequency hopping (FH) cannot support the higher speeds without violating current FCC regulations. The implication is that the 802.11b system will interoperate with 1 and 2 Mbps 802.11 DSSS systems, but will not work with 1 and 2 Mbps FHSS systems.

The original version of the 802.11 specifies in the DSSS standard an 11-bit chipping, called a *Barker sequence,* to encode all data sent over the air. Each 11-chip sequence represents a single data bit (1 or 0), and is converted to a waveform, called a symbol, that can be sent over the air. These symbols are transmitted at a one million symbols per second (Msps) rate using binary phase shift keying (BPSK). In the case of 2 Mbps, a more sophisticated implementation based on quadrature phase shift keying (QPSK) is used. This doubles the data rate available in BPSK, via improved efficiency in the use of the radio bandwidth.

Table 5.11 802.11b Data Rate Specification.

Data Rate	Code Length	Modulation 6-1	Symbol Rate	Bits/Symbol
1 Mbps	11 (Barker Sequence)	BPSK	1 Msps	1
2 Mbps	11 (Barker Sequence)	QPSK	1 Msps	2
5.5 Mbps	8 (CCK)	QPSK	1.375 Msps	4
11 Mbps	8 (CCK)	QPSK	1.375 Msps	8

To increase the data rate in 802.11b standard, advanced coding techniques are employed. Rather than the two 11-bit Barker sequences, 802.11b specifies complementary code keying (CCK). CCK allows for multichannel operation in the 2.4 GHz band by using existing 1 and 2 Mbps DSSS channelization schemes. CCK consists of a set of 64 8-bit code words. As a set, these code words have unique mathematical properties that allow them to be correctly distinguished from one another by a receiver even in the presence of substantial noise and multipath interference. The 5.5 Mbps rate uses CCK to encode four bits per carrier, while the 11 Mbps rate encodes eight bits per carrier. Both speeds use QPSK modulation and a signal at 1.375 Msps. This is how the higher data rates are obtained. Table 5.11 lists the specifications.

To support very noisy environments as well as extended ranges, 802.11b WLANs use dynamic rate shifting, allowing data rates to be automatically adjusted to compensate for the changing nature of the radio channel. Ideally, users connect at a full 11 Mbps rate. However, when devices move beyond the optimal range for 11 Mbps operation, or if substantial interference is present, 802.11b devices will transmit at lower speeds, falling back to 5.5, 2, and 1 Mbps. Likewise, if a device moves back within the range of a higher-speed transmission, the connection will automatically speed up again. Rate shifting is a PHY mechanism transparent to the user and upper layers of the protocol stack.

5.10 IEEE 802.11n

In response to growing market demand for higher-performance WLANs, the IEEE formed the task group 802.11n. The scope of this task group is to define modifications to the PHY and MAC layer to deliver a minimum of 100 Mbps throughput at the MAC service AP (SAP).

802.11n employs an evolutionary philosophy reusing existing technologies where practical, while introducing new technologies where they provide effective performance improvements to meet the needs of evolving applications. Reuse of legacy technologies such as OFDM, FEC coding, interleaving, and quadrature amplitude modulation mapping have been maintained to keep costs down and ease backward compatibility.

There are three key areas that need to be considered when addressing increases in WLAN performance. First, improvements in radio technology are needed to increase the physical transfer rate. Second, new mechanisms implementing the effective management of enhanced

PHY performance modes must be developed. Third, improvements in data transfer efficiency are needed to reduce the improvements achieved with an increase in physical transfer rate.

The emerging 802.11n specification differs from its predecessors in that it provides for a variety of optional modes and configurations that dictate different maximum raw data rates. This enables the standard to provide baseline performance parameters for all 802.11n devices, while allowing manufacturers to enhance or tune capabilities to accommodate different applications and price points. WLAN hardware does not need to support every option to be compliant with the standard.

The first requirement is to support an OFDM implementation that improves upon the one employed in 802.11a/g standards, using a higher maximum code rate and slightly wider bandwidth. This change improves the highest attainable raw data rate to 65 Mbps from 54 Mbps in the existing standards.

Multi-input, multi-output (MIMO) technology is used in 802.11n to evolve the existing OFDM physical interface presently implemented with legacy 802.11a/g. MIMO harnesses multipath with a technique known as space-division multiplexing (SDM). The transmitting WLAN device splits a data stream into multiple parts, called spatial streams, and transmits each spatial stream through separate antennas to corresponding antennas on the receiving end. The current 802.11n provides for up to four spatial streams, even though compliant hardware is not required to support that many.

Doubling the number of spatial streams from one to two effectively doubles the raw data rate. There are trade-offs, however, such as increased power consumption and, to a lesser extent, cost. The 802.11n specification includes an MIMO power-save mode, which mitigates power consumption by using multiple paths only when communication would benefit from the additional performance. The MIMO power-save mode is a required feature in the 802.11n specification.

There are two features in the specification that focus on improving MIMO performance: (1) beam-forming and (2) diversity. Beam-forming is a technique that focuses radio signals directly on the target antenna, thereby improving range and performance by limiting interference. Diversity exploits multiple antennas by combining the outputs of or selecting the best subset of a larger number of antennas than required to receive a number of spatial streams. The 802.11n specification supports up to four antennas.

Another optional mode in the 802.11n effectively doubles data rates by doubling the width of a WLAN communications channel from 20 to 40 MHz. The primary trade-off is fewer channels available for other devices. In the case of the 2.4-GHz band, there is enough room for three nonoverlapping 20-MHz channels. A 40-MHz channel does not leave much room for other devices to join the network or transmit in the same air space. This means intelligent, dynamic management is critical to ensuring that the 40-MHz channel option improves overall WLAN performance by balancing the high-bandwidth demands of some clients with the needs of other clients to remain connected to the network.

One of the most important features in the 802.11n specification to improve mixed-mode performance is aggregation. Rather than sending a single data frame, the transmitting client bundles several frames together. Thus, aggregation improves efficiency by restoring the percentage of time that data is being transmitted over the network.

The 802.11n specification was developed with previous standards in mind to ensure compatibility with more than 200 million Wi-Fi (802.11b) devices currently in use. An 802.11n AP will communicate with 802.11a devices on the 5-GHz band as well as 802.11b and 802.11g hardware on 2.4-GHz frequencies. In addition to basic interoperability between devices, 802.11n provides for greater network efficiency in mixed mode over what 802.11g offers.

Table 5.12 lists the major components of 802.11n. Table 5.13 compares the primary IEEE 802.11 specifications.

Because it promises far greater bandwidth, better range, and reliability, 802.11n is advantageous in a variety of network configurations. And as emerging networking applications take hold in the home, a growing number of consumers will view 802.11n not just as an enhancement to their existing network, but as a necessity. Some of the current and emerging applications that are driving the need for 802.11n are voice over IP (VoIP), streaming video and music, gaming, and network attached storage.

Table 5.12 Major Components of IEEE 802.11n.

Feature	Definition	Status
Better	OFDM supports wider bandwidth and higher code rate to bring maximum data rate to 65 Mbps.	Mandatory
Space-division multiplexing (SDM)	Improve performance by parsing data into multiple streams transmitted through multiple antennas.	Optional for up to four antennas
Diversity	Exploits the existence of multiple antennas to improve range and reliability. Typically employed when the number of antennas on the receiving end is higher than the number of streams being transmitted.	Optional for up to four antennas
MIMO power save	Limits power consumption penalty of MIMO by utilizing multiple antennas only on as-needed basis.	Required
40 MHz channels	Effectively doubles data rates by doubling channel width from 20 to 40 MHz.	Optional
Aggregation	Improves efficiency by allowing transmission bursts of multiple data packets between overhead communications.	Required
Reduced interframe spacing (RIFS)	Designed to improve efficiency by providing a shorter delay between OFDM transmissions than in 802.11a or g.	Required
Greenfield mode	Improves efficiency by eliminating support for 802.11a/b/g devices in an all 802.11n network.	Optional

Table 5.13 Primary IEEE 802.11 Specifications and Their Comparisons.

	802.11a	802.11b	802.11g	802.11n
Approval date	July 1999	July 1999	June 2003	August 2006
Maximum data rate	54 Mbps	11 Mbps	54 Mbps	600 Mbps
Modulation	OFDM	DSSS or CCK	DSSS or CCK or OFDM	DSSS or CCK or OFDM
RF band	5 GHz	2.4 GHz	2.4 GHz	2.4 or 5 GHz
Number of spatial streams	1	1	1	1, 2, 3, or 4
Channel width	20 MHz	20 MHz	20 MHz	20 or 40 MHz

5.11 Other WLAN Standards

The high performance radio LAN (HIPERLAN) committee in ETSI, referred to as Radio and Equipment Systems (RES) 10, worked with the European Conference of Postal and Telecommunications Administration (CEPT, a committee of PTT and other administration representatives) to identify its target spectrum. The CEPT identified the 5.15–5.25 GHz band (this allocation allows three channels), with an optional expansion to 5.30 GHz (extension to five channels). Any country in the CEPT area (which covers all of Europe, as well as other countries that implement CEPT recommendations) may decide to implement this recommendation. Most of the CEPT countries permit HIPERLAN systems to use this 5 GHz band. In the United States, the FCC followed the European model roughly. The unlicensed National Information Infrastructure (U-NII) band covers approximately 300 MHz in three different bands between 5.1 and 5.8 GHz. The regulators in Japan are likely to align with the 5 GHz band also. In addition, a second band from 17.1 to 17.3 GHz was identified by CEPT but so far no systems have been defined to use this band.

5.11.1 HIPERLAN Family of Standards

HIPERLAN/1 is aligned with the IEEE 802 family of standards and is very much like a modern wireless Ethernet. HIPERLAN/1, a standard completed and ratified in 1996, defines the operation of the lower portion of the OSI reference model, namely the DLL and PHY [13,14]. The DLL is further divided into two parts, the channel access control (CAC) sublayer and MAC sublayer. The CAC sublayer defines how a given channel access attempt will be made depending on whether the channel is busy or idle and at what priority level an attempt will be made. The HIPERLAN MAC layer defines the various protocols which provide the HIPERLAN/1 features of power conservation, security, and multihop routing (i.e., support for forwarding), as well as the data transfer service to the upper layers of protocols. HIPERLAN/1 uses the same modulation technology that is used in GSM, Gaussian minimum shift keying (GMSK). It has an over air data rate of 23.5 Mbps and maximum user data rate (per channel) of over 18 Mbps. The range in a typical indoor environment is 35 to 50 m. HIPERLAN/1 provides QoS, which lets critical traffic be prioritized.

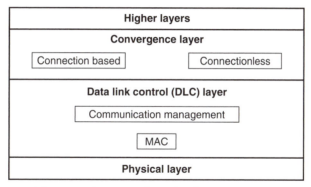

Figure 5.18 Protocol stack of HIPERLAN/2.

Table 5.14 A Comparison of HIPERLAN/2 and IEEE 802.11.

Characteristic	IEEE 802.11	HIPERLAN/2
Spectrum	2.4 GHz	5 GHz
Max. physical rate	2 Mbps	54 Mbps
Max. data rate, layer-3	1.2 Mbps	32 Mbps
Medium access control/ media sharing	CSMA/CA	Central resource control, TDMA/TDD
Access scheme	DCF/PCF	Elimination yield non-preemptive priority multiple access
Connectivity	Connectionless	Connection-oriented
Multicast	Yes	Yes
QoS support	PCF	ATM/802.1p/Resource reSerVation Protocol/ Differential service (full control)
Frequency selection	Frequency hopping or DSSS	Single carrier with dynamic frequency selection
Authentication	No	Network access identifier/IEEE address/X.509
Encryption	40-bit RC4	Data Encryption Standard (DES), triple DES
Handover support	No	No
Fixed network support	Ethernet	Ethernet, IP, ATM, UMTS, Firewire, PPP
Management	802.11 MIB	HIPERLAN/2 MIB
Radio link quality control	No	Link adaptation

HIPERLAN/2 has many characteristics of IEEE 802.11 WLAN. HIPERLAN/2 has three basic layers: PHY, data link control layer (DLC), and convergence layer (CL) (see Figure 5.18). The protocol stack is divided into a control plane and a user plane. The user plane includes functions for transmission of traffic over established connections, and the control plane performs functions of connection establishment, release, and supervision. The transmission format on the PHY is a burst consisting of a preamble part and a data part. The data part originates from each of the transport layers within DLC. A key feature of the PHY is to provide several modulation and coding schemes according to current radio link quality and meet the requirements for different PHY modes as defined by transport channels within DLC. Table 5.14 provides a comparison of the IEEE 802.11 WLAN with HIPERLAN/2.

The faster HIPERLANs include the high-performance radio access (HIPERACCESS) and high-performance metropolitan area network (HIPERMAN). Both HIPERACCESS and HIPERMAN are designed for broadband speeds and greater ranges than HIPERLAN/2. HIPERACCESS provides up to 100 Mbps in the 40.5–43.5 GHz band whereas HIPERMAN is designed for a WMAN in 2 and 11 GHz bands.

The DLC layer constitutes the logical link between an AP and mobile terminals (MTs). The DLC includes functions for medium access and transmission as well as terminal/user connection handling. The DLC layer consists of MAC, error control (EC), radio link control (RLC), DLC connection control (DCC), radio resource control (RRC), and association control function (ACF) (see Figure 5.19). Compared to IEEE 802.11 WLAN, medium access in HIPERLAN/2 is based on the time-division duplex/time-division multiple access (TDD/TDMA) and uses a MAC frame of 2 ms duration. An AP provides centralized control and informs the mobile terminals at which point in time in the MAC frame they are allowed to transmit their data. Time slots are allocated dynamically depending on the need for transmission resources.

HIPERLAN/2 operates as a connection-oriented wireless link. It supports different QoS levels required for the transmission of various traffic types. The CL between the DLL and network layer provides QoS. The role of the CL is two-fold—it maps the service requirements of the higher layer to the service offered by the data link control layer, and converts packets received from the core network to the format expected at the lower layers. There are two types of CL. One is cell-based and the other is packet-based. We focus only on the packet-based CL,

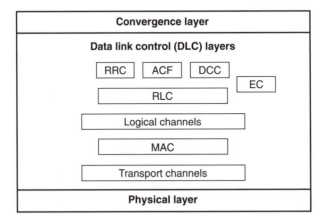

RRC: Radio resource control
ACF: Association control function
DCC: DLC connection control
EC: Error control
RLC: Radio link control
MAC: Medium access control

Figure 5.19 Relation between logical and transport channels in HIPERLAN/2.

which can be further divided into a common part and a service-specific part. The packet-based service-specific convergence sublayer (SSCS) is for switched Ethernet and IEEE 1394 Firewire. Broadband radio access for IP-based networks (BRAIN) focuses on the specifications of an innovative SSCS dedicated to provide support to IP traffic in a mobile environment. The architecture of the CL makes HIPERLAN/2 suitable as a radio access for different types of fixed networks, e.g., Ethernet, IP, ATM, UMTS, etc. The main function of the common part is to segment packets received from the SSCS, and reassemble segmented packets received from the data link control layer before they are handed over to the SSCS. The Ethernet SSCS makes the HIPERLAN/2 network look like a wireless segment of a switched Ethernet.

HIPERLAN/2 supports two QoS schemes: the best-effort scheme and IEEE 802.1p-based priority scheme. The connection-oriented nature of HIPERLAN/2 allows implementation of QoS. Each connection is assigned a specific QoS in terms of bandwidth, delay, jitter, BER, and so on. Also a simple approach is used where each connection is assigned a priority level relative to other connections. The QoS support with high data rate facilitates the transmission of many different types of data streams, e.g., video, voice, and data.

5.11.1.1 QoS in HIPERLAN/2

QoS deals with the ability of a network to provide service for specific network traffic over various underlying wireline or wireless technologies. Compared to end-to-end IP network QoS, wireless network may provide QoS only for one or two hops of an end-to-end connection. The cellular radio access in the BRAIN uses HIPERLAN/2 and supports QoS on a per connection basis.

An IP CL is used to provide the functions required for mapping the QoS requirements of the individual connection to the QoS parameters available in DLC connections. The CL offers a QoS interface to support different IP QoS schemes. By using IP QoS parameters, the CL establishes DLC connections in which IP QoS parameters are mapped into DLC connections for priority, radio bandwidth reservation, appropriate ARQ scheme, and handover strategy. This procedure is realized by mapping IP packets into different DLC connection queues based on respective code point and DA fields. The CL associates a specific link scheduling priority, discarding time and/or bandwidth reservation to each DLC queue. The CL segments IP traffic to fixed length packets. The segmentation and reassembly causes extra complexity in the CL but enables a better bandwidth reservation policy.

MAC enables full rescheduling in every 2 ms and dynamically adjusts uplink and downlink capacity. Radio link control (RLC) provides connection-oriented secured link service to the CL. There are up to 63 unicast data connections per terminal that can be supported with various QoS parameters. Error correction (EC) provides a selective repeat ARQ mode for each connection. Alternatively, for delay intolerant and multicast services a repetition mode can be used. Thus, DLC provides means for executing several IP QoS techniques such as prioritizing, on-demand-based bandwidth reservation, and delay guarantee. DLC also provides dynamic frequency selection (DFS), link adaptation, power control, and power saving.

The PHY uses OFDM to combat frequency-selective fading and randomize the burst errors caused by a wide band fading channel. There are seven modes with different coding and modulation schemes available in PHY; all of them can be adapted dynamically by a link adaptation scheme. There is a strong interaction between the PHY modes, retransmission load and utilization of the radio link, delay, and overall throughput.

The OFDM transmits broadband, high data rate information by dividing the data into several interleaved, parallel bit streams, and lets each one of them modulate on a separate subcarrier. Various coding and modulation schemes are used by a link adaptation mechanism. This is to adapt to current radio link quality and meet the requirements for different PHY properties as defined by the transport channels within DLC. Table 5.15 provides the different PHY modes and their transmission rates. The seven PHY modes use BPSK, QPSK, and 16-QAM as mandatory subcarrier modulation schemes whereas 64-QAM is optional. FEC is performed by a convolutional code of a rate of 1/2 and a constraint length of 7. Other code rates of 3/4 and 9/16 can be obtained by puncturing.

The DLC scheduling algorithm deals with the properties of the HIPERLAN/2 radio access that are dependent on ARQ and link adaptation. ARQ reacts on transmission errors and initiates retransmission. When the error check bit detects error(s) in the transmission, ARQ sends a request for retransmission of the error packet data unit (PDU). Thus, for a poor radio link, retransmission will cause large transmission delay. Selective repeat ARQ uses a transmission window at the transmitter and receiver. The receiver notifies the transmitter of the sequence number below which all PDUs are received correctly and points out which PDU is not correct.

Table 5.15 Physical Modes and Transmission Rates of HIPERLAN/2.

Mode	Modulation	Coding Rate R	Nominal Bit Rate (Mbps)	Coded Bit Rate Per Subcarrier	Coded Bits Per OFDM Symbol	Data Bit Per OFDM Symbol
1	BPSK	1/2	6	1	48	24
2	BPSK	3/4	9	1	48	36
3	QPSK	1/2	12	2	96	48
4	QPSK	3/4	18	2	96	72
5	16-QAM (HIPERLAN/2 only)	9/16	27	4	192	108
6	16-QAM (IEEE only)	1/2	24	4	192	96
7	16-QAM	3/4	36	4	192	144
8	64-QAM	3/4	54	6	288	216

Based on the current radio link conditions, the link adaptation in the DLC layer assigns a specific PHY mode to the PDU dedicated to a connection. Each connection and its direction are addressed individually and the assignment varies from one MAC frame to another. The link adaptation scheme adapts the PHY mode based on link quality measurements. ARQ and link adaptation reduce packet loss rate but introduce additional overhead and delay to the radio access system.

Total system throughput, transmission delay, and BER are the important parameters in determining the performance of the HIPERLAN/2 radio access. There is a strong interaction between PHY modes and these parameters.

The MAC protocol functions are used for organizing the access and transmission of data on the radio link. Since HIPERLAN/2 uses a central resource controlled TDD/TDMA scheme, MAC frame (MF) is allowed to simultaneously communicate via a number of DLC connections in both downlink and uplink directions. Each MF allocates time slots for broadcast channel (BCH), frame channel, access feedback channel (ACH), random channel (RCH), downlink (DL) phase, uplink (UL) phase, and directlink (DiL) phase. Data is grouped as PDU trains. There are two kinds of PDU, one is long PDU (LCH PDU) of 54 bytes and another is short PDU (SCH PDU) of 9 bytes. The PDU error ratio refers to the error rate of LCH PDU.

5.11.2 Multimedia Access Communication—High-Speed Wireless Access Network

Multimedia access communication (MMAC)—high-speed wireless access network (HiSWAN)—started in Japan in 1996. It uses two frequency bands: 5 GHz for HiSWANa and 25 GHz for HiSWANb. The HiSWAN uses the 5 GHz license-free frequency band and is closely aligned with the HIPERLAN/2. HiSWAN uses the OFDM PHY to provide a standard speed of 27 Mbps and 6 to 36 Mbps by link adaptation. However, MMAC-HiSWANa differs from the HIPERLAN/2 in radio network functions due to the differences in regional frequency planning and regulations. Instead of DFS in HIPERLAN/2, carrier sense functions of APs are mandatory in MMAC-HiSWANa. Also, inter-AP synchronizations are specified to avoid interference among APs and to use four available channels in Japan for wide coverage. Table 5.16 summarizes various WLANs.

■ Example 5.5

Consider the HIPERLAN/2 that uses BPSK and $R = 3/4$ codes for 9 Mbps information transmission and 16-QAM with the same coding for the actual payload data-transmission rate of 36 Mbps. Calculate the coded symbol transmission rate per subcarrier for each of the two modes. What is the bit-transmission rate per subcarrier for each of the two modes?

Solution

- User data-transmission rate per carrier with $R = 3/4$ convolution encoder (refer to Table 5.11):

$$\text{Mode I (9 Mbps)} = \frac{9 \times 10^6}{48} = 187.5\,\text{kbps}$$

$$\text{Mode II (36 Mbps)} = \frac{36 \times 10^6}{48} = 750\,\text{kbps}$$

- Carrier transmission rate with $R = 3/4$ convolutional encoder:

$$\text{Mode I} = \frac{187.5}{(3/4)} = 250\,\text{kbps}$$

$$\text{Mode II} = \frac{750}{(3/4)} = 1000\,\text{kbps}$$

- Carrier symbol rate:

$$\text{Mode I (BPSK)} = 250\,\text{ksps}$$

$$\text{Mode II (16-QAM)} = \frac{1000}{4} = 250\,\text{ksps}$$

■

Table 5.16 Comparisons of Various WLAN Standards.

	IEEE 802.11	IEEE 802.11b	IEEE 802.11a	IEEE 802.11g	HIPERLAN/1	HIPERLAN/2	MMAC HiSWAN
Rectification	June 1997	Sept. 1999	Sept. 1999	June 2003	Early 1993	Feb. 2000	April 1997
RF bandwidth (GHz)	2.4	2.4	5.0	2.4	5	5	5
Max. data rate (Mbps)	2	11	54	54	23.5	54	27
Physical layer (PHY)	FHSS, DSSS, IR	DSSS	OFDM	OFDM	GMSK	OFDM	OFDM
Range (m)	50–100	50–100	50–100	50–100	50	50 indoor, 300 outdoor	100–150

■ Example 5.6

What is the user data rate for HIPERLAN/2 with 64-QAM modulation with $R = 3/4$ convolutional coder?

Solution

Carrier symbol rate $= 250$ ksps; bits per symbol for 64-QAM $= 6$. The user data rate is given by

$$\text{User data rate} = 250 \times \frac{3}{4} \times 6 \times 48 = 54\,\text{Mbps}$$

■

5.12 Performance of a Bluetooth Piconet in the Presence of IEEE 802.11 WLANs

Due to its global availability, the 2.4 GHz ISM unlicensed band is a popular frequency band to low-cost radios. Bluetooth and the IEEE 802.11 WLAN both operate in this band. Therefore, it is anticipated that some interference will result from both these systems operating in the same environment. Interference may lead to significant performance degradation. In this section, we evaluate Bluetooth MAC layer performance in the presence of neighboring Bluetooth piconets and neighboring IEEE 802.11 WLANs.

A packet collision occurs when a desired Bluetooth packet [15–17] overlaps the interfering packets in time and frequency. In Bluetooth, the duration of a single slot packet is 366 ms and the duration of the slot is 625 ms. The time between the end of the transmission of the packet and the start of the next slot is the idle time. Similarly, the duration of one 802.11 packet traffic time includes packet transmission time and a backoff period.

To simplify the analysis, we make the following assumptions:

- The link is continuously established and the collocated systems are sufficiently close to each other such that the Bluetooth packet will be corrupted completely by the interference packets even if they overlap by a single bit.

- The desired Bluetooth packet will not be destroyed by another piconet if it is hit during the idle time.

- The desired Bluetooth packet will not be destroyed by an IEEE 802.11 network during the IEEE 802.11 backoff period.

- In Bluetooth, the hopping patterns are 100% uncorrelated.

- For a long enough observation time, a given transmitter uses the 79 hopping channels equally.

- There are also 79 channels spaced 1 MHz apart in the IEEE 802.11 FH system.

- Each station's signal hops from one modulating frequency to another in a predetermined pseudo-random sequence.

The collision probability of Bluetooth to the IEEE 802.11 FH system is 1/79. In the IEEE 802.11 DS, the data stream is converted into a symbol stream which spreads over a relatively wide band channel of 22 MHz, so the interference on a Bluetooth packet from IEEE 802.11 DS system is much higher than that from the 802.11 FH system. It is because the bandwidth of a channel in DS is 22 times as wide as Bluetooth one channel. The collision probability of Bluetooth to the IEEE 802.11 DS system is 22/79.

5.12.1 Packet Error Rate (PER) from N Neighboring Bluetooth Piconets

- *Synchronous mode:* The probability that one interfering Bluetooth piconet selects the same channel as the desired piconet is 1/79. The probability for a Bluetooth packet to be transferred successfully for synchronous mode is $(1 - 1/79) = 78/79$.

- *Asynchronous mode:* The duration of a single slot packet is 366 μs and the duration of a slot is 625 μs. If r is equal to 366/625, there is a probability of $2(1 - r)$ that only the preceding or the following slot is vulnerable and a probability of $(2r - 1)$ that both preceding and following slots are vulnerable. Hence the probability of the desired piconet not being disturbed by one advisory piconet is given as:

$$P_s^{UR} = 2(1 - r) \times \left(\frac{78}{79}\right) + (2r - 1) \times \left(\frac{78}{79}\right)^2 \tag{5.1}$$

The PER due to N neighboring Bluetooth piconets for synchronous and asynchronous modes are given as:

$$(\text{PER})_{\text{syn}} = 1 - \left(\frac{78}{79}\right)^N \tag{5.2}$$

$$(\text{PER})_{\text{asyn}} = 1 - \left[2(1 - r) \times \left(\frac{78}{79}\right) + (2r - 1) \times \left(\frac{78}{79}\right)^2\right]^N = 1 - \left(P_s^{UR}\right)^N \tag{5.3}$$

5.12.2 PER from M Neighboring IEEE 802.11 WLANs[1]

Under IEEE 802.11 FH, the probability of M IEEE 802.11 induced collisions on a Bluetooth packet is given as [17]

$$\text{PER} = 1 - \left\{ \left[\left(1 - \frac{|G|}{L} \right) \times \left(\frac{78}{79} \right)^{\lceil H/L \rceil} + \frac{|G|}{L} \times \left(\frac{78}{79} \right)^{\lceil H/L \rceil - G/|G|} \right] \right\}^{M} \tag{5.4}$$

Under IEEE 802.11 DS, the probability of M IEEE 802.11 induced collisions on a Bluetooth packet is given as:

$$\text{PER} = 1 - \left\{ \left[\left(1 - \frac{|G|}{L} \right) \times \left(\frac{57}{79} \right)^{\lceil H/L \rceil} + \frac{|G|}{L} \times \left(\frac{57}{79} \right)^{\lceil H/L \rceil - G/|G|} \right] \right\}^{M} \tag{5.5}$$

where H is the duration of a Bluetooth packet, L the dwell period of an IEEE 802.11 transmission, T_w the packet duration of IEEE 802.11, G is $\lceil H/L \rceil L - T_w - H$, $\lceil x \rceil$ is the least integer greater than or equal to x.

The collision probability of a Bluetooth piconet where there are N neighboring Bluetooth piconets and M IEEE 802.11 WLANs will be:

$$(\text{PER})_{\text{syn}} = 1 - \left[\left(\frac{78}{79} \right)^{N} \times (P_s)^{M} \right] \tag{5.6}$$

$$(\text{PER})_{\text{asyn}} = 1 - \left(P_s^{\text{UR}} \right)^{N} (P_s)^{M} \tag{5.7}$$

5.12.3 Aggregated Throughput

The aggregated throughput of successfully transmitted packets in all piconets can be expressed as $S_a(n) = nP_s(n,m)$, where n is the number of Bluetooth piconets, m is the number of IEEE 802.11 WLANs, and $P_s(n,m)$ is the probability that a Bluetooth packet is free from other piconets and 802.11 network collisions. The aggregate throughput for different cases is given in Table 5.17.

---

[1] Refer to [17] for the derivation of equations and details.

Table 5.17 Aggregated Throughputs for Different Cases.

Case	n	m	$P_s(n, m)$	$S_a(n)$
Synchronous	$N + 1$	$0\ (78/79)^N$	$(N + 1)(78/79)^N$	
	$N + 1$	M	$(78/79)^N P_s^{\ M}$	$(N + 1)(78/79)^N P_s^{\ M}$
Asynchronous	$N + 1$	0	$(P_s^{\ UR})^N$	$(N + 1)\ (P_s^{\ UR})^N$
	$N + 1$	M	$(P_s^{\ UR})^N P_s^{\ M}$	$(N + 1)(P_s^{\ UR})^N P_s^{\ M}$

■ Example 5.7

Determine the collision probability of 1000 bytes IEEE 802.11 FH packet at 2 Mbps and Bluetooth. Assume a dwell period of an 802.11 transmission to be 3 ms. What is the PER with an IEEE 802.11 DS packet? Duration of Bluetooth packet = 0.625 ms.

Solution

$$T_w = \frac{1000 \times 8}{2 \times 10^6} = 4\,\text{ms}$$

$$\left\lceil \frac{H}{L} \right\rceil = \left\lceil \frac{0.625}{3} \right\rceil = 1$$

$$G = 3 - 4 - 0.625 = -1.625\,\text{ms}$$
$$|G| = 1.625\,\text{ms}$$

$$(\text{PER})_{\text{FH}} = 1 - \left\{ \left(1 - \frac{1.625}{3}\right)\left(\frac{78}{79}\right) + \frac{1.625}{3} \times \left(\frac{78}{79}\right)^{1+1} \right\} = 0.0195 \approx 2\%$$

$$(\text{PER})_{\text{DS}} = 1 - \left\{ \left(1 - \frac{1.625}{3}\right) \times \left(\frac{57}{79}\right) + \frac{1.625}{3} \times \left(\frac{57}{79}\right)^{2} \right\} = 0.3873 \approx 38.73\%$$

Note the collision probability with 802.11 DS is much higher than with 802.11 FH. ■

5.13 Interference Between Bluetooth and IEEE 802.11

Interference range is the distance between two devices in order to interfere if they operate at the same frequency and at the same time. The interference range depends on propagation characteristics of the environment, processing gains of receivers, and transmitted power from different devices. Figure 5.20 shows an interference scenario between a transmitting Bluetooth (BT-1) device and a receiving IEEE 802.11 FH device (MS) collocated in the same

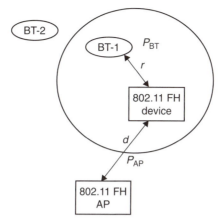

Figure 5.20 First interference scenario between Bluetooth and IEEE 802.11 FH device.

area [11]. Since IEEE 802.11 AP is usually located on the wall to provide better coverage, it is less likely to be interfered with by the BT. Interference occurs when the MS receives information from the AP and BT-1 transmits information to BT-2; or when the MS transmits and BT-1 receives. We assume the interference from the AP to the BT devices and the interference of the BT-2 to the IEEE 802.11 device are negligible. When the MS is receiving and BT-1 is transmitting, the signal-to-interference ratio (SIR) at the MS will be:

$$\text{SIR} = \frac{S}{I} = \frac{KP_{\text{AP}}d^{-\gamma}}{KP_{\text{BT}}r^{-\gamma}} = \frac{P_{\text{AP}}}{P_{\text{BT}}} \times \left(\frac{r}{d}\right)^{\gamma} \tag{5.8}$$

$$r_{\max} = d\left[(\text{SIR})_{\min} \times \left(\frac{P_{\text{BT}}}{P_{\text{AP}}}\right)\right]^{1/\gamma} \tag{5.9}$$

where P_{AP} and P_{BT} is the transmitted power by the AP and Bluetooth devices, respectively, γ the path loss exponent, d the distance between AP and IEEE 802.11 device, r the distance between Bluetooth device and IEEE 802.11 device, $r_{\max}$ the range of interference between Bluetooth and 802.11 device, and $(\text{SIR})_{\min}$ the minimum signal-to-interference ratio.

In the second scenario, the MS transmits to the AP and BT-1 receives from BT-2 (see Figure 5.21), then

$$R_{\max} = d\left[(\text{SIR})_{\min}\left(\frac{P_{\text{MS}}}{P_{\text{BT}}}\right)\right]^{1/\gamma} \tag{5.10}$$

where P_{MS} is the transmitted power of the IEEE 802.11 device.

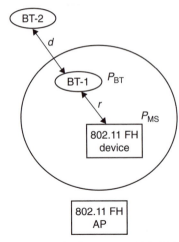

Figure 5.21 Second interference scenario between IEEE 802.11 FH device and Bluetooth.

If instead of the IEEE 802.11 FH system, the IEEE 802.11 DS system is used in the scenario of Figure 5.20, the minimum required received SIR at the mobile terminal is reduced by the processing gain, G_P, of the DSSS. The interference range r_{max} will be:

$$r_{max} = d\left[(SIR)_{min}\left(\frac{P_{BT}}{\{P_{AP}G_P\}}\right)\right]^{1/\gamma} \tag{5.11}$$

Similarly, the interference range for the second scenarios of Figure 5.21 with the IEEE 802.11 DSSS system will be:

$$r_{max} = d\left[(SIR)\left\{\frac{P_{MS}}{(P_{BT}G_P)}\right\}\right]^{1/\gamma} \tag{5.12}$$

■ Example 5.8

Consider the Bluetooth and IEEE 802.11 FH interference scenario (refer to Figure 5.20):

(a) Assuming that the acceptable error probability for the mobile terminal is 10^{25}, find $(SIR)_{min}$ that supports this error rate, and (b) using $(SIR)_{min}$ from (a) calculate r_{max} for $d = 10\,m$, $\gamma = 4$, $P_{BT} = 20\,dBm$ and $P_{AP} = 40\,dBm$.

Solution

$$P_e = 0.5e^{-0.5E_b/N_0}$$

$$10^{-5} = 0.e^{-0.5E_b/N_0}$$

$$\frac{E_b}{N_0} = 21.6 = 13.35\text{dB}$$

$$r_{max} = 10\left[\frac{21.6 \times 20}{40}\right]^{1/4} = 18.13\,\text{m}$$

■ Example 5.9

Calculate r_{max} for the interference scenarios (see Figure 5.21) using S_{min} from Example 5.8 and $d = 10\,\text{m}$, $\gamma = 4$, $P_{BT} = 20\,\text{dBm}$, and $P_{MS} = 40\,\text{dBm}$.

Solution

$$r_{max} = 10\left[\frac{21.6 \times 40}{20}\right] = 25.6\,\text{m}$$

■ Example 5.10

Repeat Problems 5.8 and 5.9, if the IEEE 802.11 FH device is replaced by the IEEE 802.11 DS device ($G_P = 11$).

Solution

$$r_{max} = 10\left[\frac{21.6 \times 20}{40 \times 11}\right]^{1/4} = 9.95\,\text{m}$$

$$r_{max} = 10\left[\frac{21.6 \times 20}{20 \times 11}\right]^{1/4} = 14.08\,\text{m}$$

Note the interference ranges are smaller for the IEEE 802.11 DS device compared to the IEEE 802.11 FH device.

5.14 IEEE 802.16

The IEEE 802.16 standard delivers performance comparable to traditional cable, DSL, or T1 offerings. The principal advantages of systems based on 802.16 are multifold: faster provisioning of service, even in areas that are hard for wired infrastructure to reach; lower

Table 5.18 Road Map of IEEE 802.16 Standards.

Standards	Features
802.16 (2001)	Air interface for fixed broadband wireless access system, MAC and PHY specification for 10–66 GHz (LOS)
802.16a (January 2003)	Amendment to 802.16; MAC modifications and additional PHY specifications for 2–11 GHz (NLOS); three physical layers—OFDM, OFDMA, single carrier; additional MAC functions; mesh topology support; ARQ
802.16d (July 2004)	Combine 802.16 and 802.16a, some modification to MAC and PHY
802.16e (December 2005)	Amendment to 802.16d, MAC modifications for limited mobility

installation cost; and ability to overcome the physical limitations of the traditional wired infrastructure. 802.16 technology provides a flexible, cost-effective, standard-based means of filling gaps in broadband services not envisioned in a wired world. For operators and service providers, systems built upon the 802.16 standard represent an easily deployable "third pipe" capable of delivering flexible and affordable last-mile broadband access for millions of subscribers in homes and businesses throughout the world [3, 4].

The 802.16a is an extension of the 802.16 originally designed for 10–66 GHz. It covers frequency bands between 2 and 11 GHz and enables NLOS operation, making it an appropriate technology for last-mile applications where obstacles such as trees and buildings are often present and where base stations may need to be unobtrusively mounted on the roofs of homes or buildings rather than towers on mountains.

The 802.16a has a range of up to 30 miles with a typical cell radius of 4 to 6 miles. Within the typical cell radius NLOS performance and throughputs are optimal. In addition, the 802.16a provides an ideal wireless backhaul technology to connect 802.11 WLAN and commercial 802.11 hotspots with the Internet. Table 5.18 provides a road map of IEEE 802.16 standards.

Applications of the 802.16 are cellular backhaul, broadband on-demand, residential broadband, and best-connected wireless service (see Figure 5.22). The 802.16 delivers high throughput at long ranges with a high spectral efficiency. Dynamic adaptive modulation allows base stations to trade off throughput for range. The 802.16 supports flexible channel bandwidths to accommodate easy cell planning in both licensed and unlicensed spectra worldwide. The 802.16 includes robust security features and QoS needed to support services that require low latency, such as voice and video. The 802.16 voice service can either be TDM voice or VoIP. Privacy and encryption features are also included to support secure transmission and data encryption.

The *Worldwide Interoperability for Microaccess, Inc.* (WiMAX) forum, an industry group, focused on creating system profiles and conformance programs to ensure operability among devices based on the 802.16 standard from different manufacturers. For more details see [3, 4].

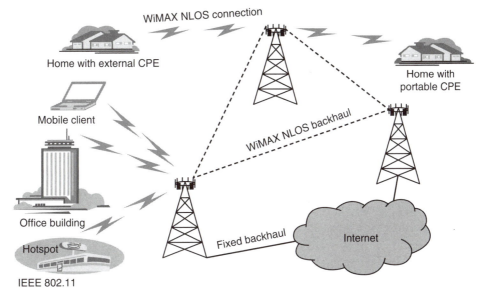

CPE: Customer premises equipment

Figure 5.22 Applications of IEEE 802.16 (WiMax).

5.15 World Interoperability for MicroAccess, Inc. (WiMAX)

WiMAX is an advanced technology solution based on an open standard, designed to meet the need for very high speed wide area Internet access, and to do so in a low-cost, flexible way. It aims to provide business and consumer broadband service on the scale of the metropolitan area network (MAN). WiMAX networks are designed for high-speed data and will spur innovation in services, content, and new mobile devices. WiMAX is optimized for IP-based high-speed wireless broadband which will provide for a better mobile wireless broadband Internet experience.

The WiMAX product certification program ensures interoperability between WiMAX equipment from vendors worldwide. The certification program also considers interoperability with (HIPERMAN), the European telecommunication standards institute's MAN standard.

With its large range and high transmission rate, WiMAX can serve as a backbone for 802.11 hotspots for connecting to the Internet. Alternatively, users can connect mobile devices such as laptops and handsets directly to WiMAX base stations without using 802.11. Mobile devices connected directly can achieve a range of four to six miles, because mobility makes links vulnerable. The WiMAX technology can also provide fast and cheap broadband access to markets that lack infrastructure (fiber optics or copper wire), such as rural areas and unwired countries. WiMAX can be used in disaster recovery scenes where the wired networks have broken down. It can be used as backup links for broken wired links.

WiMAX can typically support data rates from 500 kbps to 2 Mbps. WiMAX also has clearly defined QoS classes for applications with different requirements such as VoIP, real-time video streaming, file transfer, and web traffic. A cellular architecture similar to that of mobile phone systems can be used with a central base station controlling downlink/uplink traffic (see Figure 5.22).

WiMAX is a family of technologies based on IEEE 802.16 standards. There are two main types of WiMAX today: *fixed WiMAX* (IEEE 802.16d—2004) and *mobile WiMAX* (IEEE 802.16e—2005). Fixed WiMAX is a point-to-multipoint technology, whereas mobile WiMAX is a multipoint-to-multipoint technology, similar to that of a cellular infrastructure. Both solutions are engineered to deliver ubiquitous high-throughput broadband wireless service at a low cost. Mobile WiMAX uses orthogonal frequency division multiple access (OFDMA) technology which has inherent advantages in latency, spectral efficiency, advanced antenna performance, and improved multipath performance in an NLOS environment. Scalable OFDMA (SOFDMA) has been introduced in IEEE 802.16e to support scalable channel bandwidths from 1.25 to 20 MHz. Release 1 of mobile WiMAX will cover 5, 7, 8.75, and 10 MHz channel bandwidths for licensed worldwide spectrum allocations in 2.3, 2.5, 3.3, and 3.5 GHz frequency bands. Also, next generation 4G wireless technologies are evolving toward OFDMA and IP-based networks as they are ideal for delivering cost-effective high-speed wireless data services.

The WiMAX specification improves upon many of the limitations of the Wi-Fi standard (802.11b) by providing increased bandwidth and stronger encryption. Table 5.19 provides comparisons of Wi-Fi and WiMAX.

The 802.16 standard was designed mainly for point-to-multipoint topologies, in which a base station distributes traffic to many subscriber stations that are mounted on rooftops. The point-to-multipoint configuration uses a scheduling mechanism that yields high efficiency because stations transmit in their scheduled slots and do not contend with one another. WiMAX does not require stations to listen to one another because they encompass a larger area. This scheduling design suits WiMAX networks because subscriber stations might aggregate

Table 5.19 Comparison of Wi-Fi and WiMAX.

Wi-Fi	WiMAX
802.11a—OFDM, maximum rate = 54 Mbps	802.16—OFDM, maximum rate = 50 Mbps
802.11b—DSSS, maximum rate = 11 Mbps	802.16e—OFDM, maximum rate = 30 Mbps
802.11g—OFDM, maximum rate = 54 Mbps	
Range < 100 m	A few kilometers non-line-of-sight, more with line-of-sight
Indoor environment	Outdoor environment
No admission control, no load balancing	Admission control and load balancing
No quality of service (QoS)	Five QoS classes enforced by base station

traffic from several computers and have steady traffic, unlike terminals in 802.11 hotspots, which usually have bursty traffic. The 802.16 also supports a mesh mode, where subscriber stations can communicate directly with one another. The mesh mode can help relax the LOS requirement and ease the deployment costs for high-frequency bands by allowing subscriber stations to relay traffic to one another. In this case, a station that does not have LOS with the base station can get its traffic from another station (see Figure 5.23).

Mobile WiMAX systems offer scalability in both radio access technology and network architecture, thus providing a great deal of flexibility in network deployment options and service offerings. Some of the salient features supported by WiMAX are:

- *High data rates:* The inclusion of MIMO antenna techniques along with flexible subchannelization schemes, advanced coding, and modulation all enable the mobile WiMAX technology to support peak downlink data rates of 63 Mbps per sector and peak uplink data rates of up to 28 Mbps per sector in a 10 MHz channel.

- *QoS:* The fundamental premise of the IEEE 802.16 MAC architecture is QoS. It defines service flows which can map to DiffServ code points or MPLS flow labels that enable end-to-end IP-based QoS. Additionally, sub-channelization and MAP-based signaling schemes provide a flexible mechanism for optimal scheduling of space, frequency, and time resources over the air interface on a frame-by-frame basis.

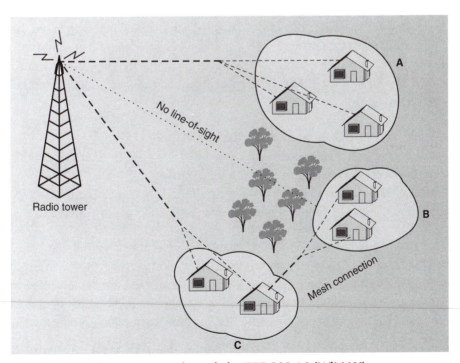

Figure 5.23 Mesh mode in IEEE 802.16 (WiMAX).

- *Scalability:* Mobile WiMAX is designed to be able to scale to work in different channelization from 1.25 to 20 MHz to comply with varied worldwide requirements as efforts proceed to achieve spectrum harmonization in the longer term.

- *Security:* Support for a diverse set of user credentials exists including SIM/USIM cards, smart cards, digital certificates, and user name/password schemes based on the relevant extensible authentication protocol (EAP) methods for the credential type.

- *Mobility:* Mobile WiMAX supports optimized handoff schemes with latencies less than 50 ms to ensure that real-time applications such as VoIP can be performed without service degradation. Flexible key management schemes assure that security is maintained during handoff.

5.15.1 WiMAX PHY

The 802.16 PHY supports TDD and full and half-duplex frequency-division duplex (FDD) operations; however, the initial release of mobile WiMAX only supports TDD. Other advanced PHY features include adaptive modulation and coding (AMC), hybrid ARQ (HARQ), and fast channel feedback (CQICH) to enhance coverage and capacity of WiMAX in mobile applications.

For the bands in the 10–66 GHz range, 802.16 defines one air interface called Wireless MAN-SC. The PHY design for the 2–11 GHz range (both licensed and unlicensed bands) is more complex because of interference. Hence, the standard supports burst-by-burst adaptability for modulation and coding schemes and specifies three interfaces. The adaptive features at the PHY allow trade-off between robustness and capacity. The three air interfaces for the 2–11 GHz range are:

- Wireless MAN—SCa uses single carrier modulation.
- Wireless MAN—OFDM uses a 256-carrier OFDM. This air interface provides multiple access to different stations through TDMA.
- Wireless MAN—OFDM uses a 2048-carrier OFDM scheme. The interface provides multiple access by assigning a subset of the carriers to an individual receiver.

Support for QPSK, 16-QAM, and 64-QAM are mandatory in the downlink with mobile WiMAX. In the uplink 64-QAM is optional. Both convolutional code and turbo code with variable code rate and repetition coding are supported. The combinations of various modulation and code rates provide a fine resolution of data rates. The frame duration is 5 ms. Each frame has 48 OFDM symbols with 44 OFDM symbols available for data transmission.

The base station (BS) scheduler determines the appropriate data rate for each burst allocation based on the buffer size, channel propagation conditions at the receiver, etc. A channel quality indicator (CQI) channel is used to provide channel state information from the user terminals to the BS scheduler.

WiMAX provides signaling to allow fully asynchronous operation. The asynchronous operation allows variable delay between retransmissions which gives more flexibility to the scheduler at the cost of additional overhead for each retransmission. HARQ combined with CQICH and AMC provides robust link adoption in the mobile environment at vehicular speeds in excess of 120 km/h.

5.15.2 WiMAX Media Access Control (MAC)

The IEEE 802.16 MAC is significantly different from IEEE 802.11b Wi-Fi MAC. In Wi-Fi, the MAC uses contention access—all subscribers wishing to pass data through an AP compete for the AP's attention on a random basis. This can cause distant nodes from the AP to be repeatedly interrupted by less sensitive, closer nodes, greatly reducing their throughput. This makes services, such as VoIP or IPTV which depend on a determined level of QoS, difficult to maintain for large numbers of users.

The MAC layer of 802.16 is designed to serve sparsely distributed stations with high data rates. Subscriber stations are not required to listen to one another because this listening might be difficult to achieve in the WiMAX environment. The 802.16 MAC is a scheduling MAC where the subscriber only has to compete once (for initial entry into the network). After that it is allocated a time slot by the base station. The time slot can enlarge and constrict, but it remains assigned to the subscriber, meaning that other subscribers are not supposed to use it but take their turn. This scheduling algorithm is stable under overload and oversubscription. It is also more bandwidth-efficient. The scheduling algorithm allows the BS to control QoS by balancing the assignment among the needs of subscribers.

Duplexing, a station's concurrent transmission and reception, is possible through TDD and FDD. In TDD, a station transmits then receives (or vice versa) but not at the same time. This option helps reduce subscriber station costs, because the radio is less complex. In FDD, a station transmits and receives simultaneously on different channels.

The 802.16 MAC protocol is connection-oriented and performs link adaptation and ARQ functions to maintain target BER while maximizing the data throughput. It supports different transport technologies such as IPv4, IPv6, Ethernet, and ATM. This lets service providers use WiMAX independently of the transport technology they support.

The recent WiMAX standard, which adds full mesh networking capabilities, enables WiMAX nodes to simultaneously operate in "subscriber" and "base station" mode. This blurs the initial distinction and allows for widespread adoption of WiMAX-based mesh networks and promises widespread WiMAX adoption. Mobile WiMAX with OFDMA and scheduled MAC allows wireless mesh networks to be much more robust and reliable.

5.15.3 Spectrum Allocation for WiMAX

The IEEE 802.16 specification applies across a wide swath of RF spectrum. There is no uniform global licensed spectrum for WiMAX in the United States. The biggest segment available is around 2.5 GHz and is already assigned—primarily to Sprint Nextel. Elsewhere in the world, the most likely bands used will be around 3.5 GHz, 2.3/2.5 GHz, or 5 GHz, with 2.3/2.5 GHz probably being most important in Asia.

There is some prospect that some of a 700 MHz band might be made available for WiMAX in the United States, but it is currently assigned to analog TV and awaits the complete rollout of HD digital TV before it can become available, likely by 2009. There are several variants of 802.16, depending on local regulatory conditions and thus of which spectrum is used.

Mobile WiMAX based on the 802.16e standard will most likely be in 2.3 and 2.5 GHz frequencies—low enough to accommodate the NLOS conditions between the base station and mobile devices. The key technologies in 802.16e on PHY levels are OFDMA and SOFDMA. OFDMA uses a multicarrier modulation in which the carriers are divided among users to form subchannels (see Figure 5.24). For each subchannel, the coding and modulation are adapted separately, allowing channel optimization on a smaller scale (rather than using

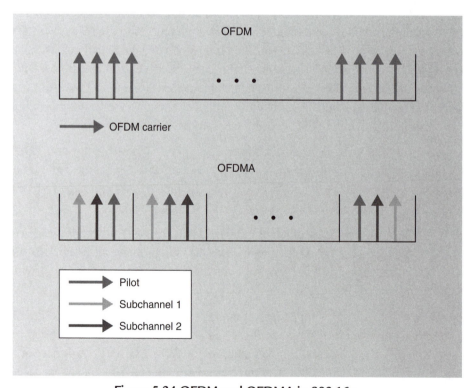

Figure 5.24 OFDM and OFDMA in 802.16e.

the same parameters for the whole channel). This technique optimizes the use of spectrum resources and enhances indoor coverage by assigning a robust scheme to vulnerable links. SOFDMA is an enhancement of OFDMA that scales the number of subcarriers in a channel with possible values of 128, 512, 1024, and 2048.

802.16e includes power-saving and sleep modes to extend the battery life of mobile devices. 802.16e also supports hard and soft handoffs to provide users with seamless connections as they move across coverage areas of adjacent cells. Other improvements for mobile devices include a real-time polling service to provide QoS, HARQ scheme to retransmit erroneous packets, and private key-management schemes to help with the distribution of encryption keys.

5.16 Summary

In this chapter we provided an overview of the wireless LANs (WLANs). We divided WLAN standards into IEEE 802.11 connectionless and ETSI HIPERLAN/2 connection-oriented networks. HIPERLAN/2 is useful for variable QoS support. IEEE 802.11 WLAN uses FHSS and DSSS techniques to offer data rates up to 11 Mbps.

Bluetooth is a digital wireless data transmission standard in the 2.4 GHz ISM band aimed at providing a short-range, wireless link between laptops, mobile phones, and other devices. The IEEE 802.11 WLANs also operate in this frequency band. Since both systems operate in the same frequency band, there is interference between them. We evaluated the performance of the Bluetooth MAC layer when Bluetooth radio operates in close proximity of other Bluetooth piconets and IEEE 802.11 WLANs. A probabilistic approach was suggested to obtain the packet error rate (PER) of a Bluetooth piconet and the aggregated throughput of N collocated piconets.

The chapter concluded by providing a brief description of the IEEE 802.16 standard for metropolitan area networks (MANs) and highlighting the features of the WiMAX.

Problems

5.1 What are the application fields of a WLAN?

5.2 Discuss WLAN topologies.

5.3 What are the two network architectures for the WLAN defined in the IEEE 802.11 standard? Discuss them briefly.

5.4 What is CSMA/CA protocol?

5.5 What are the hidden and exposed node problems in a WLAN? Discuss them briefly.

5.6 What is a Wi-Fi? Discuss briefly.

5.7 What is IEEE 802.11n? Discuss briefly.

5.8 Discuss the exponential backoff algorithm used in a WLAN.

5.9 What is the HiSWAN? Discuss briefly.

5.10 In the HIPERLAN/2 PHY layer, 64-subchannel implementation is used. 48 subcarriers are used for information transmission, 4 subcarriers for pilot tones used for synchronization, and 12 subcarriers reserved for other purposes. The HIPERLAN/2 standard uses 16-QAM with $R = 9/16$ coding for an actual payload data-transmission rate of 27 Mbps. Calculate the coded symbol transmission rate per subcarrier. What is the bit-transmission rate per subcarrier?

5.11 In a DSSS WLAN how many simultaneous data users at 38.4 kbps can be supported by an AP so that an average bit error data rate of 10^{-3} is maintained for each user? Assume the following data: spreading rate = 3.84 Mcps, power control efficiency = 0.8, interference factor from other terminals = 0.67, 3-sector antenna gain = 2.55, and cell loading = 70%. Assuming that each user transmits on average eight packets per second, what is the average packet length that can be used in the system?

5.12 An FHSS WLAN system uses a 50 kHz channel over a continuous 20 MHz spectrum. Fast frequency hopping is used in which two hops occur for each bit. If binary frequency shift keying (BFSK) is the modulation scheme used in the system, determine (a) number of hops per second if each user transmits 25 kbps data and (b) probability of error for a single user operating at E_b/N_0 equal to 10 dB.

5.13 If we switch from 36 Mbps mode to 9 Mbps mode in WLAN, how much more (in dB) of the path loss can be afforded? If the system covers 50 m with 36 Mbps, what would be the coverage with 9 Mbps?

5.14 Consider the Bluetooth and IEEE 802.11 FH interference scenario (refer to Figure 5.20). If the acceptable error probability for the mobile terminal is 10^{-4}, find (a) $(SIR)_{min}$ that supports this error rate and (b) calculate r_{max} for $d = 12$ m, $\gamma = 4.3$, $P_{BT} = 23$ dBm, and $P_{AP} = 43$ dBm. What is r_{max} if the IEEE 802.11 FH device is replaced by the IEEE 802.11 DS device?

5.15 Find the collision probability of 1200 bytes IEEE 802.11 FH packet at 2 Mbps and the Bluetooth. Assume dwell period of an 802.11 transmission to be 3 ms and Bluetooth packet duration 0.625 ms. What is PER with IEEE 802.11 DS?

5.16 Discuss WiMax.

5.17 What are the main differences between the IEEE 802.11b (Wi-Fi) and WiMax?

References

[1] Intermec Technologies Corporation, Guide to Wireless Technologies. http://www. intermec.com/datactr/wlan_wp.pdf.

[2] Z. Abichar, Y. Peng, M. Chang, WiMAX: the emergence of wireless broadband. IT Pro July/August (2006) 44–48.

[3] http://www.ieee802.org/16.

[4] http://www.wimaxforum.org.

[5] Breeze Wireless Communications, Inc., Network Security in a Wireless LAN. http://www.breezecom.com/pdfs/security.pdf.

[6] D.F. Bantz, Wireless LAN design alternative. IEEE Network (March/April) (1994) 43–53.

[7] IEEE, Wireless Medium Access Control (MAC) and Physical Layer (PHY) Specifications. P. 802.11D6.2, July 1998.

[8] Intel Corporation, IEEE 802.11b High Rate Wireless LAN. http://www.intel. com/-network/white.paper/wirelesslan/.

[9] R. Jain, Wireless local area network recent developments, Wireless Seminar Series Electrical and Computer Engineering Department. Ohio State University, February 19, 1998.

[10] K. Pahlavan, Trends in local wireless networks. IEEE Commun. Mag. March (1995) 88–95.

[11] K. Pahlavan, P. Krishnamurthy, Principle of Wireless Networks—A Unified Approach, Prentice Hall, Upper Saddle River, NJ, 2002.

[12] Proxim, Inc., What is a Wireless LAN. http://www.proxim.com/wireless/whiteppr/ whatwlan.shtml.

[13] M. Jonsson, HiperLan2—The Broadband Radio Transmission Technology Operating in the 5 GHz Frequency Band. HIPERLAN-2 Global Forum White Paper.

[14] JTC Technical Report on RF Channel Characterization and Deployment Model. Air Interface Standards, September 1994.

[15] J.C. Haartsen, S. Mattisson, Bluetooth—A new low-power radio interface providing short range connectivity. Proc. IEEE 88(10) (2000).

[16] N.J. Muller, Bluetooth Demystified, McGraw Hill, New York, 2000.

[17] F. Wang, A. Nallanathan, H.K. Garg, Performance of a Bluetooth Piconet in the Presence of IEEE 802.11 WLANs.

[18] Amre El-Hoiydi, Interference between Bluetooth network-upper bound on the packet error rate. IEEE Commun. Lett., 5(6) (2001).

[19] NDC Communications, Inc., Wireless LAN Systems—Technology and Specifications. http://networking.ittoolbox.com/peer/.

CHAPTER 6

Fourth-Generation Systems and New Wireless Technologies

Vijay K. Garg

6.1 Introduction

With the rapid development of wireless communication networks, it is expected that fourth-generation (4G) mobile systems will be launched within a decade. 4G mobile systems focus on seamless integration of existing wireless technologies including wireless wide area network (WWAN), wireless local area network (WLAN), and Bluetooth (see Figure 6.1). This is in contrast with third-generation (3G) mobile systems, which merely focuses on developing new standards and hardware. The recent convergence of the Internet and mobile radio has accelerated the demand for "Internet in the pocket," as well as for radio technologies that increase data throughput and reduce the cost per bit. Mobile networks are going multimedia, potentially leading to an explosion in throughput from a few bytes for the short message service (SMS) to a few kilobits per second (kbps) for the multimedia messaging service (MMS) to several 100 kbps for video content. In addition to wide-area cellular systems, diverse wireless transmission technologies are being deployed, including digital audio broadcast (DAB) and digital video broadcast (DVB) for wide-area broadcasting, local multipoint distribution service (LMDS), and multichannel multipoint distribution service (MMDS) for fixed wireless access. IEEE 802.11b, 11a, 11g, 11n, and 11h standards for WLANs are extending from the enterprise world into public and residential domains. Because they complement cellular networks, these new wireless network technologies and their derivatives may well prove to be the infrastructure components of the future 4G mobile networks when multistandard terminals become widely available. This is already the case for Wi-Fi in the public "hotspots," which is being deployed by mobile operators around the world with the aim to offer seamless mobility with WWANs.

The 4G systems will encompass all systems from various networks, public to private, operator-driven broadband networks to personal areas, and ad hoc networks. The 4G systems will be interoperable with second-generation (2G) and 3G systems, as well as with digital (broadband) broadcasting systems. The 4G intends to integrate from satellite broadband

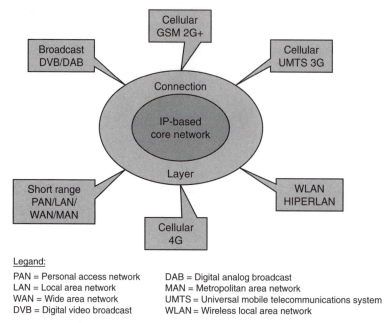

Figure 6.1 Seamless connections of networks.

Table 6.1 Comparison of Key Parameters of 4G with 3G.

Details	3G Including 2.5G (EDGE)	4G
Major requirement driving architecture	Predominantly voice-driven, data were always add on	Converge data and voice over IP
Network architecture	Wide area cell based	Hybrid-integration of WLAN (Wi-Fi, Bluetooth) and wireless wide-area networks
Speeds	384 kbps to 2 Mbps	20–100 Mbps in mobile mode
Frequency band	Dependent on country or continent (1.8–2.4 GHz)	Higher frequency bands (2–8 GHz)
Bandwidth	5–20 MHz	100 MHz or more
Switching design basis	Circuit and packet	All digital with packetized voice
Access technologies	WCDMA, cdma2000	OFDM and multicarrier (MC)-CDMA
Forward error correction	Convolutional codes rate 1/2, 1/3	Concatenated coding schemes
Component design	Optimized antenna design, multiband adapters	Smart antenna, software-defined multiband and wideband radios
Internet protocol (IP)	Number of airlink protocol including IPv5.0	All IP (IPv6.0)
Mobile top speed	200 km/h	200 km/h

to high altitude platform to cellular 2G and 3G systems to wireless local loop (WLL) and broadband wireless access (BWA) to WLAN, and wireless personal area networks (WPANs), all with IP as the integrating mechanism. Table 6.1 provides a comparison of key parameters of 4G with 3G systems.

6.2 4G Vision

The 4G systems are projected to solve the still-remaining problems of 3G systems [1–3]. They are designed to provide a wide variety of new services, from high-quality voice to high-definition video to high-data-rate wireless channels. The term 4G is used broadly to include several types of BWA communication systems, not only cellular systems. 4G is described as MAGIC—Mobile multimedia, Anytime anywhere, Global mobility support, Integrated wireless solution, and Customized personal service (see Figure 6.2). The 4G systems will not only support the next generation mobile services, but also will support the fixed wireless networks. The 4G systems are about seamlessly integrating terminals, networks, and applications to satisfy increasing user demands.

Accessing information anywhere, anytime, with a seamless connection to a wide range of information and services, and receiving a large volume of information, data, pictures, video, and so on, are the keys of the 4G infrastructure. The future 4G systems will consist of a set of various networks using IP as a common protocol. 4G systems will have broader bandwidth, higher data rate, and smoother and quicker handoff and will focus on ensuring seamless service across a multiple of wireless systems and networks. The key is to integrate the 4G capabilities with all the existing mobile technologies through the advanced techniques of digital communications and networking.

6.3 4G Features and Challenges

Some key features (primarily from users' points of view) of 4G mobile networks are as follows (see Figure 6.3):

- High usability: anytime, anywhere, and with any technology;
- Support for multimedia services at low transmission cost;
- Personalization;
- Integrated services.

4G networks will be all-IP-based heterogeneous networks that will allow users to use any system anytime and anywhere. Users carrying an integrated terminal can use a wide range of applications provided by multiple wireless networks.

4G systems will provide not only telecommunications services, but also data and multimedia services. To support multimedia services, high-data-rate services with system reliability will be provided. At the same time, a low per-bit-transmission cost will be maintained by an improved spectral efficiency of the system.

Personalized service will be provided by 4G networks. It is expected that when 4G services are launched, users in widely different locations, occupations, and economic classes will use

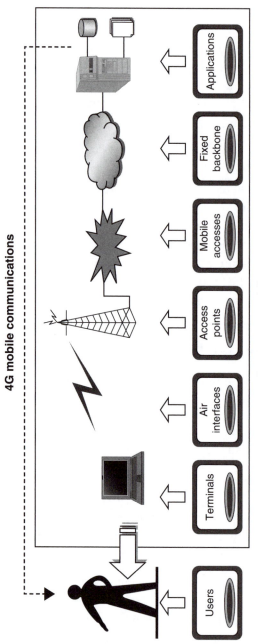

4G mobile communications

Users

Terminals

Air interfaces

Access points

Mobile accesses

Fixed backbone

Applications

Figure 6.2 4G visions.

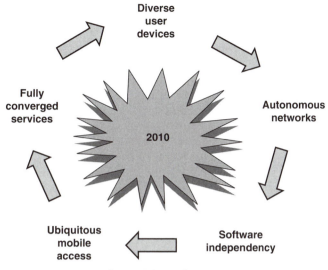

Figure 6.3 4G features.

the services. In order to meet the demands of these diverse users, service providers will design personal and customized service for them. 4G systems will also provide facilities for integrated services. Users can use multiple services from any service provider at the same time.

To migrate current systems to 4G with the above-mentioned features, we have to face a number of challenges. Table 6.2 lists the key challenges and their proposed solutions. Figure 6.4 shows the carrier migration from 3.5G to 4G systems.

6.4 Applications of 4G

The following are some of the applications of the 4G system:

- *Virtual presence:* 4G will provide user services at all times, even if the user is off-site.

- *Virtual navigation:* 4G will provide users with virtual navigation through which a user can access a database of streets, buildings, etc., of a large city. This requires high-speed transmission.

- *Tele-medicine:* 4G will support the remote health monitoring of patients via video conference assistance for a doctor anytime and anywhere.

- *Tele-geo-processing applications:* 4G will combine geographical information systems (GIS) and global positioning systems (GPS) in which a user will get location querying.

- *Education:* 4G will provide a good opportunity to people anywhere in the world to continue their education on-line in a cost-effective manner.

Table 6.2 4G Key Challenges and Their Proposed Solutions.

	Key Challenges	Proposed Solutions
Mobile Station		
Multimode user terminals	To design a single-user terminal that can operate in different wireless networks and overcome design problems such as limitations in device size, cost power consumption, and backward compatibilities to systems.	A software-defined radio approach can be used: the user terminal adapts itself to the wireless interfaces of the networks.
Wireless system discovery	To discover available wireless systems by processing the signals sent from different wireless systems (with different access protocols and incompatible with each other).	User- or system-initiated discoveries, with automatic download of software modules for different wireless systems.
Wireless system selection	Every wireless system has its unique characteristics and role. The proliferation of wireless technologies complicates the selection of the most suitable technology for a particular service at a particular time and place.	The wireless system can be selected according to the best possible fit of user QoS requirements, available network resources, or user preferences.
System		
Terminal mobility	To locate and update the locations of the terminals in various systems. Also, to perform horizontal (within the same system) and vertical (within different systems) handoff as required with minimum handover latency and packet loss.	Signaling schemes and fast handoff mechanisms are proposed.
Network infrastructure and QoS support	To integrate the existing non-IP-based and IP-based systems, and to provide QoS guarantee for end-to-end services that involves different systems.	A clear and comprehensive QoS scheme for the UMTS system has been proposed. This scheme also supports interworking with other common QoS technologies.
Security	The heterogeneity of wireless networks complicates the security issue. Dynamic reconfigurable, adaptive, and lightweight security mechanisms should be developed.	Modifications in existing security schemes may be applicable to heterogeneous systems. Security handoff support for application sessions is also proposed.
Fault tolerance and survivability	To minimize the failures and their potential impacts in any level of tree-like topology in wireless networks.	Fault-tolerant architectures for heterogeneous networks and failure recovery protocols are proposed.
Service		
Multioperators and billing system	To collect, manage, and store the customers' accounting information from multiple service providers. Also, to bill the customers with simple but detailed information.	Various billing and accounting frameworks are being proposed to achieve this goal.
Personal mobility	To provide seamless personal mobility to users without modifying the existing servers in heterogeneous systems.	Personal mobility frameworks are proposed. Most of them use mobile agents, but some do not.

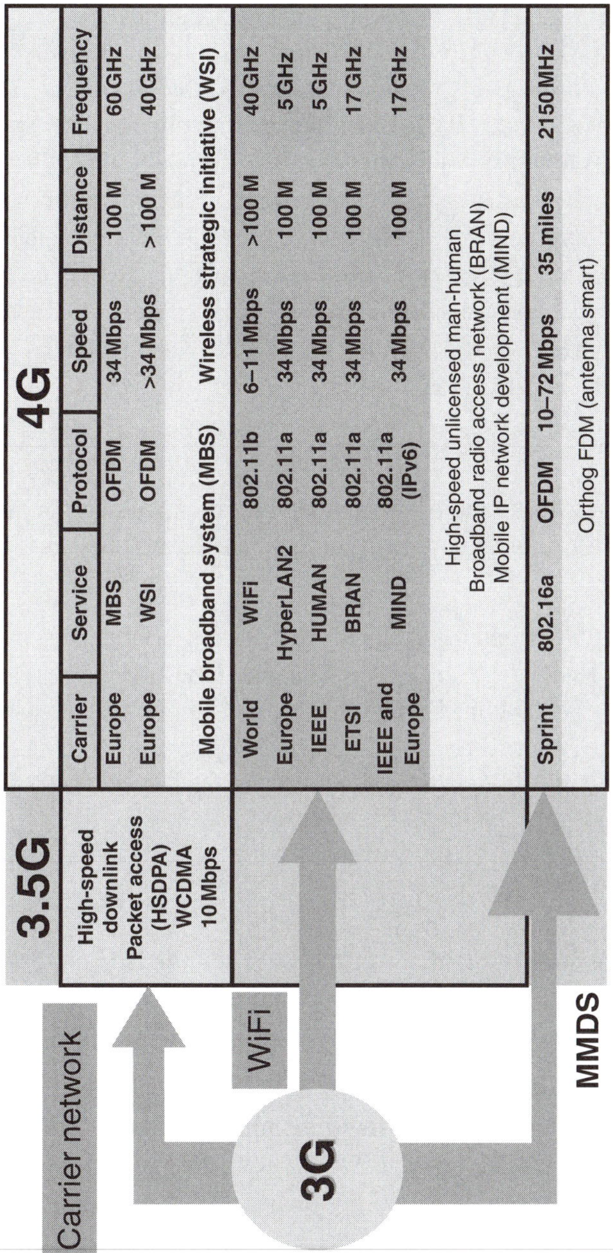

3.5G	4G					
High-speed downlink Packet access (HSDPA) WCDMA 10 Mbps	**Carrier**	**Service**	**Protocol**	**Speed**	**Distance**	**Frequency**
	Europe	MBS	OFDM	34 Mbps	100 M	60 GHz
	Europe	WSI	OFDM	>34 Mbps	>100 M	40 GHz
	Mobile broadband system (MBS)			Wireless strategic initiative (WSI)		
	World	WiFi	802.11b	6–11 Mbps	>100 M	40 GHz
	Europe	HyperLAN2	802.11a	34 Mbps	100 M	5 GHz
	IEEE	HUMAN	802.11a	34 Mbps	100 M	5 GHz
	ETSI	BRAN	802.11a	34 Mbps	100 M	17 GHz
	IEEE and Europe	MIND	802.11a (IPv6)	34 Mbps	100 M	17 GHz
			High-speed unlicensed man–human Broadband radio access network (BRAN) Mobile IP network development (MIND)			
	Sprint	802.16a	OFDM	10–72 Mbps	35 miles	2150 MHz
			Orthog FDM (antenna smart)			

Carrier network

WiFi

3G

MMDS

(multi-channel multipoint distribution service)

Reference: Presentation notes taken from presentation by Carl Burnett, for Spring Standards and Protocols Class, June 2002

Figure 6.4 Carrier migration from 3.5G to 4G.

6.5 4G Technologies

6.5.1 Multicarrier Modulation

Multicarrier modulation (MCM) is a derivative of frequency-division multiplexing. It is not a new technology. Forms of multicarrier systems are currently used in DSL modems and digital audio/video broadcast (DAB/DVB). MCM is a baseband process that uses parallel equal bandwidth subchannels to transmit information and is normally implemented with fast Fourier transform (FFT) techniques. MCM's advantages are better performance in the intersymbol-interference environment and avoidance of single-frequency interferers. However, MCM increases the peak-to-average ratio of the signal, and to overcome intersymbol interference a cyclic extension or guard band must be added to the data. The difference, D, of the peak-to-average ratio between MCM and a single carrier system is a function of the number of subcarriers, N, as:

$$D(\text{dB}) = 10 \log N \qquad (6.1)$$

Any increase in the peak-to-average ratio of a signal requires an increase in linearity of the system to reduce distortion. Linearization techniques can be used, but they increase the cost of the system.

If L_b is the original length of block and the channel's response is of length L_c, the cyclically extended symbol has a new length $L_b + L_c - 1$. The new symbol of length $L_b + L_c - 1$ sampling periods has no intersymbol interference. The cost is an increase in energy and uncoded bits are added to the data. At the MCM receiver, only L_b samples are processed and $L_c - 1$ samples are discarded, resulting in a loss in signal-to-noise ratio (SNR) as:

$$(\text{SNR})_{\text{loss}} = 10 \log \frac{L_b + L_c - 1}{L_b} (\text{dB}) \qquad (6.2)$$

Two different types of MCM are likely candidates for 4G. These include multicarrier code division multiple access (MC-CDMA) and orthogonal frequency-division multiplexing (OFDM) using time-division multiple access (TDMA). MC-CDMA is actually OFDM with a CDMA overlay.

Similar to single-carrier CDMA systems, the users are multiplexed with orthogonal codes to distinguish users in MC-CDMA. However, in MC-CDMA, each user can be allocated several codes, where the data is spread in time or frequency. Either way, multiple users simultaneously access the system.

In OFDM with TDMA, the users are assigned time slots to transmit and receive data. Typically MC-CDMA uses quadrature phase shift keying (QPSK) for modulation, while OFDM with TDMA could use more high-level modulations, such as multilevel quadrature amplitude modulation (M-QAM) (where $M = 4$ to 256). However, to optimize overall performance, adaptive modulation can be used, where the level of QAM for all subcarriers is chosen based on measured parameters. In OFDM the subcarrier pulse shape is a square wave. The task of pulse forming and modulation is performed by a simple inverse FFT (IFFT) which can be implemented very efficiently. To decode the transmission, a receiver needs only to implement FFT.

The OFDM divides a broadband channel into many parallel subchannels. The subchannel pulse shape is a square wave (see Figure 6.5). The OFDM receiver senses the channel and corrects distortion on each subchannel before the transmitted data can be extracted. In OFDM, each of the frequencies is an integer multiple of a fundamental frequency. This ensures that even though subchannels overlap, they do not interfere with each other (see Figure 6.6).

6.5.2 Smart Antenna Techniques

Smart antenna techniques, such as multiple-input multiple-output (MIMO) systems, can extend the capabilities of the 3G and 4G systems to provide customers with increased data

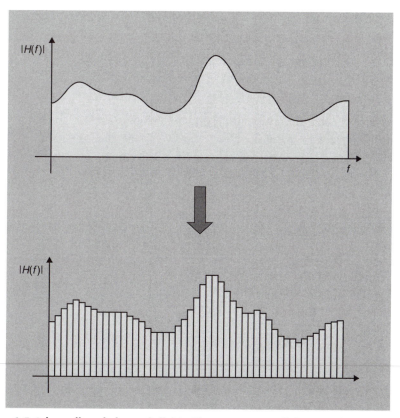

Figure 6.5 A broadband channel divided into many parallel narrowband channels.

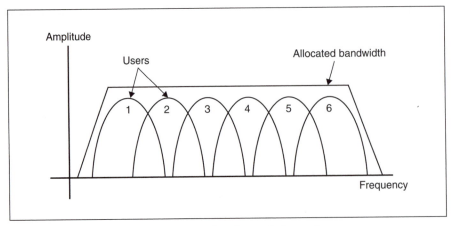

Figure 6.6 Overlapping subchannels.

throughput for mobile high-speed data applications. MIMO systems use multiple antennas at both the transmitter and the receiver to increase the capacity of the wireless channel (see Figure 6.7). With MIMO systems, it may be possible to provide in excess of 1 Mbps for 2.5G wireless TDMA EDGE and as high as 20 Mbps for 4G systems.

With MIMO, different signals are transmitted out of each antenna simultaneously in the same bandwidth and then separated at the receiver. With four antennas at the transmitter and receiver, this has the potential to provide four times the data rate of a single antenna system without an increase in transmit power or bandwidth.

MIMO techniques can support multiple independent channels in the same bandwidth, provided the multipath environment is rich enough. What this means is that high capacities are theoretically possible, unless there is a direct line-of-sight between the transmitter and receiver.

The number of transmitting antennas is M, and the number of receiving antennas is N, where $N \geq M$. We examine four cases:

- Single-input, single-output (SISO);
- Single-input, multiple-output (SIMO);
- Multiple-input, single-output (MISO);
- Multiple-input, multiple-output (MIMO).

6.5.2.1 Single-Input, Single-Output

If the channel bandwidth is B, the transmitter power is P_t, the signal at the receiver has an average SNR of SNR_0, then the Shannon limit on channel capacity C is

$$C \approx B \log_2(1 + SNR_0) \tag{6.3}$$

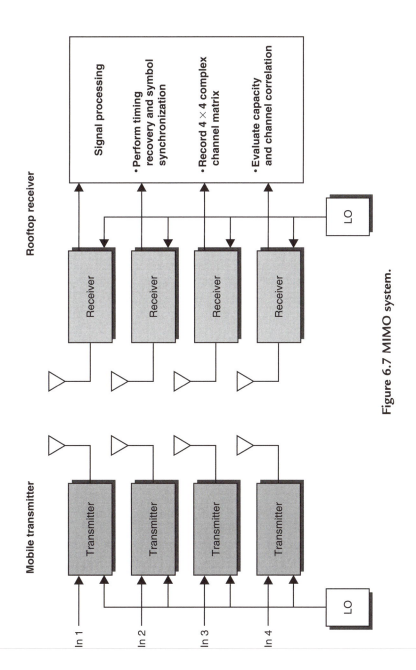

Figure 6.7 MIMO system.

6.5.2.2 Single-Input, Multiple-Output

There are N antennas at the receiver. If the signals received on the antennas have on average the same amplitude, then they can be added coherently to produce an N^2 increase in signal power. There are N sets of noise sources that are added coherently and result in an N-fold increase in noise power. Hence, the overall increase in SNR will be:

$$\text{SNR} \approx \frac{N^2 \times (\text{signal power})}{N \times (\text{noise})} = N \times \text{SNR}_0 \qquad (6.4)$$

The capacity for this channel is approximately equal to

$$C \approx B \log_2(1 + N \times \text{SNR}_0) \qquad (6.5)$$

6.5.2.3 Multiple-Input, Single-Output

We have M transmitting antennas. The total power is divided into M transmitter branches. If the signals add coherently at the receiving antenna, we get an M-fold increase in SNR as compared to SISO. Because there is only one receiving antenna, the noise level is the same as SISO. The overall increase in SNR is approximately

$$\text{SNR} \approx \frac{M^2 \times [(\text{signal power})/M]}{\text{noise}} = M \times \text{SNR}_0 \qquad (6.6)$$

6.5.2.4 Multiple-Input, Multiple-Output

MIMO systems can be viewed as a combination of MISO and SIMO channels. In this case, it is possible to achieve approximately an MN-fold increase in the average SNR_0 giving a channel capacity equal to

$$C \approx B \log_2(1 + M \times N \times \text{SNR}_0) \qquad (6.7)$$

Assuming $N \geqslant M$, we can send different signals using the same bandwidth and still be able to decode correctly at the receiver. Thus, we are creating a channel for each one of the transmitters. The capacity of each one of these channels is roughly equal to

$$C_{\text{single}} \approx B \log_2\left(1 + \frac{N}{M} \times \text{SNR}_0\right) \qquad (6.8)$$

Since we have M of these channels (M transmitting antennas), the total capacity of the system is

$$C \approx MB \log_2\left(1 + \frac{N}{M} \times \text{SNR}_0\right) \qquad (6.9)$$

Table 6.3 Comparison of Channel Capacity for Different Channel Types.

Channel Type	Capacity (Mbps)	Normalized Capacity with Respect to SISO
SISO	3.45 B	1.0
SIMO	5.66 B	1.64
MISO	5.35 B	1.55
MIMO (with same input)	7.64 B	2.21
MIMO (with different input)	15 B	4.35

We get a linear increase in capacity with respect to the transmitting antennas. As an example we assume SNR_0 is equal to 10 dB, $M = 4$, $N = 5$, and bandwidth B (MHz), and list the system capacity for each channel type in Table 6.3.

6.5.3 OFDM–MIMO Systems

OFDM and MIMO techniques can be combined to achieve high spectral efficiency and increased throughput. The OFDM–MIMO system transmits independent OFDM modulated data from multiple antennas simultaneously. At the receiver, after OFDM demodulation, MIMO decodes each subchannel to extract data from all transmit antennas on all the subchannels.

6.5.4 Adaptive Modulation and Coding with Time-Slot Scheduler

In general, TCP/IP is designed for a highly reliable transmission medium in wired networks where packet losses are seldom and are interpreted as congestion in the network [4]. On the other hand, a wireless network uses a time-varying channel where packet losses may be common due to severe fading. This is misinterpreted by TCP as congestion which leads to inefficient utilization of the available radio link capacity. This results in significant degradation of the wireless system performance.

There is a need for a system with efficient packet data transmission using TCP in 4G [5–7]. This can be achieved by using a suitable automatic repeat request (ARQ) scheme combined with an adaptive modulation and coding system, and a time-slot scheduler that uses channel predictions. This way, the lower layers are adapted to channel conditions while still providing some robustness through retransmission. The time-slot scheduler shares the spectrum efficiently between users while satisfying the quality-of-service (QoS) requirements.

If the channel quality for each radio link can be predicted for a short duration (say about 10 ms) into the future and accessible by the link layer, then ARQ along with an adaptive modulation and coding system can be selected for each user to satisfy the bit error rate (BER) requirement and provide high throughput. The scheduler uses this information about individual data streams (along with predicted values of different radio links and selected modulation and coding systems by the link layer) and distributes the time slots among the users. The planning is done so that the desired QoS and associated priority to different users are guaranteed while channel spectrum is efficiently utilized.

6.5.5 Bell Labs Layered Space Time (BLAST) System

BLAST is a space-division multiplexing (SDM)-based MIMO system. It provides the best trade-off between system performance (spectral efficiency and capacity) and system implementation complexity. The spectral efficiency of BLAST ranges from 20 to 40 bps/Hz. It uses a zero-forcing (ZF) nonlinear detection algorithm based on a spatial nulling process combined with symbol cancellation to improve system performance. The BLAST exploits multipath by using scattering characteristics of the propagation environment to enhance transmission accuracy. Figure 6.8 shows the architecture of the BLAST system.

6.5.5.1 Transmitter

The data stream of a user is divided into multiple substreams. An array of transmit antennas (M) is used to simultaneously launch parallel data substreams. Each substream is mapped to a symbol by the same constellation and sent to its transmit antenna. All substreams are transmitted in the same frequency band and are independent of one another. Effective transmission rate is increased roughly in proportion to the number of transmit antennas used. The individual transmitter power is scaled by $1/M$, so that the total power remains constant and independent of the number of transmitters.

6.5.5.2 Receiver

An array of antennas ($N \geq M$) is used to receive multiple transmitted substreams and their scattered images. Since substreams originate from different transmit antennas, they are located at different points in space. Using sophisticated signal processing, the substreams are identified and recovered.

6.5.5.3 Model

Each time sequence $s_j(t), j = 1, 2, ..., M$ is referred to as a layer. At the receiver, the signal $r_i(t)$ is received at time t. It is a noisy superposition of the M transmitted signal respectively corrupted by noise $n_i(t)$:

$$r_i(t)\sum_{j=1}^{M}h_{ij}(t)s_i(t) + n_i(t) \quad i = 1, 2, 3, ..., N \quad\quad (6.10)$$

where $h_{ij}(t)$ is the channel gain (complex transfer function) from transmit antenna j to receive antenna i at any time t.

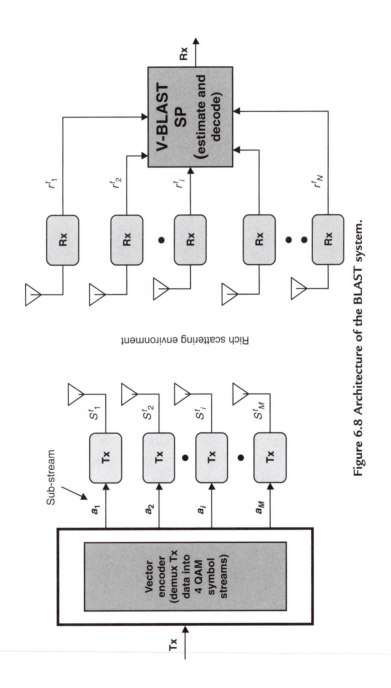

Figure 6.8 Architecture of the BLAST system.

We make the following assumptions:

- Quasi-static flat fading channel. That is, channel gain $h_{ij}(t)$ remains constant over a block of time, and then changes block by block in an independent manner.

- Channel is rich scattering. This is true if antenna spacing is sufficient (i.e., several times of wavelength). This condition provides a large number of local scatters around transmitter or receiver and supports that the channel gains are complex Gaussian and independent of one another.

Equation (6.10) can be written as

$$[r] = [h] \times [s] + [n] \tag{6.11}$$

where

$$[r] = \begin{bmatrix} r_1 \\ r_2 \\ . \\ . \\ r_N \end{bmatrix}; [n] = \begin{bmatrix} n_1 \\ n_2 \\ . \\ . \\ n_N \end{bmatrix}; [s] = \begin{bmatrix} s_1 \\ s_2 \\ . \\ . \\ s_M \end{bmatrix} \text{ and } [h] = \begin{bmatrix} h_{11} & h_{12} & . & . & h_{1M} \\ h_{21} & h_{22} & . & . & h_{2M} \\ . & . & . & . & . \\ h_{N1} & h_{N2} & . & . & h_{NM} \end{bmatrix}$$

6.5.5.4 Signal Processing Algorithm

At the bank of the receiving antennas, high-speed signal processors look at signals from all the receiving antennas simultaneously, first extracting the strongest substream from the morass, then proceeding with the remaining weaker signals, which are easier to recover once the stronger signals have been removed as a source of interference. Maximum-likelihood (ML) detection is optimal for BLAST, but it is too complex to implement. As an example, with six transmit antennas and QPSK modulation, a total of $4^6 = 4096$ comparisons have to be made for each transmitted symbol. A low complexity suboptimal detection algorithm called ZF is used. At each symbol time, the strongest layer (transmitted signal) is first detected and its effect is cancelled for each received signal. We then proceed to detect the strongest of the remaining layers and so on. The ZF algorithm consists of four recursive steps:

1. *Ordering*: Determine the optimal detection order.

2. *Nulling*: Choose the nulling vector to null out all the weaker transmit signals and obtain the strongest transmit signal.

3. *Slicing*: Detect the estimated value of the strongest signal by slicing to the nearest value in the signal constellation.

4. *Cancellation*: Cancel the effect of the strongest signal from the received signal vector to reduce the detection complexity for the remaining transmit signal. Go to step 2—nulling process.

6.5.5.5 Implementation

Each transmitter is a QAM transmitter and operates with synchronized symbol timing, i.e., the collection of transmitters comprises a vector-valued transmitter. 16-QAM signal constellation is used for each transmitter. The total transmitted power is kept constant. BLAST algorithm in three different architectures 4×8, 8×12, and 12×16 have been used. Results are shown in Figures 6.9–6.11.

BLAST shows promising results in enhancing spectral efficiency. Further gain in spectral efficiency can be obtained by using high-level M-QAM and OFDM.

6.5.6 Software-Defined Radio

A software-defined radio (SDR) system is a radio communication system which uses software for the modulation and demodulation of radio signals. An SDR performs significant amounts

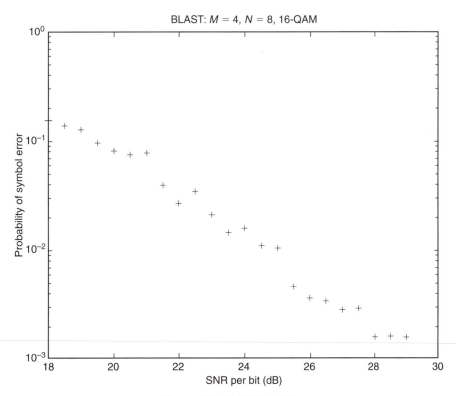

Figure 6.9 BLAST 4 × 8.

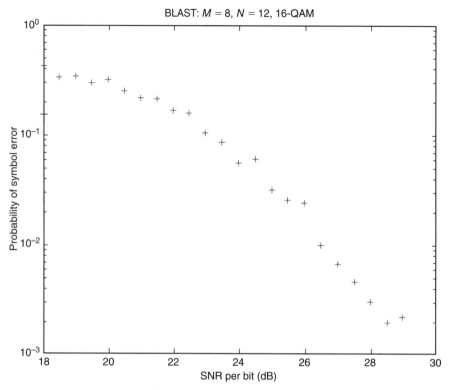

Figure 6.10 BLAST 8 × 12.

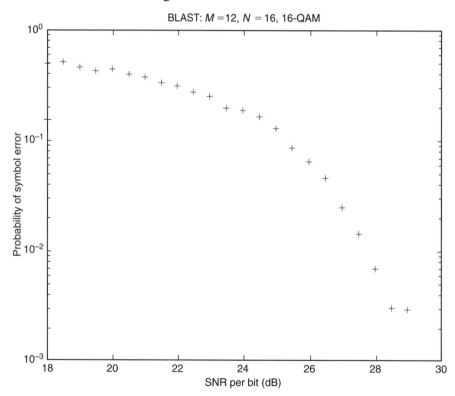

Figure 6.11 BLAST 12 × 16.

of signal processing in a general-purpose computer, or a reconfigurable piece of digital electronics. The goal of this design is to produce a radio that can receive and transmit a new form of radio protocol just by running new software.

SDRs have significant utility for cell phone services, which must serve a wide variety of changing radio protocols in real time. The hardware of an SDR typically consists of a superheterodyne RF front end which converts RF signals from and to analog RF signals, and analog to digital converters and digital to analog converters which are used to convert digitized intermediate frequency (IF) signals from and to analog form, respectively. SDR can currently be used to implement simple radio modem technologies. In the long run, SDR is expected to become the dominant technology in radio communications. The following are some of the things that SDR can do that have not been possible before:

- SDRs can be reconfigured "on-the-fly," i.e., the universal communication device would reconfigure itself appropriately for the environment. It could be a cordless phone one minute, a cell phone the next, a wireless Internet gadget the next, and a GPS receiver the next.

- SDRs can be quickly and easily upgraded with enhanced features. In fact, the upgrade could be delivered over-the-air.

- SDRs can talk and listen to multiple channels at the same time.

- New kinds of radios can be built that have never before existed. Smart radios or cognitive radios (CRs) can look at the utilization of the RF spectrum in their immediate neighborhood and configure themselves for the best performance.

6.5.7 Cognitive Radio

With the CR paradigm, spectrum can be efficiently shared in a more flexible fashion by a number of operators/users/systems. The CR can be viewed as an enabling technology that will benefit several types of users by introducing new communications and networking models for the whole wireless world, creating better business opportunities for the incumbent operators and new technical dimensions for smaller operators, and helping shape an overall more efficient approach regarding spectrum requirements and usage in the next generation of wireless networks.

The CR can be regarded as an extension of SDR. In 2003, the IEEE Committee on Communications and Information Policy (CCIP) recommended CR for consideration by the FCC as a means to conserve valuable spectrum utilization. The CR focuses on applying software capabilities that have been developed to support algorithm control across a wide spectrum of signal processing technologies to add smarts to the software that allows it to determine when frequencies are free to use and then use them in the most efficient manner possible.

Most of the research work currently is focusing on spectrum-sensing cognitive radio—particularly on the utilization of TV bands for communication. The essential problem of spectrum-sensing CR is the design of high quality sensing devices and algorithms for exchanging spectrum-sensing data between nodes. It has been shown in [8] that a simple energy detector cannot guarantee accurate detection of signal presence. This calls for more sophisticated spectrum-sensing techniques and requires that information about spectrum sensing be exchanged between nodes regularly.

It is not implicit that a CR must be SDR. It is possible to implement CR features—the ability to detect and avoid (protect) incumbent users—while using relatively conventional radio transmitter/receiver architectures and techniques. The goal of CR is to relieve radio spectrum overcrowding, which actually translates to a lack of access to full radio spectrum utilization.

6.6 Summary

The 4G system was conceived by the Defense Advanced Research Projects Agency (DARPA). DARPA selected the distributed architecture, end-to-end Internet protocol (IP), and peer-to-peer networking in which every device is both a transceiver and a router for other devices in the network eliminating the spoke-and-hub weakness of 2G and 3G cellular systems. In the 4G system network coverage/capacity will change dynamically to accommodate changing user patterns. Users will automatically move from congested routes to allow the network to dynamically self-balance. The 4G technologies will include instantaneous channel condition estimations of several users to distribute transmission load, better access methods than 3G, adaptive antenna, adaptive coding and modulation, adaptive channel/code allocation, and scheduling among sectors and users. Applications of 4G will be virtual presence, virtual navigation, tele-medicine, tele-geo-processing applications, and online education. 4G is still in a formative stage. Its commercial application is likely to be in 2010. The ITU-WG 8F has started to consider 4G requirements.

Problems

6.1 Define the role of the 4G system.

6.2 Compare the 3G and 4G systems.

6.3 Discuss multicarrier modulation (MCM).

6.4 What is a multiple-input multiple-output (MIMO) system? Explain.

6.5 How are higher spectral efficiency and increased throughput achieved in the OFDM–MIMO system?

6.6 What is the BLAST system? Explain.

6.7 What is the software-defined radio system?

6.8 What is cognitive radio?

6.9 List some of the new technologies that will be used in the 4G system.

References

[1] B.G. Evans, K. Baughan, Visions of 4G, Electron. Commun. J., December (2002).

[2] H. Huomo, Nokia, Fourth generation mobile, presented at ACTS Mobile Summit 99, Sorrento, Italy, June 1999.

[3] J.M. Pereira, 4G: now, it is personal, in: Proc. 11th IEEE International Symposium on Personal Indoor and Mobile Radio Communication, London, UK, September 2000.

[4] H. Balakrishnan et al., Improving TCP/IP performance over wireless network, in: Proc. Mo-BICOM, 1995, Berkeley, CA, pp. 2–11.

[5] S.T. Chung, A.J. Goldsmith, Degree of freedom in adaptive modulation: a unified view, IEEE Transac. Commun. 49 (9) (2001) 1561–1571.

[6] N.C. Ericsson, Adaptive modulation and scheduling of IP traffic over fading channels, in: Proc. IEEE Vehicular Technical Conference, Amsterdam, The Netherlands, September 1999, pp. 849–853.

[7] S. Falahati, A. Svensson, Hybrid type-II ARQ schemes with adaptive modulation systems for wireless channels, in: Proc. IEEE Vehicular Technical Conference, Amsterdam, The Netherlands, September 1999, pp. 2691–2695.

[8] N. Hoven et al., Some fundamental limits on cognitive radio, Wireless Foundations, EECS, University of California, Berkeley, February 11, 2005.

CHAPTER 7

Mesh Networks: Optimal Routing and Scheduling

Anurag Kumar
D. Manjunath
Joy Kuri

In this chapter, we consider wireless mesh networks (WMNs) or wireless multihop networks and will study the supporting of point-to-point flows in the mesh networks. We will also consider the optimal routing of these flows and scheduling of the transmissions on the wireless links.

7.1 Overview

In this section we first describe the communication graph of a wireless network deployed in a given geographical area. Constraints on the simultaneous transmissions based on SINR, protocol-model, and the network graph are then described. In Section 7.2, for a given set of allowable link activation vectors, we obtain the network stability region, the set of end-to-end packet arrival rates for which the queues in all the network nodes will be stable. In Section 7.3, we consider the joint optimal routing of a set of end-to-end open-loop packet flows and the corresponding link scheduling. A static link schedule using graph coloring techniques is derived. In Section 7.4 we develop the important dynamic, queue-length based, backpressure algorithm for joint routing and transmission scheduling on the links. This algorithm is optimal in the sense that it can stabilize any stabilizable end-to-end arrival rate vector. The algorithm is a maximum weight scheduling algorithm and the stability proof makes use of stochastic Lyapunov functions. In Section 7.5 we consider end-to-end elastic traffic and, for a given set of users, we obtain the jointly optimal routing of the packet flows and the transmission schedule on the links. In this case, a utility function on the allocated rate is defined for each user and the sum of the total utilities of all the users is maximized. Using convex programming and Lagrangian duality we obtain optimal joint packet flow rate allocation, routing, and link scheduling policies. In this section, we also consider optimal scheduling of one-hop packet flows in a slotted Aloha network. In the optimal algorithm the nodes update their transmission probabilities using local information to maximize the sum of link utility functions.

7.2 Network Topology and Link Activation Constraints

In this chapter we begin considering networks in which there is no such association between the wireless stations and any fixed infrastructure.

In WMNs, information transport services are built over a set of arbitrarily located nodes, which are possibly mobile. Every node behaves both like a mobile host and as a wireless router. There are many obvious applications for such networks, such as providing communication services in emergency situations like in areas affected by storms, floods, and earthquakes. A WMN can also provide connectivity to fleets of vehicles operating in areas with no networking infrastructure. Of course, there are also many military applications. In all these applications, we can identify a set of point-to-point packet flows between the nodes in the network with each packet flow having its own quality-of-service (QoS) requirement, e.g., a minimum throughput requirement and, possibly, an average end-to-end packet delay requirement. In this chapter, we analyze the ability of a given network to support a set of throughput requirements and the mechanisms to support them.

Consider a wireless network of N nodes deployed in a two-dimensional area. Let x_i be the coordinate vector of the location of Node i. A wireless link (i, j), $i, j \in \{1, 2, ..., N\}$ exists in the network if, in the absence of any other transmission in the network, the transmission from Node i can be decoded by the receiver of j; i.e., the SNR for the signal from Node i is above the threshold, say β. This also means that x_j is in the decode region of the transmitter at x_i.

A wireless network formed by the N nodes can be represented by a directed graph $G = (V, \mathcal{E})$ with the vertex set V representing the N nodes and the edge set $\mathcal{E}$ representing the set of E wireless links in the network. In general, G is not a fully connected graph and the network is a multihop wireless network; packets of end-to-end flows may need to pass through one or more intermediate nodes.

Denote the transmitter and receiver of edge $e \in \mathcal{E}$ by T_e and R_e, respectively. A simple model that is often used in obtaining $\mathcal{E}$ is to assume that the decode region around transmitter i is a circle of radius r_i; $(i, j) \in \mathcal{E}$ if $d_{i,j} := ||x_i - x_j|| < r_i$. Here r_i is a function of the transmission power. A further simplification that is often made is that $r_i = r$ for all i.

7.2.1 Link Activation Constraints

A multihop mesh network exploits spatial reuse; transmissions can occur simultaneously on links that are sufficiently separated in space. We now examine the various models that are used in specifying the set of links that can have simultaneous transmissions. We assume time-slotted networks; all nodes are synchronized in time and time is divided into slots. New transmissions occur at the beginning of a slot and all transmissions are completed at the end of the slot. The transmission rate on the links is assumed to be such that all packets fit into a slot. All scheduling decisions are taken at the beginning of the slot and, if a transmission is scheduled on a link in a slot, exactly one packet is transmitted in the slot.

As we have just mentioned, the edges in G can be grouped into subsets such that the edges in a subset can be active in the same slot; the receiver of each active edge can decode the transmission from the transmitter of the edge. When such a set, say S, is activated, one packet can be sent across each edge in S. These sets must respect any radio operation constraints and interference constraints. We will use the term *link activation set* to refer to such a set. Let us now consider some models that usually are used to obtain the link activation sets of a network.

Recall that the receiver has a minimum SINR requirement to decode the received signal. Let $S \subset \mathcal{E}$ denote a set of links along which transmissions can occur in the same slot. For $e \in S$, let P_{T_e} be the transmit power used by T_e. Let $L(x, y)$ be the path loss function between a transmitter at x and a receiver at y, N_0 the thermal noise spectral density at the receivers, and W the bandwidth allocated to the network. For all $e \in S$, at the receiver R_e, the following minimum SINR requirement should be satisfied:

$$\frac{P_{T_e} L(x_{T_e}, x_{R_e})}{WN_0 + \gamma \sum_{\substack{e_1 \in S \\ e_1 \neq e}} P_{T_{e_1}} L(x_{T_{e_1}}, x_{R_e})} \geq \beta \tag{7.1}$$

where γ is called the orthogonality factor and it satisfies $0 \leq \gamma \leq 1$. If the signals are all perfectly orthogonal, $\gamma = 0$ and there is no interference. $\gamma = 1$ corresponds to the *physical model*. The simplest model for $L(x, y)$ is the far field attenuation where we assume that the attenuation is inversely proportional to a power of the distance; i.e., $L(x, y) = (1/\|x - y\|^\alpha)$, where α is called the path loss exponent.

We can also specify the link activation sets using geometric constraints. A simple criterion is to specify that for each $e \in S$, R_e should be further from all the other transmitters in S than it is from T_e. Intuitively, this is to ensure that the interference is lower than the received signal power. For a given $\Delta > 0$, this can be specified as follows. For all $e, e_1 \in S$ and $e_1 \neq e$, we have

$$\|x_{T_{e_1}} - x_{R_e}\| \geq (1 + \Delta)\|x_{T_e} - x_{R_e}\|$$

Here Δ specifies a guard region that should not contain another transmitter. This is called the *protocol model* and is illustrated in Figure 7.1.

A third type of constraint could be those derived from the graph G. Once again, there are many possibilities. The simplest constraint is to ensure that for all $e \in S$, R_e should not be receiving from another node and T_e should not be transmitting to another node. This is called the *primary conflict* constraint. For example, in Figure 7.2, this means that when A is transmitting to B, A should not be transmitting to any other node and B should not be

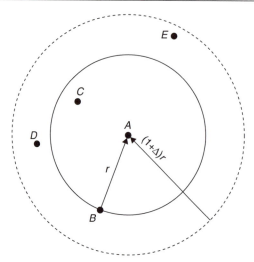

Figure 7.1 Illustrating the guard zone of the protocol model. When *B* is transmitting to *A*, no subset of nodes *C*, *D* and *E*, should be transmitting simultaneously.

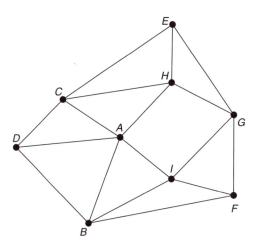

Figure 7.2 Example of a network graph. Vertices represent the nodes in the network. An undirected edge corresponds to directed edges in both directions. For example, undirected edge *AB* implies directed edges *AB* and *BA*; edges represent the half duplex wireless links.

receiving from any other node; when there is communication along directed edge *AB*, there should be no communication along directed edges *AD*, *AC*, *AH*, *AI*, *DB*, *IB*, and *FB*. An alternative constraint is as follows. For all $e \in S$, no other neighbor (an in-neighbor if *G* is a directed graph; if (i, j) is a directed edge, then *i* is called an in-neighbor of *j*) of R_e should be transmitting. For example, in Figure 7.2, when *A* is transmitting to *B*, nodes *D*, *I*, and *F* should not be transmitting at the same time. This is also called the *receiver conflict* constraint. A third type of constraint is the *transmitter–receiver conflict* constraint. Here, in addition to the receiver conflict constraint, we also add the constraint that the neighbors of T_e should not be simultaneously transmitting. As an example, under this constraint, for the network of Figure 7.2, when A is transmitting to B, in addition to D, I and F, C and H should also not transmit. This is useful in IEEE 802.11 like protocols where the transmitter expects a link-layer acknowledgment from the receiver after the packet has been transmitted.

In general, a link activation set S can be represented by an E-dimensional vector of nonnegative rates, with r_e specifying the link-layer data rate for the edge e when the set S is active. The modulation scheme can be adapted to suit the interference (from the active links) and the noise. In much of this chapter we will assume only one transmission rate on all the links. This means that for a desired bit error rate and a given modulation scheme (this fixes the link transmission rate), the SINR requirement is given by Equation (7.1). In this case, the link activation set only specifies whether a link is allowed to transmit or not allowed to transmit and it suffices to describe S using an E-dimensional 0/1 column vector $[\mu_1, \mu_2, \ldots, \mu_E]^T$. We will work with this model in the rest of this chapter. $\mathcal{S}$ will denote the set of all possible link activation vectors, including the all-zero vector, and will be called the *link activation constraint set* of the network.

If the network topology is changing with time, $\mathcal{S}$ could also be a function of time. In this chapter we will consider only static wireless networks; the geographical location of the nodes is assumed fixed.

7.3 Link Scheduling and Schedulable Region

Let S_t denote the link activation vector for slot t. Of course, $S_t \in \mathcal{S}$ for $t = 0, 1, 2, \ldots$. A sequence $\{S_t\}_{t \geq 0}$ is called a *schedule*. The schedule in a network could be static (predetermined) or it could be dynamic. Static scheduling is usually a periodic schedule and is analogous to a time-division multiplexed (TDM) link. A set of T slots form a frame and S_t is defined for $0 \leq t \leq (T - 1)$. The sequence is repeated in every frame. In dynamic scheduling a schedule is decided for each slot. The schedule could be computed in a centralized manner in which a central entity decides the transmission schedule and distributes it to all the nodes in the network. The schedule could also be computed in a distributed manner in which each node executes a distributed algorithm that will determine the schedule. A centralized dynamic scheduling algorithm would typically use the complete network topology information and the queue length information at every node at the beginning of every slot. The scheduling decision for a slot could use the current state of the network and, possibly, the recent history.

Consider an arbitrary schedule Π. Let $\phi_S(\Pi)$, $S \in \mathcal{S}$, represent the fraction of time that the link activation set S is used in the schedule Π; i.e.,

$$\phi_S(\Pi) := \lim_{\tau \to \infty} \frac{1}{\tau} \sum_{t=0}^{\tau-1} I_{\{S_t = S\}} \tag{7.2}$$

where $I_{\{X\}}$ is the indicator function for the event X. Define $\Phi(\Pi)$ to be the $|\mathcal{S}|$-dimensional vector with elements $\phi_S(\Pi)$. Schedules for which the limit in Equation (7.2) exists for all $S \in \mathcal{S}$ will be called *ergodic schedules* and we will only consider such schedules. In this case, $0 \le \phi_S(\Pi) \le 1$ and $\Sigma_{S \in \mathcal{S}} \phi_S(\Pi) = 1$.

We can also construct a randomized schedule; S_t could be chosen according to a probability distribution. In this case, the schedule can be thought of in terms of the probabilities ϕ_S, $S \in \mathcal{S}$. In fact, given a probability vector $\tilde{\Phi}$ on $\mathcal{S}$, it is easy to see that we can obtain a schedule by simply choosing activation set S with probability ϕ_S in a slot independently of the activation set chosen in all the other slots. This is a static randomized schedule. Note that in this case $\Phi = \tilde{\Phi}$.

The *packet-flow capacity* of an edge $e \in \mathcal{E}$ is the maximum rate at which packets can flow along the edge. For an ergodic schedule, this capacity can be obtained as follows. Consider a schedule Π and for this schedule define $C_e(\Pi)$ as follows:

$$C_e(\Pi) := \sum_{\{S:e \in S\}} \phi_S(\Pi)$$

$C_e(\Pi)$ is the long-term fraction of time that transmissions are scheduled on edge e. Thus $C_e(\Pi)$ is the maximum rate at which packets can flow along edge e under the ergodic schedule Π; i.e., it is the packet-flow capacity of edge e in the ergodic schedule Π; $\mathbf{C}(\Pi) := [C_e(\Pi)]_{\{e \in \mathcal{E}\}}$ is the vector of edge capacities for schedule Π. This means that to transport packet flows in the network using schedule Π, the flow rate allocated to edge e can be no more than C_e. Thus, for a given schedule, we can think of the wireless network as a *capacitated network,* which we represent by $G(\mathcal{V}, \mathcal{E}, \mathbf{C}(\Pi))$. Thus, unlike wireline networks where the link capacities are fixed and given, in wireless networks they depend on the schedule. For a given network graph $G(\mathcal{V}, \mathcal{E})$ and the set of possible link activation vectors $\mathcal{S}$, the set of possible schedules Π defines the set of possible link capacities. The schedule is therefore an important variable in the optimization of a wireless network.

Let us now characterize the set of edge capacity vectors that can arise from all possible ergodic schedules. Let $\mathbf{C} := [C_e]_{\{e \in \mathcal{E}\}}$ be a vector of link capacities realized by an ergodic schedule. Consider a two-link network shown in the top part of Figure 7.3. In a slot only one of the two links can be activated: $S_1 = [1, 0]$ and $S_2 = [0, 1]$. Of course $[0, 0]$ is also possible. Consider a requirement that capacities on the two links must be C_1 and C_2 packets per slot, respectively. Assume C_1 and C_2 are rational numbers. We can then express $C_1 = m_1/m$ and $C_2 = m_2/m$ for integers m_1, m_2, and m, and construct a periodic schedule with a frame of m slots in which S_1 is activated in m_1 slots and S_2 is activated in m_2 slots. Notice that if $(m_1 + m_2) > m$ then the link capacity requirement cannot be satisfied. The requirement that C_1 and C_2 be rational was for convenience of illustration. In Problem 7.1 we devise a mechanism to allocate capacity to a link that is an irrational number.

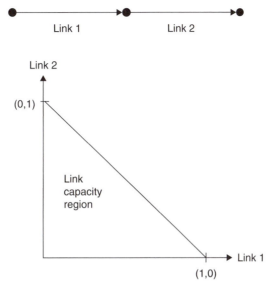

Figure 7.3 Illustrating the link capacity region for the two link network shown in the top part of the figure.

In the previous example, observe that an ergodic schedule can be constructed to achieve any link capacity that satisfies

$$C_1 \geq 0, \quad C_2 \geq 0 \quad \text{and} \quad C_1 + C_2 \leq 1 \tag{7.3}$$

This means that any capacity vector that is less than or equal to a convex combination of [1, 0] and [0, 1] can be achieved by an ergodic schedule. Thus we can say that the region in R^2 specified by Equation (7.3) is the *link capacity region* for the network. This is illustrated in Figure 7.3.

Generalizing this notion, for a given $\mathcal{S}$ and a schedule Π,

$$\mathbf{C}(\Pi) = \sum_{S \in \mathcal{S}} \phi_S(\Pi) S$$

Thus $\mathbf{C}(\Pi)$ is a convex combination of the elements of $\mathcal{S}$. If we now consider the set of all possible ergodic schedules, we get the set of all possible link capacities. This in turn is the set of all convex combinations of $S \in \mathcal{S}$. This is the *convex hull* of $\mathcal{S}$ and is denoted by $\mathrm{Co}(\mathcal{S})$. We can thus state the following result.

■ Lemma 7.1

For a wireless network with link activation constraint $\mathcal{S}$, the set of link capacities C that can be achieved by an ergodic schedule is the same as $\mathrm{Co}(\mathcal{S})$. ■

We reiterate that any link-capacity vector that is in $\text{Co}(S)$ can be achieved by a stationary randomized schedule.

We have just described the service capacity of the links in the wireless network that can be achieved by a schedule. We next describe the arrival rates of packets that can be stabilized by these service rates.

7.3.1 Stability of Queues

Consider a discrete time packet queuing system. Assume that the server capacity in each slot is a random sequence. Let $A(t)$ be the number of packets that arrive in slot t, $\mu(t)$ the server capacity (the number of packets that the server could have served) in slot t, and $Q(t)$ the number of packets in the queue at the beginning of slot t, just after the arrival instant. The number of departures in slot t would be less than or equal to $\mu(t)$. This queue is unlike that in a traditional queuing system analysis where $\mu(t)$ is assumed constant for all t. In fact, $\mu(t)$ could even depend on arrivals and queue occupancies up to time t. Similarly, $A(t)$ could also depend on the queue occupancies up to time t. We need to consider this generalization because, in a wireless mesh network, the arrival and service processes of packets at the nodes depend on the schedule and would have such dependencies.

Let $A(t) \le A_{\max}$ for all $t \ge 0$ and

$$\lim_{T \to \infty} \frac{1}{T} \sum_{t=0}^{T-1} \mathbf{E}(A(t)) = \lambda$$

Similarly, let $\mu(t) \le \mu_{\max}$ for all $t \ge 0$ and

$$\lim_{T \to \infty} \frac{1}{T} \sum_{t=0}^{T-1} \mathbf{E}(\mu(t)) = \mu$$

λ and μ correspond to the arrival rate and service rate, respectively, for the queue. Let $H(t)$ represent the history of the queue up to and including time t; i.e., the sequence of arrivals into and service from the queue up to time t. Knowing $A(t)$ and $\mu(t)$ implies knowing $Q(t)$. We also impose the following restriction on the arrival and service processes. For any $\epsilon_1 > 0$, there exists an interval of T slots such that for every t_0 the following property is satisfied:

$$\mathbf{E}\left(\frac{1}{T} \sum_{t=t_0}^{t_0+T-1} A(t) \mid H(t_0)\right) \le \lambda + \epsilon_1$$

$$\mathbf{E}\left(\frac{1}{T} \sum_{t=t_0}^{t_0+T-1} \mu(t) \mid H(t_0)\right) \ge \mu - \epsilon_1$$

(7.4)

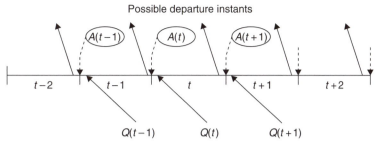

Possible departure instants

Figure 7.4 Observing the queue. Arrivals occur at the beginning of the slot, departures at the end of the slot, and the queue is observed at the beginning of the slot just after the instant at which an arrival could occur.

This is not a very restrictive property and is satisfied, e.g., if $A(t)$ and $\mu(t)$ are i.i.d. sequences. Informally, this means that the conditional time average of the arrival and service rates have the same limit as the unconditional rates. We are imposing a restriction on how this convergence to the limit occurs.

Let us assume that arrivals occur at the beginning of the slot, departures at the end of the slot, and the queue is observed at the beginning of the slot, just after the arrival instant. This is shown in Figure 7.4. We can see that $Q(t)$ evolves as follows:

$$Q(t + 1) = \max(Q(t) - \mu(t), 0) + A(t + 1)$$

For the queue to provide useful service, the queue should be *stable.* Informally, stability of $Q(t)$ means that it does not grow to infinity with time. There are many ways in which the notion of stability can be formalized. For example, if $Q(t)$ evolves as a Markov chain, then $Q(t)$ is stable if it is positive recurrent. In this chapter, we will use the following notion: $Q(t)$ is said to be *strongly stable* if

$$\limsup_{T \to \infty} \frac{1}{T} \sum_{t=0}^{T-1} \mathbf{E}(Q(t)) < \infty \tag{7.5}$$

Let us first obtain a sufficient condition for $Q(t)$ to be strongly stable. Recall our analysis of the stability of the s-Aloha protocol using the *drift* from a state. There the drift from a state was defined as the conditional expectation of the one-step change in the state. We generalize that notion and define a *Lyapunov drift*. Define a nonnegative function $L(\cdot)$ from the integers (the values that $Q(t)$ can take) to the reals that is increasing to ∞ in its argument; $L(Q(t)) : \mathcal{Z}_+ \to R_+$. $\mathcal{Z}_+$ is the set of nonnegative integers and R_+ is the set of nonnegative reals. Let $0 < B < \infty$ and $\epsilon_2 > 0$ be constants such that

$$\mathbf{E}(L(Q(t + 1)) - L(Q(t)) \mid Q(t)) \leq B - \epsilon_2 Q(t) \tag{7.6}$$

for all timeslots t. Taking expectations, we obtain the following:

$$\mathbf{E}(L(Q(t+1))) - \mathbf{E}(L(Q(t))) \leq B - \epsilon_2 \mathbf{E}(Q(t))$$

Summing over slots $t = 0, \ldots, T - 1$ we get

$$\mathbf{E}(L(Q(T))) - \mathbf{E}(L(Q(0))) \leq BT - \epsilon_2 \sum_{t=0}^{T-1} \mathbf{E}(Q(t))$$

Dividing by T, rearranging the terms, and noting that $L(Q(T)) \geq 0$ we get

$$\frac{1}{T} \sum_{t=0}^{T-1} \mathbf{E}(Q(t)) \leq \frac{B}{\epsilon_2} + \frac{1}{T\epsilon_2} \mathbf{E}(L(Q(0)))$$

Taking lim sup as $T \to \infty$, we get

$$\limsup_{T \to \infty} \frac{1}{T} \sum_{t=0}^{T-1} \mathbf{E}(Q(t)) \leq \frac{B}{\epsilon_2} < \infty$$

This means that $Q(t)$ is strongly stable if Equation (7.6) is satisfied; i.e., $Q(t)$ is strongly stable if we can find a scalar function of the state space for which the expected drift in a slot is strictly negative for all large queue lengths and is finite for the remaining queue lengths. The negativity requirement essentially means that queue length is being pushed back toward the lower values when it becomes too large. The finiteness ensures that on the average, the process does not jump to very large values in one step when the queue lengths are small.

Now consider the queue at timeslot t_0. Along the lines of the one-slot Lyapunov drift defined earlier, we can define a T-slot Lyapunov drift as follows:

$$\mathbf{E}(L(Q(t_0 + T)) - L(Q(t_0)) \mid Q(t_0))$$

The arguments leading to Equation (7.6) being a sufficient condition for stability of $Q(t)$ can be extended to obtain the following T-slot stability condition. If there exists a T such that $\mathbf{E}(Q(t)) < \infty$ for $t = 0, \ldots, T - 1$, and there exist constants $B > 0$ and $\epsilon_3 > 0$ such that

$$\mathbf{E}(L(Q(t_0 + T)) - L(Q(t_0)) \mid Q(t_0)) \leq B - \epsilon_3 Q(t_0) \tag{7.7}$$

then $Q(t)$ is strongly stable. Equation (7.7) is essentially generalizing Equation (7.6) to allow a negative drift over T slots rather than over one slot.

We will need the following identity in our analyses. Let W, X, Y, and Z be four nonnegative numbers.

If
$$W \leq \max\{X - Y, 0\} + Z \tag{7.8}$$

then
$$W^2 \leq X^2 + Y^2 + Z^2 - 2X(Y - Z) \tag{7.9}$$

To show this, we need to consider two cases. First, consider the case of $(X - Y) > 0$. For this case,

$$
\begin{aligned}
W^2 &\leq (X - Y + Z)^2 \\
&= X^2 + Y^2 + Z^2 - 2X(Y - Z) - 2YZ
\end{aligned}
$$

Since Y and Z are nonnegative, $2YZ > 0$ and Equation (7.9) follows. Now consider the second case of $(X - Y) \leq 0$.

$$
\begin{aligned}
W^2 &\leq Z^2 \\
&\leq Z^2 + ((X - Y)^2 + 2XZ) \\
&= X^2 + Y^2 + Z^2 - 2X(Y - Z)
\end{aligned}
$$

The second inequality follows because $((X - Y)^2 + 2XZ)$ is the sum of two nonnegative quantities.

Let us now get back to analyzing $Q(t)$. Our objective is to obtain a condition on $A(t)$ and $\mu(t)$ that will make $Q(t)$ stable. Consider the evolution of $Q(t)$ over T slots. An upper bound on $Q(t_0 + T)$ can be obtained as follows. Assume that in slots $t_0, \ldots, t_0 + T - 1$, we serve only packets that were present at t_0. In a slot, most $\mu(t)$ packets depart. Therefore $Q(t_0)$ can decrement by at most $\left(\sum_{t_0}^{t_0 + T - 1} \mu(t)\right)$ packets in T slots. All packets that have arrived in slots $t_0 + 1, \ldots, t_0 + T$ will be in the queue at the beginning of timeslot $(t_0 + T)$. We thus have

$$Q(t_0 + T) \leq \max\left(Q(t_0) - \sum_{t=t_0}^{t_0+T-1} \mu(t), \, 0\right) + \sum_{t=t_0+1}^{t_0+T} A(t)$$

We will use the Lyapunov function $L(Q(t)) = Q^2(t)$. Using Equations (7.7) and (7.9), and simplifying, we get

$$
\begin{aligned}
Q^2(t_0 + T) \leq \; &Q^2(t_0) + T^2\mu_{\max}^2 + T^2A_{\max}^2 \\
&- 2TQ(t_0)\left(\frac{1}{T}\sum_{t=t_0}^{t_0+T-1} \mu(t) - \frac{1}{T}\sum_{t=t_0+1}^{t_0+T} A(t)\right)
\end{aligned}
$$

Taking conditional expectation on $Q(t_0)$ we get

$$
\begin{aligned}
\mathbf{E}(Q^2(t+T) - Q^2(t_0) \mid Q(t_0)) \leq T^2\mu_{\max}^2 + T^2 A_{\max}^2 \\
- 2TQ(t_0)\left[\mathbf{E}\left(\frac{1}{T}\sum_{t=t_0}^{t_0+T-1}\mu(t) \mid Q(t_0)\right) - \mathbf{E}\left(\frac{1}{T}\sum_{t=t_0+1}^{t_0+T}A(t) \mid Q(t_0)\right)\right]
\end{aligned}
\tag{7.10}
$$

Let $\lambda < \mu$ (i.e., $\mu = \lambda + \epsilon_4$ where $\epsilon_4 > 0$). For $\epsilon_3 > 0$, if we choose $\epsilon_1 = (\epsilon_3/4T)$ in Equation (7.4) and $\epsilon_4 = (\epsilon_3/T)$ we see that there exists a T such that

$$
\mathbf{E}\left(\frac{1}{T}\sum_{t=t_0}^{t_0+T-1}\mu(t) \mid Q(t_0)\right) - \mathbf{E}\left(\frac{1}{T}\sum_{t=t_0+1}^{t_0+T}A(t) \mid Q(t_0)\right) \geq \frac{\epsilon_2}{2T}
$$

From this and writing $B = T^2\mu_{\max}^2 + T^2 A_{\max}^2$ in Equation (7.10), we see that Equation (7.7) is satisfied. Thus $\lambda < \mu$ ensures that $Q(t)$ is stable.

It can also be shown that if $\lambda > \mu$ then the queue is unstable. An informal argument is that the rate at which packets exit the queue is lower than the rate at which they arrive and eventually the queue will build up.

With this background on the stability of a single queue, we now consider the stability of the network of queues in the wireless network.

7.3.2 Link Flows and Link Stability Region

Consider a WMN in which there are J users indexed by j, $1 \leq j \leq J$, each with their end-to-end packet flows that need to be transported by the network. (In the rest of this chapter, the terms user, flow, and session will be used synonymously.) User j has source node s_j and destination node d_j. We will assume that the packet flows are open-loop flows; i.e., they have an intrinsic arrival rate. Let $A_j(t)$ denote the number of new packets of User j arriving at node s_j in slot t. We assume that $A_j(t)$ are i.i.d. for each j, $\mathbf{E}(A_j(1)) = \lambda_j$, and $\mathbf{E}((A_j(1))^2) < \infty$, for $1 \leq j \leq J$. λ_j is the packet arrival rate of User j in packets per slot. Let $\lambda = [\lambda_1, \lambda_2, \ldots, \lambda_J]^T$ be the column vector of the packet arrival rates of the J users. Let us assume that each packet can be transported to its destination over any route in the network that begins at the source and ends at the destination.

A *routing policy* determines the sequence of links to be traversed by the packet. We will be interested in *ergodic routing policies*, i.e., policies that route the packets such that we can define an arrival rate for the packets that arrive at the transmitting node of a link. Thus, for a given λ, the routing policy determines the rate at which packets arrive at the transmitter of a link. Now consider a routing policy $\mathcal{R}$ that routes the user flows with arrival rates λ such that $f_{e,j}(\mathcal{R})$ is the rate at which packets of User j are to be transmitted on edge e. Define

$$\mathbf{f}(\mathcal{R},j) := [f_{1,j}(\mathcal{R}), f_{2,j}(\mathcal{R}), \ldots, f_{E,j}(\mathcal{R})]^T$$

to be the E-dimensional column vector indicating the rate of User j on link e, $1 \leq e \leq E$. $f_{e,j}(\mathcal{R})$ also depends on λ but we do not express the dependence explicitly. Let

$$\hat{\mathbf{f}}(\mathcal{R}) := \sum_{j=1}^{J} \mathbf{f}(\mathcal{R},j) = [\hat{f}_1(\mathcal{R}), \hat{f}_2(\mathcal{R}), \ldots, \hat{f}_E(\mathcal{R})]^T$$

be the column vector of total flows on the links; $\hat{f}_e(\mathcal{R})$ is the total flow on link e under routing policy $\mathcal{R}$. Also define

$$\mathbf{f}(\mathcal{R}) := [\mathbf{f}(\mathcal{R},1)^T, \mathbf{f}(\mathcal{R},2)^T, \ldots, \mathbf{f}(\mathcal{R},J)^T]^T$$

This is simply a column vector whose first E elements specify the link-flow vector for User 1, the next E elements specify the link-flow vector for User 2, ..., and the last E elements specify the link-flow vector for User j. Thus, it is a column vector of dimension $JE \times 1$. To simplify the notation, many a time, we will drop the reference to $\mathcal{R}$ when referring to the flow vectors; the dependence will be implicit.

Since we are considering a multihop network, and also since packet arrivals are random, nodes will need to store packets of different users before forwarding them on the next hop toward the destination. Let $Q_{i,j}(t)$ denote the number of packets of User j that are in the queue at node i at the beginning of slot t. Let $\mathbf{Q}(t) := [Q_{1,1}(t), \ldots, Q_{1,J}(t), \ldots, Q_{N,J}(t)]^T$. We say that $\mathbf{Q}(t)$ is strongly stable if $Q_{i,j}(t)$ for $1 \leq i \leq N$ and $1 \leq j \leq J$ are strongly stable.

The arrival rate of packets of User j to be transmitted on link e will be $f_{e,j}(\mathcal{R})$. The total arrival rate of packets at node T_e to be transmitted on link e is $\hat{f}_e(\mathcal{R}) = \Sigma_{j=1}^{J} f_{e,j}(\mathcal{R})$. Let $C_{e,j}(\Pi)$ be the capacity allocated to packets of User j on link e. Let Λ_1 denote the set of all λ for which there exists a routing $\mathcal{R}$ and a schedule Π such that

$$f_{e,j}(\mathcal{R}) < C_{e,j}(\Pi) \tag{7.11}$$

Similarly, let $\bar{\Lambda}_1$ denote the set of all λ for which there exists a routing $\mathcal{R}$ and a schedule Π such that

$$f_{e,j}(\mathcal{R}) \leq C_{e,j}(\Pi) \tag{7.12}$$

It can be shown that $\bar{\Lambda}_1$ is the closure of the set Λ_1.

Since the set of feasible link capacities are in Co($\mathcal{S}$), a feasible routing policy will result in link flows that are in Co($\mathcal{S}$).

Let **P** denote a *routing and scheduling policy*, a set of rules that determines the routing and scheduling of the packets in each slot for a realization of a random process of packet arrivals into the network. Let Λ denote the set of all λ for which there exists a **P** such that **Q**(t) is stable; Λ is called the *schedulable region* for the network.

It can be shown that if $\lambda \notin \bar{\Lambda}_1$, then **Q**($t$) is unstable, i.e., $\Lambda \subset \bar{\Lambda}_1$. Informally, this is because if $\lambda \notin \bar{\Lambda}_1$, then for every **P**, there will be at least one link, say e_1, for which the arrival rate of User j packets is strictly greater than the capacity allocated to User j on the link (i.e., $f_{e1,j}(\mathbf{P}) > C_{e1,j}(\mathbf{P})$ for all **P**). Hence, at Node T_{e1}, the queue of User j packets that are to be transmitted on link e_1 will build up leading to instability of $Q_{Te,j,}$ and hence of **Q**(t). In Section 7.4 we will develop the maximum weight routing and scheduling algorithm, for which the network will be stable if $\lambda \in \Lambda_1$. This implies $\Lambda_1 \subset \Lambda$. We can thus say the following.

■ Lemma 7.2

If $\lambda \in \Lambda_1$, then **Q**(t) is schedulable with the maximum weight schedule and hence $\Lambda_1 \subset \Lambda$. If $\lambda \notin \bar{\Lambda}$, then **Q**($t$) is unstable and hence $\Lambda \subset \bar{\Lambda}$. Thus,

$$\Lambda_1 \subset \Lambda \subset \bar{\Lambda}_1$$

■

■ Exercise 7.1

Show that Λ is a convex set, and that if $\lambda \in \Lambda$ then for any λ' such that $\lambda'_j < \lambda_j$, for all j, $\lambda' \in \Lambda$.

■

Given λ and a schedule Π (and hence $\mathbf{C}(\Pi)$), the problem of determining the optimal link flows $f_{e,j}$ is well known and is called the *multicommodity flow* problem. (The flow from each user is treated as a distinct commodity; hence the name.) There are many candidates for optimality: maximize the minimum spare capacity on the links, minimize the maximum flow allocated to a link, minimize the average delay, and so on. Alternatively, given λ and $\mathcal{R}$ for which a schedule exists, it may be possible to obtain the schedule from graph coloring techniques. We will discuss one such technique in the next section. The most general case, of course, is to find both simultaneously. In the rest of this chapter we will consider three basic kinds of problems in which we need to obtain $\mathcal{R}$ and Π simultaneously.

- First, we consider the case of a given λ for which we obtain the routing and a static scheduling scheme.

- Second, we consider the case when λ is unknown but we assume that $\lambda \in \Lambda_1$. For this we devise a dynamic routing and scheduling algorithm that is guaranteed to stabilize the network.

- Finally we consider elastic flows in which User j will define a utility function on λ_j. We will choose $\lambda \in \bar{\Lambda}_1$ to maximize the sum of the utility functions of all the users, over all possible $\mathcal{R}$ and Π and also derive the corresponding optimal $\mathcal{R}$ and Π.

7.4 Routing and Scheduling a Given Flow Vector

In this section we consider the scheduling and routing of a given flow vector λ in a network with the *primary conflict constraint*. The packets of User j arriving at Node s_j are routed over multiple paths toward the destination d_j. The routing problem will determine the fraction of User j packets that will be transported on each of the edges. The sum of such fractions from all the flows on an edge is the flow assignment for the edge. Recall that the edge flows should be in $\text{Co}(\mathcal{S})$. The cardinality of $\mathcal{S}$ is usually very large and it is hard to check for $\hat{\mathbf{f}} \in \text{Co}(\mathcal{S})$. We therefore obtain a sufficient condition that ensures $\hat{\mathbf{f}} \in \text{Co}(\mathcal{S})$ and use this sufficient condition as a constraint in a multicommodity routing problem formulation.

Let us first see how to find the elements of $\mathcal{S}$. Since determining $\mathcal{S}$ is hard, we will just obtain a subset of $\mathcal{S}$. Recall that under the primary conflict constraint, in a slot, a node can be either receiving from one transmitter or transmitting to one receiver. Edges that have a node in common are called *adjacent* edges—if two edges e_1 and e_2 are adjacent then one or more of the following are satisfied:

$$T_{e_1} = T_{e_2} \quad T_{e_1} = R_{e_2}$$
$$R_{e_1} = R_{e_2} \quad R_{e_1} = T_{e_2}$$

Color the edges of G using a minimum number of colors $1, 2, \ldots$, such that no two adjacent edges have the same color. Two edges that have the same color satisfy the primary conflict constraint and can transmit simultaneously. Thus, a link activation vector can be obtained by doing the following for each color c. If edge e is colored c, then set $\mu_e = 1$, otherwise set $\mu_e = 0$. Each color gives us one activation vector. Using fewer colors corresponds to higher spatial reuse. Let $\chi(G)$ be the number of colors used. The minimum $\chi(G)$ is called the *edge-chromatic number* of G. A flow of at least $1/\chi(G)$ is possible on each link. See Problem 7.3 to see how there could be some links with capacity more than $1/\chi(G)$. Thus, a total flow allocation of less than $1/\chi(G)$ on all the links is a sufficient condition for the schedulability of a flow assignment. We can thus formulate an optimal routing problem with this capacity constraint. In this scheme no link gets a capacity more than $1/\chi(G)$. There will surely be some $\lambda \in \Lambda_1$ that may require that the flow on some of the edges be greater than $1/\chi(G)$. Thus this capacity constraint on the links will not be able to route and schedule all $\lambda \in \Lambda_1$.

Further, it is very restrictive in its allocation of link capacity. We therefore look for alternate sufficient conditions for achievable link flows. Also note that there is no unique edge coloring. Thus another coloring of the graph would give us another set of link activation sets. To obtain S we need to find all possible colorings of G. This is, in general, a hard problem.

For now assume that we know the edge flows. Let $\hat{f}_e$ be the required total flow on edge e; the vector of link flows will be denoted by $\hat{\mathbf{f}}$. We will first consider the scheduling of the links into a static schedule to satisfy a specified link flow vector $\hat{\mathbf{f}}$.

Let $\mathcal{N}_{in}(v)$ and $\mathcal{N}_{out}(v)$, respectively, denote the set of in-neighbors and set of out-neighbors [if there is an edge (i, j) in G, i is the in-neighbor of j and j is the out-neighbor of i] of node v, and $\mathcal{N}(v)$ the set of neighbors of v:

$$\mathcal{N}_{in}(v) = \{v_1 : T_e = v_1 \text{ and } R_e = v\}$$
$$\mathcal{N}_{out}(v) = \{v_1 : R_e = v_1 \text{ and } T_e = v\}$$
$$\mathcal{N}(v) = \mathcal{N}_{in}(v) \cup \mathcal{N}_{out}(v)$$

From the primary conflict assumption, in a slot, a node can be transmitting on at most one edge or receiving on at most one edge but not both. Hence, it is necessary that for all $v \in \mathcal{V}$ the following inequality is satisfied:

$$\sum_{e:T_e=v} \hat{f}_e + \sum_{e:R_e=v} \hat{f}_e \leq 1 \tag{7.13}$$

The resource here is a timeslot; in every clique of the graph G, in any timeslot, at most one node can be active in a slot. Note that Equation (7.13) is not a sufficient condition.

To achieve a specified $\hat{\mathbf{f}}$, we will assume that all $\hat{f}_e$ are rational and find an integer τ such that we can express all $\hat{f}_e$ as

$$\hat{f}_e = \frac{w_e}{\tau}$$

where w_e is also an integer. This essentially says that we can achieve a link flow vector $\hat{\mathbf{f}}$ with a periodic schedule using a frame of τ slots, and, in each frame, edge e is activated at least w_e times. Let us now see how to construct such a schedule. In the process we will be able to obtain sufficient conditions for $\hat{\mathbf{f}}$ to be schedulable that will be easy to use as a constraint in an optimization problem.

We will once again use graph coloring techniques to obtain the schedule. First convert the network graph G into a *scheduling multigraph* $G_1(\mathcal{V}_1, \mathcal{E}_1)$ as follows. A multigraph is a graph in which there can be multiple edges between two nodes. The vertex set of G and G_1 will be the same, i.e., $\mathcal{V}_1 = \mathcal{V}$. Corresponding to every edge $e \in \mathcal{E}$, $\mathcal{E}_1$ will have w_e edges (T_e, R_e).

Let D denote the maximum degree, D_{out} the maximum out-degree, and D_{in} the maximum in-degree of G_1:

$$D = \max_v \sum_{e \in \mathcal{N}(v)} w_e$$

$$D_{\text{out}} = \max_v \sum_{e \in \mathcal{N}_{\text{out}}(v)} w_e$$

$$D_{\text{in}} = \max_v \sum_{e \in \mathcal{N}_{\text{in}}(v)} w_e$$

Now color the edges of G_1 using a minimum number of colors $1, 2, \ldots$, using the adjacency constraint that we used earlier. Let $\chi(G_1)$ denote the chromatic number of the multigraph G_1.

Let us now interpret the colored graph. Like in the example of the two-link network of the previous section, consider a frame of $\chi(G_1)$ slots. For $1 \le t \le \chi(G_1)$, let the edges that are colored t transmit in slot t. Consider any node v in the network. From the coloring constraint, we see that none of the incoming or outgoing edges of v have the same color. Hence, in a slot, node v will either be receiving from a node or transmitting to a node or neither. Thus the primary conflict constraint is satisfied by the schedule. From this we can conclude that a link flow vector $\hat{\mathbf{f}}$ is schedulable if $\chi(G_1) \le \tau$. This is because the activation of every color over a frame of length $\chi(G_1)$ achieves $\hat{\mathbf{f}}_e \ge (w_e/\tau)$.

For a given G_1, let us now characterize $\chi(G_1)$. Since the edges that have a vertex in common cannot have the same color, $\chi(G_1)$ is lower bounded by the maximum degree of G_1; $\chi(G_1) \ge D$. It can also be shown that $\chi(G_1)$ is upper bounded by $3D/2$. We thus have

$$D \le \chi(G_1) \le \frac{3D}{2} \tag{7.14}$$

We can now use this discussion to determine a sufficient condition for $\hat{\mathbf{f}}$ to be schedulable on G. $\hat{\mathbf{f}}$ is schedulable if $\tau \ge \chi(G_1)$. This is the same as saying that the following be satisfied for all $v \in \mathcal{V}$.

$$\frac{3}{2} \left(\sum_{e: T_e = v} w_e + \sum_{e: R_e = v} w_e \right) \le \tau$$

Divide both sides of this inequality by τ and observe that $w(e)/\tau$ is the flow rate on edge e in packets per slot. We can therefore say that if for all $v \in \mathcal{V}$,

$$\left(\sum_{e: T_e = v} \hat{f}_e + \sum_{e: R_e = v} \hat{f}_e \right) < \frac{2}{3}$$

then $\hat{\mathbf{f}}$ is schedulable. This condition implies that a flow assignment in which each node is active (receiving or transmitting) for at most two-thirds of the slots is achievable. We thus have a sufficient condition for a flow assignment $\hat{\mathbf{f}}$ to be schedulable and also a mechanism to obtain this schedule.

Comparing with Equation (7.13), we have a gap between the necessary and sufficient conditions for the schedulability of $\hat{\mathbf{f}}$. In the rest of the discussion we will use the sufficient condition to determine the link flow allocation. We will comment on reducing the gap between the necessary and sufficient conditions in practice later in the section.

We are now ready to formulate the optimal route assignment problem. We assume that the packets from each flow may be split arbitrarily across all possible paths between the source and the destination. This assumption allows a simple formulation. An alternative is to define a set of paths for User j and then split the flow across these paths, but we will not pursue that.

We need some more notations. The network graph G can be summarized using its *node-link incidence matrix* $\mathbf{A}$. $\mathbf{A}$ is an $N \times E$ matrix with a row for each node and a column for each edge. Let $A_{i,e}$ represent the (i,e)-th element of $\mathbf{A}$. Let $\mathbf{A}_{i,\cdot}$ represent the i-th row of $\mathbf{A}$ and $\mathbf{A}_{\cdot,e}$ represent the e-th column of $\mathbf{A}$. Then, the column corresponding to edge e has the following entries:

$$
A_{i,e} = \begin{cases} +1 & \text{if } i = T_e \\ -1 & \text{if } i = R_e \\ 0 & \text{otherwise} \end{cases}
$$

Consider the product $\mathbf{Af}(j)$. The product is a column vector with N elements. The i-th element of this vector is the product of the row $\mathbf{A}_{i,\cdot}$ and the vector $\mathbf{f}(j)$. It can be seen that $\mathbf{A}_{i,\cdot} \cdot \mathbf{f}(j)$ is the *net outgoing traffic* of User j at Node i.

At any Node i other than s_j and d_j, the net outgoing traffic corresponding to User j will be zero because such a node neither sources nor sinks packets of User j. The same argument shows that when $i = s_j$, the product $\mathbf{A}_{i,\cdot} \cdot \mathbf{f}(j)$ should be λ_j, and when $i = d_j$, the product $\mathbf{A}_{i,\cdot} \cdot \mathbf{f}(j)$ should be $-\lambda_j$. These *flow conservation equations* are

$$
\mathbf{A}_{i,\cdot}\mathbf{f}(j) = \begin{cases} \lambda_j & \text{if } i = s_j \\ -\lambda_j & \text{if } i = d_j \\ 0 & \text{otherwise} \end{cases}
$$

If we now consider all the rows of $\mathbf{A}$ together, then we have the following compact equation:

$$
\mathbf{Af}(j) = \mathbf{v}(j) \tag{7.15}
$$

where $\mathbf{v}(j)$ is an $N \times 1$ vector with the following entries:

$$v_i(j) = \begin{cases} \lambda_j & \text{if } i = s_j \\ -\lambda_j & \text{if } i = d_j \\ 0 & \text{otherwise} \end{cases}$$

From what we just saw, $\mathbf{v}(j)$ is a vector specifying the amount of net User j traffic from each node in the network.

Equation (7.15) holds for all j, $1 \leq j \leq J$. Thus, there are J equations of the form of equation (7.15), one for each $j = 1,2,\ldots,J$. We can obtain a single compact equation that expresses the J equalities together. Consider the matrix

$$\mathbb{A} = \begin{bmatrix} \mathbf{A} & 0 & 0 & \cdots & 0 \\ 0 & \mathbf{A} & 0 & \cdots & 0 \\ \vdots & \vdots & \vdots & \ddots & \vdots \\ 0 & 0 & \cdots & 0 & \mathbf{A} \end{bmatrix}$$

There are J block-elements in each row and J block-elements in each column. $\mathbf{A}$ is the node-link incidence matrix defined earlier and is of dimension $N \times E$. 0 is also a matrix of dimension $N \times E$. Hence $\mathbb{A}$ is a matrix of dimension $JN \times JE$.

With these definitions, consider the equation

$$\begin{bmatrix} \mathbf{A} & 0 & 0 & \cdots & 0 \\ 0 & \mathbf{A} & 0 & \cdots & 0 \\ \vdots & \vdots & \vdots & \ddots & \vdots \\ 0 & 0 & \cdots & 0 & \mathbf{A} \end{bmatrix} \begin{bmatrix} \mathbf{f}(1) \\ \mathbf{f}(2) \\ \vdots \\ \mathbf{f}(J) \end{bmatrix} = \begin{bmatrix} \mathbf{v}(1) \\ \mathbf{v}(2) \\ \vdots \\ \mathbf{v}(J) \end{bmatrix} \tag{7.16}$$

Since $\mathbf{v}(j)$ is a vector of dimension $N \times 1$ for each $j \in \{1, 2, \ldots, J\}$, the vector on the right-hand side is of dimension $JN \times 1$. This is what we expect when a $JN \times JE$ matrix is multiplied with a $JE \times 1$ vector. Equation (7.16) is the compact flow conservation equation we were looking for. Clearly, it is nothing but J equations of the form $\mathbf{A}\mathbf{f}(j) = \mathbf{v}(j)$, with $1 \leq j \leq J$.

Now consider any node in the network. Recall from our earlier discussion that for a feasible routing, if the sum of all flows into and out of a node is less than 2/3 packets per slot, then the link-flow assignment is schedulable. Let ρ denote an N element column vector with every element being equal to 2/3. ρ is analogous to the capacity vector of a multicommodity flow problem or the capacity vector of a routing problem of wireline networks. However, note that unlike in traditional routing problems, the capacity is defined in terms of the nodes and not in terms of the links. Let

$$\psi(j) = |\mathbf{A}| \, \mathbf{f}(j) = [\psi_1(j), \psi_2(j), \ldots, \psi_N(j)]^T$$

where $|\mathbf{A}|$ is obtained by taking the magnitudes of the corresponding elements of $\mathbf{A}$. Notice that $\psi(j)$ is an $N \times 1$ column vector and $\psi_i(j)$ denotes the sum of the incoming and outgoing rates of User j at Node i. Define

$$\mathbf{\Phi} := \sum_{j=1}^{J} \psi(j) = \sum_{j=1}^{J} |\mathbf{A}| \mathbf{f}(j) = [\phi_1, \phi_2, \ldots, \phi_N]^T$$

We see that ϕ_i is the sum of the incoming and outgoing flows at Node i.

The vector of *spare node-capacities*, denoted by $\mathbf{z}$, is given by

$$\mathbf{z} = \rho - \mathbf{\Phi}$$

Let $z := \min_{1 \le i \le N} z_i$ be the *smallest* spare node-capacity corresponding to a given feasible routing. Then, the following inequality holds:

$$\mathbf{\Phi} \le \rho - z\mathbf{1}$$

where $\mathbf{1}$ is a column vector of N elements, all of which are 1.

For a given network and a set of end-to-end flow rate vectors of the J users, there may be many feasible routings. To choose one routing from this set, we need to define an *objective function* and then choose the routing that optimizes this objective function. There are many objective functions possible. Let us define the objective function as the quantity z earlier; the objective function is the smallest spare capacity at a node resulting from a routing. Then, an optimal routing would be that which maximizes the smallest spare capacity. Defining an optimal routing in this way is reasonable because *any* node in the network has a spare capacity of at least z. This increases the chance that a future demand between any pair of nodes in the network would find sufficient free capacity. In other words, we avoid routings that lead to a bottleneck node with very little spare capacity. Further, this objective promotes a balanced utilization of capacity and does not create hot spots.

Putting together all these elements, we have the following optimization problem:

Max z is subject to

$$\begin{bmatrix} \mathbf{A} & 0 & 0 & \cdots & 0 \\ 0 & \mathbf{A} & 0 & \cdots & 0 \\ \vdots & \vdots & \vdots & \ddots & \vdots \\ 0 & 0 & \cdots & 0 & \mathbf{A} \end{bmatrix} \begin{bmatrix} \mathbf{f}(1) \\ \mathbf{f}(2) \\ \vdots \\ \mathbf{f}(J) \end{bmatrix} = \begin{bmatrix} \mathbf{v}(1) \\ \mathbf{v}(2) \\ \vdots \\ \mathbf{v}(J) \end{bmatrix} \qquad (7.17)$$

$$\sum_{j=1}^{J} |\mathbf{A}| \mathbf{f}(j) + z \cdot \mathbf{1} \le \rho \tag{7.18}$$

$$\mathbf{f}(j) \ge 0, \quad 1 \le j \le J, \quad z \ge 0$$

We can see that this is a linear program, with the variables being $\mathbf{f}(j)$, $1 \le j \le J$, and z. The objective is a linear function of the variables, with z being the sole variable determining its value. This is the final form of the optimization problem that defines the optimal routing. Since this is a linear program, efficient algorithms for computing its solution are available and one can actually obtain the optimal routing. We will not discuss the solution technique.

7.5 Discussion

1. If the linear program results in a solution in which the flow allocation to some of the nodes is not rational, we will have to round it to the next rational number. Further, this method will not be able to route and schedule all $\lambda \in \Lambda_1$.

2. Recall that there is a significant gap between the sufficient and necessary conditions for a set of node flows to be feasible. Also, from Exercise 7.3 we know that link flows greater than that derived from the sufficient condition can be supported. Thus it has been advocated that one could use $\rho = [1, \dots, 1]$ rather than $\rho = [2/3, \dots, 2/3]$. In this case, it is possible that the clique constraint is not satisfied. Thus, this is only a heuristic and does not guarantee a flow allocation for which a schedule can be obtained.

3. The optimal routing problem that we formulated earlier is just one example of the many alternative formulations possible. One other popular formulation is based on the cost of the utilization of a link. We describe this briefly.

   Let $\mathcal{D}_e(x)$ be a cost function associated with edge e when the rate of packet flow on the edge is x. Let P_j be the set of paths on which the User j packets can be routed. Each path $p \in P_j$ is a sequence of connected edges starting at the source s_j and ending at the destination d_j of User j. Let $\mathcal{P} := \cup_{j=1}^{J} P_j$ denote the set of all paths defined in the network. The total flow λ_j is to be split among the paths in P_j with $x_j(p)$ allocated to path p subject to the link flow constraints. Let y_e be the total traffic rate on link e. y_e is just the sum of rates $(x_j(p))$ allocated to the paths that use link e. For a given path allocation $\mathbf{x} := \{x_j(p) : j = 1, \dots, J, p \in \mathcal{P}\}$, the sum of the inflow into and outflow from node v in the network, denoted by $\phi_v(\mathbf{x})$, will be given by

$$\phi_v(\mathbf{x}) = \sum_{\{e:T_e=v\}} y_e + \sum_{\{e:R_e=v\}} y_e$$

The first term is the inflow into the node and the second term is the outflow from the node. The optimal routing problem is thus

Minimize

$$\sum_{e \in \varepsilon} D_e(y_e)$$

subject to

$$x_j(p) \geq 0 \qquad \text{for } p \in P_j, j = 1,\ldots,J$$

$$\sum_{p \in P_j} x_j(p) = \lambda_j \quad \text{for } 1 \leq j \leq J$$

$$\phi_v(\mathbf{x}) \leq \frac{2}{3} \qquad \text{for } 1 \leq v \leq N$$

This is a well-known optimal routing problem except for additional linear constraints on the variables from $\phi_v(\mathbf{x})$. These constraints just restrict the state-space. We can use well-known methods (e.g., flow deviation method) to obtain the optimal link-flow assignment vector.

7.6 Maximum Weight Scheduling

In the previous section we considered a static routing and scheduling algorithm for scheduling user flow rates $\lambda \in \Lambda_1$. We assumed λ was known. In this section we assume that λ is unknown but is in the open set Λ_1. We will derive a dynamic routing and scheduling algorithm for which the network will be strongly stable. This provides a constructive proof to show that $\Lambda_1 \subset \Lambda$.

It would seem that if the end-to-end flow vectors are known to be in the schedulable region, finding the optimal routes for the flows and a corresponding static link activation schedule would be possible. We saw in the previous section that even for a simple constraint, this is not easy. Although we could convert the network constraint into a set of necessary and sufficient conditions for the link flows, there is still a significant gap between the two.

In this section, we will study a dynamic routing and scheduling algorithm to route a $\lambda \in \Lambda_1$. We will show that an *optimal centralized, dynamic scheduling, and routing algorithm* exists that will stabilize the network for any $\lambda \in \Lambda_1$. Interestingly, we do not even need to know λ. Before we develop this important algorithm, we will need some assumptions and notations.

We begin with some notations. Let $A_{i,j}(t)$ denote the number of packets of User j arriving into the network at Node i in slot t. $A_{i,j}(t)$ are bounded i.i.d. random variables; $A_{i,j}(t) \leq A_{\max} < \infty$ for all $t > 0$ and $1 \leq j \leq J$ and $\mathbf{E}(A_{i,j}(1)) = \lambda_{i,j}$. Note that we are allowing new packets of User j to arrive into more than one node in the network. This is a generalization from the previous (and the next) section where each user has only one source node. Packets of User j have destination d_j.

Each packet can be transported to its destination over any route in the network that begins at the source and ends at the destination. In each slot, either exactly one packet or no packet is transmitted on a link. Further, in a slot, each node receives at most one packet or transmits at most one packet. In the rest of the section it is convenient to represent a directed edge from Node i to Node k by (i,k) and we will follow this notation. Let $\mu_{(i,k),j}(t)$ be the indicator variable for the transmission of a packet of User j being scheduled on link (i,k) in slot t; $\mu_{(i,k),j}(t) \in \{0,1\}$ and $\sum_{j=1}^{J} \mu_{(i,k),j}(t) = \mu_{(i,k)}(t)$ where $\mu_{(i,k)}(t)$ is the indicator variable for a packet transmission on link (i,k) in slot t. The sum will have at most one nonzero term because, in a slot, we serve one full packet from at most one queue. Thus $\mu_{(i,k)}(t) \in \{0,1\}$. It will be implicit that $\mu_{(i,k),j}(t) = 0$ if $(i,k) \notin \mathcal{E}$.

The sequence $\{\mu_{(i,k),j}(t)\}_{t \geq 0}$ represents the routing and scheduling of packets of User j on link (i,k) and is governed by the routing and scheduling policy **P**. If $\mu_{(i,k),j}(t) = 1$, then one packet of User j is transmitted from Node i and received at Node k at the end of slot t. If $k = d_j$ then the packet is removed from the network. Otherwise, the packet is queued at Node k. In this section, we will develop an optimum policy to choose $\mu_{(i,k),j}(t)$.

Each node maintains a separate queue for packets of User j; i.e., there are NJ queues in the network with $Q_{i,j}(t)$ denoting the number of packets of User j queued at Node i at the beginning of slot t. Collect the $Q_{i,j}(t)$ into the vector $\mathbf{Q}(t) := [Q_{1,1}(t), \ldots, Q_{1,J}(t), \ldots, Q_{N,J}(t)]$. Figure 7.5 illustrates the queues and links in a network with four nodes and six links.

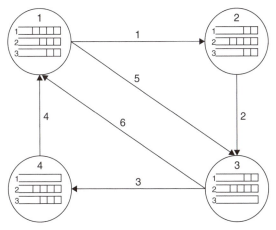

Figure 7.5 Illustrating the variables for dynamic scheduling in a WMN with six links and 3 flows of packets. The link number is marked against the links. The queue occupancies at the beginning of a slot are shown. Some example values for the variables are $Q_{1,1} = 4$, $Q_{2,1} = 2$, $Q_{1,2} = 3$, $Q_{4,3} = 3$, $w_{1,1} = 4 - 2 = 2$, $w_{1,2} = 3 - 4 = -1$, $w_{1,3} = 2 - 2 = 0$, $w_1 = 2$.

7.6.1 Multicommodity Flow Criteria

From our discussion in Section 7.3, the packet flow rates on each of the links should satisfy the following flow conservation equation for $1 \leq j \leq J$ and $1 \leq i \leq N, i \neq d_j$:

$$\sum_{k \in \mathcal{N}_{out}(i)} f_{(i,k),j} - \sum_{k \in \mathcal{N}_{in}(i)} f_{(k,i),j} = \lambda_{i,j} \tag{7.19}$$

In addition, we will require that

- Flows $f_{(k,i),j}$ are all nonnegative and positive flows are not assigned to nonexistent links.
- Packets that have reached the destination are not injected back into the network.

We can show the following lemma.

■ Lemma 7.3

If $\lambda \in \Lambda_1$ then there exists a stationary randomized algorithm to choose $\mu_{(i,k),j}(t)$ independent of the history of the arrivals and departures up to timeslot t, such that

$$E\left(\sum_{k \in \mathcal{N}_{out(i)}} \mu_{(i,k),j}(t) - \sum_{k \in \mathcal{N}_{in(i)}} \mu_{(k,i),j}(t) \right) > \lambda_{i,j} \tag{7.20}$$

for all $1 \leq i \leq N$, and $1 \leq j \leq J$.

■

The following is an informal proof. Recall that any link capacity vector in $Co(\mathcal{S})$ can be achieved by a stationary randomized schedule that chooses the link activation vector in each slot independently of all previous selections and the current state of the network. From the definition, Λ_1 is the set of λ for which the link flow rate vectors are in the interior of $Co(\mathcal{S})$. If there exist flows $f_{(i,k),j}$ that satisfy Equation (7.19) and the corresponding $\hat{\mathbf{f}}$ is in the interior of $Co(\mathcal{S})$, then there is a link capacity vector $\mathbf{C}$ that is equal to these flows that can be achieved by a stationary randomized schedule. Since Λ_1 is an open set, there exists another capacity vector $\mathbf{C}_1$ in which every edge has capacity strictly larger than the capacity of the same edge in $\mathbf{C}$. The $\mu_{(i,k),j}(t)$ in Equation (7.20) can be thought of as coming from the stationary randomized schedule for $\mathbf{C}_1$.

7.6.2 Lyapunov Stability of a Network of Queues

Our interest is in ensuring the stability of the vector of queue lengths $\mathbf{Q}(t)$. We will use the Lyapunov technique introduced in Section 7.2.1 to derive the conditions for the strong stability of $\mathbf{Q}(t)$. The stability conditions will yield a routing and scheduling policy.

Like in Section 7.2.1 for single queues, we can define a nonnegative, increasing and unbounded Lyapunov function on the vector $\{\mathbf{Q}(t)\}$. $L(\cdot) : \mathcal{Z}_+^{NJ} \to R_+$. $L(\cdot)$ defines a scalar value for every value that $\mathbf{Q}(t)$ can take. Along the same lines as the derivation of Equation (7.6), we can make the following claim. If there exist constants $B > 0$ and $\epsilon > 0$ such that

$$\mathbf{E}(L(\mathbf{Q}(t+1)) - L(\mathbf{Q}(t)) \mid \mathbf{Q}(t)) \leq B - \epsilon \sum_{i=1}^{N} \sum_{j=1}^{J} Q_{i,j}(t) \tag{7.21}$$

then $\mathbf{Q}(t)$ is stable.

■ Exercise 7.2

Show that if Equation (7.21) is satisfied, then the queues $Q_{i,j}(t)$, for $1 \leq i \leq N$ and $1 \leq j \leq J$, are all stable.   ■

In our analysis, we will be using the following quadratic Lyapunov function:

$$L(\mathbf{Q}(t)) := \sum_{i,j} (Q_{i,j}(t))^2$$

This is just the sum of the squares of the queue occupancies at the beginning of a slot.

7.6.3 The Algorithm and Its Analysis

Our goal in this section is to develop a centralized dynamic routing and scheduling algorithm that will stabilize all $\lambda \in \Lambda_1$. The routes for the packets of the users and the sequence of activation vectors will not be statically determined. The centralized algorithm will decide both of these—the link activation vector to be used in a slot (scheduling) and the packets to be transmitted on the activated links (routing)—dynamically in every slot. We will consider a policy in which the routing and scheduling decision depends on the queue occupancies at the nodes in the network. Further, we will only consider stationary policies in which the scheduling algorithm is the same in every slot.

At nodes $i \neq d_j$, in each slot, $Q_{i,j}(t)$ is incremented by the packets of User j transmitted to i by its neighbors and also by the new User j packets arriving into the network at Node i. $Q_{i,j}(t)$ is decremented by a transmission of User j packets by Node i to its neighbors in slot t. We can thus write the following inequality for $Q_{i,j}(t)$:

$$Q_{i,j}(t+1) \leq \max\left\{ Q_{i,j}(t) - \sum_{k \in \mathcal{N}_{\text{out}}(i)} \mu_{(i,k),j}(t), 0 \right\}$$

$$+ \left[A_{i,j}(t+1) + \sum_{k \in \mathcal{N}_{\text{in}}(i)} \mu_{(k,i),j}(t) \right] \tag{7.22}$$

There is no queue for User j at d_j and the preceding equation applies only for $i \neq d_j$. We will now see what it takes to make $\{\mathbf{Q}(t)\}$, and hence the network, strongly stable.

We begin by analyzing the Lyapunov drift for our network. Recognizing the analogy between the variables of Equation (7.7) and those of the queue evolution in Equation (7.22) and applying Equation (7.9) we can write

$$(Q_{i,j}(t+1))^2 \leq (Q_{i,j}(t))^2 + \left(\sum_{k \in \mathcal{N}_{\text{out}}(i)} \mu_{(i,k),j}(t) \right)^2 + \left(A_{i,j}(t+1) + \sum_{k \in \mathcal{N}_{\text{in}}(i)} \mu_{(k,i),j}(t) \right)^2$$
$$- 2Q_{i,j}(t) \left(\sum_{k \in \mathcal{N}_{\text{out}}(i)} \mu_{(i,k),j}(t) - A_{i,j}(t+1) - \sum_{k \in \mathcal{N}_{\text{in}}(i)} \mu_{(k,i),j}(t) \right)$$

Summing over $1 \leq j \leq J$ and $1 \leq i \leq N$, we get

$$\sum_{i=1}^{N} \sum_{j=1}^{J} ((Q_{i,j}(t+1))^2 - (Q_{i,j}(t))^2) \leq \sum_{i=1}^{N} \sum_{j=1}^{J} \left(\sum_{k \in \mathcal{N}_{\text{out}}(i)} \mu_{(i,k),j}(t) \right)^2$$
$$+ \sum_{i=1}^{N} \sum_{J=1}^{J} \left(A_{i,j}(t+1) + \sum_{k \in \mathcal{N}_{\text{in}}(i)} \mu_{(k,i),j}(t) \right)^2$$
$$- \sum_{i=1}^{N} \sum_{j=1}^{J} 2Q_{i,j}(t) \left(\sum_{k \in \mathcal{N}_{\text{out}}(i)} \mu_{(i,k),j}(t) - A_{i,j}(t+1) - \sum_{k \in \mathcal{N}_{\text{in}}(i)} \mu_{(k,i),j}(t) \right)$$

Recall the following from our discussion earlier on the properties of $\mu_{(i,k),j}(t)$: In a slot, at most one packet can be transmitted by a node, at most one packet can be received by a node, and at most A_{max} packets of User j will arrive into the network at Node i. We, can therefore, say

$$\sum_{j=1}^{J} \left(\sum_{k \in \mathcal{N}_{\text{out}}(i)} \mu_{(i,k),j}(t) \right)^2 \leq 1$$

$$\sum_{j=1}^{J} \left(A_{i,j}(t+1) + \sum_{k \in \mathcal{N}_{\text{in}}(i)} \mu_{(k,i),j}(t) \right)^2 \leq J(A_{\text{max}} + 1)^2$$

Writing

$$B := \sum_{i=1}^{N} (1 + J(A_{\text{max}} + 1)^2) = N(1 + J(A_{\text{max}} + 1)^2)$$

and rearranging the terms, we get

$$\sum_{i=1}^{N}\sum_{j=1}^{J}((Q_{i,j}(t+1))^2 - (Q_{i,j}(t))^2) \leq B + 2\sum_{i=1}^{N}\sum_{j=1}^{J}(Q_{i,j}(t)A_{i,j}(t+1))$$

$$- 2\sum_{i=1}^{N}\sum_{j=1}^{J}\left(Q_{i,j}(t)\left(\sum_{k\in\mathcal{N}_{\text{out}}(i)}\mu_{(i,k),j}(t) - \sum_{k\in\mathcal{N}_{\text{in}}(i)}\mu_{(k,i),j}(t)\right)\right)$$

$$(7.23)$$

Now consider the last term in this inequality. Since the summation is over all $1 \leq i, k \leq N$, $\mu_{(i,k),j}$ appears twice in the sum—once multiplied by $Q_{i,j}(t)$ and another time multiplied by $-Q_{k,j}(t)$. Further, all the edges appear in the summation. We can see this more easily by letting k range from 1 to N and changing the order of the summation. From this observation we can rewrite the last term in the preceding inequality as

$$2\sum_{i=1}^{N}\sum_{j=1}^{J}Q_{i,j}(t)\left(\sum_{k=1}^{N}\mu_{(i,k),j}(t) - \sum_{k=1}^{N}\mu_{(k,i),j}(t)\right)$$

$$= 2\sum_{i=1}^{N}\sum_{k=1}^{N}\sum_{j=1}^{J}Q_{i,j}(t)\mu_{(i,k),j}(t) - \sum_{i=1}^{N}\sum_{k=1}^{N}\sum_{j=1}^{J}\mu_{(k,i),j}(t)Q_{i,j}(t)$$

$$= 2\sum_{i=1}^{N}\sum_{k=1}^{N}\sum_{j=1}^{J}(\mu_{(i,k),j}(t)(Q_{i,j}(t) - Q_{k,j}(t)))$$

$$(7.24)$$

Using Equation (7.24) and taking conditional expectation in Equation (7.23) we get

$$E(L(\mathbf{Q}(t+1)) - L(\mathbf{Q}(t)) \mid \mathbf{Q}(t))$$

$$\leq B + 2E\left[\sum_{i=1}^{N}\sum_{j=1}^{J}Q_{i,j}(t)A_{i,j}(t+1) \mid \mathbf{Q}(t)\right]$$

$$- 2E\left[\sum_{i=1}^{N}\sum_{k=1}^{N}\sum_{j=1}^{J}\mu_{(i,k),j}(t)(Q_{i,j}(t) - Q_{k,j}(t)) \mid \mathbf{Q}(t)\right]$$

Since $A_{i,j}(t+1)$ are independent of $Q_{i,j}(t)$, the second term on the right-hand side of the preceding inequality is simplified as follows:

$$2E\left[\sum_{i=1}^{N}\sum_{j=1}^{J}Q_{i,j}(t)A_{i,j}(t+1) \mid \mathbf{Q}(t)\right] = 2\sum_{i=1}^{N}\sum_{j=1}^{J}Q_{i,j}(t)E(A_{i,j}(t+1))$$

$$= 2\sum_{i=1}^{N}\sum_{j=1}^{J}Q_{i,j}(t)\lambda_{i,j}$$

We thus get

$$\mathbf{E}(L(\mathbf{Q}(t+1)) - L(\mathbf{Q}(t)) \mid \mathbf{Q}(t)) \leq B + 2\sum_{i=1}^{N}\sum_{j=1}^{J}Q_{i,j}(t)\lambda_{i,j}$$

$$- 2\mathbf{E}\left[\sum_{i=1}^{N}\sum_{k=1}^{N}\sum_{j=1}^{J}(\mu_{(i,k),j}(t)(Q_{i,j}(t) - Q_{k,j}(t))) \mid \mathbf{Q}(t)\right] \tag{7.25}$$

The last term in Equation (7.25) involves the routing and link scheduling algorithm. If we choose an algorithm that makes

$$\sum_{i=1}^{N}\sum_{k=1}^{N}\sum_{j=1}^{J}(\mu_{(i,k),j}(t)(Q_{i,j}(t) - Q_{k,j}(t)))$$

as large as possible in every slot, then the expectation in the last term in Equation (7.25) will also be large, and hence the right-hand side of Equation (7.25) will be made small. This can lead to the queues being stable for larger values of $\lambda_{i,j}$. We now describe a routing and scheduling algorithm that achieves this.

For slot t, define the weight, $w_{(i,k)}(t)$, of each edge $(i,k) \in \mathcal{E}$ as follows. First we define

$$w_{(i,k),j}(t) := \begin{cases} Q_{i,j}(t) - Q_{k,j}(t) & \text{if } k \neq d_j \\ Q_{i,j}(t) & \text{if } k = d_j \end{cases}$$

This is illustrated in Figure 7.5. From this, define the weight of link (i,k) as follows:

$$w_{(i,k)}(t) := \max_{j} w_{(i,k),j}(t)$$

Thus the weight of a link is the maximum of the difference in the queue lengths of User j packets at the transmitter and receiver of the link. For each $S \in \mathcal{S}$ calculate W_S, the weight of S, and use it to choose the link activation vector for slot t, $S^*(t)$. This is done as follows:

$$W_S(t) = \sum_{(i,k)\in\mathcal{E}} w_{(i,k)}(t)\mu_{(i,k)}(S)$$

$$S^*(t) = \arg\max_{S\in\mathcal{S}} W_S(t)$$

Here $\mu_{(i,k)}(S)$ is the value of $\mu_{(i,k)}$ in the link activation vector $\mathbf{S}$. This decides the scheduling of the link transmissions in slot t. To decide the routing, we need to determine which of the J

flows are to be transmitted on each of the active links. On each active link $(i,k) \in S^*(t)$, select the j for which $w_{(i,k),j}(t)$ is maximum.

The routing and scheduling algorithm that we just described is called the *maximum weight scheduling* (MWS) algorithm. Since the weights are chosen based on the queue lengths in the *NJ* queues in each slot, this is a *queue-length-based* scheduling algorithm. Notice that the packets do not move forward toward the destination if the queues ahead have a higher occupancy. Thus we can see that a queue exerts a backpressure toward the source until its backlog is cleared. Hence this is also called a *queue-length-based backpressure* (QLB) algorithm.

Let $\mu^*_{(i,k),j}(t)$ denote the scheduling in slot t in the MWS algorithm. Using this notation in Equation (7.25), we can write

$$
\begin{aligned}
\mathbf{E}(L(\mathbf{Q}(t+1)) - L(\mathbf{Q}(t)) \mid \mathbf{Q}(t)) \le{}& B + 2\sum_{i=1}^{N}\sum_{j=1}^{J} Q_{i,j}(t)\lambda_{i,j} \\
& - 2\mathbf{E}\left(\sum_{i=1}^{N}\sum_{k=1}^{N}\sum_{j=1}^{J} \mu^*_{(i,k),j}(t)(Q_{i,j}(t) - Q_{k,j}(t)) \mid \mathbf{Q}(t) \right)
\end{aligned}
\tag{7.26}
$$

Let $\tilde{\mu}_{(i,j),k}(t)$ be any other routing and scheduling algorithm that selects the activation vector and the packet to transmit on each link according to our assumptions made in the beginning of the section. From our choice of $\mu^*_{(i,k),j}(t)$ we can say the following:

$$
\begin{aligned}
\mathbf{E}&\left(\sum_{i=1}^{N}\sum_{k=1}^{N}\sum_{j=1}^{J} \mu^*_{(i,k),j}(t)(Q_{i,j}(t) - Q_{k,j}(t)) \mid \mathbf{Q}(t) \right) \\
&= \mathbf{E}\left(\sum_{i=1}^{N}\sum_{k=1}^{N} \mu^*_{(i,k)}(t)w_{(i,k)}(t) \mid \mathbf{Q}(t) \right) \\
&\ge \mathbf{E}\left(\sum_{i=1}^{N}\sum_{k=1}^{N} \tilde{\mu}_{(i,k),j}(t)w_{(i,k)}(t)\mathbf{Q}(t) \right)
\end{aligned}
$$

The first equality is obtained from the definition of $w_{(i,k)}(t)$, and from our assumption that $\tilde{\mu}_{(i,k),j} \in \{0,1\}$ and $\sum_{j=1}^{J} \tilde{\mu}_{(i,k),j} = \tilde{\mu}_{(i,k)}$. Using the same reasoning we also see that the following is true:

$$
w_{(i,k)}(t)\tilde{\mu}^*_{(i,k)}(t) \ge \sum_{j=1}^{J} (Q_{i,j}(t) - Q_{k,j}(t))\tilde{\mu}^*_{(i,k),j}(t)
$$

Using this and continuing with our previous calculations, we get

$$
\mathbf{E}\left(\sum_{i=1}^{N}\sum_{k=1}^{N}\sum_{j=1}^{J}\mu^{*}_{(i,k),j}(t)(Q_{i,j}(t) - Q_{k,j}(t)) \mid \mathbf{Q}(t)\right)
$$

$$
\geq \mathbf{E}\left(\sum_{i=1}^{N}\sum_{k=1}^{N}\sum_{j=1}^{J}\tilde{\mu}_{(i,k),j}(t)(Q_{i,j}(t) - Q_{k,j}(t)) \mid \mathbf{Q}(t)\right)
$$

$$
= \mathbf{E}\left(\sum_{i=1}^{N}\sum_{j=1}^{J}Q_{i,j}(t)\left(\sum_{k=1}^{N}\tilde{\mu}_{(i,k),j} - \sum_{k=1}^{N}\tilde{\mu}_{(k,i),j}\right) \mid \mathbf{Q}(t)\right)
$$

$$
= \sum_{i=1}^{N}\sum_{j=1}^{J}Q_{i,j}(t)\left(\mathbf{E}\left(\left(\sum_{k=1}^{N}\tilde{\mu}_{(i,k),j} - \sum_{k=1}^{N}\tilde{\mu}_{(k,i),j}\right) \mid \mathbf{Q}(t)\right)\right)
$$

The first equality is obtained by switching the order of the summation and rearranging like we did in Equation (7.24).

From Lemma 7.3, we know that if $\lambda \in \Lambda_1$, then there exists a stationary randomized schedule that satisfies Equation (7.20) and is not dependent on $\mathbf{Q}(t)$. Let $\tilde{\mu}_{(i,k),j}(t)$ in the preceding discussion come from such a schedule. Then, from Equation (7.20), we have

$$
\mathbf{E}\left(\left(\sum_{k=1}^{N}\tilde{\mu}_{(i,k),j} - \sum_{k=1}^{N}\tilde{\mu}_{(k,i),j}\right) \mid \mathbf{Q}(t)\right) = \mathbf{E}\left(\sum_{k=1}^{N}\tilde{\mu}_{(i,k),j} - \sum_{k=1}^{N}\tilde{\mu}_{(k,i),j}\right) \geq \lambda_{i,j} + \epsilon
$$

for some $\epsilon > 0$, $1 \leq i \leq N$, and $1 \leq j \leq J$. Resuming our earlier calculations, we get

$$
\mathbf{E}\left(\sum_{i=1}^{N}\sum_{k=1}^{N}\sum_{j=1}^{J}\mu^{*}_{(i,k),j}(t)(Q_{i,j}(t) - Q_{k,j}(t)) \mid \mathbf{Q}(t)\right) \geq \sum_{i=1}^{N}\sum_{j=1}^{J}Q_{i,j}(t)(\lambda_{i,j} + \epsilon)
$$

Using this last relation in Equation (7.26), we get

$$
\mathbf{E}(L(\mathbf{Q}(t+1)) - L(\mathbf{Q}(t)) \mid \mathbf{Q}(t))
$$

$$
\leq B + 2\sum_{i=1}^{N}\sum_{j=1}^{J}Q_{i,j}(t)\lambda_{i,j} - 2\sum_{i=1}^{N}\sum_{j=1}^{J}Q_{i,j}(t)(\lambda_{i,j} + \epsilon)
$$

$$
- B - 2\epsilon\sum_{i=1}^{N}\sum_{j=1}^{J}Q_{i,j}(t)
$$

Thus we see that Equation (7.21) is satisfied. When $\sum_{i=1}^{N}\sum_{j=1}^{J}Q_{i,j}(t) > (B/2\epsilon)$ the right-hand side becomes negative and the drift is negative pushing the queues toward smaller values. Thus the maximum weight scheduling algorithm stabilizes $\lambda \in \Lambda_1$.

7.6.4 Discussion

- In deriving the scheduling algorithm, we could also consider the error probability on the link. Of course, if the probability of a packet error on a link is nonzero, then the stability region and also the queue evolution equation would need to be changed. However, the MWS algorithm is only slightly different. This is explored in Problem 7.9.

- With a suitable choice of edge weights, the MWS routing and scheduling algorithm is applicable in considerably more general scenarios. For example, we could use the same algorithm when the topology is time-varying in a manner that a time average probability for a link to exist can be defined.

- The elements of the link activation vectors **S** could be nonnegative real numbers. Recall that the transmission bit rate could be a function of the SINR at the receiver. This in turn depends on the transmission power used by the transmitters in the link activation vector. Thus corresponding to a transmission rate vector **S**, we also need to specify the transmission powers. In such cases, an obvious optimization criterion could be to minimize the energy or power consumption.

- The MWS algorithm is complex to implement. Further, what we have described is a centralized algorithm that requires complete knowledge of the network state. Hence this is not quite a practical algorithm. Many distributed and randomized algorithms have been proposed in the literature.

- The MWS algorithm is a significantly general algorithm and can be applied to a large class of problems. The most notable use is in developing maximum throughput scheduling algorithms in input queued switches.

7.7 Routing and Scheduling for Elastic Traffic

In the discussion in the previous two sections our concern had been to support a given end-to-end flow rate requirement λ through appropriate routing and link scheduling. We assumed that a requirement of λ exists due to applications involving stream traffic like interactive voice and streaming video. Much of the traffic in networks is due to client–server based data exchanges like those of ftp and http applications. Figure 7.6 shows a network with several application sessions between http or ftp servers and clients. The servers could be directly connected to the WMN or they could be connected via a node that in turn connects to a wireline network. These data transfer sessions are elastic sessions and there is no intrinsic rate that the applications demand.

In this section we assume that a number of elastic sessions are sharing the network resources and that *each session is transferring a single file with infinitely large volume of data*. This is the file transfer abstraction in analyzing a network with elastic sessions. Of course, in practice,

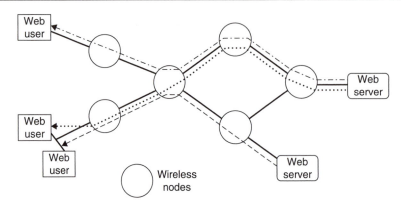

Figure 7.6 Elastic transfers between web servers and clients over a multihop wireless network.

sessions have finite lifetimes, and sessions arrive and depart. Hence even if the network topology and routing do not change, the session topology is constantly changing. Thus, in a sense, we are considering a situation in which the session topology and the network variations occur over a timescale that is slower than the file transfer time. However, we will assume that the stabilization of the dynamics of the congestion control scheme is on a faster timescale than the file transfer time. This simplifying assumption helps us develop an understanding of some of the basic issues in bandwidth sharing and congestion control in wireless networks.

Fair bandwidth sharing in a network is a complex issue. The complexity is compounded in wireless networks because the link capacity is itself a variable. Further, there are many notions of fairness that can be defined as being desirable or achievable by specific resource sharing mechanisms. Of course, the network will also need to allocate bandwidth *efficiently* while being fair. Once again many definitions of efficiency are possible.

Fair sharing and efficiency have been studied extensively in wireline networks. As we have mentioned earlier, an important difference between wireline and wireless networks is that in the latter, link capacity is a variable in the bandwidth sharing algorithm. To illustrate this difference, consider the two-link network shown in Figure 7.7. Assume that the physical layer transmission rates on the links are equal, which we think of as unity. If it were a wireline network, assigning equal rates to the sessions could lead to a rate of one-third being assigned to each session, thus having unutilized bandwidth on link 1. However, if it were a time-slotted wireless network, with the primary conflict constraint, each session could be scheduled once in every five slots, and hence would be allocated a rate of 0.2 packets per slot. In doing so, links 1 and 2 have been allocated capacities 0.4 and 0.6, respectively. Since each clique has unit capacity, this implies that the clique capacity is not wasted.

Allocating equal rates to all the flows will not always be efficient from the network point of view. To illustrate, consider the network and sessions shown in Figure 7.8. Assuming the primary conflict scheduling constraint we have $S_1 = [1,0,1]$ and $S_2 = [0,1,0]$ as the link

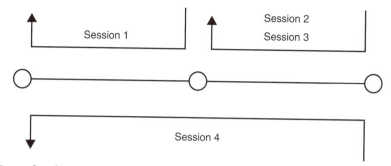

Figure 7.7 Example of a network and flows in which equal rate allocation to all flows is possible in wireless networks but not in wireline networks.

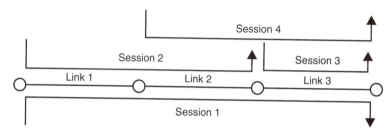

Figure 7.8 Fair sharing is not equal sharing in a network of links and transfers.

activation vectors. Let ϕ_1 and ϕ_2 be fractions of time that, respectively, S_1 and S_2 are activated. Let x_i be the rate allocated to Session i. The x_i need to satisfy the following inequalities:

$$\phi_1 + \phi_2 \leq 1$$
$$x_1 + x_2 \leq \phi_1$$
$$x_1 + x_2 + x_4 \leq \phi_2$$
$$x_1 + x_3 + x_4 \leq \phi_1$$

With equal rate allocation to all the sessions (i.e., $x_i = x$ for all i), these inequalities reduce to

$$x \leq \frac{\phi_1}{2} \quad x \leq \frac{\phi_2}{3} \quad x \leq \frac{\phi_1}{3}$$

and $x \leq (1/3)\ \min(\phi_1, \phi_2)$. Since $\phi_1 + \phi_2 \leq 1$ we get $x = (1/6)$ as the largest possible solution such that all x_i are equal. Clearly, allocating equal rates would be inefficient because while Session 4 is using link c, link a could be underutilized. Once again many notions of efficiency are possible. A simple efficiency objective could be that of *Pareto efficiency*, which, somewhat informally, is defined as follows: *An allocation of resources in a system is Pareto efficient if there does not exist another allocation in which some individual is better off while no individual is worse off.*

The preceding examples illustrate another point. In the example of Figure 7.7, notice that with the rate allocation of 0.2 packets per slot, Session 4 requires resources from both links; hence for each unit of Session 4 traffic carried we take away a unit of bandwidth from each of the two links. Yet, we need to be fair in some sense between the various sessions.

As in the previous sections, we will assume J users but each of them now has an infinite backlog of data to send. The network will have to decide the rate to be allocated to User j, say x_j; $\mathbf{x} := [x_1, \ldots, x_J]^T$. We thus have added a third dimension to the problem of routing and scheduling—determining the optimal fair rates for the users that can be routed and scheduled on a network with network graph G and link activation vector set S. We are, of course, constrained that the flow allocation be within the feasible region determined by the graph G and the link activation vector set S. An obvious question that arises now is the definition of fair sharing of the network capacity by the different users.

Max–min fairness (MMF) is a popular fairness notion. In a network represented by the network graph G and the constraint S, a stabilizable rate vector $\mathbf{x}$ is **MMF** if it is not possible to increase the rate of a User j, *while maintaining the feasibility property,* without reducing the rate of some session j_1 with $x_{j_1} \leq x_j$.

An important property of the MMF allocation is the following: Consider a feasible rate vector and look at the smallest rate in this vector. The MMF rate vector has the largest value of this minimum rate. Further, among all feasible rate vectors with this value of the minimum rate, consider the next larger rate. The MMF rate vector has the largest value of the next larger rate as well and so on.

Another important and more general approach to achieve fairness is to assume that each flow j has a *utility function* $U_j(x_j)$ that defines the utility that User j obtains when it is allocated a flow rate of x_j. Then, if the assigned rate vector is $\mathbf{x} = [x_1, x_2, \ldots, x_J]^T$, the total utility of all the users in the network is $\sum_{j=1}^{J} U_j(x_j)$. For simplicity in the discussion, let us assume that all sources have the same utility function $U(\cdot)$. The following is a popular utility function:

$$U(x) := \log(x)$$

An important property of this utility function is that it is a nondecreasing and concave function of x. Concavity is related to the practical fact that any incremental value of additional rate decreases with increasing rate that a user already has—the law of diminishing returns. In this framework, the optimal bandwidth sharing is provided by the solution of the following utility maximization problem:

$$\max \sum_{j=1}^{J} U(x_j)$$

is subject to

$$X \in \Lambda \tag{7.27}$$

If the flows and capacity allocations are all deterministic, then we can replace Λ by $\bar{\Lambda}_1$. In this section we will consider the utility function approach to fair sharing of wireless network resources by elastic flows. We will first consider single hop flows in Aloha networks and then consider multihop flows.

7.7.1 Fair Allocation for Single Hop Flows

We begin with a simple network in which all users have end-to-end flows that are just one hop; i.e., we have only single-hop sessions. Consider a network with all the edges that have flows. We will assume that the network uses the s-Aloha protocol at the MAC layer.

The s-Aloha is a distributed MAC protocol in which if a node has a packet to transmit, it just transmits it. If another neighboring node of the receiver also transmits in the same slot, then there is a collision and the receiver cannot decode the packet that was transmitted to it. The assumption is that a node will have a packet to transmit in a slot with some probability. Since we are considering elastic flows in which all the sources are infinitely backlogged, a node always has a packet to transmit to all its neighbors. Further, there is a backlog on all the links and a node can transmit on at most one link in a slot. We cannot have the nodes transmitting all the time. We therefore assign a transmission probability to every edge. The probability that the packet was decoded successfully at the receiver without a collision is the flow rate on the link. Thus the scheduling decision essentially consists of choosing the transmission probability in a slot for each link. Since all flows are from single-hop sessions, we do not need to consider routing. Also, only single-hop sessions mean that the flow rate allocated to a link is the rate allocated to the session. Thus, this is a simple example of distributed fair scheduling in wireless networks.

In the following, we will assume that in each slot, every node transmits independently of other nodes and also independently of its own previous transmission attempts. Further, given that a node transmits, we will also assume that it chooses a receiver from among its neighbors independently. We thus have an attempt probability along each edge. Let $G_{(i,k)}$ be the attempt probability for edge (i,k); $\mathbf{G}$ is the vector of the edge attempt probabilities. From our assumptions, the attempt probability for Node i, $\hat{G}_i$, is then given by

$$\hat{G}_i = \sum_{k \in \mathcal{N}_{out}(i)} G_{(i,k)}$$

of course, $0 \le G_{(i,k)} \le 1$ and $0 \le \hat{G}_i \le 1$.

Consider the network shown in Figure 7.2. If node A transmits to B, for B to successfully decode this transmission, neither B nor any of its neighbors should be transmitting in the slot. Generalizing, for a transmission on edge (i,k) to be successfully decoded, k should not be transmitting and none of the neighbors of k (except i) should be transmitting in the slot.

As we have said earlier, the flow rate on edge (i,k), denoted by $x_{i,k}$, is equal to the probability of a successful transmission along edge (i,k). Thus we have

$$x_{(i,k)} = G_{(i,k)}(1 - \hat{G}_k) \prod_{\substack{m \in \mathcal{N}_{\text{in}}(k) \\ m \neq k}} (1 - \hat{G}_m)$$

If we use the logarithmic utility function introduced earlier for the links, then the network utility, which is the sum of the edge utilities, is given by

$$\sum_{(i,k) \in \mathcal{E}} \log(x_{(i,k)})$$

Let $G_{(i,k)}^*$ be the optimum edge attempt probabilities and let $\mathbf{G}^*$ denote the vector of $G_{(i,k)}^*$. $\mathbf{G}^*$ is obtained as

$$\arg \max_{\substack{0 < G_{(i,k)} < 1 \\ (i,k) \in \mathcal{E}}} \left(\sum_{(i,k) \in \mathcal{E}} \log(x_{(i,k)}) \right)$$

■ Exercise 7.3

Note the strict inequality in the range for $G_{(i,k)}$. What are the implications of allowing $G_{(i,k)} = 0$ and $G_{(i,k)} = 1$? ■

Let us now consider the network utility function $U(\mathbf{G})$ given as

$$U(\mathbf{G}) = \sum_{(i,k) \in \mathcal{E}} \log \left(G_{(i,k)}(1 - \hat{G}_k) \prod_{\substack{m \in \mathcal{N}_{\text{in}}(k) \\ m \neq i}} (1 - \hat{G}_m) \right)$$

$$= \sum_{(i,k) \in \mathcal{E}} \left(\log(G_{(i,k)}) + \log(1 - \hat{G}_k) + \sum_{\substack{m \in \mathcal{N}_{\text{in}}(k) \\ m \neq i}} \log(1 - \hat{G}_m) \right) \tag{7.28}$$

■ Exercise 7.4

Show that $\log(G_{(i,k)})$ and $\log(1 - \hat{G}_i) = \log\left(1 - \sum_{k \in \mathcal{N}_{\text{out}}(i)} G_{(i,k)}\right)$ are strictly concave functions in $G_{(i,k)}$. ■

From Exercise 7.4 we see that $U(\mathbf{G})$ is a sum of concave functions and hence it also is concave with a unique maximum. Hence, the value of $\mathbf{G}$ which maximizes $U(\cdot)$, $\mathbf{G}^*$, can be obtained by observing that a strict concave function over a compact set has a unique maximum. Let us now obtain $G^*_{(i,k)}$. Since

$$1 - \hat{G}_i = 1 - \sum_{k_1 \in \mathcal{N}_{out}(i)} G_{(i,k_1)},$$

we have

$$\frac{\partial(\log(1 - \hat{G}_i))}{\partial G_{(i,k)}} = -\frac{1}{1 - \hat{G}_i}$$

Let us now see the terms that will have $G_{(i,k)}$ when the summation in Equation (7.27) is expanded. The second term in Equation (7.27) corresponds to the receiver not transmitting. Thus $(1 - \hat{G}_i)$ will appear in terms that correspond to any of the in-neighbors of I transmitting. Hence we will have $|\mathcal{N}_{in}(i)|$ terms of the form $-1/(1 - \hat{G}_i)$. The third term in Equation (7.27) corresponds to the in-neighbors of the receiver not transmitting. Thus $(1 - \hat{G}_i)$ will appear whenever the out-neighbors of i have to receive. Hence we have $\sum_{m \in \mathcal{N}_{out}(i)} |\mathcal{N}_{in}(m)| - |\mathcal{N}_{out}(i)|$ terms of the form $-1/(1 - \hat{G}_i)$. We subtract $|\mathcal{N}_{out}(i)|$ because i should not be counted. Thus

$$\frac{\partial U}{\partial G_{(i,k)}} = \frac{1}{G_{(i,k)}} - \left(\frac{1}{1 - \hat{G}_i}\right)\left(|\mathcal{N}_{in}(i)| + \sum_{m \in \mathcal{N}_{out}(i)} |\mathcal{N}_{in}(m)| - |\mathcal{N}_{out}(i)|\right)$$

$$G^*_{(i,k)} = \frac{1 - \hat{G}^*_i}{|\mathcal{N}_{in}(i)| + \sum_{m \in \mathcal{N}_{out}(i)} |\mathcal{N}_{in}(m)| - |\mathcal{N}_{out}(i)|}$$

Now observe that $G^*_{(i,k)}$ is independent of k and, for a given i, it is the same for all k; i.e., all outgoing edges are activated with equal probability. Therefore $G^*_{(i,k)} = G^*_i / \mathcal{N}_{out}(i)$. Substituting in the preceding and simplifying we get

$$G^*_{i,k} = \frac{1}{|\mathcal{N}_{in}(i)| + \sum_{m \in \mathcal{N}_{out}(i)} |\mathcal{N}_{in}(m)|} \tag{7.29}$$

■ Exercise 7.5

Verify that $G^*_{i,j}$ obtained in Equation (7.29) is a valid probability by verifying that $0 \le G^*_{(i,k)} \le 1$ for $(i,k) \in \mathcal{E}$ and $0 \le \hat{G}^*_i \le 1$ for $1 \le i \le N$.

Observe that the attempt probabilities for each edge can be conveniently obtained by the transmitter of the edge using local information, the in-degree of the node, and the in-degrees of the neighbors. This means that even when the topology of the network is changing, the optimum attempt probabilities can be obtained quickly and the network can quickly settle into its optimum operating point. This is an important requirement in networking protocols in general and in wireless networks in particular because of the dynamic nature of the topology. We will also be seeking such capability in the algorithms that we will explore next.

7.7.2 Fair Allocation for Multihop Flows

Let us now consider multihop flows. Our interest will be in determining a routing and a schedule to support this fair allocation. As in Section 7.3, we will assume that the flows can be routed along any possible path in the network and follow the same notation. The optimization that we consider is similar to that in Section 7.3 except that we are maximizing the network utility and not the "minimum spare capacity"; i.e., we have

$$\max U = \sum_{j=1}^{J} U(x_j)$$

subject to

$$\mathbf{x} \in \Lambda$$

$$(7.30)$$

Here x_j is the flow rate allocated to User j. Since all users have only elastic traffic and the flow volume allocated to a user is variable, we will use x rather than λ to indicate the flow rate.

The constraint is the schedulability constraint for the user rates. Previously, we have also referred to Λ as the *capacity region*. Note that this is not a linear program. The objective function is a sum of concave functions and is hence concave. The constraints also define a convex region. Thus this is a convex program.

Recall that the capacity region Λ is the set of user rates $\mathbf{x}$ ($\mathbf{x} = (x_1, x_2, \ldots, x_J)^T$) such that for each such vector in the set, there exists a scheduling and routing that ensures that the vector can feasibly be carried in the network. It is also worth recalling that if $\mathbf{x} \notin \Lambda$, then there is *no* scheduling and routing such that the rate vector $\mathbf{x}$ can be transported through the network.

What is the capacity region for our problem? This can be defined in terms of a *capacitated network*; recall from Section 7.2 that given an ergodic schedule Π, each link e in the wireless network has an effective capacity $C_e(\Pi)$ that is determined by the fraction of slots in which e gets activated in the schedule.

Let $C_{e,j} \geq 0$, $e \in \varepsilon$, $1 \leq j \leq J$ denote the capacity (as yet unknown) that is earmarked for User j traffic on link e. Then the capacity region Λ is characterized by the following: $\Lambda = \{\mathbf{x} = (x_1, x_2, \ldots, x_J)^T \geq 0\}$ such that there exist capacity vectors $C_{e,j} \geq 0$, $e \in \mathcal{E}$, $1 \leq j \leq J$ satisfying

$$\sum_{\{e:R_e=i\}} C_{e,j} + x_j I_{\{i=s_j\}} \leq \sum_{\{e:T_e=i\}} C_{e,j},$$

$$\text{for } 1 \leq j \leq J \text{ and } 1 \leq i \leq N, i \neq d_j \qquad (7.31)$$

$$\left(\sum_{j=1}^{J} C_{e,j} \right)_{\{e\in\mathcal{E}\}} \in Co(\mathcal{S}) \tag{7.32}$$

The first inequality is written for all users (indexed by j) and all nodes (indexed by i) except the destination node of User j, d_j. The first term on the left-hand side of Equation (7.31) gives the sum of the capacities allocated for User j traffic on all *incoming* edges terminating at Node i; similarly, the term on the right gives the sum of User j capacities allocated on all *outgoing* edges leaving Node i. Therefore, the inequality asserts that the total incoming User j capacity at Node i plus the rate injected into the network by User j (if Node i is the source node of j, viz., s_j) must be less than the total outgoing User j capacity at Node i.

When $i \neq s_j$, there is no User j traffic inserted into the network at Node i, so the second term on the left in Equation (7.31) disappears. When $i = s_j$, we do not need to allocate any capacity for j on the incoming edges at Node i, so the first term on the left in Equation (7.31) may actually be suppressed. However, as $C_{e,j} \geq 0$, allocating $C_{e,j} = 0$ on the incoming links achieves the same effect. Hence we retain the first term on the left in Equation (7.31) even when $i = s_j$.

We note that in Equation (7.31), we do not insist on strict inequality, as was done earlier in Equation (7.11). In writing Equation (7.11), we considered *open-loop* stochastic traffic. For ensuring stability with open-loop stochastic traffic, it is necessary to allocate, on each link, strictly higher capacity than the average aggregate traffic on that link, so that the queues in the network are stable. In this section, however, we consider *elastic* traffic that is subject to closed-loop control. Elastic traffic sources react to feedback signals from the network. As long as the feedback from the network remains unchanged, traffic is injected at constant rates. Because the input traffic is not varying stochastically, it is possible to allocate outgoing capacity that is not just strictly less than but even *equal to* the aggregate inflow into a node.

The second constraint of Equation (7.32) says that the aggregate link capacity vector (with $|\mathcal{E}|$ elements), obtained after adding all the allocated User j capacities on each link, must belong to the convex hull of all the possible link activation vectors in the set $\mathcal{S}$. This ensures that an ergodic schedule can be found that achieves the desired aggregate link capacities.

Another point worth noting about the equations characterizing Λ is that for every $j \in \{1, 2, ..., J\}$, Equation (7.31) is written for all nodes i except d_j. Why do we omit the Node d_j? First, by omitting Node d_j, we are not omitting any links. This is because every link e has an associated transmitting node and a receiving node (T_e and R_e, respectively), and the incoming links at d_j have been considered when we wrote the equations for the corresponding transmitting nodes. Second, we know that the rate of User j traffic leaving the network at d_j cannot be more than the sum of the j capacities of the incoming links at d_j. But this conclusion already follows from the equations written for the other nodes, and hence presents no new information.

To solve the optimization problem Equation (7.30), we will proceed as follows. Let $\mathbf{p}(j) := [p_{1,j}, \ldots, p_{N,j}]^T$, with $p_{dj,j} = 0$. We define $\mathbf{p} := [\mathbf{p}^T(1), \ldots, \mathbf{p}^T(J)]^T \geq 0$. $p_{i,j}$, $1 \leq i \leq N$, $1 \leq j \leq J$ are the *Lagrangian* or *dual* variables. Relaxing the $J \times (N-1)$ constraints in Equation (7.31) that define Λ, we get the following Lagrangian function:

$$
\begin{aligned}
L(\mathbf{x}, \mathbf{p}) = {}& \sum_{j=1}^{J} U(x_j) - \sum_{j=1}^{J} \sum_{i=1, i \neq d_j, i \neq s_j}^{N} p_{i,j} \left(\sum_{\{e:R_e=i\}} C_{e,j} - \sum_{\{e:T_e=i\}} C_{e,j} \right) \\
& - \sum_{j=1}^{J} p_{s_j,j} \left(\sum_{\{e:R_e=s_j\}} C_{e,j} + x_j - \sum_{\{e:T_e=s_j\}} C_{e,j} \right) \\
= {}& \sum_{j=1}^{J} (U(x_j) - p_{s_j,j} x_j) - \sum_{j=1}^{J} \sum_{i=1, i \neq d_j}^{N} p_{i,j} \left(\sum_{\{e:R_e=s_i\}} C_{e,j} - \sum_{\{e:T_e=s_i\}} C_{e,j} \right) \\
= {}& \sum_{j=1}^{J} (U(x_j) - p_{s_j,j} x_j) + \sum_{j=1}^{J} \sum_{e \in \mathcal{E}} (p_{T_{e,j}} - p_{R_{e,j}}) C_{e,j}
\end{aligned}
$$

In arriving at the last line, we have computed the sum

$$
\sum_{i=1, i \neq d_j}^{N} p_{i,j} \left(\sum_{\{e:R_e=i\}} C_{e,j} - \sum_{\{e:T_e=i\}} C_{e,j} \right)
$$

by collecting together terms referring to the same edge. As each edge e has a transmitting node T_e and a receiving node R_e, we get the second term in the last line.

Thus, the relaxed problem is

$$
\max \sum_{j=1}^{J} (U(x_j) - p_{s_j,j} x_j) + \sum_{j=1}^{J} \sum_{e \in \mathcal{E}} \left(p_{T_{e,j}} - p_{R_{e,j}} \right) C_{e,j}
$$

subject to

$$
\left(\sum_{j=1}^{J} C_{e,j} \right)_{\{e \in \mathcal{E}\}} \in \mathrm{Co}(\mathcal{S}), \quad \mathbf{x} \geq 0 \tag{7.33}
$$

In this problem, the maximization is carried out over x_j, $1 \leq j \leq J$ and $C_{e,j}$, $e \in \mathcal{E}$, $1 \leq j \leq J$. The quantity to be maximized in this problem is just the Lagrangian that we obtained before; let us denote the maximum value by $D(\mathbf{p})$. This notation is justified because after the maximization, the objective becomes a function of $\mathbf{p}$ only. It may be noted that the constraint has changed from $\mathbf{x} \in \Lambda$ to $(\sum_{j=1}^{J} C_{e,j})_{\{e \in \mathcal{E}\}} \in \mathrm{Co}(\mathcal{S})$ after the relaxation. Recall also that $\mathrm{Co}(\mathcal{S})$ is a convex set.

It is interesting to note that in the relaxed problem, the constraint $\mathbf{x} \geq 0$ can affect the first term (the summation) only; the constraint $(\sum_{j=1}^{J} C_{e,j})_{\{e \in \mathcal{E}\}} \in Co(\mathcal{S})$ can affect the second term only. Further, the constraint $x_j \geq 0$ can affect the j-th term in the summation only. Thus, there is a nice decomposition of the relaxed problem into several subproblems. For a given vector of dual variables $\mathbf{p}$, we can therefore solve the flow control problem for each User j, $1 \leq j \leq J$, and the scheduling problem independently.

The relaxed problem suggests a simple interpretation of the dual variables $\mathbf{p}$. Consider the j-th flow control problem. The term $p_{s_j,j} x_j$ can be thought of as the total cost that User j has to pay for sending x_j amount of traffic into the network. It is as if upon entry into the network via node s_j, User j pays a *price* of $p_{s_j,j}$ for every unit of traffic that it sends into the network. Thus, given $p_{s_j,j}$, User j's flow control problem is to maximize the *net utility*, where the latter is defined as the difference between the utility $U(x_j)$ and the total cost $p_{s_j,j} x_j$.

Consider now the last subproblem, which is the scheduling subproblem. We can think of $(p_{T_{e,j}} - p_{R_{e,j}})$ as the price associated with link e for User j traffic, and the term $(p_{T_{e,j}} - p_{R_{e,j}})C_{e,j}$ becomes the *weighted* capacity allocated to j on link e, with the weight being the link price. Thus, given $p_{i,j}$, $1 \leq i \leq N$, $1 \leq j \leq J$, the last subproblem asks us to find $C_{e,j}$, $e \in \mathcal{E}$, $1 \leq j \leq J$, such that $(\sum_{j=1}^{J} C_{e,j})_{e \in \mathcal{E}}$ lies in $Co(\mathcal{S})$, and the sum of weighted link capacities over all j and over all links in the network is maximized.

From the preceding discussion, given $\mathbf{p}$, the network needs to solve the scheduling problem, with the objective being to maximize the sum of weighted link capacities, while each user needs to solve its individual net utility maximization problem. We note that according to this simple view, the solution of the scheduling problem must be found by a centralized entity that is aware of *all* prices $p_{i,j}$ and *all* possible capacity allocations $C_{e,j}$.

Now if we solve the subproblems independently for an *arbitrary* $\mathbf{p} \geq 0$, are we sure to get a feasible solution to the original problem in Equation (7.30)? The answer is no. What comes to our rescue, however, is the fact that there *is* at least one particular value of the price vector $\mathbf{p}$ such that *a* solution of the relaxed problem in Equation (7.33) is, indeed, feasible for the original problem in Equation (7.30); moreover, that solution is *optimal* for the original problem in Equation (7.30). This conclusion is based on the Strong Duality Theorem, which is applicable here because

- The objective function in Equation (7.30) is concave, and therefore, the negative of the objective function is convex.
- The first constraint in Equation (7.31) is *linear* in the variables x_j, $1 \leq j \leq J$, and $C_{e,j}$, $e \in \mathcal{E}$, $1 \leq j \leq J$, and thus trivially convex.
- The vector of unknowns $[x_j, C_{e,j}]_{\{e \in \mathcal{E}, 1 \leq j \leq J\}}$ lies in a convex set.

■ Exercise 7.6

Given that $[x_j]_{\{1 \leq j \leq J\}}$ lies in a convex set and $[C_{e,j}]_{\{e \in \mathcal{E}, 1 \leq j \leq J\}}$ lies in a convex set, show that the vector $[x_j, C_{e,j}]_{\{e \in \mathcal{E}, 1 \leq j \leq J\}}$ lies in a convex set also.   ■

This motivates us to consider the *Dual Problem*

$$\min D(\mathbf{p})$$

subject to   (7.34)

$$\mathbf{p} \geq 0$$

The Strong Duality Theorem assures us that there is no *duality gap*, and therefore, the objective function values of the primal and dual problems are equal. Moreover, if we can find an optimal price vector $\mathbf{p}^*$ at which $D(\mathbf{p})$ is minimized, then we just need to solve the relaxed problem in Equation (7.33) for *that* $\mathbf{p}^*$, and the optimal solution to the original problem in Equation (7.30) will be obtained.

Let us consider the problem in Equation (7.33) again. As we noted before, for a given $\mathbf{p}$, the problem is decomposed into several subproblems that can be solved independently. For a given $\mathbf{p}$, the maximizing $\mathbf{x}$, denoted by $\mathbf{x}^*(\mathbf{p})$, can be obtained without difficulty when each User j solves its individual net utility maximization problem independently. For solving the scheduling problem, let us consider some aggregate capacity vector $(C_e)_{e \in \mathcal{E}} \in \mathrm{Co}(\mathcal{S})$. For each $e \in \mathcal{E}$, the first question is about how C_e should be split into $C_{e,j}$, $1 \leq j \leq J$. For this, we need to note the value of j for which $(pT_{e,j} - pR_{e,j})$ is largest. Letting

$$j^*(e,\mathbf{p}) = \arg \max_{1 \leq j \leq J} \left(pT_{e,j} - pR_{e,j} \right)$$

the best split is given by

$$C_{e,j} = C_e \quad \text{for } j = j^*(e,\mathbf{p})$$
$$C_{e,j} = 0 \quad \text{for } j \neq j^*(e,\mathbf{p})$$

In other words, the best split is obtained by allocating, on edge e, the entire capacity C_e to *that* flow $j^*(e, \mathbf{p})$ that exhibits the largest price differential between the transmitter and receiver nodes of e. With this observation, the objective function of the scheduling problem becomes

$$\sum_{e \in \mathcal{E}} \left(pT_{e,j^*(e,\mathbf{p})} - pR_{e,j^*(e,\mathbf{p})} \right) C_e$$

(7.35)

Hence, to maximize the weighted sum of link capacities, it is necessary to select a vector $(C_e)_{e \in \mathcal{E}}$ in $\mathrm{Co}(\mathcal{S})$ such that this sum is maximized. We observe that this problem is actually a linear program because we are maximizing a linear function of C_e, $e \in \mathcal{E}$, over the convex hull of $\mathcal{S}$, the set of all link activation vectors. Hence, an optimizing vector can always be found at some extreme point of $\mathrm{Co}(\mathcal{S})$, i.e., at some vector in $\mathcal{S}$ itself. Denoting such a vector by $(C_e^*(\mathbf{p}))_{e \in \mathcal{E}}$, the optimal solution to the scheduling problem is seen to be

$$C_{e,j}^*(\mathbf{p}) = C_e^*(\mathbf{p}) \quad \text{for } j = j^*(e, \mathbf{p})$$
$$C_{e,j}^*(\mathbf{p}) = 0 \qquad \text{for } j \neq j^*(e, \mathbf{p}) \tag{7.36}$$

As remarked before, if we solve the scheduling and flow control problems for an arbitrary price vector $\mathbf{p}$, there is no guarantee that the solution so obtained will even be feasible for the original problem. The question that arises then is how to get the "right" price vector $\mathbf{p}^*$. Such a price vector $\mathbf{p}^*$ would constitute the *optimal dual variables*. What we need is an algorithm that, starting from some initial price vector $\mathbf{p}(0)$ at slot 0, updates the price vector in each slot such that $\mathbf{p}(t)$ converges to $\mathbf{p}^*$. Such an algorithm is

$$p_{i,j}(k+1) =$$

$$\left(p_{i,j}(k) - h_k \left[\sum_{\{e:T_e=i\}} C_{e,j}^*(\mathbf{p}(k)) - \sum_{\{e:R_e=i\}} C_{e,j}^*(\mathbf{p}(k)) - I_{\{i=s_j\}} x_j^*(\mathbf{p}(k)) \right] \right)^+ \tag{7.37}$$

where $C_{e,j}^*(\mathbf{p})$ are obtained from Equation (7.36) and h_k, $k = 1, 2, \ldots$ is a sequence of positive step-sizes. The factor multiplying h_k is known as the *subgradient* of the dual objective function $D(\mathbf{p})$ at $\mathbf{p}$. It can be shown that if the sequence h_k satisfies the two conditions

1. $h_k \to 0$ as $k \to \infty$

2. $\sum_k h_k = \infty$

then the iteration in Equation (7.37) converges to the optimal price vector $\mathbf{p}^*$. For example, the sequence $h_k = 1/k$ satisfies the two preceding conditions. Finally, solving the relaxed problem in Equation (7.33) with this $\mathbf{p}^*$ yields the optimal solution to the original problem in Equation (7.30).

7.8 Discussion

We provide an overview here of how the solution to the problem of sum-utility maximization for elastic flows is obtained. In slot k, we have the price vector $\mathbf{p}(k)$. Using this, the network solves the scheduling problem. For $\mathbf{p}(k)$, the optimal aggregate capacity vector $(C_e^*(\mathbf{p}(k))_{e \in \mathcal{E}}$

is obtained by solving the linear program whose objective function is given in Equation (7.35), and the optimal split of this among the Users j is obtained as in Equation (7.36). The price vector $\mathbf{p}(k)$ is now fed back to the users, and each user now solves its own net utility maximization problem, yielding $\mathbf{x}^*(\mathbf{p}(k))$.

Accordingly, in slot k, users j, $1 \leq j \leq J$ inject the appropriate amounts of traffic into the network. The network activates the links in the vector $(C_e^*(\mathbf{p}(k))_{e \in \mathcal{E}}$ and transfers data from the users $j^*(e, \mathbf{p}(k))$ over the duration of slot k. At the end of slot k, the network evaluates the right-hand side of Equation (7.37) and new price variables for slot $(k + 1)$ are obtained.

An interesting conclusion follows from Equation (7.37). Consider a Node i and a User j for which the factor multiplying h_k in Equation (7.37) is negative. This means that the total inflow rate of User j traffic into Node i is more than the corresponding outflow rate; i.e., packets of User j are queuing up at Node i. Under these circumstances, $p_{i,j}(k + 1)$ is more than $p_{i,j}(k)$. This means that in slot $(k + 1)$, the pair (i, j) is likely to be part of the vector that maximizes the weighted sum of link capacities. In that case, the network would schedule this node and user pair in slot $(k + 1)$, thereby depleting the queue of User j packets that had started to build up in Node i. Thus, the schedule computed by the network tends to keep queue lengths small.

The observation that queue lengths tend to be small also suggests that the schedule computed by the network leads *implicitly* to a routing in which traffic from the sources does, ultimately, reach the respective destinations. If this were not true, then somewhere in the network, queues would start building up.

We have an iterative process in which the network computes prices and informs these to the users, who react by sending traffic into the network. Next, the network schedules links according to the prevailing prices and users' traffic gets transferred across links. At the end of this, the network computes fresh prices, and the cycle repeats. It can be shown that if this process is allowed to run for many slots, then, as long as the conditions on h_k are satisfied, the price vector $\mathbf{p}$ and the users' rate vector $\mathbf{x}$ both converge to their respective optimal values. After convergence, we would therefore have a vector of user rates that can be transported through the network, and, at the same time, achieve sum-utility maximization, which was our original objective.

Another conclusion from Equation (7.37) is as follows. Consider Equation (7.37) *after convergence*, and suppose $p_{i,j}^*(\infty)$ is positive. This implies that on the right-hand side of Equation (7.37), the factor multiplying h_k must be zero. This says that the total rate of traffic from User j coming into and going out of Node i are equal; the first constraint in Equation (7.31) of the original problem is satisfied with equality. We note that this is exactly the same conclusion that follows from the Complementary Slackness conditions.

In the case where open-loop traffic was to be transported, the problem for the network was to determine a schedule and routing such that traffic could be carried in the network. The input traffic was stochastically characterized and given. In the case of elastic traffic, we recall that the input traffic to the network was *not given*. We just had an objective stating that the sum of users' utilities was to be maximized, subject to the constraint that the users' injected traffic should be supportable by the network. In contrast to the wired network case where link capacities are given and fixed, in the wireless network, not even the link capacities are known; in fact, they depend on the scheduling strategy followed by the network. It is somewhat remarkable that the method outlined in this section is able to provide a scheduling, routing, and rate control that manages to actually achieve the original objective of sum-utility maximization.

7.9 Notes on the Literature

Much of the recent work on optimization in wireless networks has its roots in the work of Tassiulas and Ephremides [1–3]. The schedulable region or the stability region of a wireless mesh network is characterized in [2]. A less general version of the schedulable region is used in [4]. The discussion on the stability of queues is adapted from [5].

Hajek and Sasaki [4] first addressed the problem of simultaneous routing and scheduling in wireless networks. The optimal routing formulation is adapted from Chapter 14 of [6].

The maximum weight scheduling algorithm of Section 7.4 was first described in [2]. This has been considerably generalized and many new applications found. The analysis in [2] assumes that the arrival of new packets into the network is i.i.d. in every slot. Since the routing and scheduling in a slot in the MWS algorithm depends only on the queue occupancies at the beginning of the slot, positive recurrence of the resulting Markov chain implies stability of the queues. This is shown using a technique similar to what is described here. Neely, Modiano, and Rohrs [7] consider significant generalizations, e.g., non-i.i.d. arrivals and stationary time-varying network topology. Georgiadis, Neely, and Tassiulas [5] provide a comprehensive overview of the recent developments and generalizations. Our discussion of Sections 7.2.1 and 7.4 is based on [5]. We have made some simplifying assumptions for pedagogical convenience but the results can be generalized using the framework that we have provided. An important application of the MWS algorithm is in the maximum weight matching algorithm for input queued switches [8].

Ever since the proportional-fairness paradigm for congestion control in wireline networks was introduced by Kelly, Maulloo, and Tan [9], there has been significant interest in extending that to wireless networks. Kar et al. [10] apply this congestion control principle to select the transmission probabilities to optimize single-hop flows in Aloha networks. This is an interesting introduction to this problem. This discussion is adapted from there. Extending it to multihop flows has been the focus of Lin and Shroff [12] and Lo Presti [11] among others. The discussion in Section 7.5.2 is based on [12]. Lin, Shroff, and Srikant [13] provide an excellent tutorial on these techniques.

Since the optimizations involve multiple layers of the network stack, these are also called *cross-layer optimizations.* Kawadia and Kumar [14] provide important insights into the pitfalls that could accompany cross-layer optimizations.

Problems

7.1 Consider a network in which the frames are not equal. Let T_k be the number of slots in the k-th frame and B_k the number of slots allocated to a link in the k-th frame. Find the expression for the bandwidth allocated to the link. The continued fraction expansion of $(1 + \sqrt{2})$ is given by

$$2 + \cfrac{1}{(2 + 1/(2 + 1/(2 + \cdots)))}$$

Using this, identify suitable T_k and B_k so that the link is allocated a bandwidth of $1/(1 + \sqrt{2})$. Since every irrational number can be expressed as a continued fraction, this gives you a method to allocate irrational capacities to links. Explore irrational allocations using this method.

7.2 Given a network graph G, describe a graph coloring algorithm for each of the three graph-based constraints that determine the schedule. Let $\chi(G)$ be the vertex-chromatic number of G, the minimum number of colors required to color the vertices such that adjacent vertices have different colors. Let $\Delta(G)$ and $\omega(G)$ be the maximum vertex degree and the clique number, respectively. It can be shown that $\omega(G) \leq \chi(G) \leq \Delta(G) + 1$. Derive the corresponding inequalities for each of the three graph-based constraints.

7.3 Devise a greedy algorithm for edge-coloring of a graph. For the network of Figure 7.1, perform a greedy coloring and use the coloring to devise a scheme to provide all edges a capacity greater than $1/C_1$ where C_1 is the number of colors used. Observe that the coloring is not unique. Perform a second distinct coloring of this network. If C_2 is the number of colors required for the second coloring, number the colors $C_1 + 1, \ldots,$ $C_1 + C_2$. Comment on the change in $\text{Co}(\mathcal{S})$.

7.4 Consider a routing and scheduling policy, say **P**, in a slotted WMN. Let $\Lambda_{\mathbf{P}}$ denote the set of arrival rate vectors λ that are stabilized by this policy. Let $\mathbf{P}_0$ denote the queue-length-based centralized scheduling policy discussed in Section 7.4. Argue that $\Lambda_{\mathbf{P}_0} = U_{\mathbf{P}} \Lambda_{\mathbf{P}}$. This means that if there exists any policy that stabilizes the queues under the arrival rate vector λ, then the queues will be stable for this arrival rate vector under policy $\mathbf{P}_0$.

7.5 Construct an example to illustrate that Equation (7.13) is not a sufficient condition.

7.6 Consider a two-link network. Let $S_1 = [1, 0]$, $S_2 = [0, 1]$, $S_3 = [0.25, 0.75]$, and $S_4 = [0.75, 0.25]$ be the four possible schedules in the network. Draw the link-layer capacity region for this network.

7.7 Consider a two-link network. The links operate in a fading environment and in each slot, link i is either available with probability P_i or not available with probability $(1 - p_i)$, independently of the other link and of its availability in other slots. Characterize the link-capacity region for this system.

7.8 Consider the network shown in Figure 7.1. Choose 10 arbitrary source-destination pairs and designate them as users $1, \ldots, 10$. Assume $A_{i,j}(t)$ to be i.i.d. Bernoulli with probability of arrival λ in every slot. Write a program to simulate MWS algorithm on this network. Let $h_j(\lambda)$ be the average hop length for User j. Compare $h_j(\lambda)$ with the minimum hop distance.

7.9 Consider the MWS algorithm in a network in which there are link errors. Let $p_{(i,k)}$ be the packet error probability on link (i, k). Find the link capacity region for this network. Adapt the MWS algorithm for this case and show that it will stabilize the network for all $\lambda \in \Lambda_1$.

7.10 Consider a network in which all flows are single hop flows. All flows are to be routed over the single-hop path from the source to the destination. Given a network graph G obtain a schedule that maximizes the total utility.

7.11 Consider the single-hop s-Aloha network with N nodes. In each slot, all nodes transmit independently with probability p. Derive the proportionally fair p when all nodes have the same utility function. Generalize to the case when Node i has utility function $a_i \log(x_i)$.

References

[1] L. Tassiulas, A. Ephremides, Jointly optimal routing and scheduling in packet ratio networks, IEEE Trans. Inform. Theory 38 (1) (1992) 165–168.

[2] L. Tassiulas, A. Ephremides, Stability properties of constrained queueing systems and scheduling policies for maximum throughput in multihop radio networks, IEEE Trans. Auto. Control 37 (12) (1992) 1936–1948.

[3] L. Tassiulas, A. Ephremides, Dynamic server allocation to parallel queues with randomly varying connectivity, IEEE Trans. Inform. Theory 39 (2) (1993) 466–478.

[4] B. Hajek, G. Sasaki, Link scheduling in polynomial time, IEEE Trans. Inform. Theory 34 (5, Part 1) (1988) 910–917.

[5] L. Georgiadis, M.J. Neely, L. Tassiulas, Resource allocation and cross layer control in wireless networks, Foundations and Trends in Networking 1 (1) (2006) 1–144.

[6] A. Kumar, D. Manjunath, J. Kuri, Communication Networking: An Analytical Approach. Morgan-Kaufmann (an imprint of Elsevier), San Francisco, May 2004.

[7] M.J. Neely, E. Modiano, C.E. Rohrs, Dynamic power allocation and routing for time varying wireless networks, in: Proc. IEEE INFOCOM, San Francisco, CA, USA, 2003.

[8] N. McKeown, A. Mekkittikul, V. Anantharam, J. Walrand, Achieving 100% throughput in an input queued switch, IEEE Trans. Commun. 47 (8) (1999) 1260–1267.

[9] F.P. Kelly, A. Maulloo, D. Tan, Rate control for communication networks: shadow price proportional fairness and stability, J. Op. Res. Soc. 49 (1998) 237–252.

[10] K. Kar, S. Sarkar, L. Tassiulas, Achieving proportional fairness using local information in aloha networks, IEEE Trans. Auto. Control 49 (10) (2004) 1858–1863.

[11] F. Lo Presti, Joint congestion control: routing and media access control optimization via dual decomposition for ad hoc wireless networks, in: Proc. 8th ACM International Symposium on Modeling, Analysis and Simulation of Wireless and Mobile Systems (WiOpt), 2005.

[12] X.J. Lin, N.B. Shroff, Joint rate control and scheduling in multihop wireless networks, in: Proc. IEEE Conference on Decision and Control, Paradise Island, Bahamas, December 2004, pp. 1484–1489.

[13] X. Lin, N.B. Shroff, R. Srikant, A tutorial on cross-layer optimization in wireless networks, IEEE J. Select. Areas Commun. 24 (8) (2006) 1452–1463.

[14] V. Kawadia, P.R. Kumar, A cautionary perspective on cross layer design, IEEE Wireless Commun. Mag. 12 (1) (2005) 3–11.

CHAPTER 8

Ad Hoc Wireless Sensor Networks

Anurag Kumar
D. Manjunath
Joy Kuri

Advances in microelectronics technology have made it possible to build inexpensive, low-power, miniature sensing devices. Equipped with a microprocessor, memory, radio, and battery, such devices can now combine the functions of sensing, computing, and wireless communication into miniature *smart sensor nodes*, also called *motes*. Since smart sensors need not be tethered to any infrastructure because of on-board radio and battery, their main utility lies in being ad hoc, in the sense that they can be rapidly deployed by randomly strewing them over a region of interest. Several applications of such wireless sensor networks have been proposed, and there have also been several experimental deployments. Example applications are:

- *Ecological Monitoring:* wild-life in conservation areas, remote lakes, forest fires.

- *Monitoring of Large Structures:* bridges, buildings, ships, and large machinery, such as turbines.

- *Industrial Measurement and Control:* measurement of various environment and process parameters in very large factories, such as continuous process chemical plants.

- *Navigation Assistance:* guidance through the geographical area where the sensor network is deployed.

- *Defense Applications:* monitoring of intrusion into remote border areas; detection, identification, and tracking of intruding personnel or vehicles.

The ad hoc nature of these wireless sensor networks means that the devices and the wireless links will not be laid out to achieve a planned topology. During the operation, sensors would be difficult or even impossible to access and hence their network needs to operate autonomously. Moreover, with time it is possible that sensors fail (one reason being battery drain) and cannot be replaced. It is, therefore, essential that sensors *learn about each other* and *organize into a network* on their own. Another crucial requirement is that since sensors may often be deployed randomly (e.g., simply strewn from an aircraft), in order to be useful, the devices need to determine their locations. In the absence of a centralized control, this whole process of self-organization needs to be carried out in a distributed fashion.

In a sensor network, there is usually a *single, global objective* to be achieved. For example, in a surveillance application, a sensor network may be deployed to detect intruders. The global objective here is intrusion detection. This can be contrasted with multihop wireless *mesh networks*, where we have a collection of source–destination pairs, and each pair is interested in optimizing its *individual* performance metric. Another characteristic feature of sensor networks appears in the *packet scheduling* algorithms used. Sensor nodes are battery-powered and the batteries cannot be replaced. Hence, energy-aware packet scheduling is of crucial importance.

A smart sensor may have only modest computing power, but the ability to communicate allows a group of sensors to collaborate to execute tasks more complex than just sensing and forwarding the information, as in traditional sensor arrays. Hence, they may be involved in online processing of sensed data in a distributed fashion so as to yield partial or even complete results to an observer, thereby facilitating control applications, interactive computing, and querying. A distributed computing approach will also be energy-efficient as compared to mere data dissemination since it will avoid energy consumption in long haul transport of the measurements to the observer; this is of particular importance since sensors could be used in large numbers due to their low cost, yielding very high resolutions and large volumes of sensed data. Further, by arranging computations among only the neighboring sensors the number of transmissions is reduced, thereby saving transmission energy. A simple class of distributed computing algorithms would require each sensor to periodically exchange the results of local computation with the neighboring sensors. Thus the design of distributed signal processing and computation algorithms, and the mapping of these algorithms onto a network, is an important aspect of sensor network design.

Design and analysis of sensor networks must take into account the native capabilities of the nodes, as well as architectural features of the network. We assume that the sensor nodes are *not mobile*. Further, nodes are *not equipped with position-sensing technology*, like the *Global Positioning System* (GPS). However, each node can set its transmit power at an appropriate level—each node can exercise *power control*. Further, each node has an associated *sensing radius*; events occurring within a circle of this radius centered at the sensor can be detected.

In general, a sensor network can have multiple sinks, where the traffic generated by the sensor sources leaves the network. We consider networks in which only a *single sink* is present. Further, we will be concerned with situations in which sensors are *randomly deployed*. In many scenarios of practical interest, preplanned placing of sensors is infeasible, leaving random deployment as the only practical alternative; e.g., consider a large terrain that is to be populated with sensors for surveillance purposes. In addition, random deployment is a convenient assumption for analytical tractability in models. Our study will also assume a simple *path loss model*, with no shadowing and no fading in the environment.

8.1 Overview

In this chapter, we will be concerned with the question of how sensor nodes should set their transmit powers; specifically, how should transmit powers be set so that the randomly deployed network is *connected* with high probability? After this brief look at *communication coverage*, we will consider the problem of *sensing coverage*. Each sensor can sense events within a certain radius of itself. All points within the disk of this radius are said to be covered by the sensor. If the sensor deployment is random, it is not clear that every point within the deployment region can be covered by at least one sensor. We are interested in finding the *density* of deployment that ensures complete sensing coverage with high probability.

The next problem we consider is that of *localization*. A group of sensors called *anchors* are aware of their own positions and transmit this information to others via beacons. The problem is for the nonanchor nodes to estimate their own locations utilizing the information provided by the anchors. Next, we turn to the problem of *routing* in the sensor network. We discuss *face routing*, where the estimated node location information is used, and also *attribute-based routing*, which does not depend on the knowledge of node locations. *Directed Diffusion* (DD) is a prominent example of attribute-based routing. Sensor networks are deployed with specific objectives and usually, some kind of inference about a phenomenon is desired. The inference is based on measurements and subsequent computation of some function of the measurements.

We consider the generic problem of *function computation* next. Our interest is in understanding the maximum rate at which a particular type of function computation can be carried out. Lastly, we briefly describe two *Medium Access Control* (MAC) *scheduling algorithms* that have been designed, keeping the resource-constrained nature of the sensors in mind.

8.2 Communication Coverage

Formally, we will view the network as a graph, with the motes being the vertices of the graph. If two motes can hear each other *in the absence of interference from other nodes*, then there will be an edge between the corresponding vertices. Essentially, this corresponds to the receiver being within the *decode region* of the transmitter.

In this graph model, which is obtained when only the decode regions are considered, it is desirable that each vertex have a path to the vertex corresponding to the sink. This assures us that there *is* a way for a sensor node *i* to communicate its measurements to the sink. This is because one can think of a strategy in which *i* is the *only* node that transmits in a time slot, thereby passing its information to a neighbor within its decode region. Similarly, in the next slot, the neighbor is the only node that transmits. This naive strategy, albeit inefficient, will succeed in transferring information from *i* to the sink, over several time slots, *if* there is a path in the graph model from *i* to the sink.

Let us enlarge the requirement slightly and ask that there be a path between *any* pair of nodes. Thus, we are asking the question: What is the minimum power at which the nodes should transmit so that the graph obtained is *connected?*

In passing, we recall that *not all* the edges in a path from a vertex to the sink can be active *simultaneously.* In this section, we will consider only the question of connectivity of the graph obtained by considering just the decode regions.

Now for a random placement of nodes, the right question to ask is: What is the minimum power at which the nodes should transmit so that the graph is connected *with a given high probability?* For a given number of motes N, this question is hard to answer. Rather, answers have been found in the asymptotic regime where N tends to ∞.

Suppose that N sensors are deployed in a square region of unit area. Each sensor is located independently of any other, and the location is chosen by sampling the uniform distribution. Further, let $r_c(N)$ be the *range* of each of the nodes, i.e., if nodes i and j are separated by a distance less than or equal to $r_c(N)$, then they can decode each other's transmission. We note that $r_c(N)$ is being regarded as a function of the total number of nodes N; this suggests that the range changes as N varies. In fact, we would be interested in understanding how to set $r_c(N)$ for a given N, so that the sensor network remains connected.

As N increases, it is expected that the range required to maintain connectivity decreases; $r_c(N)$ is a decreasing function of N. Suppose we consider a range such that

$$\pi r_c^2(N) = \frac{\ln N + c(N)}{N}$$

where $c(N)$ is some function of N that we will discuss later. Note that this range assignment essentially means that a disk of area $\ln N + c(N)/N$ is within reach of a node. Let $P_d(N, r_c(N))$ be the probability that, with this $r_c(N)$, the graph $\mathcal{G}(N, r_c(N))$ is disconnected.

The following has been shown:

$$\liminf_{N \to \infty} P_d(N, r_c(N)) \geq e^{-c}(1 - e^{-c})$$

where $c = \limsup_{N \to \infty} c(N)$. Also,

$$\limsup_{N \to \infty} P_d(N, r_c(N)) \leq 2e^{-c}$$

8.3 Discussion

Let us consider the implication of these results. Suppose we set the range $r_c(N)$ such that

$$\pi r_c^2(N) = \frac{\ln N + c(N)}{N}$$

The first result says: As $N \rightarrow \infty$, suppose $c = \lim \sup_{N \rightarrow \infty} c(N)$ is finite; then, the probability that the network is disconnected is positive. The second result says: As $N \rightarrow \infty$, suppose $c = \lim \sup_{N \rightarrow \infty} c(N)$ is infinite; then, the probability that the network is disconnected goes to zero.

Together, the two results provide a necessary and sufficient condition: As $N \rightarrow \infty$, with the range assignment as shown, the probability that the network remains connected approaches 1 if and only if $\lim \sup_{N \rightarrow \infty} c(N) = \infty$.

The significance of this result is that if we simply set the range such that $\pi r_c^2(N) = (\ln N/N)$, then, *with positive probability*, we would get a disconnected network as N increases. This range assignment decreases too rapidly as N increases. It is necessary to ensure that the decrease is not so rapid; this can be done, e.g., by adding a term $c(N) = \sqrt{N}$ to the numerator, so that we have $\pi r_c^2(N) = (\ln N + \sqrt{N}/N)$. Another example is given by $c(N) = \varepsilon \ln N$, so that we get $\pi r_c^2(N) = ((1 + \epsilon) \ln N/N)$. Even $c(N) = \ln(\ln N)$ suffices to ensure connectivity with high probability as $N \rightarrow \infty$. In all cases, it is still true that the range $r_c(N)$ decreases as N increases; however the decrease is slow enough to ensure connectedness with probability approaching 1.

8.4 Sensing Coverage

Next, let us turn to the question of sensing coverage. We recall that the question here is essentially this: Given an area to be monitored and given a sensing disk around each sensor, how many sensors are required? Now as the node deployment process is random, as a first step, we assume that the nodes are deployed as a two-dimensional spatial Poisson process of intensity λ points per unit area. The significance of the Poisson assumption is that in two nonoverlapping areas, the numbers of sensors are independent random variables. Further, in an area $\mathcal{A}$, the number of sensors is Poisson-distributed with parameter λA, where A is the area of $\mathcal{A}$.

This question must be refined as follows: What is the minimum intensity λ such that the probability that every point in the monitoring region is covered by at least k nodes is close to 1?

Let r_s denote the *sensing radius* of each disk. Let us choose the unit of area such that each sensor covers unit area: $\pi r_s^2 = 1$. Let us define V_k to be the total area that is *not* k-covered. This means that each point in the area V_k is at most $(k - 1)$-covered. V_k is referred to as the *k-vacancy value*. Clearly, V_k is a nonnegative random variable that depends on the particular instance of the Poisson deployment process.

First, it can be shown that no finite λ, no matter how large, can ensure that each point in the monitoring area is covered by at least k nodes. To see this, let $I_k(x)$ denote the indicator function corresponding to k-vacancy at location x. That is,

$$I_k(x) = \begin{cases} 1 & \text{if at most } k - 1 \text{ nodes cover point } x \\ 0 & \text{else} \end{cases}$$

If the point x is covered by at most $(k - 1)$ sensors, then it is within the sensing distance r_s from at most that many sensors. Equivalently, if we draw a circle of radius r_s centered at x, then there are at most $(k - 1)$ sensors within it. Recalling that the deployment process is Poisson with intensity λ and that r_s has been chosen such that the area of a circle with radius r_s is unity, we have

$$\mathbf{Pr}(I_k(x) = 1) = e^{-\lambda} \sum_{i=0}^{k-1} \frac{\lambda^i}{i!}$$

(8.1)

Now V_k can be written as

$$V_k = \int_A I_k(x) dx$$

Then

$$\mathbf{E}(V_k) = \int_A \mathbf{E}(I_k(x)) dx$$
$$= A \mathbf{Pr}(I_k(x) = 1)$$
$$= a^2 e^{-\lambda} \sum_{i=0}^{k-1} \frac{\lambda^i}{i!}$$
$$> 0$$

where we have assumed that $\mathcal{A}$ is a square region with each side of length a. In arriving at the second line, we have used the fact that $\mathbf{Pr}(I_k(x) = 1)$ does not depend on x. We note that $\mathbf{E}(V_k) > 0$ for any finite λ, no matter how large it is. But $\mathbf{E}(V_k) > 0$ implies that $\mathbf{Pr}(V_k = 0)$ cannot be 1. Thus, for any finite λ no matter how large, we see that $\mathbf{Pr}(V_k > 0) > 0$; we cannot ensure that each point in the area is covered by at least k nodes.

■ **Exercise 8.1**

Show that as $\lambda \to \infty$, $\mathbf{E}(V_k) \to 0$. ■

From this exercise, as λ increases, $\mathbf{E}(V_k)$ goes to zero. In other words, $\mathbf{Pr}(V_k = 0) \to 1$ as $\lambda \to \infty$. This agrees with intuition: Given a finite monitoring area, as the intensity of the Poisson process increases, it is expected that the probability of the whole area being k-covered (i.e., covered by at least k or more sensors) will increase to 1.

However, it turns out that even more can be shown. Consider the square area $\mathcal{A}$ with sides of length a. Let $a \to \infty$ and, along with this, let $\lambda \to \infty$ in a certain way to be discussed later.

It can then be shown that even when the monitoring area grows to infinity (i.e., becomes the whole first quadrant), $\mathbf{Pr}(V_k > 0) \to 0$ as $\lambda \to \infty$ in that particular way.

We will say that a point in $\mathcal{A}$ is covered by a sensor if it lies *strictly* within the sensing circle of the sensor, which is the circle of radius r_s centered at it. Consider the sensing circles around the Poisson-distributed sensors in $\mathcal{A}$. Let us define a *crossing* as an intersection point of the boundaries of two or more sensing circles, or an intersection of the boundary of a circle with the boundary of $\mathcal{A}$.

■ Lemma 8.1

If all crossings in $\mathcal{A}$ are k-covered, then $\mathcal{A}$ is k-covered.
                                                                              ■

Figure 8.1 shows a square monitoring region $\mathcal{A}$ with the sensing circles of several sensors. It can be seen that the set of sensing circles *partitions* $\mathcal{A}$ into several coverage patches. Each patch is bounded by the arcs of sensing circles and/or the boundary of $\mathcal{A}$. Some patches are 1-covered, some are 2-covered, and some are 0-covered. If a patch is k-covered, we will also say that the *coverage degree* of the patch is k. It can be seen that *all* points in a patch have the same coverage degree.

Now suppose that all crossings are k-covered. Let us recall that each sensing circle is *open*. Consider a point x whose coverage degree is the *least* in $\mathcal{A}$, say m. If possible, let $m < k$. Let us now consider the patch $\mathcal{S}$ within which x lies. One can claim that the boundary of $\mathcal{S}$ cannot be that of a sensing circle.

Suppose that the boundary of $\mathcal{S}$, the patch with the least coverage degree, is a circle. Then no other sensing circle can overlap with any part of $\mathcal{S}$ since that would break up $\mathcal{S}$ into smaller patches. So, other sensing circles can, at best, touch $\mathcal{S}$ at some points on its circumference.

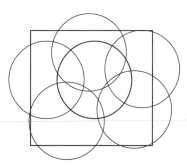

Figure 8.1 Sensor nodes are distributed randomly in a square area. The radius of each circle is r_s, the sensing radius. Several crossings can be seen. The circles define a *partition* of the area.

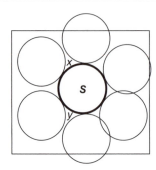

Figure 8.2 The dark circle in the center represents $\mathcal{S}$ (if possible). Other sensing circles cannot overlap with any part of $\mathcal{S}$; at best, the other circles can touch $\mathcal{S}$s circumference. In such a situation, there are points like x, y where the coverage degree is lower than that in $\mathcal{S}$.

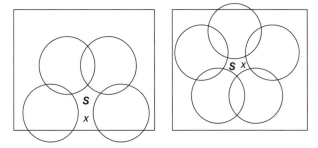

Figure 8.3 Different possibilities for the coverage patch $\mathcal{S}$. When $\mathcal{S}$ is not circular, points on its boundary *can* be crossing points. In these examples, $\mathcal{S}$ is 0-covered. The crossings are 0-covered because they are not *strictly* inside any sensing circle.

Thus, we can at best have $\mathcal{S}$ surrounded by some other sensing circles; see Figure 8.2. The dark circle in the center represents $\mathcal{S}$ (if possible). In such a situation, geometry shows us that there are always points like x, y, in the interstitial spaces, where the coverage degree is lower than that in $\mathcal{S}$. But this leads to a contradiction, because the coverage degree cannot be lower than that in $\mathcal{S}$, where it is lowest. Hence, the boundary of $\mathcal{S}$ cannot be that of a sensing circle.

The possibilities that remain are shown in Figure 8.3. It can be seen that when $\mathcal{S}$ is *not* circular, at least one point on the boundary of $\mathcal{S}$ is a crossing point.

Let us now go back and show by contradiction that if all crossings are k-covered, then $\mathcal{A}$ is also k-covered. As before, let x be a point in $\mathcal{S}$, the coverage patch with the least coverage degree m, with $m < k$. Now, recalling that sensing circles are *open*, a crossing on the boundary of $\mathcal{S}$ cannot have the same coverage degree as the sensing circle on whose circumference it lies; in other words, the crossing is not covered by the circle since it is not strictly inside the circle. Then the coverage degree of the crossing must be the same as that of

$\mathcal{S}$, viz., m. But $m < k$, and this means that not all crossings are k-covered—a contradiction. Therefore, if all crossings are k-covered, it must be true that $\mathcal{A}$ is also k-covered.

Equivalently, Lemma 8.1 states that the event $\{\mathcal{A}$ is not k-covered$\}$ implies the event $\{$there is at least one disk with two or more less-than-k-covered crossings on its boundary$\}$. We use this to proceed with the analysis. Let M_k denote the total number of less-than-k-covered crossings in $\mathcal{A}$. Recalling that V_k is the random variable representing the total area that is not k-covered, we have

$$\mathbf{Pr}(V_k > 0) \leq \mathbf{Pr}(M_k \geq 2)$$

■ Exercise 8.2

Show that

$$\Pr(M_k \geq 2) \leq \frac{E(M_k)}{2}$$

■

Using this, we have $\mathbf{Pr}(V_k > 0) \leq (\mathbf{E}(M_k)/2)$, and we will now proceed to find an upper bound on $\mathbf{E}(M_k)/2$.

Let us consider first the crossings created by two disks intersecting. If two nodes are within a distance of $2r_s$ from each other, their coverage disks intersect. So, given a particular node, the expected number of crossings due to it is twice the expected number of nodes within $2r_s$ of this node, and hence, is given by

$$2\lambda\pi(2r_s)^2$$

where we have used the fact that sensors are distributed according to a Poisson process. The factor 2 in the expression arises because two disks intersect at two points.

■ Exercise 8.3

Show that if N_1 represents the total number of crossings created by two disks intersecting in the square area of side a and $\pi r_s^2 = 1$ (as assumed before), then

$$\mathbf{E}(N_1) = 4\lambda^2 a^2$$

■

Next, we consider the crossings created by coverage disks intersecting the boundary of the deployment area. If a node is within a distance r_s from the boundary, then two crossings are created. Let N_2 denote the number of such crossings in the area.

■ **Exercise 8.4**

Show that

$$\mathbf{E}(N_2) \le 4\lambda ar_s$$

■

Let us recall from Equation (8.1) that the probability that a given crossing is not k-covered is

$$e^{-\lambda} \sum_{i=0}^{k-1} \frac{\lambda^i}{i!}$$

Here, we recall that a crossing is *not* covered by any of the circles that intersect at the crossing. So, as far as k-coverage is concerned, a crossing is just like any other location x in the area. Then we have

$$\mathbf{E}(M_k) = (\mathbf{E}(N_1) + \mathbf{E}(N_2))e^{-\lambda} \sum_{i=0}^{k-1} \frac{\lambda^i}{i!}$$

$$\le (4\lambda^2 a^2 + 4\lambda ar_s)e^{-\lambda} \sum_{i=0}^{k-1} \frac{\lambda^i}{i!}$$

$$\le (4\lambda^2 a^2(1 + o(1)))e^{-\lambda} \sum_{i=0}^{k-1} \frac{\lambda^i}{i!}$$

where, as usual, $o(1)$ indicates a function $f(\lambda)$ such that $\lim_{\lambda \to \infty} f(\lambda) = 0$.

■ **Exercise 8.5**

Show that

$$\frac{\mathbf{E}(M_k)}{2} \le 2a^2 e^{-\lambda} \frac{\lambda^{k+1}}{(k-1)!}(1 + o(1))$$

■

Using these results, we arrive at the following inequality:

$$\mathbf{Pr}(V_k > 0) \le 2a^2 e^{-\lambda} \frac{\lambda^{k+1}}{(k-1)!}(1 + o(1))$$

Now our task is to see how λ should increase with a so that the right-hand side of the expression goes to zero as $a \to \infty$. To this end, consider

$$\lambda = \ln a^2 + (k+1)\ln(\ln a^2) + c(a) \tag{8.2}$$

where $c(a) = o(\ln a^2)$. This means that $\lambda = \ln a^2 + o(\ln a^2)$. Then we have

$$e^{-\lambda} = e^{-\ln a^2} e^{-(k+1)\ln(\ln a^2)} e^{-c(a)}$$

$$= \frac{1}{a^2} \frac{1}{(\ln a^2)^{k+1}} \frac{1}{e^{c(a)}}$$

$$\therefore \frac{\mathbf{E}(M_k)}{2} \leq \frac{2}{(k-1)!} \left(\frac{\lambda}{\ln a^2}\right)^{k+1} \frac{(1+o(1))}{e^{c(a)}}$$

Now $\lambda = \ln a^2 + o(\ln a^2)$ implies that

$$\frac{\lambda}{\ln a^2} \to 1$$

as $a \to \infty$, and we can write $(\lambda/\ln a^2) = 1 + o(1)$. Therefore, we get

$$\frac{\mathbf{E}(M_k)}{2} \leq \frac{2(1+o(1))}{e^{c(a)}(k-1)!}$$

From this expression, we can see that if $c(a) \to \infty$ as $a \to \infty$, then the upper bound on $\mathbf{Pr}(V_k > 0)$ goes to zero as the length of the square goes to ∞. If we did not have the term $c(a)$ in the expression for λ [Equation (8.2)], then we would not be able to assert that $\mathbf{Pr}(V_k > 0) \to 0$ as $a \to \infty$. Thus, a sufficient condition on λ, to ensure that $\mathbf{Pr}(V_k > 0) \to 0$ as $a \to \infty$, *demands* that the term $c(a)$ be present and increase to infinity. As an example, we could have $c(a) = \sqrt{\ln a}$.

Actually, it can be shown that $c(a) \to \infty$ as $a \to \infty$ is not only a sufficient condition for $\mathbf{Pr}(V_k > 0) \to 0$ as $a \to \infty$, but also *necessary*. This means that if $c(a)$ is bounded above as $a \to \infty$, then $\mathbf{Pr}(V_k > 0)$ remains strictly positive.

8.5 Discussion

We began this section with the question: How dense should the deployment of sensors be so that an entire area $\mathcal{A}$ is k-covered? To get quantitative answers, we modeled the distribution process as a spatial Poisson process with rate λ. Our first observation was that in a finite area we cannot ensure that each point is k-covered, no matter how large λ is. However, it *is* true that as λ increases, the probability of a nonzero less-than-k-covered area tends to zero; with high probability, the entire area becomes k-covered.

Next, we considered $\mathcal{A}$ to be a square area of side a, and allowed a to increase to infinity. The question was: How should λ change so that, as in the finite case, the entire first quadrant is

k-covered with arbitrarily high probability? It is, of course, expected that λ should increase to infinity; however, the increase has to satisfy some criterion, as Equation (8.2) shows.

8.6 Localization

In many situations of practical interest, sensor nodes are strewn randomly over the deployment area. Consequently, the position of each sensor node is not known a priori. Position information, however, is crucial in many situations; e.g., to report *where* an event has occurred. Moreover, knowledge of node positions can be exploited in routing also, as in *geographic routing*. Hence, localization is an important problem in sensor networks.

Let us consider several sensors distributed over an area. A small fraction of these are *anchor* devices that know their own positions. They could be GPS-enabled, or they could have been placed precisely at particular positions, with the position information being programmed into them. The problem is to localize the other sensors with help from these anchors.

A crude idea of the distance from an anchor node can be obtained by noting the strength of the signal received from the anchor and the transmit power of the anchor. The quality of a distance estimate obtained in this way depends on the accuracy of the model of signal attenuation used. Further, the transmit power used by an anchor may not be easily available to a sensor. For this reason, let us consider "range-free" localization, where we do not calculate distances from anchors based on the received signal strength.

Suppose each anchor sends out messages including its own position and including a hop count parameter. The anchor initializes the hop count to 1. A sensor (i.e., nonanchor node) receiving the message notes down the anchor's position and the hop count contained in the packet. Next, it increments the hop count value and broadcasts the packet again.

In this way, a wave of packets originates from an anchor and spreads outward. If a sensor receives a packet with a hop count value that is greater than the one stored locally, it ignores the received packet.

The hop count from the i-th anchor, stored at a sensor, is a crude measure of its distance from the anchor. As the density of sensor deployment increases, the distance estimate indicated by the hop count becomes more reliable. As the density increases, sensors at the same hop count from an anchor tend to form concentric rings, of annular width approximately r_c, where r_c is the communication range of a sensor. Thus, if h_i is the hop count from anchor i, then the sensor is at a distance approximately $h_i r_c$ from anchor i.

After obtaining several node–anchor distance estimates as before, nodes follow the multilateration technique. Suppose a node has heard from M anchors, and the anchors' positions are, respectively, (x_i, y_i), $1 \le i \le M$. The sensor node j is located at position (x_j, y_j), and this information is not available to it. The actual distance between node j and anchor i is given by

$$d_{j,i} = \sqrt{(x_j - x_i)^2 + (y_j - y_i)^2}$$

which, of course, is unknown in j. The estimate of this distance that *is* available to j is $\hat{d}_{j,i} := h_i r_c$. Then, a natural criterion that can be used to determine the unknown (x_j, y_j) is the total *localization error* E_j, defined as

$$E_j = \sum_{i=1}^{M} (d_{j,i} - \hat{d}_{j,i})^2$$

$$= \sum_{i=1}^{M} \left(\sqrt{(x_j - x_i)^2 + (y_j - y_i)^2} - \hat{d}_{j,i} \right)^2$$

■ Exercise 8.6

Show that the partial derivatives of E_j with respect to x_j and y_j are given by

$$\frac{\partial E_j}{\partial x_j} = 2\sum_{i=1}^{M} (x_j - x_i)\left(1 - \frac{\hat{d}_{j,i}}{d_{j,i}}\right) \quad \text{and} \quad \frac{\partial E_j}{\partial y_j} = 2\sum_{i=1}^{M} (y_j - y_i)\left(1 - \frac{\hat{d}_{j,i}}{d_{j,i}}\right)$$

■

Using these expressions, we can get an iterative procedure to obtain x_j and y_j. We start with some initial guess of the position of $j : (x_j^{(0)}, y_j^{(0)})$. This allows us to calculate $d_{j,i}$ approximately, and also evaluate $\partial E_j / \partial x_j$ and $\partial E_j / \partial y_j$. Then, *updates* to the initial guessed position can be obtained as

$$\Delta x_j = -\alpha \frac{\partial E_j}{\partial x_j} \quad \text{and} \quad \Delta y_j = -\alpha \frac{\partial E_j}{\partial y_j} \frac{dy}{dx}$$

where α is a small positive fraction. It can be seen that the sign of the update Δx_j is always opposite that of $\partial E_j / \partial x_j$; a similar conclusion follows for the update Δy_j. The updated position is obtained by taking a small step in the direction of the *negative gradient* of error with respect to the current position. Therefore, the iterative process of updating positions is such that the error tends to decrease.

Essentially, this method estimates distance from an anchor by the hop count from that anchor. In a dense deployment of sensors, this estimate is reasonable. Thus, it can be expected that the quality of the localization obtained from this method is critically dependent on the density of sensor deployment. Further, the method also assumes that the communication range r_c is known.

8.6.1 Convex Position Estimation

We now discuss an alternative approach to sensor localization in which a *convex* position estimation problem is formulated and solved. As before, it is assumed that the positions of anchors are known. A sensor node wishing to localize itself notes the identities of the anchors it can hear and computes its position as follows.

If a sensor node j can hear an anchor i, then j must be within a distance r_c from i. In other words, j can be localized to within a circle of radius r_c around i. Let us assume that the *boundary* of the circle of radius r_c is out of bounds, and the distance between i and j should be *strictly* less than r_c. Formally, we have

$$||\mathbf{i} - \mathbf{j}||_2 < r_c \tag{8.3}$$

where $\mathbf{i} = (x_i, y_i)$ and $\mathbf{j} = (x_j, y_j)$ are the positions of anchor i and node j, respectively, in the two-dimensional plane, and $||\mathbf{i} - \mathbf{j}||_2$ represents the Euclidean norm of $(\mathbf{i} - \mathbf{j})$, i.e.,

$$||\mathbf{i} - \mathbf{j}||_2 = \sqrt{(x_i - x_j)^2 + (y_i - y_j)^2}$$

This constraint can be represented in terms of a *Linear Matrix Inequality* (LMI), as we discuss now. The motivation for formulating the constraint in these terms comes from the availability of powerful numerical methods for solving such problems.

Let us recall how a *positive definite* matrix $\mathbf{F}$ is defined. Suppose $\mathbf{F}$ is a real and symmetric $N \times N$ matrix. Then $\mathbf{F}$ is positive definite if for every *nonzero N vector* $\mathbf{u} \in \mathbb{R}^N$, $\mathbf{u}^T \mathbf{F} \mathbf{u} > 0$, where $\mathbf{u}^T$ denotes the transpose of $\mathbf{u}$.

We note the following facts. Let

$$\mathbf{G} = \begin{bmatrix} \mathbf{G}_1 & \mathbf{G}_2 \\ \mathbf{G}_3 & \mathbf{G}_4 \end{bmatrix} \tag{8.4}$$

be a positive definite $N \times N$ matrix, where $\mathbf{G}_1$ is an $M \times M$ matrix, $\mathbf{G}_4$ is an $(N - M) \times (N - M)$ matrix, and the dimensions of $\mathbf{G}_2$ and $\mathbf{G}_3$ are evident ($\mathbf{G}_2$ and $\mathbf{G}_3$ are not necessarily square matrices). Then it is known that

- $\mathbf{G}_1$ and $\mathbf{G}_4$ are both positive definite.

- $\mathbf{G}_4 - \mathbf{G}_3\mathbf{G}_1^{-1}\mathbf{G}_2$ is also positive definite. ($\mathbf{G}_4 - \mathbf{G}_3\mathbf{G}_1^{-1}\mathbf{G}_2$ is called the *Schur complement* of $\mathbf{G}_1$ in $\mathbf{G}$.)

To see how this is used, consider the real, symmetric matrix

$$\mathbf{F} = \begin{bmatrix} r_c\mathbf{I}_2 & \mathbf{i} - \mathbf{j} \\ (\mathbf{i} - \mathbf{j})^T & r_c \end{bmatrix}$$

where $\mathbf{I}_2$ is the 2×2 identity matrix. By correspondence with Equation (8.4), $N = 3$ and $M = 2$ here. Suppose that $\mathbf{F}$ is positive definite. Then, considering the Schur complement of $r_c\mathbf{I}_2$ in $\mathbf{F}$, we have

$$\mathbf{G}_4 - \mathbf{G}_3\mathbf{G}_1^{-1}\mathbf{G}_2 = r_c - (\mathbf{i} - \mathbf{j})^T \frac{1}{r_c}\mathbf{I}_2^{-1}(\mathbf{i} - \mathbf{j})$$

$$= r_c - \frac{1}{r_c}\|\mathbf{i} - \mathbf{j}\|_2^2$$

As $\mathbf{F}$ is positive definite, so is the Schur complement, and therefore we have $(r_c - (1/r_c)\|\mathbf{i} - \mathbf{j}\|_2^2) > 0$, as positive definiteness reduces to simple positivity for a 1×1 matrix. Thus, we get

$$\|\mathbf{i} - \mathbf{j}\|_2 < r_c$$

as in Equation (8.3). Here $\mathbf{i}$ represents the position of the anchor, which is known. The position of the node is unknown, which means that $\mathbf{j}$ is unknown. The matrix $\mathbf{F}$ can be regarded as a function of the unknowns x_j, y_j; thus, $\mathbf{F} = \mathbf{F}(x_j, y_j)$. What we saw earlier can be rephrased as follows: If $\mathbf{j}$ is such that $\mathbf{F}(x_j, y_j)$ is positive definite, then $\|\mathbf{i} - \mathbf{j}\|_2 < r_c$. Thus, if we *define* the set of *feasible positions* for node j as the set

$$\{j : \mathbf{F}(x_j, y_j) \text{ is positive definite}\}$$

then we are assured that the constraint $\|\mathbf{i} - \mathbf{j}\|_2 < r_c$ is respected. It may be noted that this definition is *sufficient* for the condition in Equation (8.3) to hold. Hence, by this definition, we get a *smaller* feasible set than that indicated by Equation (8.3). The smaller feasible set is the price we pay when we formulate the problem in terms of a LMI.

■ Exercise 8.7

Show that the preceding set, viz.,

$$\{j : \mathbf{F}(x_j, y_j) \text{ is positive definite}\}$$

is convex; i.e., the set of feasible positions for node j is a convex set. This is why this approach is referred to as convex position estimation.

In the previous discussion, we have considered the situation when node j hears only one anchor, viz., anchor i. What happens when j hears from M anchors? The LMI approach readily extends to cover this situation. For this, we have to define a number of matrices $\mathbf{F}^{(i)}(x_j, y_j)$, $i = 1, 2, ..., M$, as follows:

$$\mathbf{F}^{(i)}(x_j, y_j) = \begin{bmatrix} r_c \mathbf{I}_2 & \mathbf{i} - \mathbf{j} \\ (\mathbf{i} - \mathbf{j})^T & r_c \end{bmatrix}$$

For each $i = 1, 2, ..., M$, the arguments of $\mathbf{F}^{(i)}$ are the same: the unknowns (x_j, y_j). One can arrange these matrices in block-diagonal form to get a large block-diagonal matrix $\mathbf{F}(x_j, y_j)$:

$$\mathbf{F}(x_j, y_j) = \begin{bmatrix} \mathbf{F}^{(1)} & 0 & \cdots & 0 & 0 \\ 0 & \mathbf{F}^{(2)} & 0 & \cdots & 0 \\ & & \cdots & & \\ 0 & 0 & \cdots & 0 & \mathbf{F}^{(M)} \end{bmatrix}$$

■ Exercise 8.8

Show that this block-diagonal matrix $\mathbf{F}(x_j, y_j)$ is positive definite if and only if each block matrix $\mathbf{F}^{(i)}(x_j, y_j)$, $i = 1, 2, ..., M$, is also positive definite.   ■

Suppose we require $\mathbf{F}(x_j, y_j)$ to be positive definite. Then, by virtue of the preceding exercise, $\mathbf{F}^{(i)}(x_j, y_j)$ is also positive definite for $i = 1, 2, ..., M$. This, in turn, allows us to conclude that if $\mathbf{j} = (x_j, y_j)$ is feasible, then $\|\mathbf{i} - \mathbf{j}\| < r_c$ for each anchor $i = 1, 2, ..., M$. Thus, if a feasible point exists, it is guaranteed to be in the intersection of the circular discs of radius r_c around each anchor.

Thus, for each sensor j that needs to be localized, we can pose the problem: Find $\{\mathbf{j}: \mathbf{F}(x_j, y_j)$ is positive definite$\}$, where M represents the number of anchors that j hears from. As we saw, this will give a convex feasible set to which j can be localized.

Further, the feasible set obtained can be bounded within a rectangle. For this, consider a two-element vector $\mathbf{c}$, and consider the following semidefinite program (SDP):

$$\min c^T \mathbf{j}$$
subject to
$$\mathbf{F}(x_j, y_j) \succ 0$$

where $\mathbf{F}(x_j, y_j) \succ 0$ means $\mathbf{F}(x_j, y_j)$ is positive definite. An SDP is a generalization of a linear program in which the objective function is linear in the unknowns, but the constraints are expressed in terms of a positive/negative definite/semidefinite matrix. As mentioned before, efficient computational methods for solving SDPs are available.

In this formulation, $\mathbf{c}$ represents the cost of the position estimation (x_j, y_j) that we are interested in. Suppose we choose $\mathbf{c} = (1, 0)^{\mathrm{T}}$. Then, the SDP corresponds to finding the *smallest* x_j that is consistent with the feasibility constraint. On the other hand, consider $\mathbf{c} = (-1, 0)^{T}$; now the SDP corresponds to finding the *largest* x_j that is consistent with the feasibility constraint. Similarly, by choosing appropriate values of $\mathbf{c}$, we can obtain bounds on y_j, too.

8.7 Discussion

This approach leads to the conclusion that it is possible to obtain a rectangular bounding box within which each sensor j can be localized (see Figure 8.4). In this way, each sensor can be localized to a rectangular box within which it must lie. As long as the feasible set is nonempty, the dimensions of the box provide estimates of location errors along the x and y axes.

The convex position estimation approach discussed previously also requires knowledge of the communication radius r_c, just as the first method did. However, in contrast to the first method, the convex position estimation method does not demand dense sensor deployment. Further, the first method was iterative, but the second method discussed is not. On the other hand, the LMI-based approach can place a significant computational burden on the sensors.

8.7.1 Routing

Standard table-driven routing approaches are often not attractive in the sensor network context. Route discovery and route maintenance are periodic and energy-intensive tasks, and

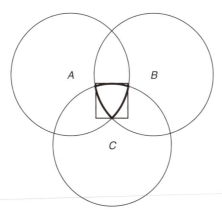

Figure 8.4 A sensor node *j* which hears from three anchor nodes will lie in the intersection of the three circles. Thus, the closed region *ABC* is the feasible set. The dark rectangle around *ABC* gives the bounding box within which the feasible region must lie.

typical sensor nodes are severely constrained in energy, memory, and computing power. Thus, alternate approaches have been considered in the literature.

Let us consider routing ideas referred to as geographic or geometric or position-based routing. Its characteristic features are: (1) every node knows its own position and the positions of its neighbors; (2) the source knows the position of the destination; (3) there are no routing tables stored in the nodes; (4) the additional information stored in a packet is bounded above by a constant times the number of nodes in the graph; the additional information is $o(|\mathcal{V}|)$, where $\mathcal{V}$ is the vertex set of the graph $\mathcal{G}(\mathcal{V},\mathcal{E})$ representing the sensor network. Because of the memory restrictions, geometric routing is known also as $o(1)$-memory routing. Evidently, geometric routing is based entirely on local information. We will assume that nodes have *acquired knowledge of their own positions.*

The simplest approach is for a source node s to forward data to a neighbor who is closer to t. Basically, this is a *greedy* approach—a packet is passed to a neighbor who is closest to the destination.

As can be expected, however, the greedy approach does not always work: What if none of the neighbors of a node i is closer to the destination t than i itself? An example is shown in Figure 8.5.

As mentioned before, we will consider the sensor network as a graph, with the node positions being the vertices and a link between two nodes being an edge. For simplicity, we will assume that all nodes transmit at the same power, so that the communication radius r_c is the same for all nodes. This means that any two nodes at a distance less than or equal to r_c can communicate directly with each other. If r_c is defined as the unit of distance, then we have what is called a *Unit Disk Graph* (UDG).

In a dense network, it is clear that a UDG will give rise to numerous edges. Typically, in a graph with a large number of edges, significant computational effort is required to find routes

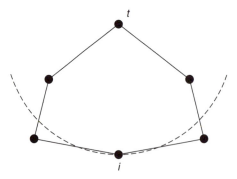

Figure 8.5 Scenario where greedy routing fails. Neither of the neighbors of *i* is closer to the destination *t* than *i* itself.

between pairs of nodes. In a resource-constrained sensor network, one can ill-afford this energy expenditure.

This suggests that *removing* some edges from the UDG, while retaining graph connectivity, is an option worth exploring. However, removing edges also means that path lengths between pairs of nodes increase; e.g., if the direct link between i and j is removed, then evidently, these nodes are connected through a multihop path instead of the earlier single-hop one. Now higher bit rates may be achievable over paths with fewer hops. Clearly, we are trading off bit rate for computational efficiency here.

A *planar* graph is one that *can* be drawn such that no edges intersect on the plane. When it *is* drawn in such a way, what we get is a plane graph. Planar graphs are of interest because they are usually sparse, as we will see later. The energy and computation overhead of finding routes can be expected to be significantly less on a sparse graph.

It is noteworthy that a given graph may *appear* to have edge intersections, but it may be possible to distort the given graph, while ensuring that each edge connects the same pair of nodes as before, so that in the new drawing there are no edge crossings on the plane. For example, the graph on the left in Figure 8.6 can be redrawn as shown on the right, keeping all edges between the same pair of nodes in both cases.

How would one obtain a planar graph from a UDG? One possibility is to start with the node positions of the original UDG, eliminate all edges in the UDG, and then reintroduce some edges appropriately. Several standard geometric constructions are used to get planar graphs in this way. The basic idea is to introduce an edge between nodes i and j, say $i \rightarrow j$, if a suitable region around $i \rightarrow j$ (called the *witness region*) is free of other nodes.

Let $d(i, j)$ be the geometric or Euclidean distance between nodes i and j. Consider two circles of radius $d(i, j)$ centered around the nodes i and j (see Figure 8.7). The intersection of the two circles is called the *lune*. Suppose we introduce the edge $i \rightarrow j$ if the lune is free of other nodes. If we do this for every pair of nodes, we get the *Relative Neighborhood Graph* (RNG).

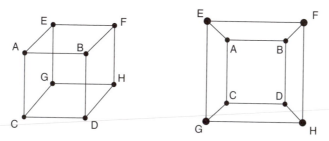

Figure 8.6 The graph on the left is planar because it can be redrawn as shown on the right, keeping all node adjacencies unchanged.

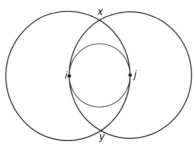

Figure 8.7 Obtaining the Relative Neighborhood Graph (RNG) and the Gabriel Graph (GG) from the node positions. To get the RNG, we introduce edge $i \rightarrow j$ if the lune *ixjy* is free of other nodes. To get the GG, we introduce edge $i \rightarrow j$ if the circle of diameter $d(i, j)$ within the lune is free of other nodes.

On the other hand, suppose we introduce the edge $i \rightarrow j$ if the circle of diameter $d(i, j)$ within the lune is free of other nodes. Doing this for every pair of nodes gives us the *Gabriel Graph* (GG). For the RNG, the witness region is the lune; for the GG, the witness region is the circle within the lune.

It is known that both the RNG and the GG are planar graphs. Further, it is also evident that the RNG is a subgraph of the GG. It turns out that both of these planar graphs can be computed using local algorithms, involving exchange of information among a node and its neighbors only.

We observe that a planar graph induces a partitioning of the plane into a set of regions with disjoint interiors. Each such region is called a face. The outer unbounded region is also regarded as a face.

To get around the problem encountered with greedy routing, consider a strategy that routes along the boundaries of the faces that are crossed by the straight line between the source and the destination. Figure 8.8 shows an example.

In Figure 8.8, we see four faces, $F1$, $F2$, $F3$, and $F4$, in the planar graph. The source s and the destination t are also marked. $F1$ is the face that contains s and the line s, t intersects $F1$. To begin with, say the boundary of $F1$ is explored, in the clockwise direction. This is indicated by the thin solid arrows in Figure 8.8. As the boundary is traversed, the algorithm notes all points where the line s, t intersects the boundary, and the point closest to t is stored for future use. In Figure 8.8, there is only one such point, viz., $p1$. After traversing the whole boundary and reaching s again, a second traversal (along the dashed line) is started. This time, when $p1$ is reached, the face $F2$ is explored in a similar manner. We may refer to the point $p1$ as a switch point.

In this way, faces are explored successively, with a new face being taken up at switch points closest to t. It can be shown that on simple planar graphs, face routing terminates in $o(N)$

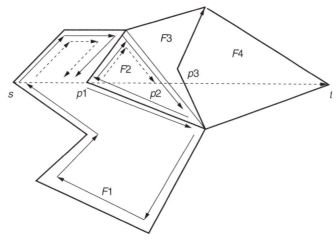

Figure 8.8 A planar graph with four faces—F1, F2, F3, and F4—is shown. s and t are the source and the destination, respectively. p1, p2, and p3 are the points at which the straight line from s to t intersects the edges between the corresponding faces. The solid lines with arrows indicate the first circumnavigation around a face, and the dashed lines indicate the second traversal until the switch point. After the switch point is reached, the packet retraces its path and starts moving around an adjacent face.

steps, where N is the number of nodes. Essentially, the idea is to show that in the course of the execution of the face routing algorithm, each edge is traversed *at most* a constant number of times. Then, a theorem about planar graphs is applied; this theorem says that the number of edges $|\mathcal{E}|$ in a connected plane graph with at least three vertices satisfies

$$|\mathcal{E}| \leq 3|\mathcal{V}| - 6$$

This relation is significant, because it indicates that planar graphs are basically sparse graphs. In a fully connected graph, the number of edges is $o(|\mathcal{V}|^2)$, whereas the relation asserts that in a planar graph, the upper bound is only a linear function of $|\mathcal{V}|$.

Using this relationship, it follows that face routing terminates in $o(N)$ steps, as $|\mathcal{V}| = N$. Thus, we are assured that face routing works correctly. Nevertheless, face routing may select a path that is considerably longer than the shortest path between a pair of nodes.

This description provides the principle underlying the face routing algorithm. In practice, nodes will need to deduce the locations of the switch points p_1, p_2, and p_3. This is possible because each node knows its own position and the positions of its neighbors, as well as the positions of the source s and destination t, because the latter are carried in the packet header.

In summary, we note that face routing requires very little memory and computation, but the price to be paid is the knowledge of nodes' own positions, as well as the positions of their neighbors. Not unexpectedly, face routing is sensitive to the accuracy of position information, and large errors in position may cause face routing to fail.

8.7.2 Attribute-Based Routing

In the previous section, we considered a routing approach that relied upon nodes knowing their own positions. In this section, we consider a routing strategy that is oblivious to the nodes' positions and even addresses. In fact, the routing scheme to be discussed here does not even *attempt* to reach a specific node from another; it uses a completely different philosophy.

In a deployed sensor network, a specific type of event may be of interest. For example, in a sensor network used for environment monitoring, observations of a particular type of animal may be of interest. The strategy in *attribute-based* routing schemes is to launch a query that *describes the data of interest*. As this query propagates through the network, it encounters nodes that have observed the event of interest. Such nodes now provide replies that move back toward the original node issuing the query. Thus, attribute-based routing provides a way for information seekers and information gatherers to "meet," *without* knowing one another beforehand.

Data are described by *attribute-value* pairs that characterize the information that is of interest. For example, a query can be expressed as a *record* consisting of multiple attribute-value pairs:

```
type = animal
instance = leopard
rectangle = [0, 400, 0, 400]
```

In the first line, "type" is the attribute and "animal" is the value; similarly, "instance" is the attribute and "leopard" is the value. The third line specifies an area (in some coordinate system) within which the observation is sought; a rectangle of size 400×400 is shown here, with the ranges along the x and y axes specified.

A prominent example of attribute-based routing is provided by a scheme known as *Directed Diffusion* (DD). In DD terminology, the node issuing the query is called a *sink*, while the nodes providing the observation are called *sources*. The query itself is referred to as the *interest*. In the following paragraphs, we provide a high-level description of how DD finds paths between sources and sinks.

To begin with, the sink broadcasts the interest. As shown in the previous example, the interest is a collection of several attribute-value pairs, among which are the attributes *duration*, *interval*, and *update*. The duration attribute specifies the period of time for which the interest is valid. The interval attribute specifies the intervals at which the observation is to be reported. Implicit in this attribute is the characteristic of DD that *repeated observations* of the event of interest are important. Further, the duration attribute indicates that the interest persists for some time. Both attributes suggest that the sink is not satisfied with just one observation of the event; rather observations extended over time are important. This allows DD to amortize the cost of finding paths between sources and sinks over the duration of the communication. The use of the update attribute is discussed shortly.

The interest generated originally by the sink passes through nodes in the network. A node that receives the interest checks if it has any event record that matches the interest. If it does, then it becomes a source and proceeds to relay the information back to the sink; we will see this in more detail shortly. If it does not, then it forwards the received interest to its neighbors.

Each node maintains an *interest cache*, where valid interests are stored. Along with each interest, the node notes down the neighbor from which the interest was received. It is noteworthy that this is strictly *local information*; the sink that generated the interest in the first place is not tracked.

A particular interest may be received at a node from a number of neighbors because, initially, the interest is flooded through the network and may arrive at the node via multiple paths. All such neighbors are stored in the interest cache. How often should each neighbor receive a report of the observed event? This is determined by the *update* attribute of the interest received from that neighbor. The smaller the value of update, the more frequently the neighbor receives a report. In fact, the update attribute determines what is called a *gradient* toward a neighbor, where gradient is defined as the reciprocal of the update value.

In this way, utilizing neighbors and the gradient toward each neighbor, an observed event record makes its way back toward the sink. As in the forward pass when the interest was making its way into the network, the requested information may arrive back at the sink over multiple paths. In the DD scheme, the update attribute is now used in a clever way to reinforce good quality paths.

To do this, the sink observes the returned reports received from various neighbors. The neighbor from which the *first* report was received is likely to lie on the least-delay path from the source to the sink. The sink now resends the interest to *this* particular neighbor, with a smaller update attribute. This leads to higher gradients being set up all along the backward path from the source to the sink. In this way, DD provides a way of adaptively selecting preferred paths. Similarly, the update interval toward a nonpreferred neighbor can be increased, so that ultimately, that particular path from source to sink is suppressed.

It is worth noting that DD is inherently robust to node failures, because if the currently preferred path becomes unavailable (due to node failure, say), then an alternate path (which was currently not preferred) may be picked up and reinforced by update attribute manipulation.

8.8 Function Computation

Let us imagine a situation where N sensors have been distributed uniformly and independently in a square area A. These sensors have self-organized to form a network. In particular, the transmission range of each has been set to a value $r_c(N)$ such that the network $\mathcal{G}(N, r_c(N))$ is *connected* asymptotically; the probability that $\mathcal{G}(N, r_c(N))$ is connected goes to 1 as N goes to infinity. As we have seen before, this will happen when

$$r_c(N) = \sqrt{\frac{\ln N + c(N)}{\pi N}} \tag{8.5}$$

with $\limsup_{N \to \infty} c(N) = \infty$.

The sensors make periodic measurements. There is a single sink in the network where some function of the sensors' measurements is to be computed. The function, in general, would depend on the inference problem that the sensor network has been designed to solve. For example, in an event-detection application, the function could be the conditional probability of the sensor output being in a certain range, given that there has been no event (the *null* hypothesis). In statistics, such a function is referred to as a *likelihood* function, and it is extensively used in event detection.

One naive way to compute the function is to forward *all* the measured data to the sink, which then computes the function. This is a centralized model of computation. However, this fails to take advantage of the processing capability of the sensors. An alternative approach is *in-network processing*, where the sensors compute intermediate results and forward these to the sink. This aggregation helps in reducing the amount of data to be forwarded to the sink, and thus helps in easing congestion as well as prolonging battery life.

For example, consider a linear network of $(N + 1)$ sensors as shown in Figure 8.9, with s denoting the sink. Suppose that each sensor measures the temperature in its neighborhood and the objective is to compute the maximum temperature. If all measurements are simply forwarded to the sink, then the communication effort is $o(N^2)$; sensor 1 data requires N hops to reach the sink, sensor 2 data requires $(N - 1)$ hops, and so on. On the other hand, an alternate strategy is one in which node i compares received data with its own measurement and forwards the maximum of the two. In this strategy, in-network processing is being done, and the communication effort drops to just $o(N)$.

Figure 8.9 A linear network of $(N + 1)$ sensors is shown. Each sensor makes measurements, and the maximum of all measurements is desired at the sink s.

Suppose that the N sensors make periodic measurements. Let each sensor reading belong to a discrete set χ. Let time be slotted. $\mathbf{X}^{(t)}$ denotes the vector of N sensor readings at discrete time slot t. Let us also assume that readings over a period $t = 1, 2, \ldots, T$ are available with each sensor; here T is the block length over which measurements have been collected. The $N \times T$ matrix $\mathbf{X}$ represents the complete data set, across sensors as well as across the block length, that is available. $\mathbf{X}_i$, the i-th row of the matrix, represents the readings of the i-th sensor over the block. Correspondingly, the t-th column $\mathbf{X}^{(t)}$ represents the readings across the sensors at time t. The objective is to compute the function $f(\mathbf{X}^{(t)})$, for every $t \in \{1, 2, \ldots, T\}$.

Generally, if $\mathcal{C}$ is a subset of sensors, then $f(\mathbf{X}_{\mathcal{C}}^{(t)})$ is the function computed by taking the readings of sensors in the set $\mathcal{C}$ at time t.

We have tacitly assumed that the function to be computed admits distributed computation in a divide-and-conquer fashion, in which the result of a partial computation by some sensors is forwarded to others, which then repeat the process. To formally state the property that we assumed, we introduce the notion of *divisible functions*.

Let $\mathcal{C}$ be a subset of $\{1, 2, \ldots, N\}$, and let $\pi := \{\mathcal{C}_1, \mathcal{C}_2, \ldots, \mathcal{C}_s\}$ be a *partition* of $\mathcal{C}$. The function $f(\cdot)$ is said to be divisible, if for any $\mathcal{C} \subset \{1, 2, \ldots, N\}$ and any partition $\pi = \{\mathcal{C}_1, \mathcal{C}_2, \ldots, \mathcal{C}_s\}$ of $\mathcal{C}$, there exists a function $g^{(\pi)}(\cdot)$ such that

$$f(\mathbf{X}_{\mathcal{C}}^{(t)}) = g^{(\pi)}(f(\mathbf{X}_{\mathcal{C}_1}^{(t)}), f(\mathbf{X}_{\mathcal{C}_2}^{(t)}), \ldots, f(\mathbf{X}_{\mathcal{C}_s}^{(t)}))$$

This says that if we know the values of the function $f(\cdot)$ evaluated over the sets in any partition π of $\mathcal{C}$, then we can combine these values, using the function $g^{(\pi)}(\cdot)$, to obtain $f(\cdot)$ evaluated over $\mathcal{C}$. Thus, it is possible to compute $f(\mathbf{X}_{\mathcal{C}}^{(t)})$ in a divide-and-conquer fashion.

■ Exercise 8.9

Let each sensor reading belong to a discrete set $\mathcal{X}$. Consider the function $\tau(\mathbf{X}^{(t)})$ that gives the frequency histogram or "type vector" corresponding to the sensor readings $\mathbf{X}^{(t)}$ at time t. This function is a vector with $|\mathcal{X}|$ elements, where $|\mathcal{X}|$ denotes the size of the set $\mathcal{X}$:

$$\tau : \mathcal{X}^N \rightarrow \{0, 1, 2, \ldots, N\}^{|\mathcal{X}|}$$

Show that $\tau(\cdot)$ is a divisible function.   ■

■ Exercise 8.10

Show that the function that provides the *second largest value* in a set of sensor measurements is *not* divisible.   ■

Let $\mathcal{R}(f)$ denote the range of the function; let us recall that the range of a function $f : \mathcal{X} \to \mathcal{Y}$ is defined as

$$f(\mathcal{X}) := \{y \in \mathcal{Y} : \exists x \in \mathcal{X} \text{ with } f(x) = y\}$$

■ Exercise 8.11

In Exercise 8.9, is $\mathcal{R}(\tau) = \{0,1,2,...,N\}^{|\mathcal{X}|}$? ■

Now the sensors together compute $f(\mathbf{X}^{(t)})$ for $t = 1, 2, ..., T$, by passing messages among one another according to some scheme. Let $\mathcal{U}_{N,T}$ denote such a scheme. Further, let $\mathcal{T}(\mathcal{U}_{N,T})$ denote the *maximum* time (in slots) taken to complete the computation of the function for all times in $t = 1, 2, ..., T$, where the maximum is taken over all possible values of $\mathbf{X}(t)$, $t = 1, 2, ..., T$. This is the time at which the *sink* in the network is able to obtain the values $f(\mathbf{X}^{(t)})$, $t = 1, 2, ..., T$.

With the previous notation, the *rate* of function computation when scheme $\mathcal{U}_{N,T}$ is defined, in computation/slot, as

$$R(\mathcal{U}_{N,T}) = \frac{T}{\mathcal{T}(\mathcal{U}_{N,T})}$$

Considering the maximum of $R(\mathcal{U}_{N,T})$ over all possible schemes and all possible block lengths T, we obtain the *maximum rate of function computation* for a given divisible function, written as $R_{max}^{(N)}$. The value of $R_{max}^{(N)}$ is specific to the N-sensor network; the superscript in $R_{max}^{(N)}$ is intended to serve as a reminder of this fact.

How large can $R_{max}^{(N)}$ be? To compute $f(\mathbf{X}^{(t)})$, $t = 1, 2, ..., T$, the sink must receive the results of the partial computations carried out by outlying sensors and complete the task using its own data. Considering the protocol model, it is clear that only one link terminating at the sink can be active at any instant. If the maximum possible bit rate on a link is W bits per slot, then the sink cannot receive more than W bits in a slot.

On the other hand, to identify the specific function value $f(\mathbf{X}^{(t)})$, we would need $\log_2 |\mathcal{R}(f)|$ bits, where we have assumed that the discrete set $\mathcal{R}(f)$ has 2^m elements for some $m \geq 1$. This leads to the following upper bound on $R_{max}^{(N)}$:

$$R_{max}^{(N)} \leq \frac{W}{\log_2 |R(f)|}$$

Before proceeding further, let us suppose that N nodes are placed uniformly and independently in the unit square. Let us denote by $\mathcal{G}(N, \phi_N)$ the graph that results when each node is connected to its ϕ_N *nearest neighbors*. Then, $\mathcal{G}(N, \phi_N)$ is connected with high probability if and only if $\phi_N = \Theta(\ln N)$. Specifically, there are two constants $0 < c_1 < c_2$ such that

$$\lim_{N \to \infty} \mathbf{Pr}(\mathcal{G}(N, c_1 \ln N) \text{ is disconnected}) = 1$$

$$\lim_{N \to \infty} \mathbf{Pr}(\mathcal{G}(N, c_2 \ln N) \text{ is connected}) = 1$$

Thus, by selecting a transmission range such that a node connects to at least $c_2 \ln N$ nearest neighbors, we are assured of getting a connected graph with high probability. Also, we note that the *degree* of the resulting graph is $o(\ln N)$ with high probability.

Let us now consider the N-sensor network with the transmission range $r_c(N)$ set appropriately (as before), so that each node has enough numbers of neighbors for the graph to be connected with high probability. Consider a tessellation of the unit square into small squares (called cells) of side $r_c(N)/\sqrt{2}$. This implies that nodes within a cell are always within range of one another.

Let us now define a *cell graph*. Each nonempty cell of the tessellation (see Figure 8.10) is a vertex in the cell graph. Further, two vertices c_1 and c_2 of the cell graph are defined to be adjacent (i.e., to have an edge between them), if we can find a node inside cell c_1 and a node inside cell c_2 such that the nodes are neighbors.

Figure 8.10 shows a cell graph corresponding to a number of sensors deployed randomly in a unit square. The small rectangle inside the cell in the middle represents the sink of the network. Corresponding to each nonempty cell in this tessellation, we have a vertex in the cell graph. Further, as shown in Figure 8.10, we can find a node in cell c_1 and a node in cell c_2 such that these nodes are neighbors (indicated by the line joining them); hence, vertices c_1 and c_2 are adjacent in the cell graph. The figure also shows relay nodes in a cell and relay parents; we define these later.

Let us consider a spanning tree on the cell graph, rooted at the cell containing the sink. It is possible to obtain such a spanning tree because the underlying network of nodes is connected, and, therefore, so is the cell graph.

Consider a cell c and its parent cell in the spanning tree. A node i in cell c will be called the *relay node* in that cell if (1) it has at least one neighbor in cell c, and (2) it collects data from all neighbors in cell c, runs a partial computation on the data, and forwards the result to a node j in an adjacent cell. This node j will be called the *relay parent* of relay i. By definition, a relay node in cell c cannot serve as a relay parent for any other cell.

This definition implies that a cell has a relay node in it only if there are two or more nodes in it. If a cell has only one node, then we will *not* consider that node to be a relay node.

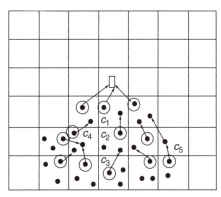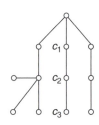

Figure 8.10 On the left panel, a random deployment of sensors is shown. The nodes with a circle around them are the relay nodes. The arrow pointing away from a relay node identifies the corresponding relay parent, located in a parent cell. Cell c_4 has *two* relay parents and one relay, and cell c_2 has one relay, one relay parent, and also a node that is neither a relay nor a relay parent. The cell graph for this deployment would be obtained by considering a vertex for every nonempty cell; two vertices would be adjacent if each of the corresponding cells has a node within communication range of the other. The right panel shows a spanning tree on the cell graph.

However, it will, of course, make measurements and pass them to some other node in an adjacent cell. It can also *receive* measurements from nodes in adjacent cells and pass them on. Thus, the single node *may* behave as a relay parent for relays in adjacent cells. In Figure 8.10, the cell c_5 has a single node in it, and this node behaves as a relay parent; however, it is not considered a relay node.

In summary, a relay node collects data from other nodes in its *own* cell only, whereas a relay parent collects data from relay nodes in *other* cells only. A node can be either a relay or a relay parent, but not both. Of course, it is possible that a node is neither a relay nor a relay parent.

In Figure 8.10, the node with a circle around it is the relay node in that cell, and the arrow indicates its relay parent. As Figure 8.10 shows, there is one relay node in each cell and possibly several relay parents. A node that has neither a circle around it nor an arrow pointing to it is neither a relay node nor a relay parent.

For computing function values, data need to be collected at the sensors and sent toward the sink. On the way, partial function computations can be carried out. In Figure 8.10, the process would start with the sensor nodes in the leaf cells. Next, we outline an approach that makes distributed function computation possible.

Suppose a divisible function $f(\cdot)$ is to be computed at T epochs. Let us divide time into T rounds. For $n = 1, 2, \ldots, T$, round n consists of T_1 slots, where T_1 will be specified later.

In round 1, all *nonrelay* nodes in the leaf cells in Figure 8.10 transmit to the relay node the result of a partial computation of $f(\cdot)$, where the function is evaluated at a node's *own* sensor measurements. For example, in cell c_3 in Figure 8.10, each of the two nonrelay nodes transmits the result of its computation to the relay node in c_3. No other transmission occurs in c_3 or in any other cell.

In round 2, the *relay node* of cell c_3 carries out a partial computation based on the values it received in the previous round, as well as its own sensor reading. The result is transmitted to its *relay parent* in cell c_2. Further, in round 2, the nonrelay nodes in cell c_3 again transmit computed function values to their relay node. No transmissions occur in other cells.

Consider the situation in round 3. Before round 3 begins, the cells that are one hop closer to the sink than the leaf-cells, like cell c_2, have received the results of some particular partial computations. Specifically, before round 3 begins, a relay parent in c_2 already has the result of a partial computation based on the measurements made by a subset of sensors below it. Hence, during round 3, the relay parent is in a position to include its own measurement, carry out the function evaluation, and transmit the result to the relay in c_2; at the end of round 3, we have the result of a partial computation based on the measurements of sensors constituting a *subtree* rooted at the relay parent in c_2. Further, during round 3, the nonrelay nodes in cell c_3 are again occupied in transmitting their results to the relay node in c_3. Similarly, in round 4, it is the relay node in c_2 that carries out a computation and transmits the result to *its* relay parent in c_1.

We can see that intermediate results progress toward the sink along the spanning tree on the cell graph in a *pipeline*. Nodes occurring lower in the tree deposit their computed results with a node that is higher up. In turn, the node that is higher up in the tree picks up the result, includes its own measurement, carries out a fresh partial computation, and passes the result upward. Moreover, as we go up the tree, partial computation and transmission are initiated *later*, once all the necessary inputs have arrived.

Our discussion is summarized in Figure 8.11, for an example cell graph of depth 2. It can be seen that several transmissions need to occur in the same round. How can we be sure that these transmissions can be arranged in time and space such that they do not interfere? In other words, how do we know that a *feasible schedule* exists?

The following observation is critical in showing the existence of a feasible schedule:

> Each cell has a bounded number of *interfering cell-neighbors* (say k_2), where two cells c_1 and c_2 are interfering cell-neighbors if there exist a node in c_1 and a node in c_2 separated by a distance less than the bound imposed by the Protocol Model. This means that interfering cell-neighbors cannot support simultaneous transmissions.

According to the Protocol Model, if node i is transmitting to node j, then other transmitters that can *interfere* with successful reception at node j must be located within a disk of radius $(1 + \Delta)d_{i,j}$ around node j, where $d_{i,j}$ is the distance between nodes i and j. Here, Δ is a parameter used in the Protocol Model.

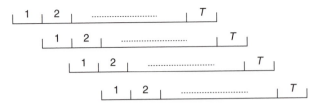

Figure 8.11 Sketch showing *T* rounds of computation and transmission at various nodes. The two rows at the top correspond to the activities of the nonrelay nodes and the relay node, respectively, at the leaf-cells of the cell graph. The two rows at the bottom refer to the actions of the nonrelay nodes and relay node, respectively, in a cell that is one hop closer to the sink. It may be noted that the rounds are *staggered* according the nodes' positions in the cell graph. Computation and transmission are pipelined.

As the number of nodes N increases, the communication range $r_c(N)$ decreases, and so the cells in the tessellation shrink, since the cell side is of length $r_c(N)/\sqrt{2}$. Therefore, interferers must be located within disks of smaller radii around the receivers. This argument leads to the conclusion that the number of interfering cell neighbors is *uniformly bounded*; the bound k_2 does not depend on N. With this, a graph coloring argument (see Exercise 8.8) is used to show that there exists a schedule in which each cell receives 1 out of every $(1 + k_2)$ slots to transmit.

Hence, in an interval of T_1 slots constituting one round, each cell can be allotted $T_1/(1 + k_2)$ slots. Each relay parent j in the cell requires at most $\log_2|\mathcal{R}(f)|$ bits to communicate the result of the partial function computation based on data received from its children. Further, each cell in the cell graph has a uniformly bounded number of children, say k_3, and therefore, it follows that there are *at most* k_3 relay parents per cell.

Similarly, a relay node also requires at most $\log_2|\mathcal{R}(f)|$ bits. A node that is neither a relay parent nor a relay node requires at most $\log_2|\mathcal{X}|$ bits because it merely transmits its own readings.

To get an upper bound on the total number of bits that a cell needs to transmit, we need to bound the number of nodes in a cell. This is where the degree of the sensor node graph plays a role. Let us *assume* that the degree of the sensor node graph $d(\mathcal{G}(N, r_c(N)))$ is bounded above by

$$d(\mathcal{G}(N,r_c(N))) \le k_1 \log_2|R(f)|$$

for some $k_1 > 0$. Clearly, then, the number of nodes in a single cell cannot be more than $k_1 \log_2|\mathcal{R}(f)|$, because, by construction, all nodes in a cell are within communication range. Hence, the total number of bits that a cell needs to transmit per computation is bounded above by

$$k_3 \log_2|\mathcal{R}(f)| + \log_2|\mathcal{R}(f)| + \log_2|\mathcal{X}| \times k_1 \log_2|\mathcal{R}(f)| = (k_3 + 1 + k_1 \log_2|\mathcal{X}|)\log_2|\mathcal{R}(f)|$$

Recalling that in the feasible schedule mentioned earlier, a cell gets $T_1/(1 + k_2)$ slots in an interval of T_1 slots, and also that at most W bits can be sent in a slot, we can see that the transmissions can be feasibly scheduled if

$$\frac{T_1}{1 + k_2} = \frac{(k_3 + 1 + k_1 \log_2 |\mathcal{X}|)\log_2 |R(f)|}{W}$$

We can now get an upper bound on the total time required for the function computation to be completed. Extending the idea depicted in Figure 8.11, it can be seen that for the scheme described, by time $(T + 2\delta_{max})T_1$, the sink can complete T computations (here, δ_{max} is the maximum depth of the spanning tree on the cell graph). This implies that

$$R_{max}^{(N)} \geq \lim_{T \to \infty} \left(\frac{T}{T + 2\delta_{max}} \right)\frac{1}{T_1}$$

$$= \frac{1}{T_1}$$

$$= \frac{W}{(1 + k_2)(k_3 + 1 + k_1 \log_2 |\mathcal{X}| \log_2 |\mathcal{R}(f)|)}$$

Thus, we see that the maximum rate of function computation satisfies

$$\frac{W}{\{(1 + k_2)(k_3 + 1 + k_1 \log_2 |\mathcal{X}|)\}\log_2 |\mathcal{R}(f)|} \leq R_{max}^{(N)} \leq \frac{W}{\log_2 |\mathcal{R}(f)|}$$

and hence

$$R_{max}^{(N)} = \Theta\left(\frac{W}{\log_2 |\mathcal{R}(f)|} \right)$$

8.9 Discussion

We started by noting the communication range $r_c(N)$ that ensures, with high probability, that the graph $\mathcal{G}(N, r_c(N))$ is connected. Then we considered a divisible discrete-valued function $f(\cdot)$, with $\mathcal{R}(f)$ denoting its range. What we found is that *if* the degree of the graph, $d(\mathcal{G}(N, r_c(N)))$, satisfies

$$d(\mathcal{G}(N, r_c(N))) \leq k_1 \log_2 |\mathcal{R}(f)|$$

then the maximum rate of function computation $R_{\text{max}}^{(N)}$ satisfies

$$R_{\text{max}}^{(N)} = \Theta\left(\frac{W}{\log_2|R(f)|}\right)$$

It is worth noting that the proof of the result is constructive, in that a scheme for function computation has been obtained. As the supportable bit rate W increases, it is expected that the rate of function computation will increase, because the network's communication capability has increased. Also, if the range of the function is larger, more bits will be required to specify its value at a particular argument, and hence the rate of computation would decrease. We see that both these aspects are captured in the expression

$$R_{\text{max}}^{(N)} = \Theta\left(\frac{W}{\log_2|\mathcal{R}(f)|}\right).$$

Consider the simple scenario where all measured data simply are uploaded to the sink. In this extreme case, there is no in-network processing at all. For this case, we can consider $f(X^{(t)}) = X^{(t)}$; $f(\cdot)$ is just the *identity function*. Since each sensor measurement takes values in the discrete set $\mathcal{X}$, we have

$$\mathcal{R}(f) = \mathcal{X}^N$$

Thus, $\log_2|\mathcal{R}(f)| = N\log_2|\mathcal{X}|$, i.e., $\log_2|\mathcal{R}(f)|$ is *linear* in N. Therefore, to apply the previous result, we need to check if the degree of the graph is bounded above by a linear function of N. But this is true for *any* connected graph. Hence, applying the result, we then conclude that there *is* a scheme that allows us to communicate $f(\cdot)$, the identity function, at rate $o(1/N)$. Thus, for large sensor networks, straightforward data uploading to the sink will lead to very low rates of extracting information.

8.10 Scheduling

Sensor nodes share the wireless medium. Therefore, they need a MAC protocol to coordinate access. However, in a sensor network, energy efficient MACs are extremely important, and this forces us to look at MAC protocols closely.

Even when a sensor node is not transmitting but merely listening to the medium, significant energy is spent. This is because the electronic circuitry in the radio transceiver has to be kept ON. Studies have shown that the ratio of energy spent in transmitting a packet to a receiver at unit distance to that spent in receiving a packet and to that spent in *listening* for the same length of time is 3:1.05:1. (Of course, when the receiver is far away, a transmitter would use more power and therefore, the energy spent would be more.) The notable point here is that a sensor spends the same order of energy in simply listening on the medium as in actually receiving a packet.

Since saving energy is so important, we need to understand how energy can be *wasted*. The following causes can be discerned.

- *Idle Listening:* If the medium is idle and yet a sensor node's radio transceiver is ON, then it is spending energy unnecessarily.

- *Collision:* If transmissions collide, then all packets involved are garbled, leading to waste of energy all around.

- *Overhearing:* Overhearing occurs when a node receives a packet that is not addressed to it.

- *Control Packet Overhead:* From an application's point of view, energy spent in carrying information bits is energy usefully spent. It is desirable that the energy spent on control path activities, like channel reservation, acknowledgment, and route discovery, be as small as possible.

A good sensor MAC protocol leads to savings on all four of these fronts.

Sensor MAC protocols are significantly different from other wireless MAC protocols (like IEEE 802.11) because they can put the sensors into the *sleep state*. In this state, the radio transceiver is turned OFF completely. Nodes wake up periodically, listen on the medium for a short while, and then go back to sleep. This reduces idle listening drastically, and is a major reason for energy savings.

However, it is also immediate that as a result of the cycling between sleep and wake states, the latency in transferring information across nodes can be considerably increased. A transmitter has to hold on to the information it must send until it is certain that the receiver is ready and listening. Nevertheless, in many application scenarios, the increase in latency does not cause difficulties. For example, in an intrusion detection application, the speed at which the network transfers information is orders of magnitude higher than that of an intruder's movements, even when additional latency due to sleep–wake duty cycling is considered.

8.10.1 S-MAC

The protocol sensor-MAC (S-MAC) is one of the first to use the notion of sleep–wake duty cycles heavily. It aims to ensure a low duty cycle operation on the network. It introduces the notion of *coordinated sleeping*, in which clusters of nodes synchronize their sleep schedules so that all of them sleep together. This ensures that when a node wakes up and wishes to transmit to a neighbor node in its cluster, the neighbor node will be awake to receive the transmission.

S-MAC reduces the energy wasted due to collisions by using the same approach as in IEEE 802.11, viz., distributed channel reservation by RTS–CTS exchange. It is worth recalling that the exchange of RTS and CTS by the transmitter and receiver results in a silent neighborhood around each, allowing the transmission to complete successfully. This means that collisions involving long data packets are avoided at the small additional energy expense due to the short control packets.

Further, S-MAC utilizes the information available in the RTS and CTS packets to reduce overhearing by nodes. The RTS/CTS packet structure includes a duration field, which informs listeners of the interval for which the medium will be busy with the impending packet transfer. All nodes other than the transmitter and receiver can now afford to switch off their radios for this interval.

Finally, S-MAC reduces control packet overhead by resurrecting the old technique of *message passing*. Link layer frames normally have a maximum frame size, and a long message needs to be fragmented into pieces of the largest possible size. Now if each resulting fragment is transmitted as a separate entity, then each must be preceded by the RTS–CTS exchange. To reduce the control overhead, S-MAC proposed that the RTS–CTS exchange be carried out *only once* at the beginning, and the multiple fragments be sent in a burst, one after the other. The reservation interval indicated in the RTS–CTS packets correspond to not just one fragment but the total time required to transmit *all* the fragments.

It is apparent that message passing allows one node to hog the channel and thereby cause unfairness in channel access opportunities among nodes. However, in a sensor network context, node-level unfairness over a *short time interval* is not a matter of concern. As mentioned before, a sensor network is not a collection of nodes that are interested in data transfer in a peer-to-peer fashion. Rather, the network has a single objective and all nodes collaborate toward achieving the same. However, over longer time intervals, we do need fairness because otherwise, distributed computation of functions can get held up.

S-MAC forms a flat, peer-to-peer topology. Thus, unlike clustering protocols, there is no cluster-head to coordinate channel access. We will see that some sensor MACs, like the IEEE 802.15.4 MAC, do require the presence of a coordinator. S-MAC also builds reliability into unicast data transfer by using explicit acknowledgements. Recall that we have seen the same idea before in the context of IEEE 802.11.

Because coordinated sleeping is so important in S-MAC, nodes need to exchange schedules before data transfer can begin. The *SYNC* packet is used for this purpose. The transmission time for a SYNC packet is called the *synchronization period*. Each node maintains a *schedule table* that stores the schedules of all its neighbors.

To choose a schedule, a node first listens for at least the synchronization period. If no SYNC packet is heard within this time, then the node chooses its own schedule and starts to follow it. It also broadcasts its schedule by transmitting its own SYNC packet.

If the node does receive a SYNC packet within the initial listen interval, then it sets its own schedule to the received one. Thus, synchronization with a neighbor is achieved. As before, it announces its schedule by transmitting its own SYNC packet later.

However, the following can also happen: After a node chooses and announces its own schedule, it receives a new and different schedule. What it does now depends on how many neighbors it heard from. If the node had no neighbors, then it discards its original schedule and switches to the new schedule just received. If the node had one or more neighbors, it adopts *both* schedules, by waking up at the listen times of both. Such behavior typically is found among nodes that are located at the borders of two virtual clusters and facilitates communication between the two.

8.10.2 IEEE 802.15.4 (Zigbee)

The other sensor MAC protocol that has received wide attention is the IEEE 802.15.4 MAC. The protocol was introduced first in the context of Low-Rate Wireless Personal Area Networks (LR-WPANs). The physical (PHY) and MAC layers in LR-WPANs are defined by the IEEE 802.15.4 group, whereas the higher layers are defined by the Zigbee alliance.

IEEE 802.15.4 defines two types of devices: a *Full Function Device* (FFD) and a *Reduced Function Device* (RFD). The FFDs are capable of playing the role of a *network coordinator*, but RFDs are not. FFDs can talk to any other device, while RFDs can only talk to an FFD. Thus, one mode of operation of the IEEE 802.15.4 MAC is based on a hierarchy of nodes, with one FFD and several RFDs connected in a *star* topology (see Figure 8.12). The FFD at the hub, which is a network coordinator, plays the role of a cluster-head, and all communication is controlled by it. In the *peer-to-peer* topology, however, all nodes are equally capable; all are FFDs.

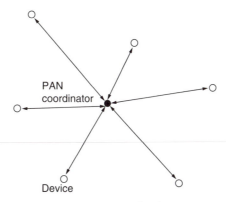

Figure 8.12 IEEE 802.15.4 nodes in a star topology.

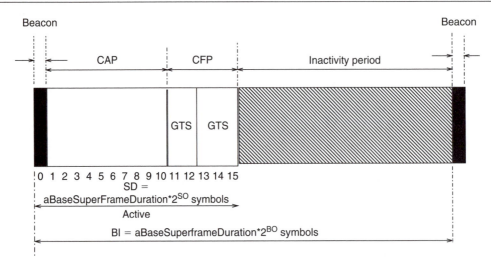

Figure 8.13 The Zigbee MAC superframe structure. CAP and CFP stand for Contention Access Period and Contention Free Period, respectively. GTS means Guaranteed Time Slot. The other parameters in the figure are defined in [16].

Figure 8.13 shows the superframe structure defined for IEEE 802.15.4. The superframe begins with a beacon. Nodes hearing the beacon can set their local clocks appropriately, so that they go to sleep and wake up at the same time. This means *synchronized operation*.

The superframe is divided into an *active* and an *inactive* period. During the inactive period, nodes sleep. The active period consists of at most three parts—beacon transmission interval, the *Contention Access Period* (CAP) and an optional *Contention Free Period* (CFP). During the CAP, nodes contend using slotted CSMA/CA, as in IEEE 802.11. In the CFP, a node can be allotted *Guaranteed Time Slots* (GTSs) by the network coordinator. Nodes request for GTS allocation by sending explicit GTS allocation *requests*. Transmitted frames are always followed by *Inter-Frame Spacings*.

8.11 Notes on the Literature

We began our discussion with a question about the transmission range to be used by sensor nodes such that the network is connected. As the number of nodes increases to infinity, we discussed a necessary and sufficient condition on the transmission range such that the probability that the network remains connected approaches 1. This result is due to Gupta and Kumar [1]. Our discussion of sensing coverage is based on the work of Zhang and Hou [2]. The notion of crossings that we used in analyzing the sensing coverage problem appeared in Wang et al. [3]. Our initial discussion of localization follows Nagpal et al. [4]; the convex position estimation approach follows Doherty et al. [5]. A detailed discussion of Linear Matrix Inequalities, with many applications, can be found in Boyd et al. [6].

The first geographic routing algorithms were greedy, as in Takagi and Kleinrock [7]. West [8] provides a very readable introduction to graph theory and associated algorithms. The notions of Unit Disk Graph, Gabriel Graph, Relative Neighborhood Graph, and Delaunay Triangulation are extensively discussed in books on Computational Geometry, for example, the one by de Berg et al. [9]. The survey article by Jaromczyk and Toussaint [10] also discusses these ideas. Face routing was introduced for the first time by Kranakis, Singh, and Urrutia [11], albeit under a different name. Several refinements are due to Kuhn et al. [12]. Directed Diffusion was proposed by Intanagonwiwat et al. in [13]. Our treatment of function computation follows Giridhar and Kumar [14]. The S-MAC protocol, due to Ye et al., appeared in [15]. See our brief discussion of the IEEE 802.15.4 standard uses in [16].

Problems

8.1 Sensors are deployed according to a Poisson process of rate λ. Assume that each sensor covers a circular area of radius 1 unit. Consider two points x and y. Let C_x be the indicator variable that x is covered by at least one sensor. Find $\mathbf{E}(C_x C_y)$ and $\mathbf{E}((1 - C_x)(1 - C_y))$.

8.2 Sensors are deployed according to a Poisson process of rate λ. Assume that each sensor covers a circular area of radius 1 unit. Now consider an arbitrary straight line path through the sensor field. Find the distribution of the segment of the line covered by a sensor.

8.3 Consider a one-dimensional sensor field in which the sensors are deployed according to a Poisson process on a straight line. Each sensor covers a random segment whose mean is $\bar{X}$. What is the probability that a point is covered by exactly k sensors?

8.4 Consider the sensing coverage problem discussed in Section 8.2. Suppose that the coverage degree of a patch is k. Is the patch an open set or a closed set in $\mathbb{R}^2$?

8.5 Consider the first sensor localization method discussed in Section 8.3. Is it possible that the true distance of sensor j from anchor i, viz., $d_{j,i}$ is equal to the estimated distance $\hat{d}_{j,i}$, for $i = 1, 2, \ldots, M$, but the position of sensor j, as concluded by the algorithm, is incorrect?

8.6 Consider N nodes connected according to a complete graph; that is, all nodes can decode every other node's transmission. All communication channels are independent binary symmetric channels with error probability $0 \le q \le 0.5$. Each node has a bit and it is required that all the nodes know the parity of the N bits. Each node transmits its bit M times and every receiver uses the majority rule to decode; that is, a bit is decoded as 1 if more that $M/2$ transmissions are decoded as 1. Find $p_c(N, M)$, the probability that *all* the N nodes have the correct parity. Investigate the asymptotics of $p_c(N, M)$ when $M = \log_2 N$ and $N \to \infty$.

8.7 Consider N nodes connected according to a complete graph; that is, all nodes can decode every other node's transmission. Assume that the Aloha MAC protocol is used and each node transmits in a slot with probability p. Each node has a bit and it is required that all the nodes know the parity of the N bits. Assume that there is no channel error. If p is to be fixed, find the expectation and variance of the time at which all the nodes have transmitted once and all know the parity. If p can be dynamic, i.e., it can be changed in possibly every slot, design an algorithm that will minimize the expected time to complete the computation. Find the corresponding variance.

8.8 Consider the function computation problem discussed in Section 8.5. For a specific choice of $r_c(N)$, consider the cells of the cell graph as nodes of a new graph. Define two cells to be adjacent—having an edge between them—if they are interfering neighbors. The degree of such a graph is clearly $\leq k_2$, see Section 8.5. Our objective is to *color* the vertices of this graph using the *minimum* number of colors, subject to the constraint that no two adjacent vertices have the same color. Show that the minimum number of colors is $\leq (1 + k_2)$.

Note: After the coloring is done, nodes having the same color correspond to cells that can support simultaneous transmissions. Therefore, the result above says that within an interval of length $(1 + k_2)$ slots, *every* cell gets a transmission opportunity.

References

[1] P. Gupta, P.R. Kumar, Critical Power for Asymptotic Connectivity in Wireless Networks, in: W.M. McEneaney, G. Yin, Q. Zhang (Eds.), Stochastic Analysis, Control, Optimization and Applications: A Volume in Honor of W. H. Fleming, Birkhauser, Boston, MA, 1998.

[2] H. Zhang, J. Hou, On deriving the upper bound of α-lifetime for large sensor networks, in: Proc. ACM MobiHoc, 2004, pp. 121–132.

[3] X. Wang, G. Xing, Y. Zhang, C. Lu, R. Pless, C. Gill, Integrated coverage and connectivity configuration in wireless sensor networks, in: Proc. ACM SENSYS, November 2003, pp. 28–39.

[4] R. Nagpal, H. Shrobe, J. Bachrach, Organizing a global and coordinate system from local information on an ad hoc sensor network, in: Proc. IPSN, Lecture Notes in Computer Science 2634, April 2003.

[5] L. Doherty, K. Pister, L. El Ghaoui, Convex position estimation in wireless sensor networks, in: Proc IEEE INFOCOM, 2001, pp. 1663–1665.

[6] S. Boyd, L. El Ghaoui, E. Feron, V. Balakrishnan, Linear Matrix Inequalities in System and Control Theory. SIAM (1994).

[7] H. Takagi, L. Kleinrock, Optimal transmission ranges for randomly distributed packet radio terminals, IEEE Transact. Commun. 32 (3) (1984) 246–257.

[8] D.B. West, Introduction to Graph Theory, second ed., Pearson Education, Prentice Hall, 2006.

[9] M. de Berg, M. van Kreveld, M. Overmars, O. Schwarzkopf, Computational Geometry: Algorithms and Applications, first ed., Springer-Verlag, 1997.

[10] J.W. Jaromczyk, G.T. Toussaint, Relative neighbourhood graphs and their relatives, Proc. IEEE 80 (9) (1992) 1502–1517.

[11] E. Kranakis, H. Singh, J. Urrutia, Compass routing on geometric networks, in: Proc. 11th Canadian Conference on Computational Geometry, August 1999, pp. 51–54.

[12] F. Kuhn, R. Wattenhofer, Y. Zhang, A. Zollinger, Geometric ad-hoc routing: of theory and practice, in: Proc. ACM Symposium on the Principles of Distributed Computing (PODC), 2003, pp. 63–72.

[13] C. Intanagonwiwat, R. Govindan, D. Estrin, J. Heidemann, Directed diffusion for wireless sensor networking, IEEE/ACM Transact. Networking 11 (1) (2003) 2–16.

[14] A. Giridhar, P.R. Kumar, Computing and communicating functions over sensor networks, IEEE J. Select. Areas Commun. 23 (4) (2005) 755–764.

[15] W. Ye, J. Heidemann, D. Estrin, Medium access control with coordinated adaptive sleeping for wireless sensor networks, IEEE/ACM Transact. Networking 12 (3) (2004) 493–506.

[16] IEEE. IEEE std. 802.15.4, Part 15.4: Wireless MAC and PHY Specifications for Low-Rate Wireless Personal Area Networks. IEEE, New York, May 2003.

CHAPTER 9

Sensor Network Platforms and Tools

Feng Zhao
Leonidas Guibas

In previous chapters, we discussed various aspects of sensor networks, including sensing and estimation, networking, infrastructure services, sensor tasking, and data storage and query. A real-world sensor network application most likely has to incorporate all these elements, subject to energy, bandwidth, computation, storage, and real-time constraints. This makes sensor network application development quite different from traditional distributed system development or database programming. With ad hoc deployment and frequently changing network topology, a sensor network application can hardly assume an always-on infrastructure that provides reliable services such as optimal routing, global directories, or service discovery.

There are two types of programming for sensor networks, those carried out by end users and those performed by application developers. An end user may view a sensor network as a pool of data and *interact* with the network via queries. Just as with query languages for database systems like SQL, a good sensor network programming language should be expressive enough to encode application logic at a high level of abstraction, and at the same time be structured enough to allow efficient execution on the distributed platform. Ideally, the end users should be shielded away from details of how sensors are organized and how nodes communicate.

On the other hand, an application developer must provide end users of a sensor network with the capabilities of data acquisition, processing, and storage. Unlike general distributed or database systems, collaborative signal and information processing (CSIP) software comprises reactive, concurrent, distributed programs running on ad hoc, resource-constrained, unreliable computation and communication platforms. Developers at this level have to deal with all kinds of uncertainty in the real world. For example, signals are noisy, events can happen at the same time, communication and computation take time, communications may be unreliable, battery life is limited, and so on. Moreover, because of the amount of domain knowledge required, application developers are typically signal and information processing specialists, rather than operating systems and networking experts. How to provide appropriate programming abstractions to these application writers is a key challenge for sensor network software development. In this chapter, we focus on software design issues to support this type of programming.

To make our discussion of these software issues concrete, we first give an overview of a few representative sensor node hardware platforms (Section 9.1). In Section 9.2, we present the challenges of sensor network programming due to the massively concurrent interaction with the physical world. Section 9.3 describes TinyOS for Berkeley motes and two types of node-centric programming interfaces: an imperative language, nesC, and a dataflow-style language, TinyGALS. Node-centric designs are typically supported by node-level simulators such as ns-2 and TOSSIM, as described in Section 9.4. State-centric programming is a step toward programming beyond individual nodes. It gives programmers platform support for thinking in high-level abstractions, such as the state of the phenomena of interest over space and time. An example of state-centric platforms is given in Section 9.5.

9.1 Sensor Node Hardware

Sensor node hardware can be grouped into three categories, each of which entails a different set of trade-offs in the design choices.

- *Augmented general-purpose computers:* Examples include low-power PCs, embedded PCs (e.g., PC104), custom-designed PCs (e.g., Sensoria WINS NG nodes),[1] and various personal digital assistants (PDAs). These nodes typically run off-the-shelf (OTS) operating systems such as Win CE, Linux, or real-time operating systems and use standard wireless communication protocols such as Bluetooth or IEEE 802.11. Because of their relatively higher processing capability, they can accommodate a wide variety of sensors, ranging from simple microphones to more sophisticated video cameras.

  Compared with dedicated sensor nodes, PC-like platforms are more power hungry. However, when power is not an issue, these platforms have the advantage that they can leverage the availability of fully supported networking protocols, popular programming languages, middleware, and other OTS software.

- *Dedicated embedded sensor nodes:* Examples include the Berkeley mote family [1], the UCLA Medusa family [2], Ember nodes,[2] and MIT μAMP [3]. These platforms typically use commercial OTS (COTS) chip sets with emphasis on small form factor, low power processing and communication, and simple sensor interfaces. Because of their COTS CPU, these platforms typically support at least one programming language, such as C. However, in order to keep the program footprint small to accommodate their small memory size, programmers of these platforms are given full access to hardware but barely any operating system support. A classical example

---

[1] See http://www.sensoria.com/ and http://www.janet.ucla.edu/WINS/.

[2] See http://www.ember.com.

is the TinyOS platform and its companion programming language, nesC. We will discuss these platforms in Sections 9.3.1 and 9.3.2.

- *System-on-chip (SoC) nodes:* Examples of SoC hardware include smart dust [4], the BWRC picoradio node [5], and the PASTA node.[3] Designers of these platforms try to push the hardware limits by fundamentally rethinking the hardware architecture trade-offs for a sensor node at the chip design level. The goal is to find new ways of integrating CMOS, MEMS, and RF technologies to build extremely low power and small footprint sensor nodes that still provide certain sensing, computation, and communication capabilities. Since most of these platforms are currently in the research pipeline with no predefined instruction set, there is no software platform support available.

Among these hardware platforms, the Berkeley motes, due to their small form factor, open source software development, and commercial availability, have gained wide popularity in the sensor network research community. In the following section, we give an overview of the Berkeley MICA mote.

9.1.1 Berkeley Motes

The Berkeley motes are a family of embedded sensor nodes sharing roughly the same architecture. Figure 9.1 shows a comparison of a subset of mote types.

Let us take the MICA mote as an example. The MICA motes have a two-CPU design, as shown in Figure 9.2. The main microcontroller (MCU), an Atmel ATmega103L, takes care of regular processing. A separate and much less capable coprocessor is only active when the MCU is being reprogrammed. The ATmega103L MCU has integrated 512 KB flash memory and 4 KB of data memory. Given these small memory sizes, writing software for motes is challenging. Ideally, programmers should be relieved from optimizing code at assembly level to keep code footprint small. However, high-level support and software services are not free. Being able to mix and match only necessary software components to support a particular application is essential to achieving a small footprint. A detailed discussion of the software architecture for motes is given in Section 9.3.1.

In addition to the memory inside the MCU, a MICA mote also has a separate 512 KB flash memory unit that can hold data. Since the connection between the MCU and this external memory is via a low-speed serial peripheral interface (SPI) protocol, the external memory is more suited for storing data for later batch processing than for storing programs. The RF communication on MICA motes uses the TR1000 chip set (from RF Monolithics, Inc.)

---

[3] See http://pasta.east.isi.edu.

Mote type			WeC	Rene	Rene2	Mica	Mica2	Mica2Dot
Example picture								
MCU		Chip	AT90LS8535	ATmega163L		ATmega103L	ATmega128L	
		Type	4 MHz, 8 bit	4 MHz, 8 bit		4 MHz, 8 bit	8 MHz, 8 bit	
		Program memory (KB)	8	16		128	128	
		RAM (KB)	0.5	1		4	4	
External nonvolatile storage		Chip	24LC256			AT45DB014B		
		Connection type	I2C			SPI		
		Size (KB)	32			512		
Default power source		Type	Coin cell	2xAA				Coin cell
		Typical capacity (mAh)	575	2850				1000
RF		Chip	TR1000				CC1000	
		Radio frequency	868/916 MHz				868/916 MHz, 433, or 315 MHz	
		Raw speed (kbps)	10			40	38.4	
		Modulation type	On/Off key			Amplitude shift key	Frequency shift key	

Figure 9.1 A comparison of Berkeley motes.

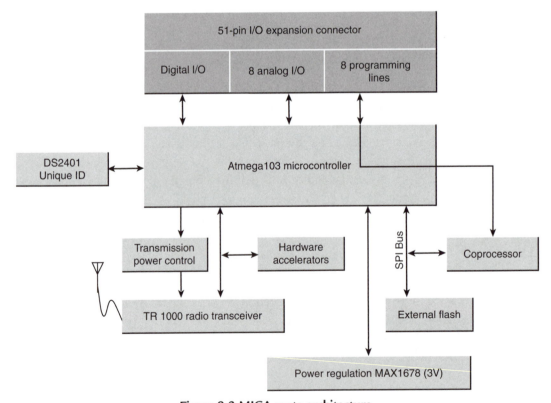

Figure 9.2 MICA mote architecture.

Component	Rate	Startup time	Current consumption
MCU active	4 MHz	N/A	5.5 mA
MCU idle	4 MHz	1 µs	1.6 mA
MCU suspend	32 kHz	4 ms	<20 µA
Radio transmit	40 kHz	30 ms	12 mA
Radio receive	40 kHz	30 ms	1.8 mA
Photoresister	2000 Hz	10 ms	1.235 mA
Accelerometer	100 Hz	10 ms	5 mA/axis
Temperature	2 Hz	500 ms	0.150 mA

Figure 9.3 Power consumption of MICA motes.

operating at 916 MHz band. With hardware accelerators, it can achieve a maximum of 50 kbps raw data rate. MICA motes implement a 40 kbps transmission rate. The transmission power can be digitally adjusted by software through a potentiometer (Maxim DS1804). The maximum transmission range is about 300 feet in open space.

Like other types of motes in the family, MICA motes support a 51 pin I/O extension connector. Sensors, actuators, serial I/O boards, or parallel I/O boards can be connected via the connector. A sensor/actuator board can host a temperature sensor, a light sensor, an accelerometer, a magnetometer, a microphone, and a beeper. The serial I/O (UART) connection allows the mote to communicate with a PC in real time. The parallel connection is primarily for downloading programs to the mote.

It is interesting to look at the energy consumption of various components on a MICA mote. As shown in Figure 9.3, a radio transmission bears the maximum power consumption. However, each radio packet (e.g., 30 bytes) only takes 4 ms to send, while listening to incoming packets turns the radio receiver ON all the time. The energy that can send one packet only supports the radio receiver for about 27 ms. Another observation is that there are huge differences among the power consumption levels in the active mode, the idle mode, and the suspend mode of the MCU. It is thus worthwhile from an energy-saving point of view to suspend the MCU and the RF receiver as long as possible.

9.2 Sensor Network Programming Challenges

Traditional programming technologies rely on operating systems to provide abstraction for processing, I/O, networking, and user interaction hardware, as illustrated in Figure 9.4. When applying such a model to programming networked embedded systems, such as sensor

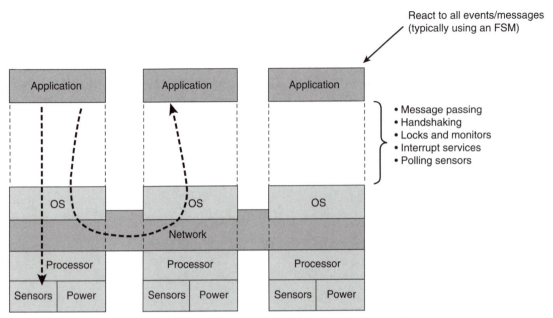

Figure 9.4 Traditional embedded system programming interface.

networks, the application programmers need to explicitly deal with message passing, event synchronization, interrupt handing, and sensor reading. As a result, an application is typically implemented as a finite state machine (FSM) that covers all extreme cases: unreliable communication channels, long delays, irregular arrival of messages, simultaneous events, and so on. In a target tracking application implemented on a Linux operating system and with directed diffusion routing, roughly 40% of the code implements the FSM and the glue logic of interfacing computation and communication [6].

For resource-constrained embedded systems with real-time requirements, several mechanisms are used in embedded operating systems to reduce code size, improve response time, and reduce energy consumption. Microkernel technologies [7] modularize the operating system so that only the necessary parts are deployed with the application. Real-time scheduling [8] allocates resources to more urgent tasks so that they can be finished early. Event-driven execution allows the system to fall into low-power sleep mode when no interesting events need to be processed. At the extreme, embedded operating systems tend to expose more hardware controls to the programmers, who now have to directly face device drivers and scheduling algorithms, and optimize code at the assembly level. Although these techniques may work well for small, stand-alone embedded systems, they do not scale up for the programming of sensor networks for two reasons.

- Sensor networks are large-scale distributed systems, where global properties are derivable from program execution in a massive number of distributed nodes.

Distributed algorithms themselves are hard to implement, especially when infrastructure support is limited due to the ad hoc formation of the system and constrained power, memory, and bandwidth resources.

- As sensor nodes deeply embed into the physical world, a sensor network should be able to respond to multiple concurrent stimuli at the speed of changes of the physical phenomena of interest.

In the rest of the chapter, we give several examples of sensor network software design platforms. We discuss them in terms of both *design methodologies* and *design platforms*. A design methodology implies a conceptual model for programmers, with associated techniques for problem decomposition for the software designers. For example, does the programmer think in terms of events, message passing, and synchronization, or does he/she focus more on information architecture and data semantics? A design platform supports a design methodology by providing design-time (precompile time) language constructs and restrictions, and run-time (postcompile time) execution services.

There is no single universal design methodology for all applications. Depending on the specific tasks of a sensor network and the way the sensor nodes are organized, certain methodologies and platforms may be better choices than others. For example, if the network is used for monitoring a small set of phenomena and the sensor nodes are organized in a simple star topology, then a client–server software model would be sufficient. If the network is used for monitoring a large area from a single access point (i.e., the base station), and if user queries can be decoupled into aggregations of sensor readings from a subset of sensor nodes, then a tree structure that is rooted at the base station is a better choice. However, if the phenomena to be monitored are moving targets, then neither the simple client–server model nor the tree organization is optimal. More sophisticated design methodologies and platforms are required.

9.3 Node-Level Software Platforms

Most design methodologies for sensor network software are node-centric, where programmers think in terms of how a node should behave in the environment. A node-level platform can be a node-centric operating system, which provides hardware and networking abstractions of a sensor node to programmers, or it can be a language platform, which provides a library of components to programmers.

A typical operating system abstracts the hardware platform by providing a set of services for applications, including file management, memory allocation, task scheduling, peripheral device drivers, and networking. For embedded systems, due to their highly specialized applications and limited resources, their operating systems make different trade-offs when providing these services. For example, if there is no file management requirement then a file system is obviously not needed. If there is no dynamic memory allocation then memory management can be simplified. If prioritization among tasks is critical then a more elaborate priority scheduling mechanism may be added.

TinyOS [1] and TinyGALS [9] are two representative examples of node-level programming tools that we will cover in detail in this section. Other related software platforms include Maté [10], a virtual machine for the Berkeley motes. Observing that operations such as polling sensors and accessing internal states are common to all sensor network application, Maté defines virtual machine instructions to abstract those operations. When a new hardware platform is introduced with support for the virtual machine, software written in the Maté instruction set does not have to be rewritten.

9.3.1 Operating System: TinyOS

TinyOS aims at supporting sensor network applications on resource-constrained hardware platforms, such as the Berkeley motes.

To ensure that an application code has an extremely small footprint, TinyOS chooses to have no file system, supports only static memory allocation, implements a simple task model, and provides minimal device and networking abstractions. Furthermore, it takes a language-based application development approach, to be discussed later, so that only the necessary parts of the operating system are compiled with the application. To a certain extent, each TinyOS application is built into the operating system.

Like many operating systems, TinyOS organizes components into layers. Intuitively, the lower a layer is, the "closer" it is to the hardware; the higher a layer is, the "closer" it is to the application.

In addition to the layers, TinyOS has a unique component architecture and provides as a library a set of system software components. A component specification is independent of the component implementation. Although most components encapsulate software functionalities, some are just thin wrappers around hardware. An application, typically developed in the nesC language covered in the next section, *wires* these components together with other application-specific components.

Let us consider a TinyOS application example—FieldMonitor, where all nodes in a sensor field periodically send their temperature and photosensor readings to a base station via an ad hoc routing mechanism. A diagram of the FieldMonitor application is shown in Figure 9.5, where blocks represent TinyOS components and arrows represent function calls among them. The directions of the arrows are from callers to callees.

To explain in detail the semantics of TinyOS components, let us first look at the Timer component of the FieldMonitor application, as shown in Figure 9.6. This component

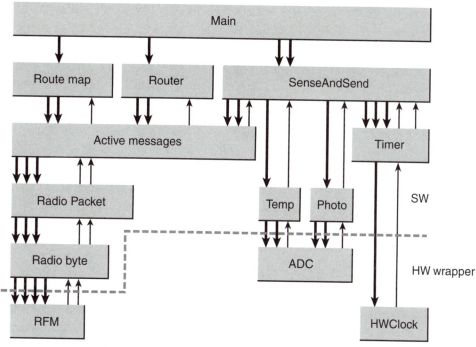

Figure 9.5 The `FieldMonitor` **application for sensing and sending measurements.**

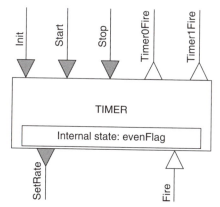

Figure 9.6 The `Timer` **component and its interfaces.**

is designed to work with a clock, which is a software wrapper around a hardware clock that generates periodic interrupts. The method calls of the `Timer` component are shown in the figure as arrowheads. An arrowhead pointing into the component is a method of the component that other components can call. An arrowhead pointing outward is a method that this component requires another layer component to provide. The absolute directions of the arrows, up or down, illustrate this component's relationship with other layers. For example, the Timer depends on a lower layer HWClock component. The Timer can set the rate of the clock, and in response to each clock interrupt it toggles an internal Boolean flag, evenFlag, between true (or 1) and false (or 0). If the flag is 0, the Timer produces a timer0Fire event to trigger other components; otherwise, it produces a timer1Fire event. The Timer has an init() method that initializes its internal flag, and it can be enabled and disabled via the start and stop calls.

A program executed in TinyOS has two contexts, *tasks* and *events*, which provide two sources of concurrency. Tasks are created (also called *posted*) by components to a task scheduler. The default implementation of the TinyOS scheduler maintains a task queue and invokes tasks according to the order in which they were posted. Thus tasks are deferred computation mechanisms. Tasks always run to completion without preempting or being preempted by other tasks. Thus tasks are nonpreemptive. The scheduler invokes a new task from the task queue only when the current task has completed. When no tasks are available in the task queue, the scheduler puts the CPU into the sleep mode to save energy.

The ultimate sources of triggered execution are events from hardware: clock, digital inputs, or other kinds of interrupts. The execution of an interrupt handler is called an *event context*. The processing of events also runs to completion, but it preempts tasks and can be preempted by other events. Because there is no preemption mechanism among tasks and because events always preempt tasks, programmers are required to chop their code, especially the code in the event contexts, into small execution pieces, so that it will not block other tasks for too long.

Another trade-off between nonpreemptive task execution and program reactiveness is the design of split-phase operations in TinyOS. Similar to the notion of asynchronous method calls in distributed computing, a split-phase operation separates the initiation of a method call from the return of the call. A call to a split-phase operation returns immediately, without actually performing the body of the operation. The true execution of the operation is scheduled later; when the execution of the body finishes, the operation notifies the original caller through a separate method call. An example of a split-phase operation is the packet send method in the Active Messages (AM) component, used in Figure 9.5. Sending a packet is a long operation, involving converting the packets to bytes, then to bits, and ultimately driving the RF circuits to send the bits one by one. Without a split-phase execution, sending a packet will block the entire system from reacting to new events for a significant period of time. In the TinyOS implementation, the send() command in the AM component returns immediately. However, it is the caller's responsibility to remember that the packet has not yet been sent. When the packet is indeed sent, the AM component will notify its caller by a sendDone() method call. Only at this time is the AM component ready to accept another packet.

In TinyOS, resource contention is typically handled through explicit rejection of concurrent requests. All split-phase operations return Boolean values indicating whether a request to perform the operation is accepted. In the above example, a call of send(), when the

AM component is still sending the first packet, will result in an error signaled by the AM component. To avoid such an error, the caller of the AM component typically implements a *pending* lock to remember not to request further sendings until the sendDone() method is called. To avoid loss of packets, a queue should be incorporated by the caller if necessary.

In summary, many design decisions in TinyOS are made to ensure that it is extremely lightweight. Using a component architecture that contains all variables inside the components and disallowing dynamic memory allocation reduces the memory management overhead and makes the data memory usage statically analyzable. The simple concurrency model allows high concurrency with low thread maintenance overhead. As a consequence, the entire FieldMonitor system shown in Figure 9.5 takes only 3 KB of space for code and 226 bytes for data. However, the advantage of being lightweight is not without cost. Many hardware idiosyncrasies and complexities of concurrency management are left for the application programmers to handle. Several tools have been developed to give programmers language-level support for improving programming productivity and code robustness. We introduce in the next two sections two special-purpose languages for programming sensor network nodes. Although both languages are designed on top of TinyOS, the principles they represent may apply to other platforms.

9.3.2 Imperative Language: nesC

nesC [11] is an extension of C to support and reflect the design of TinyOS v1.0 and above. It provides a set of language constructs and restrictions to implement TinyOS components and applications.

9.3.2.1 Component Interface

A component in nesC has an interface specification and an implementation. To reflect the layered structure of TinyOS, interfaces of a nesC component are classified as *provides* or *uses* interfaces. A provides interface is a set of method calls exposed to the upper layers, while a uses interface is a set of method calls hiding the lower layer components. Methods in the interfaces can be grouped and named. For example, the interface specification of the Timer component in Figure 9.6 is listed in Figure 9.7. The interface, again, independent of the implementation, is called TimerModule.

Although they have the same method call semantics, nesC distinguishes the *directions* of the interface calls between layers as *event* calls and *command* calls. An event call is a method call from a lower layer component to a higher layer component, while a command is the opposite. Note that one needs to know both the type of the interface (provides or uses) and the direction of the method call (event or command) to know exactly whether an interface method is implemented by the component or is required by the component.

```
module TimerModule {
  provides {
     interface StdControl;
     interface Timer01;
  }
  uses interface Clock as Clk;
}

interface StdControl {
  command result_t init();
}

interface Timer01 {
  command result_t start(char type, uint32_t interval;
  command result_t stop();
  event result_t timer0Fire();
  event result_t timer1Fire();
}

interface Clock {
  command result_t setRate(char interval, char scale);
  event result_t fire();
}
```

Figure 9.7 The interface definition of the `Timer` **component in nesC.**

The separation of interface type definitions from how they are used in the components promotes the reusability of standard interfaces. A component can provide and use the same interface type, so that it can act as a filter interposed between a client and a service. A component may even use or provide the same interface multiple times. In these cases, the component must give each interface instance a separate name, as shown in the `Clock` interface in Figure 9.7.

9.3.2.2 Component Implementation

There are two types of components in nesC depending on how they are implemented: *modules* and *configurations*. Modules are implemented by application code (written in a C-like syntax). Configurations are implemented by connecting interfaces of existing components.

The implementation part of a module is written in C-like code. A command or an event `bar` in an interface `foo` is referred as `foo.bar`. A keyword `call` indicates the invocation of a command. A keyword `signal` indicates the triggering by an event. For example, Figure 9.8 shows part of the implementation of the `Timer` component, whose interface is defined in Figure 9.7. In a sense, this implementation is very much like an object in object-oriented programming without any constructors.

```
module Timer {
  provides {
    interface StdControl;
    interface Timer01;
  }
  uses interface Clock as Clk;
}
implementation {
  bool evenFlag;

  command result_t StdControl.init() {
    evenFlag = 0;
    return call Clk.setRate(128, 4); //4 ticks per second
  }

  event result_t Clk.fire() {
    evenFlag = !evenFlag;
    if (evenFlag) {
      signal Timer01.timer0Fire();
    } else {
      signal Timer01.timer1Fire();
    }
    return SUCCESS;
  }
  ...
}
```

Figure 9.8 The implementation definition of the Timer **component in nesC.**

Configuration is another kind of implementation of components, obtained by connecting existing components. Suppose we want to connect the Timer component and a hardware clock wrapper, called HWClock, to provide a timer service, called TimerC. Figure 9.9 shows a conceptual diagram of how the components are connected and Figure 9.10 shows the corresponding nesC code.

First of all, notice that the keyword configuration in the specification indicates that this component is not implemented directly as a module. In the implementation section of the configuration, the code first includes the two components and then specifies that the interface StdControl of the TimerC component is the StdControl interface of the TimerModule; similarly for the Timer01 interface. The connection between the Clock interfaces is specified using the -> operator. Essentially, this interface is hidden from upper layers.

nesC also supports the creation of several instances of a component by declaring *abstract components* with optional parameters. Abstract components are created at compile time in configurations.

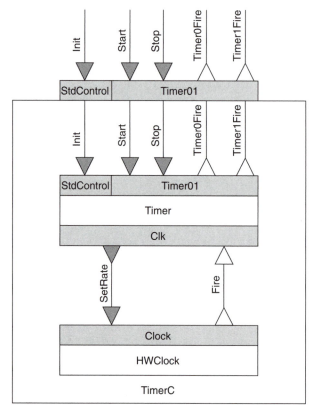

Figure 9.9 The TimerC **configuration implemented by connecting** Timer **with** HWClock.

```
configuration TimerC {
  provides {
    interface StdControl;
    interface Timer01;
  }
}
implementation {
  components TimerModule, Clock;

  StdControl = TimerModule.StdControl;
  Timer = TimerModule.Timer;

  TimerModule.Clk -> HWClock.Clock;
}
```

Figure 9.10 The implementation definition of the TimerC **configuration in nesC.**

Recall that TinyOS does not support dynamic memory allocation, so all components are statically constructed at compile time.

A complete application is always a configuration rather than a module. An application must contain the Main module, which links the code to the scheduler at run time. The `Main` has a single `StdControl` interface, which is the ultimate source of initialization of all components.

9.3.2.3 Concurrency and Atomicity

The language nesC directly reflects the TinyOS execution model through the notion of command and event contexts. Figure 9.11 shows a section of the component `SenseAndSend` to illustrate some language features to support concurrency in nesC and the effort to reduce race conditions. The `SenseAndSend` component is intended to be built on top of the `Timer` component (described in the previous section), an analog-to-digital conversion (ADC) component, which can provide sensor readings, and a communication component, which can send (or, more precisely, broadcast) a packet. When responding to a `timer0Fire` event, the `SenseAndSend` component invokes the ADC to poll a sensor reading. Since polling a sensor reading can take a long time, a split-phase operation is implemented for getting sensor readings. The call to `ADC.getData()` returns immediately, and the completion of the operation is signaled by an `ADC.dataReady()` event. A busy flag is used to explicitly reject new requests while the ADC is fulfilling an existing request. The `ADC.getData()` method sets the flag to true, while the `ADC.dataReady()` method sets it back to false. Sending the sensor reading to the next-hop neighbor via wireless communication is also a long operation. To make sure that it does not block the processing of the `ADC.dataReady()` event, a separate task is posted to the scheduler. A task is a method defined using the task keyword. In order to simplify the data structures inside the scheduler, a task cannot have arguments. Thus the sensor reading to be sent is put into a sensorReading variable.

There is one source of race condition in the `SenseAndSend`, which is the updating of the busy flag. To prevent some state from being updated by both scheduled tasks and event-triggered interrupt handlers, nesC provides language facilities to limit the race conditions among these operations.

In nesC, code can be classified into two types:

- *Asynchronous code (AC):* Code that is reachable from at least one interrupt handler.
- *Synchronous code (SC):* Code that is only reachable from tasks.

Because the execution of TinyOS tasks are nonpreemptive and interrupt handlers preempt tasks, an SC is always atomic with respect to other SCs. However, any update to shared state from AC, or from SC that is also updated from AC, is a potential race condition. To reinstate atomicity of updating shared state, nesC provides a keyword atomic to indicate that the execution of a block of statements should not be preempted. This construction can be efficiently implemented by turning OFF hardware interrupts. To prevent blocking the interrupts for too long and affecting the

```
module SenseAndSend{
  provides interface StdControl;
    uses interface ADC;
    uses interface Timer:
    uses interface Send;
}

implementation {
  bool busy;
  norace uint16_t sensorReading;

  command result_t StdControl.init() {
    busy = FALSE;
  }

  event result_t Timer.timer0Fire() {
    bool localBusy;
    atomic {
      localBusy = busy;
      busy = TRUE;
    }
    if (!localBusy} {
      call ADC.getData(); //start getting sensor reading
      return SUCESS;
    } else {
      return FAILED;
    }
  }

  task void sendData() { // send sensorReading
    adcPacket.data = sensorReading;
    call Send.send(&adcPacket, sizeof adcPacket.data};
    return SUCESS;
  }

  event result_t ADC.dataReady(uinit16_t data) {
    sensorReading = data;
    post sendData();
    atomic {
      busy = FALSE;
    }
    return SUCCESS;
  }
  ...
}
```

Figure 9.11 A section of the implementation of SenseAndSend, **illustrating the handling of concurrency in nesC.**

responsiveness of the node, nesC does not allow method calls in atomic blocks. In fact, nesC has a compiler rule to enforce the accessing of shared variables to maintain the race-free condition. If a variable x is accessed by an AC, then any access of x outside of an atomic statement is a compile-time error. This rule may be too rigid in reality. When a programmer knows for sure that a data race is not going to occur, or does not care if it occurs, then a no race declaration of the variable can prevent the compiler from checking the race condition on that variable.

Thus, to correctly handle concurrency, nesC programmers need to have a clear idea of what is synchronous code and what is asynchronous code. However, since the semantics is hidden away in the layered structure of TinyOS, it is sometimes not obvious to the programmers where to add atomic blocks.

9.3.3 Dataflow-Style Language: TinyGALS

Dataflow languages [12] are intuitive for expressing computation on interrelated data units by specifying data dependencies among them. A dataflow program has a set of processing units called *actors*. Actors have ports to receive and produce data, and the directional connections among ports are first-in, first-out (FIFO) queues that mediate the flow of data. Actors in dataflow languages intrinsically capture concurrency in a system, and the FIFO queues give a structured way of decoupling their executions. The execution of an actor is triggered when there are enough input data at the input ports.

Asynchronous event-driven execution can be viewed as a special case of dataflow models, where each actor is triggered by every incoming event. The *globally asynchronous and locally synchronous* (GALS) mechanism is a way of building event-triggered concurrent execution from thread-unsafe components. TinyGALS is such a language for TinyOS.

One of the key factors that affect component reusability in embedded software is the component composability, especially concurrent composability. In general, when developing a component, a programmer may not anticipate all possible scenarios in which the component may be used. Implementing all access to variables as atomic blocks incurs too much overhead. At the other extreme, making all variable access unprotected is easy for coding but certainly introduces bugs in concurrent composition. TinyGALS addresses concurrency concerns at the system level rather than at the component level as in nesC. Reactions to concurrent events are managed by a dataflow-style FIFO queue communication.

9.3.3.1 TinyGALS Programming Model

TinyGALS supports all TinyOS components, including its interfaces and module implementations.[4] All method calls in a component interface are synchronous method

---

[4] Although posting tasks is not part of the TinyGALS semantics, the TinyGALS compiler and run time are compatible with it.

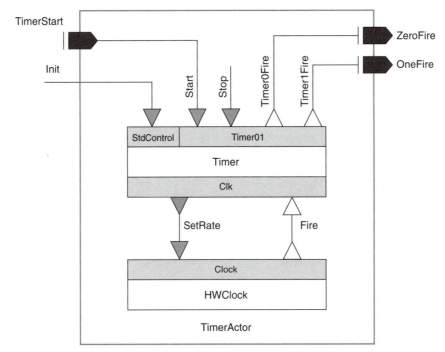

Figure 9.12 Construction of a `TimerActor` **from a** `Timer` **component and a clock component.**

calls—i.e., the thread of control enters immediately into the callee component from the caller component. An application in TinyGALS is built in two steps: (1) constructing asynchronous actors from synchronous components,[5] and (2) constructing an application by connecting the asynchronous components through FIFO queues.

An actor in TinyGALS has a set of input ports, a set of output ports, and a set of connected TinyOS components. An actor is constructed by connecting synchronous method calls among TinyOS components. For example, Figure 9.12 shows a construction of `TimerActor` from two TinyOS components (i.e., nesC modules), `Timer` and `Clock`. Figure 9.13 is the corresponding TinyGALS code. An actor can expose one or more initialization methods. These methods are called by the TinyGALS run time before the start of an application. Initialization methods are called in a nondeterministic order, so their implementations should not have any cross-component dependencies.

At the application level, the asynchronous communication of actors is mediated using FIFO queues. Each connection can be parameterized by a queue size. In the current implementation

---

[5] In the implementation of TinyGALS as described in [9], which is based on TinyOS 0.6.1 and predates nesC, the asynchronous actors are called *modules*, and asynchronous connections are represented as "→." To avoid the confusion with nesC, we have modified some of the TinyGALS syntax for inclusion in this section.

```
Actor TimerActor {
  include components {
    TimerModule;
    HWClock;
  }
  init {
    TimerModule.init;
  }
  port in {
    timerStart;
  }
  port out {
    zeroFire;
    oneFire;
  }
}
implementation {
  timerStart -> TimerModule.Timer.start;
  TimerModule.Clk -> HWClock.Clock;
  TimerModule.Timer.timer0Fire -> zeroFire;
  TimerModule.Timer.timer1Fire -> oneFire;
}
```

Figure 9.13 Implementation of the `TimerActor` **in TinyGALS.**

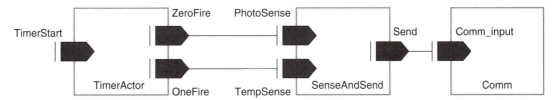

Figure 9.14 Triggering, sensing, and sending actors of the `FieldMonitor` **in TinyGALS.**

of TinyGALS, events are discarded when the queue is full. However, other mechanisms such as discarding the oldest event can be used. Figure 9.14 shows a TinyGALS composition of timing, sensing, and sending part of the `FieldMonitor` application in Figure 9.5.

Figure 9.15 is the TinyGALS specification of the configuration in Figure 9.14. We omit the details of the `SenseAndSend` actor and the Comm actor, whose ports are shown in Figure 9.14. The symbol $=>$ represents a FIFO queue connecting input ports and output ports. The integer at the end of the line specifies the queue size. The command START@ indicates that the TinyGALS run time puts an initial event into the corresponding port after all initialization is finished. In our example, an event inserted into the `timerStart` port starts the `HWClock`, and the rest of the execution is driven by clock interrupt events.

```
Application FieldMonitor {
  include actors {
    TimerActor;
    SenseAndSend;
    Comm;
  }
  implementation {
    zeroFire => photoSense 5;
    oneFire => tempSense 5;
    send => comm_input 10;
  }
  START@ timerStart;
}
```

Figure 9.15 Implementation of the `FieldMonitor` **in TinyGALS.**

The TinyGALS programming model has the advantage that actors become decoupled through message passing and are easy to develop independently. However, each message passed will trigger the scheduler and activate a receiving actor, which may quickly become inefficient if there is a global state that must be shared among multiple actors. TinyGUYS (Guarded Yet Synchronous) variables are a mechanism for sharing global state, allowing quick access but with protected modification of the data.

In the TinyGUYS mechanism, global variables are guarded. Actors may read the global variables synchronously (without delay). However, writes to the variables are asynchronous in the sense that all writes are buffered. The buffer is of size one, so the last actor that writes to a variable wins. TinyGUYS variables are updated by the scheduler only when it is safe (e.g., after one module finishes and before the scheduler triggers the next module).

TinyGUYS have global names defined at the application level which are mapped to the parameters of each actor and are further mapped to the external variables of the components that use these variables. The external variables are accessed within a component by using special keywords: `PARAM_GET` and `PARAM_PUT`. The code generator produces thread-safe implementation of these methods using locking mechanisms, such as turning OFF interrupts.

9.3.3.2 TinyGALS Code Generation

TinyGALS takes a generative approach to mapping high-level constructs such as FIFO queues and actors into executables on Berkeley motes. Given the highly structured architecture of TinyGALS applications, efficient scheduling and event-handling code can be automatically generated to free software developers from writing error-prone concurrency control code. The rest of this section discusses a code-generation tool that is implemented based on TinyOS v0.6.1 for Berkeley motes.

Given the definitions for the components, actors, and application, the code generator automatically generates all of the necessary code for (1) component links and actor connections, (2) application initialization and start of execution, (3) communication among actors, and (4) global variable reads and writes.

Similar to how TinyOS deals with connected method calls among components, the TinyGALS code generator generates a set of aliases for each synchronous method call. The code generator also creates a system-level initialization function called `app_init()`, which contains calls to the `init()` method of each actor in the system. The `app_init()` function is one of the first functions called by the TinyGALS run-time scheduler before executing the application. An application start function `app_start()` is created based on the @start annotation. This function triggers the input port of the actor defined as the application starting point.

The code generator automatically generates a set of scheduler data structures and functions for each asynchronous connection between actors. For each input port of an actor, the code generator generates a queue of length n, where n is specified in the application definition. The width of the queue depends on the number of arguments of the method connected to the port. If there are no arguments, then as an optimization, no queue is generated for the port (but space is still reserved for events in the scheduler event queue).

For each output port of an actor, the code generator generates a function that has the same name as the output port. This function is called whenever a method of a component wishes to write to an output port. The type signature of the output port function matches that of the method that connects to the port. For each input port connected to the output port, a `put()` function is generated which handles the actual copying of data to the input port queue. The output port function calls the input port's `put()` function for each connected input port. The `put()` function adds the port identifier to the scheduler event queue so that the scheduler will activate the actor at a later time.

For each connection between a component method and an actor input port, a function is generated with a name formed from the name of the input port and the name of the component method. When the scheduler activates an actor via an input port, it first calls this generated function to remove data from the input port queue and then passes it to the component method.

For each TinyGUYS variable declared in the application definition, a pair of data structures and a pair of access functions are generated. The pair of data structures consists of a data storage location of the type specified in the module definition that uses the global variable along with a buffer for the storage location. The pair of access functions consists of a `PARAM_GET()` function that returns the value of the global variable and a `PARAM_PUT()` function that stores a new value for the variable in the variable's buffer. A generated flag indicates whether the scheduler needs to update the variables by copying data from the buffer.

Since most of the data structures in the TinyGALS run-time scheduler are generated, the scheduler does not need to worry about handling different data types and the conversion among them. What are left in the run-time scheduler are merely event-queuing and function-triggering mechanisms. As a result, the TinyGALS run-time scheduler is very lightweight. The scheduler itself takes 112 bytes of memory, comparable with the original 86-byte TinyOS v0.6.1 scheduler.

9.4 Node-Level Simulators

Node-level design methodologies are usually associated with simulators that simulate the behavior of a sensor network on a per-node basis. Using simulation, designers can quickly study the performance (in terms of timing, power, bandwidth, and scalability) of potential algorithms without implementing them on actual hardware and dealing with the vagaries of actual physical phenomena.

A node-level simulator typically has the following components:

- *Sensor node model:* A node in a simulator acts as a software execution platform, a sensor host, as well as a communication terminal. In order for designers to focus on the application-level code, a node model typically provides or simulates a communication protocol stack, sensor behaviors (e.g., sensing noise), and operating system services. If the nodes are mobile then the positions and motion properties of the nodes need to be modeled. If energy characteristics are part of the design considerations then the power consumption of the nodes needs to be modeled.

- *Communication model:* Depending on the details of modeling, communication may be captured at different layers. The most elaborate simulators model the communication media at the physical layer, simulating the RF propagation delay and collision of simultaneous transmissions. Alternately, the communication may be simulated at the MAC layer or network layer, using, e.g., stochastic processes to represent low-level behaviors.

- *Physical environment model:* A key element of the environment within which a sensor network operates is the physical phenomenon of interest. The environment can also be simulated at various levels of detail. For example, a moving object in the physical world may be abstracted into a point signal source. The motion of the point signal source may be modeled by differential equations or interpolated from a trajectory profile. If the sensor network is passive—i.e., it does not impact the behavior of the environment—then the environment can be simulated separately or can even be stored in data files for sensor nodes to read in. If, in addition to sensing, the network also performs actions that influence the behavior of the environment, then a more tightly integrated simulation mechanism is required.

- *Statistics and visualization:* The simulation results need to be collected for analysis. Since the goal of a simulation is typically to derive global properties from the execution of individual nodes, visualizing global behaviors is extremely important. An ideal visualization tool should allow users to easily observe on demand the spatial distribution and mobility of the nodes, the connectivity among nodes, link qualities, end-to-end communication routes and delays, phenomena and their spatio-temporal dynamics, sensor readings on each node, sensor node states, and node lifetime parameters (e.g., battery power).

A sensor network simulator simulates the behavior of a subset of the sensor nodes with respect to time. Depending on how the time is advanced in the simulation, there are two types of execution models: *cycle-driven (CD) simulation* and *discrete-event (DE) simulation*. A CD simulation discretizes the continuous notion of real time into (typically regularly spaced) ticks and simulates the system behavior at these ticks. At each tick, the physical phenomena are first simulated, and then all nodes are checked to see if they have anything to sense, process, or communicate. Sensing and computation are assumed to be finished before the next tick. Sending a packet is also assumed to be completed by then. However, the packet will not be available for the destination node until the next tick. This split-phase communication is a key mechanism to reduce cyclic dependencies that may occur in CD simulations. That is, there should be no two components such that one of them computes $y_k = f(x_k)$ and the other computes $x_k = g(y_k)$ for the same tick index k. In fact, one of the most subtle issues in designing a CD simulator is how to detect and deal with cyclic dependencies among nodes or algorithm components. Most CD simulators do not allow interdependencies within a single tick. Synchronous languages [13], which are typically used in control system designs rather than sensor network designs, do allow cyclic dependencies. They use a fixed-point semantics to define the behavior of a system at each tick.

Unlike CD simulators, DE simulators assume that the time is continuous and an event may occur at any time. An event is a 2-tuple with a value and a time stamp indicating when the event is supposed to be handled. Components in a DE simulation react to input events and produce output events. In node-level simulators, a component can be a sensor node and the events can be communication packets; or a component can be a software module within a node and the events can be message passings among these modules. Typically, components are *causal*, in the sense that if an output event is computed from an input event, then the time stamp of the output event should not be earlier than that of the input event. Noncausal components require the simulators to be able to roll back in time, and, worse, they may not define a deterministic behavior of a system [14]. A DE simulator typically requires a global event queue. All events passing between nodes or modules are put in the event queue and sorted according to their chronological order. At each iteration of the simulation, the simulator removes the first event (the one with the earliest time stamp) from the queue and triggers the component that reacts to that event.

In terms of timing behavior, a DE simulator is more accurate than a CD simulator, and, as a consequence, DE simulators run slower. The overhead of ordering all events and computation, in addition to the values and time stamps of events, usually dominates the computation time. At an early stage of a design when only the asymptotic behaviors rather than timing properties are of concern, CD simulations usually require less complex components and give faster simulations. Partly because of the approximate timing behaviors, which make simulation results less comparable from application to application, there is no general CD simulator that fits all sensor network simulation tasks. We have come across a number of homegrown simulators written in Matlab, Java, and C++. Many of them are developed for particular applications and exploit application-specific assumptions to gain efficiency.

DE simulations are sometimes considered as good as actual implementations, because of their continuous notion of time and discrete notion of events. There are several open-source or commercial simulators available. One class of these simulators comprises extensions of classical network simulators, such as ns-2,[6] J-Sim (previously known as JavaSim),[7] and GloMoSim/QualNet.[8] The focus of these simulators is on network modeling, protocols stacks, and simulation performance. Another class of simulators, sometimes called *software-in-the-loop simulators*, incorporate the actual node software into the simulation. For this reason, they are typically attached to particular hardware platforms and are less portable. Examples include TOSSIM [15] for Berkeley motes and Em* (pronounced *em star*) [16] for Linux-based nodes such as Sensoria WINS NG platforms.

9.4.1 The ns-2 Simulator and Its Sensor Network Extensions

The simulator ns-2 is an open-source network simulator that was originally designed for wired, IP networks. Extensions have been made to simulate wireless/mobile networks (e.g., 802.11 MAC and TDMA MAC) and more recently sensor networks. While the original ns-2 only supports logical addresses for each node, the wireless/mobile extension of it (e.g., [17]) introduces the notion of node locations and a simple wireless channel model. This is not a trivial extension, since once the nodes move, the simulator needs to check for each physical layer event whether the destination node is within the communication range. For a large network, this significantly slows down the simulation speed.

There are at least two efforts to extend ns-2 to simulate sensor networks: SensorSim from UCLA[9] and the NRL sensor network extension from the Navy Research Laboratory.[10]

---

[6] Available at http://www.isi.edu/nsnam/ns.

[7] Available at http://www.j-sim.org.

[8] Available at http://pcl.cs.ucla.edu/projects/glomosim.

[9] Available at http://nesl.ee.ucla.edu/projects/sensorsim/.

[10] Available at http://pf.itd.nrl.navy.mil/projects/nrlsensorsim/.

SensorSim aims at providing an energy model for sensor nodes and communication, so that power properties can be simulated [18]. SensorSim also supports hybrid simulation, where some real sensor nodes, running real applications, can be executed together with a simulation. The NRL sensor network extension provides a flexible way of modeling physical phenomena in a discrete event simulator. Physical phenomena are modeled as network nodes which communicate with real nodes through physical layers. Any interesting events are sent to the nodes that can sense them as a form of communication. The receiving nodes simply have a sensor stack parallel to the network stack that processes these events.

The main functionality of ns-2 is implemented in C++, while the dynamics of the simulation (e.g., time-dependent application characteristics) is controlled by Tcl scripts. Basic components in ns-2 are the layers in the protocol stack. They implement the *handlers* interface, indicating that they handle events. Events are communication packets that are passed between consecutive layers within one node or between the same layers across nodes.

The key advantage of ns-2 is its rich libraries of protocols for nearly all network layers and for many routing mechanisms. These protocols are modeled in fair detail, so that they closely resemble the actual protocol implementations. Examples include the following:

- *TCP:* reno, tahoe, vegas, and SACK implementations;
- *MAC:* 802.3, 802.11, and TDMA;
- *Ad hoc routing:* Destination sequenced distance vector (DSDV) routing, dynamic source routing (DSR), ad hoc on-demand distance vector (AODV) routing, and temporally ordered routing algorithm (TORA).
- *Sensor network routing:* Directed diffusion, geographical routing (GEAR), and geographical adaptive fidelity (GAF) routing.

9.4.2 The Simulator TOSSIM

TOSSIM is a dedicated simulator for TinyOS applications running on one or more Berkeley motes. The key design decisions on building TOSSIM were to make it scalable to a network of potentially thousands of nodes, and to be able to use the actual software code in the simulation. To achieve these goals, TOSSIM takes a cross-compilation approach that compiles the nesC source code into components in the simulation. The event-driven execution model of TinyOS greatly simplifies the design of TOSSIM. By replacing a few low-level components, such as the ADC, the system clock, and the radio front end, TOSSIM translates hardware interrupts into discrete-event simulator events. The simulator event queue delivers the interrupts that drive the execution of a node. The upper-layer TinyOS code runs unchanged.

TOSSIM uses a simple but powerful abstraction to model a wireless network. A network is a *directed* graph, where each vertex is a sensor node and each directed edge has a bit-error rate. Each node has a private piece of state representing what it hears on the radio channel. By setting connections among the vertices in the graph and a bit-error rate on each connection, wireless channel characteristics, such as imperfect channels, hidden terminal problems, and asymmetric links, can be easily modeled. Wireless transmissions are simulated at the bit level. If a bit error occurs, the simulator flips the bit.

TOSSIM has a visualization package called TinyViz, which is a Java application that can connect to TOSSIM simulations. TinyViz also provides mechanisms to control a running simulation by, e.g., modifying ADC readings, changing channel properties, and injecting packets. TinyViz is designed as a communication service that interacts with the TOSSIM event queue. The exact visual interface takes the form of plug-ins that can interpret TOSSIM events. Beside the default visual interfaces, users can add application-specific ones easily.

9.5 Programming Beyond Individual Nodes: State-Centric Programming

Many sensor network applications, such as target tracking, are not simply generic distributed programs over an ad hoc network of energy-constrained nodes. Deeply rooted in these applications is the notion of states of physical phenomena and models of their evolution over space and time. Some of these states may be represented on a small number of nodes and evolve over time, while others may be represented over a large and spatially distributed number of nodes, as in tracking a temperature contour.

A distinctive property of physical states, such as location, shape, and motion of objects, is their continuity in space and time. Their sensing and control is typically done through sequential state updates. System theories, the basis for most signal and information processing algorithms, provide abstractions for state update, such as:

$$\mathbf{X}_{k+1} = f(\mathbf{X}_k, u_k) \tag{9.1}$$

$$\mathbf{y}_k = g(\mathbf{X}_k, u_k) \tag{9.2}$$

where $\mathbf{X}$ is the state of a system, u are the inputs, $\mathbf{y}$ are the outputs, k is an integer update index over space and/or time, f is the state update function, and g is the output or observation function. This formulation is broad enough to capture a wide variety of algorithms in sensor fusion, signal processing, and control (e.g., Kalman filtering, Bayesian estimation, system identification, feedback control laws, and finite-state automata).

However, in distributed real-time embedded systems such as sensor networks, the formulation is not so clean as represented in those equations. The relationships among subsystems can be highly complex and dynamic over space and time. The following concerns, not explicitly raised in Equations (9.1) and (9.2), must be properly addressed during the design to ensure the correctness and efficiency of the resulting systems:

- Where are the state variables stored?
- Where do the inputs come from?
- Where do the outputs go?
- Where are the functions f and g evaluated?
- How long does the acquisition of inputs take?
- Are the inputs in u_k collected synchronously?
- Do the inputs arrive in the correct order through communication?
- What is the time duration between indices k and $k + 1$? Is it a constant?

These issues, addressing *where* and *when*, rather than *how*, to perform sensing, computation, and communication, play a central role in the overall system performance. However, these "nonfunctional" aspects of computation, related to concurrency, responsiveness, networking, and resource management, are not well supported by traditional programming models and languages. State-centric programming aims at providing design methodologies and frameworks that give meaningful abstractions for these issues, so that system designers can continue to write algorithms like Equations (9.1) and (9.2) on top of an intuitive understanding of where and when the operations are performed. This section introduces one such abstraction, namely, collaboration groups.

9.5.1 Collaboration Groups

A collaboration group is a set of entities that contribute to a state update. These entities can be physical sensor nodes or they can be more abstract system components such as virtual sensors or mobile agents hopping among sensors. In this context, they are all referred to as *agents*.

Intuitively, a collaboration group provides two abstractions: its *scope* to encapsulate network topologies and its *structure* to encapsulate communication protocols. The scope of a group defines the membership of the nodes with respect to the group. For the discussion of collaboration groups in this chapter, we broaden the notion of nodes to include both physical sensor nodes and virtual sensor nodes that may not be attached to any physical sensor. In this broader sense of node, a software agent that hops among the sensor nodes to track a target is a virtual node. Limiting the scope of a group to a subset of the entire space of all agents improves scalability. The scope of a group can be specified existentially or by a membership function (e.g., all nodes in a geometric extent, all nodes within a certain number of hops from an anchor node, or all nodes that are "close enough" to a temperature contour). Grouping nodes according to some physical attributes rather than node addresses is an important and distinguishing characteristic of sensor networks.

The *structure* of a group defines the "roles" each member plays in the group, and thus the flow of data. Are all members in the group equal peers? Is there a "leader" member in the group that consumes data? Do members in the group form a tree with parent and children relations? For example, a group may have a leader node that collects certain sensor readings from all followers. By mapping the leader and the followers onto concrete sensor nodes, we effectively define the flow of data from the hosts of followers to the host of the leader. The notion of roles also shields programmers from addressing individual nodes either by name or address. Furthermore, having multiple members with the same role provides some degree of redundancy and improves robustness of the application in the presence of node and link failures.

Formally, a group is a 4-tuple:

$$G = (A, L, p, R)$$

where A is a set of agents; L is a set of labels, called *roles*; $p: A \rightarrow L$ is a function that assigns each agent a role; $R \subseteq L \times L$ are the connectivity relations among roles.

Given the relations among roles, a group can induce a lower-level connectivity relation E among the agents, so that for $a, b \in A$, if $(p(a), p(b)) \in R$, then $(a, b) \in E$. For example, under this formulation, the leader–follower structure defines two roles, $L = \{leader, follower\}$, and a connectivity relation, $R = \{(follower, leader)\}$, meaning that the follower sends data to the leader. Then, by specifying one leader agent and multiple follower agents within a geographical region (i.e., specifying a map p from a set of agents in A to labels in L), we have effectively specified that all followers send data to the leader without addressing the followers individually.

At run time, the scope and structural dynamics of groups are managed by group management protocols, which are highly dependent on the types of groups. A detailed specification of group management protocols is beyond the scope of this section. Some examples of these protocols are discussed here at a high level.

9.5.1.1 Examples of Groups

Combinations of scopes and structures create patterns of groups that may be highly reusable from application to application. Here, we give several examples of groups, though by no means is it a complete list. The goal is to illustrate the wide variety of the kinds of groups, and the importance of mixing and matching them in applications.

Geographically Constrained Group. A geographically constrained group (GCG) consists of members within a prespecified geographical extent. Since physical signals, especially the ones from point targets, may propagate only to a limited extent in an environment, this kind of group naturally represents all the sensor nodes that can possibly "sense" a phenomenon. There are many ways to specify the geographic shape, such as circles, polygons, and their unions and intersections. A GCG can be easily established by geographically constrained flooding. Protocols such as Geocasting [19], GEAR [20], and Mobicast [21] may be used to support the communication among members even in the presence of communication "holes" in the region. A GCG may have a leader, which fuses information from all other members in the group.

N-hop Neighborhood Group. When the communication topology is more important than the geographical extent, hop counts are useful to constrain group membership. An *n*-hop neighborhood group (*n*-HNG) has an anchor node and defines that all nodes within *n* communication hops are members of the group. Since it uses hop counts rather than Euclidean distances, local broadcasting can be used to determine the scope. Usually, the anchor node is the leader of the group, and the group may have a tree structure with the leader as the root to optimize for communication. If the leader's behavior can be decomposed into suboperations running on each node, then the tree structure also provides a platform for distributing the computation.

There are several useful special cases for *n*-HNG. For example, 0-HNG contains only the anchor node itself, 1-HNG comprises the one-hop neighbors of the anchor node, and ∞-HNG contains all the nodes reachable from the root. From this point of view, TinyDB [22] is built on a ∞-HNG group.

Publish/Subscribe Group. A group may also be defined more dynamically by all entities that can provide certain data or services or that can satisfy certain predicates over their observations or internal states. A publish/subscribe group (PSG) comprises consumers expressing interest in specific types of data or services and producers that provide those data or services. Communication among members of a PSG may be established via rendezvous points, directory servers, or network protocols such as directed diffusion.

Acquaintance Group. An even more dynamic kind of group is the acquaintance group (AG), where a member belongs to the group because it was "invited" by another member in the group. The relationships among the members may not depend on any physical properties at the current time but may be purely logical and historical. A member may also quit the group without requiring permission from any other member. An AG may have a leader, serving as the rendezvous point. When the leader is also fixed on a node or in a region, GPSR [23], ad hoc routing trees, or directed diffusion types of protocols may facilitate the communication between the leader and the other members. An obvious use of this group is to monitor and control mobile agents from a base station. When all members in the group are mobile, there is no leader member, and any member may wish to communicate to one or more other members—the maintenance of connectivity among the group members can be nontrivial. The roaming hub (RoamHBA) protocol is an example of maintaining connectivity among mobile agents [24].

9.5.1.2 Using Multiple Types of Groups

Mixing and matching groups is a powerful technique for tackling system complexity by making algorithms much more scalable and resource efficient without sacrificing conceptual clarity. One may use highly tuned communication protocols for specific groups to reduce latency and energy costs.

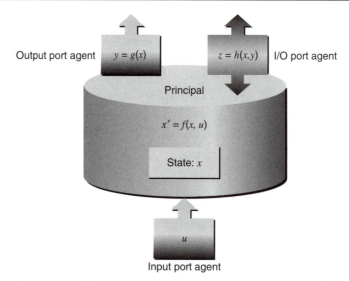

Figure 9.16 Principal and port agents (adapted from [25]).

There are various ways to compose groups. They can be composed in parallel to provide different types of input for a single computational entity. Note that one may use a GCG to gather sensor measurements, while using a 1-HNG to select the potential next leader. Groups may also be composed hierarchically, such that a group (or its representative member) is contained by another group. For example, while using multiple groups to compute target trajectories, all tracking leaders of various targets may form a PSG with a base station to report the tracking result to.

9.5.2 PIECES: A State-Centric Design Framework

PIECES (Programming and Interaction Environment for Collaborative Embedded Systems) [25] is a software framework that implements the methodology of state-centric programming over collaboration groups to support the modeling, simulation, and design of sensor network applications. It is implemented in a mixed Java-Matlab environment.

9.5.2.1 Principals and Port Agents

PIECES comprises *principals* and *port agents*. Figure 9.16 shows the basic relations among principals and port agents.

A principal is the key component for maintaining a piece of *state*. Typically, a principal maintains state corresponding to certain aspects of the physical phenomenon of interest.[11]

---

[11] From a computational perspective, a port agent as an object certainly has its own state. But the distinction here is that the states of port agents are *not* about physical phenomena.

The role of a principal is to update its state from time to time, a computation corresponding to evaluating function f in Equation (9.1). A principal also accepts other principals' queries of certain views on its own state, a computation corresponding to evaluating function g in Equation (9.2).

To update its portion of the state, a principal may gather information from other principals. To achieve this, a principal creates port agents and attaches them onto itself and onto the other principals. A port agent may be an input, an output, or both. An output port agent is also called an *observer*, since it computes outputs based on the host principal's state and sends them to other agents. Observers may be active or passive. An active observer pushes data autonomously to its destination(s), while a passive observer sends data only when a consumer requests it. A principal typically attaches a set of observers to other principals and creates a local input port agent to receive the information collected by the remote agents. Thus port agents capture communication patterns among principals.

The execution of principals and port agents can be either time-driven or event-driven, where events may include physical events that are pushed to them (i.e., data-driven) or query events from other principals or agents (i.e., demand-driven). Principals maintain state, reflecting the physical phenomena. These states can be updated, rather than rediscovered, because the underlying physical states are typically continuous in time. How often the principal states need to be updated depends on the dynamics of the phenomena or physical events. The executions of observers, however, reflect the demands of the outputs. If an output is not currently needed, there is no need to compute it. The notion of "state" effectively separates these two execution flows.

To ensure consistency of state update over a distributed computational platform, PIECES requires that a piece of state, say $\mathbf{x}_s$, can only be maintained by exactly one principal. Note that this does not prevent other principals from having local caches of $\mathbf{x}_s$ for efficiency and performance reasons; nor does it prevent the other principals from locally updating the values of cached $\mathbf{x}_s$. However, there is only one "master copy" for $\mathbf{x}_s$; all local updates should be treated as "suggestions" to the master copy, and only the principal that owns $\mathbf{x}_s$ has the final word on its values. This asymmetric access of variables simplifies the way shared variables are managed.

9.5.2.2 Principal Groups

Principals can form groups. A principal group gives its members a means to find other relevant principals and attaches port agents to them. A principal may belong to multiple groups. A port agent, however, serving as a proxy for a principal in the group, can only be associated with one group.

The creation of groups can be delegated to port agents, especially for leader-based groups. The leader port agent, typically of type input, can be created on a principal, and the port agent can take group scope and structure parameters to find the other principals and create follower port agents on them. Groups can be created dynamically, based on the collaboration needs of principals. For example, when a tracking principal finds that there is more than one target in its sensing region, it may create a classification group to fulfill the need of classifying the targets. A group may have a limited time span. When certain collaborations are no longer needed, their corresponding groups can be deleted.

The structure of a group allows its members to address other principals through their role, rather than their name or logical address. For example, the only interface that a follower port agent in a leader–follower structured group needs is to send data to the leader. If the leader moves to another node while a data packet is moving from a follower agent to the leader, the group management protocol should take care of the dangling packet, either delivering it to the leader at the new location or simply discarding it. The group management protocol may be built on top of data-centric routing and storage services such as diffusion routing and GHT.

9.5.2.3 Mobility

A principal is hosted by a specific network node at any given time. The most primitive type of principal is a *sensing principal*, which is fixed to a sensor node. A sensing principal maintains a piece of (local) state related to the physical phenomenon, based solely on its own local measurement history. Although a sensing principal is constrained to a physical node, other principals may be implemented as software agents that move from host to host, depending on information utility, performance requirements, time constraints, and resource availability. A principal P may also be *attached* to another principal Q in the sense that P moves with Q. When a principal moves, it carries its state to the new location and the scope of the group it belongs to may be updated if necessary.

Mobile principals bring additional challenges to maintaining the state. For example, a principal should not move while it is in the middle of updating the state. To ensure this, PIECES imposes the restriction that whenever an agent is triggered, its execution must have reached a quiescent state. Such a trigger is called a *responsible trigger*. Only at these quiescent states can principals move to other nodes in a well-defined way, carrying a minimum amount of information representing the phenomena.

9.5.2.4 PIECES Simulator

PIECES provides a mixed-signal simulator that simulates sensor network applications at a high level. The simulator is implemented using a combination of Java and Matlab. An event-driven engine is built in Java to simulate network message passing and agent execution at the collaboration-group level. A continuous-time engine is built in Matlab to simulate target trajectories, signals and noise, and sensor front ends. The main control flow is in Java, which maintains the global notion of time. The interface between Java and Matlab also makes it possible to implement functional algorithms such as signal processing and sensor fusion in

Matlab, while leaving their execution control in Java. A three-tier distributed architecture is designed through Java registrar and RMI interfaces, so that the execution in Java and Matlab can be separately interrupted and debugged.

Like most network simulators such as ns-2, the PIECES simulator maintains a global event queue and triggers computational entities—principals, port agents, and groups—via timed events. However, unlike network simulators that aim to accurately simulate network behavior at the packet level, the PIECES simulator verifies CSIP algorithms in a networked execution environment at the collaboration-group level. Although groups must have distributed implementations in real deployments, they are centralized objects in the simulator. They can internally make use of instant access to any member of any role, although these services are not available to either principals or port agents. This relieves the burden of having to develop, optimize, and test the communication protocols concurrently with the CSIP algorithms. The communication delay is estimated based on the locations of sender and receiver and the group management protocol being used. For example, if an output port of a sensing principal calls `sendToLeader(message)` on its container group, then the group determines the sensor nodes that host the sensing principal and the destination principal, computes the number of hops between the two nodes specified by the group management protocol, and generates a corresponding delay and a bit error based on the number of hops. A detailed example of using this simulator is given in the next section.

9.5.3 Multitarget Tracking Problem Revisited

Using the state-centric model, programmers decouple a global state into a set of independently maintained pieces, each of which is assigned a principal. To update the state, principals may look for inputs from other principals, with sensing principals supporting the lowest-level sensing and estimation tasks. Communication patterns are specified by defining collaboration groups over principals and assigning corresponding roles for each principal through port agents. A mobile principal may define a utility function, to be evaluated at candidate sensor nodes, and then move to the best next location, all in a way transparent to the application developer. Developers can focus on implementing the state update functions as if they are writing centralized programs.

Recall that, the tracking of two crossing targets can be decomposed into three phases:

- When the targets are far apart, the tracking problem can be treated as a set of single-target tracking subproblems.

- When the targets are in proximity of each other, they are tracked jointly due to signal mixing.

- After the targets move apart, the tracking problem becomes two single-target tracking subproblems again.

To summarize, there are two kinds of target information that the user cares about in this context: target positions and target identities. In the third phase above, in addition to the problem of updating track locations, there is a need to sort out ambiguity regarding which track corresponds to which target. We refer to this problem as the *identity management* problem. Specifically, one must keep track of how the identities mix when targets cross over, and update identity information at the other node when credible target identity evidence is available to one node. The identity information may be obtained by a local classifier or by an identity management protocol across tracks. In PIECES, the system is designed as a set of communicating target trackers (MTTrackers), where each tracker maintains the trajectory and identity information about a target or a set of spatially adjacent targets. An MTTracker is implemented by three principals: a *tracking principal*, a *classification principal*, and an *identity management principal*, as shown in Figure 9.17. In the first phase, the identity state of the track is trivial; thus no classification and identity management principals are needed.

A tracking principal updates the track position state periodically. It collects local individual position estimates from sensors close to the target by a GCG with a leader–follower relation. The tracking principal is the leader, and all sensing principals within a certain geographical extent centered about the current target position estimate are the followers. The tracking principal also makes hopping decisions based on its current position estimate and the node characteristic information collected from its one-hop neighbors via a 1-HNG. When the principal is initialized, it creates the agents and corresponding groups. Behind the scene, the groups create follower agents with specific types of output, indicated by the sensor modalities. Without further instructions from the programmer, the followers periodically report their outputs to the input port agents. Whenever the leader principal is activated by a time trigger, it updates the target position using the newly received data from the followers and selects the next hosting node based on neighbor node characteristics.

Both the classification principal and the identity management principal operate on the identity state, with the identity management principal maintaining the "master copy" of the state. In fact, the classification principal is created only when there is a need for classifying targets. The classification principal uses a GCG to collect class feature information from nearby sensing principals in the same way that tracking principals collect location estimates. The identity management principal forms an AG with all other identity management principals that may have relevant identity information. They become members of a particular identity group only when targets intersect and their identities mix. Both classification principals and identity management principals are *attached* to the tracking principal for their mobility decisions. However, the formation of an AG among these three principals also provides the flexibility that they can make their own hopping decisions without changing their interaction interface.

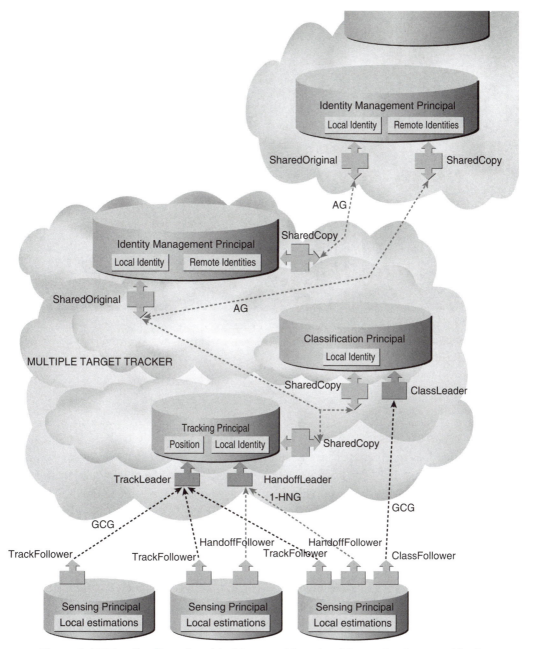

Figure 9.17 The distributed multi-object tracking algorithm as implemented in the state-centric programming model, using distributed principals and agents as discussed in the text. Notice that the state-centric model allows an application developer to focus on key pieces of state information the sensor network creates and maintains, thus raising the abstraction level of programming (adapted from [25]).

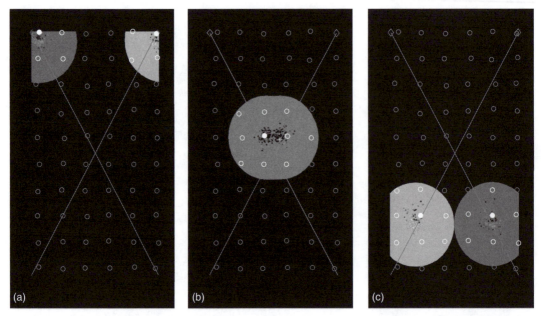

Figure 9.18 (a, b, c) Simulation snapshots: sensor nodes are indicated by small circles, and the crossing lines indicate the true trajectories of the two targets. One geographically constrained group is created for each target. When the two targets cross over, their groups merge into one.

9.5.3.1 Simulation Results

Figure 9.18 shows the progression of tracking two crossing targets. Initially, when the targets are well separated, as in Figure 9.18a, each target is tracked by a tracker whose sensing group is pictured as a shaded disk. The hosting node of the tracking principal is plotted in solid white dots, and the hosts for corresponding sensing principals are plotted in small, empty white circles inside the shaded disks. Since the targets are well separated, each identity group contains only one member—the identity management principal of a tracker. As the targets move toward the center of the sensor field, the sensing groups move with their respective track positions. In Figure 9.18b, the two separate tracking groups have merged. A joint tracking principal updates tracks for both targets. The reason for the merge is that when the two targets approach each other, it is more accurate to track the targets jointly, rather than independently, due to the effect of signal mixing. Finally, as the targets move away from each other, the merged tracking group splits into two separate single-target tracking groups that proceed to track each target separately, as shown in Figure 9.18c. At this point, the identities of the targets are mixed, so that an identity group is created to contain the two identity management principals from both trackers.

Figure 9.19 shows a snapshot of a more complicated multitarget crossover scenario. Three tracks (A, B, and D) have crossed one another at some point in time; hence the identities of

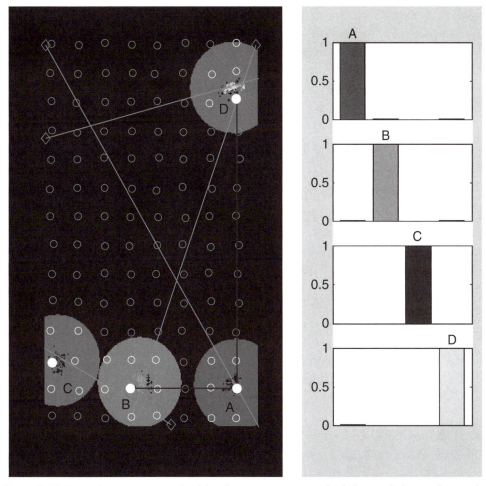

Figure 9.19 Acquaintance group for identity management: the left panel shows the tracker group and tracking results and the right panel shows the identity of each track as bar charts. On the right panel, each subfigure represents the identity belief of each tracker. For example, in the first subfigure, the identity management principal—the one near the bottom right on the left panel—believes that the track it is maintaining is most likely that of the target A, with a much smaller probability of being target B or target D.

these tracks are mixed. The corresponding identity management principals form an identity group. Now, one identity management principal (the one at the bottom-right corner) collects classification information and identifies the track as belonging to the red target, as shown in the figure. Hence, it communicates with its peers in the identity management group (top-right and bottom-middle principals) to update the identity of their respective targets as well. The updated identity is shown in the right-hand-side bar chart in Figure 9.19. Defining the acquaintance group and its interface in this way allows these spatially distributed identity management principals to communicate with one another, thus providing the application developer the necessary abstraction for focusing on the functional aspect of identity management algorithms without worrying about the communication details.

9.6 Summary

This chapter has provided an overview of sensor network hardware and software platforms and application design methodologies. Although most of the existing platforms are tightly bound to particular hardware designs, the design principles covered in this chapter can be generalized to other hardware platforms as well. We described TinyOS, nesC, and TinyGALS, as examples of node-level operating systems and programming languages based on the Berkeley mote hardware. The node-centric platforms typically employ a message-passing abstraction of communication between nodes. Interfaces for these protocols include the active messaging of TinyOS and the publish/subscribe interface of directed diffusion.

Programming distributed systems beyond individual nodes has been traditionally handled by middleware technologies such as CORBA [26]. However, these are not directly suitable for ad hoc resource-constrained sensor networks. State-centric programming is aimed at providing domain-specific programming models for information processing applications in sensor networks. This allows programmers to think in terms of high-level abstractions such as the state of the physical phenomena of interest, rather than the behaviors of individual nodes. Ultimately, in a dense sensor network, the behavior of each individual node is not as important, and sensor network applications should be robust to individual node failures. It is the collective behavior that makes sensor networks viable and interesting.

Programming methodologies and tools for sensor networks is a new area of research, as new network organization principles and new programming abstractions emerge and as more sensor network applications are built. Just as hardware-description languages (e.g., VHDL and Verilog) have served the VLSI designs, and as control languages (e.g., Signal [27], Esterel [28], and Giotto [29]) and architectures (e.g., time-triggered architecture [30]) have supported real-time control system designs, domain-specific programming models and tools will be key to the development and deployment of large-scale sensor network applications.

References

[1] J. Hill, R. Szewcyk, A. Woo, D. Culler, S. Hollar, K. Pister, System architecture directions for networked sensors, in: Proc. 8th International Conference on Architectural Support for Programming Languages and Operating Systems (ASPLOS IV), Cambridge, MA, 2000, pp. 93–104.

[2] A. Savvides, M.B. Srivastava, A distributed computation platform for wireless embedded sensing, in: Proc. International Conference on Computer Design (ICCD02), Freiburg, Germany, September 2002, pp. 220–225.

[3] A. Chandrakasan, R. Min, M. Bhardwaj, S.-H. Cho, A. Wang, Power aware wireless microsensor systems, in: Proc. 32nd European Solid-State Device Research Conference (ESSDERC02), Florence, Italy, September 2002.

[4] J.M. Kahn, R.H. Katz, K. Pister, Next century challenges: mobile networking for "smart dust," in: Proc. 5th International Conference on Mobile Computing and Networking (MobiCom 1999), Seattle, WA, ACM Press, August 1999, pp. 271–278.

[5] J. Rabaey, J. Ammer, J. da Silva, D. Patel, S. Roundy, Picoradio supports ad-hoc ultra-low power wireless networking. IEEE Computer Magazine (2002) 42–48.

[6] J.J. Liu, J. Liu, J. Reich, P. Cheung, F. Zhao, Distributed group management for track initiation and maintenance in target localization applications, in: Proc. 2nd International Workshop on Information Processing in Sensor Networks (IPSN03), Palo Alto, CA, Springer, April 2003, pp. 113–128.

[7] A. Silberschatz, P.B. Galvin, G. Gagne, Operating System Concepts, sixth ed., John Wiley & Sons, Hoboken, NJ, 2003.

[8] G. Buttanzo, Hard Real-Time Computing Systems, Kluwer Academic Publishers, The Netherlands, 1997.

[9] E. Cheong, J. Liebman, J. Liu, F. Zhao, TinyGALS: a programming model for event-driven embedded systems, in: Proc. 18th Annual ACM Symposium on Applied Computing (SAC '03), Melbourne, FL, March 2003, pp. 698–704.

[10] P. Levis, D. Culler, Maté: a tiny virtual machine for sensor networks, in: Proc. 10th International Conference on Architectural Support for Programming Languages and Operating Systems (ASPLOS X), San Jose, CA, October 2002, pp. 85–95.

[11] D. Gay, P. Levis, R. von Behren, M. Welsh, E. Brewer, D. Culler, The nesC language: a holistic approach to network embedded systems, in: Proc. ACM SIGPLAN 2003 Conference on Programming Language Design and Implementation (PLDI), San Diego, CA, June 2003, pp. 1–11.

[12] W.B. Ackerman, Data flow languages, IEEE Comp. 15 (2) (1982) 15–22.

[13] N. Halbwachs, Synchronous Programming of Reactive Systems, Kluwer International Series in Engineering and Computer Science, 215, Kluwer Academic Publishers, The Netherlands, 1993.

[14] E.A. Lee, Modeling concurrent real-time processes using discrete events, Ann. Software Eng. 7 (1999) 25–45.

[15] P. Levis, N. Lee, M. Welsh, D. Culler, TOSSIM: accurate and scalable simulation of entire TinyOS applications, in: Proc. 1st ACM Conference on Embedded Networked Sensor Systems (SenSys2003), Los Angeles, CA, November 2003, pp. 126–137.

[16] J. Elson, S. Bien, N. Busek, V. Bychkovskiy, A. Cerpa, D. Ganesan, L. Girod, B. Greenstein, T. Schoellhammer, T. Stathopoulos, D. Estrin, EmStar: an environment for developing wireless embedded systems software, Cens Technical Report 0009, University of California, Los Angeles, March 2003.

[17] J. Broch, D.A. Maltz, D.B. Johnson, Y.-C. Hu, J. Jetcheva, A performance comparison of multi-hop wireless ad hoc network routing protocols, in: Proc. 4th Annual International Conference on Mobile Computing and Networking (MobiCom 1998), Dallas, TX, ACM Press, October 1998, pp. 85–97.

[18] S. Park, A. Savvides, M.B. Srivastava, SensorSim: a simulation framework for sensor networks, in: Proc. 3rd ACM International Workshop on Modeling, Analysis and Simulation of Wireless and Mobile Systems (MSWiM 2000), Boston, MA, ACM Press, August 2000, pp. 104–111.

[19] Y.-B. Ko, N.H. Vaidya, Geocasting in mobile ad hoc networks: location based multicast algorithms, in: Proc. IEEE Workshop on Mobile Computing Systems and Applications, New Orleans, LA, February 1999, pp. 101–110.

[20] Y. Yu, R. Govindan, D. Estrin, Geographical and energy aware routing: a recursive data dissemination protocol for wireless sensor networks. Technical Report UCLA/CSD-TR-01-0023, UCLA Computer Science Department, May 2001.

[21] Q. Huang, C. Lu, G.-C. Roman, Mobicast: just-in-time multicast for sensor networks under spatiotemporal constraints, in: Proc. 2nd International Workshop on Information Processing in Sensor Networks (IPSN03), Palo Alto, CA, Springer, April 2003, pp. 442–457.

[22] S. Madden, M. Franklin, J. Hellerstein, W. Hong. TAG: a tiny aggregation service for ad-hoc sensor networks, in: Proc. 5th Symposium on Operating Systems Design and Implementation (OSDI 2002), Boston, MA, ACM Press, December 2002, pp. 131–146.

[23] B. Karp, H.T. Kung, GPSR: greedy perimeter stateless routing for wireless networks, in: Proc. 6th Annual International Conference on Mobile Computing and Networking (MobiCom 2000), ACM Press, 2000, pp. 243–254.

[24] Q. Fang, J. Liu, L. Guibas, F. Zhao, Roam HBA: maintaining group connectivity in sensor networks, in: Proc. 3rd International Symposium on Information Processing in Sensor Networks (IPSN 2004), Berkeley, CA, April 2004, pp. 151–160.

[25] J. Liu, M. Chu, J.J. Liu, J. Reich, F. Zhao, State-centric programming for sensor and actuator network systems, IEEE Pervasive Computing Magazine (2003) 50–62.

[26] Object Management Group, The common object request broker: architecture and specification, Technical Report, Object Management Group, June 1999.

[27] P. Le Guernic, T. Gautier, M. Le Borgne, C. Le Maire, Programming real-time applications with signal, Proc. IEEE 79 (9) (1991) 1321–1336.

[28] G. Berry, G. Gonthier, The Esterel synchronous programming language: design, semantics, implementation, Sci. Comput. Progr. 19 (2) (1992) 87–152.

[29] T.A. Henzinger, B. Horowitz, C.M. Kirsch, Giotto: a time-triggered language for embedded programming, Lecture Notes Comp. Sci. 2211 (2001) 166–185.

[30] H. Kopetz, The time-triggered model of computation, in: Proc. 19th IEEE Real-Time Systems Symposium (RTSS98), December 1998, pp. 168–177.

CHAPTER 10

Mobile IP

Adrian Farrel

Today's computers are smaller and more mobile than they once were. Processing power that used to take up a whole air-conditioned room can now be easily carried around and used anywhere. At the same time, connectivity to the Internet has become easier and more diverse. A user may now disconnect his computer in the office and reconnect from another site within the same office or elsewhere. Connectivity may be achieved through established networking technologies such as Ethernet, through dial-up lines, or using wireless networking. In the latter case, the point of attachment may change even while the user is connected since the user may travel between base stations of a wireless local area network (LAN) or a mobile phone system.

The infrastructure to support IP telephony and IP over dial-up links is discussed in subsequent sections of this chapter. This section examines the problems and solutions for handling IP when a host's physical location changes.

10.1 The Requirements of Mobile IP

Mobile IP allows a node to change its point of attachment to the Internet without needing to change its IP address. This is not simply a configuration simplification, but can facilitate continuous application-level connectivity as the node moves from point to point.

A possible solution to this problem would be to distribute routes through the network to declare the node's new location and to update the routing tables so that packets can be correctly dispatched. This might, at first, seem attractive, but it is a solution that scales very poorly since it would be necessary to retain host-specific routes for each mobile host. As the number of mobile hosts in the Internet increases (and the growth of web access from mobile devices such as cell phones and palm-tops is very rapid), it would become impractical to maintain such tables in the core of the Internet.

The solution developed by the IETF involves protocol extensions whereby packets targeted at a mobile host are sent to its home network (as if the host were not mobile) and passed to a static (nonmobile) node called the node's *home agent*. The mobile host registers its real location with the home agent, which is responsible for forwarding the packets to the host.

If the mobile host is at home (attached to its home network), forwarding is just plain old IP forwarding, but if the host is roving, packets must be tunneled across the Internet to a *care-of address* where the host has registered its attachment to a *foreign agent*. At the care-of address (the end of the tunnel) the packets are forwarded to the mobile host. This is illustrated in Figure 10.1.

Note that this tunneling process is only required in one direction. Packets sent by the mobile host may be routed through the network using the standard IP procedures.

It is worth observing that although mobile IP can be used to address any IP mobility issue, its use within wireless LANs and mobile phone networks might be better served by link-layer (i.e., sub-IP) procedures such as link-layer handoff. These processes are typically built into the link-layer mechanisms and involve less overhead than mobile IP. Such processes do, however, require that the mobile host remains logically connected within the IP subnet to which its address belongs—it becomes the responsibility of the link layer to maintain connections or virtual connections into that subnet.

An alternative to tunneling in mobile IP might be to use source routing within IP. IPv4 has been enhanced with optional extensions to support source routing. However, since the source routing extensions to IPv4 are a relatively new development and are in any case optional, many (or even most) deployed IPv4 nodes do not support them. This means that they are not a lot of use for developing mobile IP services over existing IPv4 networks. They may be

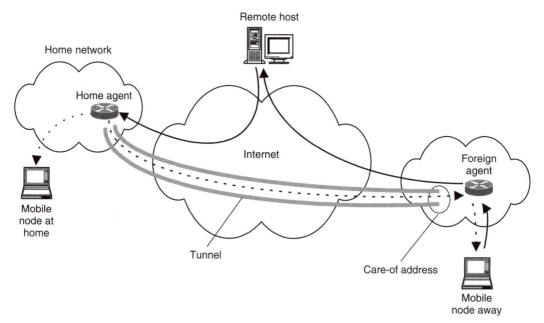

Figure 10.1 If the mobile node is away from home, IP traffic is sent to a home agent and tunneled across the Internet to a foreign agent for delivery to the mobile node.

of more use in new networks that are being constructed for the first time since the Service Providers can insist on these extensions from their equipment vendors.

IPv6 offers some alternatives to tunneling for mobile IP by using the routing extension header. In this way the mobile node can establish communications with its home agent and then use information learned to directly route packets to the destination, bypassing the home agent. Since this feature is built into IPv6 and so supported by all IPv6 implementations, it makes IPv6 a popular option for mobile IP deployments.

10.2 Extending the Protocols

Specific protocol exchanges are necessary to allow the mobile node to register with either its home agent or some remote foreign agent. Similarly, once a mobile node has registered with a foreign agent, a further registration process with the home agent is needed to get it to redirect traffic and to supply the care-of address. Additionally, foreign agents may advertise their capabilities so that mobile nodes that connect to them know that registration for mobile IP is an option. The messages to support these functions are described in RFC 3344.

Mobile nodes discover available home and foreign agents through extensions to the ICMP router discovery process. The agents advertise their mobile IP capabilities through new TLVs, shown in Figure 10.2, that follow the Router Advertisement fields in an ICMP Router Advertisement Message. The TLVs give the capabilities of the agent and list a set of useable care-of addresses and the length of validity of the registration. The meanings of the capabilities bit flags are shown in Table 10.1.

Note that regardless of the capability set advertised, a foreign agent must always support IP in IP encapsulation as defined in RFC 2003. This is the favored tunneling mechanism.

A mobile node tells its home agent about its care-of address using a registration procedure built as a new miniprotocol that uses UDP as its transport. The UDP port number 434 is reserved for agents to listen on for incoming registration requests from mobile nodes. The registration is a simple request–reply exchange using the messages shown in Figure 10.3.

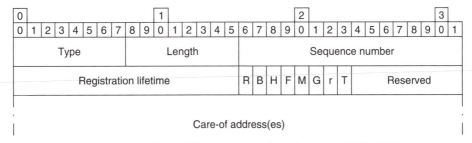

Figure 10.2 The mobile IP agent advertisement ICMP TLV.

Table 10.1 The Agent Capability Flags Within the Mobile IP Agent Advertisement ICMP TLV.

Flag	Meaning
R	The mobile nodes must complete registration procedures to make use of this foreign agent.
B	The agent is busy and will not accept registrations from additional mobile nodes.
H	This agent offers service as a home agent on the link on which this Agent Advertisement message was sent.
F	This agent offers service as a foreign agent on the link on which this Agent Advertisement message was sent.
M	This agent supports receiving tunneled datagrams (from the home agent) that use minimal encapsulation as defined in RFC 2004.
G	This agent supports receiving tunneled datagrams (from the home agent) that use GRE encapsulation as defined in RFC 2784.
r	Reserved (must be zero).
T	This agent supports reverse tunneling as defined in RFC 3024.

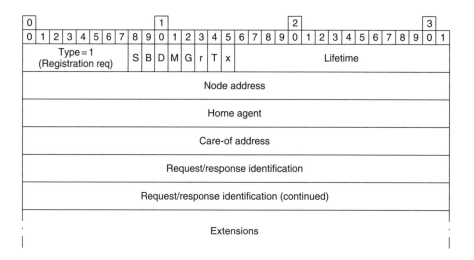

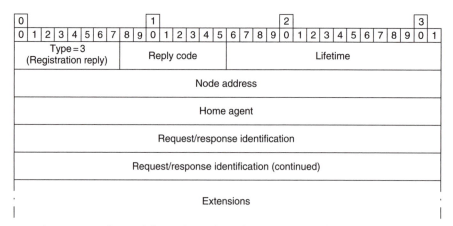

Figure 10.3 The mobile node registration request and reply messages.

The capability bits in the Registration message are inherited with some modification from the ICMP Advertisement message flags shown in Table 10.1—their precise meanings are given in Table 10.2. The Request/Response Identification is a 64-bit random number used by the requester to prevent replay attacks by malicious agents. The Reply Code in the Reply message indicates the success or failure of the request—a host of rejection reasons are allowed, as shown in Table 10.3.

Extensions to the Request and Reply messages exist to convey authentication details. The extensions are defined as TLVs for use in communication between the different components of the mobile IP network. Thus, there are extensions for Mobile-Home Authentication, Mobile-Foreign Authentication, and Foreign-Home Authentication.

10.3 Reverse Tunneling

In some environments, routers examine not only the destination IP address, but also the source IP address, when making a decision about how to forward a packet. This processing allows the router to make some attempts to filter out spoofed packets. However, in mobile IP, the source IP address of a packet sent by the mobile node may be unexpected within the context of the foreign network and may be discarded by a router. This undesirable problem is overcome by tunneling packets from the mobile node back to the home agent, and having the home agent forward them from there. This process, known as reverse tunneling, effectively reverses the path of packets that are sent to the mobile node.

Ideally, reverse tunnels would be established by the mobile nodes; however, this only works if the mobile node is colocated with the care-of address. If a foreign agent is used to provide

Table 10.2 The Capability Flags Within the Mobile IP Registration Request Message.

Flag	Meaning
S	This bit indicates that the mobile node is requesting that this binding supplement the previous binding rather than replacing it.
B	The mobile node requests that broadcast datagrams be tunneled to it along with any datagrams that are specifically addressed to it.
D	The mobile node will itself decapsulate datagrams that are tunneled to the care-of address. That is, the mobile node is colocated with the care-of address.
M	The mobile node requests the use of minimal encapsulation tunneling as defined in RFC 2004.
G	The mobile node requests the use of GRE encapsulation tunneling as defined in RFC 2784.
r	Reserved (must be zero).
T	The mobile node requests the use of reverse tunneling as defined in RFC 3024 (see below).
x	Reserved (must be zero).

Table 10.3 Mobile IP Registration Reply Message Reply Codes.

Reply Code	Meaning
0	Registration accepted
1	Registration accepted, but simultaneous mobility bindings unsupported
Rejections from the Foreign Agent	
64	Reason unspecified
65	Administratively prohibited
66	Insufficient resources
67	Mobile node failed authentication
68	Home agent failed authentication
69	Requested lifetime too long
70	Poorly formed Request
71	Poorly formed Reply
72	Requested encapsulation unavailable
73	Reserved and unavailable
74	Requested reverse tunnel unavailable
75	Reverse tunnel is mandatory and T-bit not set
76	Mobile node too distant
77	Invalid care-of address
78	Registration timeout
79	Delivery style not supported
80	Home network unreachable (ICMP error received)
81	Home agent host unreachable (ICMP error received)
82	Home agent port unreachable (ICMP error received)
88	Home agent unreachable (other ICMP error received)
Rejections from the Home Agent	
128	Reason unspecified
129	Administratively prohibited
130	Insufficient resources
131	Mobile node failed authentication
132	Foreign agent failed authentication
133	Registration Identification mismatch
134	Poorly formed Request
135	Too many simultaneous mobility bindings
136	Unknown home agent address
137	Requested reverse tunnel unavailable
138	Reverse tunnel is mandatory and T-bit not set
139	Requested encapsulation unavailable

the care-of address, the reverse tunnel is managed by the foreign agent. There are two options:

1. In the Direct Delivery style of reverse tunneling, the mobile node sends packets directly to the foreign agent as its default router and lets the foreign agent intercept them, and tunnel them to the home agent.

2. In the Encapsulating Delivery style of reverse tunneling, the mobile node sends packets to the foreign agent using a tunnel. The foreign agent decapsulates the packets and retunnels them to the home agent.

Signaling extensions for reverse tunneling are defined in RFC 3024 and basically involve the use of the T-bit shown in Tables 10.1 and 10.2, and the reply codes 74–76, 79, and 137–139 shown in Table 10.3.

10.4 Security Concerns

The standards for mobile IP mandate the use of strong authentication cryptography for the registration process between a mobile node and its home agent. This is the most vulnerable part of the mobile IP process and might, if intercepted or spoofed, cause the interception or diversion of all traffic sent from the home agent to the mobile node on behalf of the remote point of contact. Strong authentication may also be used between the mobile node and the foreign agent and between the foreign agent and the home agent. Agent discovery messages are not subject to authentication because there is currently no IP-based authentication key distribution protocol.

The data exchanged between hosts participating in mobile IP may also be encrypted. Any of the standard approaches may be used, giving rise to three models. In the first, the source of the data encrypts it and sends it through the home agent to the mobile node, which decrypts it. In the second model, the home agent chooses whether to encrypt the data it forwards according to whether the mobile node is away from or at home—in this way data forwarded to a roving mobile node is encrypted across the unknown part of the network and is decrypted by the mobile node. In the final model, IPsec is used as the tunneling protocol between the home agent and the foreign agent and the mobile node does not need to have encryption/decryption capabilities.

Further Reading

Mobile IP

Mobile IP is discussed by the Mobile IP Working Group of the IETF. Their web site is http://www.ietf.org/html.charters/mobileip-charter.html. Some key RFCs are:

- RFC 2005—Applicability Statement for IP Mobility Support.
- RFC 2794—Mobile IP Network Access Identifier Extension for IPv4.
- RFC 3024—Reverse Tunneling for Mobile IP.
- RFC 3344—IP Mobility Support for IPv4.

Media gateway control is worked on by the Megaco Working Group located at http://www.ietf.org/html.charters/megaco-charter.html.

Some important RFCs are:

- RFC 2824—Call Processing Language Framework and Requirements.
- RFC 2871—A Framework for Telephony Routing over IP.
- RFC 3219—Telephony Routing over IP (TRIP).
- RFC 3216—SIP: Session Initiation Protocol.
- RFC 3312—Integration of Resource Management and Session Initiation Protocol (SIP).
- RFC 3428—Session Initiation Protocol (SIP) Extension for Instant Messaging.
- RFC 2805—Media Gateway Control Protocol Architecture and Requirements.
- RFC 3015—Megaco Protocol Version 1.0.
- RFC 3054—Megaco IP Phone Media Gateway Application Profile.

CHAPTER 11

Mobile IPv6

Qing Li
Jinmei Tatuya
Keiichi Shima

11.1 Introduction

Mobile IPv6 is a mobility support protocol for IPv6 at the network layer. The specification was standardized at the IETF in June 2004. The standardization process was quite slow compared to the basic IPv6 specification. The initial working group draft of Mobile IPv6 was submitted in 1996, which compares favorably with the first IPv6 draft specification which was proposed to the IPng working group in 1995. The reason for the delay in the standardization of Mobile IPv6 was the need to solve security issues associated with the protocol. Mobile IPv6 enables IPv6 nodes to send or receive packets whose source address does not match the network prefix to which they are currently attached. That is, nodes have to use a type of source spoofing technique. In the early version of the specification, the protocol required the use of IPsec to ensure that the source address was valid. However, when we consider the real situation—a mobile node may communicate with many other nodes for which it does not have any identification information—using IPsec is almost impossible.

The IESG rejected the proposal from the Mobile IPv6 working group to standardize the protocol specification at that time, and insisted the working group propose a procedure to securely validate the source address of a mobile node. The Mobile IPv6 working group started a discussion to solve the problem in 2000 and finally developed a loose address ownership mechanism called the return routability procedure (discussed in Section 11.5.1) in 2002. The specification was accepted by the IESG and published as [1] in 2004.

The KAME project originally used the Mobile IPv6 stack that was contributed by Ericsson. The project started to implement its own Mobile IPv6 stack in 2001 during the middle of the second term of the KAME activity. KAME implemented several versions of Mobile IPv6 to follow and validate the latest specification. The code discussed in this chapter is based on the KAME snapshot released in July 2004. At that time, the specification had already been accepted as an RFC and the code was mature.

After KAME completed the first version of their Mobile IPv6 code, they started to redesign the architecture of the mobility stack. In the new architecture most of the signal processing tasks are moved to user space, compared to the first version of Mobile IPv6 where the code was implemented in the kernel. The design is similar to the BSD Routing Socket mechanism, which separates the routing information exchange and forwarding mechanisms, with exchanging routing information in the user space and forwarding in the kernel space. There are many benefits to this design. It makes it easier to develop complicated signal processing code since developers can utilize many advanced debugging programs and techniques, while the packet processing performance is not reduced, since it is done in the kernel. Extending or replacing some of the signal processing mechanisms is also easier, which makes it possible to add support for new mobility protocols or to adapt some part of the functions to user needs. Reducing the amount of kernel modification is important when we consider merging the developed code into the original BSDs.

In this chapter, we first introduce the basic procedures of Mobile IPv6. Next, we discuss how the KAME Mobile IPv6 stack implements the specification in detail and briefly explain the usage of the stack.

11.2 Mobile IPv6 Overview

Mobile IPv6 adds the mobility function to IPv6. Mobile IPv6 is specified in [1, 2]. An IPv6 host which supports the Mobile IPv6 function can move around the IPv6 Internet.[1] The host which supports Mobile IPv6 can change its point of attachment to the IPv6 Internet whenever it wants. If a host does not support Mobile IPv6, all the existing connections on the host are terminated when it changes its point of attachment. A connection between two nodes is maintained by the pairing of the source address and the destination address. Since the IPv6 address of an IPv6 node is assigned based on the prefix of the network, the assigned address on a given network becomes invalid when the host leaves that network and attaches itself to another network. The reason for this problem came from the nature of IP addresses. An IP address has two meanings: one is the identifier of the node and the other is the location information of the node. It would not be a big problem as long as IP nodes do not move around the Internet frequently, because, in that case, the location information would not change frequently and we could use location information as the identifier of a node. However, recent progress of communication technologies and small computers made it possible for IP nodes to move around. It is getting harder and harder to treat location information as an identifier, because the location information frequently changes.

---

[1] There is ongoing work to extend the Mobile IPv6 specification to support the IPv4 Internet [MIP6-NEMO-V4TRAVERSAL]. With this extension, a Mobile IPv6 mobile node can attach to the IPv4 Internet keeping the existing connections with its IPv6 peer nodes. In addition, the mobile node can use a fixed IPv4 address to communicate with other IPv4 nodes regardless of the IP version of the network to which the node is attached.

As such the basic idea of Mobile IPv6 is to provide a second IPv6 address to an IPv6 host as an identifier in addition to the address that is usually assigned to the node from the attached network as a locator. The second address is fixed to the home position of the host and never changes even if the host moves. The fixed address is called a "home address." As long as the host uses its home address as its connection information, the connection between the host and other nodes will not be terminated when the mobile host moves.

The concept of a home address provides another useful feature to a host that supports Mobile IPv6. Any IPv6 nodes on the Internet can access a host which supports Mobile IPv6 by specifying its home address, regardless of the location of the host. Such a feature will make it possible to create a roaming server. Since the home address of the roaming server never changes, we can constantly reach the server at the home address. For example, anyone could run a web server application on a notebook computer which supports Mobile IPv6 and everyone could access it without any knowledge of where the computer is located.

11.2.1 Types of Nodes

The Mobile IPv6 specification defines three types of nodes. The first type is the *mobile node*, which has the capability of moving around IPv6 networks without breaking existing connections while moving. A mobile node is assigned a permanent IPv6 address called a *home address*. A home address is an address assigned to the mobile node when it is attached to the *home network* and through which the mobile node is always reachable, regardless of its location on an IPv6 network. Because the mobile node is always assigned the home address, it is always logically connected to the home link. When a mobile node leaves its home network and attaches to another network, the node will get another address called a *care-of address*, which is assigned from the newly attached network. This network, which is not a home network, is called a *foreign network* or a *visited network*. A mobile node does not use a care-of address as an endpoint address when communicating with other nodes, since the address may change when the mobile node changes its point of attachment.

A second Mobile IPv6 node type is the *home agent*, which acts as a support node on the home network for Mobile IPv6 mobile nodes. A home agent is a router which has a proxy function for mobile nodes while they are away from home. The destination addresses of packets sent to mobile nodes are set to the home addresses of the mobile nodes. A home agent intercepts all packets which are addressed to the mobile node's home address, and thus delivered to the home network on behalf of the mobile nodes.

This forwarding mechanism is the core feature provided by the Mobile IPv6 protocol. All IPv6 nodes which want to communicate with a mobile node can use the home address of the mobile node as a destination address, regardless of the current location of the mobile node. Those packets sent from an IPv6 node to the home address of a mobile node are delivered to the home network by the Internet routing mechanism where the home agent of the mobile node receives the packets and forwards the packets appropriately. For the reverse direction, a mobile node uses its home address as a source address when sending packets. However, a mobile cannot directly send packet nodes whose source address is a home address from its current location if it is away from home, since source addresses are not topologically correct. Sending a packet whose source address is out of the range of the network address of the sender node is a common technique when an attacker tries to hide its location when he is attacking a specific node. Such a packet may be considered as an attack. Because of this reason, the first hop router may drop such topologically incorrect packets to avoid the risk of the source spoofing attack. To solve this problem, a mobile node uses the IPv6 in IPv6 encapsulation technology. All packets sent from a mobile node while away from home are sent to its home agent using the encapsulation mechanism. The home agent decapsulates the packets and forwards them as if the packets were sent from the home network.

A third type of Mobile IPv6 node is called the *correspondent node*. A correspondent node is an IPv6 node that communicates with a mobile node. A correspondent node does not have to be Mobile IPv6-capable, other than supporting the IPv6 protocol; any IPv6 node can be a correspondent node. Since the Mobile IPv6 specification provides a backward compatibility to all IPv6 nodes which do not support Mobile IPv6, all IPv6 nodes can communicate with mobile nodes without any modification. However, as we have described in the previous paragraph, all packets between a mobile node and a correspondent node must be forwarded basically by the home agent of the mobile node. This process is sometimes redundant, especially when a correspondent node and a mobile node are located on topologically near networks. To solve this redundancy, Mobile IPv6 provides an optimization mechanism called the *route optimization* mechanism which a correspondent node may support. A mobile node can send packets directly to a correspondent node using the care-of address of the mobile node as a source address. The information of the home address of a mobile node is carried by the newly defined option for the Destination Options Header. Also, a correspondent node can send packets directly to the care-of address of a mobile node. In this case, the information of the home address is carried by the Routing Header.

A correspondent node may itself be a mobile node. In this case, two moving nodes can communicate with each other without terminating their sessions regardless of their points of attachment to the Internet.

11.2.2 Basic Operation of Mobile IPv6

A mobile node uses a home address when communicating with other nodes. When a mobile node moves from one network to another network, the node sends a message called a *Binding Update* (BU) to its home agent. The message includes the care-of address and the home address of the mobile node. Such information is called *binding information*, since it binds a care-of address to the home address of a mobile node.

When a home agent receives the message and accepts the contents of the message, the home agent replies with a *Binding Acknowledgment* (BA) message to indicate that the BU message is accepted. The home agent creates a bi-directional tunnel connection from its address to the care-of address of the mobile node. A mobile node also creates a bi-directional tunnel connection from its care-of address to the home agent when it receives the acknowledgment message. After the successful tunnel creation, all packets sent to the home address of the mobile node are intercepted by the home agent at the home network and tunneled to the mobile node. Also, all packets originated at the mobile node are tunneled to its home agent and forwarded from its home network to destination nodes. Figure 11.1 shows the concept.

The communication path between a mobile node and a peer node described in Figure 11.1 sometimes may not be optimal. Figure 11.2 shows the worst case: A mobile node and a correspondent node are on the same network. The packets exchanged between them are always sent to the home network of the mobile nodes, even if they are directly accessible to each other using the local network. For example, when two people whose mobile nodes are originally located in Japan visit the United States, their traffic always traverses the Pacific Ocean.

If a peer node supports the route optimization mechanism defined in the Mobile IPv6 specification, the mobile node and the peer node can communicate directly without detouring through the home agent. To optimize the route, the mobile node sends a BU message to the peer node. After it receives the message, the peer node sends packets directly to the care-of address of the mobile node. The packets also contain a Routing Header which specifies their

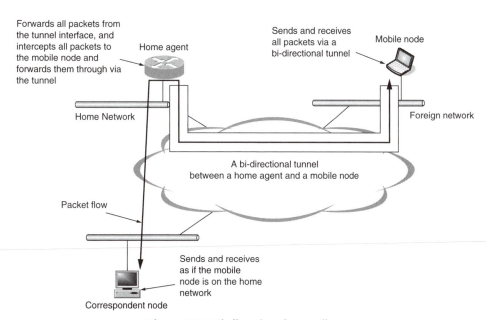

Figure 11.1 Bi-directional tunneling.

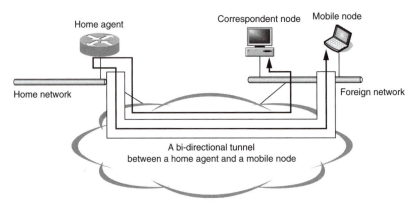

Figure 11.2 The worst case of bi-directional tunneling.

final destination which is set to the home address of the mobile node. The packets are routed directly to the care-of address of the mobile node. The mobile node receives the packets and finds the packets have a Routing Header and performs Routing Header processing, which involves swapping the destination address in the packets' IPv6 header and the home address carried in the Routing Header. The mobile node forwards the packets to the final destination which is the home address at this point, and the packets are delivered to the mobile node itself. When the mobile node sends packets to the peer node, the mobile node sets its care-of address as a source address of the packets and inserts its home address into a Destination Options Header. The peer node swaps the care-of address and the home address when it receives those packets, and processes the packets as if they were sent from the home address. Figure 11.3 shows the procedure.

As you may notice, a BU message is quite a dangerous message. If a node accepts the message without any verification, an attacker can easily redirect packets sent to the mobile node to the attacker. To prevent this attack, the message is protected in the following two ways:

- A BU message to a home agent is protected by the IPsec mechanism.

- A BU message to a correspondent node is protected by the return routability procedure described in Section 11.5.1.

The IPsec mechanism is strong enough to prevent this type of attack and we can use the technology between a mobile node and a home agent. However, it is difficult to use the IPsec mechanism between a mobile node and a correspondent node, since the IPsec mechanism requires both nodes to be in the same administrative domain. We can assume that a home agent and a mobile node can share such a secret since they are managed by the same administrative domain in most cases. However, there is usually no such relationship between a mobile node and a correspondent node.

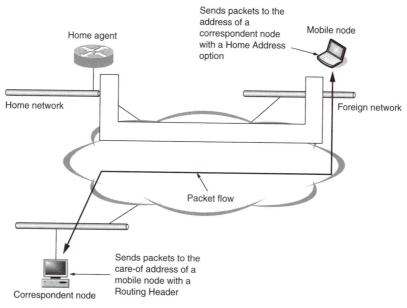

Figure 11.3 Optimized communication between a mobile node and a correspondent node.

There is an ongoing action to use the IPsec mechanism between a mobile node and a correspondent node [MIP6-CN-IPSEC].

The Mobile IPv6 specification defines a new method of creating a shared secret between a mobile node and a correspondent node. The procedure is called the *return routability* procedure. When a mobile node sends a BU message, the most important thing is to provide a way to prove to the correspondent node that the care-of address and home address are owned by the same mobile node. The return routability procedure provides such an address ownership proof mechanism.

A mobile node sends two messages: One message is sent from its home address and the other message is sent from its care-of address. Respectively, the messages are called a *Home Test Init* (HoTI) message and a *Care-of Test Init* (CoTI) message. A correspondent node replies to both messages with a *Home Test* (HoT) message to the first and a *Care-of Test* (CoT) message to the second. These reply messages include values for tokens which are computed from addresses of the mobile node and secret information which is only kept in the correspondent node. A mobile node generates a shared secret from the token values and puts a signature in a BU message using the shared secret. This mechanism ensures that the home address and the care-of address are assigned to the same mobile node. Figure 11.4 shows the procedure. Section 11.4 contains a detailed discussion of Mobile IPv6 operation.

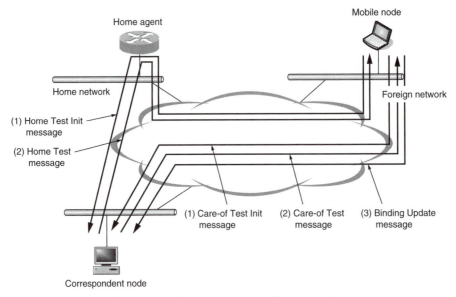

Figure 11.4 The return routability procedure.

11.3 Header Extension

Reference [1] defines new extension headers and several new types and options for existing headers for Mobile IPv6. The specification also defines some header formats of Neighbor Discovery [3] which are modified for Mobile IPv6. The following is a list of new or modified headers and options. The detailed description of each header and option will be discussed in Sections 11.3.2 to 11.3.7.

- *Home Address Option:* The Home Address option is a newly defined destination option which carries the home address of a mobile node when packets are sent from a mobile node.

- *Type 2 Routing Header:* The Type 2 Routing Header is a newly defined routing header type which carries a home address of a mobile node when packets are sent from a home agent or a correspondent node to a mobile node.

- *Mobility Header:* The Mobility Header is a newly defined Extension Header which carries the signaling information of the Mobile IPv6 protocol.

- *Router Advertisement Message:* The Router Advertisement message is modified to include a flag which indicates whether a router has the home agent function or not.

- *Prefix Information Option:* The Prefix Information option is one of the Neighbor Discovery options used to distribute prefix information of a network from a router to other nodes connected to the network. In Mobile IPv6, a home agent includes its address in this option as a part of the prefix information. All home agents on the same home network can know all addresses of home agents of the network by listening to this option.

- *Home Agent Information Option:* The Home Agent Information option is a newly defined Neighbor Discovery option which carries the lifetime and preference information of a home agent.

- *Advertisement Interval Option:* The Advertisement Interval option is a newly defined Neighbor Discovery option which carries the interval value between unsolicited Router Solicitation messages sent from a router.

- *Dynamic Home Agent Address Discovery Request/Reply Messages:* The Dynamic Home Agent Address Discovery Request and Reply messages are newly defined ICMPv6 message types which provide the mechanism to discover the addresses of home agents for a mobile node when the mobile node is away from home.

- *Mobile Prefix Solicitation/Advertisement Messages:* The Mobile Prefix Solicitation and Advertisement messages are newly defined ICMPv6 message types used to solicit/deliver the prefix information of a home network to a mobile node while the mobile node is away from home.

11.3.1 Alignment Requirements

Some Extension Headers and Options have alignment requirements when placing these headers in a packet. Basically, the header or option fields are placed at a natural boundary, i.e., fields of n bytes in length are placed at multiples of n bytes from the start of the packet. The reason for such a restriction is for performance; accessing the natural boundary is usually faster. For example, the Home Address option (Figure 11.5) has $8n + 6$ alignment requirements that put the home address field on an 8-byte boundary.

11.3.2 Home Address Option

The *Home Address* option is a newly defined Destination option. The alignment requirement of the Home Address option is $8n + 6$. The format of the Home Address option is shown in Figure 11.5. This option is used to specify the home address of a mobile node when the mobile node sends packets while it is away from home. It is used in the following three cases:

- When a mobile node sends a BU message;

- When a mobile node communicates with peers with route optimization;

- When a mobile node sends a Mobile Prefix Solicitation message.

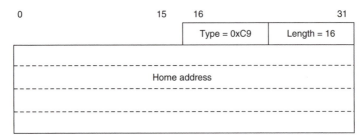

Figure 11.5 Home Address option.

A mobile node never sends packets with its source address set to its home address directly while it is away from home, since such a source address is topologically incorrect and may be dropped by an intermediate router because of the Ingress Filtering posed on that router. When sending a packet, a mobile node needs to perform one of following procedures:

- Send a packet using a bi-directional tunnel created between a mobile node and its home agent.

- Use the Home Address option which includes the home address of the mobile node with the source address of the packet set to the care-of address of the mobile node.

The *Type* field is $0 \times C9$. The first two bits of an option type number determine the action taken on the receiving node when the option is not supported. In this case, the first two bits are both set. This means that if a node does not recognize the option, the following actions must be taken:

- The packet that includes the option must be dropped.

- An ICMPv6 Parameter Problem message must be sent if the destination address of the incoming packet is not a multicast address.

This provides a mechanism to detect whether a peer supports the Home Address option. If the peer does not support the option, the mobile node cannot use the route optimization mechanism.

The *Length* field is set to 16. The *Home Address* field contains a home address of a mobile node.

11.3.3 Type 2 Routing Header

The *Type 2 Routing Header* is a newly defined routing header type for Mobile IPv6. This Routing Header is used by a home agent or a correspondent node to carry a home address of

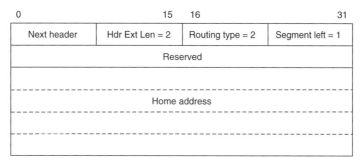

Figure 11.6 Type 2 Routing Header.

a mobile node when packets are sent to the mobile node. The format of the Type 2 Routing Header is shown in Figure 11.6.

The Type 2 Routing Header is used in the following three cases:

- When a node sends a BA message;

- When a home agent or a correspondent is performing route optimization;

- When a home agent sends a Mobile Prefix Advertisement message.

A packet whose destination address is a home address of a mobile node is never delivered to the mobile node directly when the mobile node is away from home. Such a packet is delivered to the home network of the mobile node.

A node needs to use a Type 2 Routing Header if it wants to send packets directly to a mobile node which is away from home. In this case, the destination address of the packet is set to the care-of address of the mobile node. The home address is carried in the Type 2 Routing Header. A packet is delivered directly to the care-of address of the mobile node, and the mobile node processes the Type 2 Routing Header and delivers the packet to the home address, which is the mobile node itself.

The *Next Header* field is set to the protocol number of the following header. The *Hdr Ext Len* field is fixed at 2, since the length of the Type 2 Routing Header is fixed. The *Routing Type* field is set to 2. The *Segments Left* field is initialized to 1. The *Home Address* field contains one IPv6 address which is the home address of the mobile node. The usage of this header is very restrictive. We can only specify one intermediate node as a home address. A mobile node which receives this header drops the packet if there is more than one intermediate node specified. Also, the address in the Type 2 Routing Header and the destination address of the IPv6 packet must belong to the same mobile node. That is, the packet can only be forwarded to the mobile node itself.

A new type number is required for Mobile IPv6 in order to make it easy to support Mobile IPv6 on firewall software. In the early stages of the Mobile IPv6 standardization, a Type 0 Routing Header was used instead of a Type 2 Routing Header. However, many people thought that it would be difficult to distinguish between using a Type 0 Routing Header for carrying a Mobile IPv6 home address or carrying a Routing Header that is being used as a method to perform source routing. We need to pay attention to the usage of source routing, since such forwarding is sometimes used as a method for attacking other nodes. Firewall vendors may drop all packets with a Type 0 Routing Header to decrease the risk of such attacks. It is much easier for those vendors to pass only Mobile IPv6 data if we have a new routing header type number for the exclusive use of Mobile IPv6.

11.3.4 Mobility Header

The *Mobility Header* is a newly introduced extension header to carry Mobile IPv6 signaling messages. The format of the Mobility Header is shown in Figure 11.7. The format of the header is based on the usual extension header format.

The *Payload Proto* field indicates the following header. The field is equivalent to the Next Header field of other extension headers; however, the current specification does not allow the Mobility Header to be followed by other extension headers or by transport headers. That is, the Mobility Header must always be the last header in the header chain of an IPv6 packet. The reason for this restriction is to simplify the interaction between the IPsec mechanism and Mobile IPv6. Some signaling messages used by the Mobile IPv6 protocol must be protected by the IPsec mechanism. It is impossible to protect the Mobility Header if other headers follow it, because with the current IPsec specification we cannot apply IPsec policies to the intermediate extension headers. Currently, the *Payload Proto* field is always set to 58 (IPV6-NONXT) which indicates there is no next header. The *Header Len* field indicates the length of a Mobility Header in units of 8 bytes excluding the first 8 bytes. The *MH Type* field indicates the message type of the Mobility Header. Currently, eight kinds of Mobility Header types are defined. Table 11.1 shows all Mobility Header types. The *Reserved* field is reserved for future use. The *Checksum* field stores the checksum value of a Mobility Header message.

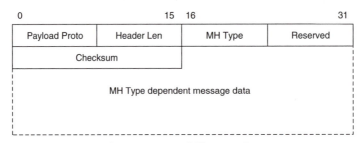

Figure 11.7 Mobility Header.

The algorithm used to compute the checksum value is the same as is used for ICMPv6. The rest of the header is defined depending on the Mobility Header type value. Also, the Mobility Header may have some options called *mobility options*.

11.3.4.1 Binding Refresh Request Message

The *Binding Refresh Request* (BRR) message is used when a correspondent needs to extend the lifetime of binding information for a mobile node. A mobile node that has received a BRR message should send a BU message to the correspondent node to update the binding information held in the correspondent node. The format of the BRR message is shown in Figure 11.8.

The BRR message is sent from a correspondent node to a mobile node. The source address of the IPv6 packet is the address of the correspondent node which is sending the BRR message. The destination address of the IPv6 packet is the home address of a mobile node, which is requested to resend a BU message. The BRR message must have neither a Type 2 Routing Header nor a Home Address option. That is, the message is tunneled by the home agent to the destination mobile node, if the destination mobile node is away from home. Currently, no mobility options are defined for the BRR message.

Table 11.1 Mobility Header Types.

Type	Description
0	Binding Refresh Request: requests a mobile node to resend a Binding Update message to update binding information.
1	Home Test Init: starts the return routability procedure for a home address of a mobile node.
2	Care-of Test Init: starts the return routability procedure for a care-of address of a mobile node.
3	Home Test: a response message to the Home Test Init message.
4	Care-of Test: a response message to the Care-of Test Init message.
5	Binding Update: sends a request to create binding information between a home address and a care-of address of a mobile node.
6	Binding Acknowledgment: a response message to the Binding Update message.
7	Binding Error: notifies an error related to the signal processing of the Mobile IPv6 protocol.

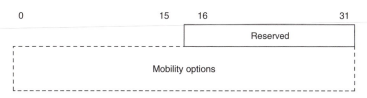

Figure 11.8 Binding Refresh Request message.

11.3.4.2 Home Test Init Message

The *HoTI* message is used to initiate the return routability procedure. The format of the HoTI message is shown in Figure 11.9.

The HoTI message is sent from a mobile node to a correspondent node when the mobile node wants to optimize the path between itself and the correspondent node. The source address of the IPv6 packet is the home address of the mobile node and the destination address of the IPv6 packet is the address of the correspondent node.

The *Home Init Cookie* field is filled with a random value generated in the mobile node. The cookie is used to match a HoTI message and a HoT message, which is sent from a correspondent node in response to the HoTI message. The HoTI message must have neither a Type 2 Routing Header nor a Home Address option. The HoTI message is always tunneled from a mobile node to its home agent and forwarded to a correspondent node. Currently, no mobility options are defined for the HoTI message.

11.3.4.3 Care-of Test Init Message

The *CoTI* message is used to initiate the return routability procedure. The format of the CoTI message is shown in Figure 11.10.

The CoTI message is sent from a mobile node to a correspondent node when a mobile node wants to optimize the path between itself and the correspondent node. The source address of

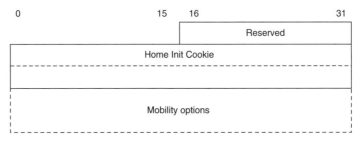

Figure 11.9 Home test Init message.

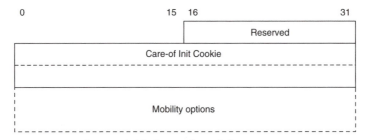

Figure 11.10 Care-of test Init message.

the IPv6 packet is the care-of address of the mobile node and the destination address of the IPv6 packet is the address of the correspondent node.

The *Care-of Init Cookie* is filled with a random value generated in the mobile node. The cookie is used to match a CoTI message and a CoT message, which is sent from the correspondent node in response to the CoTI message. A CoTI message must have neither a Type 2 Routing Header nor a Home Address option. A CoTI message is always directly sent from a mobile node to a correspondent node. Currently, no mobility options are defined for the CoTI message.

11.3.4.4 Home Test Message

The *HoT* message is used as a reply to a HoTI message sent from a mobile node to a correspondent node. This message includes a token which is used to compute a shared secret to protect the BU message. The format of the HoT message is shown in Figure 11.11.

The HoT message is sent from a correspondent node to a mobile node as a response to a HoTI message which was previously sent from the mobile node. The source address of the IPv6 packet is the address of the correspondent node and the destination address is the home address of the mobile node.

The *Home Nonce Index* indicates an index value of the nonce value in the home nonce array which is maintained in the correspondent node. The *Home Init Cookie* is a copy of the value of the *Home Init Cookie* field of the corresponding HoTI message. A mobile node can match a previously sent HoTI message and the received HoT message by comparing the cookie values. If there is no corresponding HoTI message, the received HoT message is dropped. The *Home Keygen Token* is a token value which is used to compute a shared secret to secure the BU message. The algorithm used is described in Section 11.5.1. Currently, no mobility options are defined for the HoT message.

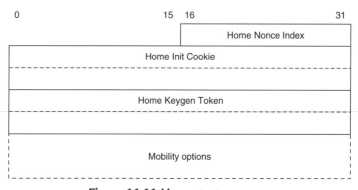

Figure 11.11 Home test message.

11.3.4.5 Care-of Test Message

The CoT message is used as a reply to a CoTI message sent from a mobile node to a correspondent node. This message includes a token value which is used to compute a shared secret to protect the BU message. The format of the CoT message is shown in Figure 11.12.

The CoT message is sent from a correspondent node to a mobile node as a response to the CoTI message which was previously sent from the mobile node. The source address of the IPv6 packet is the address of the correspondent node and the destination address is the care-of address of the mobile node.

The *Care-of Nonce Index* indicates the index value of the nonce value in the care-of nonce array which is maintained in the correspondent node. The *Care-of Init Cookie* is a copy of the value of the *Care-of Init Cookie* field of the corresponding CoTI message. A mobile node can match a previously sent CoTI message and the received CoT message by comparing the cookie values. The *Care-of Keygen Token* is a token value which is used to compute a shared secret to secure the BU message later. The algorithm used is described in Section 11.5.1. Currently, no mobility options are defined for the CoT message.

11.3.4.6 Binding Update Message

The *BU* message is used by a mobile node to notify a correspondent node or a home agent of the binding information of a care-of address and a home address of the mobile node. A mobile node sends the BU message with its care-of address and its home address whenever it changes its point of attachment to the Internet and changes its care-of address. The node which receives the message will create an entry to keep the binding information. Figure 11.13 shows the BU message.

The BU message is sent from a mobile node to a home agent or a correspondent node. The source address of the IPv6 packet is the care-of address of the mobile node and the destination address is the address of the home agent or the correspondent node. To include the

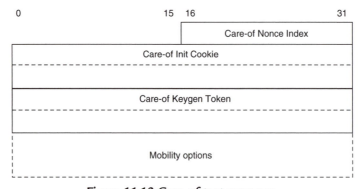

Figure 11.12 Care-of test message.

information of the home address of the mobile node, the BU message contains a Destination Options Header which has a Home Address option as described in Section 11.3.2.

The *Sequence Number* field contains a sequence number for a BU message to avoid a replay attack. The *flag* fields of the BU message may contain the flags described in Table 11.2.

The *Lifetime* field specifies the proposed lifetime of the binding information. When a BU message is used for home registration, the value must not be greater than the remaining lifetime of either the home address or the care-of address of the mobile node which is sending the BU message. The value is in units of 4 sec.

The BU message may have the following mobility options.

- The Alternate Care-of Address option;

- The Nonce Indices option;

- The Binding Authorization Data option.

Each option is described in Section 11.3.5.

11.3.4.7 Binding Acknowledgment Message

The BA message is sent as a response to a BU message sent from a mobile node. The format of the BA message is shown in Figure 11.14.

Figure 11.13 Binding Update message.

Table 11.2 The Flags of the Binding Update Message.

Flag	Description
A	Acknowledge: requires a Binding Acknowledgment message as a response to a Binding Update message. When the H flag is set, the A flag must be set. Note that a Binding Acknowledgment message may be sent to indicate an error even if the A flag is not set.
H	Home Registration: means that this Binding Update message is a message for home registration.
L	Link-local Address Compatibility: means that the link-local address of a mobile node has the same interface ID with its home address.
K	Key Management Mobility Capability: means the IKE SA information survives on movements.

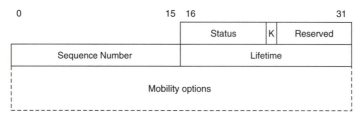

Figure 11.14 Binding Acknowledgment message.

Table 11.3 The Status Codes of the Binding Acknowledgment Message.

Code	Description
0	Binding Update accepted
1	Accepted but prefix discovery necessary
128	Reason unspecified
129	Administratively prohibited
130	Insufficient resources
131	Home registration not supported
132	Not home subnet
133	Not home agent for this mobile node
134	Duplicate Address Detection failed
135	Sequence number out of window
136	Expired home nonce index
137	Expired care-of nonce index
138	Expired nonces
139	Registration type change disallowed

A BA message is sent from a home agent or a correspondent node to a mobile node. The source address of the BA message is the address of the home agent or the correspondent node and the destination address is the care-of address of the mobile node. To deliver a BA message to the home address of a mobile node which is away from home, a Type 2 Routing Header, which contains the home address of the mobile node, is necessary.

The *Status* field specifies the result of the processing of the received BU message. Table 11.3 is a list of currently specified status codes. The field immediately after the *Status* field is the flag field. Currently only the K flag is defined. Table 11.4 describes the K flag. The *Sequence Number* field indicates the copy of the last valid sequence number which was contained in the last BU message. The field is also used as an indicator of the latest sequence number when a mobile node sends a BU message with a smaller sequence number value. This situation may occur when a mobile node reboots and loses the sequence number information of recent binding information. The *Lifetime* field indicates the approved lifetime for the binding information. Even if a mobile node requests a large lifetime value in the *Lifetime* field in the BU message, the requested lifetime is not always approved by the receiving node. The actual lifetime can be determined by the node which receives the BU message.

Table 11.4 The Flag of the Binding Acknowledgment Message.

Flag	Description
K	Key Management Mobility Capability means the IKE SA information cannot survive on movements.

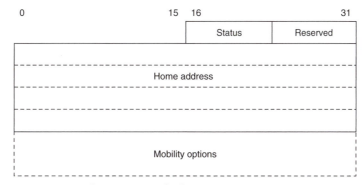

Figure 11.15 Binding Error message.

Table 11.5 The Status Value of a Binding Error Message.

Status	Description
1	A Home Address option is received without existing binding information.
2	Unrecognized Mobility Header type value is received.

The BA message may have the following mobility options:

- The Binding Refresh Advice option;

- The Binding Authorization Data option.

Each option is described in Section 11.3.5.

11.3.4.8 Binding Error Message

The *Binding Error* (BE) message is used to indicate an error which occurs during the mobility signaling processing. The format of a BE message is shown in Figure 11.15.

The BE message is sent from a node which supports Mobile IPv6. The source address of the IPv6 packet is the address of the node which sends the BE message. The BE message must have neither a Type 2 Routing Header nor a Home Address option.

The *Status* field indicates the kind of error as described in Table 11.5. The *Home Address* field contains the home address of a mobile node if the packet which causes the error is sent from a mobile node. Otherwise, the field contains an unspecified address. Currently, no mobility options are defined for the BE message.

11.3.5 Mobility Options

The Mobility Options are the options used with the Mobility Header to provide supplemental information. Figure 11.16 shows the format of the Mobility Option.

The Mobility Option format is the same format used by the Hop-by-Hop options and Destination options. The first byte indicates the type of the option. The second byte indicates the length of the following data. Currently six options are defined as described in Table 11.6.

11.3.5.1 Pad1 Option

The *Pad1* option is used when one byte of padding is needed to meet the alignment requirements of other Mobility Options. This option does not have any effect and must be ignored on the receiver side. The format of the Pad1 option is a special format which does not meet the standard format described in Figure 11.16. Figure 11.17 shows the format of the Pad1 option.

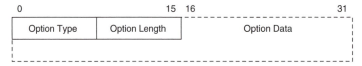

Figure 11.16 Mobility Option.

Table 11.6 Mobility Options.

Type	Description
0	Pad1
1	PadN
2	Binding Refresh Advice
3	Alternate Care-of address
4	Nonce indices
5	Binding Authorization data

Figure 11.17 Pad1 option.

11.3.5.2 PadN Option

The *PadN* option is used when two or more bytes of padding are needed to meet the alignment requirements of other Mobility Options. This option does not have any effect and must be ignored on the receiver side. The format of the PadN option is described in Figure 11.18.

The *Option Length* field is set to the size of the required padding length minus 2. The *Option Data* field consists of a zero cleared byte stream whose length is the required padding size minus 2. A receiver must ignore the contents of the *Option Data* field when processing this option.

11.3.5.3 Binding Refresh Advice Option

The *Binding Refresh Advice* option is used to specify the recommended interval between BU messages for updating the binding information. The option is used with the BA message which is sent from a home agent to a mobile node which the home agent serves. The format of the Binding Refresh Advice option is shown in Figure 11.19. The alignment requirement of the Binding Refresh Advice option is $2n$.

The *Length* field is set to 2. The *Refresh Interval* field indicates the interval value. The value is specified in units of 4 sec.

11.3.5.4 Alternate Care-of Address Option

The *Alternate Care-of Address* option is used in two cases with the BU message. The first case is when a mobile node wants to bind its home address to an address other than the source address of the BU message. Usually, the source address of the IPv6 packet is used as a care-of address, if the Alternate Care-of Address option does not exist. The second case is to protect the care-of address information from on-path attackers. The BU message for home registration must be protected by an IPsec ESP or AH. However, the ESP does not protect the IPv6 header itself. That is, the source address, which is used as a care-of address, is not

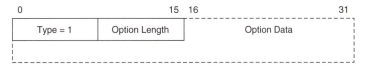

Figure 11.18 PadN option.

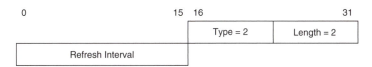

Figure 11.19 Binding Refresh Advice option.

protected by the ESP. Adding this option to a BU message will protect the care-of address information, since this option is included in a Mobility Header and the Mobility Header is covered by the ESP. If we use the AH, the option can be omitted. The format of the Alternate Care-of Address option is shown in Figure 11.20. The alignment requirement of the Alternate Care-of Address option is $8n + 6$.

The *Length* field is set to 16 which is the length of an IPv6 address. The *Alternate Care-of Address* field contains the address which should be used as a care-of address instead of the source address of the BU message.

11.3.5.5 Nonce Indices Option

The *Nonce Indices* option is used to specify nonce values which are used to compute the Authenticator value specified by the Binding Authorization Data option. This option is used with the Binding Authorization Data option. The alignment requirement of the Nonce Indices option is $2n$. The format of the Nonce Indices option is shown in Figure 11.21.

The *Length* field is set to 4. The value of the *Home Nonce Index* and *Care-of Nonce Index* fields are copied from the *Home Nonce Index* field of the HoT message and *Care-of Nonce Index* field of the CoT message which a mobile node has previously received.

11.3.5.6 Binding Authorization Data Option

The *Binding Authorization Data* option stores a hash value computed over the BU or the BA message. The option does not have any alignment requirement; however, because it has to be placed at the end of the message, it eventually has an $8n + 2$ requirement. The format of the Binding Authorization Data option is shown in Figure 11.22.

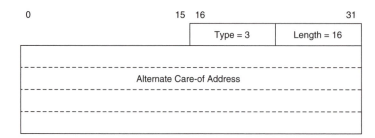

Figure 11.20 Alternate Care-of Address option.

Figure 11.21 Nonce Indices option.

The *Length* field depends on the length of the *Authenticator* field. At this moment, the length is 12 because the procedure to compute the authenticator produces a 96-bit authenticator value.

11.3.6 Neighbor Discovery Messages

The Mobile IPv6 specification modifies the Router Advertisement message and the Prefix Information option so that we can distribute information about a home agent. Two new Neighbor Discovery options are introduced.

11.3.6.1 Router Advertisement Message

The *Router Advertisement* message is modified to include the newly defined Home Agent flag. Figure 11.23 shows the modified Router Advertisement message.

The H flag in the flags field is added. A router which is acting as a Mobile IPv6 home agent must specify the H flag so that other home agents can detect there is another home agent on the same network. This information is used on each home agent when creating a list of home agent addresses. The mechanism is described in Section 11.7. A mobile node may use this option to create the list of home agents when it is at home.

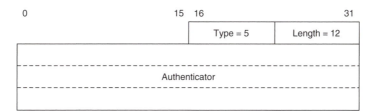

Figure 11.22 Binding Authorization Data option.

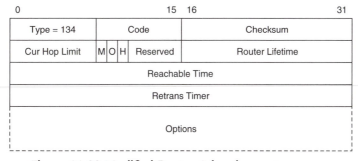

Figure 11.23 Modified Router Advertisement message.

11.3.6.2 Prefix Information Option

The *Prefix Information* option is an option defined in [3]. The option is used with the Router Advertisement message to distribute the prefix information to the nodes on the attached network. Figure 11.24 shows the format of this option.

In [3], this option only carries the information of the prefix part. In the Mobile IPv6 specification, the option is modified to include the address of the home agent including the interface identifier part. The R flag is added in the flags field for that purpose. If the R flag is set, the Prefix field includes a full IPv6 address of the home agent, not only the prefix part. A node which receives this option with the R flag can discover the address of a home agent on the network. This information is used when each home agent creates a list of home agent addresses. The mechanism is described in Section 11.7.

11.3.6.3 Advertisement Interval Option

The *Advertisement Interval* option is used to supply the interval at which Router Advertisement messages are sent from a home agent. The Router Advertisement message is used as a hint of the reachability of the router. A mobile node assumes it has not moved to other networks as long as the same router is reachable on the attached network. A mobile node can detect the unreachability of a router by listening for the Router Advertisement message, since a router periodically sends these messages. However, such detection is usually difficult since the interval between Router Advertisement messages varies on each network. This option explicitly supplies the interval between Router Advertisement messages. The interval is set to a lower value than the usual IPv6 Router Advertisement messages. A mobile node can determine a router is unreachable if the router does not send a Router Advertisement message for the period specified in this option. The format of the Advertisement Interval option is shown in Figure 11.25.

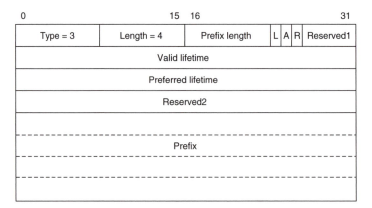

Figure 11.24 Prefix Information option.

The *Type* field is set to 7. The *Length* field is fixed at 1. The *Reserved* field must be cleared by the sender and must be ignored by the receiver. The *Advertisement Interval* field is a 32-bit unsigned integer which specifies the interval value between Router Advertisement messages in units of 1 sec.

11.3.6.4 Home Agent Information Option

The *Home Agent Information* option is a newly defined Neighbor Discovery option to distribute the information of a home agent. This option is used with the Router Advertisement message sent from a home agent. The format of the Home Agent Information option is shown in Figure 11.26.

The *Type* field is set to 8. The *Length* field is fixed at 1. The *Reserved* field must be cleared by the sender, and must be ignored by the receiver. The *Home Agent Preference* field specifies the preference value of a home agent which sends this option. The value is a 16-bit unsigned integer. Higher values mean the home agent is more preferable. This value is used to order the addresses of the home agent list which is maintained on each home agent on the home network. The home agent list is sent to a mobile node when the mobile node requests the latest list of home agents. The *Home Agent Lifetime* field contains the lifetime of the home agent. The value is a 16-bit unsigned integer and stored in units of 1 sec. This value specifies how long the router can provide the home agent service. If there is no Home Agent Information option sent by a home agent, the preference value is considered 0 and the lifetime is considered the same value as the router lifetime.

11.3.7 ICMPv6 Messages

The Mobile IPv6 specification defines four new types of the ICMPv6 message.

11.3.7.1 Dynamic Home Agent Address Discovery Request

A mobile node sometimes requests the latest list of home agents on its home network. When requesting the list, a mobile node sends the *Dynamic Home Agent Address Discovery Request*

0	15	16	31
Type = 7	Length = 1	Reserved	
Advertisement Interval			

Figure 11.25 Advertisement Interval option.

0	15	16	31
Type = 8	Length = 1	Reserved	
Home Agent Preference		Home Agent Lifetime	

Figure 11.26 Home Agent Information option.

message, which is a newly defined ICMPv6 message. The format of the Dynamic Home Agent Address Discovery Request message is shown in Figure 11.27.

The source address of the IPv6 packet is the care-of address of a mobile node. The destination address is the *home agent anycast address*. The algorithm to construct the home agent anycast address is shown in Figure 11.28. There are two patterns to compute the anycast address: One is for the prefix whose prefix length is 64 and the other is for the prefix whose prefix length is not 64. The home agent anycast address is a combination of a prefix and the anycast identifier `ffff:ffff:ffff:ffff:ffff:ffff:ffff:fffe`, which is reserved for the home agent anycast address. The important point when generating the anycast address is if the prefix length is 64, the interface identifier part of the generated anycast address must satisfy the EUI-64 requirements. That is, the universal/local bit must be cleared since the anycast address may

0		15	16		31
Type = 144		Code = 0	Checksum		
Identifier			Reserved		

Figure 11.27 Dynamic Home Agent Address Discovery Request message.

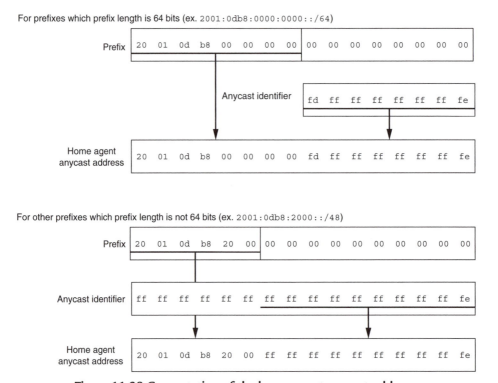

Figure 11.28 Computation of the home agent anycast address.

be assigned to multiple home agents. In this case we must use `fdff:ffff:ffff:fffe` as an anycast identifier. The interface identifier of the home agent anycast address is defined in [4].

The *Type* field is set to 144. The *Code* field is set to 0. No other code value is defined. The *Checksum* field is a checksum value computed as specified in the ICMPv6 specification [5]. The *Identifier* field contains an identifier to match the request message and the reply message. The *Reserved* field must be cleared by the sender and must be ignored by the receiver. The procedure of Dynamic Home Agent Address Discovery is discussed in Section 11.7.

11.3.7.2 Dynamic Home Agent Address Discovery Reply

The *Dynamic Home Agent Address Discovery Reply* message is used as a response message to the Dynamic Home Agent Address Discovery Request message. Each home agent maintains the list of home agents on its home network by listening to Router Advertisement messages sent by other home agents and updating the list as necessary. When a home agent receives a Dynamic Home Agent Address Discovery Request message, the node will reply to the mobile node that has sent the request message with a Dynamic Home Agent Address Discovery Reply message including the latest list of home agents. The format of the Dynamic Home Agent Address Discovery Reply message is shown in Figure 11.29.

The source address of the IPv6 packet is set to one of the addresses of the home agent which replies to this message. The source address must be an address recognized as the home agent's address because a mobile node may use the source address as the home agent's address in the following Mobile IPv6 signaling process. The destination address is copied from the source address field of a Dynamic Home Agent Address Discovery Request message.

The *Type* field is set to 145. The *Code* field is set to 0. No other code values are defined. The *Checksum* field is a checksum value computed as specified in the ICMPv6 specification [5]. The value of the *Identifier* field is copied from the *Identifier* field of the corresponding Dynamic Home Agent Address Discovery Request message. The *Reserved* field must be cleared by the sender and must be ignored by the receiver. The *Home Agent Addresses* field

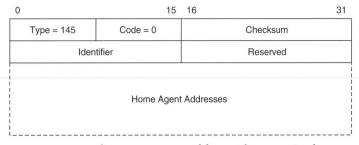

Figure 11.29 Dynamic Home Agent Address Discovery Reply message.

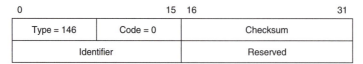

Figure 11.30 Mobile Prefix Solicitation message.

contains the list of addresses of home agents on the home network. The order of the list is decided based on the preference value of each home agent. To avoid fragmentation of the message, the maximum number of addresses in the list is restricted to not exceed the path MTU value from a home agent to a mobile node. The procedure of Dynamic Home Agent Address Discovery is discussed in Section 11.7.

11.3.7.3 Mobile Prefix Solicitation

The *Mobile Prefix Solicitation* message is a newly defined ICMPv6 message which is sent when a mobile node wants to know the latest prefix information on its home network. This message is typically sent to extend the lifetime of the home address before it expires. The format of the Mobile Prefix Solicitation message is shown in Figure 11.30.

The source address of the IPv6 packet is set to the current care-of address of the mobile node. The destination address is set to the address of the home agent with which the mobile node is currently registered. This message must contain the Home Address option to carry the home address of the mobile node. This message should be protected by the IPsec ESP header to prevent the information from being modified by attackers.

The *Type* field is set to 146. The *Code* field is set to 0. No other code values are defined. The *Checksum* field is a checksum value computed as specified in the ICMPv6 specification [5]. The *Identifier* field contains a random value which is used to match the solicitation message and the advertisement message. The *Reserved* field is cleared by the sender and must be ignored by the receiver.

11.3.7.4 Mobile Prefix Advertisement

The *Mobile Prefix Advertisement* message is a newly defined ICMPv6 message which is used to supply the prefix information of a home network to mobile nodes. This message is used as a response message to a Mobile Prefix Solicitation message sent from a mobile node. Also, this message may be sent from a home agent to each mobile node which has registered with the home agent to notify the mobile node of updates to the prefix information of the home network, even if the mobile nodes do not request the information explicitly. The format of the Mobile Prefix Advertisement message is shown in Figure 11.31.

The source address of the IPv6 packet is one of the addresses of the home agent. The destination address is copied from the source address field of the Mobile Prefix Solicitation

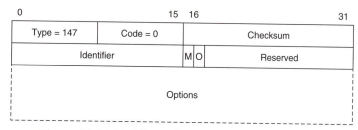

Figure 11.31 Mobile Prefix Advertisement message.

message if the message is in response to a solicitation message. Otherwise, the destination address is the registered care-of address of a mobile node. A Type 2 Routing Header must be included in this message to contain the home address of a mobile node. This message should be protected by the IPsec ESP header to prevent being modified by attackers.

The *Type* field is set to 147. The *Code* field is set to 0. No other code values are defined. The *Checksum* field is a checksum value computed as specified in the ICMPv6 specification [5]. If this message is in response to a solicitation message, the value of the *Identifier* field is copied from the *Identifier* field of the Mobile Solicitation message. If the message is not a response message, this field can be set to any value. A mobile node that receives a Mobile Prefix Advertisement which has an unmatched identifier should send the Mobile Prefix Solicitation message to confirm the prefix information. The M and O flags are copied from the configuration of a home network. That is, if the home network is being operated with a managed address configuration mechanism (e.g., DHCPv6), the M flag is set. Also if the home network provides stateful configuration parameters (e.g., DNS server addresses via DHCPv6), the O flag is set. Currently, the exact processing procedure of these flags is not defined in the Mobile IPv6 specification. A future document will define the exact processing mechanism. The *Reserved* field must be cleared by the sender and must be ignored by the receiver. This message will have the modified Prefix Information option described in Section 11.3.6.

11.4 Procedure of Mobile IPv6

In this section, we discuss the detailed procedure of the Mobile IPv6 protocol operation.

11.4.1 Protocol Constants and Variables

Table 11.7 shows a list of the variables used in the Mobile IPv6 protocol. Some of these variables are constant while others may have their values modified.

11.4.2 Home Registration

When a mobile node is at home, the node acts as a fixed IPv6 node. Figure 11.32 shows the situation.

Table 11.7 Protocol Constants and Variables.

Name	Description
INITIAL_DHAAD_TIMEOUT	The initial timeout value when retransmitting a Dynamic Home Agent Address Discovery Request message (constant: 3 sec).
DHAAD_RETRIES	The maximum number of retries for a Dynamic Home Agent Address Discovery Request message (constant: 4 times).
InitialBindackTimeoutFirstReg	The initial timeout value when retransmitting a Binding Update message when a mobile node moves from a home network to a foreign network for the first time (configurable: default to 1.5 sec).
INITIAL_BINDACK_TIMEOUT	Update message when updating the existing binding information of a peer node (constant: 1 sec).
MAX_BINDACK_TIMEOUT	The maximum timeout value for retransmitting a Binding Update message (constant: 32 sec).
MAX_UPDATE_RATE	The maximum number of Binding Update messages which a mobile node can send in 1 sec (constant: 3 times).
MAX_NONCE_LIFETIME	The maximum lifetime of nonce values (constant: 240 sec).
MAX_TOKEN_LIFETIME	The maximum lifetime of Keygen Token values (constant: 210 sec).
MAX_RR_BINDING_LIFETIME	The maximum lifetime for binding information created by the Return Routability procedure (constant: 420 sec).
MaxMobPfxAdvInterval	The maximum interval value between Mobile Prefix Advertisement messages (modifiable: default to 86,400 sec).
MinMobPfxAdvInterval	The minimum interval value between Mobile Prefix Advertisement messages (modifiable: default to 600 sec).
PREFIX_ADV_TIMEOUT	The timeout value when retransmitting a Mobile Prefix Advertisement message (constant: 3 sec).
PREFIX_ADV_RETRIES	The maximum number of retransmissions of Mobile Prefix Advertisement messages (constant: 3 times).
MinDelayBetweenRAs	The minimum interval value between Router Advertisement messages (modifiable: default to 3 sec, minimum 0.03 sec).

A mobile node gets its IPv6 addresses from its home network. The addresses assigned on the home network are called home addresses. When a mobile node sends a packet, the source address of the packet is set to one of the home addresses of the mobile node. The destination address of the packet is the address of the peer node. When the peer node sends a packet to the mobile node, the source and the destination address are set to the peer address and the home address respectively.

When a mobile node moves to a foreign network, the mobile node will get address(es) from the foreign network. These addresses are called care-of addresses. If the mobile node detects that it is on a foreign network, the node creates an entry that keeps the state of the mobile node and maintains it. The entry is called a *binding update list* entry. It contains the information of the home address and one of the care-of addresses of the node, the lifetime of the entry, and so on.

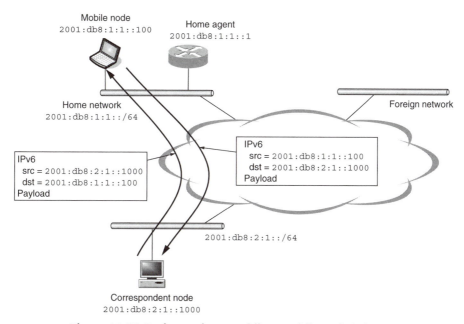

Figure 11.32 Packet exchange while a mobile node is home.

The mobile node sends a BU message to its home agent to notify the home agent of its current location. The source address of the message is set to the care-of address picked from the list of available care-of addresses. The destination address is the address of the home agent. The message also includes a Home Address option which contains the home address of the mobile node. This message must be protected by the IPsec ESP mechanism.

When a home agent receives a BU message, it adds the information to its internal database. The information kept in a home agent is called a *binding cache*. The home agent replies with a BA message in response to the BU message. If the mobile node does not receive the acknowledgment message, it resends a BU message until it gets an acknowledgment message. This procedure is called *Home registration*. Figure 11.33 shows the procedure.

A BU message includes a sequence number. If a home agent already has a corresponding binding cache entry and the sequence number of the received BU message is smaller than the sequence number kept in the cache entry, the home agent returns a BA message with an error status of 135 and the latest sequence number. The mobile node resends a BU message with a correct sequence number to complete home registration. The comparison of sequence numbers is based on modulo 216, since the sequence number is represented as a 16-bit variable. For example, if the current sequence number is 10015, then the numbers 0 through 10014 and 42783 through 65535 are considered less than 10015 (Figure 11.34).

A mobile node must set the H and A flags to indicate that it is requesting home registration when it registers its current location with its home agent. In addition to the flags, a mobile

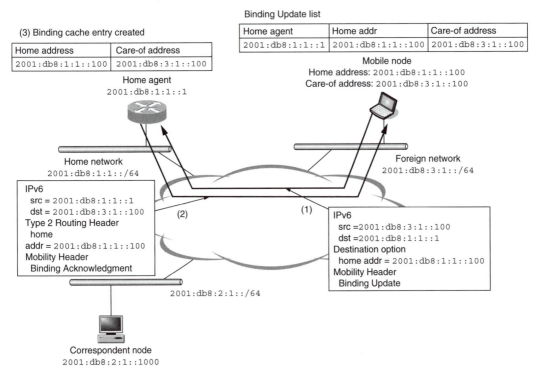

(3) Binding cache entry created

Home address	Care-of address
2001:db8:1:1::100	2001:db8:3:1::100

Home agent
2001:db8:1:1::1

Binding Update list

Home agent	Home addr	Care-of address
2001:db8:1:1::1	2001:db8:1:1::100	2001:db8:3:1::100

Mobile node
Home address: 2001:db8:1:1::100
Care-of address: 2001:db8:3:1::100

Home network
2001:db8:1:1::/64

Foreign network
2001:db8:3:1::/64

IPv6
  src = 2001:db8:1:1::1
  dst = 2001:db8:3:1::100
Type 2 Routing Header
  home
addr = 2001:db8:1:1::100
Mobility Header
  Binding Acknowledgment

(2)

(1)

IPv6
  src =2001:db8:3:1::100
  dst =2001:db8:1:1::1
Destination option
  home addr = 2001:db8:1:1::100
Mobility Header
  Binding Update

2001:db8:2:1::/64

Correspondent node
2001:db8:2:1::1000

Figure 11.33 Sending binding messages.

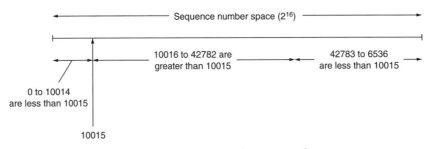

Sequence number space (2^{16})

10016 to 42782 are
greater than 10015

42783 to 6536
are less than 10015

0 to 10014
are less than 10015

10015

Figure 11.34 Sequence number comparison.

node must set the L flag if the home address of the mobile node has the same interface identifier as is used in its link-local address. Setting the L flag will create a binding cache entry for the link-local address of the mobile node and protect that address from being used by other nodes on its home network.

When a mobile node sets the A flag, the node resends a BU message until it receives a BA message. The initial retransmission timeout value is determined based on whether this registration is the first home registration or if it is updating the home registration entry. If the message is for the first home registration, the initial retransmission timeout is set to

`InitialBindackTimeoutFirstReg` seconds. Otherwise, the initial retransmission timeout is `INITIAL_BINDACK_TIMEOUT` seconds. The difference is due to running the DAD procedure at the home agent. The first time a mobile node registers its location, the home agent must make sure that the home address (and the link-local address, if the L flag is set) is not used on the home network by some other node by performing the DAD procedure. Usually the DAD procedure takes 1 sec. This is why the initial timeout must be greater than 1 sec. The timeout value is increased exponentially on every retransmission with the maximum retransmission timeout being `MAX_BINDACK_TIMEOUT` seconds. If a mobile node does not receive a BA after the last retransmission, the mobile node may perform a Dynamic Home Agent Address Discovery to find another home agent on the home network.

A BU message includes an Alternate Care-of Address option to protect the care-of address information. The BU message is protected by an ESP IPsec header, but the ESP header does not cover the source address field of an IPv6 header which contains the care-of address of a mobile node. A mobile node needs to put its care-of address in the Alternate Care-of Address option as a part of the BU message in order for it to be covered by the ESP header.

The lifetime field of a BU message is set to the smaller lifetime of either the care-of address or the home address of a mobile node. If a home agent accepts the requested lifetime, the acknowledgment message includes the same value. A home agent can reduce the lifetime based on the local policy of the home agent. A BA message may include a Binding Refresh Advice option.

A mobile node maintains its BU list entry for home registration by sending a BU message periodically.

11.4.3 Bi-Directional Tunneling

When a mobile node and a home agent complete the exchange of the binding information, these nodes create a tunnel connection between them. The endpoint addresses of the tunnel connection are the address of the home agent and the care-of address of the mobile node. This tunnel connection is used to hide the location of the mobile node from correspondent nodes. The peer node does not notice whether the mobile node is at home or in any foreign networks. Note that the packets sent to the link-local address of the mobile node are not forwarded to the mobile node even if the L flag is set in the BU message from the mobile node. The flag is used to protect the link-local address to be used with other nodes on the home link but not to be used to forward the link-local packets to other links.

A mobile node usually uses its home address as a logical endpoint address when sending packets. This ensures that the communication between a mobile node and other nodes survives when the mobile node moves from one network to another network, since a home address never changes. However, a mobile node cannot simply send a packet with its source

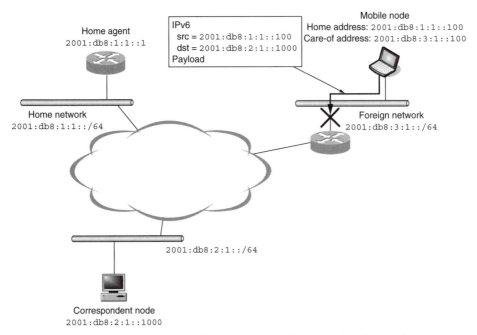

Figure 11.35 Topologically incorrect packets may be dropped.

address set to the home address of the node. Such a packet is topologically incorrect and the router which serves the foreign network may discard the packet based on its local security policy. Figure 11.35 shows the procedure.

To avoid this problem, a mobile node sends packets whose source address is the home address of the node by using the tunnel connection created between the mobile node and its home agent. Figure 11.36 shows the procedure.

A packet is encapsulated within another IPv6 header whose source and destination addresses are the care-of address of the mobile node and the address of mobile node's home agent respectively. The packet is de-capsulated at the home agent, and the home agent forwards the packet to the final destination. The packet looks as if it is being sent from a node which is attached to the home network.

When a correspondent node sends packets to the mobile node, the tunnel connection is also used in reverse direction. All packets whose destination address is the home address of the mobile node are delivered to the home network of the mobile node. These packets are intercepted by the home agent of the mobile node, if the home agent has a valid binding cache entry for the mobile node, and sent to the mobile node using IPv6 in IPv6 tunneling. The source and destination addresses of the outer IPv6 header are the address of the home agent and the care-of address of the mobile node respectively. Figure 11.37 shows the flow.

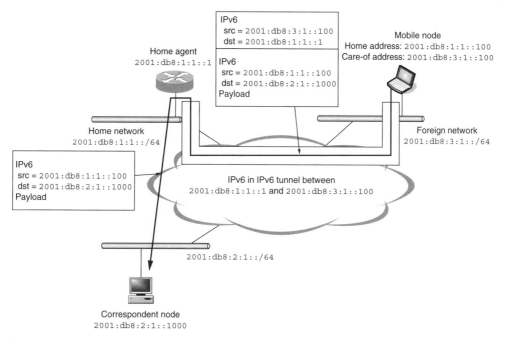

Figure 11.36 Sending packets by a tunnel connection from a mobile node to a home agent.

11.4.4 Intercepting Packets for a Mobile Node

A home agent needs to intercept packets sent to a mobile node which the home agent is serving, and then needs to forward these packets using a tunnel connection between the home agent and the mobile node.

To receive packets which are sent to a mobile node, a home agent utilizes the proxy Neighbor Discovery mechanism. When a home agent creates a binding cache entry after receiving a BU message from a mobile node, the home agent starts responding to Neighbor Solicitation messages sent to the home address or the solicited node multicast address of the home address. The home agent replies with a Neighbor Advertisement message in response to these solicitation messages. In the advertisement message, the home agent includes its own link-layer address as a target link-layer address. As a result, all packets sent to the home address of the mobile node are sent to the link-layer address of the home agent. The home agent forwards the received packets to the tunnel connection constructed between the home agent and the mobile node as described in the previous section. Figure 11.38 shows the behavior of the proxy Neighbor Discovery mechanism.

11.4.5 Returning Home

When a mobile node returns home, it must clear any of its binding information registered on a home agent and correspondent nodes. The procedure to de-register binding information is

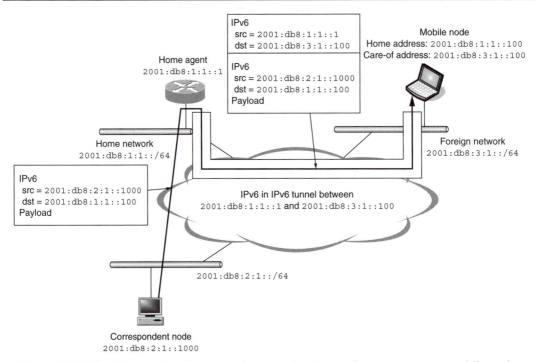

Figure 11.37 Sending packets by a tunnel connection from a home agent to a mobile node.

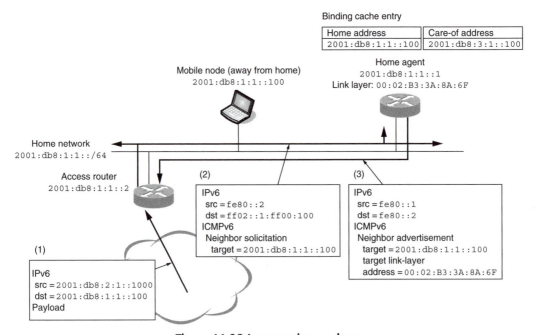

Figure 11.38 Intercepting packets.

almost the same as that of registering the information. The message used to de-register the binding is a BU message.

First of all, a mobile node must send a BU message to its home agent. The source address of the message must be a care-of address of a mobile node; however, in this case, the source address is set to the home address of a mobile node, since the care-of address and the home address are the same when a mobile node is home. The message also contains a Home Address option which contains the home address. The lifetime field is set to 0 to indicate de-registration. Also, the message contains an Alternate Care-of Address option to hold a care-of address (which is a home address in this case). The message must be protected by the IPsec ESP mechanism.

In some situations, a mobile node may not know the link-layer address of its home agent, which is necessary when sending a packet to the home agent. In this case, a mobile node must perform the Neighbor Discovery procedure, but we need to take care of one thing. If a home agent has a valid binding cache entry for the mobile node's link-local address, the mobile node cannot use its link-local address during the Neighbor Discovery procedure because the home agent is acting as a proxy server of the address. Such usage may be considered address duplication. When a mobile node needs to resolve the link-layer address of its home agent when returning home, it sends a Neighbor Solicitation message from an unspecified address. When the home agent receives such a solicitation message, it replies with a Neighbor Advertisement message to an all-node multicast address as described in the Neighbor Discovery specification [3]. A mobile node can learn the link-layer address of the home agent by listening to the advertisement message.

If a home agent accepts the BU message, it replies with a BA message. A home agent also stops its proxy function for the mobile node and shuts down the tunnel connection between the home agent and the mobile node. Finally it removes the binding cache entry for the mobile node.

A mobile node also shuts down the tunnel connection between itself and its home agent after receiving a BA message from its home agent. This procedure is called *home de-registration*.

There is a possibility that the signaling messages may be dropped because of communication errors. If a BU message sent from a mobile node for de-registration is lost, the mobile node will resend another BU message until it receives a BA message. If a BA message is lost, the situation is slightly complicated, because the binding cache entry for the mobile node which sent a de-registration message has already been removed from the home agent when the BA message was sent. The mobile node will resend a BU message because it has not received a corresponding BA message. When a home agent receives a BU message for de-registration from a mobile node but it does not have a corresponding binding cache entry, it will reply to the mobile node with a BA message with status code 133. When a mobile node which has returned home receives a BA message with status code 133, the mobile node should consider that the acknowledgment message has been lost and complete the de-registration procedure.

A mobile node may de-register its address from its home agent even when it does not return to home (e.g., when the mobile node stops its mobility function on a foreign network). In this case, a similar procedure is used to de-register the address. The BU message sent from the mobile node will have a different home address and care-of address but the lifetime field will be set to 0. The home agent will remove its binding cache entry and stop intercepting packets for the mobile node.

11.5 Route Optimization

When a mobile node communicates with other nodes, all packets are forwarded by a home agent if the mobile node is away from home. This causes a communication delay, especially if the mobile node and its peer node are located on networks that are topologically close and the home agent is far away. The worst case is when both nodes are on the same network.

The Mobile IPv6 specification provides a solution for this problem. If the peer node supports the Mobile IPv6 correspondent node function, the path between a mobile node and the peer node can be optimized. To optimize the path, a mobile node sends a BU message to the correspondent node. The message must not have the H and L flags set because the message is not requesting home registration. The A flag may be set; however, it is not mandatory. If the A flag is set, a correspondent node replies with a BA message in response to the BU message. Note that even if the A flag is not set, a correspondent node must reply to the mobile node with a BA message when an error occurs during the message processing except in the authentication error case.

A BU message must be protected by the return routability procedure, discussed in the next section. The message must contain a Binding Authorization Data option. The option contains a hash value of the BU message, which is computed with the shared secret generated as a result of the return routability procedure. If the hash value is incorrect, the message is dropped. Similarly, a BA message sent from a correspondent node must include a Binding Authorization Data option to protect the contents.

Once the exchange of a BU message (and a BA message, if the A flag is set) has completed, a mobile node starts exchanging route optimized packets with a correspondent node. The source address field of the packets is set to the care-of address of the mobile node. The mobile node cannot set the source address to its home address directly, since intermediate routers may drop a packet whose source address is not topologically correct to prevent source spoofing attacks. The home address information is kept in a Home Address option of a Destination Options header of the packet.

When a correspondent node receives a packet which has a Home Address option, it checks to see if it has a binding cache entry related to the home address. If there is no such entry, the correspondent node responds with a BE message with status code 0. A mobile node needs to resend a BU message to create a binding cache entry in the correspondent node if it receives a

BE message. This validation procedure prevents any malicious nodes from using forged care-of addresses on behalf of the legitimate mobile node.

If the Home Address option is valid, the correspondent node accepts the incoming packet and swaps the home address in the option and the source address of the packet. As a result, the packets passed to the upper layer protocols have the home address as the source address. The upper layer protocols and applications need not care about any address changes for the mobile node since this address swap is done in the IPv6 layer.

When a correspondent node sends a packet to a mobile node, it uses the Type 2 Routing Header. A home address of a mobile node is put in the Routing Header and the destination address of the IPv6 packet is set to the care-of address of the mobile node. The packet does not go to the home network. Instead, the packet is routed to the foreign network where the mobile node is currently attached, since the destination address is set to the care-of address. The processing of a Type 2 Routing Header is similar to the processing of a Type 0 Routing Header except for some validation checks. A mobile node checks that the Routing Header contains only one address in the intermediate nodes field and ensures that the address is assigned to the mobile node itself. If the address specified in the Routing Header is not an address of the mobile node, the mobile node discards the packet, as the packet may be an attempt to force the mobile node to forward the packet. A mobile node drops any packets which contain an invalid Type 2 Routing Header.

11.5.1 Return Routability

A mobile node and a correspondent node need to share secret information before exchanging binding information. When a mobile node sends a BU message, it computes a hash value of the message, using the shared information, and puts the value in the message. A correspondent node verifies the hash value by recomputing it, and drops the packet if the value computed on the correspondent node and the value specified in the message are different. In the same manner, a BA message sent from a correspondent node to a mobile node is protected by the hash mechanism. The shared information is created by the return routability procedure. In this section, we discuss the detailed procedure of the return routability mechanism.

11.5.2 Sending Initial Messages

Only a mobile node can initiate the return routability procedure. When a mobile node wants to start route optimized communication, it sends two initial messages. One is a HoTI message and the other is a CoTI message. There is no strict specification as to when a mobile node should send these messages. A mobile node can initiate the procedure whenever it needs to optimize the route. In the KAME implementation, e.g., a mobile node sends these messages when the mobile node receives a packet from a correspondent node via a bi-directional tunnel between the mobile node and its home agent.

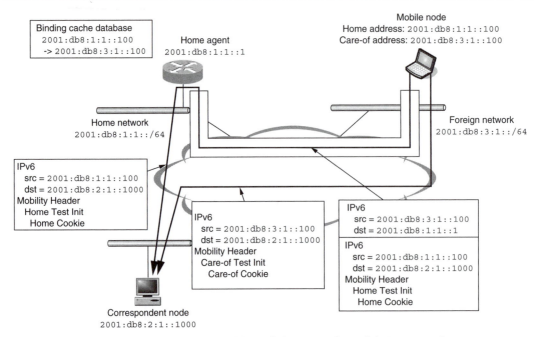

Figure 11.39 The home test init and the care-of test init message flow.

A HoTI message is sent from the home address of a mobile node. As we discussed already, such a packet whose source address is a home address cannot be sent directly from a foreign network. A HoTI message is sent through a tunnel connection between a mobile node and its home agent. A correspondent node will receive the message as if it were sent from the home network of the mobile node.

A CoTI message is sent from the care-of address of a mobile node. This message can be sent directly from a foreign network.

Both messages contain a random value called a cookie. The cookie in a HoTI message is called the Home Init Cookie and the cookie in a CoTI message is called the CoTI Cookie. These cookie values are used to match messages which a mobile node receives in response to the HoTI/CoTI messages from the correspondent node.

Figure 11.39 shows the packet flow of the HoTI and CoTI message.

11.5.3 Responding to Initial Messages

When a correspondent node which supports the return routability procedure receives a HoTI or a CoTI message from a mobile node, the correspondent node replies to the mobile node with a HoT message and a CoT message.

A HoT message is sent to the home address of a mobile node. The message is delivered to the home network of the mobile node and intercepted by the home agent of the mobile node. The mobile node receives the message from a tunnel connection between the node and its home agent.

A CoT message is sent to the care-of address of a mobile node directly.

Both messages contain a copy of the cookie value which is contained in the HoTI/CoTI message, so that a mobile node can check to see if the received messages are sent in response to the initial messages.

A HoT and a CoT message have two other pieces of information: the nonce index and the Keygen Token. A correspondent node keeps an array of nonce values and node keys. The nonce index values specify the nonce values in the array. The nonce values and the node key values are never exposed outside of a correspondent node. This information must be kept in the correspondent node. The Keygen Token is computed from a nonce value and a node key using the following algorithms.

Home Keygen Token = First(64, HMAC_SHA1(K_{cn} (the home address of a mobile node |the nonce specified by the home nonce index |0)))

Care-of Keygen Token = First(64, HMAC_SHA1(K_{cn} (the care-of address of a mobile node |the nonce specified by the care-of nonce index |1)))

where "|" denotes concatenation, First (x, y) function returns the first x bits from y, HMAC_SHA1(key, data) function returns a HMAC SHA-1 hash value against "data" using "key" as a key, K_{cn} is a node key of a correspondent node.

These tokens are used to generate a shared secret which is used to compute the hash values of a BU message on a mobile node and a BA message on a correspondent node. To prevent a replay attack, a correspondent node must generate a new nonce value and node key and revoke the old nonce value and node key periodically. The maximum lifetime of all nonce values is restricted to `MAX_NONCE_LIFETIME` seconds. The lifetime of generated tokens is also restricted to `MAX_TOKEN_LIFETIME` seconds.

The array that keeps the nonce values and node keys are shared between mobile nodes with which the correspondent node is communicating. In theory, it is possible to use different values per mobile node; however, it introduces vulnerability in management of the values. That is, a malicious node can easily consume the memory of the correspondent node sending bogus HoTI or CoTI messages with a lot of fake mobile node's addresses.

When a mobile node sends a BU message, it includes nonce index values. A correspondent node must keep the history of these values and must be able to regenerate Keygen Tokens from the index values.

Figure 11.40 shows the packet flow of the HoT and the CoT messages.

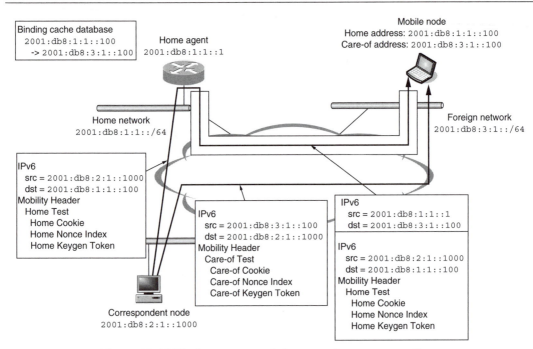

Figure 11.40 The home test and the care-of test message flow.

11.5.4 Computing a Shared Secret

A shared secret is computed as follows:

$$K_{bm} = \text{SHA1}(\text{home keygen token} \mid \text{care-of keygen token})$$
... (if a mobile node is at a foreign network)

or

$$K_{bm} = \text{SHA1}(\text{home keygen token})$$
... (if a mobile node is at home)

where "|" denotes concatenation of data, K_{bm} is a shared secret computed from token values, *SHA*1(*data*) computes a SHA-1 hash value against "*data*."

Depending on the location of a mobile node, the shared secret is computed differently. If a mobile node is in a foreign network, the secret is computed from both a Home Keygen Token and a Care-of Keygen Token. If a mobile node is at home, only a Home Keygen Token is used, because the home address and the care-of address of the mobile node are the same. In this case, we need to check only one of them. The procedure when returning to home is discussed in Section 11.5.7.

A mobile node computes a hash value using the secret information computed above. The algorithm is as follows:

$$\text{Mobility Data} = \text{the care-of address of a mobile node}$$
$$| \text{ the address of a correspondent node}$$
$$| \text{ the Mobility Header message}$$
$$\text{Authenticator} = \text{First}(96, \text{HMAC\_SHA1}(K_{bm}, \text{Mobility Data}))$$

where "|" denotes concatenation of data, "the Mobility Header message" is either a BU or a BA message, First(x, y) function returns the first x bits from y, *HMAC_SHA*1(*key, data*) computes a HMAC SHA-1 hash value against "*data*" using "*key*" as a key.

The hash value is called an Authenticator. The original data of the hash value consists of a care-of address, a home address, and a Mobility Header message. When sending a BU message, the Mobility Header message is the content of the BU message. When computing the hash value, all mobility options are included as a part of the Mobility Header, except the Authenticator field of the Binding Authorization Data option. The checksum field of a Mobility Header message is considered zero and it must be cleared before computing the hash value.

11.5.5 Verifying Message

A mobile node sends a BU message with a Binding Authorization Data option which includes the Authenticator value computed by the procedure described in the previous paragraph and a Nonce Index option which contains the home nonce index and the care-of nonce index which have been used when generating a shared secret to compute the Authenticator. When creating a BU message as a result of the return routability procedure, the lifetime of the binding information is limited to MAX_RR_BINDING_LIFETIME seconds.

When a correspondent node receives a BU message, it first checks the existence of a Binding Authorization Data option and a Nonce Index option. If these options do not exist, the message is dropped.

The correspondent node generates a Home Keygen Token and a Care-of Keygen Token from the nonce index values included in the Nonce Index option of the incoming BU message. From the tokens, the correspondent node can generate the shared secret which was used by the mobile node when it created the BU message. A correspondent node verifies the message by computing a hash value of the message using the same algorithm described previously. If the result is different from the Authenticator value of the Binding Authorization Data option which was computed in the mobile node, the incoming message is dropped.

In some cases, a mobile node may use older nonce index values which a correspondent node has not kept any more. In this case, the correspondent node replies with a BA message with a status code 136 to 138 (see Table 11.3) which indicates the specified nonce index is not valid.

The mobile node which receives such an error status performs the return routability procedure to get the latest nonce values.

If the incoming BU message is valid, the correspondent node creates a binding cache entry for the mobile node and, if the A flag is set in the BU message, replies with a BA message. The BA message also includes a Binding Authorization Data option and a Nonce Index option to protect the message. Figure 11.41 describes the packet flow of the BU and the BA messages between a mobile node and a correspondent node.

11.5.6 Security Considerations

The return routability procedure provides an authorization mechanism for mobile nodes to inject binding cache entries to correspondent nodes. A correspondent node can ensure that the home address and the care-of address provided by a BU message are bound to a single mobile node. But it cannot determine who the mobile node is.

For the purpose of route optimization, the provided feature is sufficient. The problem when creating a binding cache entry is that if an attacker can create a binding cache entry with the home address of a victim mobile node and the care-of address of the attacker, all traffic to the victim node is routed to the attacker. The return routability procedure at least prevents this problem.

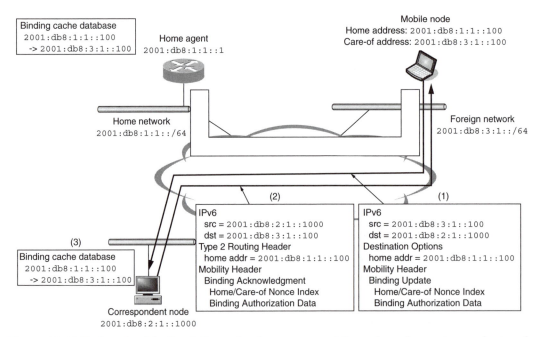

Figure 11.41 Exchanging binding information between a mobile node and a correspondent node.

The messages exchanged between a mobile node and a correspondent node are protected by a hash function. The tokens used to generate a shared secret are exchanged by the HoT and CoT messages. That means anyone can generate the shared secret once he/she acquires these tokens. The Mobile IPv6 specification stipulates that the tunnel connection between a mobile node and a home agent used to send or receive the HoTI and the HoT messages must be protected by the IPsec ESP mechanism. This is done by using the IPsec tunnel mode communication between them. As a result, an attacker cannot eavesdrop on the contents of the HoT message that includes a Home Keygen Token value; however, the path between the home network of the mobile node and the correspondent node is not protected. If the attacker is on this path, the Home Keygen Token value can be examined.

To generate a shared secret, an attacker must get both a Home Keygen Token and a Care-of Keygen Token. One possible way to get both the tokens is to attach to the network between the home agent and the correspondent node of the victim mobile node. In this case, the attacker can eavesdrop on the Home Keygen token sent to the victim and can request a Care-of Keygen token by sending a faked CoTI message from the attacker's address. However, even if the attacker can get access to such a network, the situation is no worse than the normal IPv6 (not Mobile IPv6) communication. If the attacker can get access between two nodes, it can do more than just examine traffic, as with a man-in-the-middle attack.

11.5.7 De-Register Binding for Correspondent Nodes

After successful home de-registration as discussed in Section 11.4.5, a mobile node may perform the return routability procedure for all correspondent nodes for which it has BU list entries. The return routability procedure from a home network is slightly different from the procedure done in a foreign network since the care-of address and the home address of a mobile node are the same. In this case, a mobile node and correspondent nodes only exchange a HoTI and a HoT message and a shared secret is generated only from a Home Keygen Token as described in Section 11.5.4. These messages are not tunneled to the home agent because the tunnel link has already been destroyed by the home de-registration procedure performed before this return routability procedure.

11.5.8 Backward Compatibility

When we consider deploying a new technology, we need to take care of the backward compatibility with legacy nodes. Mobile IPv6 will not be deployed if it cannot communicate with many old IPv6 nodes that do not understand it.

To ensure backward compatibility, the Mobile IPv6 specification defines a tunnel mechanism. A mobile node can send and receive packets using a tunnel between a mobile node and its home agent, as if the mobile node were at home. As long as a mobile node uses the tunnel, no backward compatibility issues occur.

However, as we have already discussed, a mobile node may initiate the return routability procedure to optimize the route between itself and a correspondent node. A mobile node cannot know beforehand if the peer node, with which the mobile node is currently communicating, supports Mobile IPv6. So, a mobile node may send a HoTI or a CoTI message even if the peer node does not support Mobile IPv6. These messages use the Mobility Header, which is a new extension header introduced by the Mobile IPv6 specification. The old IPv6 nodes do not know of the extension header and cannot recognize the protocol number (in this case, 135). When a node receives an unrecognized protocol number, the node will generate an ICMPv6 Parameter Problem message with code 2 indicating that the incoming packet has an unrecognized next header value. The ICMPv6 message also indicates the position where an error occurred. In this case, the error messages point to the next header field of the header located before the Mobility Header. The generation of an ICMPv6 message for an unrecognized header is defined in the IPv6 base specification. We can assume all IPv6 nodes have this functionality.

If a mobile receives an ICMPv6 Parameter Problem message with code 2 and the error position indicates the protocol number of a Mobility Header, the mobile node stops performing the return routability procedure and uses only tunnel communication. Figure 11.42 shows the packet exchange.

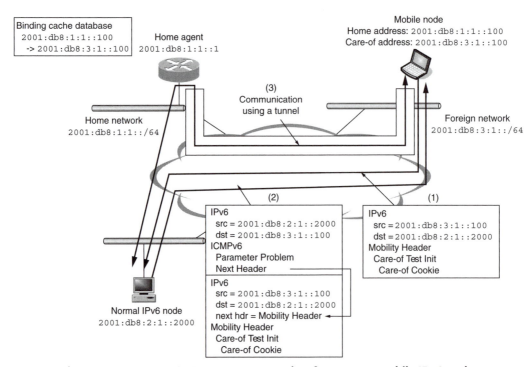

Figure 11.42 An ICMPv6 message generation from a non-mobile IPv6 node.

11.6 Movement Detection

When a mobile node attaches to a network, it must detect whether or not it has moved. There are several pieces of information which can be used to detect the movement of a node. The Mobile IPv6 specification talks about a basic movement detection method which uses Neighbor Unreachability Detection of a default router of a mobile node. As described in the Neighbor Discovery specification, an IPv6 node keeps a list of default routers on the attached network. If the routers become unreachable, it can be assumed that the node is attached to a different network.

When performing Neighbor Unreachability Detection for default routers, we need to take care of one thing. The Neighbor Unreachability Detection is done by sending a Neighbor Solicitation message to the target router. Usually, the address of the target router is a link-local address, since a normal Router Advertisement does not contain the global address of the router. A node usually does not know the global address of routers. However, a link-local address is unique only on a single link. This means that even if a mobile node moves from one network to another network, the mobile node may not be able to detect the unreachability of the default router if routers on the different links use the same link-local address. A mobile node needs to utilize other information as much as possible.

One of the other pieces of information which can be used for the unreachability detection is a global address from a Prefix Information option which is extended by the Mobile IPv6 specification. If a Router Advertisement message contains the extension, a mobile node should perform Neighbor Unreachability Detection against the global address. Of course, this can be used only with routers that support Mobile IPv6 extension.

Another method is collecting all prefix information on a network. The prefix value is unique to each network. In this method, a mobile node keeps collecting prefix information. If prefix information which was advertised before can no longer be seen, the node may have moved to another network. The important thing is that the mobile node must not decide its movement by receiving only one advertisement message because there may be several routers which advertise different prefix information on the network. In that case, a single router advertisement does not show the entire network information.

There is no standard way of detecting movement of a mobile node. It is highly implementation dependent.

The IETF DNA working group is trying to enhance the detection mechanism so that mobile nodes can detect their location or movement faster and more precisely.

11.7 Dynamic Home Agent Address Discovery

A mobile node may not know the address of its home agent when it wants to send a BU message for home registration. For example, if a mobile node reboots on a foreign network, there is no information about the home agent unless such information is pre-configured.

The Dynamic Home Agent Address Discovery mechanism is used to get the address information of home agents when a mobile node is in a foreign network. A mobile node sends a Dynamic Home Agent Address Discovery request message when it needs to know the address of its home agent. The source address of the message is a care-of address of a mobile node and the destination address of the message is a home agent anycast address which can be computed from the home prefix. This message does not contain a Home Address option, since this message may be sent before the first home registration is completed. A mobile node cannot use its home address before home registration is completed.

On the home network, home agents maintain the list of global addresses of all home agents on the home network by listening to each other's Router Advertisement messages. As described in Section 11.3.6, a home agent advertises its global address with a modified Prefix Information option. Figure 11.43 shows the concept.

Every home agent has a special anycast address called a home agent anycast address which is computed as described previously in Figure 11.28. A Dynamic Home Agent Address Discovery request message is delivered to one of the home agents in a home network thanks to the anycast address mechanism. The home agent that receives the message will reply to the mobile node with a Dynamic Home Agent Address Discovery reply message containing all of the home agent addresses which the home agent currently knows. The address list is ordered by the preference value of each home agent. If there are multiple home agents with the same preference value, the addresses should be ordered randomly every time for load balancing. To avoid packet fragmentation, the total length of the message must be smaller than the path MTU to the mobile node. If the list is too long to include in one packet, the home agents which have low preference values are excluded from the reply message. Figure 11.44 shows the procedure.

If a mobile node does not receive a reply message, the node will resend a request message. The initial timeout value for the retransmission is `INITIAL_DHAAD_TIMEOUT` seconds. The timeout value is increased exponentially at every retransmission. The maximum number of retransmissions is restricted to `DHAAD_RETRIES` times.

In theory, the Home Agent Address Discovery mechanism can be used as a mechanism to notify mobile nodes of available home agents on its home network. However, as we discuss in Section 11.9, adding/removing the home agent causes IPsec configuration problems. In the recent discussion at the IETF, the dynamic home agent assignment and security setup are considered as part of other infrastructure-based mechanisms [6].

11.8 Mobile Prefix Solicitation/Advertisement

An IPv6 address has a lifetime value. The lifetime is derived from the lifetime of the prefix. If the home address of a mobile node is going to expire, the mobile node sends a Mobile

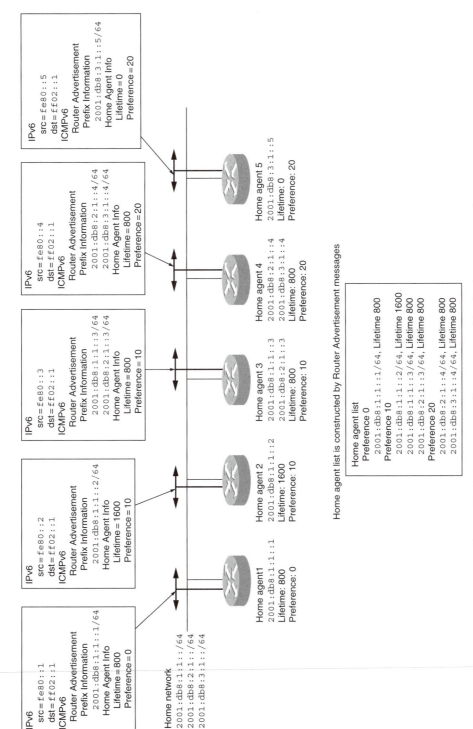

Figure 11.43 Home agent list generated in the home network.

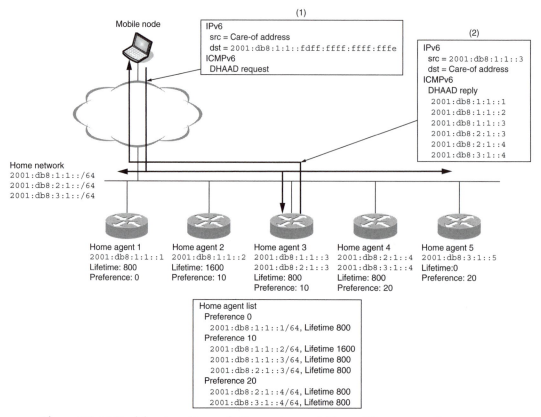

Figure 11.44 Replying to a Dynamic Home Agent Address Discovery reply message.

Prefix Solicitation message to get the latest information about home prefixes. The source address of the message is set to the care-of address of the mobile node. The destination of the message is the address of the home agent with which the mobile node is currently registered. The message must include a Home Address option which contains the home address of the mobile node (i.e., a Mobile Prefix Solicitation message can be sent only after successful home registration). Since the home registration procedure requires the information of a home network, this prefix discovery mechanism cannot be used to find the home prefixes when a mobile node is booting up on a foreign network, but can only be used to know new home prefixes or deprecated home prefixes.

When a home agent receives a Mobile Prefix Solicitation message from a mobile node, the node must reply to the mobile node with a Mobile Prefix Advertisement message. The source address of the message must be the destination address of the corresponding solicitation message. The destination address of the message must be the source address of the corresponding solicitation message, that is, the care-of address of a mobile node. A Type 2 Routing Header that contains the home address of a mobile node must exist. The list of modified Prefix Information options follows the advertisement message header.

Unlike the Router Advertisement messages, the list of Prefix Information options sent from the home agents on the same home network must be consistent. To make sure of the consistency, every home agent must be configured to have the same prefix information of its home network, or must listen to Router Advertisement messages from other home agents and construct a merged list of prefix information. A mobile node sends a solicitation message to the home agent with which the mobile node is currently registered. If the prefix information returned in response to the solicitation message differs for each home agent, the mobile node may incorrectly consider that some prefix information has disappeared.

A home agent may send a Mobile Prefix Advertisement message even if a mobile node does not request the prefix information in the following cases:

- The state of the flags of the home prefix which a mobile node is using changes.

- The valid or preferred lifetime of a home prefix is reconfigured.

- A new home prefix is added.

- The state of the flags or lifetime values of a home prefix which is not used by any mobile node changes.

When either of the first two conditions occurs, a home agent must send an unsolicited Mobile Prefix Advertisement. When the third condition occurs, a home agent should send an unsolicited Mobile Prefix Advertisement message. When the last condition occurs, a home agent may send the message. A mobile node updates its prefix information and home addresses derived from updated prefixes when it receives this unsolicited Mobile Prefix Advertisement.

When sending an advertisement message, a home agent must follow the following scheduling algorithm to avoid network congestion:

- If a mobile node sends a solicitation message, a home agent sends an advertisement message immediately.

- Otherwise, a home agent schedules the next transmission time as follows:

MaxScheduleDelay = MIN(MaxMobPfxAdvInterval, preferred lifetime)

RandomDelay = MinMobPfxAdvInterval

+ (*RANDOM*()%

ABS(MaxScheduleDelay − MinMobPfxAdvInterval))

where *MIN(a, b)* returns the smaller of *a* or *b*, *RANDOM()* generates a random value from 0 to the maximum possible integer value, *ABS(a)* returns an absolute value of *a*.

The next advertisement will be sent after *RandomDelay* seconds.

When a mobile node receives an unsolicited Mobile Prefix Advertisement message, it must send a Mobile Prefix Solicitation message as an acknowledgment of that message. Otherwise, a home agent will resend the unsolicited advertisement message every `PREFIX_ADV_TIMEOUT` seconds. The maximum number of retransmissions is restricted to `PREFIX_ADV_RETIRES` times. The Mobile Prefix Solicitation and Advertisement message should be protected by the IPsec mechanism.

In theory, the Mobile Prefix Solicitation/Advertisement mechanism can be used as a mechanism to renumber the home network of mobile nodes, however, as discussed in Section 11.9, renumbering the home addresses has IPsec configuration problems. A mobile node and its home agent must negotiate which home address should be used and the IPsec policy database on both nodes need to be updated because the database has home address information. The Mobile IPv6 specification does not specify any address transition procedure in its base specification.

11.9 Relationship with IPsec

Mobile IPv6 uses the IPsec mechanism to protect the Mobile IPv6 signaling messages. The specifications on how to protect messages are defined in [2].

The messages directly exchanged between a mobile node and a home agent are protected by the IPsec transport mode mechanism. The BU and BA messages must be protected by the IPsec ESP or AH header. The Mobile Prefix Solicitation and Advertisement messages should be protected by the IPsec mechanism.

The messages exchanged between a mobile node and a correspondent node, and relayed by the home agent, are protected by the IPsec tunnel mode mechanism. The HoTI and HoT messages must be protected by the IPsec ESP header with the IPsec tunnel mode. As we will show in this section, the tunnel mode policy entries must be able to support the Mobility Header type specific policy rule. More precisely, it must be able to send and receive the HoTI and HoT messages only via the IPsec tunnel. This is necessary when two mobile nodes communicate with route optimization. If a mobile node cannot specify the HoTI/HoT messages as policy specification, a BU message to the other mobile node (this node is actually treated as a correspondent node) is incorrectly tunneled to the home agent of the mobile node that is sending the BU message.

Note that the Dynamic Home Agent Address Discovery Request and Reply messages cannot be protected because the mobile node does not know the home agent address before exchanging these messages. The address information is required to set up the IPsec security policy database to protect messages.

Tables 11.8 and 11.9 summarize the policy entries required for a mobile node and a home agent.

The Security Associations for each policy can be configured by a manual operation. The IKE mechanism can be used to create these Security Associations dynamically, however, it requires a modification to the IKE program. Usually, the addresses of a Security Association IKE configures are derived from the addresses which are used to perform the IKE negotiation. In the Mobile IPv6 case, when a mobile node moves from its home network to a foreign

Table 11.8 Security Policy Entries Required for a Mobile Node.

Mode	IPsec Protocol	Target Source	Target Destination	Target Protocol	Tunnel Source	Tunnel Destination
Transport	ESP (or AH)	Home address	Home agent	MH (Binding Update)	–	–
Transport	ESP (or AH)	Home agent	Home address	MH (Binding Acknowledgment)	–	–
Transport	ESP (or AH)	Home address	Home agent	ICMPv6 (Mobile Prefix Solicitation)	–	–
Transport	ESP (or AH)	Home agent	Home address	ICMPv6 (Mobile Prefix Advertisement)	–	–
Tunnel	ESP	Home address	Any	MH (Home Test Init)	Care-of address	Home agent
Tunnel	ESP	Any	Home address	MH (Home Test)	Home agent	Care-of address

Table 11.9 Security Policy Entries Required for a Home Agent.

Mode	IPsec Protocol	Target Source	Target Destination	Target Protocol	Tunnel Source	Tunnel Destination
Transport	ESP (or AH)	Home agent	Home address	MH (Binding Update)	–	–
Transport	ESP (or AH)	Home address	Home agent	MH (Binding Acknowledgment)	–	–
Transport	ESP (or AH)	Home agent	Home address	ICMPv6 (Mobile Prefix Solicitation)	–	–
Transport	ESP (or AH)	Home address	Home agent	ICMPv6 (Mobile Prefix Advertisement)	–	–
Tunnel	ESP	Any	Home address	MH (Home Test Init)	Home agent	Care-of address
Tunnel	ESP	Home address	Any	MH (Home Test)	Care-of address	Home agent

network, the home address cannot be used until the home registration procedure has been completed. But we need a Security Association between the home address and the home agent address to complete the home registration procedure. The IKE program must use a care-of address for IKE negotiation and create a Security Association for addresses which are not used in the IKE negotiation. Currently, few IKE implementations support this function.

There are other problems which are caused by the design of the IPsec policy configuration mechanism. The IPsec policy configuration is usually static; however in the Mobile IPv6 operation we need to change policies in the following situations:

- When a new home agent is installed a mobile node needs to install new transport and tunnel mode policy entries for the new home agent

- When a renumbering occurs a mobile node and a home agent need to update their home prefix information in xx the policy database

The use of IPsec with Mobile IPv6 has many unresolved issues. More research is required to achieve flexible operation of the combination of these technologies.

References

[1] D. Johnson et al., Mobility Support in IPv6, RFC3775, June 2004.

[2] J. Arkko et al., Using IPsec to Protect Mobile IPv6 Signaling Between Mobile Nodes and Home Agents, RFC3776, June 2004.

[3] T. Narten et al., Neighbor Discovery for IP version 6 (IPv6), RFC2461, December 1998.

[4] D. Johnson, S. Deering, Reserved IPv6 Subnet Anycast Addresses, RFC2526, March 1999.

[5] A. Conta, S. Deering, Internet Control Message Protocol (ICMPv6) for the Internet Protocol version 6 (IPv6) Specification, RFC2463, December 1998.

[6] A. Patel, G. Giaretta, Problem Statement for Bootstrapping Mobile IPv6 (MIPv6), RFC4640, September 2006.

CHAPTER 12

Security and Survivability of Wireless Systems

Yi Qian,
Prashant Krishnamurthy
David Tipper

12.1 Introduction

Recent trends indicate that the next-generation wireless networks will consist of hybrid wireless access networks and wireless sensor networks (WSNs) [1–3]. The wireless access networks will be hybrid, i.e., they will consist of wide-area mobile data services providing extensive coverage but lower data rates and wireless local area networks (WLANs) for covering local area hot spots with much higher data rates [2]. Wireless ad hoc connections can assist with missing connections between a wireless device and the rest of a network [1, 3]. WSNs are becoming increasingly relevant for sensing physical phenomenon for a variety of applications (e.g., structural health monitoring, sampling soil quality). All of these wireless networks are expected to be interconnected in the future.

Already, the public's demand for and dependence on mobile services makes existing wireless networks a part of the nation's critical network infrastructure (CNI), and ongoing development of next-generation wireless networks only increases their importance. The continually increasing reliance on wireless networks by businesses, the general public, and government services, and their role in the CNI of the country make it imperative to have information assurance (IA) built into them. IA for wireless networks is an emerging research area with relatively little literature in comparison to wired networks. While individual wireless technologies currently incorporate some in-built security features, these have been implemented in a largely uncoordinated manner. Availability features for wireless systems are either nonexistent or not well understood [4]. Moreover, IA techniques employed in wired networks have limited direct applicability in wireless networks because of the unique aspects of wireless networks (e.g., user mobility, wireless communication channel, power conservation, limited computational power in mobile nodes, security at the link layer). IA in WSNs is unique in that the faults and threats that need to be considered are quite different from those in other kinds of networks or distributed systems. Sensor networks consist of perhaps thousands of low-cost, battery-operated units with limited computational power and memory that need to communicate potentially with one another and some sink or base station using wireless links. Consequently, scalability (because of the sheer numbers of nodes), energy efficiency, necessity of lightweight cryptographic protocols, and methods to overcome wireless vulnerabilities are important. Also, it is not possible to assume that sensor units will not be compromised or tampered with for the same reasons. Hence, it is important to consider both outsider and insider threats in sensor networks. Low-cost sensor nodes are likely to fail randomly or stop working due to limited battery life.

Finally, to the best of our knowledge, there is very little literature on how the components of IA, namely availability and security, interact with each other in a wireless network environment. Component failures or coordinated physical/cyber attacks on network equipment will result in security breaches and impact network performance simultaneously. Thus, there is a need to study the coupling between network survivability and security and create design strategies consistent with both sets of requirements [5, 6].

In this chapter, we investigate the security and survivability issues for wireless systems and networks. We first provide a background of hybrid wireless access networks and sensor networks (Section 12.2). We discuss the current survivability and security approaches in hybrid wireless infrastructure networks in Sections 12.3 and 12.4. We then present a preliminary study on the design of security and survivability for wireless ad hoc and sensor networks in Section 12.5. We also discuss with two case studies the issues that relate to the interaction between security and survivability in hybrid wireless access networks and sensor networks in Section 12.6.

12.2 Background

In this section, we give a brief discussion on hybrid wireless access networks, wireless ad hoc and sensor networks, and security and survivability for wireless networks in general.

Traditionally, wireless networks have been homogeneous with limited or no interoperability between various technologies. However, no single wireless technology is capable of supporting all the various application requirements such as coverage, data rates, error rates, mobility, and so on. The evolutionary trend is toward a mixture of various technologies and networks that must coexist and interoperate to provide required services [2]. Cellular service providers are currently deploying such hybrid architectures in the United States and Europe. As an example, a WLAN may be employed for local coverage, low mobility, and high data rates while an overlaid mobile data network (such as the General Packet Radio Service, GPRS, or Third-Generation Universal Mobile Telecommunications Service, 3G-UMTS) is used for wide-area coverage and high mobility, but lower data rates [7]. Figure 12.1 shows the architecture of a future hybrid wireless network with 3G-UMTS, IEEE 802.11 infrastructure

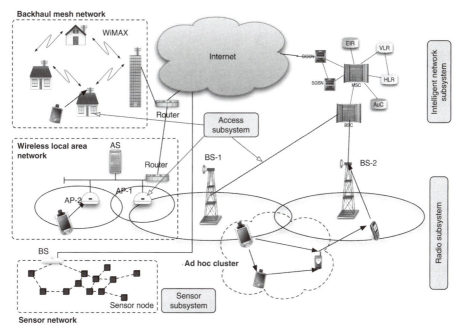

Figure 12.1 A hybrid wireless network architecture.

WLANs, a backhaul mesh network (perhaps using 802.16 WiMAX), a single ad hoc network cluster, and a sensor network. MSs participating in such a hybrid network must have the capability to operate with multiple technologies and possess the intelligence to appropriately switch among technologies and networks. Entities in Figure 12.1 are grouped into different subsystems (such as the access subsystem), which are considered in more detail later in the chapter.

In Figure 12.1, the mobile switching center (MSC) in conjunction with several databases—the home and visitor location registers (HLR/VLR), the equipment identity register (EIR), and the authentication center (AuC)—manage access control (via authentication) and mobility for MSs. The base station/radio network controller (BSC/RNC) is involved in allocating and deallocating radio channels, handoff decisions, transmit powers, and so on. GPRS support nodes (GSNs) that support data traffic also play a role in mobility management. The serving GSN (SGSN) handles communications to and from MSs in its service area and is similar to the foreign agent (FA) in the mobile Internet Protocol (mobile IP). The gateway GSN (GGSN) is similar to the home agent (HA) in mobile IP. WLANs do not have the full range of mobility and radio resource management functions as the cellular network and rely on the AP (or mobile IP) to provide some of these services. Since LANs are broadcast in nature (there is no need to track MS locations) and based on carrier sensing, they do not require sophisticated management techniques. Authentication using 802.1X or RADIUS servers is also possible in WLANs and this is now a standard (802.11i). In backhaul mesh networks, *mesh routers* form a network through self-configuration and may also provide connectivity to isolated base stations or access points [8]. Mesh networking is possible using 802.11 WLAN technology or 802.16 WiMAX technology. Mobile stations in ad hoc clusters communicate in peer-to-peer fashion directly or in multihop fashion using mobile ad hoc networks (MANET) routing protocols.

Wide-area cellular systems are far more sophisticated than their local area, metro-area, and ad hoc counterparts. There are little or no mechanisms or entities (like the HLR/VLR, BSC, or AuC) to handle mobility management, radio resources management, billing, or security in WLANs or ad hoc networks. For seamless operation between different technologies, some interworking functions are required [2, 7] that are not discussed here in great detail. Five different approaches for roaming between GPRS and WLANs were suggested in [2]. The approaches can be broadly considered as using an emulator entity that makes the WLAN look like a location area or routing area of a UMTS network, using mobile IP or a proxy mobility gateway to reconcile the two networks. A network where the cellular operator owns the WLAN is considered in [7]. A loose coupling approach where the WLAN is complementary to GPRS and only uses the GPRS databases (for authentication and subscriber information) but not the GPRS interfaces is proposed. The WLAN directly transports data to the Internet in this case. A tight coupling approach where data from a WLAN first go through the GPRS core network is also proposed in [7]. In this case, the WLAN looks like a GPRS radio access network with a different air interface. These two approaches are similar to the ones proposed in [2] but include more operational details. Details of the messages and protocols used in these approaches can be found in [2] and [7]. Similarly, mesh routers with gateway bridges are used for interworking with base stations or MSs in mesh networks [8].

Recently, interconnecting MANETs and infrastructure wireless networks has been considered in [9] where the primary motivation is to allow MSs that have poor connectivity to a base station to get higher throughputs by using intermediate relays or proxies that have better connectivity. In this work, greedy and on-demand algorithms have been developed for discovering the proxies with the best connectivity and routing between the MSs. While the greedy algorithm generates lesser overhead on the cellular uplink, it results in larger energy consumption at the MSs compared to the on-demand algorithm. However, this work does not consider survivability or interworking aspects of the hybrid network.

WSNs consist of hundreds of sensor nodes deployed over the environment to be sensed. Typically, a high-power, high-capability base station communicates with all the nodes through broadcast messages for network activities such as synchronization, querying, topology control, transmission schedules, and so on [3]. Sensor nodes have low transmission powers, so they have to use multihop communications to report sensed data to sensor nodes closest to the base station. These closest nodes then relay the information (perhaps fused, aggregated, or processed cooperatively by all the sensor nodes) to the base station, which may be connected to the Internet. We consider a different kind of sensor network with heterogeneous sensor nodes and no base station in Section 12.6.3.

12.3 Current Security Approaches in Wireless Networks

Unlike wired networks that have some degree of physical security, physical security in wireless networks is impossible to achieve on wireless links (because of their broadcast nature) and, therefore, security attacks on information flow can be widespread (e.g., passive interception of data, active injection of traffic, and overloading the access point with garbage packets). Modification of information is possible because of the nature of the channel and the mobility of nodes.

The radio channel is harsh and subject to interference, fading, multipath, and high error rates. As a result, packet losses are common even without security threats. An opponent can make use of these natural impairments to modify information and also render the information unavailable.

Most wireless networks use mild variations of wired security mechanisms. The primary vulnerabilities in the past were fraud and exposure of information and, thus, only confidentiality (privacy of voice calls) and identification (entity authentication) are given importance in second-generation (2G) wireless networks. For this, they employ challenge–response schemes [10]. The key sizes range from 40–128 bits, in many cases being insufficient for good security. The security mechanisms are not designed from the perspective of *data integrity* or potential attacks like replay or overload. The drawbacks of existing security in wireless networks, ranging from the flaws in encryption algorithms in the Global System for Mobile Communications (GSM), Cellular Digital Packet Data (CDPD), Bluetooth, and IEEE 802.11 to the more obvious protocol flaws, are discussed in many papers (e.g., see [11] for attacks on RC-4 used in CDPD and IEEE 802.11). Third-generation wireless systems and emerging standards address some of these drawbacks. The Kasumi algorithm (for confidentiality) and the Milenage algorithm (for authentication) employed by the 3G partnership project (3GPP) use larger key sizes (128 bits long) and stronger algorithms [12]. There are also mechanisms for data integrity and message authentication. In CDPD and in 3GPP, two sets of identification information are maintained: the latest update and the previous one in case the latest update is lost due to bad radio conditions [12]. The IEEE 802.11i standard proposes the use of the advanced encryption standard (AES) in one of its many modes of operation (countermode) for WLANs with 802.1X entity authentication for IEEE 802.11 WLANs [13]. Key management makes use of preinstalled master keys (or passwords) that are used with nonces to generate fresh session keys. Research groups have also suggested the use of IPSec at the network layer for all IP traffic on the air. Very little work exists in the evaluation of security of backhaul wireless mesh networks.

Security for sensor networks is still in the research stage. Threats to sensor networks can be at the physical layer (e.g., jamming), eavesdropping of sensed data, attacks against routing of data through multiple hops, corruption of fused or aggregated data by compromised nodes, and so on. The IEEE 802.12.4 low-rate wireless personal area networking standard employs mechanisms similar to IEEE 802.11i (AES countermode and cipher-block chaining message authentication code) for security. However, key distribution and management in sensor networks is not simple (see the case study in Section 12.6.3). The interested reader is referred to [14] for a survey of security issues in the superset of ad hoc networks; to [15] for security in low-rate wireless networks; and to [16] for a discussion of design issues for security in sensor networks.

12.4 Current Survivability Approaches in Wireless Networks

Survivability of wireless networks has recently begun to receive attention, mainly focusing on database survivability tailored to the cellular network databases (HLR and VLR) architecture [17–19]. This work focuses on the development of checkpoint algorithms and authentication techniques for the fault recovery of database contents. Literature on the design of a survivable landline topology for wireless networks [20–23] concentrates on formulating various optimization models for single-link failure survivable landline mesh-topology and capacity allocation design. However, the approach and assumptions used are identical to techniques used for wired backbone network design. None of the unique aspects of wireless networks are incorporated into the models. In [24], the importance of survivability for wireless networks is discussed and the difficulty in applying standard wired metrics for quantifying wireless survivability is shown.

We believe that survivability approaches for wired networks are not entirely applicable to the mobile and wireless domain. Consider that the failure of nodes and links is a primary survivability consideration. Wired networks are characterized by relatively high-speed, highly reliable, fixed-capacity links serving fixed users. The number of physical cables and their interconnection configuration influences system capacity. Diversity techniques often consist of adding spare capacity by the addition of physical cables, which are primarily subject to cost constraints. In contrast, the wireless domain is characterized by variable capacity and unreliable links serving mobile users. Wireless link capacity is influenced by the continually changing network conditions such as cell congestion, environmental factors, and interference. Diversity techniques are constrained by cost and a regulated frequency spectrum. Spectrum is a scarce resource in wireless networks and allocating spare capacity is much more difficult since, unlike wired networks, duplicating the medium is not easy. Furthermore, wireless network survivability approaches must account for user mobility and radio resource management. It has been shown that *user mobility worsens transient conditions* as disconnected users move among geographical areas to attempt to reconnect to the wireless access network [25–27]. In [25–27], the results of a sample survivability analysis of a typical GSM cellular network are presented using simulation. The steady-state and transient behavior of standard performance metrics, such as the call-blocking rate and location registration delay, were measured for a variety of failure cases. One significant result from these studies is that the *impact of failure is larger than the failed area*. For example, the failure of a BSC knocking out a group of four adjacent cells (in a network of 100) results in the mean time to process a location update for the entire group of 100 cells to exceed (by a factor of 10) the recommended International Telecommunications Union (ITU) benchmark value, resulting in protocol timeouts. Further, the magnitude and duration of a failure impact depend on a complex set of factors including the location of the failure (e.g., center or edge of location area), shape of the failed area (e.g., adjacent or disjoint cells), user mobility patterns, and user behavior in attempting reconnection. Thus, the network design should consider transient conditions in the capacity allocation and restoration techniques must consider *spatial* and *temporal* properties and address both the *transient* and steady-state periods. Current literature also does not consider the impact a failure in the wireless access networks has on the signaling network. In fact, our studies [26, 27] show that radio-level failure (e.g., loss of a base station, BS) causes a large increase in transient congestion in the signaling network. Similar results from network measurement on a GSM after an earthquake have been reported in the IST Caution Project [28]. Incorporating such transient effects into the network topology design was recently proposed in [29].

A framework for cellular network survivability at the access layer, transport layer, and intelligent layer is presented in [4, 25] along with potential survivability approaches at each layer. An extension of this framework to packet-based 3G cellular networks was presented in [30]. Note that hybrid wireless networks offer alternatives to restoration schemes by enabling the use of overlays or underlays after failure of components of one particular technology. However, such schemes have also not been studied extensively for their benefits.

An overview of survivability issues and possible approaches for mobile ad hoc networks was presented in [31], including store-and-forward when end-to-end paths do not exist and store-and-haul in which nodes physically transport data. More recently, work on delay tolerant networking [32] has developed an architecture that has led to work in disruption-tolerant networking. Disruption-tolerant networking addresses the problem of how to communicate when wireless channel environments and mobility are so severe that stable end-to-end paths never exist and conventional communication that assumes routing convergence breaks down. In sensor networks, partitioning of the network due to failed sensor nodes (either hardware failure or battery exhaustion) can lead to the sensor network being unable to sense data or transmit the sensed data reliably to the base station. Work has been done to reduce the energy consumption in WSNs and load balancing among sensor nodes, but this is primarily at the academic research level.

12.5 Framework for Wireless Network Survivability and Security

In light of the limitations indicated by the current literature, we have developed a framework for the comprehensive treatment of the problems of IA in hybrid wireless access networks. To facilitate the work, a hybrid wireless access network survivability/security framework [5] is developed similar to the approaches in [33] for wired backbone networks. The wireless access network is viewed as having radio, sensor, access, and intelligent layers, as shown in Figure 12.1, with survivability/security strategies possible at each layer as detailed in [4], [5], and [26]. The components and functions supported at each layer are listed in Table 12.1. The radio network subsystem (RNS) includes the APs, BSs, BSC/RNC, and radio resource management schemes. The sensor subsystem (SenS) consists of a sensor network of sensor nodes with a base station connected to the Internet. The access network subsystem (ANS) supports packet switching, connection management, call management, and mobility management functions using the wired interconnection of APs, BSs, BSC, and MSC. The MSC, HLR, and VLR at the transport layer use the signaling network and services provided by service data management functions, implemented at the intelligent layer, to support connection and mobility management. The intelligent network subsystem (INS) supports security, location, service data and mobility management functions.

Given the framework above to conduct a survivability analysis, performance-oriented *survivability metrics* along with techniques for evaluating the metrics over various *modes of operation* are identified. The modes of operation include normal, single-failure, and multiple-failure/attack/disaster modes. Table 12.2 lists examples of possible *survivability metrics* and *failure conditions* at each layer in the framework, as well as some of the potential *impacts* of a failure in terms of the area affected and network service disruption. The survivability of a particular network is based on the ability of the network to meet performance goals stated in terms of *service thresholds* for each survivability metric, over each operational mode. For example, a performance goal with respect to packet delivery may be 1% packet loss for all cells during normal operation and 2% steady-state packet loss for cells adjacent to or near a failed cell with a maximum transient peak of 10% packet

Table 12.1 Wireless Network Subsystems for Survivability and Security.

Subsystem	Components	Communication Links	Function
RNS	MS, BS, ad hoc clusters, WLAN AP, and BSC	Digital radio channels with TDMA, FDMA, or CDMA, wireline links, and/or terrestrial microwave	Define physical interface for radio communication, BS cluster management, radio channel management, and MAC signaling
ANS	BS, BSC, MSC, WAP, SGSN, GGSN, and signaling network	Wireline links and/or terrestrial microwave	Connection management and mobility management
INS	MSC, HLR, VLR, EIR, AuC, mobile IP signaling, and RADIUS	Wireline links and/or terrestrial microwave	Service management, security, location services, and mobility management
SenS	Sensor nodes and BS	Wireless multihop links on the uplink and broadcast wireless downlink	Deliver sensed data to BS and broadcast control messages for network operation to sensor nodes

loss. While many of the survivability metrics listed in Table 12.2 have target mean and 0.95 percentile values recommended by ITU [34] for voice, no corresponding values exist for data.

For a network to be fault-tolerant, alternate routes must exist between the network components or spare components must be provisioned (e.g., spare link between the BS-BSC with automatic protection switching at the end points). At the ANS and INS levels, traditional survivability strategies such as a mesh-type architecture (at least two connected) are feasible. For example, all of the base stations in a cluster together with their associated BSC could be connected with a self-healing ring.

Table 12.3 lists examples of the types of survivable network design strategies that can be implemented. In addition, specific network controls (e.g., routing) are required to support the restoration of service to connections disrupted by a failure/attack, while maintaining network performance goals. This should enable a network to provide service continuity if possible, while minimizing network congestion. Table 12.3 also lists examples of the type of restoration technique for a given redundancy approach at a particular layer. As an example, a *self-healing ring* (SHR) at the ANS layer is shown in Figure 12.2. The SHR can provide full restoration capability against a single cable cut and equipment failure. Each node in the SHR uses one add/drop multiplexer (ADM) to access either the primary (outer) ring or the secondary (inner) ring. In normal operation, the system uses the primary ring for both transmitting and receiving data, and the secondary ring is served as a protection system. In the ANS, the SHR could be used to connect a BS and a BSC, a BSC and an MSC, or

Table 12.2 Typical Failure Scenarios and Survivability Metrics at Each Layer.

Subsystem	Failure Scenario	Potential Impact	Possible Metrics
RNS	Loss of AP or BS/Node B	Partial/full-service loss in cell and increased traffic in cells adjacent to failure; increased signaling	Packet loss rate, TCP session timeout, connection blocking probability, forced connection termination probability, throughput, and handover request rate
ANS	Loss of BSC-MSC or AP link	Partial/full-service loss in a cell or cluster of cells and increased traffic in cells adjacent to failure; increased signaling	Packet loss rate, TCP session timeout, connection blocking probability, forced connection termination probability, connection setup/release delay, and paging/location update/registration delays
INS	Loss of VLR	Loss of roaming service in a coverage area or network/subnetwork	Lost user load (Erlangs or packets), database access delay, and information accuracy probability
SenS	Failure of sensor nodes or links	Partitioning of network leading to more energy consumption for data delivery, or congestion	Network lifetime, throughput, delay, packet delivery ratio, and energy efficiency

Table 12.3 Typical Survivability Strategies.

Subsystem	Robustness and Redundancy	Traffic Restoration
RNS	Spare RF components, NICs, overlapping/ scaleable cells, corner excited overlapping cells, ad hoc relays, spare BS-BSC links, dual-homing APs, multihoming BS to BSCs, and ring topology for BS-BSC interconnect	Load-sharing protocols, dynamic channel allocation, adaptive channel quality protocols, MANET routing protocols, automatic protection switching, dynamic rerouting protocols, and self-healing rings
ANS	Spare BSC-MSC link, ring topology for BSC-MSC interconnect, multihoming BSC to MSCs, and dual-homing APs	Automatic protection switching, self-healing rings, dynamic rerouting, call gapping/ selective packet dropping
INS	Physical diversity in signal networking links and physical database diversity	Dynamic routing and checkpoint protocols
SenS	Spare sensor nodes with alternating sleep and waking schedules and multipath routing	Creating new routes upon failure and control messaging from BS for restoring routes and time synchronization

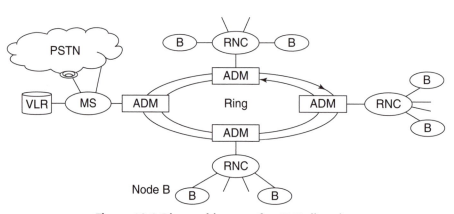

Figure 12.2 Ring architecture for ANS diversity.

multiple MSCs as a ring topology. Figure 12.2 illustrates an example of employing SHR between an MSC and multiple BSCs in a mobile cellular network. The SHR is simple, fast, and provides full-capacity restoration. However, it can protect a system from failures that occur only in its physical rings and ADMs. Also, it is expensive to implement.

Thus far we have considered failure conditions. In Table 12.4 we look at the layers of Table 12.1 from a security standpoint. At each layer, the messages and protocols are identified that have security implications and the types of security attacks that are possible at each layer. Currently in WLANs, the only repository of the shared key is the AP (or Authentication Server) and the MS. In cellular networks, different entities have possession of different secrets. The subscriber identity is kept in the HLR, MS, and SGSN. For random nonces used in session key generation, the challenge messages are known to the HLR, SGSN, BSC, MS, and BS. Only the MS and AuC know the master key. The AuC maintains a different

Table 12.4 Wireless Network Layers and Security Implications.

Subsystem	Network Components	Secret Information	Messages	Information to Be Secured
RNS	MS, BS, ad hoc clusters WLAN AP, and BSC	Subscriber identity, shared secret master key, session key(s), random nonces	Signaling messages (RRM, MM), challenge, response voice/data traffic	Beacon needs to be checked for integrity; challenge, response, nonces to be authenticated; and voice/data traffic confidentiality
ANS	BS, BSC, MSC, WAP, SGSN, GGSN, and signaling network	Shared keys between entities for each session, and random nonces	Signaling messages, voice/data traffic	All traffic needs authentication especially nonces and RRM and MM messages
INS	MSC, HLR, VLR, EIR, AuC, mobileIP signaling, and RADIUS	Certificates, shared secret master key, subscriber ID, session keys, and nonces	Challenge, response, session key, and nonces	Session key to be confidential; challenge, response, and nonces need to be tested for integrity and authentication
SenS	Sensor nodes and BS	Predistributed secret keys and public keys	Sensed/fused/data, routing control data, and broadcast control messages	Authenticity and confidentiality of different types of information (control and data)

master key for each MS that belongs to its network. This master key is utilized for securely generating session keys for encrypting voice calls. Table 12.5 shows examples of security breaches at each level and the impact on a network. In a hybrid wireless access network, several security features will have to be in place to prevent or quickly detect security attacks such as those listed in Table 12.5. Table 12.6 provides some typical security features and mechanisms (and network entities that need to share secret information) that can prevent or detect the attacks in Table 12.5.

12.6 Interaction Between Survivability and Security in Wireless Networks

A major area of research that has been neglected is the interaction between survivability and security. Survivability and security have been usually studied separately. A system may be survivable under component failures but may make itself vulnerable to security attacks because of the restoration mechanisms employed. Also, automatic recovery from a security breach in wireless networks is not very well understood. Very few works exist in the literature that consider the two aspects together even for wired networks. Furthermore, in wireless

Table 12.5 Typical Security Breaches and Potential Impacts.

Subsystem	Attack Scenario	Potential Impact
RNS	Modify beacon or BCCH to falsify information	Loss of access, changed sleep times, and false signal strength measurements
ANS	Replay nonce	Creation of wrong session key, exposure of session key, and failure to detect replayed data
INS	Man-in-the-middle attack for session key generation	Interception of traffic on-air link and modification of traffic on-air link
SenS	Eavesdropping and jamming, fabricated messages	Loss of confidential information, partition of network, lifetime reduction, delivered data are unreliable, data delivery impacted, and network operations fail

Table 12.6 Typical Security Features and Mechanisms That Need to Be in Place.

Subsystem	Attack Scenario	Entities Involved	Security Feature/ Mechanism	Required Shared Secret
RNS	Modify beacon or BCCH to falsify information	MS and BS	Message authentication code, encryption algorithm/hash, and digital signature	Shared secret key > 80 bits, known algorithm like AES and nonce, and authenticated public key of BS/network through certificate
ANS	Replay nonce	BSC and BS	Message authentication code and encryption algorithm/hash	Shared secret key > 80 bits
INS	Man-in-the-middle attack	AuC, BSC/BS, AuC, and AP	Authenticated and secure key establishment	Public key certificates at both ends (not secret)
SenS	Eavesdropping or jamming fabrication	Sensor nodes and BS	Encryption, obfuscation, broadcast and unicast authentication	Secret keys between sensor node pairs and sensor nodes-BS pairs

networks, the two aspects are closely related because of the need to secure the broadcast wireless link and also keep a network survivable. Recent activities in Network Reliability and Interoperability Council (NRIC) VI Wireless Network Reliability Focus Group indicate that network interoperability and security are considered to the extent that they can impact network survivability. In addition, access to remote wireless network elements (e.g., cell sites) for restoration of service can often be delayed due to security concerns. The security and survivability and their interoperability in the wireless networks need to be improved [35].

12.6.1 Extending the Framework to Include Interactions Between Security and Survivability

The framework for security and survivability in the last section can also be used to understand the interaction between security and survivability in wireless networks. A range of issues

Table 12.7 Typical Survivability and Security Features and Mechanisms That Need to Be in Place.

Subsystem	Failure/Attack Scenario	Impact	Survivability Measures Related to Security	Security Measures Related to Survivability
RNS	Loss of BS/Node B	Service loss requiring MSs to move to neighboring cell	Generate spare keys for failure scenario	Need authentication of failure and reconnect messages
	Compromise of BCCH	Loss of access to cell and potential impact on signal strength measurements	Generate redundant BCCH	Quick detection of compromise, and authenticate the updated BCCH to MS
ANS	Loss of BSC-SGSN link and compromise of SGSN	Partial/full-service loss in a cell or cluster of cells, increased traffic in cells adjacent to failure, and loss of data integrity and exposure of session keys	Hold spare session keys in SGSNs targeted for handoff and in neighboring clusters and reroute traffic to another SGSN from a BSC	Need authentication of messages to MSs asking them to defer new calls and set up of new session keys and authentication of new session between BSC and secondary SGSN
INS	Loss of VLR	Loss of roaming service in a coverage area or network/subnetwork	VLR with physical diversity must have a spare subset of nonces and keys	Need to authenticate the spare VLR and ensure that new nonces and keys replace the spare subset rapidly
	Compromise of HLR-VLR link	Man-in-the-middle attack exposes the session key	Physically separate spare link	Detection of compromise and check integrity of spare link
SenS	Failed sensor node(s) and compromise of sensor nodes	Network partition or impact on data delivery, and false data injected into the network	Wake up sleeping nodes to fill holes, wake up additional nodes to verify sensed data, and rekeying protocols	Woken nodes need to establish secure links (check for nodes that they share keys with), and detection of compromise and check integrity of received data

exists such as the impact of node and link failures and restoration schemes on the security architecture and the impact of attacks on components of the survivability strategies and methods of recovery. Table 12.7 shows some examples of each case at the RNS, ANS, INS, and SenS levels. At each of the levels, possible failure/attack scenarios, the impact of the failure/attack scenarios, survivability measures related to security, and security measures related to survivability are identified.

At the RNS level, an example of a failure/attack scenario is the loss of a BS/Node B or compromise of the BCCH message in a cell. When a BS or Node B fails, several MSs will try to reconnect to nearby Node Bs that may have overlapping coverage. The survivability measures related to security are now required to generate spare keys for the failure scenario, while the security measures related to survivability now need to perform authentication of failure and reconnect messages. When the attack scenario is the compromise of the BCCH, MSs will likely lose access to the cell, and it also has potential impact on signal strength measurements. Now the survivability measures related to security are required to generate a redundant BCCH first, perhaps sending the information through neighboring Node Bs. The security measures related to survivability need to quickly detect the compromise and authenticate the updated BCCH to the MSs.

At the ANS level, an example of a failure/attack scenario is the loss of a BSC-SGSN link or compromise of the SGSN. When a BSC-SGSN link fails, there will be partial- or full-service loss in a cell or cluster of cells, and there will be increased traffic in cells adjacent to the failed link. The survivability measures related to security are required to hold spare session keys in SGSNs targeted for handoff and in neighboring clusters, while the security measures related to survivability need authentication of messages to MSs asking them to defer new calls. When compromise of the SGSN happens, there will be loss of data integrity and exposure of session keys. Now the survivability measures related to security are required to reroute traffic to another SGSN from a BSC, while the security measures related to survivability need the set up of new session keys and authentication of a new session between the affected BSC and secondary SGSN.

At the INS level, an example of a failure/attack scenario is the loss of the VLR or compromise of the HLR-VLR link. When a VLR fails, there will be loss of roaming service in the coverage area of a network/subnetwork. The survivability measures related to security will be required to have a spare subset of nonces and keys for the VLR with physical diversity, while the security measures related to survivability need to authenticate the spare VLR and ensure that new nonces and keys rapidly replace the spare subset. When compromise of the HLR-VLR link happens, the session key could be exposed and man-in-the-middle attacks can be launched. Now the survivability measures related to security are required to physically separate the spare link, while the security measures related to survivability quickly need to detect the compromise and need to check the integrity of the spare link.

At the SenS level, one example of failure is a group of sensor nodes dying due to hardware failures or battery exhaustion. The network may be partitioned unless redundant nodes that are sleeping are woken up by broadcast messages from a BS. However, such nodes may not share keys with neighboring sensor nodes, or they may have to discover those nodes with which they share a key to secure the new links and routes created in the sensor network. Similarly, if some sensor nodes are compromised and they inject fabricated data into the network, upon detection of such compromise, other nodes in their vicinity may have to be queried to send sensed data that may be essential for the application. It may be necessary to have some restoration schemes for rekeying the sensor nodes that are not compromised if keys are revealed by the compromised nodes.

12.6.2 Case Study I: Idle Handoffs

Figure 12.3 shows another example of the interaction between survivability and security. In a UMTS-WCDMA system, an *idle handoff* occurs upon detecting a stronger pilot (when an MS moves to another cell while it is not making a call). The request from the MS is sent through the new Node B and RNC to a new MSC/VLR if necessary. The VLR contacts the HLR for an authentication request. In response, several authentication vectors (AVs) are sent to the VLR, one of which is used to authenticate the MS as a challenge and obtain the MS response. The others are kept in reserve if necessary. Suppose now a Node B fails and several MSs will try to simultaneously make idle handoffs to nearby Node Bs that may have overlapping coverage. All of these requests will congest the connection to the VLR. If AVs are instead stored in neighboring Node Bs and some time-limited authentication can be done while a traffic restoration protocol can schedule a more rigorous authentication, the performance could be improved significantly.

In a hybrid network scenario, the interaction between survivability and security becomes more complex. In the case of failure of a Node B in a cellular network, MSs may benefit from connecting to an underlay 802.11 WLAN that may be providing coverage in the same geographical area. When the MSs try to connect to the 802.11 AP, the process involved will be similar to a handoff. The only difference is that the handoff is performed to a different type of wireless access network. As part of this handoff, MSs need to be authenticated. Only then can an MS associate itself with an AP and resume communications. Even assuming loose coupling (described earlier), the time taken to authenticate an MS in a 802.11 WLAN can be

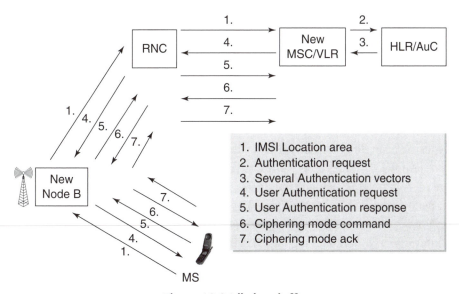

Figure 12.3 Idle handoff.

fairly large, (1) because of the time taken to obtain information about the WLAN availability through the beacon messages [36, 37] and (2) because of the numerous message exchanges and cryptographic functions.

In the case of tight coupling, this delay could be worse because of the need to communicate with the GPRS core network. Survivability and security measures will have to carefully interact to ensure that the quality of communications is maintained according to the specified metrics, while adequate security levels are maintained. Moreover, the examples of failure/ attack scenarios described above can be more complex in this case.

12.6.3 Case Study II: Key Management in Heterogeneous Sensor Networks

To understand the interaction between survivability and security of our WSN security architecture with heterogeneous sensor nodes, we conduct a case study for the key management scheme. Our study shows that the WSN can achieve higher key connectivity and higher resilience with our proposed key management scheme, with a small percentage of heterogeneous nodes that have reasonable storage, processing, and communication capabilities. We can also see the trade-off between reliability and security in some examples.

Key management is one of the most important prevention and protection schemes for security mechanisms of WSNs. To provide secure communications for WSNs, all messages should be encrypted and authenticated. Consequently, security solutions for such applications depend on the existence of strong and efficient key distribution mechanisms for uncontrolled environments of WSNs. We illustrate how to design an effective key management framework under the general heterogeneous WSN security architecture. Up to now, almost all the existing key management schemes for distributed WSNs assume that the sensor nodes are homogeneous with the same capabilities for each sensor network. Therefore, it is of significance to investigate how to design a suitable key management scheme for heterogeneous WSNs. Consequently, it is also important to address the reliability issue in the design of a key management scheme. Energy conservation is a critical issue in WSNs since batteries are the only limited-life energy source to power the sensor nodes. The key management schemes designed for WSNs should be energy aware and efficient.

Obviously, using a single shared key in a whole WSN is not a good idea because an adversary can easily obtain the key. Therefore, as a fundamental security service, pair-wise key establishment shall be used, which can enable the sensor nodes to communicate securely with each other using cryptographic techniques. However, due to resource constraints on sensor nodes, it is not feasible for sensors to use traditional pair-wise key establishment techniques such as public key cryptography and key distribution center [38]. Instead, sensor nodes can use predistributed keys directly or use keying materials to dynamically generate pair-wise keys. In such a case, the main challenge is to find an efficient way of distributing keys and keying materials to sensor nodes prior to deployment.

In this case study, we assume that there are I classes of sensor nodes in the network, with Class 1 consisting of the least powerful nodes and Class I the most powerful nodes, in terms of communication range, node processing capability, and energy level. Particularly, in terms of communication range, we assume the existence of bidirectional links between any two nodes. Let r_i denote the communication range of Class i nodes; we always have $r_m < r_n$ if $m < n$. Therefore, if a Class m node is within the range of a direct communication link of a Class n node, the Class m node might need multiple links to reach the Class n node if $m < n$. The heterogeneity of the sensor nodes are distributed in the WSN, with p_i the percentage of the Class i nodes, and $p_1 + p_2 + ... + p_I = 1$. Here, it is important to notice the fundamental difference between the heterogeneous WSNs assumed in this section and the hierarchical WSNs in [39] and [40]. In the hierarchical WSNs, the base stations (or cluster supervisors) are centralized nodes, and more importantly, they are acting like key distribution centers. In contrast, in the heterogeneous WSNs, except that the higher class nodes are more powerful in terms of communication range, node capability, and energy level, the communications between all different classes of nodes are still peer-to-peer and distributed.

The security requirements and services can be described by the following metrics: scalability, efficiency, resilience, and reliability. Scalability is the ability to support a large number of wireless sensor nodes in a network. The security mechanisms must support a large network and be flexible against a substantial increase in the size of the network even after deployment. Efficiency is the consideration of storage, processing, and communication limitations on sensor nodes. Resilience is about the resistance to node capture. A compromise of security credentials, which are stored on a sensor node or exchanged over radio links, should not reveal information about security of any other links in the WSN. A higher resilience means a lower number of compromised links. Reliability is the capability to keep the functionality of the WSN even if some sensor nodes are failed. The survivability concerns can be provided with the design goals of scalability, efficiency, key connectivity, resilience, and reliability. Key connectivity is the probability that two or more sensor nodes store the same key or keying material. Enough key connectivity must be provided for a WSN to perform its intended functionality.

The key generation in heterogeneous-distributed WSNs here is based on the random key distribution [41] and the polynomial-based key predistribution protocol [42], and is inspired by the approaches of Liu and Ning in [43]. In a manner similar to the studies in Eschenauer and Gligor [41], we consider that there are three steps in the framework to establish pair-wise keys between the sensor nodes:

- Initialization;
- Direct key setup;
- Path key setup.

The initialization step is performed to initialize the sensors by distributing polynomial shares to them, with the consideration of the heterogeneity of the sensor nodes. The direct key setup step is for any two nodes trying to establish a pair-wise key, in which they always first attempt to do so through direct key establishment. If the second step is successful, there is no need to start the third step. Otherwise, these sensor nodes may start the path key setup step, trying to establish a pair-wise key with the help of other sensors.

Our scheme uses a pool of randomly generated bivariate polynomials to establish pair-wise keys between sensor nodes, with the consideration of I classes of heterogeneity among the wireless sensor nodes. In this manner, existing distributed key management schemes can all be included in the framework. For example, if $I = 1$, which means that the sensor network is homogeneous, we have the following special cases: when all the polynomials are 0-degree ones and the sensor network is homogeneous, the polynomial pool degenerates into a key pool [41]; and when the polynomial pool has only one polynomial and the sensor network is homogeneous, the key distribution scheme degenerates into the polynomial-based key predistribution [42].

The main challenge in this scheme is how to assign polynomial shares to different classes of nodes. We can clearly observe that the major issue in our scheme is the subset assignment problem, which specifies how to determine the set of polynomials and how to assign the polynomial shared for each sensor node in group j with class i. During the key distribution procedure, a number of factors must be considered, including the probability that adjacent nodes can share a common key, the resilience of the network when it is under attack, and importantly, the nature of the heterogeneity.

The proposed new key generation scheme is essentially different from most existing schemes in that the heterogeneity features can now be taken into account. To illustrate the advantages of the new scheme, we consider a typical heterogeneous WSN that is established to collect data in a distributed scenario. In this scenario, a sensor node shall submit its observation to a sink node (or sink nodes, depending on the configuration of the network) through the sensor network in a hop-by-hop manner, as shown in Figure 12.4, in which there are two classes of sensor nodes in addition to the sink node.

Since the high-class nodes have a larger transmission range, it is natural that a low-class node will tend to utilize the link between itself and a high-class node to submit the observations.

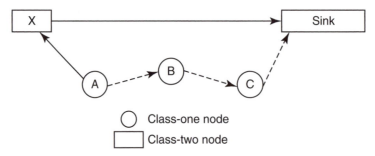

Figure 12.4 An example WSN.

For example, in Figure 12.4, class-one node A will tend to use the path "A-X-Sink" (the solid lines) to submit its report, instead of passing the message by all class-one nodes "A-B-C-Sink" (the dash lines). Clearly, a high-class node will more likely be chosen as the next hop neighbor of nearby low-class nodes to forward data. Consequently, in this heterogeneous sensor network, the connectivity between a low-class node and a high-class node will be more important than the connectivity between two low-class nodes.

We now design a special key management scheme within the new framework for the above scenario. Specifically, we consider that there are two classes of the heterogeneous sensor nodes (i.e., $I = 2$). To simplify the discussion, we also assume that there is only one group, denoted as group 0, in the network.

The special key management scheme is a key-pool-based key distribution scheme. In this scheme, we denote C_1 as the class of the less powerful sensor nodes and C_2 the class of the more powerful sensor nodes. We consider that a C_2 node X is *in the neighborhood of* a C_1 node A if A can directly receive the message from X. Since the transmission range of A is less than the transmission range of X, A may need to send messages to X through a multihop path. We define that a C_1 node is *connected to the network if it shares at least one key with C_2 nodes in its neighborhood.* We then define the key connectivity as the probability that a C_1 node is connected to the network. For simplicity, we only consider the direct key setup between a C_1 node and adjacent C_2 node.

An example of this scheme is illustrated in Figure 12.5, where node A is a C_1 node and nodes X, Y, and Z are C_2 nodes. In this example, nodes X, Y, and Z are the only C_2 neighbor nodes of node A. In addition, node A shares key K_1 with node X, K_2 with node Y, and K_1 and K_3 with node Z, respectively. In this example, node A is connected to the network through three different keys: K_1, K_2, and K_3. In such a case, if node A wants to submit new information to the sink node, it can first randomly select a key from K_1 to K_3; then, it can randomly select a

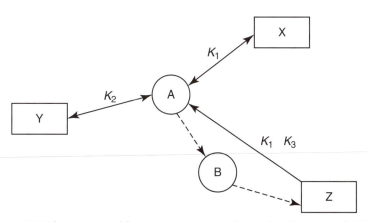

Figure 12.5 The proposed key management scheme for the example WSN.

neighbor node that shares the same key with it. For example, in Figure 12.5, if K_1 is chosen as the key, then nodes X and Z can be randomly selected. In this manner, we can see that the communication is more resilient, while the connectivity can also be maintained.

To understand the behavior of the key management scheme above, we have conducted extensive quantitative studies to evaluate the performance, in terms of key connectivity, reliability, and resilience. In our experiments, we consider a small area of WSN that consists of 200 C_1 nodes and a number of C_2 nodes, denoted as N_2. We also assume that the size of key pool is 50,000 and the number of keys in any C_2 node is fixed to 2000.

12.6.3.1 Reliability of the New Schemes: Key Connectivity of the New Schemes in Normal Conditions

According to the definition, *key connectivity* is the probability that two or more sensor nodes store the same key. Clearly, enough key connectivity must be provided for a WSN to perform its intended functionality. Figure 12.6 shows the connectivity of the proposed scheme versus the number of keys in a C_1 node with a different number of C_2 nodes. We can first observe that the connectivity can increase with the increase of the number of keys. For a fixed number of keys in each C_1 node, we can see that a small increase of the number of C_2 nodes can significantly increase the connectivity, especially when the number of keys in C_1 node is small and medium. From another perspective, we can see that, to achieve a specific connectivity, the number of keys that must be stored in each C_1 node can be decreased with

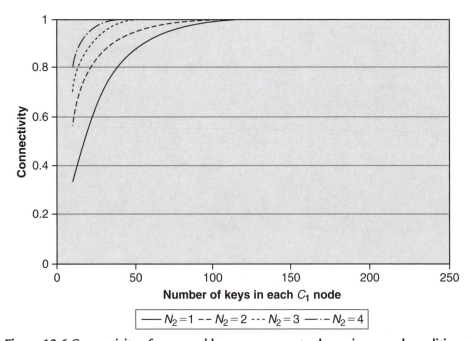

Figure 12.6 Connectivity of proposed key management scheme in normal conditions.

the increase of N_2. For instance, if the connectivity is 0.99, then about 113 keys are required for $N_2 = 1$, about 57 keys are required for $N_2 = 2$, about 38 keys are required for $N_2 = 3$, and about 29 keys are needed for $N_2 = 4$.

To highlight the impact of the number of C_2 nodes, we demonstrate in Figure 12.7 the probability distribution of the number of shared keys with different N_2. In this example, we assume the number of keys in each C_1 node is 60. We can observe that, with the increase of N_2, the shape of the distribution tends to shift to the right-hand side, which implies that a C_1 node can share more keys with neighboring C_2 nodes. With the increase of shared keys, the network becomes more reliable.

12.6.3.2 Resilience of the New Schemes: Key Connectivity of the New Schemes in Attack Conditions

To evaluate the resilience of the new schemes, we study the performance of the sensor network when some C_1 nodes are compromised. Here we assume that C_2 nodes are more tamper-resistant. In Figure 12.8, we consider the scenario in which the keys per C_1 node will be selected in a manner such that the network connectivity is 99% under normal conditions. We also assume that the compromised C_1 nodes cannot be detected. In such a scenario, the data transmission from an unaffected C_1 node may be eavesdropped by a nearby compromised node. Therefore, it is important to study the percentage of communications that are not affected. From Figure 12.5, we can see that with our schemes, a C_1 node can still

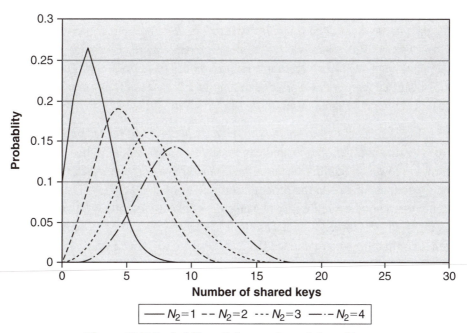

Figure 12.7 Probability of the number of shared keys.

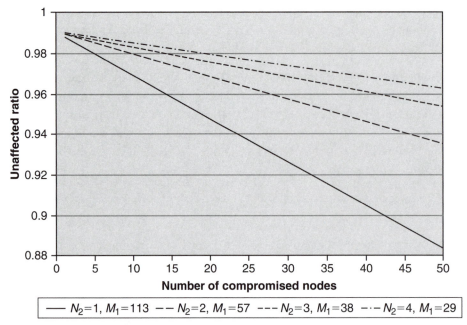

Figure 12.8 Resilience of the key management scheme in attack conditions (connectivity = 99% in normal conditions).

securely transmit data to C_2 nodes even if some of the keys are compromised. For example, if K_1 is the only key that is compromised, then we can see that node A still has a 66% chance to forward the data to any one of the C_2 nodes (with K_2 or K_3). This phenomenon can be clearly observed from Figure 12.8, where we find that a high percentage of secured communications can still be maintained even if a large number of C_1 nodes have been compromised. Moreover, we can see that more C_2 nodes can help to increase the fraction of unaffected communications, given the same number of compromised C_1 nodes.

In Figure 12.9, we consider scenarios in which we fix $N_2 = 4$ and let M_1 be 29, 38, 57, and 113, where M_1 is the number of keys that can be stored in a C_1 node. In this case, $M_1 = 29$ can represent the lowest reliability because the connectivity of the network will be less than 99% if one C_2 node is failed. On the other extreme, we notice that $M_1 = 113$ can represent the situation with the highest reliability because the connectivity of the network will be greater than 99% even if three C_2 nodes are failed. Clearly, we can first observe the trade-off between the reliability and resilience from this example. For example, if the number of compromised nodes is larger than 5, $M_1 = 29$ can have better resilience than that of $M_1 = 113$. Moreover, we also notice that, given a certain number of compromised nodes, an optimum configuration may exist that can lead to the highest resilience. For instance, if the number of compromised nodes is 20, then $M_1 = 38$ has the best performance in terms of unaffected ratio.

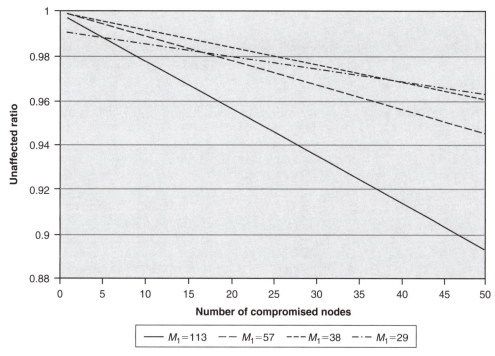

Figure 12.9 Resilience of the key management scheme in attack conditions ($N_2 = 4$).

12.7 Conclusion

IA techniques employed in wired networks have limited direct applicability in wireless networks because of the unique aspects of wireless networks (user mobility, wireless channel, power conservation, limited computational power in mobile nodes, and security at the link layer). In this chapter, we study the survivability and security in wireless networks, both for hybrid wireless infrastructure networks and wireless ad hoc and sensor networks. The issues that are related to the interaction between survivability and security in hybrid wireless infrastructure networks are discussed. We provide a framework that can be used to understand the implications of failures or security breaches on the performance and design of hybrid wireless infrastructure networks. We also address the design issues for secure and survivable WSNs, which are vulnerable to physical and network-based security attacks, accidents, and failures. Based on the study about the security requirements and survivability requirements, we develop architecture for security and survivability in WSNs with heterogeneous sensor nodes. To better understand the interactions between survivability and security, we also design and analyze a key management scheme within the architecture. The experiment results show that a good design can improve both security and survivability of WSNs. It also illustrates that there is a trade-off between security and survivability in some scenarios.

References

[1] J.J.-N. Liu, I. Chlamtac, Mobile ad-hoc networking with a view of 4G wireless: imperatives and challenges, in: S. Basagni, M. Conti, S. Giordano, I. Stojmenovic (Eds.), Mobile Ad Hoc Networking, IEEE Press, Wiley-Interscience, New York, 2004.

[2] K. Pahlavan, P. Krishnamurthy, et al., Handoff in hybrid mobile data networks, IEEE Personal Commun., April (2000).

[3] I. Akyildiz, W. Su, Y. Sankarasubramanian, E. Cayirci, A survey on sensor networks, IEEE Commun. Mag., August (2002).

[4] D. Tipper, T. Dahlberg, H. Shin, C. Charnsripinyo, Providing fault tolerance in wireless access networks, IEEE Commun. Mag., January (2002) 58–64.

[5] P. Krishnamurthy, D. Tipper, Y. Qian, The interaction of security and survivability in hybrid wireless networks, WIA 2004, in: Proc. IEEE IPCCC 2004, Phoenix, AZ, April 14–17, 2004.

[6] Y. Qian, K. Lu, D. Tipper, Towards survivable and secure wireless sensor networks, WIA 2007, in: Proc. IEEE IPCCC 2007, New Orleans, LA, April 11–13, 2007.

[7] A.K. Salkintzis, C. Fors, R. Pazhyannur, WLAN-GPRS integration for next generation mobile data networks, IEEE Wireless Commun., October (2002).

[8] I. Akyildiz, X. Wang, A survey on wireless mesh networks, IEEE Commun. Mag., September (2005) 23–30.

[9] H. Luo, R. Ramjee, P. Sinha, L. Li, S. Lu, UCAN: a unified cellular and ad hoc network architecture, ACM Mobicom, September (2003) 353–367.

[10] K. Pahlavan, P. Krishnamurthy, Principles of Wireless Networks: A Unified Approach, Prentice Hall PTR, Englewood Cliffs, NJ, 2002.

[11] S. Fluhrer, I. Martin, A. Shamir, Weaknesses in key scheduling algorithm of RC4, Eighth Annual Workshop on Selected Areas in Cryptography, August 2001.

[12] TR 33.102, 3GPP Security Architecture, 3GPP release, 1999.

[13] D. Simon, B. Aboba, T. Moore, IEEE 802.11 Security and 802.1X, IEEE 802.11 WG Document doc: IEEE 802.11–00/034r1, March 2000.

[14] D. Djenouri, L. Khelladi, N. Badache, A survey of security issues in mobile ad hoc and sensor networks, IEEE Commun. Surv. 7 (4) (2005).

[15] J. Zheng, M.J. Lee, M. Anshel, Toward secure low rate wireless personal area networks, IEEE Transac. Mobile Comput. 5 (10) (2006) 1361–1373.

[16] E. Shi, A. Perrig, Designing secure sensor networks, IEEE Wireless Commun., December (2004) 38–43.

[17] P.E. Wirth, Teletraffic implications of database architectures in mobile and personal communications, IEEE Commun. Mag., June (1995) 54–59.

[18] Y. Lin, Failure restoration of mobility databases for personal communication networks, Wireless Networks 1 (3) (1995) 365–372.

[19] Y. Lin, Per-user checkpointing for mobility database failure restoration, IEEE Transact. Mobile Comput. 4 (1) (2005).

[20] A. Hilt, P. Berzethy, Recent trends in reliable access networking for GSM systems, in: Proc. Third International Workshop on the Design of Reliable Communication Networks, Budapest, Hungary, October 2001.

[21] A. Dutta, P. Kubat, Design of partially survivable networks for cellular telecommunication systems, Eur. J. Oper. Res. 118 (1999) 52–64.

[22] L.A. Cox Jr, J.R. Sanchez, Designing least-cost survivable wireless backhaul networks, J. Heuristics 6 (2000) 525–540.

[23] P. Kubat, J.M. Smith, C. Yum, Design of cellular networks with diversity and capacity constraints, IEEE Transact. Reliab. 49 (2) (2000) 165–175.

[24] P. Snow, U. Varshney, A.D. Malloy, Reliability and survivability of wireless and mobile networks, IEEE Comp. 33 (2000) 49–55.

[25] D. Tipper, S. Ramaswamy, T. Dahlberg, PCS network survivability, in: Proc. IEEE Wireless Communications and Networking Conference (WCNC'99), New Orleans, LA, September 1999.

[26] H. Shin, C. Charnsripinyo, D. Tipper, T. Dahlberg, The effects of failures in PCS networks, in: Proc. DRCN, Budapest, Hungary, October 2001.

[27] D. Tipper, C. Charnsripinyo, H. Shin, T. Dahlberg, Survivability analysis for mobile cellular networks, in: Proc. CNDS 2002, San Antonio, TX, January 27–31, 2002.

[28] The IST Caution Project at: http://www.telecom.ntua.gr/caution/start.html.

[29] C. Charnsripinyo, D. Tipper, Topological design of 3G wireless backhaul networks for service assurance, in: Proc. Fifth IEEE International Workshop on the Design of Reliable Communication Networks (DRCN 2005), October 17–19, 2005, Ischia, Italy.

[30] T. Dahlberg, D. Tipper, B. Cao, C. Charnsripinyo, Survivability in wireless mobile networks, in: P. Stavroulakis (Ed.), Reliability, Survivability, and Quality of Large Scale Telecommunication Systems, John Wiley & Sons, London, UK, 2003, pp. 81–114.

[31] J. Sterbenz, R. Krishnan, R. Hain, A. Jackson, D. Levin, R. Ramanathan, J. Zhao, Survivable mobile wireless networks: issues, challenges, and research directions, in: Proc. ACM Wireless Security Workshop (WiSe'02), September 28, 2002, Atlanta, GA.

[32] K. Fall, A delay-tolerant network architecture for challenged Internets, in: Proc. ACM SIGCOMM 2003, Karlsruhe Germany, August 2003, pp. 27–34.

[33] A. Zolfaghari, F.J. Kaudel, Framework for network survivability performance, IEEE J. Sel. Areas Comm. 12 (1) (1994) 46–51.

[34] D. Grillo, Personal communications and traffic engineering in ITU-T: developing E.750 series of recommendations, IEEE Pers. Commun., December (1996), 16–28.

[35] NRIC, at http://www.nric.org/.

[36] M. Shin, A. Mishra, W. Arbaugh, Improving the latency of 802.11 hand-offs using neighbor graphs, in: Proc. MobiSys'04, Boston, MA, June 6–9, 2004.

[37] H. Velayos, G. Karlsson, Techniques to reduce the IEEE 802.11b handoff time, in: Proc. IEEE ICC 2004, Paris, France, June 2004.

[38] S. Avancha, J. Undercoffer, A. Joshi, J. Pinkston, Security for wireless sensor networks, in: C.S. Raghavendra, K.M. Sivalingam, T. Znati (Eds.) Wireless Sensor Networks, Kluwer Academic Publishers, New York, 2004.

[39] Y. Law, R. Corin, S. Etalle, P. Hartel, A formally verified decentralized key management for wireless sensor networks, Pers. Wireless Commun., LNCS, 2775 (2003) 27–39.

[40] S. Zhu, S. Setia, S. Jajodia, LEAP: efficient security mechanisms for large-scale distributed sensor networks, in: Proc. IEEE Symposium on Research in Security and Privacy, May 2003.

[41] L. Eschenauer, V.D. Gligor, A key-management scheme for distributed sensor networks, in: Proc. 9th ACM Conference on Computer and Communication Security, November 2002.

[42] C. Blundo, A. De Santis, A. Herzberg, S. Kutten, U. Vaccaro, M. Yung, Perfectly-secure key distribution for dynamic conferences, in: Proc. Advances in Cryptology, CRYPTO'92, LNCS 740, 1993, pp. 471–486.

[43] D. Liu, P. Ning, Establishing pairwise keys in distributed sensor networks, in: Proc. 10th ACM Conference on Computer and Communications Security, October 2003.

Index